MICHIE'S™
ANNOTATED CODE
OF THE PUBLIC GENERAL LAWS
OF MARYLAND

Criminal Law

Enacted by Chapter 26, Acts 2002

Prepared by the Editorial Staff of the Publishers

Consultants

State Department of Legislative Services

2012 Replacement Volume

*(Including Acts of the 2011 Regular and Special Sessions and annotations
taken from decisions posted as of March 2, 2012.)*

LexisNexis®

701 East Water Street, Charlottesville, VA 22902

4402411

ISBN 978-0-7698-5338-3

Preface

Contents.

The Criminal Law Article represents material repealed or transferred from other articles of the Annotated Code of Maryland that was reviewed and recompiled under the direction of the Office of Policy Analysis in the Department of Legislative Services.

This article was originally enacted by Chapter 26, Acts of 2002 and consists of fourteen titles, with Titles 8 through 14 appearing in this volume. The portion of the Criminal Law Article set forth in this volume also reflects all amendments and additions made in the article by the General Assembly through the Regular and Special Sessions of the 2011 Legislature.

Annotations.

Annotations are included based on decisions of the State and federal courts in cases arising in Maryland. Many of these cases were decided under the former statutes in effect prior to the 2002 revision. These earlier cases have been moved to pertinent sections of the revised material where they may be useful in interpreting the current statutes. This publication contains annotations taken from decisions of the Maryland Court of Appeals and the Court of Special Appeals, and the appropriate federal courts, posted on LEXIS as of March 2, 2012. These cases will be printed in the following reports:

Atlantic Reporter, 3nd Series
Supreme Court Reports
Federal Reporter, 3rd Series
Federal Supplement, 2nd Series
Federal Rules Decisions
Bankruptcy Reporter

Additionally, annotations have been taken from the following sources:

Opinions of the Attorney General: through December 21, 2011.
Maryland Law Review: through 71 Md. L. Rev. 295.
University of Baltimore Law Review: through 41 U. Balt. L. Rev. 193.
University of Baltimore Law Forum: through 41 U. Balt. Law Forum 210.

Citation.

Sections of the Criminal Law Article are to be cited as "§ ____ of the Criminal Law Article" pursuant to Article 1, § 25.

Index.

A comprehensive index to the Criminal Law Article appear at the end of the second Criminal Law Article volume.

Information, suggestions, comments and questions.

Visit our website at www.lexis.com for an online bookstore, technical support, customer support, and other company information.

For further information or assistance, please call us toll-free at (800) 833-9844, fax us toll-free at (800) 643-1280, or write to: Maryland Code Editor, LexisNexis, 701 East Water Street, Charlottesville, VA 22902.

April 2012 LexisNexis

USER'S GUIDE

In order to assist both legal professionals and lay people in obtaining the maximum benefit from Michie's Annotated Code of Maryland, a User's Guide has been included in Volume 1 of Michie's Annotated Code of Maryland. This guide contains comments and information on the many features found within Michie's Annotated Code of Maryland intended to increase the usefulness of the Code to the user.

Annotated Code of Maryland

CRIMINAL LAW.

Title 10.

Crimes Against Public Health, Conduct, and Sensibilities.

Title 14.

General Sentencing Provisions.

TITLE 8.

FRAUD AND RELATED CRIMES.

Subtitle 1. Bad Checks.

§ 8-101. Definitions.

(a) *In general.* — In this subtitle the following words have the meanings indicated.

REVISOR'S NOTE

This subsection is new language derived without substantive change from the introductory language of former Art. 27, § 140.

(b) *Check.* — "Check" means a negotiable instrument that is not postdated at the time it is issued.

REVISOR'S NOTE

This subsection is new language derived without substantive change from former Art. 27, § 140(a).

The former reference to "any check, draft, or other" negotiable instrument is deleted as included in the reference to "a negotiable instrument".

The former reference to a negotiable instrument "of any kind" is deleted as surplusage.

(c) *Drawer.* — "Drawer" means a person whose name appears on a check as the primary obligor, whether the actual signature on the check is that of the person or of another purportedly authorized to draw the check on the person's behalf.

REVISOR'S NOTE

This subsection is new language derived without substantive change from former Art. 27, § 140(b).

The reference to the signature "on the check" is added for clarity.

The reference to the signature being that "of the person" is substituted for the former reference to that "of himself" for clarity.

The former reference to the drawer "of a check" is deleted as surplusage.

Defined term:
"Person"   § 1-101

(d) *Funds.* — "Funds" means money or credit.

REVISOR'S NOTE

This subsection is new language derived without substantive change from former Art. 27, § 140(c).

(e) *Issue.* — "Issue", with respect to a check, means the act of a drawer or representative drawer who:

(1) delivers the check or causes it to be delivered to a person who acquires a right against the drawer with respect to the check as a result of the delivery; or

(2) draws the check with the intent that it be delivered to a person who on delivery would acquire a right assignable with respect to the check drawer and the check is delivered to that person.

REVISOR'S NOTE

This subsection is new language derived without substantive change from former Art. 27, § 140(j).

This subsection is restated in standard language used to define a term.

Throughout this title the references to "issu-[ing]" a check are substituted for the former references to "uttering" a check, draft, or other negotiable instrument for consistency with the Commercial Law Article and with modern commercial practice. *See, e.g.*, CL § 3-105.

The reference to issuing "with respect to" a check is added to clarify the application of the defined term.

The reference to acquiring a right "as a result of the delivery" is substituted for the former reference to acquiring a right "thereby" for clarity.

The reference to the intent that "[the check] be delivered to a person who on delivery would acquire a right assignable with respect to the check drawer" is substituted for the former reference to intent that it be "so" delivered for clarity.

Defined term:
"Person"   § 1-101

(f) *Obtain.* — "Obtain" has the meaning stated in § 7-101 of this article.

REVISOR'S NOTE

This subsection is new language derived without substantive change from former Art. 27, § 140(e).

(g) *Pass.* — "Pass", with respect to a check, means delivering the check by a payee, holder, or bearer of the check, if:

    (1) the check was or purports to have been drawn and issued by a person other than the person delivering the check; and

    (2) the delivery was made to a third person who acquires a right with respect to the check as a result of the delivery or for a purpose other than collection.

REVISOR'S NOTE

This subsection is new language derived without substantive change from former Art. 27, § 140(f).

This subsection is restated in standard language used to define a term.

The reference to passing "with respect to" a check is added to clarify the application of the defined term.

The reference to "a person other than the person delivering the check" is substituted for the former reference to "another" for clarity.

The reference to delivery made to a third person who acquires a right "or" for a purpose other than collection is added for clarity.

Defined term:

"Person"   § 1-101

(h) *Property.* — "Property" has the meaning stated in § 7-101 of this article.

REVISOR'S NOTE

This subsection is new language derived without substantive change from former Art. 27, § 140(g).

(i) *Representative drawer.* — "Representative drawer" means a person who signs a check as drawer in a representative capacity or as agent of the drawer.

REVISOR'S NOTE

This subsection is new language derived without substantive change from former Art. 27, § 140(h).

The defined term "drawer" is substituted for the former reference to "the person whose name appears thereon as principal drawer or obligor"

since by definition "a person whose name appears on a check as the primary obligor" is the "drawer".

Defined term:

"Person"   § 1-101

(j) *Service.* — "Service" includes:

    (1) labor or professional service;

    (2) telecommunication, public utility, toll facility, or transportation services;

    (3) lodging, entertainment, or restaurant service; and

    (4) the use of computers, data processing, or other equipment.

SPECIAL REVISOR'S NOTE

As enacted by Ch. 26, Acts of 2002, this subsection was new language derived without substantive change from former Art. 27, § 140(i). However, Ch. 42, Acts of 2002, added a new item (4) to this subsection, including in the definition of service "the use of computers, data processing, or other equipment".

The former words "but is not limited to" were deleted by Ch. 26 as surplusage in light of Art. 1, § 30.

The Criminal Law Article Review Committee noted, for the consideration of the General Assembly, that the definition of "service" in this subsection, though similar to that stated in § 7-101 of this article, did not explicitly include "the use of computers, data processing, or other equipment" found in § 7-101 of this article. Because other definitions in this section cross-reference parallel definitions in § 7-101 of this article, the General Assembly was asked to consider conforming this definition to the term "service" as defined in § 7-101 of this article for consistency in the treatment of theft and fraud crimes. Chapter 42 addressed this concern.

(k) *Value.* — "Value" has the meaning stated in § 7-103 of this article.

REVISOR'S NOTE

This subsection is new language derived without substantive change from former Art. 27, § 140(k).

(An. Code 1957, art. 27, § 140, 140(a)-(c), (e)-(k); 2002, ch. 26, § 2; ch. 42.)

REVISOR'S NOTE TO SECTION

The Revisor's notes in this section comprise information related to the revision by Acts 2002, ch. 26.

———

Cited in Moore v. State, 198 Md. App. 655, 18 A.3d 981 (2011).

§ 8-102. Rules of construction.

(a) *Insufficient funds.* — For purposes of this subtitle, a drawer has insufficient funds with a drawee to cover a check when the drawer has with the drawee:

(1) no account;

(2) only a closed account;

(3) no funds; or

(4) funds in an amount that is less than the amount needed to cover the check.

(b) *Insufficient funds — No account.* — A check dishonored for "no account" has been dishonored for "insufficient funds". (An. Code 1957, art. 27, § 140(d); 2002, ch. 26, § 2.)

REVISOR'S NOTE

This Revisor's note comprises information related to the revision by Acts 2002, ch. 26.

This section is new language derived without substantive change from former Art. 27, § 140(d).

In subsection (a) of this section, the introductory phrase "[f]or purposes of this subtitle" is added to clarify the scope of the subsection.

Also in subsection (a) of this section, the reference in the introductory language to "the drawer" is substituted for the former reference to the masculine pronoun "he" for clarity and gender neutrality.

Also in subsection (a) of this section, the former word "whatever" is deleted as surplusage.

Also in subsection (a) of this section, the references to funds and accounts "with the drawee" are added for clarity.

In subsection (b) of this section, the former word "also" is deleted as surplusage.

Defined terms:

"Check"	§ 8-101
"Drawer"	§ 8-101
"Funds"	§ 8-101

§ 8-103. Obtaining property or services by bad check.

(a) *Issuing check with knowledge of insufficient funds.* — A person may not obtain property or services by issuing a check if:

(1) the person knows that there are insufficient funds with the drawee to cover the check and other outstanding checks;

(2) the person intends or believes when issuing the check that payment will be refused by the drawee on presentment; and

(3) payment of the check is refused by the drawee on presentment.

(b) *Issuing check with intent to stop payment.* — A person may not obtain property or services by issuing a check if:

(1) when issuing the check, the person knows that the person or, in the case of a representative drawer, the person's principal intends, without the consent of the payee, to stop or countermand the payment of the check, or otherwise to cause the drawee to disregard, dishonor, or refuse to recognize the check; and

(2) payment is refused by the drawee on presentment.

(c) *Issuing check with intent that payment be refused — Check passed to third party.* — A person may not issue a check if:

(1) the check is in payment for services provided or to be provided by:

(i) an employee of the drawer or representative drawer; or

(ii) an independent contractor hired by the drawer or representative drawer;

(2) the drawer or representative drawer:

(i) intends or believes when issuing the check that payment will be refused by the drawee on presentment; or

(ii) knows that the drawer or, in the case of a representative drawer, the principal of the representative drawer has insufficient funds with the drawee to cover the check and other outstanding checks;

(3) the employee of the drawer or representative drawer or an independent contractor hired by the drawer or representative drawer passes the check to a third person; and

(4) payment is refused by the drawee on presentment.

(d) *Passing check with knowledge that drawer has insufficient funds.* — A person may not obtain property or services by passing a check if:

(1) the person knows that the drawer of the check has insufficient funds with the drawee to cover the check and other outstanding checks;

(2) the person intends or believes when passing the check that payment will be refused by the drawee on presentment; and

(3) payment of the check is refused by the drawee on presentment.

(e) *Passing check with knowledge of stopped payment or dishonor.* — A person may not obtain property or services by passing a check if:

    (1) the person knows that:

        (i) payment of the check has been stopped or countermanded; or

        (ii) the drawee of the check will disregard, dishonor, or refuse to recognize the check; and

    (2) payment is refused by the drawee on presentment. (An. Code 1957, art. 27, § 141; 2002, ch. 26, § 2; 2004, ch. 130.)

REVISOR'S NOTE

This Revisor's note comprises information related to the revision by Acts 2002, ch. 26.

This section is new language derived without substantive change from former Art. 27, § 141.

This section is restated in standard language used to describe a prohibited act.

In this section and throughout this subtitle, the word "when" is substituted for the former phrase "at the time of" for brevity.

Also in this section and throughout this subtitle, the references to "presentment" of a check are substituted for the former references to "presentation" of a check for consistency with provisions of the Uniform Commercial Code relating to checks and other negotiable instruments. *See, e.g.*, CL Title 3, Subtitle 5.

In subsections (a), (b), and (c) of this section, the former references to acting "[a]s a drawer or representative drawer" are deleted as surplusage in light of the definition of "issue".

In subsection (a)(1) of this section, the reference to knowing that "there are" insufficient funds is substituted for the former reference to knowing that "he or his principal, as the case may be, has" insufficient funds for clarity and brevity.

In subsection (b)(1) of this section, the reference to "the person or, in the case of a representative drawer, the person's principal" is sub-

stituted for the former reference to "he or his principal, as the case may be" for clarity and gender neutrality.

In subsection (c)(2)(i) of this section, the reference to "issuing the check" is substituted for the former reference to "utterance" for clarity.

In subsection (c)(2)(ii) of this section, the phrase "in the case of a representative drawer" is added and the former reference to the principal "of the drawer" is deleted to clarify that, with respect to a check, there is a "principal" only when the check is drawn by a "representative drawer".

In subsection (d)(1) of this section, the reference to the drawer "of the check" is substituted for the former reference to the drawer "thereof" for clarity.

Defined terms:

"Check"	§ 8-101
"Drawer"	§ 8-101
"Funds"	§ 8-101
"Issue"	§ 8-101
"Obtain"	§ 8-101
"Pass"	§ 8-101
"Person"	§ 1-101
"Property"	§ 8-101
"Representative drawer"	§ 8-101
"Service"	§ 8-101

§ 8-104. Obtaining property or services by bad check — Presumptions.

(a) *Presumption of knowledge of insufficient funds.* — The drawer or representative drawer is presumed to know that there are insufficient funds whenever the drawer of a check has insufficient funds with the drawee to cover the check and other outstanding checks when issuing the check.

(b) *Presumption of intent that check be dishonored.* — The drawer or representative drawer of a dishonored check is presumed to have intended or believed that the check would be dishonored on presentment if:

    (1) the drawer had no account with the drawee when issuing the check; or

    (2) (i) when issuing the check, the drawer had insufficient funds with the drawee to cover the check and other outstanding checks;

(ii) the check was presented to the drawee for payment not more than 30 days after the date of issuing the check; and

(iii) the drawer had insufficient funds with the drawee at the time of presentment.

(c) *Evidence of dishonor, lack of account, and insufficient funds.* — A notice of protest of a check, or a certificate under oath of an authorized representative of the drawee declaring the dishonor of a check, the drawer's lack of an account, or that the drawer had insufficient funds introduced in evidence is presumptive evidence, that:

(1) the check was dishonored by the drawee; and

(2) the drawer had:

(i) no account with the drawee when the check was issued; or

(ii) insufficient funds with the drawee at the time of presentment and issuing of the check.

(d) *Effect of intent to stop payment as evidence.* — The fact that a drawer or representative drawer, without the consent of the payee, stopped or counter-manded the payment of the check, or otherwise caused the drawee to disregard, dishonor, or refuse to recognize the check without returning or tendering the return of the property obtained, is presumptive evidence that the drawer or representative drawer had the intent when issuing the check to stop or countermand payment or otherwise cause the drawee to disregard, dishonor, or refuse to recognize the check. (An. Code 1957, art. 27, § 142; 2002, ch. 26, § 2.)

REVISOR'S NOTE

This Revisor's note comprises information related to the revision by Acts 2002, ch. 26.

This section is new language derived without substantive change from former Art. 27, § 142.

In subsections (a), (b), and (c) of this section, the references to "issuing" a check are substituted for the former references to "utterance" for clarity.

In subsections (a) and (b) of this section, the former references to a "subscribing" drawer are deleted as surplusage. Similarly, the former phrases "as the case may be" are deleted.

In subsections (a) and (c) of this section, the references to "insufficient funds" are substituted for the former references to "insuffi-ciency" for clarity and consistency of terminology within this subtitle.

In subsection (b) of this section, the former reference to "an ultimately" dishonored check is deleted as surplusage.

In subsection (c) of this section, the former reference to material "properly" introduced in evidence is deleted as surplusage.

In subsection (d) of this section, the reference to issuing "the check" is added for clarity and consistency throughout this subtitle.

Defined terms:

"Check"	§ 8-101
"Drawer"	§ 8-101
"Funds"	§ 8-101
"Issue"	§ 8-101
"Representative drawer"	§ 8-101

§ 8-105. Obtaining property or services by bad check — Limitation on prosecution.

(a) *In general — Prosecution as theft.* — A person who obtains property or services by issuing or passing a check in violation of § 8-103 of this subtitle may not be prosecuted under this article, if:

(1) other than falsely representing that there are sufficient funds with the drawee to cover the check, the issuing or passing of the check is not accompanied by a false representation; and

(2) the person who obtains the property or services makes the check good within 10 days after the drawee dishonors the check.

(b) *Delay of prosecution.* — (1) A prosecution may not be commenced against a person described in subsection (a) of this section earlier than 10 days after the drawee dishonors the check.

(2) A person who obtains property or services by issuing a check in violation of § 8-103 of this subtitle may be prosecuted immediately under this article, if the person issuing the check:

(i) is the drawer; and

(ii) did not have an account with the drawee when the check was issued.

(c) *Lesser included offense status not available unless charged.* — Unless specifically charged by the State, obtaining property or services with a value of less than $100 by issuing or passing a check in violation of § 8-103 of this subtitle, as provided in § 8-106(d) of this subtitle, may not be considered a lesser included crime of any other crime. (An. Code 1957, art. 27, § 144; 2002, ch. 26, § 2; 2004, ch. 130.)

REVISOR'S NOTE

This Revisor's note comprises information related to the revision by Acts 2002, ch. 26.

This section is new language derived without substantive change from former Art. 27, § 144.

In this section, the references to issuing or passing a check "in violation of § 8-103 of this subtitle" are added for clarity.

Also in this section, the references to "this article" are substituted for the former references to "the subheading 'theft' of this article, or. . . any other section of this article" for clarity and brevity.

In subsection (b)(1) of this section, the reference to a period of 10 days "after the drawee dishonors the check" is substituted for the former reference to "that period" for clarity.

Also in subsection (b)(1) of this section, the former reference to commencing prosecution "by warrant, information, indictment, or other charging document" is deleted as surplusage.

Defined terms:

"Check"	§ 8-101
"Drawer"	§ 8-101
"Funds"	§ 8-101
"Issue"	§ 8-101
"Obtain"	§ 8-101
"Pass"	§ 8-101
"Person"	§ 1-101
"Property"	§ 8-101
"Service"	§ 8-101

§ 8-106. Penalty.

(a) *Obtaining property or services with value of $500 or more — One check.* — A person who obtains property or services with a value of $500 or more by issuing or passing a check in violation of § 8-103 of this subtitle is guilty of a felony and on conviction is subject to imprisonment not exceeding 15 years or a fine not exceeding $1,000 or both.

(b) *Obtaining property or services with value of $500 or more — More than one check.* — A person who obtains property or services by issuing or passing more than one check in violation of § 8-103 of this subtitle is guilty of a felony and on conviction is subject to imprisonment not exceeding 15 years or a fine not exceeding $1,000 or both if:

(1) each check that is issued is for less than $500 and is issued to the same person within a 30-day period; and

(2) the cumulative value of the property or services is $500 or more.

(c) *Obtaining property or services — Value less than $500.* — Except as provided in subsections (b) and (d) of this section, a person who obtains property or services with a value of less than $500 by issuing or passing a check in violation of § 8-103 of this subtitle is guilty of a misdemeanor and on conviction is subject to imprisonment not exceeding 18 months or a fine not exceeding $100 or both.

(d) *Obtaining property or services — Value less than $100; certain defenses not available.* — (1) A person who obtains property or services with a value of less than $100 by issuing or passing a check in violation of § 8-103 of this subtitle is guilty of a misdemeanor and on conviction is subject to imprisonment not exceeding 90 days or a fine not exceeding $500 or both.

(2) It is not a defense to the crime of obtaining property or services with a value of less than $100 by issuing or passing a check in violation of § 8-103 of this subtitle that the value of the property or services at issue is $100 or more. (An. Code 1957, art. 27, § 143(a)-(c); 2002, ch. 26, § 2; 2004, ch. 130.)

REVISOR'S NOTE

This Revisor's note comprises information related to the revision by Acts 2002, ch. 26.

This section is new language derived without substantive change from former Art. 27, § 143(a) through (c).

In this section, references to issuing or passing a check "in violation of § 8-103 of this subtitle" are added for clarity.

Also in this section, the former references to "the discretion of the court" are deleted as implicit in the establishment of maximum penalties.

Defined terms:

"Check"	§ 8-101
"Issue"	§ 8-101
"Obtain"	§ 8-101
"Pass"	§ 8-101
"Person"	§ 1-101
"Property"	§ 8-101
"Service"	§ 8-101
"Value"	§ 8-101

§ 8-107. Penalty — Restoration of property; restitution; collection fee.

In addition to the penalties provided in § 8-106 of this subtitle, if a person obtains property or services by issuing or passing a check in violation of § 8-103 of this subtitle, on conviction, the court:

(1) if the property has been recovered or is in the defendant's possession or control, may order restoration of the property to any person with a property interest in it;

(2) to the extent that the property is not restored or compensation has not been provided for the services, may order restitution of the value of the property or services obtained to be paid to:

(i) any person having a property interest in the property; or

(ii) the person who provided the services; and

(3) may order the defendant to pay a collection fee of up to $35, for each check, to:

(i) any person with a property interest in the property; or

(ii) the person who provided the services. (An. Code 1957, art. 27, § 143(d); 2002, ch. 26, § 2.)

REVISOR'S NOTE

This Revisor's note comprises information related to the revision by Acts 2002, ch. 26.

This section is new language derived without substantive change from former Art. 27, § 143(d).

In this section, the reference to issuing or passing a check "in violation of § 8-103 of this subtitle" is added for clarity.

Also in this section, the former references to property or services "which has been the object of the offense" are deleted as surplusage.

Also in this section, the former reference to property recovered "from the defendant or another" is deleted as surplusage.

Defined terms:

"Check"	§ 8-101
"Issue"	§ 8-101
"Obtain"	§ 8-101
"Pass"	§ 8-101
"Person"	§ 1-101
"Property"	§ 8-101
"Service"	§ 8-101
"Value"	§ 8-101

§ 8-108. Paying court fines or costs with bad check.

(a) *Prohibited.* — A person may not pay a fine or cost imposed by a court by delivering a check issued by the person or another person if:

(1) the person knows that payment of the check has not been provided for; and

(2) payment of the check is refused by the drawee on presentment.

(b) *Penalty.* — A person who violates this section is guilty of a misdemeanor and on conviction is subject to imprisonment not exceeding 60 days or a fine not exceeding $100 or both. (2004, ch. 26, § 2.)

REVISOR'S NOTE

This Revisor's note comprises information related to the revision by Acts 2002, ch. 26.

This section is new language derived without substantive change from former Art. 38, § 4B.

This section is revised for consistency with similar provisions found in this subtitle.

In subsection (a) of this section, the defined term "check" is substituted for the former reference to a "[c]heck, draft, or other negotiable instrument of any kind" for clarity and brevity. See § 8-101(b) of this subtitle.

In subsection (a)(1) of this section, the reference to a "drawee" is substituted for the former reference to "such person or by any other person, firm, or corporation" for clarity and brevity.

Also in subsection (a)(1) of this section, the reference to "know[ing] that there are insufficient funds with the drawee to cover the check and other outstanding checks" is substituted for the former reference to "know[ing] that the bank, person, firm, or corporation is not indebted to the drawer" for clarity.

In subsection (b) of this section, the former reference to "the discretion of the court" is deleted as implicit in establishing maximum penalties.

Subtitle 2. Credit Card Crimes.

Part I. General Provisions.

§ 8-201. Definitions.

(a) *In general.* — In this subtitle the following words have the meanings indicated.

This subsection is standard language substituted for the introductory language of former Art. 27, § 145(a).

The reference to "this subtitle" is substituted for the former reference to this "section", although this subtitle is derived, in part, from material outside former Art. 27, § 145. The only uses of the terms defined in this section in material that is not derived from former § 145 are either easily distinguishable from the defined term, as in the use of "telephone credit card" in § 8-210 derived from former Art. 27, § 557A, or are consistent with the definitions in this section, as in "credit card" and "issuer" in Part II of this subtitle, derived from former CL §§ 14-1401 through 14-1405. No substantive change is intended.

(b) *Cardholder.* — "Cardholder" means the person named on the face of a credit card to whom or for whose benefit the credit card is issued by an issuer.

This subsection is new language derived without substantive change from former Art. 27, § 145(a) (1).

The former reference to an "organization" is deleted in light of the defined term "person".

Defined term:
"Person" § 1-101

(c) *Credit card.* — (1) "Credit card" means an instrument or device issued by an issuer for the use of a cardholder in obtaining money, goods, services, or anything of value on credit.

(2) "Credit card" includes:

(i) a debit card, access card, or other device for use by a cardholder to effect a transfer of funds through an electronic terminal, telephone, or computer;

(ii) a magnetic tape that orders or authorizes a financial institution to debit or credit an account; and

(iii) a code, account number, or other means of account access that is not encoded or truncated and can be used to:

1. obtain money, goods, services, or anything of value; or

2. initiate a transfer of funds.

(3) "Credit card" does not include a check, draft, or similar paper instrument.

This subsection is new language derived without substantive change from former Art. 27, § 145(a) (2) and (5).

In paragraph (2)(i) of this subsection, the reference to a device "for use by" a cardholder is substituted for the former reference to a device "used by" a cardholder for accuracy. The Criminal Law Article Review Committee calls this substitution to the attention of the General Assembly.

Also in paragraph (2)(i) of this subsection, the former reference to "instructing" a financial institution is deleted as included in the reference to "order[ing]".

The former term "payment device number" which was defined in former Art. 27, § 145(a) (5) is revised as part of the defined term "credit card", derived from former § 145(a) (2), because it was used once in former Art. 27, § 145 and only in the latter definition. The term "payment device number" in former Art. 27, § 145(a) (5) excluded an "encoded or truncated number", while the same term in former CL § 14-1401 — now in Part II of this subtitle — did not exclude them. Except as otherwise specifically provided, in Part II of this subtitle the explicit references to a "credit card number or payment device number" includes these encoded or truncated numbers.

(d) *Issuer.* — "Issuer" means a business organization or financial institution that issues a credit card or the authorized agent of the business organization or financial institution.

REVISOR'S NOTE

This subsection is new language derived without substantive change from former Art. 27, § 145(a)(3).

The second reference to "the business organization or financial institution" is substituted for the former word "its" for clarity.

The former word "duly" is deleted as implicit in the reference to an "authorized" agent.

(An. Code 1957, art. 27, § 145(a), (a)(1)-(3), (5); 2002, ch. 26, § 2.)

REVISOR'S NOTE TO SECTION

The Revisor's notes in this section comprise information related to the revision by Acts 2002, ch. 26.

Former Art. 27, § 145(a)(4) which defined "[r]eceives or receiving" to mean "acquiring possession or control of a credit card" is deleted

as unnecessary in light of the commonly understood meaning of the terms and because the substantive provisions of this subtitle are explicit with respect to receiving "a credit card". *See, e.g.,* § 8-204(a)(1)(ii), (b), and (d) of this subtitle.

§ 8-202. Rules of construction.

(a) *Course of conduct.* — If a person violates §§ 8-203 through 8-209 of this subtitle as part of one scheme or a continuing course of conduct, from the same or several sources:

(1) the conduct may be considered as one violation; and

(2) the value of money, goods, services, or things of value may be aggregated in determining if the crime is a felony or a misdemeanor.

(b) *Applicability.* — Sections 8-203 through 8-209 of this subtitle may not be construed to preclude the applicability of any other provision of the criminal law of this State that applies or may apply to any transaction that violates §§ 8-203 through 8-209 of this subtitle, unless that provision is inconsistent with §§ 8-203 through 8-209 of this subtitle. (An. Code 1957, art. 27, § 145(i), (j); 2002, ch. 26, § 2.)

REVISOR'S NOTE

This Revisor's note comprises information related to the revision by Acts 2002, ch. 26.

This section is new language derived without substantive change from former Art. 27, § 145(i) and (j).

Throughout this section, the references to "[§§] 8-203 through 8-209 of this subtitle" are substituted for the former references to "this section" to reflect the reorganization of substantive material derived from former Art. 27, § 145 in those provisions.

Former Art. 27, § 145(k), which provided for the severability of provisions of former Art. 27, § 145, is deleted in light of Art. 1, § 23, which provides that all legislation enacted after July 1, 1979 is presumed to be severable absent specific language to the contrary, and in light of the standard rule of judicial construction favoring severability even in the absence of a severability clause in the statute. *See, e.g., Turner v. State,* 299 Md. 565 (1984): "Perhaps the most important of these principles [of statutory construction] is the presumption, even in the absence of an express clause or declaration, that a legislative body generally intends its enactments to be severed if possible. Moreover, when the dominant purpose of an enactment may largely be carried out, notwithstanding the statute's partial invalidity, courts will generally hold the valid portions severable and enforce

them." 299 Md. 565, 576. The Criminal Law Article Review Committee calls this deletion to the attention of the General Assembly.

Defined term:
"Person"   § 1-101

§ 8-203. Fraud in procuring issuance of credit card.

(a) *Prohibited.* — A person may not make or cause to be made, directly or indirectly, a false statement in writing about the identity of the person or of another to procure the issuance of a credit card:

(1) knowing the statement to be false; and

(2) with the intent that the statement be relied on.

(b) *Penalty.* — A person who violates this section is guilty of a misdemeanor and on conviction is subject to imprisonment not exceeding 18 months or a fine not exceeding $500 or both. (An. Code 1957, art. 27, § 145(b), (h)(1); 2002, ch. 26, § 2.)

REVISOR'S NOTE

This Revisor's note comprises information related to the revision by Acts 2002, ch. 26.

This section is new language derived without substantive change from former Art. 27, § 145(b) and (h)(1).

In the introductory language of this section, the former reference to a "firm or corporation" is deleted in light of the defined term "person".

Defined terms:
"Credit card"   § 8-201
"Person"   § 1-101

§ 8-204. Credit card theft.

(a) *Taking credit card from another; receiving credit card taken from another with intent to sell.* — (1) A person may not:

(i) take a credit card from another, or from the possession, custody, or control of another without the consent of the cardholder; or

(ii) with knowledge that a credit card has been taken under the circumstances described in item (i) of this paragraph, receive the credit card with the intent to use it or sell or transfer it to another who is not the issuer or the cardholder.

(2) A person who violates this subsection is guilty of credit card theft.

(b) *Receiving credit card known to have been lost or misdelivered.* — (1) A person may not receive a credit card that the person knows was lost, mislaid, or delivered under a mistake as to the identity or address of the cardholder and retain possession of the credit card with the intent to use, sell, or transfer it to another who is not the issuer or the cardholder.

(2) A person who violates this subsection is guilty of credit card theft.

(c) *Buying and selling of credit cards.* — A person may not:

(1) sell a credit card unless the person is the issuer; or

(2) buy a credit card from a person other than the issuer.

(d) *Receiving credit card with knowledge of credit card theft or other violations.* — A person other than the issuer may not receive a credit card that the person knows was taken or retained under circumstances that constitute:

(1) credit card theft;

(2) a violation of § 8-203 of this subtitle; or

(3) a violation of subsection (c) of this section.

(e) *Penalty.* — A person who violates this section is guilty of a misdemeanor and on conviction is subject to imprisonment not exceeding 18 months or a fine not exceeding $500 or both. (An. Code 1957, art. 27, § 145(c)(1)-(4), (h)(1); 2002, ch. 26, § 2.)

REVISOR'S NOTE

This Revisor's note comprises information related to the revision by Acts 2002, ch. 26.

This section is new language derived without substantive change from former Art. 27, § 145(c)(1), (2), (3), and (4) and (h)(1).

In subsection (a) of this section, the reference to a credit card "taken under the circumstances described in item (i) of this paragraph" is sub-stituted for the former reference to "so taken" for clarity.

Defined terms:

"Cardholder"	§ 8-201
"Credit card"	§ 8-201
"Issuer"	§ 8-201
"Person"	§ 1-101

Merger. — Crimes of receiving a stolen credit card and theft of less than $500 share the elements of knowledge, possession of stolen property, and intention to use property to deprive the owner of its use. Since receiving a stolen credit card required an additional element that the item stolen was a credit card, defendant's theft conviction should have merged into the credit card conviction. Moore v. State, 163 Md. App. 305, 878 A.2d 678 (2005).

§ 8-205. Credit card counterfeiting.

(a) *Definitions.* — (1) In this section the following words have the meanings indicated.

(2) "Falsely emboss" means to complete a credit card without the authorization of the issuer named on the credit card by adding any of the matter, other than the signature of the cardholder, that the issuer requires to appear on a credit card before it can be used by a cardholder.

(3) "Falsely make" means:

(i) to make or draw, wholly or partly, a device or instrument that purports to be a credit card but that is not a credit card because an issuer did not authorize the making or drawing; or

(ii) to alter a credit card that was validly issued.

(b) *Falsely making or embossing credit card; transferring or possessing credit card with knowledge of falsity — Prohibited.* — A person may not, with the intent to defraud another:

(1) falsely make a purported credit card;

(2) falsely emboss a credit card; or

(3) transfer or possess:

(i) a falsely made instrument or device that purports to be a credit card, with knowledge that the instrument or device was falsely made; or

(ii) a falsely embossed credit card with knowledge that the credit card was falsely made or falsely embossed.

(c) *Signature by other than cardholder — Prohibited.* — A person other than the cardholder or one authorized by the cardholder may not sign a credit card with the intent to defraud another.

(d) *Penalty.* — A person who violates this section is guilty of the felony of credit card counterfeiting and on conviction is subject to imprisonment not exceeding 15 years or a fine not exceeding $1,000 or both. (An. Code 1957, art. 27, § 145(c)(5), (6), (h)(2); 2002, ch. 26, § 2.)

REVISOR'S NOTE

This Revisor's note comprises information related to the revision by Acts 2002, ch. 26.

This section is new language derived without substantive change from former Art. 27, § 145(c)(5) and (6) and (h)(2).

Subsection (a) of this section is revised in standard language used to define terms.

In subsection (a)(3) of this section, the reference to the credit card "of the issuer" is substituted for the former reference to "such" credit card for clarity.

In subsection (b) of this section, the former reference to "a purported issuer, a person or organization providing money, goods, services or anything else of value, or any other" person is deleted as included in the comprehensive reference to a "person". Similarly, in subsection (c) of this section, the former reference to "the issuer, or a person or organization providing money, goods, services or anything else of value, or any other" person is deleted as included in the comprehensive reference to a "person". *See* § 1-101 of this article.

In subsection (b)(3) of this section, the reference to "transfer[ring]" a false credit card is substituted for the former reference to "utter[ing]" a false credit card for clarity.

In subsection (d) of this section, the reference to credit card "counterfeiting" is substituted for the former reference to credit card "forgery" for consistency within this article.

Defined terms:

"Cardholder"	§ 8-201
"Counterfeit"	§ 1-101
"Credit card"	§ 8-201
"Issuer"	§ 8-201
"Person"	§ 1-101

§ 8-206. Obtaining property by counterfeiting, theft, or misrepresentation.

(a) *Prohibited — Use of stolen or counterfeit card.* — A person may not for the purpose of obtaining money, goods, services, or anything of value, and with the intent to defraud another, use:

(1) a credit card obtained or retained in violation of § 8-204 or § 8-205 of this subtitle; or

(2) a credit card that the person knows is counterfeit.

(b) *Prohibited — False representation.* — A person may not, with the intent to defraud another, obtain money, goods, services, or anything of value by representing:

(1) without the consent of the cardholder, that the person is the holder of a specified credit card; or

(2) that the person is the holder of a credit card when the credit card had not been issued.

(c) *Penalty.* — (1) If the value of all money, goods, services, and other things of value obtained in violation of this section exceeds $500, a person who violates this section is guilty of a felony and on conviction is subject to imprisonment not exceeding 15 years or a fine not exceeding $1,000 or both.

(2) Except as provided in paragraph (3) of this subsection, if the value of all money, goods, services, and other things of value obtained in violation of this section does not exceed $500, a person who violates this section is guilty of a misdemeanor and on conviction is subject to imprisonment not exceeding 18 months or a fine not exceeding $500 or both.

(3) If the value of all money, goods, services, and other things of value obtained in violation of this section does not exceed $100, a person who violates this section is guilty of a misdemeanor and on conviction is subject to imprisonment not exceeding 90 days or a fine not exceeding $500 or both. (An. Code 1957, art. 27, § 145(d), (h); 2002, ch. 26, § 2; 2004, ch. 130.)

REVISOR'S NOTE

This Revisor's note comprises information related to the revision by Acts 2002, ch. 26.

This section is new language derived without substantive change from former Art. 27, § 145(d) and (h).

In the introductory language of subsections (a) and (b) of this section, the former reference to "the issuer, a person or organization providing money, goods, services or anything else of value, or any other" person is deleted as included in the comprehensive reference to a "person". *See* § 1-101 of this article.

In subsection (a)(2) of this section, the reference to a "counterfeit" credit card is substituted for the former reference to a "forged" credit card for consistency within this article.

In subsection (b) of this section, the references to a "credit card" are substituted for the former references to a "card" for consistency throughout this subtitle.

Defined terms:

"Cardholder"	§ 8-201
"Counterfeit"	§ 1-101
"Credit card"	§ 8-201
"Person"	§ 1-101

Cited in Keys v. State, 195 Md. App. 19, 5 A.3d 1113 (2010).

§ 8-207. Fraud — Honoring stolen or counterfeit credit card; false representation to issuer.

(a) *Prohibited.* — If a person is authorized by an issuer to furnish money, goods, services, or anything of value on presentation of a credit card by the cardholder, the person or an agent or employee of the person may not, with the intent to defraud the issuer or cardholder:

(1) furnish money, goods, services, or anything of value on presentation of:

(i) a credit card obtained or retained in violation of § 8-204 or § 8-205 of this subtitle; or

(ii) a credit card that the person knows is counterfeit; or

(2) fail to furnish money, goods, services, or anything of value that the person represents in writing to the issuer that the person has furnished.

(b) *Penalty.* — (1) If the value of all money, goods, services, and other things of value furnished or not furnished in violation of this section exceeds $500, a person who violates this section is guilty of a felony and on conviction is subject to imprisonment not exceeding 15 years or a fine not exceeding $1,000 or both.

(2) Except as provided in paragraph (3) of this subsection, if the value of all money, goods, services, and other things of value furnished or not furnished in violation of this section does not exceed $500, a person who violates this section is guilty of a misdemeanor and on conviction is subject to imprisonment not exceeding 18 months or a fine not exceeding $500 or both.

(3) If the value of all money, goods, services, and other things of value furnished or not furnished in violation of this section does not exceed $100, a person who violates this section is guilty of a misdemeanor and on conviction is subject to imprisonment not exceeding 90 days or a fine not exceeding $500 or both. (An. Code 1957, art. 27, § 145(e), (h); 2002, ch. 26, § 2; 2004, ch. 130.)

REVISOR'S NOTE

This Revisor's note comprises information related to the revision by Acts 2002, ch. 26.

This section is new language derived without substantive change from former Art. 27, § 145(e) and (h).

In subsection (a)(1)(ii) of this section, the reference to a "counterfeit" credit card is substituted for the former reference to a "forged" credit card for consistency within this article.

Defined terms:

"Cardholder"	§ 8-201
"Counterfeit"	§ 1-101
"Credit card"	§ 8-201
"Issuer"	§ 8-201
"Person"	§ 1-101

§ 8-208. Completing credit card without consent; possessing contrivance to reproduce credit card without consent.

(a) *"Incomplete credit card" defined.* — In this section, "incomplete credit card" means a credit card that lacks any stamped, embossed, imprinted, or written matter, other than the signature of the cardholder, that an issuer requires to appear on a credit card before a cardholder can use the credit card.

(b) *Prohibited.* — (1) Without the consent of the issuer, a person other than the cardholder may not possess an incomplete credit card with the intent to complete it.

(2) A person may not possess, with knowledge of its character, machinery, plates, or any other contrivance designed to reproduce an instrument purporting to be a credit card of an issuer that has not consented to the preparation of the credit card.

(c) *Penalty.* — A person who violates this section is guilty of a felony and on conviction is subject to imprisonment not exceeding 15 years or a fine not exceeding $1,000 or both. (An. Code 1957, art. 27, § 145(f), (h)(2); 2002, ch. 26, § 2.)

REVISOR'S NOTE

This Revisor's note comprises information related to the revision by Acts 2002, ch. 26.

This section is new language derived without substantive change from former Art. 27, § 145(f) and (h)(2).

Subsection (a) of this section is revised in standard language used to define a term.

In subsection (a) of this section, the reference to the "signature" of the cardholder is substituted for the former reference to the "name" of the cardholder for clarity in light of the definition of "cardholder".

The Criminal Law Article Review Committee notes, for the consideration of the General Assembly, that the prohibition against possessing machinery, plates, or any other contrivance to make a credit card without consent of an issuer in subsection (b)(2) of this subtitle appears to preclude a person from entering into or engaging in the legitimate business of manu-facturing credit card making equipment without the prior approval of a credit card issuer.

Defined terms:

"Cardholder"	§ 8-201
"Credit card"	§ 8-201
"Issuer"	§ 8-201
"Person"	§ 1-101

§ 8-209. Receiving property by stolen, counterfeit, or misrepresented credit card.

(a) *Prohibited.* — A person may not receive money, goods, services, or anything of value if the person knows or believes that the money, goods, services, or other thing of value was obtained in violation of § 8-206 of this subtitle.

(b) *Penalty.* — (1) If the value of all money, goods, services, and other things of value obtained in violation of this section exceeds $500, a person who violates this section is guilty of a felony and on conviction is subject to imprisonment not exceeding 15 years or a fine not exceeding $1,000 or both.

(2) Except as provided in paragraph (3) of this subsection, if the value of all money, goods, services, and other things of value obtained in violation of this section does not exceed $500, a person who violates this section is guilty of a misdemeanor and on conviction is subject to imprisonment not exceeding 18 months or a fine not exceeding $500 or both.

(3) If the value of all money, goods, services, and other things of value obtained in violation of this section does not exceed $100, a person who violates this section is guilty of a misdemeanor and on conviction is subject to imprisonment not exceeding 90 days or a fine not exceeding $500 or both. (An. Code 1957, art. 27, § 145(g), (h); 2002, ch. 26, § 2; 2004, ch. 130.)

REVISOR'S NOTE

This Revisor's note comprises information related to the revision by Acts 2002, ch. 26.

This section is new language derived without substantive change from former Art. 27, § 145(g) and (h).

Defined term:

"Person"	§ 1-101

Cited in Keys v. State, 195 Md. App. 19, 5 A.3d 1113 (2010).

§ 8-210. Publishing number or code of telephone credit card.

(a) *"Publish" defined.* — In this section, "publish" means to communicate information to one or more persons:

(1) orally:

(i) in person; or

(ii) by telephone, radio, or television; or

(2) in a writing of any kind.

(b) *Prohibited.* — A person may not publish or cause to be published the number or code of an existing, canceled, revoked, expired, or nonexistent telephone credit card, or the numbering or coding system that is used in issuing telephone credit cards, with the intent that the number, code, or system be used or with knowledge that it may be used fraudulently to avoid paying a lawful toll charge.

(c) *Penalty.* — A person who violates this section is guilty of a misdemeanor and on conviction is subject to imprisonment not exceeding 12 months or a fine not exceeding $500 or both. (An. Code 1957, art. 27, § 557A; 2002, ch. 26, § 2.)

REVISOR'S NOTE

This Revisor's note comprises information related to the revision by Acts 2002, ch. 26.

This section is new language derived without substantive change from former Art. 27, § 557A.

In subsection (a) of this section, the former reference to a writing "including without limitation a letter or memorandum, circular or handbill, newspaper or magazine article, or book" is deleted as included in the reference to "a writing of any kind".

In subsection (b) of this section, the reference to "number, code, or system" is substituted for the former reference to "it" for clarity.

In subsection (c) of this section, the former phrase "in the discretion of the court" is deleted as implicit in the establishment of maximum penalties.

Defined term:
"Person"   § 1-101

§ 8-211. Prohibited defenses; lesser included crime status not available.

(a) *Certain defenses prohibited.* — It is not a defense to a crime under § 8-206, § 8-207, or § 8-209 of this subtitle involving money, goods, services, and other things of value with a value not exceeding $100 that the value of the money, goods, services, and other things of value at issue is more than $100.

(b) *Lesser included crime status not available unless charged.* — Unless specifically charged by the State, a violation of § 8-206, § 8-207, or § 8-209 of this subtitle involving money, goods, services, and other things of value with a value not exceeding $100, may not be considered a lesser included crime of any other crime. (2004, ch. 130.)

§ 8-212.

Reserved.

Part II. Credit Card Number Protection.

§ 8-213. Definitions.

(a) *In general.* — In this part the following words have the meanings indicated.

REVISOR'S NOTE

This subsection formerly was CL § 14-1401(a).

The only changes are in style.

(b) *Authorized use, disclosure, or receipt.* — "Authorized use, disclosure, or receipt" means any use, disclosure, or receipt necessary to accomplish the specific purpose for which the person issued a credit card number or payment device number, or granted to another the right to use, disclose, or receive the credit card number or other payment device number.

REVISOR'S NOTE

This subsection formerly was CL § 14-1401(b).

The conjunction "or" is added between the term "payment device number" and the phrase "granted to another" for clarity.

No other changes are made.

Defined terms:
"Credit card"	§ 8-201
"Person"	§ 1-101

(c) *Holder.* — "Holder" means a person who:

(1) has been issued a credit card number or other payment device number; or

(2) is authorized by the person who has been issued a credit card number or other payment device number to use, disclose, or receive that credit card number or payment device number.

REVISOR'S NOTE

This subsection formerly was CL § 14-1401(d).

The only changes are in style.

Defined terms:
"Credit card"	§ 8-201
"Person"	§ 1-101

(d) *Holder's signature.* — (1) "Holder's signature" means the signature of a holder in connection with a credit application or credit card transaction.

(2) "Holder's signature" includes an electronically recorded signature.

REVISOR'S NOTE

This subsection is new language derived without substantive change from former CL § 14-1401(e).

Defined term:
"Credit card"	§ 8-201

(e) *Payment device number.* — "Payment device number" means a code, account number, or other means of account access, other than a check, draft, or similar paper instrument, that can be used to obtain money, goods, services, or anything of value, or for purposes of initiating a transfer of funds.

REVISOR'S NOTE

This subsection formerly was the first sentence of CL § 14-1401(c).

The only changes are in style.

The Criminal Law Article Review Committee notes, for the consideration of the General Assembly, that the definition of "payment device number" in this subsection differs from the definition of the same term in former Art. 27, § 145(a)(5), in that the latter definition excluded an "encoded or truncated credit card number or payment device number". The distinction is that this part, derived from former

CL §§ 14-1401 through 14-1405, prohibits certain disclosures and activities relating to information about credit card and similar accounts, whereas §§ 8-203 through 8-209 of this subtitle, derived from former Art. 27, § 145, prohibit certain uses of credit cards and similar account access devices. Former § 145(a)(5) is incorporated into the term "credit card" defined in § 8-201 of this subtitle. *See* Revisor's Note to § 8-201(c) of this subtitle.

(f) *Person.* — (1) "Person" has the meaning stated in § 1-101 of this article.

(2) "Person" includes a business trust, statutory trust, estate, trust, and two or more persons having a joint or common interest.

REVISOR'S NOTE

Paragraph (1) of this subsection is new language substituted for the former reference to an "individual, corporation,... partnership, association,... or any other legal or commercial entity" in former CL § 14-1401(f) for clarity.

Paragraph (2) of this subsection is revised to incorporate the remainder of former CL § 14-1401(f) to the extent not covered by the term "person" defined in § 1-101 of this article.

Defined term:

"Person"   § 1-101

(An. Code 1957, art. CL, § 14-1401; 2002, ch. 26, § 2; 2010, ch. 611, § 2.)

REVISOR'S NOTE TO SECTION

The Revisor's notes in this section comprise information related to the revision by Acts 2002, ch. 26.

Effect of amendments. — Section 2, ch. 611, Acts 2010, effective June 1, 2010, added "statutory trust" in (f)(2).

§ 8-214. Prohibited — Unauthorized use or disclosure.

(a) *In general; exceptions.* — A person may not use or disclose any credit card number or other payment device number or holder's signature unless:

(1) the person is the holder of the credit card number or payment device number;

(2) the disclosure is made to the holder or issuer of the credit card number or payment device number;

(3) the use or disclosure is:

(i) required under federal or State law;

(ii) at the direction of a governmental unit in accordance with law; or

(iii) in response to the order of a court having jurisdiction to issue the order;

(4) the disclosure is in connection with an authorization, processing, billing, collection, chargeback, insurance collection, fraud prevention, or credit card or payment device recovery that relates to the credit card number or payment device number, an account accessed by the credit card number or payment account number, a debt for which the holder or a person authorized by the holder gave the credit card number or payment device number for purposes of identification, or a debt or obligation arising, alone or in conjunc-

tion with another means of payment, from the use of the credit card number or payment device number;

(5) except as provided in subsection (b) of this section, the disclosure is reasonably necessary in connection with:

(i) the sale or pledge, or negotiation of the sale or pledge, of any portion of a business or the assets of a business;

(ii) the management, operation, or other activities involving the internal functioning of the person making the disclosure; or

(iii) the management, operation, or other activities involving disclosures between a corporation and its subsidiaries or controlled affiliates or between the subsidiaries or the controlled affiliates;

(6) the disclosure is made to a consumer reporting agency, as defined in § 14-1201 of the Commercial Law Article;

(7) subject to subsection (d) of this section, whether or not the person is a consumer reporting agency and whether or not the disclosure is a consumer report, the disclosure is made under a circumstance specified in the credit reporting provisions of § 14-1202(3)(i), (ii), (iii), or (iv) of the Commercial Law Article; or

(8) the disclosure is allowed under § 1-303 of the Financial Institutions Article.

(b) *Disclosure for marketing against holder's direction.* — A disclosure for marketing purposes may not be made if the holder of an active credit card number or payment device number has prohibited the issuer in writing at the issuer's address from using the card or number for marketing purposes.

(c) *Notification of nondisclosure option required.* — (1) Notwithstanding subsection (a)(5)(iii) of this section, a disclosure for marketing purposes may not be made if the holder of an active credit card number or payment device number, other than an encoded credit card number or encoded payment device number, has notified the issuer in writing at an address specified by the issuer, that disclosure for marketing purposes is not allowed.

(2) The issuer shall notify each holder of an active credit card number or payment device number of the nondisclosure option and the specified address on a periodic basis at the issuer's discretion at least once each year.

(3) The issuer shall comply with the holder's election within 45 days after receiving the holder's response.

(4) The election shall remain in effect until the holder rescinds the election or until there have been no debits or credits to the credit card number or payment device number for a 12-month period.

(d) *Disclosure relating to credit reporting — Requirements.* — Notwithstanding subsection (a)(7) of this section, and except as provided in § 14-1202(3)(i) of the Commercial Law Article, a person may not furnish a report containing a credit card number or payment device number before receiving an individual written, electronic, or other tangible record of a certification from the requestor:

(1) containing the reason that the credit card number or payment device number is required; and

(2) stating that the credit card number or payment device number:

(i) cannot be obtained under a circumstance specified under this part or Title 14 of the Commercial Law Article; or

(ii) is needed for security, or loss or fraud prevention purposes. (An. Code 1957, art. CL, §§ 14-1401(c), 14-1402; 2002, ch. 26, § 2.)

REVISOR'S NOTE

This Revisor's note comprises information related to the revision by Acts 2002, ch. 26.

This section is new language derived without substantive change from former CL § 14-1402 and the second sentence of § 14-1401(c).

In subsection (a)(3)(i) of this section, the reference to a disclosure "required by" federal or State law is substituted for the former reference to a disclosure "pursuant to obligation under" federal or State law for brevity.

In subsection (c)(2) and (4) of this section, the references to a "credit card number or payment device number" are substituted for the former references to an "account" for consistency within this part.

In subsection (d)(2)(i) of this section, the reference to "this part or Title 14 of the Commercial Law Article" is substituted for the former erroneous reference to this "title" for accuracy.

For provisions on disclosures relating to consumer credit reporting agencies, *see* CL Title 14, Subtitle 12.

Defined terms:

"Credit card"	§ 8-201
"Holder"	§ 8-213
"Holder's signature"	§ 8-213
"Payment device number"	§ 8-213
"Person"	§§ 1-101, 8-213

§ 8-214.1. Use of affidavit by credit cardholder in criminal case or juvenile proceeding.

(a) *In general.* — In a criminal case or juvenile proceeding involving a violation of § 8-204, § 8-205, § 8-206, § 8-207, § 8-208, § 8-209, § 8-210, or § 8-214 of this subtitle or § 8-301 of this title, an affidavit sworn to by a lawful credit cardholder may be introduced as substantive evidence that the credit card or credit card number was taken, used, or possessed without the authorization of the credit cardholder.

(b) *Notice.* — (1) At least 10 days before a proceeding in which the State intends to introduce into evidence an affidavit as provided under this section, the State shall provide written notice to the defendant that the State intends to:

(i) rely on the affidavit; and

(ii) introduce the affidavit into evidence at the proceeding.

(2) On written demand of a defendant filed at least 5 days before the proceeding described in subsection (a) of this section, the State shall require the presence of the affiant as a prosecution witness. (2006, ch. 257; 2008, ch. 36, § 6; chs. 354, 355.)

§ 8-215. Prohibited — Possession with unlawful intent.

Repealed by Acts 2002, ch. 509, § 1, effective Oct. 1, 2002.

Cross references. — For present law, see § 8-301 of this article.

§ 8-216. Criminal penalty.

A person who violates this part is guilty of a felony and on conviction is subject to imprisonment not exceeding 15 years or a fine not exceeding $1,000 or both. (An. Code 1957, art. CL, § 14-1404; 2002, ch. 26, § 2.)

REVISOR'S NOTE

This Revisor's note comprises information related to the revision by Acts 2002, ch. 26.

This section formerly was CL § 14-1404.

The reference to this "part" is substituted for the former erroneous reference to this "title" for accuracy.

The only other changes are in style.

Defined term:

"Person"	§§ 1-101, 8-213

§ 8-217. Civil penalty; injunction.

(a) *Civil penalty.* — (1) The Attorney General may institute a civil action against a person who violates this part to recover for the State a civil penalty not exceeding $1,000 for each violation.

(2) For the purposes of this subsection, each prohibited disclosure or use of a credit card number, payment device number, or holder's signature is an independent violation.

(b) *Injunction.* — The Attorney General may seek an injunction in a civil action to prohibit a person who has engaged or is engaged in a violation of this part from engaging in the violation. (An. Code 1957, art. CL, § 14-1405; 2002, ch. 26, § 2.)

REVISOR'S NOTE

This Revisor's note comprises information related to the revision by Acts 2002, ch. 26.

This section formerly was CL § 14-1405.

In subsection (a)(1) of this section, the reference to a "civil" penalty is added for clarity.

In subsection (a)(2) of this section, the former word "other" which modified "payment device number" is deleted as surplusage.

The only other changes are in style.

Defined terms:

"Credit card"	§ 8-201
"Holder's signature"	§ 8-213
"Payment device number"	§ 8-213
"Person"	§§ 1-101, 8-213

Subtitle 3. Identity Fraud.

§ 8-301. Identity fraud.

(a) *Definitions.* — (1) In this section the following words have the meanings indicated.

(2) "Payment device number" has the meaning stated in § 8-213 of this title.

(3) "Personal identifying information" includes a name, address, telephone number, driver's license number, Social Security number, place of employment, employee identification number, mother's maiden name, bank or other financial institution account number, date of birth, personal identification number, credit card number, or other payment device number.

(4) "Re-encoder" means an electronic device that places encoded personal identifying information or a payment device number from the magnetic strip or stripe of a credit card onto the magnetic strip or stripe of a different credit card or any electronic medium that allows such a transaction to occur.

(5) "Skimming device" means a scanner, skimmer, reader, or any other electronic device that is used to access, read, scan, obtain, memorize, or store, temporarily or permanently, personal identifying information or a payment device number encoded on the magnetic strip or stripe of a credit card.

(b) *Prohibited — Obtaining personal identifying information without consent.* — A person may not knowingly, willfully, and with fraudulent intent possess, obtain, or help another to possess or obtain any personal identifying information of an individual, without the consent of the individual, in order to use, sell, or transfer the information to get a benefit, credit, good, service, or other thing of value in the name of the individual.

(c) *Prohibited — Assuming identity of another.* — A person may not knowingly and willfully assume the identity of another, including a fictitious person:

(1) to avoid identification, apprehension, or prosecution for a crime; or

(2) with fraudulent intent to:

(i) get a benefit, credit, good, service, or other thing of value; or

(ii) avoid the payment of debt or other legal obligation.

(d) *Use of re-encoder or skimming device.* — A person may not knowingly, willfully, and with fraudulent intent to obtain a benefit, credit, good, service, or other thing of value, use:

(1) a re-encoder to place information encoded on the magnetic strip or stripe of a credit card onto the magnetic strip or stripe of a different credit card or use any other electronic medium that allows such a transaction to occur without the consent of the individual authorized to use the credit card from which the personal identifying information or payment device number is being re-encoded; or

(2) a skimming device to access, read, scan, obtain, memorize, or store personal identifying information or a payment device number on the magnetic strip or stripe of a credit card without the consent of the individual authorized to use the credit card.

(e) *Possession of re-encoder or skimming device.* — A person may not knowingly, willfully, and with fraudulent intent possess, obtain, or help another possess or obtain a re-encoder device or a skimming device for the unauthorized use, sale, or transfer of personal identifying information or a payment device number.

(f) *Representation without authorization prohibited.* — A person may not knowingly and willfully claim to represent another person without the knowledge and consent of that person, with the intent to solicit, request, or take any other action to otherwise induce another person to provide personal identifying information or a payment device number.

(g) *Penalty.* — (1) A person who violates this section where the benefit, credit, good, service, or other thing of value that is the subject of subsection (b), (c), or (d) of this section has a value of $500 or greater is guilty of a felony and on conviction is subject to imprisonment not exceeding 15 years or a fine not exceeding $25,000 or both.

(2) A person who violates this section where the benefit, credit, good, service, or other thing of value that is the subject of subsection (b), (c), or (d) of this section has a value of less than $500 is guilty of a misdemeanor and on conviction is subject to imprisonment not exceeding 18 months or a fine not exceeding $5,000 or both.

(3) A person who violates this section under circumstances that reasonably indicate that the person's intent was to manufacture, distribute, or dispense another individual's personal identifying information without that individual's consent is guilty of a felony and on conviction is subject to imprisonment not exceeding 15 years or a fine not exceeding $25,000 or both.

(4) A person who violates subsection (c)(1), (e), or (f) of this section is guilty of a misdemeanor and on conviction is subject to imprisonment not exceeding 18 months or a fine not exceeding $5,000 or both.

(5) When the violation of this section is pursuant to one scheme or continuing course of conduct, whether from the same or several sources, the conduct may be considered as one violation and the value of the benefit, credit, good, service, or other thing of value may be aggregated in determining whether the violation is a felony or misdemeanor.

(h) *Statute of limitations and in banc review.* — A person described in subsection (g)(2) or (4) of this section is subject to § 5-106(b) of the Courts Article.

(i) *Restitution and costs.* — In addition to restitution under Title 11, Subtitle 6 of the Criminal Procedure Article, a court may order a person who pleads guilty or nolo contendere or who is found guilty under this section to make restitution to the victim for reasonable costs, including reasonable attorney's fees, incurred:

(1) for clearing the victim's credit history or credit rating; and

(2) in connection with a civil or administrative proceeding to satisfy a debt, lien, judgment, or other obligation of the victim that arose because of the violation.

(j) *Separate sentence.* — A sentence under this section may be imposed separate from and consecutive to or concurrent with a sentence for any crime based on the act or acts establishing the violation of this section.

(k) *Statewide jurisdiction for officers — State police.* — Notwithstanding any other law, the Department of State Police may initiate investigations and enforce this section throughout the State without regard to any limitation otherwise applicable to the Department's activities in a municipal corporation or other political subdivision.

(l) *Statewide jurisdiction for officers — Other officers.* — (1) Notwithstanding any other law, a law enforcement officer of the Maryland Transportation Authority Police, the Maryland Port Administration Police, the Park Police of the Maryland-National Capital Park and Planning Commission, or a municipal corporation or county may investigate violations of this section throughout the State without any limitation as to jurisdiction and to the same extent as a law enforcement officer of the Department of State Police.

(2) The authority granted in paragraph (1) of this subsection may be exercised only in accordance with regulations that the Department of State Police adopts.

(3) The regulations are not subject to Title 10, Subtitle 1 of the State Government Article.

(4) The authority granted in paragraph (1) of this subsection may be exercised only if an act related to the crime was committed in the investigating law enforcement agency's jurisdiction or if the complaining witness resides in the investigating law enforcement agency's jurisdiction.

(m) *Required notifications.* — If action is taken under the authority granted in subsection (l) of this section, notification of an investigation:

(1) in a municipal corporation, shall be made to the chief of police or designee of the chief of police;

(2) in a county that has a county police department, shall be made to the chief of police or designee of the chief of police;

(3) in a county without a police department, shall be made to the sheriff or designee of the sheriff;

(4) in Baltimore City, shall be made to the Police Commissioner or the Police Commissioner's designee;

(5) on property owned, leased, or operated by or under the control of the Maryland Transportation Authority, the Maryland Aviation Administration, or the Maryland Port Administration, shall be made to the respective chief of police or the chief's designee; and

(6) on property owned, leased, or operated by or under the control of the Maryland-National Capital Park and Planning Commission, to the chief of police of the Maryland-National Capital Park and Planning Commission for the county in which the property is located.

(n) *Immunities and exemptions for officers.* — When acting under the authority granted in subsection (k) or (l) of this section, a law enforcement officer:

(1) in addition to any other immunities and exemptions to which the officer may be entitled, has the immunities from liability and exemptions accorded to a law enforcement officer of the Department of State Police; but

(2) remains an employee of the officer's employing agency.

(o) *Investigation and prosecution.* — (1) A State's Attorney or the Attorney General may investigate and prosecute a violation of this section or a violation of any crime based on the act establishing a violation of this section.

(2) If the Attorney General exercises authority under paragraph (1) of this subsection, the Attorney General has all the powers and duties of a State's Attorney, including the use of a grand jury in any county or Baltimore City, to investigate and prosecute the violation.

(p) *Venue.* — Notwithstanding any other provision of law, the prosecution of a violation of this section or for a violation of any crime based on the act establishing a violation of this section may be commenced in any county in which:

(1) an element of the crime occurred; or

(2) the victim resides. (An. Code 1957, art. 27, § 231; 2002, ch. 26, § 2; ch. 19, § 10; ch. 509, § 1; 2003, ch. 21, § 1; chs. 67, 68; 2004, chs. 25, 109; 2005, ch. 25, § 1; 2006, ch. 352; 2007, ch. 447; 2008, chs. 354, 355; 2010, ch. 72; 2011, chs. 70, 71.)

SPECIAL REVISOR'S NOTE

This Special Revisor's note comprises information related to the revision by Acts 2002, ch. 26 and other chapters amending this section from the 2002 Legislative Session.

As enacted by Ch. 26, Acts of 2002, this section was new language derived without substantive change from former Art. 27, § 231. However, Ch. 509, Acts of 2002, added introductory language and a definition of "payment device number", and altered the definition of "personal identifying information" in subsection (a) of this section. Also, Ch. 509 added "possess[ion]" to the acts prohibited under subsection (b) of this section, and included avoidance of "identification [or] apprehension" under subsection (c) of this section. Also, Ch. 509 rewrote subsection (d) of this section to expand and grade penalties for violations of this section, and added subsections (h) through (k) of this section, concerning statewide jurisdiction of certain investigating units and officers, their authority, required notifications, and certain immunities and exemptions. Under the authority of Ch. 19, § 10, Acts of 2002, several stylistic and grammatical corrections have been made to provisions in subsection (d) of this section that Ch. 509 amended or added.

In subsection (a) of this section, the use of the word "means" by Ch. 26 in the definition of "personal identifying information" limited that information to the material listed. The Criminal Law Article Review Committee notes, for the consideration of the General Assembly, that in order to address other forms of personal identifying information that may become common as technology changes, it may be advisable to change "means" to "includes", thus allowing other such information to be covered by this section without requiring further legislation.

In subsections (b) and (c)(2)(i) of this section, the references to a "thing" of value were substituted by Ch. 26 for the former references to an "item" of value for consistency within this article.

In subsection (e) of this section, the reference to a violation being "subject to § 5-106(b) of the Courts Article" was substituted by Ch. 26 for the former reference to the violation subjecting the defendant to imprisonment "in the penitentiary" for clarity and consistency within this article. *See* General Revisor's Note to article.

Defined term:
"Person"   § 1-101

Effect of amendments. — Chapter 72, Acts 2010, enacted April 13, 2010, and effective from date of enactment, substituted "the Department's" for "that department's" in (k).

Chapters 70 and 71, Acts 2011, effective October 1, 2011, made identical changes. Each added "including a fictitious person" in the introductory language of (c) and reenacted (g) without change.

Identity of "another." — State did not prove that defendant used the identities of people who actually existed when defendant tried to open bank accounts with false identifications, and, thus, defendant could not be convicted of assuming the "identity of another" in violation of (c). Since the term "another" was ambiguous and consideration of the (1) legislative history, (2) case law, (3) statutory purpose, (4) statute's title, and (5) relation to other laws showed that the legislature intended for "another" to be an actual person, defendant could not be convicted under that statute since defendant's conduct did not plainly fall within the statute's terms. Ishola v. State, 404 Md. 155, 945 A.2d 1273 (2008).

Applied in Hyshaw v. State, 893 So. 2d 1239 (Ala. Crim. App. 2003).

Cited in Keys v. State, 195 Md. App. 19, 5 A.3d 1113 (2010).

§ 8-302. Blank or incorrect identification card.

(a) *"Offer for sale" defined.* — In this section, "offer for sale" includes to induce, solicit, attempt, or advertise in a manner intended to encourage a person to purchase an identification card.

(b) *Prohibited.* — Subject to subsection (c) of this section, a person may not:

(1) sell, issue, offer for sale, or offer to issue an identification card or document that contains:

(i) a blank space for a person's age or date of birth; or

(ii) a person's incorrect age or date of birth; or

(2) knowingly sell, issue, offer for sale, or offer to issue an identification card or document that contains:

    (i) an incorrect name instead of a person's true name; or

    (ii) an incorrect address for a person.

(c) *Exception.* — This section does not prohibit a manufacturer of identification cards or documents from selling or issuing identification cards or documents that contain a blank space for a person's age or date of birth to:

    (1) employers, for use as employee identification cards or documents;

    (2) hospitals, for use as patient identification cards; or

    (3) governmental units.

(d) *Penalty.* — (1) A person who violates this section is guilty of a misdemeanor and on conviction is subject to imprisonment not exceeding 2 years or a fine not exceeding $2,000 or both.

(2) Each identification card or document sold or issued and each offer in violation of this section is a crime that may be separately prosecuted.

(e) *Injunctive relief.* — The Attorney General, or the State's Attorney for a county where a violation of this section occurs, may seek an injunction to stop a sale, issue, or offer that violates this section. (An. Code 1957, art. 27, § 233E; 2002, ch. 26, § 2; 2006, ch. 486.)

REVISOR'S NOTE

This Revisor's note comprises information related to the revision by Acts 2002, ch. 26.

This section is new language derived without substantive change from former Art. 27, § 233E.

In subsection (a) of this section, the reference to advertising "in a manner" intended to encourage purchasing is added for clarity in light of the restatement of the definition of "offer for sale" as a verb phrase.

Also in subsection (a) of this section, the former reference to "printed or media" advertising is deleted as surplusage.

Also in subsection (a) of this section, the Criminal Law Article Review Committee notes, for the consideration of the General Assembly, that an "attempt" that is intended to encourage the purchase of a blank identification card appears to be redundant of "solicit[ing]" the same, and is in the nature of an attempt to attempt a sale.

In subsection (e) of this section, the former reference to seeking injunction "by application to a court of competent jurisdiction" is deleted as implicit.

Also in subsection (e) of this section, the reference to "an injunction to stop" is substituted for the former reference to "petition to enjoin" for consistency within this article.

Also in subsection (e) of this section, the former reference to the "City of Baltimore" is deleted as included in the defined term "county".

Defined terms:

"County"	§ 1-101
"Person"	§ 1-101

§ 8-303. Government identification document.

(a) *"Government identification document" defined.* — In this section, "government identification document" means one of the following documents issued by the United States government or any state or local government:

    (1) a passport;

    (2) an immigration visa;

    (3) an alien registration card;

    (4) an employment authorization card;

    (5) a birth certificate;

    (6) a Social Security card;

(7) a military identification;

(8) an adoption decree;

(9) a marriage license;

(10) a driver's license; or

(11) a photo identification card.

(b) *Prohibited.* — A person may not, with fraudulent intent:

(1) possess a fictitious or fraudulently altered government identification document;

(2) display, cause, or allow to be displayed a fictitious or fraudulently altered government identification document;

(3) lend a government identification document to another or knowingly allow the use of the person's government identification document by another; or

(4) display or represent as the person's own a government identification document not issued to the person.

(c) *Penalty.* — A person who violates this section is guilty of a misdemeanor and on conviction is subject to imprisonment not exceeding 6 months or a fine not exceeding $500 or both. (2004, ch. 288.)

§ 8-304. Report.

(a) *Contact local law enforcement agency.* — A person who knows or reasonably suspects that the person is a victim of identity fraud, as prohibited under this subtitle, may contact a local law enforcement agency that has jurisdiction over:

(1) any part of the county in which the person lives; or

(2) any part of the county in which the crime occurred.

(b) *Preparation of report.* — After being contacted by a person in accordance with subsection (a) of this section, a local law enforcement agency shall promptly:

(1) prepare and file a report of the alleged identity fraud; and

(2) provide a copy of the report to the victim.

(c) *Referring matter to another law enforcement agency.* — The local law enforcement agency contacted by the victim may subsequently refer the matter to a law enforcement agency with proper jurisdiction.

(d) *Not included as open case.* — A report filed under this section is not required to be counted as an open case for purposes including compiling open case statistics. (2005, ch. 579.)

Editor's note. — Section 2, ch. 579, Acts 2005, provides that "this Act may not be interpreted to interfere with the ability of law enforcement to allocate resources for the investigation of crimes."

§ 8-305. Identity theft passports.

(a) *Definitions.* — (1) In this section the following words have the meanings indicated.

(2) "Identity fraud" means a violation of § 8-301 of this subtitle.

(3) "Identity theft passport" means a card or certificate issued by the Attorney General that verifies the identity of the person who is a victim of identity fraud.

(b) *In general.* — A person who knows or reasonably suspects that the person is a victim of identity fraud and has filed a report under § 8-304 of this subtitle may apply for an identity theft passport through a law enforcement agency.

(c) *Processing.* — A law enforcement agency that receives an application for an identity theft passport shall submit the application and a copy of the report filed under § 8-304 of this subtitle to the Attorney General for processing and issuance of an identity theft passport.

(d) *Issuance.* — (1) The Attorney General, in cooperation with a law enforcement agency, may issue an identity theft passport to a person who is a victim of identity fraud.

(2) The Attorney General may not issue an identity theft passport to a person before completing a background check on the person.

(e) *Use.* — A person who is issued an identity theft passport under subsection (d) of this section may present the identity theft passport to:

(1) a law enforcement agency to help prevent the arrest or detention of the person for an offense committed by another using the person's personal identifying information; or

(2) a creditor to aid in the investigation of:

(i) a fraudulent account that is opened in the person's name; or

(ii) a fraudulent charge that is made against an account of the person.

(f) *Acceptance or rejection of passport.* — (1) A law enforcement agency or creditor that is presented with an identity theft passport under subsection (e) of this section has sole discretion to accept or reject the identity theft passport.

(2) In determining whether to accept or reject the identity theft passport, the law enforcement agency or creditor may consider the surrounding circumstances and available information regarding the offense of identity fraud against the person.

(g) *Confidentiality.* — An application for an identity theft passport submitted under this section, including any supporting documentation:

(1) is not a public record; and

(2) may not be released except to a law enforcement agency in this or another state.

(h) *Regulations.* — The Attorney General shall adopt regulations to carry out the provisions of this section. (2006, ch. 607.)

Editor's note. — The Department of Legislative Services reports that the contingency from § 2, ch. 607, Acts 2006 has been met.

Subtitle 4. Other Commercial Fraud.

§ 8-401. Fraudulent conversion of partnership assets.

(a) *Prohibited.* — A partner may not with fraudulent intent:

(1) convert or appropriate to the partner's own use partnership money or property;

(2) make, or cause to be made, a false entry in partnership records of a partnership transaction; or

(3) fail to make or cause to be made an entry in partnership records to show the true state of a transaction:

(i) relating to partnership business; or

(ii) involving the use of partnership money or property.

(b) *Penalty.* — A person who violates this section is guilty of a misdemeanor and on conviction is subject to imprisonment not exceeding 10 years or a fine not exceeding $5,000 or both.

(c) *Statute of limitations and in banc review.* — A person who violates this section is subject to § 5-106(b) of the Courts Article. (An. Code 1957, art. 27, § 173; 2002, ch. 26, § 2.)

REVISOR'S NOTE

This Revisor's note comprises information related to the revision by Acts 2002, ch. 26.

This section is new language derived without substantive change from former Art. 27, § 173.

In subsection (a)(1) of this section, the former references to "securities" and "assets" are deleted as included in the comprehensive reference to "property".

In subsection (a)(2) and (3) of this section, the former references to "books" are deleted as redundant in light of the references to "records".

In subsection (a)(3)(ii) of this section, the former redundant reference to "disposition" is deleted as implicit in the reference to "use".

In subsection (b) of this section, the former reference to the "house of correction" is deleted for consistency within this article. Currently, inmates are sentenced to the custody of a unit such as the Division of Correction, and then are placed into a particular facility. *See* CS § 9-103.

Also in subsection (b) of this section, the former reference to the court's "discretion" to determine the penalty is deleted as implicit in the establishment of maximum penalties.

In subsection (c) of this section, the reference to a violation being "subject to § 5-106(b) of the Courts Article" is substituted for the former reference to the violation subjecting the defendant to imprisonment "in the penitentiary" for clarity and consistency within this article. *See* General Revisor's Note to article.

Defined term:
"Person" § 1-101

§ 8-402. Fraudulent misrepresentation by corporate officer or agent.

(a) *Prohibited.* — With intent to defraud, an officer or agent of a corporation may not sign, or in any manner assent to, a statement to or a publication for the public or the shareholders that contains false representations of the corporation's assets, liabilities, or affairs, to:

(1) enhance or depress the market value of the corporation's shares or obligations; or

(2) commit fraud in another manner.

(b) *Penalty.* — A person who violates this section is guilty of a misdemeanor and on conviction is subject to imprisonment not less than 6 months and not exceeding 3 years or a fine not less than $1,000 and not exceeding $10,000 or both.

(c) *Statute of limitations and in banc review.* — A person who violates this section is subject to § 5-106(b) of the Courts Article. (An. Code 1957, art. 27, § 174; 2002, ch. 26, § 2.)

REVISOR'S NOTE

This Revisor's note comprises information related to the revision by Acts 2002, ch. 26.

This section is new language derived without substantive change from former Art. 27, § 174.

In the introductory language of subsection (a) of this section, the former reference to acting "with a view . . . to" specified ends is deleted for brevity.

In subsection (a)(2) of this section, the reference to "committing fraud in another manner" is substituted for the former reference to "in any other manner to accomplish any fraud thereby" for clarity.

In subsection (b) of this section, the former phrase "by indictment in any court of law" is deleted as surplusage.

Also in subsection (b) of this section, the former reference to imprisonment "in jail" is deleted for consistency within this article. Currently, inmates are sentenced to the custody of a unit such as the Division of Correction and then are placed in a particular facility. *See* CS § 9-103.

Also in subsection (b) of this section, the former reference to "the discretion of the court" to determine the penalty is deleted as implicit in the establishment of maximum penalties.

In subsection (c) of this section, the reference to a violation being "subject to § 5-106(b) of the Courts Article" is substituted for the former reference to the violation subjecting the defendant to imprisonment "in . . . [the] penitentiary" for clarity and consistency within this article. *See* General Revisor's Note to article.

Defined term:
"Person"   § 1-101

Cross references. — For Maryland Securities Act, see §§ 11-101 to 11-805 of the Corporations and Associations Article.

Editor's note. — Section 2, ch. 371, Acts 1991, provides that "there is no statute of limitations for a misdemeanor punishable by imprisonment in the penitentiary, notwithstanding any holding or dictum to the contrary in Massey v. State, 320 Md. 605, 579 A.2d 265 (1990)."

Maryland Law Review. — For note, "The Maryland Survey: 2001-2002: Recent Decisions: The Court of Appeals of Maryland: VII. Employment Law," see 62 Md. L. Rev. 864 (2003).

Constitutionality. — Where the constitutionality of a prior version of this section was questioned because its title on enactment in 1878 failed to meet requirements of Article III, § 29 of the Maryland Constitution, it was held that the statute had been embodied in all of the codes since its original enactment, and the Code of 1888 was a new enactment, sufficient in itself, and without dependency for its validity upon the previous enactment. State v. Coblentz, 167 Md. 523, 175 A. 340 (1934).

Construction with other laws. — A prior vserion of this section was not repealed by former Article 32A, §§ 13-19, the Blue Sky Law (now Maryland Securities Act, §§ 11-101 to 11-805 of the Corporations and Associations Article). State v. Coblentz, 167 Md. 523, 175 A. 340 (1934).

Applicability. — A prior version of this section is applicable to banking institutions. State v. Coblentz, 167 Md. 523, 175 A. 340 (1934).

Indictment. — An indictment under a prior version of this section was held sufficient where it followed substantially the words of the statute, although it failed to charge defendant with knowledge of the falsity of the statements. State v. Coblentz, 167 Md. 523, 175 A. 340 (1934).

Civil action. — The bald allegations of a complaint which do not provide a sufficient factual predicate for determining whether an employer fired an employee in order to prevent disclosure of alleged violations of a prior version of this section or any other declared mandate of public policy does not state a cause of action for wrongful discharge of an employee. Adler v. American Std. Corp., 291 Md. 31, 432 A.2d 464 (1981), superseded by statute on other grounds, Wholey v. Sears, Roebuck & Co., 803 A.2d 482 (2002).

Even construing the facts in the light most favorable to the former employee and accepting the inference that she was asked to participate in a "conspiracy to defraud stockholders" (as she suggested for the first time in her opposition motion), the employee still failed to state a viable claim of wrongful discharge in violation of public policy because she did not provide any factual details to support the general and conclusory averments regarding the illegality of the alleged activity. Terry v. Legato Sys., 241 F. Supp. 2d 566 (D. Md. 2003).

§ 8-403. Removal of personal property.

(a) *In general.* — A debtor who possesses personal property that is subject to a security interest may not secrete, hypothecate, destroy, or sell the property or remove the property from the county where it was located when the security interest attached:

    (1) without the written consent of the secured party or the secured party's assignee; and

    (2) with the intent to defraud the secured party.

    (b) *Removal by execution debtor.* — (1) A debtor who possesses personal property that is under levy pursuant to a writ of execution may not remove, secrete, hypothecate, destroy, or sell the property or remove the property from the county where it was located when the levy was made:

        (i) without the prior written consent of the judgment creditor, the judgment creditor's lawfully authorized agent, or the judgment creditor's assignee; and

        (ii) with intent to defraud the judgment creditor or the judgment creditor's assignee, and defeat the lien of the judgment creditor or the judgment creditor's assignee under the levy.

    (2) This subsection does not relieve the sheriff or other officer making the levy from responsibility to the judgment creditor for safekeeping personal property taken into possession by the sheriff or other officer making the levy.

    (c) *Removal by seller.* — A seller of personal property who possesses the personal property under a recorded bill of sale may not remove, secrete, hypothecate, destroy, or sell the property or remove the property from the county where it was located when sold:

    (1) without prior written consent in the contract of the buyer or the buyer's assignee; and

    (2) with intent to defraud the buyer.

    (d) *Penalty.* — A person who violates this section is guilty of a misdemeanor and on conviction is subject to imprisonment not exceeding 6 months or a fine not exceeding $500 or both. (An. Code 1957, art. 27, § 214; 2002, ch. 26, § 2.)

REVISOR'S NOTE

This Revisor's note comprises information related to the revision by Acts 2002, ch. 26.

This section is new language derived without substantive change from former Art. 27, § 214.

Throughout this section, the references to the person "who possesses" property are substituted for the former archaic references to being "in possession of" the property for clarity.

Also throughout this section, the former phrases "in the case of [personal property or the holder of personal property]" are deleted as surplusage.

Also throughout this section, the former references to the "city" where secured property was located when sold are deleted as surplusage.

Also throughout this section, the references to "prior written" consent are substituted for the former archaic references to consent "first had and obtained in writing" for clarity and consistency within this article.

In subsection (a) of this section, the reference to a "debtor who possesses personal property that is subject to a security interest" is substituted for the former references to a "mortgagor of personal property in possession of the same" and a "purchaser of personal property under a recorded conditional, written contract, in possession of said property" for clarity and for consistency with current terminology. Similarly, the reference to the property when "the security interest attached" is substituted for the former references to the property when "so mortgaged" and "purchased" for clarity and consistency. Similarly, the references to the "secured party" and the "secured party's assignee" are substituted for the former references to the "mortgagee", "his assigns", and "vendor" for clarity and consistency. No substantive change is intended.

Also in subsection (a) of this section, the reference to intent "to defraud the secured party" is substituted for the former archaic reference to acting "with intent as aforesaid" for clarity.

In subsection (b) of this section, the reference to a "debtor who possesses personal property that is under levy pursuant to a writ of execution" is substituted for the former reference to a "execution debtor in possession of personal property levied on and taken in execution" for clarity and for consistency with current terminology. Similarly, the reference to the property when "the levy was made" is substituted for the former references to the property when "levied on and taken in execution as aforesaid" for clarity and consistency. Similarly, the references to the "judgment creditor", the "judgment creditor's assignee", and the "judgment creditor's lawfully authorized agent" are substituted for the former references to the "execution creditor" and "his assigns or lawfully authorized agents" for clarity and consistency. No substantive change is intended.

Also in subsection (b) of this section, the reference to the intent "to defraud the judgment creditor or the judgment creditor's as-signee" is substituted for the former archaic reference to acting "with intent as aforesaid" for clarity.

In subsection (c) of this section, the reference to the intent "to defraud the buyer" is substituted for the former archaic reference to acting "with intent as aforesaid" for clarity.

In subsection (d) of this section, the former reference to "indictment" is deleted as surplusage.

Also in subsection (d) of this section, the former reference to the "city or county jail" is deleted for consistency within this article. Currently, inmates are sentenced to the custody of a unit such as the Division of Correction and then are placed in a particular facility. *See* CS § 9-103.

Also in subsection (d) of this section, the former reference to "the discretion of the court to set a penalty" is deleted as implicit in the establishment of maximum penalties.

Defined terms:
"County"   § 1-101
"Person"   § 1-101

Cross references. — As to fraudulent conveyances, see §§ 15-201 to 15-214 of the Commercial Law Article.

Malicious prosecution. — See Hooper v. Vernon, 74 Md. 136, 21 A. 556 (1891); Smith v. Brown, 119 Md. 236, 86 A. 609 (1913).

§ 8-404. Pyramid promotional schemes.

(a) *Definitions.* — (1) In this section the following words have the meanings indicated.

(2) "Compensation" includes payment based on a sale or distribution made to a person who:

(i) is a participant in a plan or operation; or

(ii) on making a payment, is entitled to become a participant.

(3) "Consideration" does not include:

(i) payment for purchase of goods or services furnished at cost for use in making sales to persons who are not participants in the scheme and who are not purchasing in order to participate in the scheme;

(ii) time or effort spent in pursuit of sales or recruiting activities; or

(iii) the right to receive a discount or rebate based on the purchase or acquisition of goods or services by a bona fide cooperative buying group or association.

(4) "Promote" means to induce one or more persons to become a participant.

(5) "Pyramid promotional scheme" means a plan or operation by which a participant gives consideration for the opportunity to receive compensation to be derived primarily from any person's introduction of others into participation in the plan or operation rather than from the sale of goods, services, or other intangible property by the participant or others introduced into the plan or operation.

(b) *Prohibited.* — A person may not establish, operate, advertise, or promote a pyramid promotional scheme.

(c) *Prohibited defenses.* — It is not a defense to a prosecution under this section that:

(1) the plan or operation limits the number of persons who may participate or limits the eligibility of participants; or

(2) on payment of anything of value by a participant, the participant obtains any other property in addition to the right to receive compensation.

(d) *Penalty.* — A person who violates this section is guilty of a misdemeanor and on conviction is subject to imprisonment not exceeding 1 year or a fine not exceeding $10,000 or both. (An. Code 1957, art. 27, § 233D; 2002, ch. 26, § 2.)

REVISOR'S NOTE

This Revisor's note comprises information related to the revision by Acts 2002, ch. 26.
This section is new language derived without substantive change from former Art. 27, § 233D.

Defined term:
"Person" § 1-101

Constitutionality. — The word "primarily," as used in the definition of "pyramid promotional scheme" in a prior version of this section, has a sufficiently definite meaning to afford a person of ordinary intelligence and experience a reasonable opportunity to know what is prohibited and provides adequate notice of the type of pyramid operations which are prohibited. The prior version is not unconstitutional for vagueness or failure to set guidelines. Schrader v. State, 69 Md. App. 377, 517 A.2d 1139 (1986), cert. denied, 309 Md. 326, 523 A.2d 1014 (1987).

§ 8-405. Wrongful disposal of vessel cargo.

(a) *Scope of section.* — This section applies only to a person employed in any capacity in the management or navigation of a vessel on a river, canal, bay, or other waters exclusively within the State whether or not the person is a co-owner of or has an interest in any of the cargo of the vessel.

(b) *Prohibited — Disposal without consent of owner.* — A person may not sell, give away, pledge, or in any manner dispose of the cargo of a vessel or an article or commodity on the vessel:

(1) without the consent of the owner; and

(2) with the intent to defraud the owner.

(c) *Same — Disposal with consent of owner — Proceeds.* — A person who sells the cargo of a vessel or an article or commodity on the vessel with the consent of the owner may not neglect or refuse to pay to the owner the consideration received by the person with the intent to defraud the owner.

(d) *Penalty.* — A person who violates this section is guilty of a misdemeanor and on conviction is subject to imprisonment not less than 6 months and not exceeding 1 year or a fine not less than $500 and not exceeding $1,000 or both. (An. Code 1957, art. 27, § 135; 2002, ch. 26, § 2.)

This Revisor's note comprises information related to the revision by Acts 2002, ch. 26.

This section is new language derived without substantive change from former Art. 27, § 135.

In subsection (b) of this section, the former reference to "vessels" is deleted in light of Art. 1, § 8, which provides that the singular generally includes the plural.

In subsection (d) of this section, the former reference to conviction "thereof in any court of this State having criminal jurisdiction" is deleted as surplusage.

Also in subsection (d) of this section, the former reference to imprisonment "in the jail of the county or city in which such conviction is had" is deleted for consistency within this article. Currently, inmates are sentenced to the custody of a unit such as the Division of Correction and then are placed in a particular facility. *See* CS 9-103.

Also in subsection (d) of this section, the former reference to the court's "discretion" to determine the penalty is deleted as implicit in the establishment of maximum penalties.

Defined term:
   "Person"   § 1-101

§ 8-406. Misuse of documents of title.

(a) *Prohibited.* — A person, on the person's own behalf or on behalf of another, who receives, accepts, or takes in trust from another a warehouse or elevator receipt, bill of lading, or document giving, or purporting to give, title to, or the right to possession of, goods, wares, merchandise, or other personal property, subject to a written contract expressing the terms and conditions of the trust, may not fail to fulfill in good faith the terms and conditions of the trust.

(b) *Penalty.* — A person who violates this section is guilty of a misdemeanor and on conviction is subject to imprisonment not less than 1 year and not exceeding 10 years or a fine not less than $500 and not exceeding $5,000 or both.

(c) *Statute of limitations and in banc review.* — A person who violates this section is subject to § 5-106(b) of the Courts Article. (An. Code 1957, art. 27, § 163; 2002, ch. 26, § 2.)

This Revisor's note comprises information related to the revision by Acts 2002, ch. 26.

This section is new language derived without substantive change from former Art. 27, § 163.

In subsection (a) of this section, the former references to a "firm, copartnership or corporation" are deleted as included in the defined term "person". *See* § 1-101 of this article.

Also in subsection (a) of this section, the former reference to acting "under . . . contract" is deleted as implicit in the reference to acting "subject to a . . . contract".

Also in subsection (a) of this section, the former reference to an "agreement" is deleted as included in the reference to a "contract".

Also in subsection (a) of this section, the former reference to "neglect[ing] or refus[ing]" is deleted in light of the reference to "fail[ing]".

Also in subsection (a) of this section, the former reference to "perform[ing]" a contract is deleted as included in the reference to "fulfill[ing]" a contract.

In subsection (b) of this section, the phrase "guilty of a misdemeanor" is added to state expressly that which was only implied in the former law. The failure to comply with the terms of a trust is a statutory offense. Because neither the common law nor the statute establishes that the failure to comply with the terms of a trust is a felony, it is considered to be a misdemeanor. *See State v. Canova*, 278 Md. 483, 490 (1976); *Bowser v. State*, 136 Md. 342, 345 (1920); *Dutton v. State*, 123 Md. 373, 378 (1914); and *Williams v. State*, 4 Md. App. 342, 347 (1968).

Also in subsection (b) of this section, the former reference to "the discretion of the court" to set a penalty is deleted as implicit in the establishment of maximum penalties.

In subsection (c) of this section, the reference to a violation being "subject to § 5-106(b) of the

Courts Article" is substituted for the former reference to the violation subjecting the defendant to imprisonment "in the penitentiary" for clarity and consistency within this article. *See* General Revisor's Note to article.

Defined term:
"Person" § 1-101

Cross references. — For provisions regarding failure to deliver documents for merchandise, see § 7-116 of this article.

For provisions of Uniform Commercial Code as to bills of lading, warehouse receipts, etc., see §§ 7-101 to 7-603 of the Commercial Law Article.

Editor's note. — Section 2, ch. 371, Acts 1991, provides that "there is no statute of limitations for a misdemeanor punishable by imprisonment in the penitentiary, notwithstanding any holding or dictum to the contrary in Massey v. State, 320 Md. 605, 579 A.2d 265 (1990)."

§ 8-407. Fraudulent conversion of leased or rented good.

(a) *Scope of section.* — This section applies to a written contract or written lease for a leased or rented good or thing of value whether or not the contract or lease contains an option to purchase the good or thing of value if the lease:

(1) does not exceed a period of 6 months; and

(2) is for a good or thing with a value of $1,500 or more.

(b) *Prohibited.* — A person may not fraudulently convert to the person's own use a good or thing of value received under a written contract or written lease entered into for the purpose of renting or leasing things for valuable consideration.

(c) *Prima facie evidence.* — The failure to return the good or thing of value to the possession of, or account for the good or thing of value with, the person who delivered the good or thing of value at the time or in the manner described in the written contract or written lease is prima facie evidence of intent to fraudulently convert the good or thing of value.

(d) *Limitation on prosecution.* — (1) A person may not be prosecuted under this section if within 10 days after a written demand for the return of the good or thing of value is mailed by certified United States mail, return receipt requested, to the person who received the good or thing of value at the last address known to the person who delivered the good or thing of value, the person returns the good or thing of value to the possession of, or accounts for the good or thing of value with, the person who delivered the good or thing of value.

(2) A prosecution may not be started until 10 days after a written demand described in paragraph (1) of this subsection is mailed.

(e) *Penalty.* — A person who violates this section is guilty of a misdemeanor and on conviction is subject to imprisonment not exceeding 60 days or a fine not exceeding $1,000 or both.

(f) *Restitution.* — A person who violates this section shall restore the good or thing of value converted to the person's own use or pay the full value to the owner or the person who delivered the good or thing of value.

(g) *Prosecution under § 7-104 of this article not precluded; merging.* — (1) A prosecution under this section does not preclude prosecution for theft under § 7-104 of this article.

(2) If a person is convicted under § 7-104 of this article and this section for the same act or transaction, the conviction under this section shall merge for sentencing purposes into the conviction under § 7-104 of this article. (An. Code 1957, art. 27, § 207; 2002, ch. 26, § 2; ch. 166; 2009, chs. 218, 219.)

SPECIAL REVISOR'S NOTE

This Special Revisor's note comprises information related to the revision by Acts 2002, ch. 26 and other chapters amending this section from the 2002 Legislative Session.

As enacted by Ch. 26, Acts of 2002, this section was new language derived without substantive change from former Art. 27, § 207. However, Ch. 166, Acts of 2002, deleted the references to a "bona fide resident of the State" enacted by Ch. 26 in subsection (d) of this section, thus extending the limitation on prosecution under that provision to all persons.

Throughout this section, the references to a "good" or a "thing" of value were substituted by Ch. 26 for the former references to "goods" or "things" of value in light of Art. 1, § 8, which provides that the singular generally includes the plural.

In subsection (c) of this section, the limitation "[s]ubject to subsection (d) of this section," was added by Ch. 26 to refer explicitly to the defense to prosecution contained in subsection (d) of this section.

In subsection (d)(1) of this section, the reference to the person "who received the good or thing of value" was substituted by Ch. 26 for the former reference to the person "who was so entrusted" for consistency with subsection (a) of this section.

Also in subsection (d)(1) of this section, the former reference to "registered" mail was deleted by Ch. 26 as included in the reference to "certified" mail. See Art. 1, § 20.

In subsection (d)(2) of this section, the reference to "a bona fide resident of the State" was added by Ch. 26 for consistency with subsection

(d)(1) of this section and to state explicitly that the prohibition against a prosecution not being started until 10 days after a written demand letter is mailed applied only to a prosecution of a resident of the State.

Also in subsection (d)(2) of this section, the former reference to prosecution "either by presentment, indictment, or otherwise" was deleted by Ch. 26 as surplusage.

The Criminal Law Article Review Committee noted, for the consideration of the General Assembly, that the Attorney General had found the limitation on prosecution of a bona fide Maryland resident, stated in subsection (d) of this section by Ch. 26, to be unconstitutional as violating both Equal Protection and the Commerce Clause of the U.S. Constitution. *See* Letter of Advice from Attorney General J. Joseph Curran, Jr. to Judge Alan M. Wilner, pp. 10-14 (October 17, 2000). It was possible to address these concerns by extending the waiting period for prosecution of a Maryland resident to all persons. It was also possible to remedy the constitutional defect by eliminating the waiting period entirely, relying instead on prosecutorial discretion in deciding whether to bring a particular case to court. Each of these options involved a substantive change. Accordingly, the General Assembly was asked to consider addressing these concerns in substantive legislation. Chapter 166 addressed this concern.

For failure to return a rental vehicle, *see* § 7-205 of this article.

Defined term:
"Person"   § 1-101

Effect of amendments. — Chapters 218 and 219, Acts 2009, effective October 1, 2009, made identical changes. Each rewrote (a); and added (g).

§ 8-408. Unlawful subleasing of motor vehicles.

(a) *Definitions.* — (1) In this section the following words have the meanings indicated.

(2) "Direct loan agreement" means an agreement between a lender and a borrower under which the lender advances funds under a loan secured by the motor vehicle purchased by the borrower.

(3) (i) "Installment sale agreement" means a contract for the sale or lease of a motor vehicle, negotiated or entered into in the State, under which:

    1. part or all of the price is payable in one or more payments after the contract is made; and

    2. the seller takes collateral security or keeps a security interest in the motor vehicle sold.

    (ii) "Installment sale agreement" includes:

    1. a prospective installment sale agreement;

    2. a purchase money security agreement;

    3. a contract for the bailment or leasing of a motor vehicle under which the bailee or lessee contracts to pay as compensation a sum that is substantially equal to or is more than the value of the motor vehicle; and

    4. a renewal, extension, or refund agreement.

    (4) "Lease contract" means a contract for or in contemplation of a lease for the use of a motor vehicle, and the purchase of services incidental to the lease, for a term of more than 4 months.

    (5) "Lessor" means a person who leases a motor vehicle to another under a lease contract.

    (6) "Motor vehicle" means a vehicle for which an owner is required to obtain a certificate of title under Title 13 of the Transportation Article.

    (7) "Motor vehicle agreement" means a lease contract, direct loan agreement, installment sale agreement, or security agreement.

    (8) "Secured party" means a person who has a security interest in a vehicle.

    (9) "Security agreement" means a written agreement that reserves or creates a security interest.

    (10) (i) "Security interest" means an interest in a vehicle that is reserved or created by agreement and that secures payment or performance of an obligation.

    (ii) "Security interest" includes the interest of a lessor under a lease intended as security.

    (11) (i) "Seller" means a person who sells or leases or agrees to sell or lease a motor vehicle under an installment sale agreement.

    (ii) "Seller" includes a present holder of an installment sale agreement.

    (b) *Prohibited.* — A person may not engage in an act of unlawful subleasing of a motor vehicle in which:

    (1) the motor vehicle is subject to a motor vehicle agreement the terms of which prohibit the transfer or assignment of a right or interest in the motor vehicle or under the motor vehicle agreement without consent of the lessor or secured party;

    (2) the person is not a party to the motor vehicle agreement;

    (3) the person:

    (i) transfers or assigns, or purports to transfer or assign, a right or interest in the motor vehicle or under a motor vehicle agreement to a person who is not a party to the motor vehicle agreement; or

    (ii) assists, causes, negotiates, attempts to negotiate, or arranges an actual or purported transfer of a right or interest in the motor vehicle or under a motor vehicle agreement from a person, other than the lessor or secured party, who is a party to the motor vehicle agreement;

(4) neither the person nor the party to the motor vehicle agreement obtains written consent to the transfer or assignment from the lessor or secured party before conducting the acts described in item (3) of this subsection; and

(5) the person receives or intends to receive a commission, compensation, or other consideration for engaging in the acts described in item (3) of this subsection.

(c) *Defense.* — (1) It is not an act of unlawful subleasing of a motor vehicle under this section if the acts under subsection (b)(3) of this section are engaged in by a person who is:

(i) a party to the motor vehicle agreement; or

(ii) a dealer or vehicle salesman licensed under Title 15 of the Transportation Article and engaged in vehicle sales who assists, causes, or arranges a transfer or assignment under the terms of an agreement for the purchase or lease of another motor vehicle.

(2) Paragraph (1) of this subsection does not affect the enforceability of a provision of a motor vehicle agreement by a party to the agreement.

(3) A party to a motor vehicle agreement may not be prosecuted under this section as an accessory to the act of unlawful subleasing of the motor vehicle that is subject to the motor vehicle agreement.

(d) *Penalty.* — A person who violates this section is guilty of a misdemeanor and on conviction is subject to imprisonment not exceeding 3 years or a fine not exceeding $5,000 or both. (An. Code 1957, art. 27, § 208(a)(1), (3)-(12), (b)-(e); 2002, ch. 26, § 2.)

REVISOR'S NOTE

This Revisor's note comprises information related to the revision by Acts 2002, ch. 26.

This section is new language derived without substantive change from former Art. 27, § 208(b) through (e) and (a)(1) and (3) through (12).

In subsection (a)(8) of this section, the former reference to a security interest "in the person's favor" is deleted as surplusage.

In subsection (c)(1) of this section, the defined term "person" is substituted for the former reference to "an individual" for consistency with subsection (b) of this section.

In subsection (c)(1)(ii) of this section, the former reference to a "bona fide" agreement is deleted as surplusage.

Former Art. 27, § 208(a)(2), which defined "buyer", is deleted because the term is not used in this section.

Defined term:
"Person"   § 1-101

Subtitle 5. Public Fraud.

Part I. Public Assistance Fraud.

§ 8-501. "Fraud" defined.

In this part, "fraud" includes:

(1) the willful making of a false statement or a false representation;

(2) the willful failure to disclose a material change in household or financial condition; or

(3) the impersonation of another. (An. Code 1957, art. 27, § 230A(b)(1); 2002, ch. 26, § 2.)

This Revisor's note comprises information related to the revision by Acts 2002, ch. 26.

This section is new language derived without substantive change from the second sentence of former Art. 27, § 230A(b)(1).

The reference to this "part" is substituted for the former reference to this "section", although this part is derived, in part, from material outside former Art. 27, § 230A. Because the term "fraud" defined here is used only in material derived from former Art. 27, § 230A, the substitution results in no substantive change.

Defined term:
"Person" § 1-101

§ 8-502. Scope of part.

This part does not apply to a violation of Part II of this subtitle. (An. Code 1957, art. 27, § 230A(a); 2002, ch. 26, § 2.)

This Revisor's note comprises information related to the revision by Acts 2002, ch. 26.

This section is new language derived without substantive change from former Art. 27, § 230A(a).

The reference to this "part" is substituted for the former reference to this "section" to reflect the reorganization of material derived from former Art. 27, § 230A, although this part is derived, in part, from material outside former Art. 27, § 230A. Because violations of Part II of this subtitle, which covers Medicaid fraud, are not violations of § 8-505 of this part, which deals with food programs and is the only provision derived from outside former Art. 27, § 230A, no substantive change is intended.

§ 8-503. Public assistance fraud.

(a) *Scope of section.* — This section applies to money, property, food stamps, or other assistance that is provided under a social or nutritional program based on need that is:

(1) financed wholly or partly by the State; and

(2) administered by the State or a political subdivision of the State.

(b) *Prohibited.* — By fraud, a person may not obtain, attempt to obtain, or help another person to obtain or attempt to obtain, money, property, food stamps, or other assistance to which the person is not entitled.

(c) *Penalty.* — A person who violates this section is guilty of a misdemeanor and on conviction is subject to imprisonment not exceeding 3 years or a fine not exceeding $1,000 or both.

(d) *Restitution.* — (1) A person who is convicted of a violation of this section shall make full restitution of the money or the value of the property, food stamps, or other assistance obtained by the person in violation of this section.

(2) Full restitution under paragraph (1) of this subsection shall be made after the person has received notice and has been given the opportunity to be heard as to the amount of payment and how it is to be made. (An. Code 1957, art. 27, § 230A(b)(1), (2); 2002, ch. 26, § 2.)

This Revisor's note comprises information related to the revision by Acts 2002, ch. 26.

This section is new language derived without substantive change from former Art. 27, § 230A(b)(2) and the first sentence of (1).

In subsection (a) of this section, the former reference to money or assistance "other than Medicaid" is deleted as redundant of the exclusion of Medical Assistance Program matters under § 8-502 of this part.

In subsection (d)(1) of this section, the reference to restitution for the value of the assistance "obtained by the person in violation of this section" is substituted for the former reference to the value of the assistance "unlawfully received" for clarity.

For general provisions governing the imposition and administration of restitution, *see* CP Title 11, Subtitle 6.

Defined terms:
"Fraud"   § 8-501
"Person"   § 1-101

Elements of offense. — The amount of money involved is no more an element of the offense than it is in a robbery. Gentry v. State, 12 Md. App. 44, 276 A.2d 673 (1971).

Proof of exact amount alleged unnecessary. — It was sufficient for the State to establish that the accused received some public assistance to which he was not entitled; whether in an amount greater or smaller than the amount charged was not material. Gentry v. State, 12 Md. App. 44, 276 A.2d 673 (1971).

The verdict of guilty was proper even though the State had not proved the exact amount alleged. Gentry v. State, 12 Md. App. 44, 276 A.2d 673 (1971).

That the amount proved is less than the amount alleged does not vitiate the conviction.

Gentry v. State, 12 Md. App. 44, 276 A.2d 673 (1971).

Double jeopardy. — Where the accused unlawfully obtained public assistance to which he was not entitled by failure to disclose a change in his household, the marriage of his daughter, but the money he received by this means was included in the amount he had unlawfully received by means of the wilfully false statement which was the basis of a prior conviction, he was twice convicted for obtaining the same money, and this was manifestly improper. Gentry v. State, 12 Md. App. 44, 276 A.2d 673 (1971).

§ 8-504. Fraudulent statement in application.

(a) *Signature required on application.* — An application for money, property, food stamps, or other assistance, under a nutritional program based on need or a social program financed in whole or in part by the State, and administered by the Department of Human Resources, the Department of Health and Mental Hygiene, or a local department of social services, whether under this or any other article of the Code, shall be in writing and signed by the applicant.

(b) *Prohibited.* — A person may not make a false or fraudulent statement with the intent to obtain money, property, food stamps, or other assistance in making and signing the application required in subsection (a) of this section.

(c) *Penalty.* — A person who violates this section is guilty of the misdemeanor of perjury and on conviction is subject to the penalties provided for perjury in § 9-101 of this article. (An. Code 1957, art. 27, § 230A(c); 2002, ch. 26, § 2.)

REVISOR'S NOTE

This Revisor's note comprises information related to the revision by Acts 2002, ch. 26.

This section is new language derived without substantive change from former Art. 27, § 230A(c).

In subsection (c) of this section, the reference to the "misdemeanor" of perjury is added for clarity and to conform to the usage in Title 9 of this article.

Also in subsection (c) of this section, the reference to the penalties "provided for perjury in § 9-101 of this article" is substituted for the former reference to the penalties "provided by law" for clarity since perjury is now codified in § 9-101 of this article.

§ 8-505. Public assistance — Conversion of donated food.

(a) *Unauthorized disposition.* — A person with intent to defraud may not make an unauthorized disposition of food donated under a program of the federal government.

(b) *Unauthorized conversion.* — A person who is not authorized to receive food donated under any program of the federal government may not convert the food to the person's own use or benefit.

(c) *Penalty.* — A person who violates this section is guilty of a misdemeanor and on conviction is subject to imprisonment not exceeding 6 months or a fine not exceeding $500 or both. (An. Code 1957, art. 27, § 191A; 2002, ch. 26, § 2.)

REVISOR'S NOTE

This Revisor's note comprises information related to the revision by Acts 2002, ch. 26.

This section is new language derived without substantive change from former Art. 27, § 191A.

In subsections (a) and (b) of this section, the former references to a food "commodity" are deleted as surplusage.

In subsection (c) of this section, the former phrase "in the discretion of the court" is deleted as implicit in the establishment of maximum penalties.

Defined term:
  "Person"   § 1-101

§§ 8-506, 8-507.

Reserved.

Part II. Medicaid Fraud.

§ 8-508. Definitions.

(a) *In general.* — In this part the following words have the meanings indicated.

REVISOR'S NOTE

This subsection formerly was Art. 27, § 230B(a).

The reference to this "part" is substituted for the former reference to this "subheading" to reflect the reorganization of material derived from former Art. 27, §§ 230B through 230H.

No other changes are made.

(b) *False representation.* — "False representation" means the knowing and willful:

    (1) concealing, falsifying, or omitting of a material fact;

    (2) making of a materially false or fraudulent statement; or

    (3) use of a document that contains a statement of material fact that the user knows to be false or fraudulent.

This subsection is new language derived without substantive change from former Art. 27, § 230B(b).

(c) *Health care service.* — (1) "Health care service" means health or medical care procedures, goods, or services that:

(i) provide testing, diagnosis, or treatment of human disease or dysfunction; or

(ii) dispense drugs, medical devices, medical appliances, or medical goods for the treatment of human disease or dysfunction.

(2) "Health care service" includes any procedure, goods, or service that is a required benefit of a State health plan.

This subsection formerly was Art. 27, § 230B(c).   No changes are made.

(d) *Representation.* — "Representation" includes an acknowledgment, certification, claim, ratification, report of demographic statistics, encounter data, enrollment claims, financial information, health care services available or rendered, and qualifications of a person rendering health care or ancillary services.

This subsection formerly was Art. 27, § 230B(d). No changes are made.

Defined term:
"Person"   § 1-101

(e) *Serious injury.* — "Serious injury" means an injury that:

(1) creates a substantial risk of death;

(2) causes serious permanent or serious protracted disfigurement;

(3) causes serious permanent or serious protracted loss of the function of any body part, organ, or mental faculty;

(4) causes serious permanent or serious protracted impairment of the function of any bodily member or organ; or

(5) involves extreme physical pain.

This subsection formerly was Art. 27, § 230B(e).   No changes are made.

(f) *State health plan.* — (1) "State health plan" includes:

(i) the State Medical Assistance Plan established in accordance with Title XIX of the federal Social Security Act of 1939;

(ii) a medical assistance plan established by the State; or

(iii) a private health insurance carrier, health maintenance organization, managed care organization as defined in § 15-101 of the Health - General

Article, health care cooperative or alliance, or other person that provides or contracts to provide health care services that are wholly or partly reimbursed by or are a required benefit of a health plan established in accordance with Title XIX of the federal Social Security Act of 1939 or by the State.

(2) "State health plan" includes a person that provides or contracts or subcontracts to provide health care services for an entity described in paragraph (1) of this subsection.

REVISOR'S NOTE

This subsection formerly was Art. 27, § 230B(f).
No changes are made.

Defined term:
"Person"   § 1-101

(An. Code 1957, art. 27, § 230B; 2002, ch. 26, § 2.)

REVISOR'S NOTE TO SECTION

The Revisor's notes in this section comprise information related to the revision by Acts 2002, ch. 26.

§ 8-509. Defrauding State health plan.

A person may not:

(1) knowingly and willfully defraud or attempt to defraud a State health plan in connection with the delivery of or payment for a health care service;

(2) knowingly and willfully obtain or attempt to obtain by means of a false representation money, property, or any thing of value in connection with the delivery of or payment for a health care service that wholly or partly is reimbursed by or is a required benefit of a State health plan;

(3) knowingly and willfully defraud or attempt to defraud a State health plan of the right to honest services; or

(4) with the intent to defraud make a false representation relating to a health care service or a State health plan. (An. Code 1957, art. 27, § 230C; 2002, ch. 26, § 2.)

REVISOR'S NOTE

This Revisor's note comprises information related to the revision by Acts 2002, ch. 26.
This section is new language derived without substantive change from former Art. 27, § 230C.

Defined terms:
"False representation"   § 8-508
"Health care service"   § 8-508
"Person"   § 1-101
"State health plan"   § 8-508

§ 8-510. Conversion.

A person who has applied for or received a benefit or payment under a State health plan for the use of another individual may not knowingly and willfully convert all or any part of a State health plan benefit or payment to a use that is not for the authorized beneficiary. (An. Code 1957, art. 27, § 230D(a); 2002, ch. 26, § 2.)

REVISOR'S NOTE

This Revisor's note comprises information related to the revision by Acts 2002, ch. 26.

This section formerly was Art. 27, § 230D(a). No changes are made.

Defined terms:
"Person"	§ 1-101
"State health plan"	§ 8-508

§ 8-511. Bribe or kickback.

A person may not:

(1) provide to another individual items or services for which payment wholly or partly is or may be made from federal or State funds under a State health plan; and

(2) solicit, offer, make, or receive a kickback or bribe in connection with providing those items or services or making or receiving a benefit or payment under a State health plan. (An. Code 1957, art. 27, § 230D(b); 2002, ch. 26, § 2.)

REVISOR'S NOTE

This Revisor's note comprises information related to the revision by Acts 2002, ch. 26.

This section is new language derived without substantive change from former Art. 27, § 230D(b).

Defined terms:
"Person"	§ 1-101
"State health plan"	§ 8-508

§ 8-512. Referral rebate.

A person may not solicit, offer, make, or receive a rebate of a fee or charge for referring another individual to a third person to provide items or services for which payment wholly or partly is or may be made from federal or State funds under a State health plan. (An. Code 1957, art. 27, § 230D(c); 2002, ch. 26, § 2.)

REVISOR'S NOTE

This Revisor's note comprises information related to the revision by Acts 2002, ch. 26.

This section is new language derived without substantive change from former Art. 27, § 230D(c).

Defined terms:
"Person"	§ 1-101
"State health plan"	§ 8-508

§ 8-513. False representation for qualification.

A person may not knowingly and willfully make, cause to be made, induce, or attempt to induce the making of a false representation with respect to the conditions or operation of a facility, institution, or State health plan in order to help the facility, institution, or State health plan qualify to receive reimbursement under a State health plan. (An. Code 1957, art. 27, § 230E; 2002, ch. 26, § 2.)

REVISOR'S NOTE

**This Revisor's note comprises informa-
tion related to the revision by Acts 2002,
ch. 26.**
This section is new language derived without
substantive change from former Art. 27,
§ 230E.

Defined terms:
"False representation"   § 8-508
"Person"   § 1-101
"State health plan"   § 8-508

§ 8-514. Obtaining benefit by fraud.

A person may not knowingly and willfully obtain, attempt to obtain, or aid another individual in obtaining or attempting to obtain a drug product or medical care, the payment of all or a part of which is or may be made from federal or State funds under a State health plan, by:

(1) fraud, deceit, false representation, or concealment;

(2) counterfeiting or alteration of a medical assistance prescription or a pharmacy assistance prescription distributed under a State health plan;

(3) concealment of a material fact; or

(4) using a false name or a false address. (An. Code 1957, art. 27, § 230F(a); 2002, ch. 26, § 2; ch. 213, § 6.)

SPECIAL REVISOR'S NOTE

**This Special Revisor's note comprises
information related to the revision by Acts
2002, ch. 26 and other chapters amending
this section from the 2002 Legislative Session.**
As enacted by Ch. 26, Acts of 2002, this
section was new language derived without substantive change from former Art. 27, § 230F(a).
However, Ch. 213, Acts of 2002, substituted the
defined term "false representation" for the term
"misrepresentation" enacted by Ch. 26 in item
(1) of this section.
In item (2) of this section, the defined term
"counterfeit[ing]" was substituted by Ch. 26 for

the former reference to "[f]orgery" for consistency within this article.
The Criminal Law Article Review Committee
noted, for the consideration of the General
Assembly, that in item (1) of this section, it was
unclear whether the word "misrepresentation"
enacted by Ch. 26 differed from the term "false
representation" defined in § 8-508 of this subtitle. Chapter 213 addressed this concern.

Defined terms:
"Counterfeit"   § 1-101
"False representation"   § 8-508
"Person"   § 1-101
"State health plan"   § 8-508

§ 8-515. Unauthorized possession of benefit card.

A person may not knowingly and willfully possess a medical assistance card or a pharmacy assistance card distributed under a State health plan or the Medical Assistance or Pharmacy Assistance Program established by Title 15 of the Health - General Article without the authorization of the person to whom the card is issued. (An. Code 1957, art. 27, § 230F(b); 2002, ch. 26, § 2.)

REVISOR'S NOTE

**This Revisor's note comprises informa-
tion related to the revision by Acts 2002,
ch. 26.**
This section is new language derived without
substantive change from former Art. 27,
§ 230F(b).

Defined terms:
"Person"   § 1-101
"State health plan"   § 8-508

§ 8-516. Criminal penalty.

(a) *Violation resulting in death.* — If a violation of this part results in the death of an individual, a person who violates a provision of this part is guilty of a felony and on conviction is subject to imprisonment not exceeding life or a fine not exceeding $200,000 or both.

(b) *Violation resulting in serious injury.* — If a violation of this part results in serious injury to an individual, a person who violates a provision of this part is guilty of a felony and on conviction is subject to imprisonment not exceeding 20 years or a fine not exceeding $100,000 or both.

(c) *Violation involving at least $500.* — If the value of the money, health care services, or other goods or services involved is $500 or more in the aggregate, a person who violates a provision of this part is guilty of a felony and on conviction is subject to imprisonment not exceeding 5 years or a fine not exceeding $100,000 or both.

(d) *Other violations.* — A person who violates any other provision of this part is guilty of a misdemeanor and on conviction is subject to imprisonment not exceeding 3 years or a fine not exceeding $50,000 or both.

(e) *Business entity violation.* — (1) In this subsection, "business entity" includes an association, firm, institution, partnership, and corporation.

(2) A business entity that violates a provision of this part is subject to a fine not exceeding:

(i) $250,000 for each felony; and

(ii) $100,000 for each misdemeanor. (An. Code 1957, art. 27, § 230H; 2002, ch. 26, § 2.)

REVISOR'S NOTE

This Revisor's note comprises information related to the revision by Acts 2002, ch. 26.

This section is new language derived without substantive change from former Art. 27, § 230H.

In subsection (e)(1) of this section, the former reference to a "copartnership" is deleted as included in the comprehensive reference to a "partnership".

Defined terms:

"Person"	§ 1-101
"Serious injury"	§ 8-508
"State health plan"	§ 8-508

§ 8-517. Civil penalty.

(a) *In general.* — A health care provider who violates a provision of this part is liable to the State for a civil penalty not more than three times the amount of the overpayment.

(b) *Additional to other penalties.* — The civil penalty provided in this section is in addition to any other penalty provided by law.

(c) *Restitution not limited.* — This section may not be construed to limit a victim's right to restitution under Title 11, Subtitle 6 of the Criminal Procedure Article. (An. Code 1957, art. 27, § 230G; 2002, ch. 26, § 2.)

REVISOR'S NOTE

This Revisor's note comprises information related to the revision by Acts 2002, ch. 26.

This section is new language derived without substantive change from former Art. 27, § 230G.

In subsection (c) of this section, the reference to "Title 11, Subtitle 6 of the Criminal Procedure Article" is substituted for the former obsolete reference to "§ 807 of this article" for accuracy.

§§ 8-518, 8-519.

Reserved.

Part III. Other Public Fraud.

§ 8-520. Fundraising.

(a) *"Public safety officer" defined.* — In this section, "public safety officer" means:

(1) a police officer;

(2) a paid or volunteer fire fighter;

(3) an emergency medical technician;

(4) a rescue squad member;

(5) the State Fire Marshal; or

(6) a sworn officer of the State Fire Marshal.

(b) *Scope of section.* — This section does not prohibit, limit, or interfere with the right of an off-duty public safety officer who is not in uniform from participating in a charitable or other fundraising campaign.

(c) *Prohibited.* — A person may not encourage, solicit, or receive contributions of money or any thing of value for, or offer any thing for sale in, a charitable or other fundraising campaign by representing to the public that the charitable or other fundraising campaign is approved by:

(1) a police or fire department in the State without the prior written consent of the chief administrative officer of the police or fire department or from the chief administrative officer's designee; or

(2) a public safety officer or member of the family of a public safety officer without the prior written consent of the public safety officer or a family member of the public safety officer.

(d) *Penalty.* — A person who violates this section is guilty of a misdemeanor and on conviction is subject to imprisonment not exceeding 60 days or a fine not exceeding $1,000 or both for each violation. (An. Code 1957, art. 27, § 233A; 2002, ch. 26, § 2.)

REVISOR'S NOTE

This Revisor's note comprises information related to the revision by Acts 2002, ch. 26.

This section is new language derived without substantive change from former Art. 27, § 233A.

In subsection (c) of this section, the references to a "thing" of value are substituted for the former references to "items" of value for clarity and consistency within this article.

Also in subsection (c) of this section, the former phrase "or to prospective donors" is deleted as included in the comprehensive reference to the "public".

Also in subsection (c) of this section, the former reference to any police or fire department "of any jurisdiction within this State" is deleted as redundant.

Also in subsection (c) of this section, the former word "donations" is deleted as included in the word "contributions".

The Criminal Law Article Review Committee notes, for the consideration of the General Assembly, that in subsection (a) of this section, the defined term "public safety officer" does not include a sheriff.

Defined term:
"Person"   § 1-101

§ 8-521. Fraudulently obtaining legal representation from Public Defender's Office.

(a) *Prohibited.* — A person may not obtain or attempt to obtain legal representation from the Office of the Public Defender by willfully and knowingly:

(1) making a false representation or false statement;

(2) failing to disclose the person's true financial condition; or

(3) using any other fraudulent means.

(b) *Penalty.* — A person who violates this section is guilty of a misdemeanor and on conviction is subject to imprisonment not exceeding 1 year or a fine not exceeding $1,000 or both. (An. Code 1957, art. 27, § 214B; 2002, ch. 26, § 2.)

REVISOR'S NOTE

This Revisor's note comprises information related to the revision by Acts 2002, ch. 26.

This section is new language derived without substantive change from former Art. 27, § 214B.

In the introductory language of subsection (a) of this section, the former reference to "falsely" is deleted as implicit in the references to "making a false representation or false statement" and "using any other fraudulent means".

In subsection (a)(3) of this section, the phrase "using any other fraudulent means" is substituted for the former phrase "in any other fraudulent manner" for clarity.

In subsection (b) of this section, the former phrase "in the discretion of the court" is deleted as implicit in the establishment of maximum penalties.

Defined term:
"Person"   § 1-101

Attorney-client privilege. — The attorney-client privilege does not prohibit disclosure of financial information given to the Public Defender's office by a prospective client when necessary to investigate an alleged fraud by the client in securing representation. 66 Op. Att'y Gen. 15 (1981).

§ 8-522. Use of simulated documents to induce payment.

(a) *Scope of section.* — This section applies to a simulated document even if the document contains a statement that it is not legal process or a government document.

(b) *Prohibited.* — (1) A person may not use, sell, or send or deliver to another, with the intent to induce the payment of a claim, a document that:

(i) simulates a summons, complaint, or other court process of any kind; or

(ii) implies that the person is a part of or associated with a unit of the federal government or a unit of the State or a county or municipal government.

(2) With intent to induce the payment of a claim, a person may not use a seal, insignia, envelope, or any other form that simulates the seal, insignia, envelope, or form of any governmental unit.

(c) *Penalty.* — A person who violates this section is guilty of a misdemeanor and on conviction is subject to a fine not exceeding:

(1) $100 for the first violation; and

(2) $500 for each subsequent violation.

(d) *Exception.* — This section does not prohibit the printing, publication, or distribution of genuine court or legal process forms in blank.

(e) *Proof of sending.* — Proof that the document was mailed or delivered to any person with the intent that it be forwarded to the intended recipient is sufficient proof of sending.

(f) *Venue.* — A person who has been charged with a violation of this section may be prosecuted in the county in which the simulated document was used, sold, sent, or delivered. (An. Code 1957, art. 27, § 199; 2002, ch. 26, § 2; ch. 43.)

SPECIAL REVISOR'S NOTE

This Special Revisor's note comprises information related to the revision by Acts 2002, ch. 26 and other chapters amending this section from the 2002 Legislative Session.

As enacted by Ch. 26, Acts of 2002, this section was new language derived without substantive change from former Art. 27, § 199. However, Ch. 43, Acts of 2002, substituted a unit of "the State or a county or municipal government" for the former reference to a unit of "a State or municipal government" in subsection (b)(1)(ii) of this section.

In subsection (b)(2) of this section, the reference to a "form" was substituted by Ch. 26 for the former reference to a "format" for accuracy.

In subsection (c) of this section, the reference to being "guilty of a misdemeanor" was added by Ch. 26 to state expressly that which was only implied in the former law. In this State, any crime that was not a felony at common law and has not been declared a felony by statute is considered to be a misdemeanor. *See State v. Canova,* 278 Md. 483, 490 (1976); *Bowser v. State,* 136 Md. 342, 345 (1920); *Dutton v. State,* 123 Md. 373, 378 (1914); and *Williams v. State,* 4 Md. App. 342, 347 (1968).

Also in subsection (c) of this section, the references to a "violation" were substituted by Ch. 26 for the former references to an "offense" for consistency within this article. *See* General Revisor's Note to article.

In subsection (d) of this section, the reference to forms "in blank" was substituted by Ch. 26 for the former reference to "blank" forms for clarity.

In subsection (f) of this section, the former reference to "Baltimore City" was deleted by Ch. 26 as included in the defined term "county". *See* § 1-101 of this article.

The Criminal Law Article Review Committee noted, for the consideration of the General Assembly, that in subsection (b)(1)(ii) of this section, a person was prohibited from using a document that implied that the person was a part of "State" or "municipal" government but not "county" government. The General Assembly was asked to consider adding a reference to "county" government. Chapter 43 addressed this concern.

Defined terms:
"County"	§ 1-101
"Person"	§ 1-101

§ 8-523. Housing assistance — Knowingly making false statement.

(a) *Definitions.* — (1) In this section the following words have the meanings indicated.

(2) "Housing agency" means an agency established to administer a housing assistance program under the Housing and Community Development Article.

(3) "Housing assistance" means financial assistance, as defined in § 1-101 of the Housing and Community Development Article, offered for the purpose of obtaining housing based on need under a program administered by a housing agency and financed wholly or partially by federal, State, or local funds.

(b) *Prohibited.* — A person may not knowingly make a false statement of a material fact for the purpose of influencing a housing agency regarding:

(1) an application for housing assistance; or

(2) an action affecting housing assistance already provided.

(c) *Penalty.* — A person who violates this section is guilty of a misdemeanor and on conviction is subject to imprisonment not exceeding 3 years or a fine not exceeding $5,000 or both. (2002, ch. 19, § 10; ch. 556; 2003, ch. 21, § 1; 2005, ch. 44, § 1; 2006, ch. 64.)

SPECIAL REVISOR'S NOTE

This Special Revisor's note comprises information related to the revision by Acts 2002, ch. 26 and other chapters amending this section from the 2002 Legislative Session.

Chapter 556, Acts of 2002, added this section.

In subsection (c) of this section, the order of imprisonment and fine has been reversed to correct a stylistic error under the authority of Ch. 19, § 10, Acts of 2002.

Subtitle 6. Counterfeiting and Related Crimes.

§ 8-601. Counterfeiting of private instruments and documents.

(a) *Prohibited.* — A person, with intent to defraud another, may not counterfeit, cause to be counterfeited, or willingly aid or assist in counterfeiting any:

(1) bond;

(2) check;

(3) deed;

(4) draft;

(5) endorsement or assignment of a bond, draft, check, or promissory note;

(6) entry in an account book or ledger;

(7) letter of credit;

(8) negotiable instrument;

(9) power of attorney;

(10) promissory note;

(11) release or discharge for money or property;

(12) title to a motor vehicle;

(13) waiver or release of mechanics' lien; or

(14) will or codicil.

(b) *Prohibited — Possession of counterfeit.* — A person may not knowingly, willfully, and with fraudulent intent possess a counterfeit of any of the items listed in subsection (a) of this section.

(c) *Penalty.* — (1) A person who violates subsection (a) of this section is guilty of a felony and on conviction is subject to imprisonment not exceeding 10 years or a fine not exceeding $1,000 or both.

(2) A person who violates subsection (b) of this section is guilty of a misdemeanor and on conviction is subject to imprisonment not exceeding 3 years or a fine not exceeding $1,000 or both.

(d) *Venue.* — Notwithstanding any other provision of law, the prosecution of an alleged violation of this section or for an alleged violation of a crime based on an act that establishes a violation of this section may be commenced in any county in which:

(1) an element of the crime occurred;

(2) the deed or other alleged counterfeit instrument is recorded in the county land records, filed with the clerk of the circuit court, or filed with the register of wills;

(3) the victim resides; or

(4) if the victim is not an individual, the victim conducts business. (An. Code 1957, art. 27, § 44(a); 2002, ch. 26, § 2; 2004, ch. 484; 2005, ch. 24; 2011, ch. 73.)

REVISOR'S NOTE

This section is new language derived without substantive change from former Art. 27, § 44(a).

In subsection (a) of this section, the defined term "counterfeit" is substituted for the former reference to "falsely mak[ing], forg[ing] or counterfeit[ing]" an instrument or document, although the defined term also includes "materially alter[ing]" such a document. Any such "materially altered" instrument or document would constitute a "counterfeit" instrument or document under current law. No substantive change is intended.

Also in subsection (a) of this section, the reference to the intent of a person to defraud "another" is substituted for the former reference to the intent of a person to defraud "any person whomsoever" for consistency within this subtitle.

Also in subsection (a) of this section, the former reference to "procur[ing]" another to commit forgery is deleted as included in the reference to "caus[ing]" another to commit forgery.

In subsection (a)(1) and (4) of this section, the former references to a "writing obligatory" are deleted as included in the references to a "bond".

In subsection (a)(3) and (4) of this section, the references to a "draft" are substituted for the former references to a "bill of exchange" for consistency with usage in the Commercial Law Article. *See* CL § 3-104 and Official Comment to that section.

In subsection (a)(4) and (7) of this section, the former references to a promissory note "for the payment of money or property" are deleted as surplusage.

In subsection (a)(8) of this section, the reference to a "release or discharge" is substituted for the former references to any "acquisition or receipt" for clarity.

In subsection (a)(10) of this section, the former reference to a "document or affidavit" of waiver or release is deleted as surplusage.

In subsection (a)(11) of this section, the former reference to a "testament" is deleted as included in the reference to a "will".

Defined terms:

"Counterfeit"	§ 1-101
"Person"	§ 1-101

Cross references. — As to indictments for forgery, see § 1-401 of this article.

Effect of amendments. — Chapter 73, Acts 2011, effective October 1, 2011, added (d)(2) and redesignated accordingly.

University of Baltimore Law Forum. — For a 2009 development, "Walker v. State: A Showing on the Record that, Under the Totality of the Circumstances, the Defendant Had Knowledge of the Jury Trial Right Satisfies the Requirement of a Knowing Waiver of the Right to a Jury Trial," see 39 U. Balt. L. F. 262 (2009).

Jurisdiction. — Jurisdiction over the subject matter may attach where acts are performed in one state with the intention of producing an illegal effect in another, or where the crime is consummated. It is not a fatal objection that there may be concurrent jurisdiction at the place where the offense is begun. Medley v. Warden of Md. House of Cor., 210 Md. 649, 123

A.2d 595, cert. denied, 352 U.S. 858, 77 S. Ct. 77, 1 L. Ed. 2d 64 (1956); Cole v. State, 232 Md. 111, 194 A.2d 278 (1963), cert. denied, 375 U.S. 980, 84 S. Ct. 503, 11 L. Ed. 2d 425 (1964).

Forgery defined. — Forgery has been defined as "the false making or material alteration, with intent to defraud, of any writing which, if genuine, might apparently be of legal efficacy or the foundation of a legal liability." Reddick v. State, 219 Md. 95, 148 A.2d 384, cert. denied, 360 U.S. 930, 79 S. Ct. 1448, 3 L. Ed. 2d 1544 (1959); Smith v. State, 7 Md. App. 457, 256 A.2d 357 (1969); Harding v. Ja Laur Corp., 20 Md. App. 209, 315 A.2d 132 (1974); Green v. State, 32 Md. App. 567, 363 A.2d 530 (1976).

Forgery is false making. Smith v. State, 7 Md. App. 457, 256 A.2d 357 (1969).

Forgery is the fraudulent making of a false writing having apparent legal significance. Smith v. State, 7 Md. App. 457, 256 A.2d 357 (1969); Banks v. State, 8 Md. App. 182, 258 A.2d 924 (1969); Harding v. Ja Laur Corp., 20 Md. App. 209, 315 A.2d 132 (1974); State v. Reese, 283 Md. 86, 388 A.2d 122 (1978).

The counterfeiting of any writing with a fraudulent intent, whereby another may be prejudiced, is forgery at common law. Smith v. State, 7 Md. App. 457, 256 A.2d 357 (1969); Reese v. State, 37 Md. App. 450, 378 A.2d 4 (1977), aff'd, 283 Md. 86, 388 A.2d 122 (1978).

Forgery involves not the making of false entries for fraudulent purposes in an otherwise genuine document but the very manufacturing of a false or spurious document itself. Reese v. State, 37 Md. App. 450, 378 A.2d 4 (1977), aff'd, 283 Md. 86, 388 A.2d 122 (1978).

Forgery, in its most fundamental character, is not an offense involving false and fraudulent writing generally but is a very specific offense in the nature of counterfeiting. Reese v. State, 37 Md. App. 450, 378 A.2d 4 (1977), aff'd, 283 Md. 86, 388 A.2d 122 (1978).

A document is not considered false for purposes of forgery merely because it contains a false statement of fact. The falsity required refers to the genuineness of the execution of the document itself; that is, there must be a false making. State v. Reese, 283 Md. 86, 388 A.2d 122 (1978).

"Counterfeit" defined. — Term "counterfeit," in common parlance, signifies the fabrication of a false image or representation; counterfeiting an instrument means falsely making it; and in its broadest sense, it means the making of a copy without authority or right and with a view to deceive or defraud by passing the copy as original or genuine. Smith v. State, 7 Md. App. 457, 256 A.2d 357 (1969).

The term "counterfeit" both by its etymology and common intendment, signifies the fabrication of a false image or representation. In its broadest sense, counterfeiting means the making of a copy without authority or right, and

with a view to deceive or defraud by passing the copy as original or genuine. As thus defined counterfeiting includes forgery. Smith v. State, 7 Md. App. 457, 256 A.2d 357 (1969).

Terms synonymous. — The terms "falsely make" and "forge" are synonymous, both describing a spurious or fictitious making relating to the genuineness of execution of an instrument. Smith v. State, 7 Md. App. 457, 256 A.2d 357 (1969); Reese v. State, 37 Md. App. 450, 378 A.2d 4 (1977), aff'd, 283 Md. 86, 388 A.2d 122 (1978).

The terms "falsely make, forge or counterfeit," as used in a prior similar provision, are virtually synonymous and were collectively intended to proscribe the crime of forgery. Smith v. State, 7 Md. App. 457, 256 A.2d 357 (1969); Bieber v. State, 8 Md. App. 522, 261 A.2d 202 (1970); Reese v. State, 37 Md. App. 450, 378 A.2d 4 (1977), aff'd, 283 Md. 86, 388 A.2d 122 (1978).

The terms "forge," "falsely make," and "counterfeit," as used in a prior similar provision, are largely synonymous and describe a spurious or fictitious making relating to the genuineness of execution of an instrument. Banks v. State, 8 Md. App. 182, 258 A.2d 924 (1969).

"Private instruments and documents" defined. — A check is a bill of exchange, and a forgery of the endorsement thereon is a felony. Hawthorn v. State, 56 Md. 530 (1881); Laird v. State, 61 Md. 309 (1884).

A certificate of indebtedness known as city stock is a bond within the meaning of a prior similar provision, and an endorsement of such certificate with fraudulent intent may be a forgery though the certificate upon its face is transferable only at the mayor's office in person or by attorney. Bishop v. State, 55 Md. 138 (1880).

A check is a bill of exchange and may be the subject of a forgery. Att'y Griev. Comm'n v. James, 333 Md. 174, 634 A.2d 48 (1993).

Deed of trust. — Deed of trust is a deed within the contemplation of this section. Bieber v. State, 8 Md. App. 522, 261 A.2d 202 (1970).

Common law offense still applicable where statute does not cover field. — Where a statute such as a prior similar provision has been enacted covering forgery, the common law offense is still applicable where the statute was not intended to cover the whole field or to repeal the common law. Reddick v. State, 219 Md. 95, 148 A.2d 384, cert. denied, 360 U.S. 930, 79 S. Ct. 1448, 3 L. Ed. 2d 1544 (1959); Green v. State, 32 Md. App. 567, 363 A.2d 530 (1976).

Where a statute has been enacted covering the crime of forgery, common law forgery subsists to the extent that the statute was not intended to preempt the entire field or repeal the common law. State v. Reese, 283 Md. 86, 388 A.2d 122 (1978).

Fact that particular class of documents is not specified not precluding prosecution. — Fact that particular class of documents is not specified in section does not preclude prosecution of an accused for forgery of an unenumerated type of instrument, if fraudulent falsification of the writing in question would have been an indictable offense at common law. State v. Reese, 283 Md. 86, 388 A.2d 122 (1978).

Elements of offense. — General Assembly did not outline elements of offense in a prior similar provision. Pearson v. State, 8 Md. App. 79, 258 A.2d 917 (1969).

The gist of the offense is false representation, whether acted on or not. Pearson v. State, 8 Md. App. 79, 258 A.2d 917 (1969).

As to the element of intent to defraud, there need not be an identified victim who suffered a pecuniary loss. Att'y Griev. Comm'n v. James, 333 Md. 174, 634 A.2d 48 (1993).

Elements of forgery. — The offense of forgery is comprised of essentially three elements: (1) There must be a writing which is the proper subject of forgery; (2) this writing must be false; (3) the writing must have been rendered false with intent to defraud. State v. Reese, 283 Md. 86, 388 A.2d 122 (1978); Att'y Griev. Comm'n v. James, 333 Md. 174, 634 A.2d 48 (1993).

One of the essential elements of forgery is a writing in such form as to be apparently of some legal efficacy, and hence, capable of defrauding or deceiving. Smith v. State, 7 Md. App. 457, 256 A.2d 357 (1969); Harding v. Ja Laur Corp., 20 Md. App. 209, 315 A.2d 132 (1974).

Forgery of any material part of instrument. — Forgery of any material part of an instrument is forgery of the instrument. Green v. State, 32 Md. App. 567, 363 A.2d 530 (1976).

Instrument valueless on its face is not subject of forgery. — If the instrument is entirely valueless on its face and of no binding force or effect for any purpose of harm, liability or injury to anyone, all authorities agree that it cannot be the subject of forgery. Smith v. State, 7 Md. App. 457, 256 A.2d 357 (1969).

A person cannot be convicted of the forgery of a paper absolutely invalid upon its face and which could not operate to the prejudice of another. Smith v. State, 7 Md. App. 457, 256 A.2d 357 (1969).

Forgery by use of assumed or fictitious name. — The offense of forgery may exist even though the name used be an assumed or fictitious one, when it is shown that it was used with the intention to defraud. Lyman v. State, 136 Md. 40, 109 A. 548 (1920); El-Masri v. State, 228 Md. 114, 178 A.2d 407 (1962).

The mere filling in of the fictitious name of the payee and the amount, might be enough to constitute forgery, even if another unauthorized person had signed the name of the pur-

ported drawer. Draper v. State, 231 Md. 423, 190 A.2d 643 (1963), cert. denied, 381 U.S. 952, 85 S. Ct. 1807, 14 L. Ed. 2d 725 (1965).

Filling out check of another to another. — Filling out check of another to another and signing held to be forgery. Draper v. State, 231 Md. 423, 190 A.2d 643 (1963), cert. denied, 381 U.S. 952, 85 S. Ct. 1807, 14 L. Ed. 2d 725 (1965).

Endorsement or negotiation of check not relevant. — That check was not endorsed or negotiated is not determinative of the question of forgery. Draper v. State, 231 Md. 423, 190 A.2d 643 (1963), cert. denied, 381 U.S. 952, 85 S. Ct. 1807, 14 L. Ed. 2d 725 (1965).

Forgery inferred from possession and uttering of forged instrument. — Forgery can be inferred from the possession and uttering of the forged instrument in the absence of a satisfactory explanation. Bieber v. State, 8 Md. App. 522, 261 A.2d 202 (1970); Green v. State, 32 Md. App. 567, 363 A.2d 530 (1976).

Possession by the accused of the forged instrument, with claim of title thereto, is prima facie evidence that he either forged it, or procured it to be forged. Bieber v. State, 8 Md. App. 522, 261 A.2d 202 (1970).

Forgery of endorsement. — Forgery of an endorsement on any of certain specified instruments is, or at least can be, a separately indictable crime. Green v. State, 32 Md. App. 567, 363 A.2d 530 (1976).

It is the separate treatment of the offenses in a prior similar provision which mandates that a person may not be convicted of forging a check when the proof shows that he forged only an endorsement. Green v. State, 32 Md. App. 567, 363 A.2d 530 (1976).

No violation shown. — Making of false entries in tax rolls may well have been fraudulent but was not a forgery where there was no manufacturing or counterfeiting of a spurious or nongenuine tax roll, but merely the making of false statements in a genuine document. Reese v. State, 37 Md. App. 450, 378 A.2d 4 (1977), aff'd, 283 Md. 86, 388 A.2d 122 (1978).

It is not forgery for an individual to make false and fictitious entries in a tax roll. State v. Reese, 283 Md. 86, 388 A.2d 122 (1978).

The making of a false entry in a tax roll is tantamount to making a false representation of fact in an otherwise genuine document. This is not forgery, despite the reprehensible nature of such conduct. State v. Reese, 283 Md. 86, 388 A.2d 122 (1978).

Separate offenses. — Proof that the defendant forged the endorsement on a bill of exchange, which is listed separately in this section, was a fatal variance from the charge of forging a bill of exchange and uttering a false or forged bill of exchange. Harris v. State, 67 Md. App. 92, 506 A.2d 655 (1986).

Convictions for false pretenses and for forgery are not inconsistent. McDuffy v. State, 6 Md. App. 537, 252 A.2d 270 (1969).

A false pretense does not require a false signature on a document and a forgery does not require the use of a credit card or an actual reliance on the false document. McDuffy v. State, 6 Md. App. 537, 252 A.2d 270 (1969).

Jury trial knowingly waived. — Convictions for violating this section were upheld because defendant's waiver of a jury trial was made knowingly and voluntarily, in compliance with the requirements of Rule 4-246(b) . Walker v. State, 406 Md. 369, 958 A.2d 915 (2008).

Attorney's misrepresentation of endorsement constituted forgery. — An attorney's misrepresentation of an endorsement constituted forgery which warranted suspension. Att'y Griev. Comm'n v. James, 333 Md. 174, 634 A.2d 48 (1993).

Cited in Moore v. State, 198 Md. App. 655, 18 A.3d 981 (2011).

§ 8-602. Issuing counterfeit private instruments and documents.

(a) *Prohibited.* — A person, with intent to defraud another, may not issue or publish as true a counterfeit instrument or document listed in § 8-601 of this subtitle.

(b) *Penalty.* — A person who violates this section is guilty of a felony and on conviction is subject to imprisonment not exceeding 10 years or a fine not exceeding $1,000 or both. (An. Code 1957, art. 27, § 44(b); 2002, ch. 26, § 2.)

REVISOR'S NOTE

This Revisor's note comprises information related to the revision by Acts 2002, ch. 26.

This section is new language derived without substantive change from former Art. 27, § 44(b).

In subsection (a) of this section, the defined term "counterfeit" is substituted for the former reference to possessing a "forged, altered, or counterfeited," instrument or document, although the defined term only includes a "materially" altered instrument or document. In order to prove fraud under current law, any such alteration must be material. No substantive change is intended.

Also in subsection (a) of this section, the reference to the intent of a person to defraud "another" is substituted for the former reference to the intent of a person to defraud "any person whomsoever" for consistency within this subtitle.

Also in subsection (a) of this section and throughout this subtitle, the reference to "issu-[ing]" an instrument or document is substituted for the former reference to "utter[ing]" an instrument or document, for consistency within this article.

Also in subsection (a) of this section and throughout this subtitle, the references to a "counterfeit" item have been substituted for the former references to a "counterfeited" item for consistency within this subtitle.

Also in subsection (a) of this section, the reference to an "instrument or document listed in § 8-601 of this subtitle" is substituted for the former reference to a "deed, title to motor vehicle, will, testament or codicil, power of attorney, bond, writing obligatory, bill of exchange, promissory note for the payment of money or property, or endorsement, or assignment of any bond, writing obligatory, bill of exchange, promissory note for the payment of money or property, acquittance or receipt for money or property, or. . . any false document of waiver or release of mechanics' lien, or any entries in a book of account or ledger" for brevity and clarity.

In subsection (b) of this section, the reference to a person being "subject to imprisonment" is substituted for the former reference to a person being "sentenced to the penitentiary" for consistency within this article. Currently, inmates are sentenced to the custody of a unit such as the Division of Correction and then are placed in a particular facility. *See* CS § 9-103.

Defined terms:

"Counterfeit"	§ 1-101
"Person"	§ 1-101

Jurisdiction. — Where one was charged in separate courts with forging and uttering, the jurisdictional requirement was satisfied by the fact that the offense of uttering occurred in the localities where the charges were laid. Medley v. Warden of Md. House of Cor., 210 Md. 649,

123 A.2d 595, cert. denied, 352 U.S. 858, 77 S. Ct. 77, 1 L. Ed. 2d 64 (1956).

As between states, forgery is deemed to be committed at the place where the false instrument is uttered. Medley v. Warden of Md. House of Cor., 210 Md. 649, 123 A.2d 595, cert. denied, 352 U.S. 858, 77 S. Ct. 77, 1 L. Ed. 2d 64 (1956); Cole v. State, 232 Md. 111, 194 A.2d 278 (1963), cert. denied, 375 U.S. 980, 84 S. Ct. 503, 11 L. Ed. 2d 425 (1964).

There is a rebuttable presumption that the instrument was forged in the county where uttered and at the date on the instrument. This presumption must be indulged, in the absence of evidence to the contrary, due to the difficulty of proving the place of the forgery. Cole v. State, 232 Md. 111, 194 A.2d 278 (1963), cert. denied, 375 U.S. 980, 84 S. Ct. 503, 11 L. Ed. 2d 425 (1964).

Venue. — As to venue, the uttering of a forged instrument in the county where the indictment was found is strong evidence in law that the forgery was committed in the same county. Cole v. State, 232 Md. 111, 194 A.2d 278 (1963), cert. denied, 375 U.S. 980, 84 S. Ct. 503, 11 L. Ed. 2d 425 (1964).

Terms defined. — The words "forged" and "counterfeited," as used in a statute creating the offense of passing forged, counterfeited or falsely altered instruments, have been held to be synonymous. Smith v. State, 7 Md. App. 457, 256 A.2d 357 (1969); Reese v. State, 37 Md. App. 450, 378 A.2d 4 (1977), aff'd, 283 Md. 86, 388 A.2d 122 (1978).

Common law offense of uttering. — At common law, uttering a forged instrument is offering as genuine an instrument known to be false, with intent to defraud. Pearson v. State, 8 Md. App. 79, 258 A.2d 917 (1969).

Knowledge that an instrument was forged was a required element of the crime of uttering at common law in this country. Pearson v. State, 8 Md. App. 79, 258 A.2d 917 (1969).

Elements of offense. — To constitute the offense of uttering, it is not necessary that the accused be the actual forger, and testimony as to the uttering of other checks may be admissible to show a common scheme or intent. Generally the mere offer of the false instrument with fraudulent intent constitutes an uttering regardless of its successful consummation and the gist of the offense is the false representation, whether acted upon or not. Levy v. State, 225 Md. 201, 170 A.2d 216, cert. denied, 368 U.S. 865, 82 S. Ct. 113, 7 L. Ed. 2d 62 (1961).

The mere offer of a false instrument with fraudulent intent constitutes an uttering regardless of its successful consummation. This would be true, even if the instrument had been entirely filled out by an unauthorized third person. Draper v. State, 231 Md. 423, 190 A.2d 643 (1963), cert. denied, 381 U.S. 952, 85 S. Ct. 1807, 14 L. Ed. 2d 725 (1965).

While a prior similar provision did not contain any requirement of prior knowledge of the instrument's falsity, or of an intention to defraud, it is plain that by making it unlawful to "utter or publish as true" a forged instrument, the General Assembly thereby intended to encompass all elements of the offense — long known in Maryland — of uttering a forged instrument. Pearson v. State, 8 Md. App. 79, 258 A.2d 917 (1969).

Prior knowledge that the instrument was a forgery is an essential ingredient of the offense of uttering. Pearson v. State, 8 Md. App. 79, 258 A.2d 917 (1969).

The factors required to constitute the crime of uttering a forged instrument as proscribed by this section are: (1) The instrument must be uttered or published as true or genuine; (2) it must be known by the party uttering or publishing it that it was false, altered, forged or counterfeited; and (3) it must be uttered or published with intent to defraud another person. Pearson v. State, 8 Md. App. 79, 258 A.2d 917 (1969); Banks v. State, 8 Md. App. 182, 258 A.2d 924 (1969); Bieber v. State, 8 Md. App. 522, 261 A.2d 202 (1970).

It is an essential element of the crime of uttering that the person uttering the forged instrument must have knowledge that it was forged or altered. Bieber v. State, 8 Md. App. 522, 261 A.2d 202 (1970).

To constitute the offense of uttering it is not necessary that the accused be the actual forger. Pearson v. State, 8 Md. App. 79, 258 A.2d 917 (1969); Bieber v. State, 8 Md. App. 522, 261 A.2d 202 (1970).

Uttering as a separate crime. — It is a separate and distinct crime to utter or publish any false, forged, altered or counterfeited instrument. Bieber v. State, 8 Md. App. 522, 261 A.2d 202 (1970).

No distinction between principals in first and second degree. — As to indictment, conviction, and punishment for forging and uttering, there is no distinction between principals in the first and second degree. Thomas v. State, 3 Md. App. 708, 240 A.2d 646 (1968).

What constitutes intent to defraud. — If the defendant at the time he uttered the instrument knew it was false, the inevitable consequence was that he intended to defraud. Pearson v. State, 8 Md. App. 79, 258 A.2d 917 (1969).

A person may pass a forged instrument without knowledge of its falsity, but with the intent to defraud, as, for example, where he undertakes to negotiate an instrument believed genuine belonging to another which he may have found or stolen or for the payment of which sufficient funds were known not to be available. In these instances, the person's intent would be fraudulent but he would not be guilty of uttering a forged instrument. Pearson v. State, 8 Md. App. 79, 258 A.2d 917 (1969).

Evidence of mens rea. — Testimony as to the uttering of other checks may be admissible to show a common scheme or intent. Pearson v. State, 8 Md. App. 79, 258 A.2d 917 (1969).

While guilty knowledge is essential to a conviction of uttering, such knowledge, like fraudulent intent, may be inferred from the facts and circumstances accompanying the particular transaction. In other words, knowledge, like intent, is a state of mind generally to be inferred from the person's conduct viewed in the light of all the accompanying circumstances. Otherwise stated, the state of one's mind is always a question of fact, and being subjective in nature, proof thereof is seldom direct, but is usually inferred from proven circumstances. Pearson v. State, 8 Md. App. 79, 258 A.2d 917 (1969).

It is not proper to infer by the mere uttering of the false instrument as valid that the person knew it was forged. In other words, the mere act of possessing a forged instrument, and attempting to utter it, cannot give rise to a conclusive inference of guilty knowledge, although it is a circumstance to be taken into consideration with all the other facts in determining whether the defendant knew of the instrument's falsity. Pearson v. State, 8 Md. App. 79, 258 A.2d 917 (1969).

In a prosecution for uttering a forged instrument, it is no more burdensome for the State to adduce proof of guilty knowledge than it is to produce proof of fraudulent intent. Pearson v. State, 8 Md. App. 79, 258 A.2d 917 (1969).

That an accused has guilty knowledge may be shown by direct evidence or it may be inferred from the facts and circumstances of the particular transaction. Bieber v. State, 8 Md. App. 522, 261 A.2d 202 (1970).

Evidence of forgery. — In indictment for forging and uttering a forged note, certain proof as to the existence and loss of the note was held sufficient to authorize introduction of parol evidence as to its contents. Brashears v. State, 58 Md. 563 (1882).

To obtain a conviction for uttering a forged instrument, the State must adduce legally sufficient evidence that the uttered instrument was in fact a forgery. Banks v. State, 8 Md. App. 182, 258 A.2d 924 (1969).

To render a verdict of guilty of forgery, the jury must find from the evidence before them that all the essential elements of forgery were established beyond a reasonable doubt. That the inference properly raised on proof that the defendant was the possessor and utterer may supply such evidence does not mean that the jury may properly convict him of forgery simply because the evidence was sufficient to convict him of uttering. Bieber v. State, 8 Md. App. 522, 261 A.2d 202, cert. denied, 258 Md. 725 (1970).

The possession of an instrument recently forged, by one claiming under it, like the possession of goods recently stolen, is evidence against the possessor. Bieber v. State, 8 Md. App. 522, 261 A.2d 202 (1970).

There is an inference arising from the possession and uttering of a forged instrument which establishes a prima facie case of guilt of forgery by the possessor. Bieber v. State, 8 Md. App. 522, 261 A.2d 202 (1970).

The rule this State has adopted is that, absent a credible nonculpable explanation, the possession and uttering of a forged instrument by one claiming under it raises an inference which provides evidence sufficient to sustain a conviction that the possessor was the forger. In other words the inference makes out a prima facie case which is rebuttable by the showing of circumstances to the contrary. This rule is to be distinguished from the presumption, in the absence of evidence to the contrary, that a forgery was committed where the forged instrument was first uttered by the defendant or found in his possession. Such presumption goes to jurisdiction or venue, not to guilt. Bieber v. State, 8 Md. App. 522, 261 A.2d 202 (1970).

The rule regarding the inference that the possessor and utterer is the forger is to be distinguished from the doctrine that when a person is charged with forgery and uttering and the evidence is sufficient to prove uttering, it would not invalidate a general verdict of guilty, even if the evidence was insufficient to prove forgery or showed that the uttered instrument was forged by someone else. Bieber v. State, 8 Md. App. 522, 261 A.2d 202 (1970).

Evidence of completed transaction. — While evidence that the offense of obtaining money by false pretenses was consummated may not sustain a conviction of attempting that offense, it does not follow that such evidence precludes a conviction of uttering, especially when there was no conviction of the offense of obtaining money by false pretenses and no merger of the uttering offense into the false pretense offense. Beard v. State, 4 Md. App. 685, 244 A.2d 906 (1968).

The presentation of a forged deed for recording among the county land records is sufficient to show an uttering of it as true or genuine. Bieber v. State, 8 Md. App. 522, 261 A.2d 202, cert. denied, 258 Md. 725 (1970).

Forgery and uttering distinguished. — In forgery the instrument must be falsely made "with intention to defraud"; in uttering, although the instrument must be falsely made, it need not be so made with an intention to defraud — if it was in fact false and published as genuine with knowledge of its falsity, the crime is committed by its publishing with intent to defraud. Bieber v. State, 8 Md. App. 522, 261 A.2d 202 (1970).

Uttering as forgery. — Where one was charged in separate counts with forging and uttering, which are both designated as offenses, proof of uttering would alone support general verdicts of guilty. Medley v. Warden of Md. House of Cor., 210 Md. 649, 123 A.2d 595, cert. denied, 352 U.S. 858, 77 S. Ct. 77, 1 L. Ed. 2d 64 (1956).

Under a general verdict a conviction of uttering will alone suffice to sustain a conviction of forgery and false pretense. This would be true, even if the instrument had been entirely filled out by an unauthorized third person. Draper v. State, 231 Md. 423, 190 A.2d 643 (1963), cert. denied, 381 U.S. 952, 85 S. Ct. 1807, 14 L. Ed. 2d 725 (1965).

In proving uttering, forgery is not necessarily proved. Bieber v. State, 8 Md. App. 522, 261 A.2d 202, cert. denied, 258 Md. 725 (1970).

Proof that a person committed uttering is not per se proof that he forged the uttered instrument. Bieber v. State, 8 Md. App. 522, 261 A.2d 202, cert. denied, 258 Md. 725 (1970).

The criminal agent in the forgery is not necessarily the criminal agent in the uttering; one person may forge the instrument and another person may utter it. Bieber v. State, 8 Md. App. 522, 261 A.2d 202, cert. denied, 258 Md. 725 (1970).

Separate offenses. — Uttering and obtaining money by false pretenses are separate and distinct crimes. Beard v. State, 4 Md. App. 685, 244 A.2d 906 (1968), cert. denied, 252 Md. 729 (1969).

Effect of acquittal of forgery or uttering particular paper. — An acquittal of forging, or uttering a particular forged paper, will not preclude the State from proving the fact of the possession or the uttering of such forged paper in another prosecution against the same party for a crime of the same character. Bell v. State, 57 Md. 108 (1881).

Merger. — Under proper circumstances, an uttering offense may merge into a false pretense offense. Beard v. State, 4 Md. App. 685, 244 A.2d 906 (1968), cert. denied, 252 Md. 729 (1969).

When defendant was convicted of issuing counterfeit currency and uttering a forged document, as well as theft and attempted theft, the issuing and uttering offenses did not have to be considered the same offenses as theft and attempted theft, for double jeopardy purposes, on the theory that the only evidence supporting the theft and attempted theft convictions was the same evidence that supported the issuing and uttering convictions, requiring the convictions and sentences for issuing and uttering to be vacated, because (1) the "actual evidence" test of merger had been rejected, (2) the theft offense contained an element not found in the issuing offense, namely, obtaining control over property of another, and (3) the attempted theft offense contained an element not found in the uttering offense, namely attempting to obtain control over property of another. Moore v. State, 198 Md. App. 655, 18 A.3d 981 (2011).

Penalty. — Sentence of three years was far below the maximum and did not constitute cruel and unusual punishment. Agner v. Warden of Md. House of Cor., 203 Md. 665, 99 A.2d 735 (1953).

Upon valid convictions of forgery and uttering any sentence on each conviction within the limit prescribed by law would be valid and would not constitute cruel and unusual punishment in violation of constitutional protections. Bieber v. State, 8 Md. App. 522, 261 A.2d 202 (1970).

§ 8-603. Possessing counterfeit title to motor vehicle.

(a) *Prohibited.* — A person may not knowingly possess, with unlawful intent, a counterfeit title to a motor vehicle.

(b) *Penalty.* — A person who violates this section is guilty of a misdemeanor and on conviction is subject to imprisonment not exceeding 3 years or a fine not exceeding $1,000 or both. (An. Code 1957, art. 27, § 44(c); 2002, ch. 26, § 2.)

REVISOR'S NOTE

This Revisor's note comprises information related to the revision by Acts 2002, ch. 26.

This section is new language derived without substantive change from former Art. 27, § 44(c).

In subsection (a) of this section, the defined term "counterfeit" is substituted for the former reference to possessing a "forged, counterfeited, or altered" title, although use of the defined term also includes a "falsely made" title. Any such "materially altered" title would constitute a "counterfeit" title under current law. In addition, the use of the defined term "counterfeit" only includes a "materially" altered title rather than any altered title. In order to prove fraud under current law, any such alteration to a title must be material. No substantive change is intended.

Defined terms:
"Counterfeit" § 1-101

§ 8-604. Counterfeiting United States currency with intent to defraud.

(a) *Prohibited.* — A person may not, with intent to defraud:

(1) manufacture United States currency;

(2) counterfeit, cause to be counterfeited, or willingly aid or assist in counterfeiting United States currency; or

(3) make, scan, record, reproduce, transmit, or have in the person's control, custody, or possession an analog, digital, or electronic image of United States currency.

(b) *Penalty.* — A person who violates this section is guilty of a felony and on conviction is subject to imprisonment not exceeding 10 years or a fine not exceeding $10,000 or both. (2003, chs. 56, 57.)

§ 8-604.1. Possessing or issuing counterfeit United States currency.

(a) *Prohibited.* — A person may not knowingly possess, with unlawful intent, or issue counterfeit United States currency.

(b) *Penalty.* — A person who violates this section is guilty of a misdemeanor and on conviction is subject to imprisonment not exceeding 3 years or a fine not exceeding $1,000 or both. (An. Code 1957, art. 27, § 44(d); 2002, ch. 26, § 2; 2003, chs. 56, 57.)

REVISOR'S NOTE

This Revisor's note comprises information related to the revision by Acts 2002, ch. 26.

This section is new language derived without substantive change from former Art. 27, § 44(d).

In subsection (a) of this section, the defined term "counterfeit" is substituted for the former reference to possessing "forged, counterfeit, or altered" currency, although use of the defined term also includes "falsely made" currency. Any such "materially altered" currency would constitute "counterfeit" currency under current law. In addition, the use of the defined term "counterfeit" only includes "materially" altered currency rather than any altered currency. In order to prove fraud under current law, any such alteration to currency must be material. No substantive change is intended.

Also in subsection (a) of this section, the word "issue" is substituted for the former word "utter" for consistency within this article.

Defined terms:

"Counterfeit"	§ 1-101
"Person"	§ 1-101

Separate crimes of possessing and issuing. — Defendant was properly convicted, under this section, of separate crimes of possessing and issuing countefeit currency because (1) the statute did not create a single offense that could be committed in two different ways but, rather, criminalized the distinct acts of possessing counterfeit currency and issuing counterfeit currency, and (2) (b), imposing a penalty of incarceration not exceeding three years, a fine not exceeding $1,000, or both for "a person who violates this section," did not require a different conclusion, as the statute only showed the General Assembly's belief that the acts of possessing or issuing counterfeit currency were worthy of equal criminal punishment. Moore v. State, 198 Md. App. 655, 18 A.3d 981 (2011).

Merger. — When defendant was convicted of violating this section by possessing and issuing counterfeit currency based on bills with different serial numbers arising from the same transaction, the convictions merged for sentencing, under the rule of lenity, because there was nothing in the language of the statute to indicate the intent of the General Assembly as to the unit of prosecution, as the statute prohibited possessing or issuing "counterfeit United States currency," and "currency" was a collective noun that could refer to either a single item or a group of items, so the issue had to be resolved in defendant's favor, and, in light of the lack of legislative intent, the rule of lenity, and analogous case law, the unit of prosecution under the statute was the transaction involving the counterfeit currency, and not the counterfeit bills with different serial numbers, nor the different denominations of such bills, so defendant's convictions and sentences as to all but one bill in a given transaction were vacated. Moore v. State, 198 Md. App. 655, 18 A.3d 981 (2011).

When defendant's convictions for violating this section by possessing and issuing counterfeit currency merged for sentencing, under the required evidence test, the convictions were not vacated because the merger was for sentencing purposes only, resulting in a single sentence, and a conviction for a merged offense survived the merger. Moore v. State, 198 Md. App. 655, 18 A.3d 981 (2011).

When defendant's convictions for violating this section by possessing and issuing counterfeit currency merged for sentencing, and, intentionally, no sentence was imposed for some offenses, the convictions as to which no sentence was imposed were not vacated because there was no need for a merger to protect defendant's rights under the double jeopardy clause, as no separate punishment was imposed, so, because the merger doctrine did not affect the conviction, the intentional imposition of no sentence was the functional equivalent of merging that conviction into the conviction for another offense for sentencing purposes. Moore v. State, 198 Md. App. 655, 18 A.3d 981 (2011).

Double jeopardy. — When defendant was convicted of issuing counterfeit currency and uttering a forged document, as well as theft and attempted theft, the issuing and uttering offenses did not have to be considered the same offenses as theft and attempted theft, for double jeopardy purposes, on the theory that the only evidence supporting the theft and attempted theft convictions was the same evidence that supported the issuing and uttering convictions, requiring the convictions and sentences for issuing and uttering to be vacated, because (1) the "actual evidence" test of merger had been rejected, (2) the theft offense contained an element not found in the issuing offense, namely, obtaining control over property of another, and (3) the attempted theft offense contained an element not found in the uttering offense, namely attempting to obtain control over property of another. Moore v. State, 198 Md. App. 655, 18 A.3d 981 (2011).

Defendant's convictions and sentences for issuing and possessing the same counterfeit currency violated double jeopardy when separate sentences were imposed for each offense because the possession and issuance of counterfeit currency in the same transaction constituted the "same offense" under the required evidence test, as one could not issue counterfeit currency without possessing it, so, to avoid offending double jeopardy principles, the convictions for possessing counterfeit currency were merged into defendant's convictions for issuing the same currency, and each merged sentence was vacated. Moore v. State, 198 Md. App. 655, 18 A.3d 981 (2011).

Evidence sufficient. — Sufficient evidence supported defendant's convictions for possessing and issuing counterfeit currency, when a store clerk could not identify defendant as the person who passed a counterfeit bill, because counterfeit bills seized from defendant the day after the incident in question bore the same serial number as the counterfeit bill retrieved from a victim after the incident in question. Moore v. State, 198 Md. App. 655, 18 A.3d 981 (2011).

§ 8-605. Counterfeiting of public documents.

(a) *Prohibited.* — (1) A person may not counterfeit, cause to be counterfeited, or willingly aid or assist in counterfeiting:

(i) a commission, patent, pardon, order for release, or other court document; or

(ii) a warrant, certificate, or other public security from which money may be drawn from the treasury of the State.

(2) A person may not write, sign, or possess a counterfeit:

(i) commission, patent, pardon, order for release, or other court document; or

(ii) warrant, certificate, or other public security from which money may be drawn from the treasury of the State.

(b) *Penalty.* — A person who violates this section is guilty of a felony and on conviction is subject to imprisonment for not less than 2 years and not exceeding 10 years. (An. Code 1957, art. 27, § 45; 2002, ch. 26, § 2; 2008, chs. 29, 30.)

REVISOR'S NOTE

This Revisor's note comprises information related to the revision by Acts 2002, ch. 26.

This section is new language derived without substantive change from former Art. 27, § 45.

In subsection (a)(1) and (2) of this section, the references to the intent to defraud "another" are substituted for the former references to the intent to defraud "any person" for consistency within this subtitle.

Also in subsection (a)(1) and (2) of this section, the former references to a person "or persons" are deleted in light of Art. 1, § 8, which provides that the singular generally includes the plural.

Also in subsection (a)(1) and (2) of this section, the defined term "counterfeit" is substituted for the former reference to "falsely mak[ing], forg[ing], or counterfeit[ing]" specified public documents, although use of the defined term also includes "falsely made" documents.

Any such "materially altered" document would constitute a "counterfeit" document under current law. No substantive change is intended.

In subsection (a)(2) of this section, the former reference to a person "be[ing] concerned in" printing, writing, signing, or passing a forged public document is deleted as implicit in the reference to a person "print[ing], writ[ing], sign[ing], or pass[ing]" the document.

In subsection (b) of this section, the reference to a person being "subject to imprisonment" is substituted for the former reference to a person being "sentenced to the penitentiary" for consistency within this article. Currently, inmates are sentenced to the custody of a unit such as the Division of Correction and then are placed in a particular facility. *See* CS § 9-103.

Defined terms:
"Counterfeit"	§ 1-101
"Person"	§ 1-101

"Commission" includes license to practice medicine and surgery. — The term "commission" in a prior similar provision could be construed to include a license to practice medicine and surgery issued by a public agency to which is delegated a part of the police power of the State. Reddick v. State, 219 Md. 95, 148 A.2d 384, cert. denied, 360 U.S. 930, 79 S. Ct. 1448, 3 L. Ed. 2d 1544 (1959).

§ 8-606. Making false entries in public records and related crimes.

(a) *Definitions.* — (1) In this section the following words have the meanings indicated.

(2) "Access" means to instruct, communicate with, store data in, or retrieve data from, or otherwise use equipment including computers and other data processing equipment or resources connected with computers or other data processing equipment.

(3) "Public record" includes an official book, paper, or record, kept on a manual or automated basis, that is created, received, or used by a unit of:

    (i) the State;

    (ii) a political subdivision of the State; or

    (iii) a multicounty agency.

(b) *Prohibited.* — A person may not or may not attempt to:

(1) willfully make a false entry in a public record;

(2) except under proper authority, willfully alter, deface, destroy, remove, or conceal a public record; or

(3) except under proper authority, willfully and intentionally access a public record.

(c) *Penalty.* — A person who violates this section is guilty of a misdemeanor and on conviction is subject to imprisonment not exceeding 3 years or a fine not exceeding $1,000 or both. (An. Code 1957, art. 27, § 45A; 2002, ch. 26, § 2.)

REVISOR'S NOTE

This Revisor's note comprises information related to the revision by Acts 2002, ch. 26.

This section is new language derived without substantive change from former Art. 27, § 45A.

In subsection (a)(2) of this section, the former reference to equipment including "but not limited to" computers is deleted as unnecessary in light of Art. 1, § 30, which provides that the term "including" is used by way of illustration and not by way of limitation.

In subsection (a)(3) of this section, the reference to a "unit" of the State is substituted for the former references to an "agency" of the State for consistency within this article. *See* General Revisor's Note to article.

Also in subsection (a)(3) of this section, the former reference to a "municipality" is deleted as included in the reference to a "political subdivision".

In subsection (c) of this section, the reference to a person "on conviction" being subject to a certain fine and term of imprisonment is added for consistency throughout this article.

Defined term:
"Person"   § 1-101

University of Baltimore Law Forum. — For a 2004 development, "Attorney Grievance Commission of Maryland v. Goodman: Disbarment Imposed in Cases Involving Intentionally Dishonest Conduct Unless Compelling Extenuating Circumstances Mitigate Against Such Sanction," see 35 U. Balt. L.F. 56 (2004).

Quoted in Att'y Griev. Comm'n v. Gansler, 377 Md. 656, 835 A.2d 548 (2003).

Cited in Att'y Griev. Comm'n v. Paul, 423 Md. 268, 31 A.3d 512 (2011).

§ 8-606.1. Forging, falsifying, or counterfeiting signature of judge, court officer, or court employee.

(a) *Prohibited.* — A person may not:

(1) forge, falsify, or counterfeit the signature of a judge, court officer, or court employee of the State; or

(2) use a document with a forged, false, or counterfeit signature of a judge, court officer, or other court employee of the State knowing the signature to be forged, false, or counterfeit.

(b) *Penalty.* — A person who violates this section is guilty of a misdemeanor and on conviction is subject to imprisonment not exceeding 5 years or a fine not exceeding $10,000 or both.

(c) *Statute of limitations and en banc review.* — A person who violates this section is subject to § 5-106(b) of the Courts Article. (2008, chs. 29, 30.)

§ 8-607. Counterfeiting public seal.

(a) *"Public seal" defined.* — In this section, "public seal" means:

(1) the great seal of the State;

(2) the seal of any court of the State; or

(3) any other public seal of the State.

(b) *Prohibited.* — A person may not:

(1) counterfeit and use a public seal;

(2) steal a public seal;

(3) unlawfully and falsely, or with evil intent, affix a public seal to a deed, warrant, or writing; or

(4) have and willfully conceal a counterfeit public seal, if the person knows that it was counterfeited.

(c) *Penalty.* — A person who violates this section is guilty of a misdemeanor and on conviction is subject to imprisonment for not less than 2 years and not exceeding 10 years.

(d) *Statute of limitations and in banc review.* — A person who violates this section is subject to § 5-106(b) of the Courts Article. (An. Code 1957, art. 27, § 46; 2002, ch. 26, § 2; 2004, ch. 25.)

REVISOR'S NOTE

This Revisor's note comprises information related to the revision by Acts 2002, ch. 26.

Subsection (a) of this section is new language added to avoid repetition of the references in former Art. 27, § 46 to "the great seal of the State, . . . or the seal of any court, or any other public seal of this State".

Subsections (b), (c), and (d) of this section are new language derived without substantive change from former Art. 27, § 46.

In subsections (a) and (b) of this section, the defined term "counterfeit" is substituted for the former references to "counterfeit[ing]" a public seal and to using, stealing, affixing, and having a "counterfeit" public seal, although use of the defined term also includes "falsely mak[ing], forg[ing], and materially alter[ing]" a public seal. Any such "falsely made", "forged", or "materially altered" public seal would constitute a "counterfeit" public seal under current law. No substantive change is intended.

In subsection (a)(1) of this section, the former reference to the great seal of the State "for the time being" is deleted as surplusage.

In subsection (a)(2) of this section, the reference to the seal of any court "of the State" is added for clarity.

In subsection (b)(2) of this section, the former reference to "true" seals is deleted as surplusage.

In subsection (b)(3) of this section, the former reference to a person "corruptly" affixing a public seal is deleted in light of the reference to a person "falsely" affixing a public seal.

In subsection (b)(4) of this section, the former reference to having a counterfeit instrument in one's "custody" is deleted as implicit in the reference to "hav[ing] a counterfeit instrument".

In subsection (c) of this section, the reference to being "guilty of a misdemeanor" is added to state expressly that which was only implied in the former law. In this State, any crime that was not a felony at common law and has not been declared a felony by statute, is considered to be a misdemeanor. *See State v. Canova*, 278 Md. 483, 490 (1976); *Bowser v. State*, 136 Md. 342, 345 (1920); *Dutton v. State*, 123 Md. 373, 378 (1914); and *Williams v. State*, 4 Md. App. 342, 347 (1968).

In subsection (d) of this section, the reference to a violation being "subject to § 5-106(b) of the Courts Article" is substituted for the former reference to the violation subjecting the defendant to imprisonment "to the penitentiary" for clarity and consistency within this article. *See* General Revisor's Note to article.

Defined terms:

"Counterfeit"	§ 1-101
"Person"	§ 1-101

§ 8-608. Counterfeiting stamp of Comptroller.

(a) *Prohibited.* — A person may not:

(1) counterfeit the stamp of the Comptroller;

(2) unlawfully use or steal the stamp of the Comptroller;

(3) unlawfully and falsely, or with evil intent, affix the stamp of the Comptroller to any written instrument; or

(4) have and willfully conceal a counterfeit stamp of the Comptroller, if the person knows that it was counterfeited.

(b) *Penalty.* — A person who violates this section is guilty of a misdemeanor and on conviction is subject to imprisonment for not less than 2 years and not exceeding 10 years.

(c) *Statute of limitations and in banc review.* — A person who violates this section is subject to § 5-106(b) of the Courts Article. (An. Code 1957, art. 27, § 47; 2002, ch. 26, § 2; 2004, ch. 25.)

REVISOR'S NOTE

This Revisor's note comprises information related to the revision by Acts 2002, ch. 26.

This section is new language derived without substantive change from former Art. 27, § 47.

In subsection (a)(1) and (4) of this section, the defined term "counterfeit" is substituted for the former references to "counterfeit[ing]" the stamp of the Comptroller and to using, stealing, affixing, and having a "counterfeit" stamp, although use of the defined term also includes "falsely mak[ing], forg[ing], and materially alter[ing]" the stamp. Any such "falsely made", "forged", or "materially altered" stamp of the Comptroller would constitute a "counterfeit" stamp under current law. No substantive change is intended.

In subsection (a)(3) of this section, the former reference to a person "corruptly" affixing the stamp of the Comptroller is deleted in light of the reference to a person "falsely" affixing the stamp of the Comptroller.

In subsection (a)(4) of this section, the former reference to a person having a counterfeit instrument in the person's "custody" is deleted as implicit in the reference to a person "hav[ing] the counterfeit instrument in the person's 'possess[ion]'".

In subsection (b) of this section, the reference to being "guilty of a misdemeanor" is added to state expressly that which was only implied in the former law. In this State, any crime that was not a felony at common law and has not been declared a felony by statute, is considered to be a misdemeanor. *See State v. Canova*, 278 Md. 483, 490 (1976); *Bowser v. State*, 136 Md. 342, 345 (1920); *Dutton v. State*, 123 Md. 373, 378 (1914); and *Williams v. State*, 4 Md. App. 342, 347 (1968).

In subsection (c) of this section, the reference to a violation being "subject to § 5-106(b) of the Courts Article" is substituted for the former reference to the violation subjecting the defendant to imprisonment "in the penitentiary" for clarity and consistency within this article. *See* General Revisor's Note to article.

Defined terms:
"Counterfeit" § 1-101
"Person" § 1-101

§ 8-609. Counterfeiting of orders for money or goods.

(a) *"Order for money or goods" defined.* — In this section, "order for money or goods" means any writing, ordering, or requesting for the payment of money or the delivery of goods.

(b) *Prohibited.* — A person may not:

(1) with intent to defraud another, cause or procure to be counterfeited, or willingly aid or assist in counterfeiting an order for money or goods;

(2) with intent to defraud another, issue, publish, or pass a counterfeit order for money or goods, if the person knows it was counterfeited; or

(3) knowingly and fraudulently obtain money or goods by means of a counterfeit order for money or goods.

(c) *Penalty.* — A person who violates this section is guilty of a felony and on conviction is subject to imprisonment for not less than 2 years and not exceeding 10 years. (An. Code 1957, art. 27, § 48; 2002, ch. 26, § 2; 2004, ch. 25.)

REVISOR'S NOTE

This Revisor's note comprises informa-tion related to the revision by Acts 2002, ch. 26.

Subsection (a) of this section is new language added to avoid repetition of the phrase in for-mer Art. 27, § 48 to "any warrant, letter or paper, writing or order, for payment of money or delivery of goods, or other valuable articles".

Subsections (b) and (c) of this section are new language derived without substantive change from former Art. 27, § 48.

In subsections (a) and (b) of this section, the former references to "other valuable articles" are deleted as implicit in the references to "goods".

In subsection (b) of this section, the defined term "counterfeit" in its various grammatical inflections is substituted for the former refer-ences to "falsely mak[ing]", "forg[ing]", and "counterfeit[ing]" for consistency within this article.

In subsection (b)(1) and (2) of this section, the reference to the intent to defraud "another" is substituted for the former reference to the intent to defraud "any person" for consistency within this subtitle.

Also in subsection (b)(1) and (2) of this sec-tion, the former phrase "whether the said war-rant or order contain a simple request to pay the said money, or deliver the said goods or other valuable articles or not" is deleted as surplusage.

In subsection (b)(3) of this section, the former reference to a person obtaining an "other thing of value" is deleted as implicit in the reference to a person obtaining "goods".

In subsection (c) of this section, the reference to a person being "subject to imprisonment" is substituted for the former reference to a person being "sentenced to the penitentiary" for con-sistency within this article. Currently, inmates are sentenced to the custody of a particular unit such as the Division of Correction and then are placed in a particular facility. *See* CS § 9-103.

Defined terms:
"Counterfeit"	§ 1-101
"Person"	§ 1-101

§ 8-610. Counterfeiting prescription.

(a) *"Prescription" defined.* — In this section, "prescription" includes an order, paper, and recipe purported to have been made by an authorized provider, as defined in § 5-101 of this article, for a drug, medicine, or alcoholic beverage.

(b) *Prohibited.* — A person may not:

(1) knowingly counterfeit, cause or procure to be counterfeited, or will-ingly aid or assist in counterfeiting a prescription;

(2) knowingly issue, pass, or possess a counterfeit prescription; or

(3) obtain or attempt to obtain a prescription drug by fraud, deceit, or misrepresentation.

(c) *Penalty.* — A person who violates this section is guilty of a misdemeanor and on conviction is subject to imprisonment not exceeding 2 years.

(d) *Prohibited defense.* — Payment or an offer or promise to pay for a drug, medicine, or alcoholic beverage obtained in violation of this section is not a defense to a violation of this section. (An. Code 1957, art. 27, § 55; 2002, ch. 26, § 2; 2003, ch. 21, § 1.)

REVISOR'S NOTE

This Revisor's note comprises informa-tion related to the revision by Acts 2002, ch. 26.

This section is new language derived without substantive change from former Art. 27, § 55.

In subsections (a) and (d) of this section, respectively, the references to an "alcoholic bev-erage" are substituted for the former archaic references to "spirituous or fermented liquors", and "spirituous liquor" and "fermented liquor", respectively.

In subsection (a) of this section, the reference to an "authorized provider, as defined in § 5-101 of this article" is substituted for the former references to a "licensed practitioner" for clar-ity.

Also in subsection (a) of this section, the former references to a "letter writing" are deleted as implicit in the reference to a "paper".

In subsection (b)(1) and (2) of this section, the defined term "counterfeit" is substituted for the former references to "falsely mak[ing], alter[ing], forg[ing] or counterfeit[ing]" a device, although the defined term only includes a "materially" altered device. In order to prove fraud under current law, any such alteration must be material. No substantive change is intended.

In subsection (c) of this section, the former reference to a conviction "in any court in this State" is deleted as surplusage.

Also in subsection (c) of this section, the former reference to imprisonment "in the dis-

cretion of the court" is deleted as implicit in setting a maximum term.

In subsection (d) of this section, the reference to drugs, medicine, or alcoholic beverages obtained "in violation of this section" is substituted for the former reference to those substances obtained "by means of the falsely made, altered, forged or counterfeited order, paper, letter writing, prescription, recipe or other device purporting to have been made by a duly licensed practitioner" for brevity.

Defined terms:

| "Counterfeit" | § 1-101 |
| "Person" | § 1-101 |

Burden of proof. — The burden is on the State to produce evidence sufficient to show, or support a rational inference, as elements of the crime charged, that the accused: (1) uttered or passed a prescription (a) purported to have been made by a regular practicing physician (b) for a drug or medicine; and (2) knew the prescription was falsely made, altered, forged or counterfeited. Goodman v. State, 2 Md. App. 473, 235 A.2d 560 (1967).

§ 8-611. Trademark counterfeiting.

(a) *Definitions.* — (1) In this section the following words have the meanings indicated.

(2) "Counterfeit mark" means:

(i) an unauthorized copy of intellectual property; or

(ii) intellectual property affixed to goods knowingly sold, offered for sale, manufactured, or distributed, to identify services offered or rendered, without the authority of the owner of the intellectual property.

(3) "Intellectual property" means a trademark, service mark, trade name, label, term, device, design, or word adopted or used by a person to identify the goods or services of the person.

(4) "Retail value" means:

(i) a trademark counterfeiter's selling price for the goods or services that bear or are identified by the counterfeit mark; or

(ii) a trademark counterfeiter's selling price of the finished product, if the goods that bear a counterfeit mark are components of the finished product.

(5) "Trademark counterfeiter" means a person who commits the crime of trademark counterfeiting prohibited by this section.

(b) *Prohibited.* — A person may not willfully manufacture, produce, display, advertise, distribute, offer for sale, sell, or possess with the intent to sell or distribute goods or services that the person knows are bearing or are identified by a counterfeit mark.

(c) *Penalty — Value at least $1,000.* — If the aggregate retail value of the goods or services is $1,000 or more, a person who violates this section is guilty of the felony of trademark counterfeiting and on conviction:

(1) is subject to imprisonment not exceeding 15 years or a fine not exceeding $10,000 or both; and

(2) shall transfer all of the goods to the owner of the intellectual property.

(d) *Penalty — Value less than $1,000.* — If the aggregate retail value of the goods or services is less than $1,000, a person who violates this section is guilty of the misdemeanor of trademark counterfeiting and on conviction:

(1) is subject to:

(i) for a first violation, imprisonment not exceeding 18 months or a fine not exceeding $1,000 or both; or

(ii) for each subsequent violation, imprisonment not exceeding 18 months or a fine not exceeding $5,000 or both; and

(2) shall transfer all of the goods to the owner of the intellectual property.

(e) *Commencement of action or prosecution.* — An action or prosecution for trademark counterfeiting in which the aggregate retail value of the goods or services is less than $1,000 shall be commenced within 2 years after the commission of the crime.

(f) *Seizure of counterfeit items.* — Any goods bearing a counterfeit mark are subject to seizure by a law enforcement officer to preserve the goods for transfer to the owner of the intellectual property either:

(1) under an agreement with the person alleged to have committed the crime; or

(2) after a conviction under this section.

(g) *Evidence of trademark or trade name.* — State or federal registration of intellectual property is prima facie evidence that the intellectual property is a trademark or trade name. (An. Code 1957, art. 27, § 48A; 2002, ch. 26, § 2.)

REVISOR'S NOTE

This Revisor's note comprises information related to the revision by Acts 2002, ch. 26.

Subsections (a)(1) through (4) and (b) through (g) of this section are new language derived without substantive change from former Art. 27, § 48A.

Subsection (a)(5) of this section is new language added to state expressly that which formerly was only implied by the use of the term "trademark counterfeiter" in former Art. 27, § 48A(a)(4).

Throughout this section, the references to a "good" or "goods" are substituted for the former references to an "item" or "items" for clarity.

In subsection (d)(1)(i) of this section, the reference to a person being subject to a fine and imprisonment "for a first violation" is added to state that which was only implied in former Art. 27, § 48A(d)(1)(ii).

In subsection (d)(1)(ii) of this section, the reference to "each" subsequent violation is substituted for the former reference to "a second or" subsequent violation for consistency within this article.

The Criminal Law Article Review Committee notes, for the consideration by the General Assembly, that in subsection (d)(1) of this section, the reference to a person being subject to a fine "or imprisonment not exceeding 18 months or both" for a subsequent violation is added to state that which only was implied in former Art. 27, § 48A(e).

Defined term:

"Person" § 1-101

Restitution for distribution of counterfeit items. — Restitution was a permissible penalty for defendant possessing for distribution or delivery from the back of his van on a public street counterfeit compact discs and digital video discs. Cunningham v. State, 397 Md. 524, 919 A.2d 30 (2007).

Cited in Grant v. State, 414 Md. 483, 995 A.2d 975 (2010).

§ 8-612. Counterfeiting and issuing of tokens.

(a) *"Token" defined.* — In this section, "token" means a ticket, coupon, coin, disc, slug, or any other thing that:

(1) is evidence of the right of an individual to enter, leave, ride on, or pass through or over any thing or place for which a fee is charged, including a building, ground, public conveyance, vessel, or bridge; and

(2) is intended or designed to be inserted into a box or machine for the collection of fees or given to a collector.

(b) *Prohibited.* — (1) A person may not counterfeit or issue, or cause to be counterfeited or issued, or aid or assist in counterfeiting or issuing a token without the permission of the person who lawfully issues, sells, or gives away the token.

(2) A person may not issue or pass a token if the person knows that it was:

(i) counterfeited; or

(ii) issued without the permission of the person who lawfully issues, sells, or gives away the token.

(c) *Penalty.* — A person who violates this section is guilty of a misdemeanor and on conviction is subject to imprisonment not exceeding 1 year. (An. Code 1957, art. 27, § 56; 2002, ch. 26, § 2.)

REVISOR'S NOTE

This Revisor's note comprises information related to the revision by Acts 2002, ch. 26.

Subsection (a) of this section is new language added to avoid repetition throughout this section of the former references in Art. 27, § 56 to tickets, coupons, tokens, coins, discs, or slugs.

Subsections (b) and (c) of this section are new language derived without substantive change from former Art. 27, § 56.

In subsections (a) and (b) of this section, the word "issue" is substituted for the former references to "utter[ing]" for consistency within this article.

In subsection (a) of this section, the former reference to a "fare" is deleted as included in the comprehensive reference to a "fee".

In subsection (a)(1) of this section, the reference to an "individual" is substituted for the former reference to a "person" because only an individual and not the other kinds of entities included in the definition of "person" can enter, leave, ride upon, or pass through or over places and things.

Also in subsection (a)(1) of this section, the former reference to a person "or persons" is deleted in light of Art. 1, § 8, which provides that the singular generally includes the plural.

In subsection (a)(2) of this section, the reference to a token intended to be "given to" a collector is substituted for the former reference to a token intended to be "taken up by" a collector for clarity.

Also in subsection (a)(2) of this section, the former reference to a token that is "used" to be inserted into a box is deleted in light of the reference to a token that is "intended or designed" to be inserted into a box.

In subsection (b) of this section, the references to "permission" are substituted for the former reference to "authority" for clarity.

Also in subsection (b) of this section, the references to a person who "lawfully" issues, sells, or gives away the token is added for clarity.

Also in subsection (b) of this section, the former references to the authority of a person "or corporation" are deleted in light of § 1-101 of this article, which provides that "person" includes a corporation.

Also in subsection (b) of this section, the defined term "counterfeit" in various grammatical inflections is substituted for the former references to "mak[ing]", "forg[ing]", or "counterfeit[ing]" for consistency within this article.

In subsection (b)(1) of this section, the former reference to "procur[ing]" another to commit counterfeiting is deleted as included in the reference to "caus[ing]" another to commit counterfeiting.

In subsection (b)(2) of this section, the former reference to a token "so issued, sold or given away by any person or corporation" is deleted as implicit in prohibiting certain acts "without the permission of the person that issues, sells, or gives away the token".

In subsection (c) of this section, the reference to a person being "subject to imprisonment" is substituted for the former reference to a person being "sentenced to the jail or house of correction" for consistency within this article. Currently, inmates are sentenced to the custody of a unit such as the Division of Correction and then are placed in a particular facility. *See* CS § 9-103.

Also in subsection (c) of this section, the former reference to a person being subject to imprisonment on conviction "in any court of this State" is deleted as implicit.

Defined terms:
"Counterfeit"	§ 1-101
"Person"	§ 1-101

§ 8-613. Unlawful operation of vending machines and related manufacture of slugs.

(a) *Definitions.* — (1) In this section the following words have the meanings indicated.

(2) "Service" includes the use of telephone or telegraph facilities, gas, electricity, or a musical instrument, phonograph, or other property.

(3) "Vending machine" includes a slot machine, pay telephone, or other receptacle designed to receive United States currency in connection with the sale or use of property or of a service.

(b) *Prohibited.* — A person may not:

(1) operate, cause to be operated, or attempt to operate or cause to be operated a vending machine by a means not lawfully authorized by the owner, lessee, or licensee of the vending machine, including by means of a slug or by counterfeit, mutilated, sweated, or foreign currency;

(2) take, obtain, or receive from or in connection with a vending machine any property or service, without depositing into the vending machine United States currency in the amount required by the owner, lessee, or licensee of the vending machine; or

(3) manufacture for sale, sell, or give away a slug or device that is intended to be deposited in a vending machine if the person:

(i) intends to defraud the owner, lessee, licensee, or other person entitled to the contents of the vending machine; or

(ii) knows that the slug or device is intended for unlawful use.

(c) *Penalty.* — A person who violates this section is guilty of a misdemeanor and on conviction is subject to imprisonment not exceeding 3 months or a fine not exceeding $500 or both. (An. Code 1957, art. 27, §§ 57, 58; 2002, ch. 26, § 2.)

REVISOR'S NOTE

This Revisor's note comprises information related to the revision by Acts 2002, ch. 26.

Subsection (a)(1) of this section is new language added as standard introductory language to a definition provision.

Subsection (a)(2) of this section is new language added to reflect that references in former Art. 27, § 57 to "goods, wares, merchandise, gas, electric current, article of value, or the use or enjoyment of any telephone or telegraph facilities or service, or of any musical instru-

ment, phonograph or other property" are meant to provide an illustration of the types of services specified by this section. This section makes the definitions in subsection (a)(2) of this section applicable to provisions to which those definitions formerly did not apply. However, the definitions generally are nonsubstantive and are intended solely to allow concise and standardized references. No substantive change is intended.

Subsection (a)(3) of this section is new language added to avoid repetition of the reference in former Art. 27, § 57 to "an[y] automatic vending machine, slot machine, coin box telephone or other receptacle, designed to receive lawful coin of the United States of America in connection with the sale, use or enjoyment of property or service", and in former Art. 27, § 58 to "any automatic vending machine, slot machine, coin box telephone or other receptacle, depository or contrivance designed to receive lawful coin of the United States of America in connection with the sale, use or enjoyment of property or service".

Subsections (b) and (c) of this section are new language derived without substantive change from former Art. 27, §§ 57 and 58.

In subsections (a)(3) and (b)(1) of this section, the references to "currency" are substituted for the former references to "coin[s]" of the United States to encompass vending machines that are operated by paper money.

In subsection (a) of this section, the reference in former Art. 27, § 58 to a "depository or contrivance" designed to receive coins is deleted as implicit in the reference to a "receptacle" designed to receive currency.

In subsection (b)(1) of this section, the former reference to an "automatic" vending machine is deleted as implicit in the reference to "machine".

Also in subsection (b)(1) of this section, the former reference to a person operating a vending machine by any means, "method, [or] trick" is deleted as implicit in the reference to a person operating a vending machine by "a means not lawfully authorized by the owner, lessee, or licensee".

In subsection (b)(2) of this section, the former reference to "wares, merchandise, . . . or article of value" is deleted as implicit in the reference to "property".

Also in subsection (b)(2) of this section, the former archaic reference to a person "surrendering" currency to a vending machine is deleted as implicit in the reference to "depositing" currency into the vending machine.

In subsection (b)(3) of this section, the former reference to a slug, device, "or substance whatsoever" is deleted as implicit in the reference to any "device".

Also in subsection (b)(3) of this section, the former reference to a device that is "calculated" to be deposited into a vending machine is deleted as implicit in the reference to a device that is "intended" to be deposited into a vending machine.

Also in subsection (b)(3) of this section, the former reference to a slug or device that is intended to be "placed" in a vending machine is deleted as implicit in the reference to a slug or device that is intended to be "deposited" in a vending machine.

In subsection (b)(3)(i) of this section, the former reference to a person's intent to "cheat" the owner of a vending machine is deleted as implicit in the reference to a person's intent to "defraud" the owner.

In subsection (c) of this section, the former reference to a person being convicted "before any court of competent jurisdiction" is deleted as implicit since only a court with criminal jurisdiction would be competent to convict a person.

Also in subsection (c) of this section, the former reference to a sentence being "in the discretion of the court" is deleted as implicit in the reference to a person being "subject to" a fine and imprisonment.

Defined terms:

"Counterfeit"	§ 1-101
"Person"	§ 1-101

GENERAL REVISOR'S NOTE TO SUBTITLE

Former Art. 27, § 53, which prohibited forgery of stock certificates issued by the State of Maryland, is repealed as obsolete. The certificates, originally issued to finance the Maryland penitentiary under legislation enacted in 1821 and 1834, are no longer outstanding. *See* Letter of Advice from Attorney General J. Joseph Curran, Jr. to Judge Alan M. Wilner, p. 17 (October 17, 2000).

Former Art. 27, § 54, which prohibited forgery or counterfeiting of cannery tokens used in agricultural and fisheries packing industries, is repealed as obsolete. *See* Letter of Advice from Attorney General J. Joseph Curran, Jr. to Judge Alan M. Wilner, p. 17 (October 17, 2000).

Subtitle 7. Crimes Against Estates.

§ 8-701. Embezzling, altering will or record.

(a) *Prohibited.* — A person may not willfully or corruptly embezzle, steal, destroy, withdraw, impair, or alter a will, codicil, deed, land patent or assignment of a land patent, or a writ of administration, return, record, or part of any of those documents if as a result of that act the estate or right of any person may be defeated, injured, or altered.

(b) *Penalty.* — A person who violates this section is guilty of a misdemeanor and on conviction is subject to imprisonment for not less than 3 years and not exceeding 7 years.

(c) *Statute of limitations and in banc review.* — A person who violates this section is subject to § 5-106(b) of the Courts Article. (An. Code 1957, art. 27, § 126; 2002, ch. 26, § 2.)

REVISOR'S NOTE

This Revisor's note comprises information related to the revision by Acts 2002, ch. 26.

This section is new language derived without substantive change from former Art. 27, § 126.

In subsection (a) of this section, the reference to a writ "of administration" is added for clarity.

Also in subsection (a) of this section, the reference to a "part of any of those documents" is substituted for the former reference to a "parcel of the same" for clarity and accuracy.

Also in subsection (a) of this section, the former reference to a "testament" is deleted as included in the reference to a "will".

Also in subsection (a) of this section, the former reference to conviction of a person violating this section "within this State" is deleted as surplusage.

Also in subsection (a) of this section, the former reference to an estate or right of a person being "in any way" altered is deleted as surplusage.

In subsection (b) of this section, the reference to being "guilty of a misdemeanor" is added to state expressly that which only was implied in the former law by the reference to a "conviction]". In this State, any crime that was not a felony at common law and has not been declared a felony by statute, is considered to be a misdemeanor. *See State v. Canova*, 278 Md. 483, 490 (1976), *Bowser v. State*, 136 Md. 342, 345 (1920), *Dutton v. State*, 123 Md. 373, 378 (1914), and *Williams v. State*, 4 Md. App. 342, 347 (1968).

In subsection (c) of this section, the reference to a violation being "subject to § 5-106(b) of the Courts Article" is substituted for the former reference to the violation subjecting the defendant to imprisonment "to the penitentiary" for clarity and consistency within this article. *See* General Revisor's Note to article.

Defined term:
    "Person"   § 1-101

Cross references. — As to defalcation by officers collecting revenue due the State or county, see § 7-114 of this article.

As to description of money in indictment, see § 4-106 of the Criminal Procedure Article.

Editor's note. — Section 2, ch. 371, Acts 1991, which amended a prior similar provision, provides that "there is no statute of limitations for a misdemeanor punishable by imprisonment in the penitentiary, notwithstanding any holding or dictum to the contrary in Massey v. State, 320 Md. 605, 579 A.2d 265 (1990)."

§ 8-702. Destroying will.

(a) *Prohibited.* — Unless the maker of a will gives instruction to the person keeping the will for safe custody, a person who receives a will for safe custody may not:

(1) destroy the will; or

(2) after the person learns of the death of the maker, willfully hide the will for a period of 6 months.

(b) *Penalty.* — A person who violates this section is guilty of a misdemeanor and on conviction is subject to imprisonment for not less than 18 months and not exceeding 15 years.

(c) *Statute of limitations and in banc review.* — A person who violates this section is subject to § 5-106(b) of the Courts Article. (An. Code 1957, art. 27, § 127; 2002, ch. 26, § 2.)

REVISOR'S NOTE

This Revisor's note comprises information related to the revision by Acts 2002, ch. 26.

This section is new language derived without substantive change from former Art. 27, § 127.

In subsection (a) of this section, the former reference to a "codicil" is deleted as included in the reference to a "will". *See* ET § 1-101.

In the introductory language of subsection (a) of this section, the reference to the "maker of a will" is substituted for the former reference to the "party making it" for clarity. Similarly, in subsection (a)(2) of this section, the reference to the "maker" is substituted for the former reference to the "party" for consistency within this subsection.

In subsection (a)(2) of this section, the phrase "after the person learns of the death of the maker" is substituted for the former phrase "after the death of the party shall be known to him" for clarity.

In subsection (b) of this section, the reference to being "guilty of a misdemeanor" is added to state expressly that which only was implied in the former law by the reference to a "conviction". In this State, any crime that was not a felony at common law and has not been declared a felony by statute, is considered to be a misdemeanor. *See State v. Canova*, 278 Md. 483, 490 (1976), *Bowser v. State*, 136 Md. 342, 345 (1920), *Dutton v. State*, 123 Md. 373, 378 (1914), and *Williams v. State*, 4 Md. App. 342, 347 (1968).

In subsection (c) of this section, the reference to a violation being "subject to § 5-106(b) of the Courts Article" is substituted for the former reference to the violation subjecting the defendant to imprisonment "to the penitentiary" for clarity and consistency within this article. *See* General Revisor's Note to article.

Defined term:
"Person" § 1-101

Subtitle 8. Financial Crimes Against Vulnerable Adults.

§ 8-801. Exploitation of vulnerable adults prohibited.

(a) *Definitions.* — (1) In this section the following words have the meanings indicated.

(2) "Deception" has the meaning stated in § 7-101 of this article.

(3) "Deprive" has the meaning stated in § 7-101 of this article.

(4) "Obtain" has the meaning stated in § 7-101 of this article.

(5) "Property" has the meaning stated in § 7-101 of this article.

(6) (i) "Undue influence" means domination and influence amounting to force and coercion exercised by another person to such an extent that a vulnerable adult or an individual at least 68 years old was prevented from exercising free judgment and choice.

(ii) "Undue influence" does not include the normal influence that one member of a family has over another member of the family.

(7) "Value" has the meaning stated in § 7-103 of this article.

(8) "Vulnerable adult" has the meaning stated in § 3-604 of this article.

(b) *Prohibited.* — (1) A person may not knowingly and willfully obtain by deception, intimidation, or undue influence the property of an individual that the person knows or reasonably should know is a vulnerable adult with intent to deprive the vulnerable adult of the vulnerable adult's property.

(2) A person may not knowingly and willfully obtain by deception, intimidation, or undue influence the property of an individual that the person knows or reasonably should know is at least 68 years old, with intent to deprive the individual of the individual's property.

(c) *Penalty.* — (1) A person convicted of a violation of this section when the value of the property is $500 or more is guilty of a felony and:

(i) is subject to imprisonment not exceeding 15 years or a fine not exceeding $10,000 or both; and

(ii) shall restore the property taken or its value to the owner, or, if the owner is deceased, restore the property or its value to the owner's estate.

(2) A person convicted of a violation of this section when the value of the property is less than $500 is guilty of a misdemeanor and:

(i) is subject to imprisonment not exceeding 18 months or a fine not exceeding $500 or both; and

(ii) shall restore the property taken or its value to the owner, or, if the owner is deceased, restore the property or its value to the owner's estate.

(d) *Sentencing.* — A sentence imposed under this section may be separate from and consecutive to or concurrent with a sentence for any crime based on the act or acts establishing the violation of this section.

(e) *Disqualification.* — (1) If a defendant fails to restore fully the property taken or its value as ordered under subsection (c) of this section, the defendant is disqualified, to the extent of the defendant's failure to restore the property or its value, from inheriting, taking, enjoying, receiving, or otherwise benefiting from the estate, insurance proceeds, or property of the victim of the offense, whether by operation of law or pursuant to a legal document executed or entered into by the victim before the defendant shall have been convicted under this section.

(2) The defendant has the burden of proof with respect to establishing under paragraph (1) of this subsection that the defendant has fully restored the property taken or its value.

(f) *Construction of section.* — This section may not be construed to impose criminal liability on a person who, at the request of the victim of the offense, the victim's family, or the court appointed guardian of the victim, has made a good faith effort to assist the victim in the management of or transfer of the victim's property. (2002, ch. 26, § 12; ch. 479, § 2; ch. 480, § 2; 2009, chs. 236, 237; 2010, chs. 72, 667.)

SPECIAL REVISOR'S NOTE

This Special Revisor's note comprises information related to the revision by Acts 2002, ch. 26 and other chapters amending this section from the 2002 Legislative Session.

Chapters 479 and 480, Acts of 2002, each added this section. Also, Chs. 479 and 480 each renumbered Title 8, Subtitle 8, as enacted by Ch. 26, to be Subtitle 9.

Effect of amendments. — Chapters 236 and 237, Acts 2009, effective October 1, 2009, made identical changes. Each added "or an individual at least 68 years old" in (a)(7)(i); added the (b)(1) designation; added (b)(2); and in (e) and (f), substituted "victim" for "vulnerable adult" or variants and added "of the offense."

Chapter 72, Acts 2010, enacted April 13, 2010, and effective from date of enactment, in subsection (a) reversed the order of the definitions of "value" and "undue influence" to conform to alphabetical order and redesignated accordingly.

Chapter 667, Acts 2010, effective October 1, 2010, rewrote (e).

Editor's note. — Section 4, ch. 72, Acts 2010, enacted April 13, 2010, and effective from date of enactment, provides that "the provisions of this Act are intended solely to correct technical errors in the law and there is no intent to revive or otherwise affect law that is the subject of other acts, whether those acts were signed by the Governor prior to or after the signing of this Act."

Section 2, ch. 667, Acts 2010, provides that "this Act shall be construed to apply only prospectively and may not be applied or interpreted to have any effect on or application to any civil action or proceeding to determine a benefit from the estate, insurance proceeds, or property of a victim that is pending before the effective date of this Act."

§§ 8-802, 8-803. [Redesignated].

Cross references. — See §§ 8-902, 8-903 of this article.

§§ 8-804, 8-805. [Redesignated].

Cross references. — See §§ 8-904, 8-905 of this article.

Subtitle 9. Miscellaneous Fraud.

§ 8-901. Livestock breed certificate not provided.

(a) *Prohibited.* — A person may not fail to furnish to the purchaser of purebred livestock a paper or certificate showing that the livestock is purebred stock within 90 days after the sale and delivery of the livestock if:

(1) the paper or certificate is a condition of sale; and

(2) payment has been made for the livestock.

(b) *Penalty.* — A person who violates this section is guilty of a misdemeanor and on conviction is subject to a fine not less than $5 and not exceeding $50 for each violation. (An. Code 1957, art. 27, § 211; 2002, ch. 26, § 2; ch. 479, § 1; ch. 480, § 1.)

SPECIAL REVISOR'S NOTE

This Special Revisor's note comprises information related to the revision by Acts 2002, ch. 26 and other chapters amending this section from the 2002 Legislative Session.

Chapter 26, Acts of 2002, enacted this section as § 8-801, which was new language derived without substantive change from former Art. 27, § 211. However, Chs. 479 and 480, § 1, Acts of 2002, each renumbered Subtitle 8 of this title to be Subtitle 9, under the amended subtitle "Subtitle 9. Miscellaneous Fraud". Accordingly, this section appears as § 8-901.

In subsection (a) of this section, the reference to "purebred" livestock was added by Ch. 26 for clarity.

Also in subsection (a) of this section, the reference to "livestock" was substituted by Ch. 26 for the former reference to a "cow, bull, calf, sheep, hog or other livestock" for brevity.

Also in subsection (a) of this section, the reference to "the livestock" was substituted by Ch. 26 for the former reference to "such animal" for consistency within this section.

Also in subsection (a) of this section, the former reference to "refusal" was deleted by Ch. 26 as implicit in the reference to "fail[ure]".

Defined term:
"Person"   § 1-101

§ 8-902. Methyl alcohol in medication.

(a) *Definitions.* — (1) In this section the following words have the meanings indicated.

(2) "Drug" means a drug, medicine, or a medicinal or chemical preparation for internal human consumption.

(3) "Prepare" means to make, mix, manufacture, or compound.

(b) *Prohibited.* — A person who is engaged in the business of preparing or dispensing a drug for internal human consumption may not prepare, dispense, sell, or deliver the drug to a person directly or through an agent or employee if:

(1) ethyl alcohol is usually used to prepare the drug; and

(2) the preparer, or the preparer's agent or employee, in any manner uses or substitutes methyl alcohol for ethyl alcohol, or puts methyl alcohol into the drug.

(c) *Penalty.* — A person who violates this section is guilty of a misdemeanor and on conviction is subject to imprisonment for not less than 3 months and not exceeding 1 year or a fine of not less than $100 and not exceeding $500 or both. (An. Code 1957, art. 27, § 230; 2002, ch. 26, § 2; ch. 479, § 1; ch. 480, § 1.)

SPECIAL REVISOR'S NOTE

This Special Revisor's note comprises information related to the revision by Acts 2002, ch. 26 and other chapters amending this section from the 2002 Legislative Session.

Chapter 26, Acts of 2002, enacted this section as § 8-802. However, Chs. 479 and 480, § 1, Acts of 2002, each renumbered Subtitle 8 of this title to be Subtitle 9, under the amended subtitle "Subtitle 9. Miscellaneous Fraud". Accordingly, this section appears as § 8-902.

Subsection (a) of this section was new language added by Ch. 26 to avoid repetition of the phrases "drug, medicine, or a medicinal or chemical preparation" and "make, mix, manufacture, or compound".

In Ch. 26, subsections (b) and (c) of this section were new language derived without substantive change from former Art. 27, § 230.

In subsection (b) of this section, the reference to "in any manner" was substituted by Ch. 26 for the former reference to "in part or in whole" for consistency within this section.

Also in subsection (b) of this section, the former redundant references to "grain" and "wood" alcohol were deleted by Ch. 26 as implicit in the references to "ethyl" and "methyl" alcohol, respectively.

In subsection (b)(2) of this section, the references to the "preparer" of a drug were substituted by Ch. 26 for the former references to the "person . . . who . . . make[s], mix[es], manufacture[s], [or] compound[s]" a drug for clarity.

In subsection (c) of this section, the former reference to "in the discretion of the court" was deleted by Ch. 26 as implicit in the establishment of maximum and minimum penalties.

The Criminal Law Article Review Committee notes, for the consideration of the General Assembly, that subsection (b) of this section does not prohibit the use of the poison methyl alcohol in a drug unless ethyl alcohol is usually used to prepare the drug.

Defined term:
"Person"   § 1-101

Civil action. — Contention in a civil suit that defendants had violated a prior version of this section was overruled where there was no evidence that they mixed, made, manufactured or compounded whiskey sold plaintiff, or that they introduced wood alcohol into it. Flaccomio v. Eysink, 129 Md. 367, 100 A. 510 (1916).

§ 8-903. Unauthorized carrier transfer ticket.

(a) *Prohibited.* — (1) A person may not intentionally issue, sell, or give to an unauthorized person a ticket or instrument for the transfer from a conveyance on one passenger line or route to a conveyance on another line or route of the same or a different carrier.

(2) Unless authorized to do so, a person may not intentionally receive a ticket or instrument for the transfer from a conveyance on one passenger line or route to a conveyance on another line or route of the same or a different carrier.

(b) *Penalty.* — A person who violates this section is guilty of a misdemeanor and on conviction is subject to:

(1) for the first violation, a fine not exceeding $100; and

(2) for each subsequent violation, imprisonment not exceeding 90 days or a fine not exceeding $500 or both. (An. Code 1957, art. 27, § 200; 2002, ch. 26, § 2; ch. 352; ch. 479, § 1; ch. 480, § 1.)

SPECIAL REVISOR'S NOTE

This Special Revisor's note comprises information related to the revision by Acts 2002, ch. 26 and other chapters amending this section from the 2002 Legislative Session.

Chapter 26, Acts of 2002, enacted this section as § 8-803, which was new language derived without substantive change from former Art. 27, § 200. However, Chs. 479 and 480, § 1, Acts of 2002, each renumbered Subtitle 8 of this title to be Subtitle 9, under the amended subtitle "Subtitle 9. Miscellaneous Fraud". Accordingly, this section appears as § 8-903. Also, Ch. 352, Acts of 2002, deleted the former minimum penalty of $10 for a first violation in subsection (b)(1) of this section, and substituted a maximum penalty of "imprisonment not exceeding 90 days or a fine not exceeding $100 or both" for

the penalty of "imprisonment not exceeding 6 months or a fine not less than $100 or both" for a subsequent violation enacted by Ch. 26 in subsection (b)(2) of this section.

In subsection (b) of this section, the references to a "violation" were substituted by Ch. 26 for the former references to an "offense" for consistency within this article. *See* General Revisor's Note to article.

The Criminal Law Article Review Committee noted, for the consideration of the General Assembly, that in subsection (b)(2) of this section, no maximum fine was provided by Ch. 26. Chapter 352 addressed this concern.

Defined term:
"Person"   § 1-101

§ 8-904. Racing horse under false name.

(a) *Prohibited.* — A person knowingly may not enter or race a horse in a running or harness race under a name or designation other than that registered with the Jockey Club or the United States Trotting Association.

(b) *Penalty.* — A person who violates this section is guilty of a misdemeanor and on conviction is subject to imprisonment not exceeding 3 years or a fine not exceeding $5,000 or both. (An. Code 1957, art. 27, § 233B; 2002, ch. 26, § 4; ch. 213, § 3; ch. 479, § 1; ch. 480, § 1.)

SPECIAL REVISOR'S NOTE

This Special Revisor's note comprises information related to the revision by Acts 2002, ch. 26 and other chapters amending this section from the 2002 Legislative Session.

Chapter 26, § 4, Acts of 2002, enacted this section as § 11-1002 of the Business Regulation Article, which was new language derived without substantive change from former Art. 27, § 233B. However, Ch. 213, § 3, Acts of 2002, transferred this section to be § 8-804 of this article. Also, Chs. 479 and 480, § 1, Acts of 2002, each renumbered Subtitle 8 of this title to be Subtitle 9 of this title, under the amended subtitle "Subtitle 9. Miscellaneous Fraud", and inserted a new Subtitle 8. Accordingly, this section appears as § 8-904.

In subsection (a) of this section, the reference to a "harness" race was substituted by Ch. 26

for the former reference to a "trotting" race for consistency with BR Title 11.

Also in subsection (a) of this section, the reference to a name other than "that" registered was substituted by Ch. 26 for the former reference to the "name or designation" registered for brevity.

Also in subsection (a) of this section, the former reference to a name or designation "assigned to the horse by" the Jockey Club or the United States Trotting Association was deleted by Ch. 26 because the Jockey Club registers, but does not name, a horse, and the United States Trotting Association assigns a name to (and then registers) a horse from a list of three names submitted by the owner.

Also in subsection (a) of this section, the former reference to "instigat[ing], engag[ing] in, or in any way further[ing]" a prohibited act

101

under this section was deleted by Ch. 26 because under Maryland law, there is no distinction between an accessory to a misdemeanor and a principal. *See, e.g., Fabian v. State*, 235 Md. 306, 317 (1963); *see, also*, CP § 4-204.

Defined term:
"Person"   § 1-101

§ 8-905. Counterfeit pari-mutuel betting tickets.

(a) *Prohibited.* — A person may not knowingly present for payoff, or give to another to present for payoff, a counterfeit or altered pari-mutuel betting ticket.

(b) *Penalty.* — A person who violates this section is guilty of a misdemeanor and on conviction is subject to imprisonment not exceeding 1 year or a fine not exceeding $1,000 or both. (An. Code 1957, art. 27, § 233C; 2002, ch. 26, § 4; ch. 213, § 3; ch. 479, § 1; ch. 480, § 1.)

SPECIAL REVISOR'S NOTE

This Special Revisor's note comprises information related to the revision by Acts 2002, ch. 26 and other chapters amending this section from the 2002 Legislative Session.

Chapter 26, § 4, Acts of 2002, enacted this section as § 11-1003 of the Business Regulation Article, which was new language derived without substantive change from former Art. 27, § 233C. However, Ch. 213, § 3, Acts of 2002, transferred this section to be § 8-805 of this article. Also, Chs. 479 and 480, § 1, Acts of

2002, each renumbered Subtitle 8 of this title to be Subtitle 9 of this title, under the amended subtitle "Subtitle 9. Miscellaneous Fraud", and inserted a new Subtitle 8. Accordingly, this section appears as § 8-905.

In subsection (a) of this section, the reference to a "betting" ticket was added by Ch. 26 for clarity and consistency with BR Title 11.

Defined terms:
"Counterfeit"   § 1-101
"Person"   § 1-101

CRIMINAL LAW

TITLE 9.

CRIMES AGAINST PUBLIC ADMINISTRATION.

103

Subtitle 1. Perjury.

§ 9-101. Perjury.

(a) *Prohibited.* — A person may not willfully and falsely make an oath or affirmation as to a material fact:

(1) if the false swearing is perjury at common law;

(2) in an affidavit required by any state, federal, or local law;

(3) in an affidavit made to induce a court or officer to pass an account or claim;

(4) in an affidavit required by any state, federal, or local government or governmental official with legal authority to require the issuance of an affidavit; or

(5) in an affidavit or affirmation made under the Maryland Rules.

(b) *Penalty.* — A person who violates this section is guilty of the misdemeanor of perjury and on conviction is subject to imprisonment not exceeding 10 years.

(c) *Contradictory statements.* — (1) If a person makes an oath or affirmation to two contradictory statements, each of which, if false, is prohibited by subsection (a) of this section, it is sufficient to allege, and for conviction to prove, that one of the statements is willfully false without specifying which one.

(2) If the two contradictory statements made in violation of paragraph (1) of this subsection are made in different counties, the violation may be prosecuted in either county.

(d) *Statute of limitations and in banc review.* — A person who violates this section is subject to § 5-106(b) of the Courts Article. (An. Code 1957, art. 27, §§ 435, 437, 439; 2002, ch. 26, § 2; 2004, ch. 105.)

REVISOR'S NOTE

This Revisor's note comprises information related to the revision by Acts 2002, ch. 26.

This section is new language derived without substantive change from former Art. 27, §§ 435, 437, and, as it related to the penalty for perjury, § 439.

In subsection (b) of this section, the phrase "is subject to imprisonment" is substituted for the former mandatory phrase "shall be sentenced" more accurately to reflect the discretionary minimum range for imprisonment for a violation.

Also in subsection (b) of this section, the reference to a person who violates this section being guilty "of the misdemeanor" of perjury is added to state expressly that which was only implied in the former law. At common law, perjury was a misdemeanor, although it was an "infamous crime" involving moral turpitude, a *crimen falsi*, which disqualified a convicted person from testifying in court. *Garitee v. Bond*, 102 Md. 379, 384 (1905); *Hourie v. State*, 53 Md. App. 62 (1982); *see, also, Murray v. State*, 27 Md. App. 404, 408 (1975) (dicta). Also, in this State, any crime that was not considered a felony at common law and has not been declared a felony by statute is considered a misdemeanor. *See State v. Canova*, 278 Md. 483, 490 (1976); *Bowser v. State*, 136 Md. 342, 354 (1920); *Dutton v. State*, 123 Md. 373, 378 (1914); and *Williams v. State*, 4 Md. App. 342, 347 (1968).

Subsection (c) of this section, derived from former Art. 27, § 437, is revised as a rule for resolving contradictory statements for purposes of indictment and conviction for clarity.

In subsection (d) of this section, the reference to a violation being "subject to § 5-106(b) of the Courts Article" is substituted for the former reference to the violation subjecting the defendant to imprisonment "in the. . . penitentiary" for clarity and consistency within this article. *See* General Revisor's Note to article.

The Criminal Law Article Review Committee notes, for the consideration of the General Assembly, that in subsection (a)(4) of this section, it is not clear whether the reference to an affidavit made to an officer of the "government" refers only to the Maryland State government, or also to an officer of the federal government, a local government, a bi-county or multi-county unit, or even to an officer of the government of another state taking an affidavit in Maryland. The General Assembly may wish to address the scope of governments and their officers covered by this provision.

Defined term:
"Person"   § 1-101

Editor's note. — Section 2, ch. 371, Acts 1991, provides that "there is no statute of limitations for a misdemeanor punishable by imprisonment in the penitentiary, notwithstanding any holding or dictum to the contrary in Massey v. State, 320 Md. 605, 579 A.2d 265 (1990)."

Legislative immunity. — Indictment charging defendant with bribery, malfeasance in office, nonfeasance in office, and perjury was properly dismissed because the General Assembly meant what the General Assembly said when the General Assembly provided in § 5-501 of the Courts Article that a criminal action could not be brought against a city council member for words spoken at a meeting of council or a committee thereof. State v. Holton, 420 Md. 530, 24 A.3d 678 (2011).

Defendant's property interest in seized property. — When defendant, after expiration of the probation imposed following defendant's guilty plea to violating a domestic protective order, sought return of the weapons seized from defendant's home, defendant's subsequent convictions for perjury, under (a)(2), and giving false information or making a material misstatement in a firearm application, under § 5-139(a) of the Public Safety Article, for stating, in an application to purchase a firearm, that defendant had never been committed to a mental institution, did not render moot defendant's appeal of the denial of defendant's motion to reconsider the denial of defendant's motion for return of the weapons because defendant still had a property interest in the weapons, under art. 24 of the Declaration of Rights, even if defendant could not lawfully possess the weapons. Furda v. State, 193 Md. App. 371, 997 A.2d 856 (2010).

Evidence sufficient. — Evidence was legally sufficient to convict defendant of perjury in connection with a firearm application despite the fact that a court in companion protective order case erred in finding that defendant's emergency evaluation constitute a commitment to a mental health institution, because the later finding of error did not change the fact that at the time the form was completed, defendant had been advised in the protective order case that the emergency evaluation constituted a commitment. Furda v. State, 194 Md. App. 1, 1 A.3d 528 (2010).

Conviction based on order that was reversed upheld. — Defendant's conviction for perjury and false information in a firearm application could be founded upon defendant's failure to disclose a court order that was later reversed; defendant was obligated to answer "yes," despite defendant's ongoing dispute with the order denying defendant's request for a return of his firearms for having been commit-

ted to a mental institution. Furda v. State, 421 Md. 332, 26 A.3d 918 (2011).

Stated in Smith v. State, 403 Md. 659, 944 A.2d 505 (2008).

§ 9-102. Subornation of perjury.

(a) *Prohibited.* — A person may not procure another to commit perjury as prohibited by § 9-101 of this subtitle.

(b) *Penalty.* — A person who violates this section is guilty of the misdemeanor of subornation of perjury and on conviction is subject to imprisonment not exceeding 10 years.

(c) *Statute of limitations and in banc review.* — A person who violates this section is subject to § 5-106(b) of the Courts Article. (An. Code 1957, art. 27, §§ 438, 439; 2002, ch. 26, § 2.)

REVISOR'S NOTE

This Revisor's note comprises information related to the revision by Acts 2002, ch. 26.

This section is new language derived without substantive change from former Art. 27, § 438 and, as it related to the penalty for subornation of perjury, § 439.

In subsection (b) of this section, the phrase "is subject to imprisonment" is substituted for the former mandatory phrase "shall be sentenced" more accurately to reflect the discretionary minimum range for imprisonment for a violation.

Also in subsection (b) of this section, the reference to a person who violates this section being guilty "of the misdemeanor" of subornation of perjury is added to state expressly that which was only implied in the former law. At common law, subornation of perjury was treated in the same manner as perjury, a misdemeanor. *See McGarvey v. McGarvey*, 286 Md.

19, 28 (1979); *see, also, Garitee v. Bond*, 102 Md. 379, 384 (1905); *Hourie v. State*, 53 Md. App. 62 (1982); *Murray v. State*, 27 Md. App. 404, 408 (1975) (dicta). Also, in this State, any crime that was not considered a felony at common law and has not been declared a felony by statute is considered a misdemeanor. *See State v. Canova*, 278 Md. 483, 490 (1976); *Bowser v. State*, 136 Md. 342, 354 (1920); *Dutton v. State*, 123 Md. 373, 378 (1914); and *Williams v. State*, 4 Md. App. 342, 347 (1968).

In subsection (c) of this section, the reference to a violation being "subject to § 5-106(b) of the Courts Article" is substituted for the former reference to the violation subjecting the defendant to imprisonment "in the. . . penitentiary" for clarity and consistency within this article. *See* General Revisor's Note to article.

Defined term:
"Person"   § 1-101

§ 9-103. Charging document.

(a) *Violations of § 9-101(a).* — An indictment, information, or other charging document for perjury in violation of § 9-101(a) of this subtitle is sufficient if it substantially states:

"(name of defendant) on (date) in (county), on examination as a witness, duly sworn to testify in (proceeding) by (court or other person administering oath) with authority to administer the oath, willfully, unlawfully, and falsely swore (facts), the matters so sworn were material, and the testimony of (name of defendant) was willfully and corruptly false, in violation of (section violated) against the peace, government, and dignity of the State.".

(b) *Violations of § 9-101(c).* — An indictment, information, or other charging document for perjury in violation of § 9-101(c) of this subtitle is sufficient if it substantially states:

"(name of defendant) in (county), on examination as a witness, duly sworn to testify in (proceeding) by (court or other person administering oath) with authority to administer the oath, on (date 1) willfully swore (facts 1) and on (date 1 or 2) (in county 1 or 2) willfully swore (facts 2), and that the matters so sworn are material, and at least one of the two contradictory statements was willfully false, in violation of (section violated) against the peace, government, and dignity of the State.". (An. Code 1957, art. 27, § 436; 2002, ch. 26, § 2; 2004, ch. 105.)

REVISOR'S NOTE

This Revisor's note comprises information related to the revision by Acts 2002, ch. 26.

This section is new language derived without substantive change from former Art. 27, § 436.

The phrase "is sufficient if it substantially states" is substituted for the former phrase "shall be sufficient to use a formula substantially to the following effect" for clarity and consistency within this article.

Also the phrase "in violation of (section violated)" is substituted for the former phrase "contrary to the form of the Act of Assembly in such case made and provided" for clarity and consistency within this article.

The Criminal Law Article Review Committee notes, for the consideration of the General Assembly, that the charging document in this section may not be sufficient to charge perjury by contradictory statements under § 9-101(c) of this subtitle. That provision requires merely that for charging and for conviction, there be two contradictory statements made under oath or affirmation, without specifying which one is false.

Defined terms:
"County"	§ 1-101
"Person"	§ 1-101

Subtitle 2. Bribery.

§ 9-201. Bribery of public employee.

(a) *Definitions.* — (1) In this section the following words have the meanings indicated.

(2) "Political subdivision" includes a:

(i) county;

(ii) municipal corporation;

(iii) bi-county or multicounty agency;

(iv) county board of education;

(v) public authority; or

(vi) special taxing district that is not a homeowner's association.

(3) (i) "Public employee" means an officer or employee of:

1. the State; or

2. a political subdivision of the State.

(ii) "Public employee" includes:

1. an executive officer of the State;

2. a judge of the State;

3. a judicial officer of the State;

4. a member or officer of the General Assembly;

5. a member of the police force of Baltimore City or the Department of State Police; and

6. a member, officer, or executive officer of a political subdivision.

(b) *Prohibited — Bribing public employee.* — A person may not bribe or attempt to bribe a public employee to influence the public employee in the performance of an official duty of the public employee.

(c) *Prohibited — Public employee demanding or receiving bribe.* — A public employee may not demand or receive a bribe, fee, reward, or testimonial to:

(1) influence the performance of the official duties of the public employee; or

(2) neglect or fail to perform the official duties of the public employee.

(d) *Penalty.* — A person who violates this section is guilty of the misdemeanor of bribery and on conviction:

(1) is subject to imprisonment for not less than 2 years and not exceeding 12 years or a fine not less than $100 and not exceeding $5,000 or both;

(2) may not vote; and

(3) may not hold an office of trust or profit in the State.

(e) *Statute of limitations and in banc review.* — A person who violates this section is subject to § 5-106(b) of the Courts Article.

(f) *Competency and immunity of witness in prosecution.* — (1) A person who violates this section:

(i) is a competent witness; and

(ii) subject to paragraph (2) of this subsection, may be compelled to testify against any person who may have violated this section.

(2) A person compelled to testify for the State under paragraph (1) of this subsection is immune from prosecution for a crime about which the person was compelled to testify. (An. Code 1957, art. 27, § 22; 2002, ch. 26, § 2; 2006, ch. 430.)

REVISOR'S NOTE

This Revisor's note comprises information related to the revision by Acts 2002, ch. 26.

This section is new language derived without substantive change from former Art. 27, § 22.

Subsection (a) of this section is revised as a definition to avoid repetition of phrases, such as "executive officer of the State of Maryland", "any judge", "or other judicial officer of this State", and "any member or officer of the General Assembly of Maryland". The former specific references to "Governor" and "mayor" are deleted as included within the illustrative examples of "public officer or employee" in subsection (a)(2) of this section.

In subsection (d) of this section, the former reference to a sentence being "in the discretion of the court" is deleted as implicit in the reference to a person being "subject to" a fine and imprisonment.

Also in subsection (d) of this section, the former reference to being "disfranchised and disqualified from holding any" office of trust or profit in the State is revised as "(2) may not vote; and (3) may not hold an" office of trust or profit in the State for clarity. *See* Md. Constitution, Art. I, § 6 and Art. III, § 50.

In subsection (e) of this section, the reference to a violation being "subject to § 5-106(b) of the Courts Article" is substituted for the former reference to the violation subjecting the defendant to imprisonment "in the penitentiary of this State" for clarity and consistency within this article. *See* General Revisor's Note to article.

In subsection (f)(2) of this section, the phrase "immune from prosecution for a crime about which the person was compelled to testify" is substituted for the former phrase "exempt from prosecution, . . . for any such crime of which such person so testifying may have been guilty or a participant therein, and about which he was so compelled to testify" for clarity.

Also in subsection (f)(2) of this section, because immunity from prosecution precludes trial and punishment, the former references to "trial" and "punishment" are deleted as unnecessary.

For provisions on testimony from convicted perjurers and from compelled witnesses generally, *see* CJ §§ 9-104 and 9-123, respectively.

The Criminal Law Article Review Committee notes, for the consideration of the General

Assembly, that subsection (f) of this section, which allows a witness to be compelled to testify and provides transactional immunity for that testimony, raises significant constitutional concerns under the 5th and 14th Amendments to the U.S. Constitution, and their State counterpart, Art. 22 of the Md. Declaration of Rights. *See, e.g., Evans v. State*, 333 Md. 660 (1994), *cert. denied*, 513 U.S. 833 (1994); *In re Criminal Investigation No. 1-162*, 307 Md. 674 (1986). The relevant constitutional provisions generally prohibit self-incrimination. The granting of some form of immunity against prosecution arising from compelled incriminating testimony does not, of itself, cure the constitutional defect. The General Assembly may wish to explore the scope of immunity that may be required to allow compelled testimony in harmony with federal and State constitutional precedent. This provision raises the same concerns as § 9-204(d) of this subtitle, *below*.

As to the authority of the legislature to enact penalties for common-law bribery and attempted bribery, *see* Md. Constitution, Art. I, § 6 and Art. III, § 50.

Defined terms:

"County"	§ 1-101
"Person"	§ 1-101

I. GENERAL CONSIDERATION.

Cross references. — For constitutional provisions as to bribery in elections, see Article I, § 6 of the Maryland Constitution.

For constitutional provision providing that the General Assembly shall provide by law for the punishment for bribery of public officers and also the acceptance of bribes by public officers, see Article III, § 50 of the Maryland Constitution.

Editor's note. — Section 2, ch. 371, Acts 1991, which amended a prior similar provision, provides that "there is no statute of limitations for a misdemeanor punishable by imprisonment in the penitentiary, notwithstanding any holding or dictum to the contrary in Massey v. State, 320 Md. 605, 579 A.2d 265 (1990)."

Maryland Law Review. — For note, "Self-Incrimination: Choosing a Constitutional Standard," see 32 Md. L. Rev. 289 (1972).

For article, "Survey of Developments in Maryland Law, 1986-87," see 47 Md. L. Rev. 739 (1988).

University of Baltimore Law Forum. — For article on permanent injunction against "chilling" Fifth Amendment rights, see 17, No. 3 . U. Balt. Law Forum 3 (1987).

University of Baltimore Law Review. — For article, "The Law Enforcement Officers' Privilege Against Compelled Self-Incrimination," see 16 U. Balt. L. Rev. 452 (1987).

Constitutionality. — There is no merit in the contention that a prior similar provision was void for vagueness under the Fourteenth Amendment to the United States Constitution and article 24 of the Maryland Declaration of Rights. Blondes v. State, 16 Md. App. 165, 294 A.2d 661 (1972), rev'd on other grounds, 273 Md. 435, 330 A.2d 169 (1975).

Former similar provision was enacted in compliance with requirements of Article III, § 50 of the Maryland Constitution.. Brown v. State, 233 Md. 288, 196 A.2d 614 (1964); State v. Comes, 237 Md. 271, 206 A.2d 124 (1965).

Former similar section contains no limiting phrases. Brown v. State, 233 Md. 288, 196 A.2d 614 (1964).

Common law. — Former similar provision was a statute declaratory of the common law and a conclusion that it is more all-inclusive than common law bribery is technically inaccurate. Blondes v. State, 16 Md. App. 165, 294 A.2d 661 (1972), rev'd on other grounds, 273 Md. 435, 330 A.2d 169 (1975).

Bribery was common law offense at time Maryland Constitution was enacted. Blondes v. State, 16 Md. App. 165, 294 A.2d 661 (1972), rev'd on other grounds, 273 Md. 435, 330 A.2d 169 (1975).

No directive was given by the Maryland Constitution that offense of bribery be provided for by statute, but rather a statute be enacted to punish that common law crime by fine, or imprisonment in penitentiary, or both, and that person convicted be forever disfranchised and disqualified from holding any office of trust or profit in this State. Blondes v. State, 16 Md. App. 165, 294 A.2d 661 (1972), rev'd on other grounds, 273 Md. 435, 330 A.2d 169 (1975).

This section embodies the basic elements of the common law without extending its boundaries to persons outside the ambit of the common law. State v. Canova, 278 Md. 483, 365 A.2d 988 (1976).

At common law, bribery and an attempt to bribe were misdemeanors. State v. Canova, 278 Md. 483, 365 A.2d 988 (1976).

As recognized by the common law, bribery is the corrupt payment or receipt of a private price for official action. State v. Canova, 278 Md. 483, 365 A.2d 988 (1976).

Maryland's definition of bribery has remained consistent; this section is merely a declaration of the common law of bribery, and is not more inclusive. Acquah v. State, 113 Md. App. 29, 686 A.2d 690 (1996).

Expansion of class of bribees to members of General Assembly under common law. — The expansion of the class of bribees under the common law from judges and jurors to members of the General Assembly was not a statutory change but an evolution of the common law firmly established in both England and the United States at the time of the adoption of the Maryland statute. Blondes v. State, 16 Md. App. 165, 294 A.2d 661 (1972), rev'd on other grounds, 273 Md. 435, 330 A.2d 169 (1975).

Briber and bribee distinguished. — With respect to the bribe-giver or briber, this section speaks of "any person," and like the common law, anyone not entirely without criminal capacity may be a briber. With respect to a bribe-taker or bribee, however, this section designates classes, and only a person within one of those classes is a potential bribee. State v. Canova, 278 Md. 483, 365 A.2d 988 (1976).

"Official duties" defined. — As to "official duties" under this section, lying between the two opposite poles of (1) duties or actions obviously prohibited and (2) official duties expressly prescribed or authorized, is a large area in which the determination of whether or not the action of a policeman is part of his official duties must depend on the particular facts. Kable v. State, 17 Md. App. 16, 299 A.2d 493, cert. denied, 268 Md. 750 (1973).

The right of a police officer in a county to recommend the nol pros of traffic cases in which he brought the original charges must be considered a responsibility implicitly authorized by custom and circumstances, amounting to an official practice and, consequently, one of his "official duties" within the language of this section. Kable v. State, 17 Md. App. 16, 299 A.2d 493, cert. denied, 268 Md. 750 (1973).

"Official duties" include those acts that bear some relation to the official duties of the State employee. Richardson v. State, 63 Md. App. 324, 492 A.2d 932 (1985).

Lack of actual authority not defense. — Defendant, a public employee, could not claim as a defense to bribery the lack of actual authority to commit an act where the act was reasonably related to defendant's official duties; the combination of defendant's official position as a deputy director of the county office of central services and defendant's comments to a subcontractor made it reasonable to view the solicitation as related to defendant's official

duties. Thomas v. State, 413 Md. 247, 992 A.2d 423 (2010).

"Municipal corporation"defined. — With respect to this section, there is no logical distinction to be made between "municipality" and "municipal corporation" as used therein and the General Assembly intended none. State v. Canova, 278 Md. 483, 365 A.2d 988 (1976).

Maryland has jurisdiction where intended result is in Maryland regardless of where bribery attempt occurred. — Since the crime charged was the corrupt offering of something of value to a Maryland police officer to influence the performance of his official duties in Maryland, the gravamen of the crime being the intended result in Maryland, a Maryland circuit court has jurisdiction over the offense, notwithstanding the fact that the actual bribery attempt occurred in the District of Columbia. Grindstaff v. State, 57 Md. App. 412, 470 A.2d 809, cert. denied, 299 Md. 655, 474 A.2d 1344 (1984).

In the light of the rule of strict construction, the view that a "quasi-municipal corporation" satisfies the classification of "municipal corporation" used in this section is not valid. State v. Canova, 278 Md. 483, 365 A.2d 988 (1976).

Status of Washington Suburban Sanitary Commission. — The Washington Suburban Sanitary Commission is not a municipality, municipal corporation or political subdivision of this State within the meaning of this section. State v. Canova, 278 Md. 483, 365 A.2d 988 (1976).

Statute of limitations. —Although bribery is not a felony, because a defendant may be imprisoned upon conviction, bribery and attempted bribery are excluded from those misdemeanors which must be prosecuted within one year after the offense was committed. State v. Canova, 278 Md. 483, 365 A.2d 988 (1976).

Bribery need not be prosecuted within one year after commission. — Bribery is among those unique misdemeanors classified as "penitentiary misdemeanors" which do not have to be prosecuted within one year after their commission. Klein v. State, 52 Md. App. 640, 452 A.2d 173 (1982), cert. denied, 295 Md. 440 (1983).

II. ELEMENTS OF OFFENSE.

Essence of crime. — The essence of the crime of bribery is the passing of money to the officer to influence the officer in the performance of his official duties. Cunningham v. State, 190 Md. 578, 59 A.2d 337 (1948); Blondes v. State, 16 Md. App. 165, 294 A.2d 661 (1972).

Requirements. — What is required under this section is to show the payment involved was not a quid pro quo for specific action, but was made with the intent to influence the conduct of the public servant in relation to his position, employment, or duty. Spector v. State, 289 Md. 407, 425 A.2d 197, cert. denied, 452 U.S. 906, 101 S. Ct. 3032, 69 L. Ed. 2d 407 (1981).

Tender not necessary. — Tender is not necessary since any expression of ability to produce the amount offered is sufficient to constitute the crime of attempted bribery. Raimondi v. State, 12 Md. App. 322, 278 A.2d 664 (1971), aff'd, 265 Md. 229, 288 A.2d 882, cert. denied, 409 U.S. 948, 93 S. Ct. 293, 34 L. Ed. 2d 219 (1972).

Public official may be guilty of both bribery and extortion. — The fact that a public official may demand money to influence the performance of his official duties, and thus be guilty of bribery, does not mean that he may not also be guilty of extortion, if the demand for money is accompanied by a threat that, unless it is paid, he will do injury to the person or property of the party upon whom the demand is made. Carey v. State, 43 Md. App. 246, 405 A.2d 293, cert. denied, 286 Md. 744 (1979), cert. denied, 445 U.S. 967, 100 S. Ct. 1660, 64 L. Ed. 2d 244 (1980).

Bribery and unfair or deceptive trade practices contrasted. — None of the constituent elements of bribery — payment to a public employee to influence him in the performance of his official duties — appear in the definition of unfair or deceptive trade practices of § 13-301 of the Commercial Law Article. Klein v. State, 52 Md. App. 640, 452 A.2d 173 (1982), cert. denied, 295 Md. 440 (1983).

Bribery requires proof of the payment of money or other benefits to a public employee for the purpose of influencing him in the performance of his official duties. It must be established that payment was received pursuant to a corrupt agreement, and the level of proof must be beyond a reasonable doubt. Unfair trade practices, on the other hand, require proof of deception, fraud, false pretense, false premise, misrepresentation, or knowing concealment, suppression, or omission of any material fact with the intent that the consumer rely on the same. There must be sufficient sworn testimony to support each violation, and the proof must be by a preponderance of the evidence. Thus, each offense contains an element which the other does not. Klein v. State, 52 Md. App. 640, 452 A.2d 173 (1982), cert. denied, 295 Md. 440 (1983).

The evidence necessary to secure a conviction of bribery and that required to support a civil judgment for engaging in unfair or deceptive trade practices are completely different. Therefore, neither can trigger the claim of double jeopardy, based on the bar against multiple punishments for the same offense. Nor is the principle of res judicata applicable since the subject matter of both actions is not the same.

Klein v. State, 52 Md. App. 640, 452 A.2d 173 (1982), cert. denied, 295 Md. 440 (1983).

Conspiracy included. — The broad language of this section referring to "any such crime of which" he "may have been guilty" should be construed as including conspiracy to violate the bribery law; but even if it were not, this gap in statutory protection would be closed by former Art. 27, § 39 (see now § 9-204 of this article). Brown v. State, 233 Md. 288, 196 A.2d 614 (1964); State v. Panagoulis, 3 Md. App. 330, 239 A.2d 145 (1968), aff'd, 253 Md. 699, 253 A.2d 877 (1969).

Conspiracy as separate offense. — Jury acquittal on bribery charge under this section held not inconsistent with a conviction for conspiracy to gain access to personal records by false pretenses, bribery, or theft under § 10-627 (a) (3) of the State Government Article. Acquah v. State, 113 Md. App. 29, 686 A.2d 690 (1996).

Promise for which bribe given does not matter. — When a bribe is taken, it does not matter whether the promise for which the bribe was given was for the performance of a legislative act or for use of influence with the Executive Branch. Blondes v. State, 16 Md. App. 165, 294 A.2d 661 (1972), rev'd on other grounds, 273 Md. 435, 330 A.2d 169 (1975).

Bribery may be deemed conduct involving moral turpitude, justifying disbarment of attorney. — Where circumstances clearly permit an inference of corrupt intent, bribery may be deemed to be conduct involving moral turpitude so as to justify disbarment of an attorney in the absence of compelling circumstances justifying a lesser sanction. Att'y Griev. Comm'n v. Spector, 293 Md. 324, 443 A.2d 965 (1982).

Bribing or attempting to bribe officer making illegal arrest not offense. — Bribing or attempting to bribe officer while making illegal arrest is not an offense under this section. Sugarman v. State, 173 Md. 52, 195 A. 324 (1937).

Even if there is any continuing vitality in the suggestion in Sugarman v. State, 173 Md. 52, 195 A. 324 (1937), that bribing or attempting to bribe a police officer while making an illegal arrest is not an offense under this section, it avails the defendant naught where the arrest is lawful. Soles v. State, 16 Md. App. 656, 299 A.2d 502 (1973), cert. denied, 415 U.S. 950, 94 S. Ct. 1473, 39 L. Ed. 2d 566 (1974).

III. IMMUNITY.

Immunity afforded displaces privilege against self-incrimination. — The statutory immunity afforded under this section is broad enough to displace the privilege against self-incrimination contained in article 22 of the

Declaration of Rights. Brown v. State, 233 Md. 288, 196 A.2d 614 (1964).

The immunity granted must be as broad as the privilege against self-incrimination which it supplants or displaces. Roll v. State, 15 Md. App. 31, 288 A.2d 605 (1972), modified, 267 Md. 714, 298 A.2d 867 (1973).

This section limits the scope of article 22 of the Declaration of Rights, if there be any conflict between them. Brown v. State, 233 Md. 288, 196 A.2d 614 (1964); State v. Panagoulis, 253 Md. 699, 253 A.2d 877 (1969).

But there is no real conflict between article 22 of the Declaration of Rights and this section. Brown v. State, 233 Md. 288, 196 A.2d 614 (1964).

Principle against self-incrimination liberally construed. — Principle against self-incrimination has always been liberally construed in order to give the fullest effect to this immunity. State v. Comes, 237 Md. 271, 206 A.2d 124 (1965).

Protection afforded adheres to the accused throughout his trial. — State v. Comes, 237 Md. 271, 206 A.2d 124 (1965).

Scope of immunity. — This section undertakes to give in full the immunity contemplated by Article III, § 50 of the Maryland Constitution, and in terms is somewhat broader, but is not beyond the constitutional authorization. Brown v. State, 233 Md. 288, 196 A.2d 614 (1964).

The immunity granted by this section to the witness compelled to testify is a broad immunity. Since it bars "prosecution," it effectively bars the use of "leads" to convict the witness of the offense as to which he testifies, and it covers the offense of attempting to bribe as well as actual bribing. Brown v. State, 233 Md. 288, 196 A.2d 614 (1964).

This section effectively bars the use of "leads" to convict the witness of the offense as to which he testifies. State v. Panagoulis, 3 Md. App. 330, 239 A.2d 145 (1968), aff'd, 253 Md. 699, 253 A.2d 877 (1969).

Indictment charging defendant with bribery, malfeasance in office, nonfeasance in office, and perjury was properly dismissed because the general assembly meant what the general assembly said when the general assembly provided in § 5-501 of the Courts Article that a criminal action could not be brought against a city council member for words spoken at a meeting of council or a committee thereof. State v. Holton, 420 Md. 530, 24 A.3d 678 (2011).

General Assembly has power to keep own house in order. — General Assembly has power to keep its own house in order under Article III, §§ 19 and 26 of the Maryland Constitution. Blondes v. State, 16 Md. App. 165, 294 A.2d 661 (1972), rev'd on other grounds, 273 Md. 435, 330 A.2d 169 (1975).

Limited constitutional mandate. — Article III, § 50 of the Maryland Constitution is a limited mandate providing for punishment of State legislators guilty of bribery if indictment and prosecution therefor can be accomplished without impinging on the legislative privilege by introducing evidence of legislative acts. Blondes v. State, 16 Md. App. 165, 294 A.2d 661 (1972), rev'd on other grounds, 273 Md. 435, 330 A.2d 169 (1975).

Constitution does not nullify speech and debate clauses. — The Maryland Constitution does not nullify speech and debate clauses in bribery prosecution of member of General Assembly. Blondes v. State, 16 Md. App. 165, 294 A.2d 661 (1972), rev'd on other grounds, 273 Md. 435, 330 A.2d 169 (1975).

Not all conduct protected under speech and debate clauses. — Not all conduct merely relating to the legislative process is protected under the speech and debate clauses. Such protection is limited to acts clearly part of the legislative process — "the due functioning of the process." Blondes v. State, 16 Md. App. 165, 294 A.2d 661 (1972), rev'd on other grounds, 273 Md. 435, 330 A.2d 169 (1975).

While the speech or debate clause recognizes speech, voting and other legislative acts as exempt from liability that might otherwise attach, it does not privilege either legislator or aide to violate an otherwise valid criminal law in preparing for or implementing legislative acts. Blondes v. State, 16 Md. App. 165, 294 A.2d 661 (1972), rev'd on other grounds, 273 Md. 435, 330 A.2d 169 (1975).

When courts may act. — Courts may act under this section if the prosecution can prove its case without inquiry into legislative acts. Blondes v. State, 16 Md. App. 165, 294 A.2d 661 (1972), rev'd on other grounds, 273 Md. 435, 330 A.2d 169 (1975).

Legislator's taking bribe not part of legislative process. — Legislator's taking bribe is, obviously, no part of legislative process or function; it is not a legislative act. Blondes v. State, 16 Md. App. 165, 294 A.2d 661 (1972), rev'd on other grounds, 273 Md. 435, 330 A.2d 169 (1975).

The closing provision of this section providing for compellable testimony, interpreted as a grant of wide immunity, should facilitate any necessary court prosecutions without impingement on the legislative privilege. Blondes v. State, 16 Md. App. 165, 294 A.2d 661 (1972), rev'd on other grounds, 273 Md. 435, 330 A.2d 169 (1975).

Legislative immunity and bribery prosecutions of legislators harmonized. — It is reasonable to harmonize legislative immunity and bribery prosecutions of legislators in accordance with the reasoning and holding of the Supreme Court in United States v. Brewster, 408 U.S. 501, 92 S. Ct. 2531, 33 L. Ed. 2d 507

(1972). Blondes v. State, 16 Md. App. 165, 294 A.2d 661 (1972), rev'd on other grounds, 273 Md. 435, 330 A.2d 169 (1975).

The United States Supreme Court's interpretation of the legislative privilege is accepted as authoritative, and applying it to article 10 of the Maryland Declaration of Rights and Article III, § 18 of the Maryland Constitution, it is plain that substantive evidence of legislative acts performed by a delegate to the General Assembly, introduced in evidence against him, over his objection, was inadmissible and, because not harmless, requires a retrial. Blondes v. State, 16 Md. App. 165, 294 A.2d 661 (1972), rev'd on other grounds, 273 Md. 435, 330 A.2d 169 (1975).

Witness does not have to assert privilege in order to get immunity. — Witness does not have to assert privilege against self-incrimination in order to obtain statutory immunity. State v. Comes, 237 Md. 271, 206 A.2d 124 (1965).

A witness need not claim his privilege in order to obtain the exemption afforded by this section. State v. Panagoulis, 253 Md. 699, 253 A.2d 877 (1969).

Subpoena not prerequisite. — A witness does not have to be compelled by subpoena to appear and testify in order to claim the statutory immunity provided for in this section. State v. Comes, 237 Md. 271, 206 A.2d 124 (1965).

A subpoena is not an indispensable factor in compelling a witness to testify. State v. Panagoulis, 253 Md. 699, 253 A.2d 877 (1969).

Where section immunized defendant from prosecution for conspiracy to bribe as well as bribery and attempted bribery, this supplied him with all the safeguards to which he was entitled. Brown v. State, 233 Md. 288, 196 A.2d 614 (1964).

Immunity afforded was not a gift. — Where defendant testified and disclosed facts which were "substantially connected" with the crimes for which he was indicted, the immunity afforded was not a gift, as the State received its "quid pro quo" for the same. State v. Comes, 237 Md. 271, 206 A.2d 124 (1965).

Applicability to grand jury proceedings. — The statutory immunity granted by this section is applicable to grand jury proceedings. Brown v. State, 233 Md. 288, 196 A.2d 614 (1964).

The exemptions mentioned in this section extend to proceedings before grand juries. State v. Comes, 237 Md. 271, 206 A.2d 124 (1965); State v. Panagoulis, 3 Md. App. 330, 239 A.2d 145 (1968), aff'd, 253 Md. 699, 253 A.2d 877 (1969).

This section applies to testimony before a grand jury. State v. Panagoulis, 253 Md. 699, 253 A.2d 877 (1969).

One who is being investigated by a grand jury has no right, constitutional or otherwise, to appear before that body. State v. Panagoulis, 253 Md. 699, 253 A.2d 877 (1969).

One who solicits the grand jury to allow him to testify in his own defense may be held in contempt. State v. Panagoulis, 253 Md. 699, 253 A.2d 877 (1969).

One who contrives to get before a grand jury to testify cannot later cloak himself with the immunity accorded by this section. State v. Panagoulis, 253 Md. 699, 253 A.2d 877 (1969).

Every person is presumed to know the law; hence, the defendant, once he got before the grand jury, whether by subpoena or otherwise, presumptively knew that he was subject to contempt proceedings and imprisonment if he refused to answer questions relative to the bribery laws, and acquiescence to or assent to what one cannot prevent does not amount to a voluntary agreement thereto. State v. Comes, 237 Md. 271, 206 A.2d 124 (1965).

Threat of federal prosecution does not render section defective. — A claim that the failure of this section to protect against prosecution for federal offenses renders it defective, would have no basis under present law. Brown v. State, 233 Md. 288, 196 A.2d 614 (1964).

Refusal to testify as contempt. — Under former Art. 27, § 298 (c) (see now § 9-123 of the Courts and Judicial Proceedings Article) an order of court is not required to make the refusal to testify a contemptuous act, the mere refusal by the terms of the act being sufficient, but under this section and former Art. 27, § 262 (see now § 9-123 of the Courts and Judicial Proceedings Article), where the witness is only designated as "compellable," there must be some order of the court to compel him in fact to testify which is disregarded by the witness to make his refusal to testify contemptuous. Roll v. State, 15 Md. App. 31, 288 A.2d 605 (1972), modified, 267 Md. 714, 298 A.2d 867 (1973).

Waiver. — Witness may waive his immunity, expressly or by his conduct. State v. Panagoulis, 3 Md. App. 330, 239 A.2d 145 (1968), aff'd, 253 Md. 699, 253 A.2d 877 (1969).

Conduct not waiver of immunity. — Conduct not mounting up to a waiver of the immunity conferred by statute. See State v. Panagoulis, 253 Md. 699, 253 A.2d 877 (1969).

Acquiescence or assent does not amount to agreement. — Acquiescence to or assent to what one cannot prevent does not amount to a voluntary agreement thereto. State v. Panagoulis, 253 Md. 699, 253 A.2d 877 (1969).

IV. INDICTMENT.

Sufficiency. — An indictment for bribery in the language of the statute is sufficient. Bosco v. State, 157 Md. 407, 146 A. 238 (1929).

There is no merit in the argument that an indictment drawn in the words of the statute is so vague and indefinite as to fail to inform a defendant of the charges against him in violation of article 21 of the Maryland Declaration of Rights. Blondes v. State, 16 Md. App. 165, 294 A.2d 661 (1972), rev'd on other grounds, 273 Md. 435, 330 A.2d 169 (1975).

Where the words of the indictments charged the accused with giving the officer money in order to influence the said officer in the performance of his official duties, the indictments were plainly laid in the words of the statute and were sufficient to inform the accused of the charge against him. It was not necessary to name the specific duty allegedly sought to be influenced. Cunningham v. State, 190 Md. 578, 59 A.2d 337 (1948); Blondes v. State, 16 Md. App. 165, 294 A.2d 661 (1972), rev'd on other grounds, 273 Md. 435, 330 A.2d 169 (1975).

Accurate designation of the class of bribee was material. — Accurate designation of the class of bribee was material in the description of the substance of the crime alleged under this section. State v. Canova, 278 Md. 483, 365 A.2d 988 (1976).

Plea bargaining agreement not breached. — Where a plea bargaining agreement contained the following language — "This agreement extends only to the specific matters discussed in this exposition and to any other crimes based upon evidence already in the possession of and fully developed by the State of Maryland as of this date" — the State's action in bringing bribery and extortion charges after having entered into the plea bargain as to unrelated charges was not a breach of the agreement merely because the State was investigating bribery and extortion charges at the time of the plea bargain. Carey v. State, 43 Md. App. 246, 405 A.2d 293, cert. denied, 286 Md. 744 (1979), cert. denied, 445 U.S. 967, 100 S. Ct. 1660, 64 L. Ed. 2d 244 (1980).

V. EVIDENCE AND JURY INSTRUCTIONS.

Prima facie case under federal statute. — To make a prima facie case under an indictment under the federal bribery statute, the government need not show any act of appellee subsequent to the corrupt promise for payment, for it is taking the bribe, not performance of the illicit compact, that is a criminal act. Blondes v. State, 16 Md. App. 165, 294 A.2d 661 (1972), rev'd on other grounds, 273 Md. 435, 330 A.2d 169 (1975).

Under the federal statute, the illegal conduct of bribery is taking or agreeing to take money for a promise to act in a certain way. Therefore, there is no need for the government to show that appellee fulfilled the alleged illegal bargain; acceptance of the bribe is the violation of the statute, not performance of the illegal promise. Blondes v. State, 16 Md. App. 165, 294 A.2d 661 (1972), rev'd on other grounds, 273 Md. 435, 330 A.2d 169 (1975).

Evidence of how a legislator acted, voted or decided in performance of official duties in relation to business before legislative body is inadmissible. Blondes v. State, 16 Md. App. 165, 294 A.2d 661 (1972), rev'd on other grounds, 273 Md. 435, 330 A.2d 169 (1975).

Instructions on attempt. — See Raimondi v. State, 12 Md. App. 322, 278 A.2d 664 (1971), aff'd, 265 Md. 229, 288 A.2d 882, cert. denied, 409 U.S. 948, 93 S. Ct. 293, 34 L. Ed. 2d 219 (1972).

§ 9-202. Bribery of juror; acceptance of bribe by juror.

(a) *Prohibited — Bribing juror.* — A person may not bribe or attempt to bribe a juror for rendering a verdict.

(b) *Prohibited — Juror accepting bribe.* — A juror may not accept a bribe for rendering a verdict.

(c) *Penalty.* — A person who violates this section is guilty of a misdemeanor and on conviction:

(1) is subject to imprisonment for not less than 18 months and not exceeding 6 years; and

(2) may not serve on a jury in the future.

(d) *Statute of limitations and in banc review.* — A person who violates this section is subject to § 5-106(b) of the Courts Article. (An. Code 1957, art. 27, § 25; 2002, ch. 26, § 2.)

REVISOR'S NOTE

This Revisor's note comprises information related to the revision by Acts 2002, ch. 26.

This section is new language derived without substantive change from former Art. 27, § 25.

In subsection (a) of this section, the reference to a "person" is substituted for the former obsolete reference to an "embracer" for clarity.

Also in subsection (a) of this section, the reference to "brib[ing] or attempt[ing] to bribe a juror" is substituted for the former reference to "procur[ing] any juror to take gain or profit" for clarity.

In subsection (b) of this section, the reference to "accept[ing] a bribe" is substituted for the former reference to "taking gain or profit" for clarity.

Subsection (c) of this section is revised to clarify that all prescribed penalties are applicable to all persons convicted under this section.

In subsection (c) of this section, the reference to a person being "guilty of a misdemeanor" is added to state expressly that which was only implied by the former reference to being "convicted". In this State, any crime that was not a felony at common law and has not been declared a felony by statute is considered a misdemeanor. *See State v. Canova*, 278 Md. 483, 490 (1976); *Bowser v. State*, 136 Md. 342, 345 (1920); *Dutton v. State*, 123 Md. 373, 378 (1914); and *Williams v. State*, 4 Md. App. 342, 347 (1968).

In subsection (d) of this section, the reference to a violation being "subject to § 5-106(b) of the Courts Article" is substituted for the former reference to the violation subjecting the defendant to imprisonment "in the penitentiary of this State" for clarity and consistency within this article. *See* General Revisor's Note to article.

For provisions on intimidating or corrupting a juror, *see* § 9-305 of this title.

Defined term:
"Person"   § 1-101

Cross references. — For constitutional provision providing that the General Assembly shall provide by law for the punishment for bribery of public officers and also the acceptance of bribes by public officers, see Article III, § 50 of the Maryland Constitution.

§ 9-203. Bribery of voter.

(a) *Prohibited.* — (1) A person, including a candidate for office, may not give or directly or indirectly promise a gift or reward to secure a vote or a ballot at an election under the Constitution and laws of the State.

(2) A person may not keep or allow to be kept a house or other accommodation in the State on an election day where, before the close of the election, the person, at the person's expense, gratuitously provides alcoholic beverages to voters.

(b) *Penalty.* — A person who violates this section is guilty of a misdemeanor and on conviction is subject to:

(1) imprisonment not exceeding 6 months or a fine not exceeding $500 or both; and

(2) any other penalties applicable under the Constitution. (An. Code 1957, art. 27, § 27; 2002, ch. 26, § 2.)

REVISOR'S NOTE

This Revisor's note comprises information related to the revision by Acts 2002, ch. 26.

This section is new language derived without substantive change from former Art. 27, § 27.

In subsection (a)(1) of this section, the former limitation "at any time before or on the day of any election" is deleted as surplusage.

Also in subsection (a)(1) of this section, the former word "bestow" is deleted as surplusage.

In subsection (a)(2) of this section, the phrase "the State" is substituted for the former phrase "any part of any district" for brevity.

Also in subsection (a)(2) of this section, the word "on" is substituted for the former phrase "at any time during the day" for brevity.

Also in subsection (a)(2) of this section, the phrase "alcoholic beverages" is substituted for the former phrase "intoxicating liquors" for style.

Also in subsection (a)(2) of this section, the former reference to a "tent [or] booth" is deleted as included in the reference to "other accommodation".

In subsection (b) of this section, the former reference to a "candidate so offending" is deleted as included in the reference to a "person".

Also in subsection (b) of this section, the former phrase "in the court of the county or city wherein such offense may be committed" is deleted as surplusage.

Also in subsection (b) of this section, the former references to a sentence being "at the discretion of the court" and "as the court may adjudge" are deleted as implicit in the reference to a person being "subject to" a fine and imprisonment.

Also in subsection (b) of this section, the reference to a person being "guilty of a misdemeanor" is added to state expressly that which only was implied by the reference, in former Art. 27, § 27, to a person being "convicted". In this State, any crime that was not a felony at common law and has not been declared a felony by statute is considered a misdemeanor. *See State v. Canova*, 278 Md. 483, 490 (1976); *Bowser v. State*, 136 Md. 342, 345 (1920); *Dutton v. State*, 123 Md. 373, 378 (1914); and *Williams v. State*, 4 Md. App. 342, 347 (1968).

For other penalties contained in the Maryland Constitution, including disfranchisement and disqualification from holding office, *see* Md. Constitution, Art. I, § 6 and Art. III, § 50.

Defined term:
"Person"   § 1-101

§ 9-204. Bribery of person participating in or connected with athletic contest.

(a) *Prohibited.* — A person may not bribe or attempt to bribe another who is participating in or connected with an athletic contest held in the State.

(b) *Penalty.* — A person who violates this section is guilty of the misdemeanor of bribery and on conviction is subject to imprisonment for not less than 6 months and not exceeding 3 years or a fine not less than $100 and not exceeding $5,000 or both.

(c) *Statute of limitations and in banc review.* — A person who violates this section is subject to § 5-106(b) of the Courts Article.

(d) *Competency and immunity of witness in prosecution.* — (1) A person:

(i) may not refuse to testify concerning a conspiracy to violate this section; but

(ii) may be compelled to testify against any person who may have conspired to violate this section.

(2) A person compelled to testify under paragraph (1) of this subsection is a competent witness.

(3) A person compelled to testify for the State under this section is immune from prosecution for a crime about which the person was compelled to testify. (An. Code 1957, art. 27, §§ 23, 39; 2002, ch. 26, § 2.)

REVISOR'S NOTE

This Revisor's note comprises information related to the revision by Acts 2002, ch. 26.

This section is new language derived without substantive change from former Art. 27, §§ 23 and 39.

In subsection (b) of this section, the reference to a person being guilty of "the misdemeanor" of bribery is added to state expressly that which was only implied by former law. In this State, any crime that was not a felony at common law and has not been declared a felony by statute is considered a misdemeanor. *See State v. Canova*, 278 Md. 483, 490 (1976); *Bowser v. State*, 136 Md. 342, 345 (1920); *Dutton v. State*, 123 Md. 373, 378 (1914); and *Williams v. State*, 4 Md. App. 342, 347 (1968).

Also in subsection (b) of this section, the former reference to a sentence being "in the discretion of the court" is deleted as implicit in the reference to a person being "subject to" a fine and imprisonment.

In subsection (c) of this section, the reference to a violation being "subject to § 5-106(b) of the Courts Article" is substituted for the former reference to the violation subjecting the defendant to imprisonment "in the penitentiary of the State" for clarity and consistency within this article. *See* General Revisor's Note to article.

In subsection (d)(1)(i) of this section, the reference to "violat[ing] of this section" is substituted for the former reference to "commit[ting] any of the offenses set forth in § 23 of this article" to reflect the reorganization of material on athletic contest bribery in this section. Similarly, in subsection (d)(1)(ii) of this section, the reference to "violat[ing] of this section" is substituted for the former reference to "commit[ting] any of the aforesaid offenses" for consistency and clarity.

In subsection (d)(1)(ii) of this section, the former reference to "persons" is deleted as included in the singular reference to "person". *See* Art. 1, § 8.

In subsection (d)(3) of this section, the reference to testifying "for the State" is added to reflect that only the State may grant immunity from prosecution.

Also in subsection (d)(3) of this section, the phrase "immune from prosecution for a crime about which the person was compelled to testify" is substituted for the former phrase "exempt from prosecution,. . . for any and all such crimes and offenses of which such person so

testifying may have been guilty or a participant or a conspirator therein and about which he was so compelled to testify" for clarity and brevity.

Also in subsection (d)(3) of this section, the former reference to "trial and punishment" is deleted because immunity from "prosecution" precludes trial and punishment.

For provisions on testimony from compelled witnesses generally, *see* CJ § 9-123.

The Criminal Law Article Review Committee notes, for the consideration of the General Assembly, that subsection (d) of this section, which allows a witness to be compelled to testify and provides transactional immunity for that testimony, raises significant constitutional concerns under the 5th and 14th Amendments to the U.S. Constitution, and their State counterpart, Art. 22 of the Md. Declaration of Rights. *See, e.g., Evans v. State*, 333 Md. 660 (1994), *cert. denied*, 513 U.S. 833 (1994); *In re Criminal Investigation No. 1-162*, 307 Md. 674 (1986). The relevant constitutional provisions generally prohibit self-incrimination. The granting of some form of immunity against prosecution arising from compelled incriminating testimony does not, of itself, cure the constitutional defect. The General Assembly may wish to explore the scope of immunity that may be required to allow compelled testimony in harmony with federal and State constitutional precedent. This provision raises the same concerns as § 9-201(f) of this subtitle, *above*.

Defined term:
"Person"   § 1-101

Maryland Law Review. — For note, "Self-Incrimination: Choosing a Constitutional Standard," see 32 Md. L. Rev. 289 (1972).

University of Baltimore Law Forum. — For article on permanent injunction against "chilling" Fifth Amendment rights, see 17, No. 3 U. Balt. Law Forum 3 (1987).

University of Baltimore Law Review. — For article, "The Law Enforcement Officers' Privilege Against Compelled Self-Incrimination," see 16 U. Balt. L. Rev. 452 (1987).

Constitutionality. — A prior similar provision was not so vague, indefinite or contradictory as to be invalid. Glickfield v. State, 203 Md. 400, 101 A.2d 229 (1953).

Construction of section. — Although under prior law bribery connoted the corrupt influencing of a public official, the General Assembly can and has removed this limitation by extending the offense to participants in athletic contests, whose duty to perform with honesty and integrity is analogous to the duty imposed by law upon persons holding public office. Glickfield v. State, 203 Md. 400, 101 A.2d 229 (1953).

"Bribe." — The word "bribe," as used in this section, implies that outcome of the contest is to be altered. Glickfield v. State, 203 Md. 400, 101 A.2d 229 (1953).

Immunity. — Brown v. State, 233 Md. 288, 196 A.2d 614 (1964).

Applicable to testimony before grand jury. — Prior version of this section applies to testimony before a grand jury. State v. Panagoulis, 253 Md. 699, 253 A.2d 877 (1969).

One who is being investigated by a grand jury has no right, constitutional or otherwise, to appear before that body. State v. Panagoulis, 253 Md. 699, 253 A.2d 877 (1969).

One who solicits the grand jury to allow him to testify in his own defense may be held in contempt. State v. Panagoulis, 253 Md. 699, 253 A.2d 877 (1969).

Earlier versions of sections granting immunity from prosecution to persons compelled to testify in lottery or gaming cases apply to testimony before a grand jury. State v. Toelle, 10 Md. App. 292, 269 A.2d 628, cert. denied, 260 Md. 722 (1970).

Providing exemplar of handwriting to grand jury not "testifying". — Person compelled to give an exemplar of his handwriting to the grand jury which indicted him for lottery and gaming offenses, did not "testify" within the meaning of the statutes granting immunity from prosecution to persons compelled to testify in such cases; therefore his constitutional privilege against self-incrimination was not violated. State v. Toelle, 10 Md. App. 292, 269 A.2d 628, cert. denied, 260 Md. 722 (1970).

Immunity afforded displaces privilege against self-incrimination. — Prior versions of this section make a witness compellable to testify against himself and thus deny him the privilege against self-incrimination provided by the Maryland Declaration of Rights and the Constitution of the United States. In return, the prior version confers upon that witness an immunity from prosecution. Such prior versions are valid only if the protection afforded is as broad as the privilege that has been removed. The prior versions here considered have been found to afford sufficient protection. State v. Panagoulis, 253 Md. 699, 253 A.2d 877 (1969).

A statute granting immunity to people compelled to testify is valid if its effect is to grant protection as broad as that afforded by the privilege it displaces. State v. Toelle, 10 Md. App. 292, 269 A.2d 628, cert. denied, 260 Md. 722 (1970).

Assent to what one cannot prevent not agreement thereto. — Acquiescence to or assent to what one cannot prevent does not amount to a voluntary agreement thereto. State v. Panagoulis, 253 Md. 699, 253 A.2d 877 (1969).

Immunity equated with compulsion. — It is quite clear that predecessors of this section equate immunity with compulsion, but it is equally clear that a witness, although compellable, gains no immunity unless he is compelled. State v. Panagoulis, 253 Md. 699, 253 A.2d 877 (1969).

Waiver of immunity. — Witness may waive his immunity, expressly or by his conduct. State v. Panagoulis, 3 Md. App. 330, 239 A.2d 145 (1968), aff'd, 253 Md. 699, 253 A.2d 877 (1969).

Conduct not amounting to waiver. — Conduct not mounting up to a waiver of the immunity conferred by prior version of this section. See State v. Panagoulis, 253 Md. 699, 253 A.2d 877 (1969).

Subpoena not indispensable factor. — A subpoena is not an indispensable factor in compelling a witness to testify. State v. Panagoulis, 253 Md. 699, 253 A.2d 877 (1969).

§ 9-205. Acceptance of bribe by person participating in or connected with athletic contest.

(a) *Prohibited.* — A person participating in or connected with an athletic contest may not accept a bribe to alter the outcome of the athletic contest.

(b) *Penalty.* — A person who violates this section is guilty of a misdemeanor and on conviction is subject to imprisonment not exceeding 3 years or a fine not exceeding $5,000 or both. (An. Code 1957, art. 27, § 24; 2002, ch. 26, § 2.)

REVISOR'S NOTE

This Revisor's note comprises information related to the revision by Acts 2002, ch. 26.

This section is new language derived without substantive change from former Art. 27, § 24.

In subsection (a) of this section, the former reference to an "amateur or professional athlete" is deleted as included in the defined term "person".

Defined term:
"Person"   § 1-101

Subtitle 3. Obstructing Justice.

§ 9-301. Definitions.

(a) *In general.* — In this subtitle the following words have the meanings indicated.

REVISOR'S NOTE

This subsection is new language derived without substantive change from former Art. 27, § 760(a).

The reference to this "subtitle" is substituted for the former reference to this "subheading", although this subtitle is derived, in part, from material outside the former "Influencing or Intimidating Victims and Witnesses" subheading of Article 27. The substitution applies the defined term "witness" to § 9-305 of this subtitle, derived from former Art. 27, § 26. Because the term is defined and used only in its ordinary meaning, no substantive change results.

(b) *Official proceeding.* — "Official proceeding" includes a criminal trial, a hearing related to a criminal trial or adjudicatory hearing, a grand jury proceeding, and any other proceeding that is part of a criminal action or juvenile delinquency case.

REVISOR'S NOTE

This subsection is new language derived without substantive change from former Art. 27, § 760(c).

(c) *Victim.* — "Victim" means a person against whom a crime or delinquent act has been committed or attempted.

REVISOR'S NOTE

This subsection is new language derived without substantive change from former Art. 27, § 760(d).

Defined term:
"Person"   § 1-101

(d) *Witness.* — "Witness" means a person who:

(1) has knowledge of the existence of facts relating to a crime or delinquent act;

(2) makes a declaration under oath that is received as evidence for any purpose;

(3) has reported a crime or delinquent act to a law enforcement officer, prosecutor, intake officer, correctional officer, or judicial officer; or

(4) has been served with a subpoena issued under the authority of a court of this State, any other state, or the United States.

REVISOR'S NOTE

This subsection is new language derived without substantive change from former Art. 27, § 760(e).

Defined terms:
"Person"   § 1-101
"State"   § 1-101

(An. Code 1957, art. 27, § 760(a), (c)-(e); 2002, ch. 26, § 2; 2003, ch. 21, § 1; 2005, ch. 461.)

REVISOR'S NOTE TO SECTION

The Revisor's notes in this section comprise information related to the revision by Acts 2002, ch. 26.

Quoted in Miller v. United States Foodservice, Inc., 405 F. Supp. 2d 607 (D. Md. 2005); Tracy v. State, 423 Md. 1, 31 A.3d 160 (2011).

Cited in King v. Marriott Int'l, Inc., 160 Md. App. 689, 866 A.2d 895 (2005).

§ 9-302. Inducing false testimony or avoidance of subpoena.

(a) *Prohibited.* — A person may not harm another, threaten to harm another, or damage or destroy property with the intent to:

(1) influence a victim or witness to testify falsely or withhold testimony; or

(2) induce a victim or witness:

(i) to avoid the service of a subpoena or summons to testify;

(ii) to be absent from an official proceeding to which the victim or witness has been subpoenaed or summoned; or

(iii) not to report the existence of facts relating to a crime or delinquent act.

(b) *Solicitation prohibited.* — A person may not solicit another person to harm another, threaten to harm another, or damage or destroy property with the intent to:

(1) influence a victim or witness to testify falsely or withhold testimony; or

(2) induce a victim or witness:

(i) to avoid the service of a subpoena or summons to testify;

(ii) to be absent from an official proceeding to which the victim or witness has been subpoenaed or summoned; or

(iii) not to report the existence of facts relating to a crime or delinquent act.

(c) *Penalty.* — (1) Except as provided in paragraph (2) of this subsection, a person who violates this section is guilty of a misdemeanor and on conviction is subject to imprisonment not exceeding 5 years or a fine not exceeding $5,000 or both.

(2) If the testimony, subpoena, official proceeding, or report involving the victim or witness relates to a felonious violation of Title 5 of this article or the commission of a crime of violence as defined in § 14-101 of this article, or a conspiracy or solicitation to commit such a crime, a person who violates this section is guilty of a felony and on conviction is subject to imprisonment not exceeding 20 years.

(d) *Sentence.* — A sentence imposed under this section may be separate from and consecutive to or concurrent with a sentence for any crime based on the act establishing the violation of this section. (An. Code 1957, art. 27, § 761; 2002, ch. 26, § 2; 2005, ch. 461.)

REVISOR'S NOTE

This Revisor's note comprises information related to the revision by Acts 2002, ch. 26.

This section is new language derived without substantive change from former Art. 27, § 761.

In subsection (a)(2)(i) and (ii) of this section, the references to "subpoena[ing]" and "subpoenaed" are added for clarity. Under Md. Rule 4-256(a), a subpoena is issued to require a witness to testify in court.

In the introductory language of subsection (a) of this section, the former reference to "injure [another]" is deleted as redundant in light of the phrase "harm another".

The Criminal Law Article Review Committee notes, for consideration of the General Assembly, that this section does not cover a person who intimidates a potential witness, other than a victim, who has not yet been subpoenaed or been issued a summons.

Defined terms:

"Official proceeding"	$ 9-301
"Person"	$ 1-101
"Victim"	$ 9-301
"Witness"	$ 9-301

Threat violated this section. — threat defendant made in a letter to an individual set to testify against defendant's brother, "I will have you harmed if you testify," was proscribed by this section. Tracy v. State, 423 Md. 1, 31 A.3d 160 (2011).

§ 9-303. Retaliation for testimony.

(a) *Prohibited.* —A person may not intentionally harm another, threaten to harm another, or damage or destroy property with the intent of retaliating against a victim or witness for:

(1) giving testimony in an official proceeding; or

(2) reporting a crime or delinquent act.

(b) *Solicitation prohibited.* — A person may not solicit another person to intentionally harm another, threaten to harm another, or damage or destroy property with the intent of retaliating against a victim or witness for:

(1) giving testimony in an official proceeding; or

(2) reporting a crime or delinquent act.

(c) *Penalty.* — (1) Except as provided in paragraph (2) of this subsection, a person who violates this section is guilty of a misdemeanor and on conviction is subject to imprisonment not exceeding 5 years or a fine not exceeding $5,000 or both.

(2) If the official proceeding or report described in subsection (a) of this section relates to a felonious violation of Title 5 of this article or the commission of a crime of violence as defined in § 14-101 of this article, or a conspiracy or solicitation to commit such a crime, a person who violates this section is guilty of a felony and on conviction is subject to imprisonment not exceeding 20 years.

(d) *Sentence.* — A sentence imposed under this section may be separate from and consecutive to or concurrent with a sentence for any crime based on the act establishing the violation of this section. (An. Code 1957, art. 27, § 762; 2002, ch. 26, § 2; 2005, ch. 461.)

REVISOR'S NOTE

This Revisor's note comprises information related to the revision by Acts 2002, ch. 26.

This section is new language derived without substantive change from former Art. 27, § 762.

In the introductory language of subsection (a) this section, the former reference to "injure [another]" is deleted as redundant in light of the phrase "harm another".

Defined terms:

"Official proceeding"	$ 9-301
"Person"	$ 1-101
"Victim"	$ 9-301
"Witness"	$ 9-301

University of Baltimore Law Review. — For article, "'Forfeiture by Wrongdoing' after Crawford v. Washington: Maryland's Approach Best Preserves the Right to Confrontation," see 37 U. Balt. L. Rev. 203 (2008).

Constitutionality. — This section was not unconstitutionally void for vagueness as the phrase "threaten to harm another" had a common and generally accepted meaning, such that persons of ordinary intelligence and experience were afforded a reasonable opportunity to know what was prohibited, such as they could modify their behavior accordingly. Parker v. State, 189 Md. App. 474, 985 A.2d 72 (2009).

Protection for employee who cooperated with ongoing investigation. — In a wrongful discharge action, the employee, who was cooperating with an ongoing government investigation into alleged accounting irregularities by the employer, was protected by the law established in Wholey, which stated that terminating an employee on the grounds that the employee (as a victim or witness) gave testimony at an official proceeding or reported a suspected crime to the appropriate law enforcement or judicial officer was wrongful and contrary to public policy. Miller v. United States Foodservice, Inc., 405 F. Supp. 2d 607 (D. Md. 2005).

"Crimes of violence" generally. — Subsection (c)(1) provides for a five-year maximum sentence. But, under (c)(2), if the official proceeding or report against which a defendant retaliated relates to a felonious violation of Title 5 of this article or the commission of a crime of violence, as defined in § 14-101 of this article, the defendant may be sentenced to a maximum of twenty years. Parker v. State, 185 Md. App. 399, 970 A.2d 968 (2009).

Threat made not covered by this section. — Defendant was entitled to reversal of a conviction for threatening harm with the intent of retaliation against a witness under this section, because the threat defendant made in a letter to an individual set to testify against defendant's brother, "I will have you harmed if you testify," was proscribed by § 9-302 of this subtitle, not this section. Tracy v. State, 423 Md. 1, 31 A.3d 160 (2011).

Accusatory instrument not defective. — Criminal Information charged defendant with retaliating against a person "for reporting Drug Activity," a violation of Title 5 of this article, and it referred specifically to (c)(2). Thus, the circumstance of drug activity was alleged in the Information supported a 20-year maximum sentence, and the Information was not defective. Parker v. State, 185 Md. App. 399, 970 A.2d 968 (2009).

Jury must find facts for sentencing enhancement. — Jury returned a guilty verdict for retaliation, a violation of this section, without deciding whether a victim's complaints concerned drug activity, which was the functional equivalent of an element of a greater offense; yet, the jury was only instructed that the State had to prove that defendant retaliated because the victim or witness either gave evidence in an official proceeding or reported a crime or delinquent act. Under Apprendi and its progeny, the question of whether the complaints related to drug activity had to be submitted to a jury, and proved beyond a reasonable doubt before the judge could sentence defendant to the greater offense of retaliation for reporting drug activity; imposition of a quadrupled sentence was of constitutional significance, and the matter of illegal drug activity was not merely a sentencing "factor." Parker v. State, 185 Md. App. 399, 970 A.2d 968 (2009).

Vacation of enhanced sentence and remand for resentencing on retaliation under this section was required. The Due Process Clause required that the circumstances allowing for an enhanced penalty should have been submitted to a jury, and proved beyond a reasonable doubt, as required by Apprendi; that did not occur. Parker v. State, 185 Md. App. 399, 970 A.2d 968 (2009).

Sufficient evidence. — Evidence supported defendant's conviction for violating this section as a detective had just testified in a trial of the mother of defendant's child and was told by defendant, on the courthouse steps, "Now that you fucked with my family, I'll be fucking with yours," and defendant confirmed that the statement was intended as a threat. Parker v. State, 189 Md. App. 474, 985 A.2d 72 (2009).

Sentencing error. — Trial court erred in sentencing appellant to twenty years for retaliation, a violation of this section. The issue pertaining to sentencing enhancement was not submitted to the jury. Parker v. State, 185 Md. App. 399, 970 A.2d 968 (2009).

Enhanced sentencing. — Trial court erred in imposing an enhanced sentence of 20 years' incarceration for the offense of retaliation for testimony under (c)(2). The issue of whether defendant's conduct related, inter alia, to "a felonious violation of Title 5," constituted an element of the offense under (c)(2); therefore, under Apprendi and its progeny, it should have been submitted to and decided by the jury. Parker v. State, 185 Md. App. 399, 970 A.2d 968 (2009).

Consecutive sentence authorized on remand. — When defendant's sentence for retaliation for testimony was vacated on appeal, a trial court imposed a consecutive sentence on remand, after defendant had been released from prison to jail after serving an assault sentence imposed at the same time, despite stating that the sentence was not consecutive, because the court stated that (1) the sentence began after defendant served the assault sentence, and (2) the sentence would have been consecutive if defendant were still in prison. Parker v. State, 193 Md. App. 469, 997 A.2d 912 (2010).

When defendant's sentence for retaliation for testimony was vacated on appeal, a trial court could impose a consecutive sentence on remand because the court (1) was entitled to impose any sentence the court could lawfully have imposed under (c)(1); and (2) the court could reconsider the entire "sentencing package" imposed for retaliation and assault and restructure the sentences to run consecutively. Parker v. State, 193 Md. App. 469, 997 A.2d 912 (2010).

§ 9-304. Court to prevent intimidation of victim or witness.

(a) *In general.* — A finding of good cause under this section may be based on any relevant evidence including credible hearsay.

(b) *Good cause.* — (1) For good cause shown, a court with jurisdiction over a criminal matter or juvenile delinquency case may pass an order that is reasonably necessary to stop or prevent:

(i) the intimidation of a victim or witness; or

(ii) a violation of this subtitle.

(2) The order may:

(i) prohibit a person from violating this subtitle;

(ii) require an individual to maintain a certain physical distance from another person specified by the court;

(iii) prohibit a person from communicating with another individual specified by the court, except through an attorney or other individual specified by the court; and

(iv) impose other reasonable conditions to ensure the safety of a victim or witness.

(3) The court may hold a hearing to determine if an order should be issued under this subsection.

(c) *Enforcement.* — (1) The court may use its contempt power to enforce an order issued under this section.

(2) The court may revoke the pretrial release of a defendant or child respondent to ensure the safety of a victim or witness or the integrity of the judicial process if the defendant or child respondent violates an order passed under this section.

(d) *Conditions of pretrial release.* — A District Court commissioner or an intake officer, as defined in § 3-8A-01 of the Courts Article, may impose for good cause shown a condition described in subsection (b)(2) of this section as a condition of the pretrial release of a defendant or child respondent. (An. Code 1957, art. 27, §§ 760(b), 763; 2002, ch. 26, § 2.)

REVISOR'S NOTE

This Revisor's note comprises information related to the revision by Acts 2002, ch. 26.

This section is new language derived without substantive change from former Art. 27, §§ 760(b) and 763.

In subsections (c) and (d) of this section, the references to a "defendant or child respondent" are substituted for the former defined term "defendant", for brevity and accuracy. The former defined term "defendant", which included both a person alleged to have committed a crime and a child alleged to have committed a delinquent act, was used only in the source material for these two subsections.

In subsection (d) of this section, the reference to "§ 3-8A-01" of the Courts Article is substituted for the former obsolete reference to "§ 3-

801(o)" of the Courts Article for accuracy. *See*   "Victim"   § 9-301
Ch. 415, Acts of 2001.   "Witness"   § 9-301

Defined terms:
"Person"   § 1-101

§ 9-305. Intimidating or corrupting juror.

(a) *Prohibited.* — A person may not, by threat, force, or corrupt means, try to influence, intimidate, or impede a juror, a witness, or an officer of a court of the State or of the United States in the performance of the person's official duties.

(b) *Solicitation prohibited.* — A person may not solicit another person to, by threat, force, or corrupt means, try to influence, intimidate, or impede a juror, a witness, or an officer of the court of the State or of the United States in the performance of the person's official duties.

(c) *Penalty.* — (1) Except as provided in paragraph (2) of this subsection, a person who violates this section is guilty of a misdemeanor and on conviction is subject to imprisonment not exceeding 5 years or a fine not exceeding $5,000 or both.

(2) If an act described in subsection (a) of this section is taken in connection with a proceeding involving a felonious violation of Title 5 of this article or the commission of a crime of violence as defined in § 14-101 of this article, or a conspiracy or solicitation to commit such a crime, a person who violates this section is guilty of a felony and on conviction is subject to imprisonment not exceeding 20 years.

(d) *Sentence.* — A sentence imposed under this section may be separate from and consecutive to or concurrent with a sentence for any crime based on the act establishing the violation of this section. (An. Code 1957, art. 27, § 26; 2002, ch. 26, § 2; 2005, ch. 461.)

REVISOR'S NOTE

This Revisor's note comprises information related to the revision by Acts 2002, ch. 26.

This section is new language derived without substantive change from former Art. 27, § 26, as it referred to intimidating or corrupting a juror.

In subsection (a) of this section, the reference to "performance" of a duty is substituted for the former reference to "discharge" of duty for consistency within this article.

Also in subsection (a) of this section, the phrase "official duties" is substituted for the former word "duty" for clarity.

In subsection (b) of this section, the former phrase "according to the nature and aggravation of the offense" is deleted in light of the generally applicable standards utilized by the courts to determine a convicted person's sentence.

Also in subsection (b) of this section, the reference to a person who violates this section being "guilty of a misdemeanor" is added to state expressly that which was only implied in the former law. In this State, any crime that was not a felony at common law and has not been declared a felony by statute is considered a misdemeanor. *See State v. Canova,* 278 Md. 483, 490 (1976); *Bowser v. State,* 136 Md. 342, 345 (1920); *Dutton v. State,* 123 Md. 373, 378 (1914); and *Williams v. State,* 4 Md. App. 342, 347 (1968).

For provisions on bribing a juror, *see* § 9-202 of this title.

Defined terms:
"Person"   § 1-101
"Witness"   § 9-301

Cross references. — For constitutional provisions regarding bribery of public officers, see Article III, § 50 of the Maryland Constitution.

Elements of offense. — Particular acts are not specified but, whatever they may be, if the acts be corrupt, or be threats or force, used in an attempt to influence, intimidate or impede any juror, witness or officer in any court of the State in the discharge of his duty, there is an obstruction of justice. Romans v. State, 178 Md. 588, 16 A.2d 642 (1940), cert. denied, 312 U.S. 695, 61 S. Ct. 732, 85 L. Ed. 1131 (1941).

Violation of statute as grounds for action against attorney under Maryland

Lawyers' Rules of Professional Conduct. — Attorney committed a criminal act that reflected adversely on his fitness as a lawyer, thereby violating Md. R. Prof. Conduct 8.4(b). He falsely represented himself to a State's trial witness in a criminal prosecution that he was a police officer, a violation of § 3-502 of the Public Safety Article, in an attempt to influence a witness, a violation of this section. Att'y Griev. Comm'n v. Smith, 405 Md. 107, 950 A.2d 101 (2008).

Quoted in Tracy v. State, 423 Md. 1, 31 A.3d 160 (2011).

§ 9-306. Obstruction of justice.

(a) *Prohibited.* — A person may not, by threat, force, or corrupt means, obstruct, impede, or try to obstruct or impede the administration of justice in a court of the State.

(b) *Penalty.* — A person who violates this section is guilty of a misdemeanor and on conviction is subject to imprisonment not exceeding 5 years or a fine not exceeding $10,000 or both. (An. Code 1957, art. 27, § 26; 2002, ch. 26, § 2.)

REVISOR'S NOTE

This Revisor's note comprises information related to the revision by Acts 2002, ch. 26.

This section is new language derived without substantive change from former Art. 27, § 26, as it related to obstructing justice.

In subsection (a) of this section, the former reference to "due" administration is deleted as surplusage.

In subsection (b) of this section, the former phrase "according to the nature and aggravation of the offense" is deleted in light of the generally applicable standards utilized by the courts to determine a convicted person's sentence.

Also in subsection (b) of this section, the reference to a person who violates this section being "guilty of a misdemeanor" is added to state expressly that which was only implied in the former law. In this State, any crime that was not a felony at common law and has not been declared a felony by statute is considered a misdemeanor. *See State v. Canova,* 278 Md. 483, 490 (1976); *Bowser v. State,* 136 Md. 342, 345 (1920); *Dutton v. State,* 123 Md. 373, 378 (1914); and *Williams v. State,* 4 Md. App. 342, 347 (1968).

Defined term:
"Person"   § 1-101

Common law. — Obstruction of justice was an indictable offense at common law. Food Fair Stores, Inc. v. Joy, 283 Md. 205, 389 A.2d 874 (1978).

Purpose of section. — This section is in aid and definition of class of criminal acts which are known to the common law as obstructions of justice. Romans v. State, 178 Md. 588, 16 A.2d 642 (1940), cert. denied, 312 U.S. 695, 61 S. Ct. 732, 85 L. Ed. 1131 (1941).

Construction of section. — Words of a prior similar version of this section were general and embraced in comprehensive terms various forms of obstruction. Romans v. State, 178 Md. 588, 16 A.2d 642 (1940), cert. denied, 312 U.S. 695, 61 S. Ct. 732, 85 L. Ed. 1131 (1941).

In light of the federal statutory scheme and the comparable language used in this section, this section may not be extended to actions that do not interfere with pending judicial proceedings. State v. Pagano, 104 Md. App. 113, 655 A.2d 55 (1995), aff'd, 341 Md. 129, 669 A.2d 1339 (1996).

Construction with federal law. — Although the language of this section criminalizes obstruction of justice by both violent and nonviolent means, any violation of this section constitutes a "violent felony" within the meaning of § 924 (e) of the Federal Armed Career Criminal Act, 18 U.S.C. § 924 (e). United States v. Cook, 26 F.3d 507 (4th Cir. 1994), cert. denied, 513 U.S. 953, 115 S. Ct. 373, 130 L. Ed. 2d 324 (1994).

Interference with due administration of justice. — An obstruction of justice charge includes interference with the due administration of justice in the courts of Maryland. State v. Pagano, 104 Md. App. 113, 655 A.2d 55 (1995), aff'd, 341 Md. 129, 669 A.2d 1339 (1996).

Elements of offense. — Although no particular acts are enumerated in this section, the conduct prohibited includes any attempt to corruptly influence, intimidate, or impede a witness in the discharge of his duty or to corruptly obstruct or impede the due administration of justice. Lee v. State, 65 Md. App. 587, 501 A.2d 495 (1985).

Forbidden act constitutes single offense. — The fact that the act denounced is at once an attempt within the meaning of both clauses of former Art. 27, § 22 (see now this section and § 9-305 of this article) forbidding certain obstructions to justice does not make the forbidden act two offenses against the State; where the acts particularly denounced are of necessity wholly within the limits of the acts generally denounced, two offenses do not arise from the same act, although it may be dealt with under alternate provisions as an obstruction to justice. Romans v. State, 178 Md. 588, 16 A.2d 642 (1940), cert. denied, 312 U.S. 695, 61 S. Ct. 732, 85 L. Ed. 1131 (1941).

Interference with preliminary police investigation. — Interference with a preliminary police investigation is conduct aimed at impeding a proceeding sanctioned by the executive arm of the government; this section does not encompass such conduct. State v. Pagano, 104 Md. App. 113, 655 A.2d 55 (1995), aff'd, 341 Md. 129, 669 A.2d 1339 (1996).

This section prohibits only actions aimed at obstructing or impeding a judicial proceeding; although a defendant's alleged actions may have obstructed a police investigation, such actions did not violate this section where there was no pending judicial proceeding which defendant sought to obstruct or impede. State v. Pagano, 341 Md. 129, 669 A.2d 1339 (1996).

Substitution of knife and giving false reports to police deemed obstruction of justice. — Where appellant's estranged wife was found dead as a result of a knife wound, appellant's actions in substituting the knife and giving false reports to the police department would have obstructed justice whether or not suicide is a crime in Maryland or whether or not the wife committed suicide. Mayne v. State, 45 Md. App. 483, 414 A.2d 1, cert. denied, 288 Md. 739 (1980), cert. denied, 450 U.S. 910, 101 S. Ct. 1347, 67 L. Ed. 2d 333 (1981).

Acts outside jurisdiction. — Where it was justice in the State of Maryland that was obstructed by defendant's act outside the boundaries of Maryland, Maryland court had jurisdiction. Pennington v. State, 308 Md. 727, 521 A.2d 1216 (1987).

Indictment. — An indictment for violation of this section was not invalid for duplicity although the offense stated came within both the particular and general terms of the denunciation of the former similar provision. Romans v. State, 178 Md. 588, 16 A.2d 642 (1940), cert. denied, 312 U.S. 695, 61 S. Ct. 732, 85 L. Ed. 1131 (1941).

Corroborating evidence. — Testimony furnished sufficient corroboration that defendant and another person conspired to obstruct justice. See Irvin v. State, 23 Md. App. 457, 328 A.2d 329 (1974), aff'd, 276 Md. 168, 344 A.2d 418 (1975).

Subtitle 4. Harboring, Escape, and Contraband.

Part I. Harboring and Escape.

§ 9-401. Definitions.

(a) *In general.* — In this subtitle the following words have the meanings indicated.

REVISOR'S NOTE

This subsection is new language derived without substantive change from former Art. 27, §§ 136(a) and 268E(a).

The reference to this "subtitle" is substituted for the former references to this "subheading"

to reflect the consolidation in this subtitle of material derived from the former "Escape and Contraband in Places of Confinement" and "Harboring" subheadings of Article 27.

(b) *Concealment.* — "Concealment" means hiding, secreting, or keeping out of sight.

REVISOR'S NOTE

This subsection formerly was Art. 27, § 268E(c).   No changes are made.

(c) *Escape.* — "Escape" retains its judicially determined meaning.

REVISOR'S NOTE

This subsection formerly was Art. 27, § 136(b).   No changes are made.

(d) *Fugitive.* — "Fugitive" means an individual for whom a felony arrest warrant has been issued and is outstanding.

REVISOR'S NOTE

This subsection is new language derived without substantive change from former Art. 27, § 268E(d).

In this subsection, the phrase "and is outstanding" is added for clarity. Otherwise, an individual could be a "fugitive" under this subtitle even if a felony arrest warrant for the individual had been quashed. The Criminal Law Article Review Committee brings this addition to the attention of the General Assembly.

(e) *Harbor.* — (1) "Harbor" includes offering a fugitive or escaped inmate:

(i) concealment;

(ii) lodging;

(iii) care after concealment; or

(iv) obstruction of an effort of an authority to arrest the fugitive or escaped inmate.

(2) "Harbor" does not include failing to reveal the whereabouts of a fugitive or an escaped inmate by a person who did not participate in the effort of the fugitive or escaped inmate to elude arrest.

REVISOR'S NOTE

This subsection is new language derived without substantive change from former Art. 27, § 268E(b).

In the introductory language of paragraph (1) and in paragraphs (1)(iv) and (2) of this subsection, the references to an "escaped inmate" are added for consistency with § 9-403 of this subtitle. The Criminal Law Article Review Committee brings these additions to the attention of the General Assembly.

Defined terms:
"Inmate"   § 1-101
"Person"   § 1-101

(f) *Hardware secure facility.* — "Hardware secure facility" means a facility that is securely locked or fenced to prevent escape.

(g) *Place of confinement.* — (1) "Place of confinement" means:

(i) a correctional facility;

(ii) a facility of the Department of Health and Mental Hygiene; or

(iii) any other facility in which a person is confined under color of law.

(2) "Place of confinement" does not include:

(i) a detention center for juveniles;

(ii) a facility for juveniles listed in § 9-226(b) of the Human Services Article;

(iii) a place identified in a juvenile community detention order; or

(iv) a privately operated, hardware secure facility for juveniles committed to the Department of Juvenile Services.

SPECIAL REVISOR'S NOTE

As enacted by Ch. 26, Acts of 2002, this subsection was new language derived without substantive change from former Art. 27, § 136(c). However, Ch. 406, Acts of 2002, added "a place identified in a juvenile community detention order" as item (5) of this subsection and renumbered the following item accordingly.

Defined terms:
"Correctional facility"	§ 1-101
"Person"	§ 1-101

(An. Code 1957, art. 27, §§ 136, 268E; 2002, ch. 26, § 2; ch. 406; 2004, ch. 358; 2007, ch. 8, § 1; 2010, ch. 123.)

REVISOR'S NOTE TO SECTION

The Revisor's notes in this section comprise information related to the revision by Acts 2002, ch. 26.

––––––––––

Effect of amendments. — Chapter 123, Acts 2010, effective October 1, 2010, added (f) and (g)(2)(iv); redesignated accordingly; and made related changes.

Concealment established. — Where defendant was advised that a felony warrant of arrest had been issued for a fugitive and that it was a punishable offense to harbor such fugitive, defendant's deceptive conduct of denying that such fugitive was present in her apartment, when he actually was, satisfied the element of "concealment" and, therefore, "harboring." Burns v. State, 80 Md. App. 252, 562 A.2d 770 (1989).

"Escape". — "Escape," as used in a prior similar provision, encompassed a departure from lawful custody from any place of confinement, by the use of force or without the use of force as known in the common law, and so includes the common law crime of prison breach. Fabian v. State, 3 Md. App. 270, 239 A.2d 100 (1968), cert. denied, 250 Md. 731 (1968); Jennings v. State, 8 Md. App. 321, 259 A.2d 547 (1969).

The statutory crime of escape encompasses both the common law "simple escape" and "breach of prison." State v. Magliano, 7 Md. App. 286, 255 A.2d 470 (1969).

Use of force not requisite. — Use of force is not requisite of escape. Meadows v. State, 3 Md. App. 441, 239 A.2d 767 (1968).

No distinction between departure by force and departure without force. — The General Assembly in proscribing escape from lawful confinement did not intend a distinction between departure by force and a departure without force. Fabian v. State, 3 Md. App. 270, 239 A.2d 100 (1968), cert. denied, 250 Md. 731 (1968).

No distinction between escape from within prison and from outside prison area. — There is no distinction between an escape from within the prison walls and one effected when the prisoner, while still in legal custody, was physically outside the prison area. Ford v. State, 237 Md. 266, 205 A.2d 809 (1965); Shifflett v. State, 4 Md. App. 227, 242 A.2d 182 (1968).

Under a prior similar provision there was no distinction between an escape from within prison walls and one effected when the prisoner was outside the prison area. Meadows v. State, 3 Md. App. 441, 239 A.2d 767 (1968).

As accused was lawfully under sentence and committed to the jail, the fact that he was physically beyond its confines when he escaped does not immunize him from prosecution under a prior similar provision. Shifflett v. State, 4 Md. App. 227, 242 A.2d 182 (1968).

Place of confinement. — Although a facility was not specifically listed in Art. 83C, § 2-117 (see now § 9-226 of the Human Services Article), this did not preclude it from being a "place of confinement" within the meaning of a prior similar provision. United States v. Minger, 976 F.2d 185 (4th Cir. 1992).

The Oak Hill Youth Center was held to be a place of confinement within the meaning of a prior similar provision. United States v. Minger, 976 F.2d 185 (4th Cir. 1992).

Escape while in constructive custody under work release program. — Escape of a prisoner while in constructive custody under a work release program constitutes an escape from a place of confinement in violation of a prior similar provision. Beasley v. State, 17 Md. App. 7, 299 A.2d 482, cert. denied, 268 Md. 745 (1973).

Patuxent Institution is "place of confinement". — Patuxent Institution, an institution for defective delinquents, is a "place of confinement" within the meaning of a prior similar provision. Caparella v. State, 214 Md. 355, 135 A.2d 311 (1957); Slagle v. State, 243 Md. 435, 221 A.2d 641 (1966).

Escape during commitment to delinquent institution but after serving burglary sentence. — A defendant was convicted under a prior similar provision for escape from Patuxent Institution. Prior to the escape the defendant had completed a sentence for burglary while under commitment to Patuxent for an indefinite period. Under those circumstances the conviction for escape did not supplant the commitment to Patuxent. Caparella v. State, 214 Md. 355, 135 A.2d 311 (1957).

Escape from Patuxent Institution punishable. — One confined in Patuxent Institution may be convicted and punished for escape. Caparella v. State, 214 Md. 355, 135 A.2d 311 (1957).

Punishment even if originating criminal sentence has expired. — If a defective delinquent convict should escape confinement, even if his originating criminal sentence has expired, he is guilty of the crime of escape under a prior similar provision. Sas v. Maryland, 334 F.2d 506 (4th Cir. 1964).

Clifton T. Perkins State Hospital is place of confinement. — Clifton T. Perkins State Hospital falls within the category of "any other place of confinement." Slagle v. State, 243 Md. 435, 221 A.2d 641 (1966).

Escape from courtroom. — In Ford v. State, 237 Md. 266, 205 A.2d 809 (1965), a defendant who was under sentence in a correctional institution and who was taken to a courtroom for trial on a subsequent charge was held to have committed the crime of escape from the correctional institution when he broke away from his guard and ran out of the courtroom, since, even though he was physically outside the prison area, he remained in legal custody. Slagle v. State, 243 Md. 435, 221 A.2d 641 (1966).

Flight from courtroom not escape prior to incarceration. — Defendant fled from the courtroom after being sentenced; his conviction for first degree escape was reversed because, at the time he fled, he was not in the actual or constructive custody of a "place of confinement": the courtroom was not a "place of confinement," and he had not yet been committed to the division of corrections. Boffen v. State, 372 Md. 724, 816 A.2d 88 (2003).

Escape from hospital. — An inmate of the penitentiary, who had been taken to a hospital for medical treatment, committed the crime of escape, within the meaning of a prior version of this section, when he walked off from the hospital, although he claimed otherwise because he was left unguarded and the hospital was not a "place of confinement." Best v. Warden of Md. Penitentiary, 235 Md. 633, 201 A.2d 490 (1964).

Escape from a hospital held an escape from the penitentiary where prisoner had been committed. Slagle v. State, 243 Md. 435, 221 A.2d 641 (1966).

Where inmate, incarcerated in the House of Correction in Anne Arundel County, was transferred to the University Hospital in Baltimore City for treatment, and while in hospital escaped, his departure constituted both escape from custody in a place of confinement and escape from constructive custody in the place of incarceration itself. Stewart v. State, 21 Md. App. 346, 319 A.2d 621 (1974), aff'd, 275 Md. 258, 340 A.2d 290 (1975).

From reformatory farm. — The mere fact that prisoner was allowed to work outside of reformatory on a farm in the daytime does not change the nature of his detention or confinement, and escape from the farm had no legal significance different from an escape from the reformatory itself. State ex rel. Johnson v. Warden of Md. Penitentiary, 196 Md. 672, 75 A.2d 843 (1950).

A prisoner working on a privately-owned farm outside a reformatory is deemed legally confined in the reformatory. Slagle v. State, 243 Md. 435, 221 A.2d 641 (1966).

From Sandy Point Correctional Camp. — Sandy Point Correctional Camp was merely an adjunct of the house of correction and a prisoner continued to be under confinement at that institution, so that escape from such camp would constitute escape from the house of correction. Taylor v. State, 229 Md. 128, 182 A.2d 52 (1962).

An escape from the Sandy Point Correctional Camp constitutes an escape from the house of correction. Slagle v. State, 243 Md. 435, 221 A.2d 641 (1966).

From maximum security area of jail. — Where accused was required to remain within the maximum security area of the jail, such area was a place of confinement and, by escaping therefrom, he violated a prior version of this section, whether or not he left the jail building. Fabian v. State, 3 Md. App. 270, 239 A.2d 100 (1968), cert. denied, 250 Md. 731 (1968).

Indictment. — Where the indictments describe the act allegedly committed by the inmates by specifying the fact of their lawful confinement, their willful departure from custody, the location of the escapes and the dates on which the escapes allegedly occurred, this information characterized the crime and sufficiently informed the inmates of the accusation against them as required by article 21 of the Maryland Declaration of Rights. State v. Morton, 295 Md. 487, 456 A.2d 909 (1983).

The State is not required in each case to set out in an indictment the details concerning the manner in which the accused escaped. A bill of particulars may be sought for that purpose. State v. Morton, 295 Md. 487, 456 A.2d 909 (1983).

Venue. — A prior similar provision by its terms permitted trial in the county in which the escape takes place, and thus, venue lies both where the departure actually occurred, and where the crime constructively took place. Stewart v. State, 21 Md. App. 346, 319 A.2d 621 (1974), aff'd, 275 Md. 258, 340 A.2d 290 (1975).

A prior similar provision did not address itself to jurisdiction but only to the place where a case is to be tried. Guarnera v. State, 23 Md. App. 525, 328 A.2d 327 (1974), cert. denied, 274 Md. 728 (1975).

To limit venue in escape cases to the place where the inmate physically happened to be when he eloped would impose impractical impediments in the administration of criminal justice. Stewart v. State, 275 Md. 258, 340 A.2d 290 (1975).

Charging the escapee in the county where the "place of confinement" is located accommodates the presentation of the evidence without requiring the attendance of witnesses and the production of documents at a place far removed from the situs of the institution to which the inmate had been committed. Stewart v. State, 275 Md. 258, 340 A.2d 290 (1975).

A prior similar provision stated that persons accused of the crime of escape are to be tried in the county where escape takes place, but where there was an escape under former Art. 27, § 700A (see now §§ 3-801 through 3-806 of the Correctional Services Article) and the defendant has been tried in the county where the institution of his place of confinement was located, rather than in the county where escape took place, the requirement of venue was satisfied. Carter v. State, 38 Md. App. 400, 381 A.2d 309, cert. denied, 282 Md. 730 (1978).

Within the terms of a prior similar provision, the crime of escape from custody "takes place": (1) In the county where the physical departure occurs, and (2) in the county of the penal institution from which the constructive departure occurs. Stewart v. State, 21 Md. App. 346, 319 A.2d 621 (1974), aff'd, 275 Md. 258, 340 A.2d 290 (1975); Stewart v. State, 275 Md. 258, 340 A.2d 290 (1975); Carter v. State, 38 Md. App. 400, 381 A.2d 309, cert. denied, 282 Md. 730 (1978).

Defenses. — A person charged with the crime of escape should have available to him the defense of necessity or compulsion if he can demonstrate to the satisfaction of the judge or jury that the facts surrounding his escape fall strictly within the required legal guidelines. Robinson v. State, 42 Md. App. 617, 402 A.2d 115 (1979).

Instructions. — The defendant's claim that his primary concern was the fear of being shot by the authorities if he surrendered was insufficient to warrant an instruction on the defense of necessity and duress. Craddock v. State, 47 Md. App. 513, 424 A.2d 168, cert. denied, 290 Md. 713 (1981).

Sufficiency of evidence. — See Williams v. State, 5 Md. App. 450, 247 A.2d 731 (1968), cert. denied, 252 Md. 731, 252 Md. 734 (1969).

Evidence, which establishes that defendant departed from the area to which he was confined, was sufficient to permit the trier of the facts to find beyond a reasonable doubt that the defendant was guilty of escape. Vucci v. State, 18 Md. App. 157, 305 A.2d 483, cert. denied, 269 Md. 767 (1973).

There was sufficient evidence from which the jury could reasonably have concluded that the defendant escaped from the penitentiary since the only basic facts necessary to be shown were that he was lawfully confined therein, that he was supposed to stay there and that he left. Hutchinson v. State, 36 Md. App. 58, 373 A.2d 50, cert. denied, 281 Md. 739 (1977).

Escape from courthouse. — Attempted escape from custody was sufficient for conviction although the prisoner never made it out of the building. Bedford v. State, 317 Md. 659, 566 A.2d 111 (1989).

Sentence. — The words "sentenced to confinement . . . for such additional period . . . as the Court may adjudge . . . " refer primarily to cases where a previous period of confinement has been fixed, but it does not follow that the imposition of a sentence for escape from confinement in the places enumerated is contingent upon a previous sentence. Baker v. State, 205 Md. 42, 106 A.2d 692 (1954); Caparella v. State, 214 Md. 355, 135 A.2d 311 (1957).

Where nothing in the questions and comments of the trial court shows that the imposition of a sentence of only 18 months out of a permissible 10 years under a prior version of (a) was dictated, not by sense of public duty, but by passion, prejudice, ill-will or any other unworthy motive, the imposition of the sentence is affirmed. Clark v. State, 284 Md. 260, 396 A.2d 243, cert. denied, 444 U.S. 858, 100 S. Ct. 119, 62 L. Ed. 2d 77 (1979).

When deadly force may be used to prevent escape of unarmed prisoner. — Deadly force may be used to prevent escape of unarmed convicted prisoner if it is reasonably likely that the prisoner would present a risk of serious harm to others, considering: (1) The nature of the institution from which the prisoner escaped; (2) the characteristics of its inmates; (3) the factors that led to their placement in the institution; and (4) the officer's personal knowledge, if any, of the particular escaping prisoner. 71 Op. Att'y Gen. 87 (1986).

Stated in Haskins v. State, 171 Md. App. 182, 908 A.2d 750 (2006).

Cited in Morris v. State, 192 Md. App. 1, 993
A.2d 716 (2010).

§ 9-402. Harboring fugitive.

(a) *Scope of section.* — This section does not apply if the warrant is for a traffic offense.

(b) *To prevent arrest.* — A person may not harbor a fugitive to prevent the fugitive's discovery or arrest after:

(1) being notified, or otherwise knowing, that a felony warrant was issued for the arrest of the fugitive; and

(2) being notified that harboring the fugitive is a crime.

(c) *To avoid prosecution, custody, or confinement.* — A person may not knowingly harbor a fugitive who is avoiding:

(1) prosecution;

(2) custody; or

(3) confinement after conviction of a felony.

(d) *Penalty.* — A person who violates this section is guilty of a misdemeanor and on conviction is subject to imprisonment not exceeding 1 year or a fine not exceeding $1,000 or both. (An. Code 1957, art. 27, § 268F; 2002, ch. 26, § 2.)

REVISOR'S NOTE

This Revisor's note comprises information related to the revision by Acts 2002, ch. 26.

This section is new language derived without substantive change from former Art. 27, § 268F.

In the introductory language of subsection (b) of this section, the reference to discovery "or" arrest is substituted for the former reference to discovery "and" arrest for clarity. The Criminal Law Article Review Committee brings this substitution to the attention of the General Assembly.

In subsection (b)(1) of this section, the word "arrest" is substituted for the former word "apprehension" for consistency within this subsection.

In subsection (b)(2) of this section, the word "crime" is substituted for the former phrase "punishable offense" for brevity.

Defined terms:

"Fugitive"	§ 9-401
"Harbor"	§ 9-401
"Person"	§ 1-101

Preemption of common law offenses. — The common law offense of hindering a police officer has not been preempted by prior version of this section. In re Antoine H., 319 Md. 101, 570 A.2d 1239 (1990).

Evidence sufficient to support conviction. — As the act of concealment occurred after notice of a felony warrant issued for fugitive's arrest, and after notice that it was a crime to harbor such fugitive, the evidence was clearly sufficient to support conviction. Burns v. State, 80 Md. App. 252, 562 A.2d 770 (1989).

§ 9-403. Harboring escaped inmate.

(a) *Prohibited.* — A person may not willfully harbor an inmate, who was imprisoned for a felony and who escaped from the custody of the Division of Correction or other correctional unit to which the inmate has been committed, after:

(1) being notified, or otherwise knowing, that the inmate escaped; and

(2) being notified that harboring the inmate is a crime.

(b) *Penalty.* — A person who violates this section is guilty of a misdemeanor and on conviction is subject to imprisonment not exceeding 1 year or a fine not exceeding $1,000 or both. (An. Code 1957, art. 27, § 268G; 2002, ch. 26, § 2.)

REVISOR'S NOTE

This Revisor's note comprises information related to the revision by Acts 2002, ch. 26.

This section is new language derived without substantive change from former Art. 27, § 268G.

In the introductory language of subsection (a) of this section, the reference to an "other correctional unit to which the inmate has been committed" is substituted for the former reference to a "place of confinement" to avoid confusion with the broader term "place of confinement" defined in § 9-401 of this subtitle and derived from former Art. 27, § 136(c) which applied to escape, not harboring. The Criminal Law Article Review Committee brings this sub-

stitution to the attention of the General Assembly.

In subsection (a) of this section, the references to the defined term "inmate" are substituted for the former references to a "person" for consistency with § 9-401(d) of this subtitle.

In subsection (a)(2) of this section, the word "crime" is substituted for the former phrase "punishable offense" for brevity and consistency within this article. *See* General Revisor's Note to article.

Defined terms:

"Escape"	§ 9-401
"Harbor"	§ 9-401
"Inmate"	§ 1-101
"Person"	§ 1-101

§ 9-404. Escape in the first degree.

(a) *Prohibited — In general.* — A person may not knowingly escape from a place of confinement.

(b) *Prohibited — From juvenile facility with assault.* — A person may not:

(1) escape from:

(i) a detention center for juveniles;

(ii) a facility for juveniles listed in § 9-226(b) of the Human Services Article;

(iii) a place identified in a juvenile community detention order; or

(iv) a privately operated, hardware secure facility for juveniles committed to the Department of Juvenile Services; and

(2) in the course of the escape commit an assault.

(c) *Penalty.* — A person who violates this section is guilty of the felony of escape in the first degree and on conviction is subject to imprisonment not exceeding 10 years or a fine not exceeding $20,000 or both. (An. Code 1957, art. 27, § 137; 2002, ch. 26, § 2; 2004, ch. 358; 2007, ch. 8, § 1; 2010, ch. 123.)

REVISOR'S NOTE

This Revisor's note comprises information related to the revision by Acts 2002, ch. 26.

Subsections (a), (c), and (d) of this section are new language derived without substantive change from former Art. 27, § 137.

Subsection (b) of this section is new language added to state explicitly that which was only implied by the former law, *i.e.* that an escape from a juvenile facility involving an assault is escape in the first degree. *See* § 9-405(a)(4) of this subtitle.

The Criminal Law Article Review Committee notes, for the consideration of the General Assembly, that the forms of home detention listed in subsection (c)(1)(ii) of this section do not cover home detention programs administered by counties or other available forms of custodial confinement. *See* Ch. 356, Acts of 2001.

Defined terms:

"Escape"	§ 9-401
"Person"	§ 1-101
"Place of confinement"	§ 9-401

Effect of amendments. — Chapter 123, Acts 2010, effective October 1, 2010, added (b)(1)(iv) and made related changes.

University of Baltimore Law Forum. — Farris v. State: Failure to Appear for a Court Mandated Weekend Detention does not Constitute the Crime of Escape in Allegany County, see 29 U. Balt. Law Forum 43 (1999).

History of section. — See Beasley v. State, 17 Md. App. 7, 299 A.2d 482, cert. denied, 268 Md. 745 (1973).

Common law. — See Fabian v. State, 3 Md. App. 270, 239 A.2d 100 (1968), cert. denied, 250 Md. 731 (1968).

An attempt to escape charged under a former version of this section constituted a common law misdemeanor. Jennings v. State, 8 Md. App. 321, 259 A.2d 547 (1969).

A prior similar provision, as adopted, represented the entire subject matter of the law of escape in Maryland, and thereby abrogated the common law of escape. Watkins v. State, 42 Md. App. 349, 400 A.2d 464 (1979).

Constitutionality. — Administrative punishment for breach of prison discipline does not cause a fine, imprisonment or other punishment meted out by a court after trial for crime of escape to amount to double jeopardy. Ford v. State, 237 Md. 266, 205 A.2d 809 (1965).

A former version of this section held not unconstitutional. Watkins v. State, 42 Md. App. 349, 400 A.2d 464 (1979).

There was nothing invidious in the former legislative distinction between escapes from the Maryland Correctional Institution-Hagerstown or the Maryland Correctional Training Center-Hagerstown and other Maryland penal institutions and that Maryland chose to treat its youthful, less serious offenders who escaped from Hagerstown in a manner that varied from the treatment afforded offenders who escaped from other places of confinement did not violate the constitutional rights of the latter. State v. Rogers, 40 Md. App. 573, 392 A.2d 1186 (1978), cert. denied, 284 Md. 747 (1979).

Severability. — A former version of this section held severable. Clark v. State, 284 Md. 260, 396 A.2d 243, cert. denied, 444 U.S. 858, 100 S. Ct. 119, 62 L. Ed. 2d 77 (1979).

Gravamen of offense. — Gravamen of the offense prohibited by a prior similar provision is the physical departure by an inmate from the "place of confinement," and although the prohibited act may physically take place in a separate geographical area, the effects of that act occur at the place of confinement. Stewart v. State, 275 Md. 258, 340 A.2d 290 (1975).

Section embraces all escapees from lawful confinement. — A prior similar provision embraces within its purview all escapes from lawful confinement, whether the escape was initiated from within or without the walls or other boundaries of a penal facility; whether the confinement was actual or constructive; whether it was effected with or without force, and without regard to the circumstances of confinement if the detention was under color of law. Robinson v. State, 18 Md. App. 438, 306 A.2d 624 (1973).

No distinction between actual or constructive custody. — There is no legal distinction between escape from actual or from constructive custody. Stewart v. State, 21 Md. App. 346, 319 A.2d 621 (1974), aff'd, 275 Md. 258, 340 A.2d 290 (1975).

A certain "gloss" has been placed upon a prior version of this section which recognizes that "constructive" custody remains in the place of confinement to which the prisoner had been committed, and it is legally indistinguishable from "actual" custody. Stewart v. State, 275 Md. 258, 340 A.2d 290 (1975).

Flight from courtroom not escape prior to incarceration. — Defendant fled from the courtroom after being sentenced; his subsequent conviction for first degree escape was reversed because, at the time he fled, he was not in the actual or constructive custody of a "place of confinement": the courtroom was not a "place of confinement," and he had not yet been committed to the division of corrections. Boffen v. State, 372 Md. 724, 816 A.2d 88 (2003).

No escape for weekend prisoner. — A convicted criminal was found not to be in custody, actual or constructive, when he failed to report to a detention center to serve a sentence consisting of several weekends; no violation of a prior version of this section occurred because the prisoner was not in custody, in that he did not leave or physically depart from any place of confinement, but rather spent the remainder of his week at home. Farris v. State, 351 Md. 24, 716 A.2d 237 (1998).

Defendant who is detained at home can be prosecuted for escape. — Trial court erred in refusing to give defendant credit against his sentence for the 240 days he served in home detention prior to trial for homicide while driving under the influence of alcohol, as he could have been prosecuted for escape. Spriggs v. State, 152 Md. App. 62, 831 A.2d 72 (2003).

Escape from custody in hospital. — Proof that defendant, an inmate, was still in legal custody while at the hospital allowed the jury to infer that defendant killed an officer to escape legal custody and thus, the evidence was sufficient to support an escape conviction. Morris v. State, 192 Md. App. 1, 993 A.2d 716 (2010).

Statutory felony. — Escape is a statutory felony. State v. Magliano, 7 Md. App. 286, 255 A.2d 470 (1969).

A prior similar provision was not declaratory of the common law crime of escape but created a new crime unknown to the common law although analogous to the common law crime of escape. Beasley v. State, 17 Md. App. 7, 299 A.2d 482, cert. denied, 268 Md. 745 (1973).

In Maryland, the crime of escape is a statutory felony, which encompasses both the common law misdemeanor of "escape" (without any act of force) and "prison breach," a felony under the common law which involved escape by the use of force. Gorman v. State, 67 Md. App. 398, 507 A.2d 1160 (1986).

Legislative intent. — It was the legislative intent under a prior similar provision to create a new crime of escape, although analogous to the common law crime. State v. Magliano, 7 Md. App. 286, 255 A.2d 470 (1969).

Assimilation by federal law. — Because a prior similar provision criminalized the precise act of escape, the unavailability of 18 U.S.C. § 751 and the general nature of a District of Columbia statute make appropriate the assimilation of this section to fill the gap present in federal law for prosecuting an escape from a youth correctional facility located on federal land in Maryland and operated by the District of Columbia. United States v. Minger, 976 F.2d 185 (4th Cir. 1992).

Applicability regardless of cause of detention. — A prior similar provision included not only unlawful escape by "an offender" but by any "person legally detained and confined" in the places enumerated, regardless of the cause of the detention. Baker v. State, 205 Md. 42, 106 A.2d 692 (1954).

Method of escape not required to be shown. — The State was not required to show how the defendant got out of the penitentiary, but only that he did get out. Hutchinson v. State, 36 Md. App. 58, 373 A.2d 50, cert. denied, 281 Md. 739 (1977).

Person illegally confined not entitled to resort to self-help. — Even if a person is illegally confined because of defects in the procedure by which he was arrested and imprisoned, he is not entitled to resort to self-help but must apply for his release through regular legal channels. Vucci v. State, 18 Md. App. 157, 305 A.2d 483, cert. denied, 269 Md. 767 (1973).

Includes principal in second degree. — Prior version of this section included principal in the second degree. State v. Magliano, 7 Md. App. 286, 255 A.2d 470 (1969).

Aiding or assisting escape. — It is a crime to aid or assist in an escape. State v. Magliano, 7 Md. App. 286, 255 A.2d 470 (1969).

Accessory after fact is offense. — Accessory after the fact to escape is a common law offense. State v. Magliano, 7 Md. App. 286, 255 A.2d 470 (1969).

Accessory before the fact. — Prior version of this section appeared to make an accessory before the fact a principal but does not make an accessory after the fact a principal. State v. Magliano, 7 Md. App. 286, 255 A.2d 470 (1969).

Sentence. — The places enumerated in a prior similar provision, escape from which is made subject to the penalty prescribed, include "station house" and "reformatory," whereas the places to which escapees may be sentenced to confinement are specified as "the penitentiary, jail or house of correction." This would seem to indicate a legislative policy that after an escape the person escaping should be sent to a place of greater security. Baker v. State, 205 Md. 42, 106 A.2d 692 (1954).

Defendant's 18-month sentence for first degree escape under this section, to be served at a local correctional facility consecutive to the one-year sentence he had been serving when he escaped, was legal. Section 9-105 of the Correctional Services Article did not bar a trial court from imposing a sentence of up to 18 months to run consecutive to a sentence for a prior, unrelated conviction. Blickenstaff v. State, 393 Md. 680, 904 A.2d 443 (2006).

Stated in Haskins v. State, 171 Md. App. 182, 908 A.2d 750 (2006).

§ 9-405. Escape in the second degree.

(a) *Prohibited.* — (1) A person who has been lawfully arrested may not knowingly depart from custody without the authorization of a law enforcement or judicial officer.

(2) A person may not knowingly fail to obey a court order to report to a place of confinement.

(3) A person may not escape from:

(i) except as otherwise punishable under § 9-404(b) of this subtitle, a detention center for juveniles or a facility for juveniles listed in § 9-226(b) of the Human Services Article;

(ii) a place identified in a home detention order or agreement;

(iii) a place identified in a juvenile community detention order; or

(iv) a privately operated, hardware secure facility for juveniles committed to the Department of Juvenile Services.

(b) *Applicability of subsection; prohibition of violating restriction of movement conditions.* — (1) This subsection applies to a person who is:

(i) temporarily released from a place of confinement;

(ii) committed to a pretrial agency;

(iii) committed to home detention by:

1. the court; or

2. the Division of Correction under Title 3, Subtitle 4 of the Correctional Services Article;

(iv) committed to a home detention program administered by a county;

(v) committed to a private home detention monitoring agency as defined in § 20-101 of the Business Occupations and Professions Article; or

(vi) ordered by a court to serve a term of custodial confinement as defined in § 6-219 of the Criminal Procedure Article as a condition of a suspended sentence or probation before or after judgment.

(2) A person may not knowingly:

(i) violate any restriction on movement imposed under the terms of a temporary release, pretrial commitment, custodial confinement, or home detention order or agreement;

(ii) fail to return to a place of confinement under the terms of a temporary release, pretrial commitment, custodial confinement, or home detention order or agreement; or

(iii) remove, block, deactivate, or otherwise tamper with a monitoring device required to be worn or carried by the person to track the person's location, including an ankle or wrist bracelet, global position satellite offender tracking technology, or comparable equipment or system.

(c) *Penalty.* — A person who violates this section is guilty of the misdemeanor of escape in the second degree and on conviction is subject to imprisonment not exceeding 3 years or a fine not exceeding $5,000 or both. (An. Code 1957, art. 27, § 137A; 2002, ch. 26, § 2; ch. 406; 2004, ch. 358; 2007, ch. 8, § 1; 2010, ch. 123.)

SPECIAL REVISOR'S NOTE

This Special Revisor's note comprises information related to the revision by Acts 2002, ch. 26 and other chapters amending this section from the 2002 Legislative Session.

As enacted by Ch. 26, Acts of 2002, this section was new language derived without substantive change from former Art. 27, § 137A. However, Ch. 406, Acts of 2002, added "a place of confinement" to subsection (a)(4) of this section and tabulated that provision.

In subsection (a)(4) of this section, the phrase "[e]xcept as otherwise punishable under § 9-404(b) of this subtitle," was added by Ch. 26 to distinguish an escape from a juvenile facility not involving an assault under this section from escaping from a juvenile facility "if the escape involves an assault" under § 9-404(b) of this subtitle.

Defined terms:

"Escape"	§ 9-401
"Person"	§ 1-101
"Place of confinement"	§ 9-401

Effect of amendments. — Chapter 123, Acts 2010, effective October 1, 2010, added (a)(3)(iv) and made related changes.

Convictions valid despite being predicated on invalid order that was part of "springing" sentence. — Convictions for escape under this section were legally valid despite the fact they were predicated on defendant's failure to obey an invalid court order to report to a place of confinement as part of deferred or "springing" sentences, because the order existed at the time defendants failed to report and any challenges had to be made through appropriate channels. Hill v. State, 419 Md. 674, 20 A.3d 780 (2011).

Stated in Haskins v. State, 171 Md. App. 182, 908 A.2d 750 (2006).

§ 9-406. Escape — Voluntary intoxication not a defense.

Voluntary intoxication is not a defense to a charge of escape under this subtitle. (An. Code 1957, art. 27, § 139(b); 2002, ch. 26, § 2.)

REVISOR'S NOTE

This Revisor's note comprises information related to the revision by Acts 2002, ch. 26.

This section is new language derived without substantive change from former Art. 27, § 139(b).

The reference to this "subtitle" is substituted for the former reference to this "subheading", although this subtitle is derived, in part, from material outside the former "Escape and Contraband in Places of Confinement" subheading of Article 27. Because the only charges of escape contained in this subtitle arise from material derived from the former "Escape and Contraband in Places of Confinement" subheading, no substantive change results.

Defined term:
"Escape"   § 9-401

§ 9-407. Escape — Sentencing terms.

A sentence imposed for a violation of § 9-404 or § 9-405 of this subtitle:

(1) shall be consecutive to any term of confinement being served or to be served at the time of the escape;

(2) may not be suspended; and

(3) may include the entry of a judgment for all reasonable expenses incurred in returning the person to the place of confinement if the person has received timely notice of and an opportunity to contest the accuracy of the expenses allegedly owed. (An. Code 1957, art. 27, § 139(a); 2002, ch. 26, § 2.)

REVISOR'S NOTE

This Revisor's note comprises information related to the revision by Acts 2002, ch. 26.

This section is new language derived without substantive change from former Art. 27, § 139(a).

Defined terms:
"Escape"   § 9-401
"Person"   § 1-101
"Place of confinement"   § 9-401

History of section. — See Beasley v. State, 17 Md. App. 7, 299 A.2d 482, cert. denied, 268 Md. 745 (1973).

Common law. — See Fabian v. State, 3 Md. App. 270, 239 A.2d 100 (1968), cert. denied, 250 Md. 731 (1968).

Construction with other laws. — Defendant's 18-month sentence for first degree escape under § 9-404 of this subtitle, to be served at a local correctional facility consecutive to the one-year sentence he had been serving when he escaped, was legal. Section § 9-105 of the Correctional Services Article did not bar a trial court from imposing a sentence of up to 18 months to run consecutive to a sentence for a prior, unrelated conviction. Blickenstaff v. State, 393 Md. 680, 904 A.2d 443 (2006).

Probation precluded. — Under a prior similar provision, the words "sentence imposed" are meant to be used in the broadest sense, and are thereby intended to preclude suspension of the execution or imposition of sentence in cases of escape. Therefore, probation, if any were to be ordered under a suspended sentence, is likewise precluded. It is equally clear that this legislative intent also extends to the more benign disposition of probation before judgment. State v. Kennedy, 320 Md. 749, 580 A.2d 193 (1990).

Suspension of sentence precluded. — The words of a prior similar provision were plain and unambiguous. The escapee is to receive an additional prison sentence, consecutive to the one already being served, no part of which can be suspended. The General Assembly intended that a person who escapes from prison should, upon being tried and found guilty, be punished. State v. Kennedy, 320 Md. 749, 580 A.2d 193 (1990).

Period of absence not credited on sentence. — A prisoner is not entitled to credit on his sentence for those periods when he willfully and voluntarily absents himself from prison without authorization. Woods v. Steiner, 207 F. Supp. 945 (D. Md. 1962).

Credit for pretrial incarceration. — An accused is not entitled to receive credit against a sentence imposed for the time he spent in jail awaiting trial on an escape charge. Gasque v. State, 45 Md. App. 471, 413 A.2d 1351 (1980).

§ 9-408. Resisting or interfering with arrest.

(a) *"Police officer" defined.* — In this section, "police officer" means an individual who is authorized to make an arrest under Title 2 of the Criminal Procedure Article.

(b) *Prohibited.* — A person may not intentionally:

(1) resist a lawful arrest; or

(2) interfere with an individual who the person has reason to know is a police officer who is making or attempting to make a lawful arrest or detention of another person.

(c) *Penalty.* — A person who violates this section is guilty of a misdemeanor and is subject to imprisonment not exceeding 3 years or a fine not exceeding $5,000 or both.

(d) *Unit of prosecution.* — The unit of prosecution for a violation of this section is based on the arrest or detention regardless of the number of police officers involved in the arrest or detention. (2004, chs. 118, 119.)

Merger. — Where a defendant is convicted of resisting arrest and second-degree assault on a law enforcement officer, those convictions do not merge for sentencing purposes under the required evidence test, as each requires proof of a fact which the other does not, and the offenses have different focuses—resisting arrest is an offense against the State of Maryland and not personally against the officer. Britton v. State, 201 Md. App. 589, 30 A.3d 236 (2011).

Sentence illegal. — Sentence for resisting arrest was illegal, as it exceeded the statutory maximum in this section. McNeal v. State, 200 Md. App. 510, 28 A.3d 88 (2011).

Cited in Pinkney v. State, 200 Md. App. 563, 28 A.3d 118 (2011).

§ 9-409.

Reserved.

Part II. Contraband — Places of Confinement.

§ 9-410. Definitions.

(a) *In general.* — In this part the following words have the meanings indicated.

This subsection is new language derived without substantive change from former Art. 27, § 138(a)(1).

In this subsection and throughout this part the references to this "part' are substituted for the former references to this "section" to reflect the reorganization of material derived from former Art. 27, § 138.

(b) *Alcoholic beverage.* — "Alcoholic beverage" means beer, wine, or distilled spirits.

This subsection formerly was Art. 27, § 138(a)(2).

No changes are made.

(c) *Contraband.* — "Contraband" means any item, material, substance, or other thing that:

(1) is not authorized for inmate possession by the managing official; or

(2) is brought into the correctional facility in a manner prohibited by the managing official.

SPECIAL REVISOR'S NOTE

As enacted by Ch. 26, Acts of 2002, this subsection formerly was Art. 27, § 138(a)(3). However, Ch. 41, Acts of 2002, amended the introductory language of this subsection by deleting the phrase "of value" following the word "thing".

No changes were made by Ch. 26.

The Criminal Law Article Review Committee noted, for the consideration of the General Assembly, that in the introductory language to this subsection, the reference to a thing "of value" was confusing and should be deleted. It was unclear whether the standard of "value" related to the prison environment or to the outside world. The General Assembly was asked to consider deleting this reference in substantive legislation. Chapter 41 addressed this concern.

Defined terms:
"Correctional facility"	§ 1-101
"Inmate"	§ 1-101

(d) *Controlled dangerous substance.* — "Controlled dangerous substance" has the meaning stated in § 5-101 of this article.

This subsection is new language derived without substantive change from former Art. 27, § 138(a)(4)(i).

The former limitation "[e]xcept as provided in subparagraph (ii) of this paragraph" is de-leted in light of the revision of former Art. 27, § 138(a)(4)(ii), which authorized certain pre-scribed inmate medications, as a scope provi-sion in § 9-411 of this part.

(e) *Managing official.* — "Managing official" means the administrator, di-rector, warden, superintendent, sheriff, or other individual responsible for the management of a place of confinement.

This subsection formerly was Art. 27, § 138(a)(5).

No changes are made.

Defined term:
"Place of confinement" §§ 9-401, 9-410

(f) *Place of confinement.* — (1) "Place of confinement" means:

(i) a correctional facility;

(ii) a facility of the Department of Health and Mental Hygiene;

(iii) a detention center for juveniles;

(iv) a facility for juveniles listed in § 9-226(b) of the Human Services Article;

(v) a place identified in a juvenile community detention order; or

(vi) any other facility in which a person is confined under color of law.

(2) "Place of confinement" does not include a place identified in a home detention order or agreement.

This subsection is new language derived without substantive change from former Art. 27, § 138(a)(6).

Paragraph (1) of this subsection is new language added to clarify that this definition of "place of confinement" restricts the general definition of the same term in § 9-401 of this subtitle.

Defined term:
"Place of confinement" §§ 9-401, 9-410

(g) *Telecommunication device.* — (1) "Telecommunication device" means:

(i) a device that is able to transmit telephonic, electronic, digital, cellular, or radio communications; or

(ii) a part of a device that is able to transmit telephonic, electronic, digital, cellular, or radio communications, regardless of whether the part itself is able to transmit.

(2) "Telecommunication device" includes a cellular telephone, digital telephone, picture telephone, and modem-equipped device.

(h) *Weapon.* — "Weapon" means a gun, knife, club, explosive, or other article that can be used to kill or inflict bodily injury.

This subsection formerly was Art. 27, § 138(a)(7).

The former reference to "maim[ing]" is deleted as included in the reference to "inflict[ing] bodily injury". The separate crime of "maiming", formerly found in Art. 27, §§ 384 through 386, was incorporated into assault. See Ch. 632, Acts of 1996.

(An. Code 1957, art. 27, § 138(a)(1)-(3), (4)(i), (5)-(7); 2002, ch. 26, § 2; ch. 41; 2004, ch. 358; 2007, ch. 8, § 1; ch. 535, § 2; ch. 536, § 2.)

The Revisor's notes in this section comprise information related to the revision by Acts 2002, ch. 26.

§ 9-411. Scope of part.

This part does not apply to a drug or substance that is legally possessed by an individual under a written prescription issued by a person authorized by law and designated by the managing official to prescribe inmate medication. (An. Code 1957, art. 27, § 138(a)(4)(ii); 2002, ch. 26, § 2.)

REVISOR'S NOTE

This Revisor's note comprises information related to the revision by Acts 2002, ch. 26.

This section is new language derived without substantive change from former Art. 27, § 138(a)(4)(ii).

It is revised as a scope provision for this part rather than as a limitation of the defined term "controlled dangerous substance" for clarity.

Defined terms:
"Inmate"	§ 1-101
"Managing official"	§ 9-410
"Person"	§ 1-101

§ 9-412. Contraband — In general.

(a) *Prohibited.* — A person may not:

(1) deliver any contraband to a person detained or confined in a place of confinement;

(2) possess any contraband with intent to deliver it to a person detained or confined in a place of confinement; or

(3) knowingly possess contraband in a place of confinement.

(b) *Penalty.* — A person who violates this section is guilty of a misdemeanor and on conviction is subject to imprisonment not exceeding 3 years or a fine not exceeding $1,000 or both. (An. Code 1957, art. 27, § 138(d); 2002, ch. 26, § 2; 2007, ch. 535, § 2; ch. 536, § 2.)

REVISOR'S NOTE

This Revisor's note comprises information related to the revision by Acts 2002, ch. 26.

This section is new language derived without substantive change from former Art. 27, § 138(d).

Defined terms:
"Contraband"	§ 9-410
"Person"	§ 1-101
"Place of confinement"	§§ 9-401, 9-410

§ 9-413. Contraband — For escape.

(a) *Prohibited.* — (1) A person may not deliver contraband to a person detained or confined in a place of confinement with the intent to effect an escape.

(2) A person may not possess contraband with the intent to deliver it to a person detained or confined in a place of confinement to effect an escape.

(3) A person may not deposit or conceal any contraband in or about a place of confinement or on any land appurtenant to the place of confinement to effect an escape.

(4) A person detained or confined in a place of confinement may not knowingly possess or receive contraband to effect an escape.

(b) *Penalty.* — A person who violates this section is guilty of a felony and on conviction is subject to imprisonment not exceeding 10 years or a fine not exceeding $5,000 or both. (An. Code 1957, art. 27, § 138(c); 2002, ch. 26, § 2; 2007, ch. 535, § 2; ch. 536, § 2.)

REVISOR'S NOTE

This Revisor's note comprises information related to the revision by Acts 2002, ch. 26.

This section is new language derived without substantive change from former Art. 27, § 138(c).

Defined terms:

"Contraband"	§ 9-410
"Escape"	§ 9-401
"Person"	§ 1-101
"Place of confinement"	§§ 9-401, 9-410

§ 9-414. Contraband — Weapon.

(a) *Prohibited.* — (1) A person may not deliver a weapon to a person detained or confined in a place of confinement.

(2) A person may not possess a weapon with the intent to deliver it to a person detained or confined in a place of confinement.

(3) A person may not deposit or conceal a weapon in or about a place of confinement or on any land appurtenant to the place of confinement to effect an escape.

(4) A person detained or confined in a place of confinement may not knowingly possess or receive a weapon.

(b) *Penalty.* — A person who violates this section is guilty of a felony and on conviction is subject to imprisonment not exceeding 10 years or a fine not exceeding $5,000 or both. (An. Code 1957, art. 27, § 138(b); 2002, ch. 26, § 2; 2007, ch. 535, § 2; ch. 536, § 2.)

REVISOR'S NOTE

This Revisor's note comprises information related to the revision by Acts 2002, ch. 26.

This section is new language derived without substantive change from former Art. 27, § 138(b).

Defined terms:

"Escape"	§ 9-401
"Person"	§ 1-101
"Place of confinement"	§§ 9-401, 9-410
"Weapon"	§ 9-410

§ 9-415. Contraband — Alcoholic beverage.

(a) *Scope of section.* — This section does not apply to an alcoholic beverage delivered or possessed in a manner authorized by the managing official.

(b) *Prohibited.* — A person may not:

(1) deliver an alcoholic beverage to a person detained or confined in a place of confinement; or

(2) possess an alcoholic beverage with the intent to deliver it to a person detained or confined in a place of confinement.

(c) *Prohibited — Knowing possession or receipt by person detained or confined.* — A person detained or confined in a place of confinement may not knowingly possess or receive an alcoholic beverage.

(d) *Penalty.* — A person who violates this section is guilty of a misdemeanor and on conviction is subject to imprisonment not exceeding 3 years or a fine not exceeding $1,000 or both. (An. Code 1957, art. 27, § 138(e); 2002, ch. 26, § 2; 2007, ch. 535, § 2; ch. 536, § 2.)

REVISOR'S NOTE

This Revisor's note comprises information related to the revision by Acts 2002, ch. 26.

This section is new language derived without substantive change from former Art. 27, § 138(e).

Defined terms:

"Alcoholic beverage"	§ 9-410
"Managing official"	§ 9-410
"Person"	§ 1-101
"Place of confinement"	§§ 9-401, 9-410

§ 9-416. Contraband — Controlled dangerous substance.

(a) *Prohibited.* — A person may not:

(1) deliver a controlled dangerous substance to a person detained or confined in a place of confinement; or

(2) possess a controlled dangerous substance with the intent to deliver it to a person detained or confined in a place of confinement.

(b) *Prohibited — Knowing possession or receipt by person detained or confined.* — A person detained or confined in a place of confinement may not knowingly possess or receive a controlled dangerous substance.

(c) *Penalty.* — A person who violates this section is guilty of a misdemeanor and on conviction is subject to imprisonment not exceeding 3 years or a fine not exceeding $1,000 or both. (An. Code 1957, art. 27, § 138(f); 2002, ch. 26, § 2; 2007, ch. 535, § 2; ch. 536, § 2.)

REVISOR'S NOTE

This Revisor's note comprises information related to the revision by Acts 2002, ch. 26.

This section is new language derived without substantive change from former Art. 27, § 138(f).

Defined terms:

"Controlled dangerous substance"	§ 9-410
"Person"	§ 1-101
"Place of confinement"	§§ 9-401, 9-410

§ 9-417. Prohibited acts; penalty.

(a) *Prohibited.* — (1) A person may not deliver a telecommunication device to a person detained or confined in a place of confinement with signs posted indicating that such conduct is prohibited.

(2) A person may not possess a telecommunication device with the intent to deliver it to a person detained or confined in a place of confinement with signs posted indicating that such conduct is prohibited.

(3) A person may not deposit or conceal a telecommunication device in or about a place of confinement with signs posted indicating that such conduct is prohibited or on any land appurtenant to the place of confinement with the intent that it be obtained by a person detained or confined in the place of confinement.

(4) A person detained or confined in a place of confinement may not knowingly possess or receive a telecommunication device.

(b) *Penalty.* — A person who violates this section is guilty of a misdemeanor and on conviction is subject to imprisonment not exceeding 3 years or a fine not exceeding $1,000 or both. (2007, ch. 5, § 7; ch. 535, § 2; ch. 536, § 2.)

Editor's note. — Section 1, chs. 535 and 536, Acts 2007, effective October 1, 2007, redesignated former § 9-417 of this subtitle to be § 9-418 of this subtitle. Section 2, chs. 535 and 536, Acts 2007, enacted a new § 9-417 in lieu thereof.

§ 9-418. Separate sentence.

A sentence imposed under this part may be separate from and consecutive to or concurrent with a sentence for any crime based on the act establishing the crime under this part. (An. Code 1957, art. 27, § 138(g); 2002, ch. 26, § 2; 2007, ch. 535, § 1; ch. 536, § 1.)

REVISOR'S NOTE

This Revisor's note comprises information related to the revision by Acts 2002, ch. 26.

This section is new language derived without substantive change from former Art. 27, § 138(g).

The Criminal Law Article Review Committee notes, for the consideration of the General Assembly, that in light of the availability of consecutive sentences under this section, the rule of lenity does not appear to apply to a conviction for violating §§ 9-412 and 9-416 of this part, relating to contraband in general and a controlled dangerous substance as contraband, respectively, and Title 5 of this article, relating to controlled dangerous substance and similar crimes.

Editor's note. — Section 1, chs. 535 and 536, Acts 2007, effective October 1, 2007, redesignated former § 9-417 of this subtitle to be § 9-418 of this subtitle. Section 2, chs. 535 and 536, Acts 2007, enacted a new § 9-417 in lieu thereof.

Subtitle 5. False Statements.

§ 9-501. False statement — To law enforcement officer.

(a) *Prohibited.* — A person may not make, or cause to be made, a statement, report, or complaint that the person knows to be false as a whole or in material part, to a law enforcement officer of the State, of a county, municipal corporation, or other political subdivision of the State, or of the Maryland-National Capital Park and Planning Police with intent to deceive and to cause an investigation or other action to be taken as a result of the statement, report, or complaint.

(b) *Penalty.* — A person who violates this section is guilty of a misdemeanor and on conviction is subject to imprisonment not exceeding 6 months or a fine not exceeding $500 or both. (An. Code 1957, art. 27, § 150(a), (c); 2002, ch. 26, § 2.)

REVISOR'S NOTE

This Revisor's note comprises information related to the revision by Acts 2002, ch. 26.

This section is new language derived without substantive change from former Art. 27, § 150(a) and (c).

In subsection (a) of this section, the term "municipal corporation" is substituted for the former term "city" to conform to usage in Md. Constitution, Art. XI-E.

Also in subsection (a) of this section, the reference to a "law enforcement" officer is substituted for the former reference to a "peace or police" officer for consistency within this article.

Defined terms:

"County"	§ 1-101
"Person"	§ 1-101

University of Baltimore Law Forum. — For article, "Contempt of Cop: Disrespect in Retrospect," see 20.2 U. Balt. Law Forum 16 (1990).

Maryland Law Review. — For note, "The Maryland Survey: 2001-2002: Recent Decisions: The Court of Appeals of Maryland: X. Statutory Interpretation," see 62 Md. L. Rev. 947 (2003).

Applicability. — The General Assembly in adopting an earlier version of this section had no intent to criminalize conduct other than the making of false reports to the police which cause the police to conduct investigations that divert them from their proper duties of preventing crime and investigating actual incidents of crime; therefore, such version would not apply to the defendant's giving false information regarding his name, address, or prior criminal record upon arrest. Johnson v. State, 75 Md. App. 621, 542 A.2d 429 (1988), cert. denied, 316 Md. 675, 561 A.2d 215 (1989).

The State failed to show that defendant violated an earlier version of this section where defendant's false statement did not initiate the police investigation because when defendant made the false statement to police, the report of the shooting at his house had already been made and the investigation had already begun. Jones v. State, 362 Md. 331, 765 A.2d 127 (2001).

Lying to police. — Neither common law nor this section clearly excludes or includes lying to the police as a crime. Thompson v. Anderson, 447 F. Supp. 584 (D. Md. 1977).

When statement may be regarded as false representation. — A statement which standing alone may be factually true but which is made under circumstances which would clearly cause it to mislead a listener may be regarded as a false representation. Sine v. State, 40 Md. App. 628, 394 A.2d 1206 (1978), cert. denied, 284 Md. 748 (1979).

The giving of false information in response to routine questioning by the police, even though it is likely to hinder or delay an investigation already underway, is not the type of false statement, report, or complaint that comes with the "false alarm" public mischief the General Assembly intended to criminalize when it enacted a prior version of this section. Johnson v. State, 75 Md. App. 621, 542 A.2d 429 (1988), cert. denied, 316 Md. 675, 561 A.2d 215 (1989).

An earlier version of this section does not proscribe a false response to police questioning after an investigation has already begun. Choi v. State, 316 Md. 529, 560 A.2d 1108 (1989).

Statements to school officials. — Twelve-year-old student's false statements to school officials regarding sexual abuse by a teacher, and false statements to police during an investigation of those allegations, were not shown to have been made with the necessary intent to violate the false reporting to police statute. In re Heather B., 369 Md. 257, 799 A.2d 397 (2002).

Sufficiency of claim against juvenile. — Trial court erred in dismissing a juvenile delinquency petition, because the petition alleging that a juvenile made a false statement to a police officer in violation of this section satisfied the requirements of art. 21 of the Declaration of Rights, the specific dictates of § 3-8A-13(a) of the Courts Article and Rule 11-103(a)(2)(c), as the petition did more than merely state the elements of the charged offense, and included specific facts concerning the alleged offense and the names and addresses of witnesses. In re Roneika S., 173 Md. App. 577, 920 A.2d 496 (2007).

Conviction as principal. — Defendant's argument that he could not be convicted as a principal in the making of a false accident report because he neither made any such reports himself nor participated in, aided, or abetted the making of any such report was rejected where the evidence was clearly sufficient to show that defendant participated in a staged accident and that he conspired with the other participants to arrange the supposed accident, and the evidence also showed that the statements made by the other participants were part and parcel of the representation that an actual accident had taken place, and, as the crime charged is a misdemeanor, all those participating in it, whether as principal or perpetrator, accessory before the fact, or aider or abettor, are chargeable as principals. Sine v. State, 40 Md. App. 628, 394 A.2d 1206 (1978), cert. denied, 284 Md. 748 (1979).

Refusal to sever from robbery offense proper. — In a prosecution on charges of robbery and making a false statement to a police officer, the trial court did not err in refusing to sever the false statement offense because evidence that defendant used a false name when questioned about the robbery was relevant to establish that he had knowledge of the offense, and defendant offered no persuasive argument that the evidence was unduly prejudicial. Harper v. State, 162 Md. App. 55, 873 A.2d 395 (2005).

Withdrawal of charges. — Trial court did not abuse its discretion by precluding defendant from impeaching a complainant with respect to her prior complaints to the police concerning unrelated events; defendant failed to establish that the complainant filed false police reports, a violation of this section, that

did not result in convictions—stets and nolle prosequis did not establish the falsity of the complaints. Without a basis for determining that the complaints were false, there was no evidence of misconduct as to which defendant could have cross examined the complainant under Rule 5-608(b). Parker v. State, 185 Md. App. 399, 970 A.2d 968 (2009).

Sufficiency of evidence. — Evidence was insufficient to support a conviction. Johnson v. State, 75 Md. App. 621, 542 A.2d 429 (1988), cert. denied, 316 Md. 675, 561 A.2d 215 (1989).

Sentence. — Where the record shows that defendant was given a sentence of one year on conviction under an earlier version of this section, this sentence must be vacated and the case remanded for resentencing. Sine v. State, 40 Md. App. 628, 394 A.2d 1206 (1978), cert. denied, 284 Md. 748 (1979).

Stated in Miller v. United States Foodservice, Inc., 405 F. Supp. 2d 607 (D. Md. 2005).

§ 9-502. False statement — When under arrest.

(a) *Prohibited.* — A person who is arrested by a law enforcement officer of the State, of a county, municipal corporation, or other political subdivision of the State, or of the Maryland-National Capital Park and Planning Police may not knowingly, and with intent to deceive, make a false statement to a law enforcement officer concerning the person's identity, address, or date of birth.

(b) *Penalty.* — A person who violates this section is guilty of a misdemeanor and on conviction is subject to imprisonment not exceeding 6 months or a fine not exceeding $500 or both. (An. Code 1957, art. 27, § 150(b), (c); 2002, ch. 26, § 2.)

REVISOR'S NOTE

This Revisor's note comprises information related to the revision by Acts 2002, ch. 26.

This section is new language derived without substantive change from former Art. 27, § 150(b) and (c).

In subsection (a) of this section, the references to a "law enforcement" officer are substi-

tuted for the former references to a "peace or police" officer for consistency within this article.

Defined terms:
"County" § 1-101
"Person" § 1-101

§ 9-503. False statement — To public official concerning crime or hazard.

(a) *Prohibited.* — A person may not make, or cause to be made, a statement or report that the person knows to be false as a whole or in material part to an official or unit of the State or of a county, municipal corporation, or other political subdivision of the State that a crime has been committed or that a condition imminently dangerous to public safety or health exists, with the intent that the official or unit investigate, consider, or take action in connection with that statement or report.

(b) *Penalty.* — A person who violates this section is guilty of a misdemeanor and on conviction is subject to imprisonment not exceeding 6 months or a fine not exceeding $500 or both. (An. Code 1957, art. 27, § 151; 2002, ch. 26, § 2.)

REVISOR'S NOTE

This Revisor's note comprises information related to the revision by Acts 2002, ch. 26.

This section is new language derived without substantive change from the initial clause of former Art. 27, § 151.

In subsection (a) of this section, the term "municipal corporation" is substituted for the former word "city" to conform to usage in Md. Constitution, Art. XI-E.

Also in subsection (a) of this section, the word "unit" is substituted for the former word "agency" for consistency within this article. *See* General Revisor's Note to article.

In subsection (b) of this section, the former reference to "the discretion of the court" is deleted as implicit in the establishment of maximum penalties.

Defined terms:
"County"	§ 1-101
"Person"	§ 1-101

§ 9-504. False statement — Concerning destructive device or toxic material.

(a) *Scope of section.* — This section does not apply to a statement made or rumor circulated by an officer, employee, or agent of a bona fide civilian defense organization or unit, if made in the regular course of the person's duties.

(b) *Prohibited.* — A person may not circulate or transmit to another, with intent that it be acted on, a statement or rumor that the person knows to be false about the location or possible detonation of a destructive device or the location or possible release of toxic material, as those terms are defined in § 4-501 of this article.

(c) *Penalty.* — A person who violates this section is guilty of a felony and on conviction is subject to imprisonment not exceeding 10 years or a fine not exceeding $10,000 or both.

(d) *Venue.* — A crime under this section committed using a telephone or other electronic means may be prosecuted:

(1) in the county in which the communication originated; or

(2) in the county in which the communication was received.

(e) *Restitution.* — (1) In addition to the penalty provided in subsection (c) of this section, a court may order a person convicted or found to have committed a delinquent act under this section to pay restitution to:

(i) the State, county, municipal corporation, bicounty unit, multicounty unit, county board of education, public authority, or special taxing district for actual costs reasonably incurred in responding to a location and searching for a destructive device as a result of a violation of this section; and

(ii) the owner or tenant of a property for the actual value of any goods, services, or income lost as a result of the evacuation of the property as a result of a violation of this section.

(2) This subsection may not be construed to limit the right of a person to restitution under Title 11, Subtitle 6 of the Criminal Procedure Article.

(3) (i) If the person convicted or found to have committed a delinquent act under this section is a minor, the court may order the minor, the minor's parent, or both to pay the restitution described in paragraph (1) of this subsection.

(ii) Except as otherwise provided in this section, the provisions of Title 11, Subtitle 6 of the Criminal Procedure Article apply to an order of restitution under this paragraph.

(f) *License suspension of minor.* — In addition to any other penalty authorized by law, if the person convicted or found to have committed a delinquent act under this section is a minor, the court may order the Motor Vehicle Administration to initiate an action, under the motor vehicle laws, to suspend the driving privilege of the minor for a specified period not to exceed:

(1) for a first violation, 6 months; and

(2) for each subsequent violation, 1 year or until the person is 21 years old, whichever is longer. (An. Code 1957, art. 27, § 151A; 2002, ch. 26, § 2; ch. 351; 2006, ch. 429.)

SPECIAL REVISOR'S NOTE

This Special Revisor's note comprises information related to the revision by Acts 2002, ch. 26 and other chapters amending this section from the 2002 Legislative Session.

As enacted by Ch. 26, Acts of 2002, this section was new language derived without substantive change from former Art. 27, § 151A. However, Ch. 351, Acts of 2002, substituted the phrase "in responding to a location and searching" for a destructive device for the phrase "due to the response to a location and search" for a device enacted by Ch. 26 in subsection (e)(1)(i) of this section.

In subsection (b) of this section, the phrase "written, printed, by any electronic means, or by word of mouth" which formerly modified "statement" or "rumor" was deleted by Ch. 26 as surplusage.

In subsection (c) of this section, the former reference to a violator being subject to imprisonment or fine "in the discretion of the court" was deleted by Ch. 26 as implicit in the establishment of maximum penalties.

Subsection (d) of this section was revised by Ch. 26 as a venue provision for clarity.

In subsection (d) of this section, the references to "communication" were substituted by Ch. 26 for the former phrase "telephone call or calls or electronic communication" for brevity.

In subsection (e)(1)(i) of this section, the word "unit" was substituted by Ch. 26 for the former word "agency" for consistency within this article. *See* General Revisor's Note to article.

In subsections (e)(3) and (f) of this section, the defined term "minor" was substituted by Ch. 26 for the former defined term "child" for consistency within this article.

In subsection (f)(2) of this section, the reference to "each" subsequent violation was substituted by Ch. 26 for the former reference to "a second or" subsequent violation for consistency within this article.

Former Art. 27, § 151A(a), which defined "child" to mean a person under the age of 18 years, was deleted by Ch. 26 as duplicative of the term "minor" defined in § 1-101 of this article.

For provisions relating to destructive devices, *see* Title 4, Subtitle 5 of this article.

Defined terms:

"County"	§ 1-101
"Minor"	§ 1-101
"Person"	§ 1-101

Gravamen of section. — The gravamen of a prior version of this section is the transmitting of a false report with respect to the location and/or possible detonation of an existing bomb, whereas the gravamen of a prior version of § 6-107 of this article is the making of the threat itself, whether it be true or false. Moosavi v. State, 355 Md. 651, 736 A.2d 285 (1999).

§ 9-505. Representation of destructive device.

(a) *Prohibited.* — A person may not manufacture, possess, transport, or place:

(1) a device or container that is labeled as containing or is intended to represent a toxic material, as defined in § 4-501 of this article, with the intent to terrorize, frighten, intimidate, threaten, or harass; or

(2) a device that is constructed to represent a destructive device, as defined in § 4-501 of this article, with the intent to terrorize, frighten, intimidate, threaten, or harass.

(b) *Penalty.* — A person who violates this section is guilty of a felony and on conviction is subject to imprisonment not exceeding 10 years or a fine not exceeding $10,000 or both.

(c) *Restitution.* — (1) In addition to the penalty provided in subsection (b) of this section, a person convicted or found to have committed a delinquent act under this section may be ordered by the court to pay restitution to:

(i) the State, county, municipal corporation, bicounty unit, multicounty unit, county board of education, public authority, or special taxing district for actual costs reasonably incurred as a result of a violation of this section; and

(ii) the owner or tenant of a property for the actual value of any goods, services, or income lost as a result of the evacuation of the property as a result of a violation of this section.

(2) This subsection may not be construed to limit the right of a person to restitution under Title 11, Subtitle 6 of the Criminal Procedure Article.

(3) (i) If the person convicted or found to have committed a delinquent act in violation of this section is a minor, the court may order the minor, the minor's parent, or both to pay the restitution described in paragraph (1) of this subsection.

(ii) Except as otherwise provided in this section, the provisions of Title 11, Subtitle 6 of the Criminal Procedure Article apply to an order of restitution under this paragraph.

(d) *License suspension of minor.* — In addition to any other penalty authorized by law, if the person convicted or found to have committed a delinquent act under this section is a minor, the court may order the Motor Vehicle Administration to initiate an action, under the motor vehicle laws, to suspend the driving privilege of the minor for a specified period not to exceed:

(1) for a first violation, 6 months; and

(2) for each subsequent violation, 1 year or until the person is 21 years old, whichever is longer. (An. Code 1957, art. 27, § 151C; 2002, ch. 26, § 2; ch. 351; 2005, ch. 201; 2006, ch. 429.)

SPECIAL REVISOR'S NOTE

This Special Revisor's note comprises information related to the revision by Acts 2002, ch. 26 and other chapters amending this section from the 2002 Legislative Session.

As enacted by Ch. 26, Acts of 2002, this section was new language derived without sub-stantive change from former Art. 27, § 151C. However, Ch. 351, Acts of 2002, substituted the reference to "responding to a location and searching for and removing" of a device for the reference to "the search for and removal" of a device enacted by Ch. 26 in subsection (c)(1)(i) of this section.

In subsection (c)(1)(i) of this section, the word "unit" was substituted by Ch. 26 for the former word "agency" for consistency within this article. *See* General Revisor's Note to article.

Also in subsection (c)(1)(i) of this section, the reference to a "device that is constructed to represent" a destructive device was substituted by Ch. 26 for the former reference to the "representation of" a destructive device for clarity and consistency within this section.

In subsections (c)(3) and (d) of this section, the defined term "minor" was substituted by Ch. 26 for the former defined term "child" for consistency within this article.

In subsection (d)(1) and (2) of this section, the references to a "violation" were substituted by Ch. 26 for the former references to an "offense" for consistency within this article. *See* General Revisor's Note to article.

In subsection (d)(2) of this section, the reference to "each" subsequent violation was substituted by Ch. 26 for the former reference to "a second or" subsequent violation for consistency within this article.

Former Art. 27, § 151C(a), which defined "child" to mean a person under the age of 18 years, was deleted by Ch. 26 as duplicative of the term "minor" defined in § 1-101 of this article.

The Criminal Law Article Review Committee noted, for the consideration of the General Assembly, that the restitution to government units under subsection (c)(1)(i) of this section only included costs "in the search for and removal of" a representation of a destructive device, whereas the restitution available to government units under § 9-504(e)(1)(i) of this subtitle includes costs "due to the response to a location and search" for a destructive device or toxic material. The General Assembly was asked to consider addressing the disparity in the restitution available to government units under these two provisions. Chapter 351 addressed this concern.

Defined terms:

"County"	§ 1-101
"Minor"	§ 1-101
"Person"	§ 1-101

§ 9-506. Maryland Higher Education Commission fund application — False or concealed material fact.

(a) *Prohibited.* — A person may not knowingly and willfully falsify or conceal a material fact in connection with an application for funds from the Maryland Higher Education Commission.

(b) *Penalty.* — A person who violates this section is guilty of a misdemeanor and on conviction is subject to imprisonment not exceeding 1 year or a fine not exceeding $5,000 or both.

(c) *Notice to applicant.* — The Maryland Higher Education Commission shall notify each applicant for funds of the conduct that constitutes a violation of this section before a State scholarship award or grant is awarded. (An. Code 1957, art. 27, § 151B; 2002, ch. 26, § 2.)

REVISOR'S NOTE

This Revisor's note comprises information related to the revision by Acts 2002, ch. 26.

This section is new language derived without substantive change from former Art. 27, § 151B.

Defined term:

"Person"	§ 1-101

§ 9-507. Common-law criminal defamation repealed.

The common-law crime of criminal defamation is repealed. (An. Code 1957, art. 27, § 150A; 2002, ch. 26, § 2.)

REVISOR'S NOTE

This Revisor's note comprises information related to the revision by Acts 2002,
ch. 26.

This section is new language derived without
substantive change from former Art. 27,
§ 150A.

The former reference to criminal defamation
being "abrogated" is deleted in light of the
reference to it being "repealed".

§ 9-508. False filings of financing statement or amendment.

(a) *"Financing statement" defined.* — In this section, "financing statement" has the meaning stated in § 9-102 of the Commercial Law Article.

(b) *Prohibition.* — A person may not file a financing statement or an amendment to a financing statement that the person knows contains false information.

(c) (1) *Penalty.* — A person who violates this section is guilty of a misdemeanor and on conviction is subject to a fine not exceeding $500.

(2) Each act of filing a financing statement or an amendment to a financing statement is a separate violation. (2010, ch. 397.)

Editor's note. — Section 2, ch. 397, Acts
2010, provides that the act shall take effect
October 1, 2010.

Subtitle 6. Interference with Government Operations.

Part I. In General.

§ 9-601. Interference with emergency communication.

(a) *"Emergency" defined.* — In this section, "emergency" means a circumstance in which:

(1) an individual is or is reasonably believed by the person transmitting the communication to be in imminent danger of death or serious bodily harm; or

(2) property is in imminent danger of damage or destruction.

(b) *Prohibited.* — A person may not:

(1) knowingly, intentionally, or recklessly interrupt, disrupt, impede, or otherwise interfere with the transmission of a two-way radio communication made:

(i) to inform or inquire about an emergency; and

(ii) on a frequency commonly used or monitored by an emergency services organization; or

(2) transmit false information about an emergency on a two-way radio frequency commonly used or monitored by an emergency services organization.

(c) *Penalty.* — A person who violates this section is guilty of a misdemeanor and on conviction is subject to imprisonment not exceeding 6 months or a fine not exceeding $1,000 or both.

(d) *Seizure and forfeiture of property.* — (1) A two-way radio and related equipment used in violation of this section is subject to seizure.

(2) On conviction of a violation of this section, any property seized under paragraph (1) of this subsection shall be forfeited to the State and no property right shall exist in the property.

(3) Any property that is forfeited under paragraph (2) of this subsection shall be turned over to the Secretary of General Services, who may:

(i) order that the property be retained for official use of State units; or

(ii) otherwise dispose of the property as the Secretary considers appropriate. (An. Code 1957, art. 27, § 125A; 2002, ch. 26, § 2.)

REVISOR'S NOTE

This Revisor's note comprises information related to the revision by Acts 2002, ch. 26.

This section is new language derived without substantive change from former Art. 27, § 125A.

In subsection (a) of this section, the former reference to a "condition" is deleted as surplusage.

Also in subsection (a) of this section, the former phrase "by the person transmitting the communication" is deleted as surplusage.

In subsections (b) and (c) of this section, the references to a "person" are substituted for the former references to an "individual" for consistency within this article.

In subsection (b) of this section, the former reference to acting "with criminal negligence" is deleted as surplusage. Criminal negligence appears to be encompassed in the reference to acting "recklessly".

In subsection (b)(1)(ii) and (2) of this section, the former references to "civilian or governmental" emergency services organizations are deleted as surplusage.

In subsection (d) of this section, the former phrase "as the Secretary may deem appropriate" is deleted as surplusage.

The Criminal Law Article Review Committee notes, for the consideration of the General Assembly, that in subsection (d)(3)(ii) of this section, the Secretary of General Services apparently has not adopted guidelines for the disposition of proceeds of property that is disposed of.

Defined term:
"Person"   § 1-101

§ 9-602. State personnel monitoring or recording telephone conversation.

(a) *Prohibited.* — (1) Except as provided in paragraph (2) of this subsection, a State official or employee may not directly or indirectly monitor or record in any manner a telephone conversation made to or from a State unit.

(2) If prior approval is granted by the Attorney General, a State official or employee may monitor or record a telephone conversation:

(i) on telephone lines used exclusively for incoming police, fire, and rescue calls; or

(ii) with recorder-connector equipment that automatically produces a distinctive recorder tone repeated at approximately 15-second intervals.

(b) *Penalty.* — A person who violates this section is guilty of a misdemeanor and on conviction is subject to a fine not exceeding $1,000.

(c) *Dismissal.* — Conviction of a violation of this section is also grounds for immediate dismissal from State employment. (An. Code 1957, art. 27, § 555B; 2002, ch. 26, § 2; 2003, ch. 21, § 1.)

REVISOR'S NOTE

This Revisor's note comprises information related to the revision by Acts 2002, ch. 26.

This section is new language derived without substantive change from former Art. 27, § 555B.

In subsection (a) of this section, the reference to authorizing a State official or employee to monitor or record a telephone conversation on telephone lines used exclusively for incoming police, fire, and rescue calls with prior approval of the Attorney General is substituted for the former qualification that on telephone lines used for incoming police, fire, and rescue calls "it is not necessary to append" a recorder tone for clarity.

Also in subsection (a) of this section, the former phrase "contains a device" is deleted as surplusage.

Subsection (a)(2) of this section is revised to require only a single approval from the Attorney General to monitor a telephone conversation generally, using a 15-second beep tone, and to monitor a line used exclusively for incoming police, fire, and rescue calls, known as a "tone waiver eligible" telephone line and on which the beep tone is not used. Former Art. 27, § 555B(a) was unclear as to whether a single approval for monitoring sufficed, or whether a second, specific approval was needed to monitor without the beep tone on a tone waiver eligible line. The Attorney General advises that the practice has been to regard the general approval to monitor as tacit approval to monitor on a tone waiver eligible line. The revision reflects the practice of the Attorney General. *See* Letter of Advice from Attorney General J. Joseph Curran, Jr. to Judge Alan M. Wilner, p. 16 (October 17, 2000).

In subsection (b) of this section, the phrase "guilty of a misdemeanor" is added to state explicitly that which was only implied by the former law. In this State, any crime that was not considered a felony at common law and has not been declared a felony by statute is considered a misdemeanor. *See State v. Canova*, 278 Md. 483, 490 (1976); *Bowser v. State*, 136 Md. 342, 354 (1920); *Dutton v. State*, 123 Md. 373, 378 (1914); and *Williams v. State*, 4 Md. App. 342, 347 (1968).

Defined term:
"Person"   § 1-101

Conversations under section and private conversations of person suspected of crime distinguished. — The conversations referred to in former Art. 27, § 555B (see now this section) are in an entirely different class from the private conversations or conduct of a person suspected of crime. In the first instance the interest sought to be protected is the public interest of the State; in the latter instance the interest involved is the personal interest of an individual suspected of crime. Avery v. State, 15 Md. App. 520, 292 A.2d 728, cert. denied, 266 Md. 733 (1972), appeal dismissed, 410 U.S. 977, 93 S. Ct. 1499, 36 L. Ed. 2d 173 (1973).

The Fourteenth Amendment does not require that private conversations or conduct of a person suspected of crime be treated equally with conversations with a State department or agency under former Art. 27, § 555B (see now this section). Avery v. State, 15 Md. App. 520, 292 A.2d 728, cert. denied, 266 Md. 733 (1972), appeal dismissed, 410 U.S. 977, 93 S. Ct. 1499, 36 L. Ed. 2d 173 (1973).

§ 9-603. Prerecorded emergency message.

(a) *Prohibited.* — Except as provided in subsection (b) of this section, a person may not use a device that dials by remote control a preprogrammed telephone number and transmits a prerecorded message communicating an existing emergency condition, including fire, illness, or crime, without written approval for the use of the device from the holder of the number dialed.

(b) *Applicability.* — This section does not apply to:

(1) a State or local law enforcement agency that is conducting an official investigation or communicating an emergency condition;

(2) a State or local emergency management agency that is communicating an emergency condition; or

(3) a person that is specifically designated by an agency described in item (1) or (2) of this subsection to participate in an official investigation or communicate an emergency condition.

(c) *Penalty.* — A person who violates this section is guilty of a misdemeanor and on conviction is subject to a fine not exceeding $50 for each violation. (An. Code 1957, art. 27, § 557B; 2002, ch. 26, § 2; 2006, ch. 386.)

REVISOR'S NOTE

This Revisor's note comprises information related to the revision by Acts 2002, ch. 26.

This section is new language derived without substantive change from former Art. 27, § 557B.

In subsection (a) of this section, the phrase "recipient of the message" is substituted for the former phrase "each holder of the telephone, which receives the prerecorded message" for clarity.

In subsection (b) of this section, the former reference to a "firm, or corporation" is deleted in light of the defined term "person".

The Criminal Law Article Review Committee notes, for the consideration of the General Assembly, that subsection (a) of this section appears to prohibit the mere attachment of remote dialing equipment rather than its use to transmit a message to a holder of the receiving telephone number. As a result, a person who attaches remote dialing equipment that dials many numbers whose holders have not approved use of the remote dialer would be chargeable only with one violation subject to a $50 fine, not: (1) $50 multiplied by the number of unapproving receiving numbers, or (2) $50 multiplied by the number of remote dialing incidents. The General Assembly may wish to address these matters in substantive legislation.

Defined term:
"Person" § 1-101

§ 9-604. False alarm.

(a) *Prohibited.* — A person may not knowingly make or cause to be made a false:

(1) fire alarm; or

(2) call for an ambulance or rescue squad.

(b) *Penalty.* — A person who violates this section is guilty of a misdemeanor and on conviction is subject to imprisonment not exceeding 5 years or a fine not exceeding $5,000 or both. (An. Code 1957, art. 27, § 156; 2002, ch. 26, § 2.)

REVISOR'S NOTE

This Revisor's note comprises information related to the revision by Acts 2002, ch. 26.

This section is new language derived without substantive change from former Art. 27, § 156.

In subsection (a) of this section, the phrase "make or cause to be made" is substituted for the former phrase "give or cause to be given" for clarity.

Also in subsection (a) of this section, the former references to a "telegraph box connected with any fire alarm telegraph or. . . telephone or telegraph system, or. . . other means or method" and to a "telephone or. . . other means or method" are deleted as surplusage.

In subsection (b) of this section, the former reference to both "fine and imprisonment" is deleted as surplusage and for consistency within this article.

Defined term:
"Person" § 1-101

GENERAL REVISOR'S NOTE TO PART

The Criminal Law Article Review Committee notes, for the consideration of the General Assembly, that many of the electronic means of conveying false messages that interfere with governmental operations today are not covered by the provisions revised in this part. Cable equipment, computer networks, and hybrid wireless devices, as examples, are all capable of being used to send false alarms and related information to governmental units. The General Assembly may wish to address the scope of this part in substantive legislation.

§§ 9-605, 9-606.

Reserved.

Part II. Alarm Systems.

§ 9-607. Definitions.

(a) *In general.* — In this part the following words have the meanings indicated.

REVISOR'S NOTE

This subsection formerly was Art. 27, § 156A(a).

The reference to this "part" is substituted for the former erroneous reference to this "subti-tle" to reflect the reorganization of material derived from the former "Burglary and Robbery False Alarm" subheading in Article 27.

No other changes are made.

(b) *Alarm system.* — "Alarm system" means a burglary alarm system, robbery alarm system, or automatic fire alarm system.

REVISOR'S NOTE

This subsection formerly was Art. 27, § 156A(c).

No changes are made.

(c) *Alarm system contractor.* — (1) "Alarm system contractor" means a person who installs, maintains, monitors, alters, or services alarm systems.

(2) "Alarm system contractor" does not include a person who only manu-factures or sells alarm systems.

REVISOR'S NOTE

This subsection is new language derived without substantive change from former Art. 27, § 156A(d).

In paragraph (1) of this subsection, the for-mer reference to an "agency that furnishes the services of a person engaged in" is deleted as included in the defined term "person".

Also in paragraph (1) of this subsection, the former phrase "engaged in" is deleted as sur-plusage.

In paragraph (2) of this subsection, the de-fined term "alarm system[s]" is substituted for the former term "alarm devices" for consistency within this part.

Also in paragraph (2) of this subsection, the former phrase "unless that person services, installs, monitors, or responds to alarm sys-tems at protected premises" is deleted as sur-plusage since such a person is included in the term "alarm system contractor" defined in paragraph (1) of this subsection.

Defined term:
"Person"   § 1-101

(d) *Alarm user.* — "Alarm user" means:

(1) a person in control of an alarm system within, on, or around any building, structure, facility, or site; or

(2) the owner or lessee of an alarm system.

REVISOR'S NOTE

This subsection is new language derived without substantive change from former Art. 27, § 156A(e).

Defined term:
"Person"   § 1-101

(e) *False alarm.* — (1) "False alarm" means a request for immediate assistance from a law enforcement unit or fire department regardless of cause that is not in response to an actual emergency situation or threatened suggested criminal activity.

(2) "False alarm" includes:

(i) a negligently or accidentally activated signal;

(ii) a signal that is activated as the result of faulty, malfunctioning, or improperly installed or maintained equipment; and

(iii) a signal that is purposely activated in a nonemergency situation.

(3) "False alarm" does not include:

(i) a signal activated by unusually severe weather conditions or other causes beyond the control of the alarm user or alarm system contractor; or

(ii) a signal activated within 60 days after a new installation of an alarm system.

REVISOR'S NOTE

This subsection is new language derived without substantive change from former Art. 27, § 156A(g)(1), (2), and (3).

(f) *Law enforcement unit.* — "Law enforcement unit" means the Department of State Police, the police department of a county or municipal corporation, and a sheriff's department or other governmental law enforcement unit having employees authorized to make arrests.

REVISOR'S NOTE

This subsection is new language derived without substantive change from former Art. 27, § 156A(f).

The word "unit" is substituted for the former word "agency" for consistency within this article. *See* General Revisor's Note to article.

The former reference to "Baltimore City Police" is deleted as included in the reference to the "police department of a county" since Baltimore City is included in the defined term "county". *See* § 1-101 of this article.

The reference to a "municipal corporation" is substituted for the former reference to an "incorporated municipality" to conform to usage in Md. Constitution, Art. XI-E.

The reference to a "governmental" law enforcement unit is added for clarity. The Criminal Law Article Review Committee brings this addition to the attention of the General Assembly.

Defined term:
"County"   § 1-101

(g) *Signal.* — "Signal" means the activation of an alarm system that requests a response by a law enforcement unit or a fire department.

REVISOR'S NOTE

This subsection is new language derived without substantive change from former Art. 27, § 156A(b).

In this subsection, the word "signal" is substituted for the former phrase "[a]larm signal" for clarity and consistency within this part.

(An. Code 1957, art. 27, § 156A(a)-(f), (g)(1)-(3); 2002, ch. 26, § 2.)

REVISOR'S NOTE TO SECTION

The Revisor's notes in this section comprise information related to the revision
by Acts 2002, ch. 26.

§ 9-608. Nonemergency activation of signal.

(a) *Prohibited.* — A person may not intentionally activate a signal for a nonemergency situation.

(b) *Penalty.* — A person who violates this section is guilty of a misdemeanor and on conviction is subject to imprisonment not exceeding 90 days or a fine not exceeding $500 or both. (An. Code 1957, art. 27, § 156B; 2002, ch. 26, § 2.)

REVISOR'S NOTE

This Revisor's note comprises information related to the revision by Acts 2002,
ch. 26.
This section is new language derived without
substantive change from former Art. 27,
§ 156B.

Defined terms:
"Person"   § 1-101
"Signal"   § 9-607

§ 9-609. Multiple false alarms.

(a) *Scope of section.* — This section does not apply:

(1) to alarm systems activated by weather conditions or causes beyond the control of the alarm user;

(2) in Frederick County if the Board of County Commissioners of Frederick County adopts regulations under Article 25, § 221A of the Code providing for the registration of alarm system contractors and alarm users, the issuance of civil citations, and penalties for a violation of a regulation;

(3) in Calvert County if the Board of County Commissioners of Calvert County adopts regulations under Article 25, § 236D of the Code providing for the registration of alarm system contractors and alarm users, the issuance of civil citations, and penalties for a violation of a regulation; or

(4) in Washington County if the Board of County Commissioners of Washington County adopts regulations under Article 25, § 236E of the Code providing for the registration of alarm system contractors and alarm users, the issuance of civil citations, and penalties for a violation of a regulation.

(b) *Rule of construction — Occurrences as single alarm.* — An alarm system that is activated more than once within a 12-hour period when a premises with an alarm system is unoccupied and that is not in response to an actual emergency situation or threatened suggested criminal activity constitutes one false alarm if:

(1) access to the building is provided to the alarm system contractor; and

(2) an alarm system contractor or an employee of an alarm system contractor responds to the activated alarm system.

(c) *Civil citation and penalty.* — (1) A law enforcement unit or fire department may issue a civil citation to an alarm user for the negligent or accidental activation of an alarm system as a result of faulty, malfunctioning, or improperly installed or maintained equipment or for a false alarm if the number of activations or false alarms to which the law enforcement unit or fire department responds exceeds:

(i) three responses within a 30-day period; or

(ii) eight responses within a 12-month period.

(2) A civil citation issued under this section shall assess a penalty of $30 for each negligent or accidental activation or false alarm. (An. Code 1957, art. 27, §§ 156A(g)(4)(i), 156C; 2002, ch. 26, § 2; 2005, ch. 25, § 1; ch. 72.)

REVISOR'S NOTE

This Revisor's note comprises information related to the revision by Acts 2002, ch. 26.

This section is new language derived without substantive change from former Art. 27, §§ 156C and 156A(g)(4)(i).

In subsection (a)(1) of this section, the former reference to "acts of God" is deleted as included in the reference to "causes beyond the control of the alarm user".

Subsection (a)(2) and (3) of this section is revised as two separate paragraphs, relating to Frederick County and Calvert County, respectively, to avoid the unintended consequence in former Art. 27, § 156C(a) that action by the board of county commissioners of either county would exempt both counties from this section.

In subsection (a)(3) of this section, the reference to Article 25, § "236D" of the Code is substituted for the former incorrect reference to "§ 237" for accuracy.

In subsection (b) of this section, the reference to an alarm system activated "more than once" within a specific period is substituted for the former reference to an alarm system activated "a second time" within a specific period for clarity.

Former Art. 27, § 156A(g)(4)(ii), which provided that failing to comply with certain conditions would result in multiple alarms being treated as such, is deleted as surplusage, since those conditions, which are revised in subsection (b) of this section, must be met before multiple alarms may be treated as a single false alarm.

Defined terms:

"Alarm system"	§ 9-607
"Alarm system contractor"	§ 9-607
"Alarm user"	§ 9-607
"False alarm"	§ 9-607
"Law enforcement unit"	§ 9-607

§ 9-610. Defective alarm system.

(a) *"Defective alarm system" defined.* — In this section, "defective alarm system" means an alarm system that activates:

(1) more than three false alarms within a 30-day period; or

(2) eight or more false alarms within a 12-month period.

(b) *Notice of defect; report.* — (1) A law enforcement unit or fire department that responds to false alarms from a defective alarm system shall provide written notice of the defective condition to the alarm user.

(2) The alarm user, within 30 days after receiving the notice, shall:

(i) 1. if qualified, inspect the alarm system; or

2. have the alarm system inspected by an alarm system contractor; and

(ii) within 15 days after the inspection, file with the law enforcement unit or fire department that issued the notice a written report that contains the:

1. result of the inspection;

2. probable cause of the false alarms; and

3. recommendations or action taken to eliminate the false alarms.

(c) *Prohibited.* — An alarm user may not use a defective alarm system after receiving a written notice under subsection (b) of this section.

(d) *Penalty.* — A person who violates subsection (c) of this section is guilty of a misdemeanor and on conviction is subject to imprisonment not exceeding 90 days or a fine not exceeding $500 or both. (An. Code 1957, art. 27, § 156D; 2002, ch. 26, § 2.)

REVISOR'S NOTE

This Revisor's note comprises information related to the revision by Acts 2002, ch. 26.

This section is new language derived without substantive change from former Art. 27, § 156D.

In subsection (b) of this section, the reference to responding to false alarms from "a defective alarm system" is substituted for the former reference to "answer[ing] to false alarms" in order to clarify the circumstances in which written notice is required.

In subsection (c) of this section, the reference to using a defective alarm system "after receiv-ing a written notice under subsection (b) of this section" is substituted for the former reference to "continu[ing] to use" a defective alarm system for clarity and consistency within this section.

Defined terms:

"Alarm system"	§ 9-607
"Alarm system contractor"	§ 9-607
"Alarm user"	§ 9-607
"False alarm"	§ 9-607
"Law enforcement unit"	§ 9-607
"Person"	§ 1-101

§ 9-611. Audible alarm system.

(a) *"Audible alarm system" defined.* — In this section, "audible alarm system" means an alarm system that, when activated, emits an audible noise from an annunciator.

(b) *Required equipment.* — An audible alarm system shall be equipped to:

(1) automatically silence the annunciator within 30 minutes after activation; and

(2) allow an accidental or negligent activation to be halted or reset.

(c) *Prohibited.* — An alarm system contractor may not sell, lease, rent, or offer to sell, lease, or rent an audible alarm system that does not comply with the requirements of this section.

(d) *Penalty.* — A person who violates this section is subject to a civil penalty of $100 for each violation. (An. Code 1957, art. 27, § 156E; 2002, ch. 26, § 2.)

REVISOR'S NOTE

This Revisor's note comprises information related to the revision by Acts 2002, ch. 26.

Subsection (a) of this section is new language added for clarity.

Subsections (b), (c), and (d) of this section are new language derived without substantive change from former Art. 27, § 156E.

Defined terms:

"Alarm system"	§ 9-607
"Alarm system contractor"	§ 9-607
"Person"	§ 1-101

Subtitle 7. Sabotage.

§ 9-701. Definitions.

(a) *In general.* — In this subtitle the following words have the meanings indicated.

REVISOR'S NOTE

This subsection formerly was Art. 27, § 535(a).

No changes are made.

(b) *Defense-related activity.* — "Defense-related activity" means:

(1) the preparation of the United States or a state for defense or war; or

(2) the prosecution of war by the United States or a country with which the United States maintains friendly relations.

REVISOR'S NOTE

This subsection formerly was Art. 27, § 535(b). No changes are made.

Defined term:
"State" § 1-101

(c) *Identification badge.* — "Identification badge" means a badge that a person wears to show the person's identity or right to be in or on any premises described in § 9-704 of this subtitle.

REVISOR'S NOTE

This subsection is new language derived without substantive change from former Art. 27, § 535(c).

In this subsection and throughout this subtitle, the references to this "subtitle" are substituted for the former references to this "sub-heading" to reflect the reorganization of material derived from the former "Sabotage and Related Crimes" subheading of Article 27.

Defined term:
"Person" § 1-101

(d) *Identification card.* — "Identification card" means a card or pass issued for the purpose of establishing the identity and the right of the person to be in or on any premises described in § 9-704 of this subtitle.

REVISOR'S NOTE

This subsection formerly was Art. 27, § 535(d).

The reference to "§ 9-704 of this subtitle" is substituted for the former reference to "§ 538 of this subheading" to reflect the reorganization of material derived from the former "Sabotage and Related Crimes" subheading of Article 27.

No other changes are made.

Defined term:
"Person" § 1-101

(An. Code 1957, art. 27, § 535(a)-(d); 2002, ch. 26, § 2.)

REVISOR'S NOTE TO SECTION

The Revisor's notes in this section comprise information related to the revision by Acts 2002, ch. 26.

§ 9-702. Injury to or interference with property — Acting with intent to hinder defense-related activity.

(a) *Prohibited.* — A person may not destroy, impair, damage, or interfere or tamper with real or personal property with intent to hinder, delay, or interfere with a defense-related activity.

(b) *Penalty.* — A person who violates this section is guilty of a felony and on conviction is subject to imprisonment not exceeding 10 years or a fine not exceeding $10,000 or both. (An. Code 1957, art. 27, § 536; 2002, ch. 26, § 2.)

REVISOR'S NOTE

This Revisor's note comprises information related to the revision by Acts 2002, ch. 26.

This section formerly was Art. 27, § 536. No changes are made.

Defined terms:
"Defense-related activity"   § 9-701
"Person"   § 1-101

§ 9-703. Defective workmanship — Acting with intent to hinder defense-related activity.

(a) *Prohibited.* — A person may not intentionally:

(1) make or cause to be made or omit to note on inspection a defect in a product to be used in connection with a defense-related activity; and

(2) act, or fail to act, with intent to hinder, delay, or interfere with a defense-related activity.

(b) *Penalty.* — A person who violates this section is guilty of a felony and on conviction is subject to imprisonment not exceeding 10 years or a fine not exceeding $10,000 or both. (An. Code 1957, art. 27, § 537; 2002, ch. 26, § 2.)

REVISOR'S NOTE

This Revisor's note comprises information related to the revision by Acts 2002, ch. 26.

This section formerly was Art. 27, § 537. No changes are made.

Defined terms:
"Defense-related activity"   § 9-701
"Person"   § 1-101

§ 9-704. Identification badges and identification cards — Certain facilities.

(a) *Application of section.* — This section applies to a person possessing an identification badge or identification card required for employment or visitation that is issued by:

(1) a unit of the State or a county, municipal corporation, special taxing district, or public corporation of the State; or

(2) a person that owns or operates in the State:

(i) a factory or warehouse or a manufacturing, printing, publishing, mechanical, or mercantile establishment or a plant of any kind;

(ii) a mine or quarry;

(iii) a railway; or

(iv) a water, sewage, gas, electric, transmission, heating, refrigerating, telephone, or other publicly owned or public service company.

(b) *Surrender required at end of employment or visit.* — A person shall surrender each identification badge or identification card to its issuer when the person's employment or authorized visit ends.

(c) *Prohibited.* — A person may not knowingly possess an identification badge or identification card after the person's employment or authorized visit ends.

(d) *Penalty.* — A person who willfully violates this section is guilty of a misdemeanor and on conviction is subject to imprisonment not exceeding 90 days or a fine not exceeding $500 or both. (An. Code 1957, art. 27, §§ 535(e), 538; 2002, ch. 26, § 2.)

REVISOR'S NOTE

This Revisor's note comprises information related to the revision by Acts 2002, ch. 26.

This section is new language derived without substantive change from former Art. 27, §§ 538 and 535(e).

In subsection (a)(1) of this section, the reference to a "county, municipal corporation, special taxing district, or public corporation of the State" is substituted for the former defined term "political subdivision" for clarity.

In subsection (b) of this section, the reference to "each" identification badge or identification card is substituted for the former reference to "an" identification badge or identification card for clarity.

Defined terms:

"County"	§ 1-101
"Identification badge"	§ 9-701
"Identification card"	§ 9-701
"Person"	§ 1-101

§ 9-705. Identification badges and identification cards — Required surrender.

A person who finds or gains possession of an identification badge or identification card required under § 9-704 of this subtitle shall surrender immediately the identification badge or identification card to the nearest police station. (An. Code 1957, art. 27, § 539(a); 2002, ch. 26, § 2.)

REVISOR'S NOTE

This Revisor's note comprises information related to the revision by Acts 2002, ch. 26.

This section is new language derived without substantive change from former Art. 27, § 539(a).

Defined terms:

"Identification badge"	§ 9-701
"Identification card"	§ 9-701
"Person"	§ 1-101

§ 9-706. Identification badges and identification cards — Unauthorized use.

(a) *Prohibited.* — To enter a place or establishment in which a person is required to have an identification badge or identification card under § 9-704 of this subtitle, a person may not willfully:

(1) make unauthorized use of an identification badge or identification card; or

(2) assist another in the unauthorized use of an identification badge or identification card.

(b) *Penalty.* — A person who violates this section is guilty of a misdemeanor and on conviction is subject to imprisonment not exceeding 90 days or a fine not exceeding $500 or both. (An. Code 1957, art. 27, § 539(b), (c); 2002, ch. 26, § 2.)

REVISOR'S NOTE

This Revisor's note comprises information related to the revision by Acts 2002, ch. 26.

This section is new language derived without substantive change from former Art. 27, § 539(b) and (c).

Defined terms:

"Identification badge"	§ 9-701
"Identification card"	§ 9-701
"Person"	§ 1-101

§ 9-706.1. Trespass or violation at nuclear power facility — Detention.

(a) *"Security officer" defined.* — In this section, "security officer" means a proprietary or contractual security officer of a license holder of a nuclear power plant facility in the State.

(b) *Authority to detain without warrant.* — Subject to subsection (c) of this section, if a nuclear power plant facility is placed under a heightened level of security condition by a federal agency pursuant to federal law, the license holder of a nuclear power plant facility in the State may authorize a security officer, without a warrant, to stop and detain any person who the owner or security officer has reasonable grounds to believe has:

(1) entered or trespassed on posted property of the nuclear power plant facility in violation of § 6-402 of this article; or

(2) violated any local, State, or federal law, regulation, or order in an area controlled by the license holder of the nuclear power plant facility.

(c) *Notice to law enforcement agency.* — A security officer who detains a person under subsection (b) of this section shall, as soon as practicable:

(1) notify an appropriate law enforcement agency about the alleged crime committed by the person; and

(2) release the person to the detention or custody of a law enforcement officer.

(d) *Release of detainee.* — If notice to a law enforcement agency is provided as required under subsection (c) of this section and the law enforcement agency determines not to investigate the alleged crime or declines to take the detained person into detention or custody, the security officer shall release the person as soon as practicable. (2002, ch. 19, § 10; ch. 100, § 2; 2003, ch. 21, § 1.)

SPECIAL REVISOR'S NOTE

This Special Revisor's note comprises information related to the revision by Acts 2002, ch. 26 and other chapters amending this section from the 2002 Legislative Session.

Chapter 100, § 2, Acts of 2002, enacted this section as § 9-704.1. However, this section was renumbered to be § 9-706.1 under the authority of Ch. 19, § 10, Acts of 2002, in order to correct improper codification.

§ 9-707. Rights of labor unaffected.

This subtitle does not impair, curtail, or destroy the rights of employees and their representatives to:

(1) self-organization;

(2) form, join, or assist labor organizations;

(3) bargain collectively through representatives of their own choosing; and

(4) strike, picket, or engage in concerted activities for the purpose of collective bargaining or other mutual aid or protection. (An. Code 1957, art. 27, § 540; 2002, ch. 26, § 2.)

REVISOR'S NOTE

This Revisor's note comprises information related to the revision by Acts 2002, ch. 26.

This section formerly was Art. 27, § 540. No changes are made.

§ 9-708. Relation to other laws.

If conduct prohibited by this subtitle is also unlawful under another law, a person may be convicted for the violation of this subtitle and the other law. (An. Code 1957, art. 27, § 541; 2002, ch. 26, § 2.)

REVISOR'S NOTE

This Revisor's note comprises information related to the revision by Acts 2002, ch. 26.

This section formerly was Art. 27, § 541. The only changes are in style.

Subtitle 8. Criminal Gang Offenses.

§ 9-801. Definitions.

(a) *In general.* — In this subtitle the following words have the meanings indicated.

(b) *Coerce.* — "Coerce" means to compel or attempt to compel another by threat of harm or other adverse consequences.

(c) *Criminal gang.* — "Criminal gang" means a group or association of three or more persons whose members:

(1) individually or collectively engage in a pattern of criminal gang activity;

(2) have as one of their primary objectives or activities the commission of one or more underlying crimes, including acts by juveniles that would be underlying crimes if committed by adults; and

(3) have in common an overt or covert organizational or command structure.

(d) *Pattern of criminal gang activity.* — "Pattern of criminal gang activity" means the commission of, attempted commission of, conspiracy to commit, or solicitation of two or more underlying crimes or acts by a juvenile that would be an underlying crime if committed by an adult, provided the crimes or acts were not part of the same incident.

(e) *Solicit.* — "Solicit" has the meaning stated in § 11-301 of this article.

(f) *Underlying crime.* — "Underlying crime" means:

(1) a crime of violence as defined under § 14-101 of this article;

(2) a violation of § 3-203 (second degree assault), § 4-203 (wearing, carrying, or transporting a handgun), § 9-302 (inducing false testimony or avoidance of subpoena), § 9-303 (retaliation for testimony), § 9-305 (intimidating or corrupting juror), § 11-303 (human trafficking), § 11-304 (receiving earnings of prostitute), or § 11-306 (a)(2), (3), or (4) (house of prostitution) of this article;

(3) a felony violation of § 3-701 (extortion), § 4-503 (manufacture or possession of destructive device), § 5-602 (distribution of CDS), § 5-603 (manufacturing CDS or equipment), § 6-103 (second degree arson), § 6-202 (first degree burglary), § 6-203 (second degree burglary), § 6-204 (third degree burglary), § 7-104 (theft), or § 7-105 (unauthorized use of a motor vehicle) of this article; or

(4) a felony violation of § 5-133 of the Public Safety Article. (2005, ch. 313; 2007, ch. 496; 2009, ch. 684; 2010, ch. 197.)

Effect of amendments. — Chapter 684, Acts 2009, effective October 1, 2009, added "§ 5-603" in (f)(2).

Chapter 197, Acts 2010, effective October 1, 2010, deleted "ongoing" following "group or" in the introductory language of (c); rewrote (c)(3); added (f)(2); redesignated accordingly; and rewrote (f)(3).

Editor's note. — Section 2, ch. 313, Acts 2005, provides that "this Act may not be construed to limit prosecution for a violation of any other provision of law with respect to any activity that constitutes a violation of this Act."

§ 9-802. Criminal gang activity.

(a) *In general.* — A person may not threaten an individual, or a friend or family member of an individual, with physical violence with the intent to coerce, induce, or solicit the individual to participate in or prevent the individual from leaving a criminal gang.

(b) *Penalties.* — A person who violates this section is guilty of a misdemeanor and on conviction is subject to imprisonment not exceeding 2 years or a fine not exceeding $1,000 or both. (2005, ch. 313; 2006, ch. 44.)

§ 9-803. Criminal gang activity — Schools.

(a) *Activities on or near school vehicles or property.* — A person may not threaten an individual, or a friend or family member of an individual, with or use physical violence to coerce, induce, or solicit the individual to participate in or prevent the individual from leaving a criminal gang:

(1) in a school vehicle, as defined under § 11-154 of the Transportation Article; or

(2) in, on, or within 1,000 feet of real property owned by or leased to an elementary school, secondary school, or county board of education and used for elementary or secondary education.

(b) *Applicability.* — Subsection (a) of this section applies whether or not:

(1) school was in session at the time of the crime; or

(2) the real property was being used for purposes other than school purposes at the time of the crime.

(c) *Penalties.* — A person who violates this section is guilty of a misdemeanor and on conviction is subject to imprisonment not exceeding 4 years or a fine not exceeding $4,000 or both.

(d) *Merger with § 9-802 conviction prohibited.* — Notwithstanding any other law, a conviction under this section may not merge with a conviction under § 9-802 of this subtitle. (2005, ch. 313.)

§ 9-804. Participation in criminal gang prohibited.

(a) *Prohibited acts.* — A person may not:

(1) participate in a criminal gang knowing that the members of the gang engage in a pattern of criminal gang activity; and

(2) knowingly and willfully direct or participate in an underlying crime, or act by a juvenile that would be an underlying crime if committed by an adult, committed for the benefit of, at the direction of, or in association with a criminal gang.

(b) *Commission of underlying crime resulting in death of victim.* — A person may not violate subsection (a) of this section that results in the death of a victim.

(c) *Penalty.* — (1) (i) Except as provided in subparagraph (ii) of this paragraph, a person who violates this section is guilty of a felony and on conviction is subject to imprisonment not exceeding 10 years or a fine not exceeding $100,000 or both.

(ii) A person who violates subsection (b) of this section is guilty of a felony and on conviction is subject to imprisonment not exceeding 20 years or a fine not exceeding $100,000 or both.

(2) (i) A sentence imposed under paragraph (1)(i) of this subsection for a first offense may be separate from and consecutive to or concurrent with a sentence for any crime based on the act establishing a violation of this section.

(ii) A sentence imposed under paragraph (1)(i) of this subsection for a second or subsequent offense, or paragraph (1)(ii) of this subsection shall be separate from and consecutive to a sentence for any crime based on the act establishing a violation of this section.

(iii) A consecutive sentence for a second or subsequent offense shall not be mandatory unless the State notifies the person in writing of the State's intention to proceed against the person as a second or subsequent offender at least 30 days before trial.

(d) *Charging documents.* — A person may be charged with a violation of this section only by indictment, criminal information, or petition alleging a delinquent act.

(e) *Authority of Attorney General.* — (1) The Attorney General, at the request of the State's Attorney for a county in which a violation or an act establishing a violation of this section occurs, may:

(i) aid in the investigation of the violation or act; and

(ii) prosecute the violation or act.

(2) In exercising authority under paragraph (1) of this subsection, the Attorney General has all the powers and duties of a State's Attorney, including the use of the grand jury in the county, to prosecute the violation.

(3) Notwithstanding any other provision of law, in circumstances in which violations of this section are alleged to have been committed in more than one county, the respective State's Attorney of each county, or the Attorney General, may join the causes of action in a single complaint with the consent of each State's Attorney having jurisdiction over an offense sought to be joined.

(f) *Powers of grand jury — Offenses in other counties.* — Notwithstanding any other provision of law and provided at least one criminal gang activity of a criminal gang allegedly occurred in the county in which a grand jury is sitting, the grand jury may issue subpoenas, summon witnesses, and otherwise conduct an investigation of the alleged criminal gang's activities and offenses in other counties. (2007, ch. 496; 2010, ch. 197; 2011, ch. 65.)

Effect of amendments. — Chapter 197, Acts 2010, effective October 1, 2010, substituted "a pattern" for "an ongoing pattern" in (a)(1); in (a)(2) deleted "the commission of" following "participate in"; in (b) substituted "violate" for "commit a violation of" and deleted "involving the commission of an underlying crime" following "section"; and rewrote (c)(2).

Chapter 65, Acts 2011, enacted April 12, 2011, and effective from date of enactment, ratified a previously made technical correction in (c)(2)(i).

§ 9-805. Criminal gang.

(a) *Prohibition.* — A person may not organize, supervise, finance, or manage a criminal gang.

(b) *Penalty.* — A person who violates this section is guilty of a felony and on conviction is subject to imprisonment not exceeding 20 years or a fine not exceeding $100,000 or both.

(c) *Separate and consecutive sentence.* — A sentence imposed under this section shall be separate from and consecutive to a sentence for any crime based on the act establishing a violation of this section. (2010, ch. 197.)

Editor's note. — Section 2, Chapter 197, Acts 2010, provides that the Act shall take effect October 1, 2010.

§ 9-806. Construction of subtitle.

Nothing in this subtitle may be construed inconsistently with the provisions relating to jurisdiction over juvenile causes contained in Title 3, Subtitle 8A of the Courts Article. (2010, ch. 197.)

Editor's note. — Section 2, Chapter 197, Acts 2010, provides that the Act shall take effect October 1, 2010.

Subtitle 1. Crimes Against Public Health and Safety.

Part I. General Provisions.

§ 10-101. Definitions.

(a) *In general.* — In this part the following words have the meanings indicated.

SPECIAL REVISOR'S NOTE

As enacted by Ch. 26, Acts of 2002, this subsection formerly was Art. 27, § 404(a)(1). However, Chs. 108 and 109, and Ch. 213, § 6, Acts of 2002, each added a new part "Part I. General Provisions" before this subsection, and substituted the reference to this "part" for the reference to this "subtitle" enacted by Ch. 26. Also, Chs. 108 and 109 each added §§ 10-113 through 10-117 under a new part "Part II. Alcoholic Beverage Consumption or Possession of Open Container in Passenger Area of Motor Vehicle". Also, Ch. 213, § 1, transferred Article 2B, §§ 22-101 through 22-108, as enacted by Ch. 26, § 4, to be §§ 10-113 through 10-120, under the new part "Part II. Alcoholic Beverages Violations". Precedence in numbering has been given to Ch. 213 as the later enactment. *See* Art. 1, § 17. Accordingly, the sections transferred by Ch. 213, § 1, appear as §§ 10-113 through 10-120 under Part II, and the sections enacted by Chs. 108 and 109 appear as §§ 10-123 through 10-127 under Part III.

In this subsection, the reference to this "subtitle" was substituted by Ch. 26 for the former reference to this "subheading" to reflect the organization of material derived from the former subheading on the sale of cigars and tobacco products to minors. Its application in Ch. 26 to the material derived from the former subheading on venereal disease remedies was not a substantive change. The defined term "tobacco product" was not used by Ch. 26 in the sections in this subtitle that dealt with venereal diseases. The word "distributed" was used in § 10-102(a)(3) of this subtitle, but the definition of "distribute" in subsection (b) of this section did not materially change the meaning of the term as used by Ch. 26 in § 10-102(a)(3) of this subtitle.

No other changes were made by Ch. 26.

(b) *Distribute.* — "Distribute" means to:

(1) give, sell, deliver, dispense, issue, or offer to give, sell, deliver, dispense, or issue; or

(2) cause or hire a person to give, sell, deliver, dispense, issue or offer to give, sell, deliver, dispense, or issue.

REVISOR'S NOTE

This subsection is new language derived without substantive change from former Art. 27, § 404(a)(3).

Defined term:
"Person"   § 1-101

(c) *Tobacco paraphernalia.* — (1) "Tobacco paraphernalia" means any object used, intended for use, or designed for use in inhaling or otherwise introducing tobacco products into the human body.

(2) "Tobacco paraphernalia" includes:

(i) a cigarette rolling paper;

(ii) a metal, wooden, acrylic, glass, stone, plastic, or ceramic pipe with or without screen, permanent screen, or punctured metal bowl;

(iii) a water pipe;

(iv) a carburetion tube or device;

(v) a smoking or carburetion mask;

(vi) an object known as a roach clip used to hold burning material, such as a cigarette that has become too small or too short to be held in the hand;

(vii) a chamber pipe;

(viii) a carburetor pipe;

(ix) an electric pipe;

(x) an air-driven pipe;

(xi) a chillum;

(xii) a bong; and

(xiii) an ice pipe or chiller.

(d) *Tobacco product.* — (1) "Tobacco product" means a substance containing tobacco.

(2) "Tobacco product" includes cigarettes, **cigars**, smoking tobacco, snuff, smokeless tobacco, and candy-like products that contain tobacco.

REVISOR'S NOTE

This subsection is new language derived without substantive change from former Art. 27, § 404(a)(2).

(e) *Venereal disease.* — "Venereal disease" includes gonorrhea, syphilis, chancroid, and any diseased condition of the human genitalia caused by, related to, or resulting from a venereal disease.

REVISOR'S NOTE

This subsection is new language derived without substantive change from the first sentences of former Art. 27, §§ 322 and 323 as they related to a description of the covered diseases.

The former references to "any other venereal disease" are deleted in light of the reference to

"includes" which indicates that the three named types of the disease are named by way of illustration and not by way of limitation. *See* Art. 1, § 30.

(An. Code 1957, art. 27, §§ 322, 323, 404(a); 2002, ch. 26, § 2; ch. 108, § 1; ch. 109, § 1; ch. 213, § 6; 2003, ch. 115; 2007, ch. 218.)

REVISOR'S NOTE TO SECTION

The Revisor's notes in this section comprise information related to the revision by Acts 2002, ch. 26.

Cross references. — As to alcoholic beverage consumption or possession of open container in passenger area of motor vehicle, *see* Title 10, Subtitle 1, Part III of this article.

As to jurisdiction in actions under Title 10, Subtitle 1, Part III of this article, concerning alcoholic beverage consumption or possession of open container in passenger area of motor vehicle, *see* § 4-401 of the Courts Article.

As to prohibition against alcoholic beverage consumption in passenger area of motor vehicle, *see* § 21-903 of the Transportation Article.

§ 10-102. Venereal disease — Advertising cure.

(a) *Scope of section.* — This section does not apply to:

(1) a government unit;

(2) a health or medical agency approved by the Secretary of Health and Mental Hygiene;

(3) a medical, pharmaceutical, or other professional publication not publicly distributed; or

(4) a news item or article published in a newspaper, magazine, or book.

(b) *Prohibited.* — A person may not advertise, allow to be advertised, or call to public attention:

(1) a drug, medicine, preparation, or substance for the treatment, alleviation, or cure of venereal disease; or

(2) a person from whom or a place where a drug, medicine, preparation, or substance for the treatment, alleviation, or cure of venereal disease may be obtained.

(c) *Penalty.* — A person who violates this section is guilty of a misdemeanor and on conviction is subject to a fine not exceeding $500 for each violation. (An. Code 1957, art. 27, § 322; 2002, ch. 26, § 2.)

REVISOR'S NOTE

This Revisor's note comprises information related to the revision by Acts 2002, ch. 26.

This section is new language derived without substantive change from former Art. 27, § 322, as it related to the prohibition of and penalty for advertising a cure for venereal disease.

In subsection (a)(1) of this section, the phrase "government unit" is substituted for the former reference to "governmental agency" for consistency within this article. *See* General Revisor's Note to article.

Also in subsection (a)(1) of this section, the former reference to a "health department" is deleted as included in the reference to a "government unit".

In subsection (a)(2) of this section, the phrase "with the approval of the Secretary of Health and Mental Hygiene" is substituted for the former phrase "approved under this section by the Secretary of Health and Mental Hygiene" to clarify that with the approval of the Secretary, the prohibitions of this section do not apply to a health or medical agency.

In subsection (a)(3) of this section, the former reference to the "sale" of certain publications is deleted in light of the defined term "distribute", which includes to "sell".

In subsection (a)(4) of this section, the former phrases "bona fide" are deleted as surplusage.

In subsection (b) of this section, the former reference to a "firm, company or corporation" is deleted in light of the defined term "person".

Also in subsection (b) of this section, the former reference to calling to public attention "in any manner whatsoever" is deleted as surplusage.

In subsection (b)(2) of this section, the phrase "treatment, alleviation, or cure of venereal disease" is added for clarity.

The Criminal Law Article Review Committee notes, for the consideration of the General Assembly, that it is unclear whether the exemptions listed in subsection (a)(3) and (4) of this section apply to publication or republication by electronic means, including the Internet, which may make available to the public advertisements that are not initially intended for public distribution.

The Criminal Law Article Review Committee also notes, for the consideration of the General Assembly, that the general prohibition on advertising or calling to public attention a treatment for venereal disease or a source for that treatment may constitute a prior restraint on speech, a content-based restriction that raises free-speech concerns under the First Amendment to the United States Constitution and Md. Decl. of Rights, Art. 40.

Defined terms:

"Distribute"	§ 10-101
"Person"	§ 1-101
"Venereal disease"	§ 10-101

§ 10-103. Venereal disease — Sale of remedy.

(a) *Scope of section.* — This section does not apply to:

(1) a physician licensed to practice medicine;

(2) a government unit; or

(3) the otherwise lawful conduct of business between commercial, medical, pharmaceutical, scientific, or government units.

(b) *Prohibited.* — Except in accordance with a prescription written by a physician licensed to practice medicine, a person may not sell, dispense, or give to another a drug, medicine, preparation, substance, or a preparation containing a sulfonamide drug to alleviate, treat, or cure venereal disease.

(c) *Requirements for prescription.* — (1) A prescription under subsection (b) of this section shall include:

(i) the physician's signature and address; and

(ii) the date the prescription was written.

(2) The person filling the prescription required under subsection (b) of this section:

(i) shall write on the prescription the date it was filled;

(ii) shall keep the prescription on file for at least 2 years after it was filled;

(iii) shall allow the prescription to be inspected by State and local health authorities; and

(iv) may not refill the prescription except on the order of the physician who wrote the prescription.

(d) *Penalty.* — A person who violates this section is guilty of a misdemeanor and on conviction is subject to a fine not exceeding:

(1) $50 for the first violation; and

(2) $250 for each subsequent violation. (An. Code 1957, art. 27, § 323; 2002, ch. 26, § 2.)

REVISOR'S NOTE

This Revisor's note comprises information related to the revision by Acts 2002, ch. 26.

This section is new language derived without substantive change from former Art. 27, § 323, as it related to the prohibition of and penalty for sale of a remedy for venereal disease.

In subsection (a)(2) and (3) of this section, the phrase "government unit[s]" is substituted for the former references to "governmental agency" and "governmental agencies" for consistency within this article. *See* General Revisor's Note to article.

In subsection (a)(2) of this section, the former reference to a "health department" is deleted as included in the reference to a "government unit".

In subsection (b) of this section, the former reference to a "firm, company or corporation" is deleted in light of the defined term "person".

Also in subsection (b) of this section, the first former reference to a "sulfonamide drug" is deleted in light of the comprehensive reference to a "drug".

Subsection (c)(2) of this section clarifies that the person who fills the prescription, who in most cases is not the physician who wrote the prescription, shall write on the prescription the date it was filled, shall keep the prescription on file for 2 years, and shall keep the prescription open for inspection.

Defined terms:

"Person"	§ 1-101
"Venereal disease"	§ 10-101

§ 10-104. Sale of nonlatex condom by vending machine.

(a) *Prohibited.* — A person may not sell or offer for sale a nonlatex condom by means of a vending machine or other automatic device.

(b) *Penalty.* — (1) A person who violates this section is guilty of a misdemeanor and on conviction is subject to a fine not exceeding $1,000 for each violation.

(2) Each vending machine or other automatic device in violation of this section is a separate violation. (An. Code 1957, art. 27, § 41; 2002, ch. 26, § 2.)

REVISOR'S NOTE

This Revisor's note comprises information related to the revision by Acts 2002, ch. 26.

This section is new language derived without substantive change from former Art. 27, § 41.

In subsection (a) of this section, the former reference to a "firm, or corporation" is deleted in light of the defined term "person".

Defined term:

"Person"	§ 1-101

§ 10-105. Sale of contraceptive by vending machine in school.

(a) *Prohibited.* — A person may not sell or offer for sale a contraceptive or a contraceptive device, whether or not advertised as a prophylactic, by means of a vending machine or other automatic device at a kindergarten, nursery school, or elementary or secondary school.

(b) *Penalty.* — (1) A person who violates this section is guilty of a misdemeanor and on conviction is subject to a fine not exceeding $1,000 for each violation.

(2) Each vending machine or other automatic device in a school is a separate violation. (An. Code 1957, art. 27, § 41A; 2002, ch. 26, § 2.)

This Revisor's note comprises information related to the revision by Acts 2002, ch. 26.

This section is new language derived without substantive change from former Art. 27, § 41A.

In subsection (a) of this section, the former definition of "school" is incorporated as part of the substantive provision because the term is only used once.

Also in subsection (a) of this section, the reference to "[a] person" is added for clarity.

In subsection (b) of this section, the former reference to a "firm, or corporation" is deleted in light of the defined term "person".

Also in subsection (b) of this section, the phrase "is guilty of a misdemeanor" is added to state expressly that which was only implied in the former law by reference to a person who is "convicted". In this State, any crime that was not a felony at common law and has not been declared a felony by statute is considered to be a misdemeanor. *See State v. Canova*, 278 Md. 483, 490 (1976), *Bowser v. State*, 136 Md. 342, 345 (1920), *Dutton v. State*, 123 Md. 373, 378 (1914), and *Williams v. State*, 4 Md. App. 342, 347 (1968).

Defined term:
"Person" § 1-101

Cited in State v. Raines, 383 Md. 1, 857 A.2d 19 (2004); Att'y Griev. Comm'n v. Tanko, 408 Md. 404, 969 A.2d 1010 (2009).

§ 10-106. Sale of clove cigarettes.

(a) *Prohibited.* — A person may not sell or offer for sale a clove cigarette.

(b) *Penalty.* — A person who violates this section is guilty of a misdemeanor and on conviction is subject to a fine of $500. (An. Code 1957, art. 27, § 40A; 2002, ch. 26, § 2.)

This Revisor's note comprises information related to the revision by Acts 2002, ch. 26.

This section is new language derived without substantive change from former Art. 27, § 40A.

In subsection (a) of this section, the former reference to the "State" is deleted as surplusage.

Defined term:
"Person" § 1-101

Cited in State v. Raines, 383 Md. 1, 857 A.2d 19 (2004).

§ 10-107. Distribution of tobacco product or paraphernalia to minor.

(a) *Scope of section.* — This section does not apply to the distribution of a coupon that is redeemable for a tobacco product, if the coupon is:

(1) contained in a newspaper, magazine, or other type of publication in which the coupon is incidental to the primary purpose of the publication; or

(2) sent through the mail.

(b) *Prohibited — By distributor of tobacco.* — (1) This subsection does not apply to the distribution of a tobacco product or tobacco paraphernalia to a minor who is acting solely as the agent of the minor's employer if the employer distributes tobacco products or tobacco paraphernalia for commercial purposes.

(2) A person who distributes tobacco products for commercial purposes, including a person licensed under Title 16 of the Business Regulation Article, may not distribute to a minor:

(i) a tobacco product;

(ii) tobacco paraphernalia; or

(iii) a coupon redeemable for a tobacco product.

(c) *Prohibited — By other person.* — A person not described in subsection (b)(2) of this section may not:

(1) purchase for or sell a tobacco product to a minor; or

(2) distribute tobacco paraphernalia to a minor.

(d) *Defense.* — In a prosecution for a violation of this section, it is a defense that the defendant examined the purchaser's or recipient's driver's license or other valid identification issued by an employer, government unit, or institution of higher education that positively identified the purchaser or recipient as at least 18 years of age.

(e) *Penalty.* — A person who violates this section is guilty of a misdemeanor and on conviction is subject to a fine not exceeding:

(1) $300 for a first violation;

(2) $1,000 for a second violation occurring within 2 years after the first violation; and

(3) $3,000 for each subsequent violation occurring within 2 years after the preceding violation.

(f) *Separate incident a violation.* — For purposes of this section, each separate incident at a different time and occasion is a violation. (An. Code 1957, art. 27, §§ 404(b)-(d), 405; 2002, ch. 26, § 2; 2003, ch. 115; 2007, ch. 218.)

REVISOR'S NOTE

This Revisor's note comprises information related to the revision by Acts 2002, ch. 26.

This section is new language derived without substantive change from former Art. 27, §§ 404(b) through (d) and 405.

In subsection (a)(1) of this section, the defined term "minor" is substituted for the former reference to "a person under 18" for clarity.

In subsection (b)(1) of this section, the phrase "if the minor's employer distributes tobacco products for commercial purposes" is substituted for the former reference to an employer "who is in the business of distributing tobacco products" for clarity.

In subsection (b)(2) of this section, the former reference to "selling" tobacco products is deleted in light of the defined term "distribute", which includes to "sell".

In subsection (c)(2) of this section, the defined term "distribute" is substituted for the former references to "sell" and "[d]eliver" for consistency within this subtitle.

In subsection (d) of this section, the phrase "government unit" is substituted for the former reference to a "governmental entity" for consistency within this article. *See* General Revisor's Note to article.

In subsection (e) of this section, the phrase "is guilty of a misdemeanor" is added to state expressly that which only was implied in the former law. In this State, any crime that was not a felony at common law and has not been declared a felony by statute is considered to be a misdemeanor. *See State v. Canova,* 278 Md. 483, 490 (1976), *Bowser v. State,* 136 Md. 342, 345 (1920), *Dutton v. State,* 123 Md. 373, 378 (1914), and *Williams v. State,* 4 Md. App. 342, 347 (1968).

In subsection (e)(3) of this section, the reference to "each" subsequent violation is substituted for the former reference to "a third or" subsequent violation for consistency within this article.

Defined terms:
    "Distribute"   § 10-101

| "Minor" | § 1-101 | "Tobacco product" | § 10-101 |
| "Person" | § 1-101 | | |

§ 10-108. Possession of tobacco product by minor; use of false identification.

(a) *"Violation" defined.* — In this section, "violation" has the meaning stated in § 3-8A-01 of the Courts Article.

(b) *Scope of section.* — This section does not apply to the possession of a tobacco product or cigarette rolling paper by a minor who is acting as the agent of the minor's employer within the scope of employment.

(c) *Prohibited.* — A minor may not:

(1) use or possess a tobacco product or cigarette rolling paper; or

(2) obtain or attempt to obtain a tobacco product or cigarette rolling paper by using a form of identification that:

(i) is falsified; or

(ii) identifies an individual other than the minor.

(d) *Penalty.* — (1) A violation of this section is a civil offense.

(2) A minor who violates this section is subject to the procedures and dispositions provided in Title 3, Subtitle 8A of the Courts Article.

(e) *Citation.* — A law enforcement officer authorized to make arrests shall issue a citation to a minor if the law enforcement officer has probable cause to believe that the minor is committing or has committed a violation of this section. (An. Code 1957, art. 27, § 406; 2002, ch. 26, § 2; 2003, ch. 115.)

REVISOR'S NOTE

This Revisor's note comprises information related to the revision by Acts 2002, ch. 26.

This section is new language derived without substantive change from former Art. 27, § 406.

Subsection (a) of this section is revised as a cross-reference to the defined term "violation" in CJ § 3-8A-01 for clarity.

In subsection (c)(2) of this section, the reference to a "form of identification" is new language added for clarity.

In subsection (c)(2)(ii) of this section, the reference to identification that "identifies an individual" is new language added for clarity.

In subsections (d) and (e) of this section, the defined term "minor" is substituted for the former references to "individual", "person", and "child" for clarity.

In subsection (d)(2) of this section, the reference to CJ "Title 3, Subtitle 8A" is substituted for the former obsolete reference to CJ "Title 3, Subtitle 8" which was rendered incorrect by the reorganization of material related to juvenile causes. *See* Ch. 415, Acts of 2001.

In subsection (e) of this section, the former reference to the "Code" is deleted as unnecessary in light of the defined term "violation".

Defined terms:
| "Minor" | § 1-101 |
| "Tobacco product" | § 10-101 |

Violation not sufficient to justify warrantless search. — Violation of this section, by defendant, a 17-year old smoking a cigarette, was a civil offense and did not justify the warrantless search of defendant for additional tobacco products; among other things, the exigent circumstances exception to the warrant requirement was not applicable as the cigarettes were not "contraband," and the search could not be justified as a legitimate stop-and-frisk under Terry because no effort was made to justify the search based on a reasonable concern for officer safety. In re Calvin S., 175 Md. App. 516, 930 A.2d 1099 (2007).

§ 10-109. Abandoned refrigerator.

(a) *Prohibited.* — A person may not place or allow to be placed outside of a building or dwelling an abandoned or discarded refrigerator, icebox, or freezer cabinet that:

(1) is in a place accessible to children;

(2) is uncrated; and

(3) has a door or a lock that cannot be released for opening from the inside.

(b) *Penalty.* — A person who violates this section is guilty of a misdemeanor and on conviction is subject to imprisonment not exceeding 30 days or a fine not exceeding $100 or both. (An. Code 1957, art. 27, § 334; 2002, ch. 26, § 2.)

REVISOR'S NOTE

This Revisor's note comprises information related to the revision by Acts 2002, ch. 26.

This section is new language derived without substantive change from former Art. 27, § 334.

The former references to a "firm or corporation" are deleted in light of the defined term "person".

In subsection (b) of this section, the former reference to a "jail" is deleted for consistency within this article. Currently, inmates are sentenced to the custody of a unit such as the Division of Correction and then are placed in a particular facility. See CS § 9-103.

Also in subsection (b) of this section, the reference to "both" a fine or imprisonment is substituted for the former reference to "in the discretion of the court" for clarity and consistency within this article.

Defined term:
  "Person"   § 1-101

§ 10-110. Litter Control Law.

(a) *Definitions.* — (1) In this section the following words have the meanings indicated.

(2) "Bi-county unit" means:

(i) the Maryland-National Capital Park and Planning Commission; or

(ii) the Washington Suburban Sanitary Commission.

(3) "Litter" means all rubbish, waste matter, refuse, garbage, trash, debris, dead animals, or other discarded materials of every kind and description.

(4) "Public or private property" means:

(i) the right-of-way of a road or highway;

(ii) a body of water or watercourse or the shores or beaches of a body of water or watercourse;

(iii) a park;

(iv) a parking facility;

(v) a playground;

(vi) public service company property or transmission line right-of-way;

(vii) a building;

(viii) a refuge or conservation or recreation area;

(ix) residential or farm property; or

(x) timberlands or a forest.

(b) *Declaration of intent.* — The General Assembly intends to:

(1) prohibit uniformly throughout the State the improper disposal of litter on public or private property; and

(2) curb the desecration of the beauty of the State and harm to the health, welfare, and safety of its citizens caused by the improper disposal of litter.

(c) *Prohibited.* — A person may not:

(1) dispose of litter on a highway or perform an act that violates the State Vehicle Laws regarding disposal of litter, glass, and other prohibited substances on highways; or

(2) dispose or cause or allow the disposal of litter on public or private property unless:

(i) the property is designated by the State, a unit of the State, or a political subdivision of the State for the disposal of litter and the person is authorized by the proper public authority to use the property; or

(ii) the litter is placed into a litter receptacle or container installed on the property.

(d) *Presumption of responsibility.* — If two or more individuals are occupying a motor vehicle, boat, airplane, or other conveyance from which litter is disposed in violation of subsection (c) of this section, and it cannot be determined which occupant is the violator:

(1) if present, the owner of the conveyance is presumed to be responsible for the violation; or

(2) if the owner of the conveyance is not present, the operator is presumed to be responsible for the violation.

(e) *Property owner not in court.* — Notwithstanding any other law, if the facts of a case in which a person is charged with violating this section are sufficient to prove that the person is responsible for the violation, the owner of the property on which the violation allegedly occurred need not be present at a court proceeding regarding the case.

(f) *Penalty.* — (1) A person who violates this section is subject to the penalties provided in this subsection.

(2) (i) A person who disposes of litter in violation of this section in an amount not exceeding 100 pounds or 27 cubic feet and not for commercial gain is guilty of a misdemeanor and on conviction is subject to imprisonment not exceeding 30 days or a fine not exceeding $1,500 or both.

(ii) A person who disposes of litter in violation of this section in an amount exceeding 100 pounds or 27 cubic feet, but not exceeding 500 pounds or 216 cubic feet, and not for commercial gain is guilty of a misdemeanor and on conviction is subject to imprisonment not exceeding 1 year or a fine not exceeding $12,500 or both.

(iii) A person who disposes of litter in violation of this section in an amount exceeding 500 pounds or 216 cubic feet or in any amount for commercial gain is guilty of a misdemeanor and on conviction is subject to imprisonment not exceeding 5 years or a fine not exceeding $30,000 or both.

(3) In addition to the penalties provided under paragraph (2) of this subsection, a court may order the violator to:

(i) remove or render harmless the litter disposed of in violation of this section;

(ii) repair or restore any property damaged by, or pay damages for, the disposal of the litter in violation of this section;

(iii) perform public service relating to the removal of litter disposed of in violation of this section or to the restoration of an area polluted by litter disposed of in violation of this section; or

(iv) reimburse the State, county, municipal corporation, or bi-county unit for its costs incurred in removing the litter disposed of in violation of this section.

(4) In addition to, or instead of, the penalties provided in paragraphs (2) and (3) of this subsection, the court may suspend for up to 7 days the license of the person to operate the type of conveyance used in the violation who is presumed to be responsible for the violation under subsection (d) of this section.

(g) *Enforcement.* — A law enforcement unit, officer, or official of the State or a political subdivision of the State, or an enforcement unit, officer, or official of a commission of the State, or a political subdivision of the State, shall enforce compliance with this section.

(h) *Receptacles to be provided; notice of provisions.* — A unit that supervises State property shall:

(1) establish and maintain receptacles for the disposal of litter at appropriate locations where the public frequents the property;

(2) post signs directing persons to the receptacles and serving notice of the provisions of this section; and

(3) otherwise publicize the availability of litter receptacles and the requirements of this section.

(i) *Disposition of fines.* — (1) Fines collected for violations of this section shall be disbursed:

(i) to the county or municipal corporation where the violation occurred; or

(ii) if the bi-county unit is the enforcement unit and the violations occurred on property over which the bi-county unit exercises jurisdiction, to the bi-county unit.

(2) Fines collected shall be used to pay for litter receptacles and posting signs as required by subsection (h) of this section and for other purposes relating to the removal or control of litter.

(j) *Authority of local governments.* — (1) The legislative body of a municipal corporation may:

(i) prohibit littering; and

(ii) classify littering as a municipal infraction under Article 23A, § 3(b) of the Code.

(2) The governing body of Prince George's County may adopt an ordinance to prohibit littering under this section and, for violations of the ordinance, may impose criminal penalties and civil penalties that do not exceed the criminal penalties and civil penalties specified in subsection (f)(1) through (3) of this section.

(k) *Short title.* — This section may be cited as the "Litter Control Law". (An. Code 1957, art. 27, § 468(a), (b), (c)(1), (2), (4), (5), (d)-(j); 2002, ch. 26, § 2; 2004, ch. 214.)

REVISOR'S NOTE

This Revisor's note comprises information related to the revision by Acts 2002, ch. 26.

This section is new language derived without substantive change from former Art. 27, § 468(a), (b), (c)(1), (2), (4), and (5), and (d) through (j).

Throughout this section, the words "dispose", "disposed", and "disposal" are substituted for various former references to "dump[ing]", "deposit[ing]", "drop[ping]", "throw[ing]", "leav[ing]", "put[ting]", and "plac[ing]" litter for clarity and brevity.

Also throughout this section, the defined term "litter" is substituted for various former references to "trash", "garbage", "junk", and "refuse" for clarity and brevity.

In subsection (a) of this section, the former definition of "commercial purpose" is deleted as unnecessary. Throughout this section, the phrase "economic gain", which was the definition of "commercial purpose", is substituted for former references to "commercial purposes" for clarity.

In subsections (a)(2), (f)(3)(iv), and (i)(1)(ii) of this section, the references to a bi-county "unit" are substituted for the former references to a bi-county "agency" for consistency within this article. *See* General Revisor's Note to article. Similarly, in subsections (c)(2)(i), (g), and (h) of this section, the references to a "unit" of the State are substituted for the former references to "agencies" of the State and State "authorit[ies]". Also similarly, in subsection (i)(1)(ii) of this section, the reference to an enforcement "unit" is substituted for the former reference to an enforcement "agency".

In subsection (b) of this section, the reference to the "General Assembly" is substituted for the former reference to the "legislature" for consistency throughout the revised articles of the Code.

Also in subsection (b) of this section, the former reference to making provision "by this section" for uniform litter control is deleted as surplusage.

In subsections (b)(1) and (c)(1) of this section, the former references to "Maryland" are deleted as unnecessary.

In subsection (b)(1) and (2) of this section, the references to "disposal of litter" are substituted for the former references to "littering" and "litter" for consistency within this section.

In subsection (b)(2) of this section, the reference to "citizens" of the State is retained. The term "citizens", however, lacks a precise legal meaning and is usually read to refer to residency. *See Crosse v. Board of Supervisors of Elections of Baltimore City*, 243 Md. 555 (1966).

In subsection (c)(2) of this section, the former reference to disposing of litter "in this State, or any waters in this State" is deleted as unnecessary in light of the defined term "public or private property", which includes a reference to "waters".

In subsection (d)(1) and (2) of this section, the former references to a "vehicle, boat, airplane or other conveyance" are deleted as included in the comprehensive references to a "conveyance".

In subsection (f)(2) of this section, the former phrases "in weight" and "in volume" are deleted as implicit in the references to particular "pounds" and "cubic feet".

In subsection (f)(2)(iii) of this section, the word "amount" is substituted for the former reference to "quantity" for consistency within the section.

In subsection (f)(3) of this section, the word "penalties" is substituted for the former reference to "sentences", because the sanctions provided in subsection (f)(2) of the section are penalties.

Subsection (f)(4) of this section clarifies that a court may order the suspension of the license to operate the conveyance.

In subsections (g) and (h) of this section, the word "shall" is substituted for the former phrases "are hereby authorized, empowered, and directed to" and "are authorized, empowered and instructed to", respectively, for clarity. If the units are "directed to" or "instructed to" enforce this section, then they are by implication "authorized [and] empowered" to do so.

In subsection (h) of this section, the reference to a "municipal corporation" is substituted for the former reference to a "city" for consistency with the usage in Md. Constitution, Art. XI-E.

In subsection (i)(2) of this section, the reference to using collected fines to "pay for litter receptacles" is substituted for the former reference to "defray[ing] the expense of establishment and maintenance of receptacles" for brevity and clarity.

In subsection (j) of this section, the former phrase "[h]owever, to permit more active enforcement of littering prohibitions within a municipality" is deleted as surplusage. There is no need to state why the municipal corporations are given the authority granted in the subsection.

Former Art. 27, § 468(c)(3), which defined "person", is revised in § 1-101 of this article.

Former Art. 27, § 468(k), which authorized the Washington County Board of County Commissioners to regulate recycling by ordinance, is revised in Art. 22, § 1-704 of the Public Local Laws of Washington County.

The Criminal Law Article Review Committee notes, for the consideration of the General Assembly, that under its over half-decade old "Maryland Parks Are Trash-Free" program, the

Department of Natural Resources has removed trash receptacles from the parks under its jurisdiction. The Department's website notes that "[v]isitors to day-use areas are provided with bags when they enter parks and are asked to take home their own refuse". Nevertheless, the Department is arguably in violation of subsection (h) of this section, notwithstanding the Department's belief in the success of the program.

Defined terms:
"County"   § 1-101
"Person"   § 1-101

Cross references. — As to disposition of fines, penalties and forfeitures collected by clerks of District Court, see § 7-302 of the Courts Article.

§ 10-111. Altering results of drug or alcohol screening test.

(a) *Definitions.* — (1) In this section the following words have the meanings indicated.

(2) "Bodily fluid" means blood, urine, saliva, or other bodily fluid.

(3) (i) "Bodily fluid adulterant" means any substance or chemical that is intended, for the purpose of altering the results of a drug or alcohol screening test, to be:

1. consumed by a person;

2. introduced into the body of a person; or

3. added to or substituted for a sample of bodily fluid.

(ii) "Bodily fluid adulterant" includes synthetic urine.

(4) "Controlled dangerous substance" has the meaning stated in § 5-101 of this article.

(5) "Drug" has the meaning stated in § 5-101 of this article.

(6) "Drug or alcohol screening test" means an analysis of a sample of bodily fluid collected from a person for the purpose of detecting the presence of alcohol, drugs, or a controlled dangerous substance in the bodily fluid of the person.

(b) *Prohibited.* — A person may not, with intent to defraud or alter the outcome of a drug or alcohol screening test:

(1) alter a bodily fluid sample;

(2) substitute a bodily fluid sample, in whole or in part, with:

(i) a bodily fluid sample of another person or animal; or

(ii) any other substance;

(3) possess or use a bodily fluid adulterant;

(4) sell, distribute, or offer to sell or distribute:

(i) any bodily fluid from a human or any animal; or

(ii) any bodily fluid adulterant; or

(5) transport into the State:

(i) any bodily fluid from a human or any animal; or

(ii) any bodily fluid adulterant.

(c) *Penalty.* — A person who violates this section is guilty of:

(1) for a first violation, a misdemeanor and on conviction is subject to imprisonment not exceeding 1 year or a fine not exceeding $1,000 or both; and

(2) for each subsequent violation, a misdemeanor and on conviction is subject to imprisonment not exceeding 3 years or a fine not exceeding $5,000 or both. (2003, ch. 97; 2005, ch. 251; 2008, ch. 311.)

§ 10-112. Dumping site surveillance systems.

(a) *Definitions.* — (1) In this section the following words have the meanings indicated.

(2) "Department" means the Baltimore City Department of Public Works.

(3) "Dumping site" means a location in Baltimore City that is:

(i) owned by the city or the State; and

(ii) identified by the Department as property that has been repeatedly used for the disposal of litter in violation of State law or a local law or ordinance.

(4) (i) "Owner" means the registered owner of a motor vehicle or a lessee of a motor vehicle under a lease of 6 months or more.

(ii) "Owner" does not include:

1. a motor vehicle rental or leasing company; or

2. a holder of a special registration plate issued under Title 13, Subtitle 9, Part III of the Transportation Article.

(5) "Surveillance image" means an image recorded by a surveillance system:

(i) on:

1. a photograph;

2. a micrograph;

3. an electronic image;

4. videotape; or

5. any other medium;

(ii) showing the front or rear of a motor vehicle, and, on at least one image or portion of the tape, clearly identifying the registration plate number of the motor vehicle; and

(iii) showing an individual committing a violation of the State litter control law or a local law or ordinance relating to the unlawful disposal of litter.

(6) "Surveillance system" means a collection of one or more cameras located at a dumping site that produces a surveillance image.

(b) *Scope.* — This section applies to a violation of the State litter control law or a local law or ordinance relating to the unlawful disposal of litter that occurs at a dumping site monitored by a surveillance system.

(c) *Power of Department to use surveillance systems.* — The Department may:

(1) place surveillance systems at dumping sites; and

(2) use surveillance images to enforce the provisions of the State litter control law or a local law or ordinance relating to the unlawful disposal of litter.

(d) *In general.* — (1) Unless the individual committing a violation received a citation from a police officer at the time of the violation, the owner of the vehicle used to commit the violation, or in accordance with subsection (g)(4) of this section, the individual committing the violation, is subject to a civil penalty if the violation and the motor vehicle used to commit the violation are recorded on a surveillance image by a surveillance system while the individual is committing a violation of the State litter control law or a local law or ordinance relating to the unlawful disposal of litter.

(2) A civil penalty under this subsection may not exceed $1,000.

(3) For purposes of this section, the District Court, in consultation with the Department, shall prescribe:

(i) a uniform citation form consistent with subsection (e)(1) of this section and § 7-302 of the Courts Article; and

(ii) a civil penalty, which shall be indicated on the citation, to be paid by persons who choose to prepay the civil penalty without appearing in District Court.

(e) *Citation.* — (1) Subject to the provisions of paragraphs (2) through (4) of this subsection, the Department shall mail to the owner liable under subsection (d) of this section a citation that shall include:

(i) the name and address of the registered owner of the vehicle;

(ii) the registration number of the motor vehicle involved in the violation;

(iii) the violation charged;

(iv) the location where the violation occurred;

(v) the date and time of the violation;

(vi) a copy of the surveillance image;

(vii) the amount of the civil penalty imposed and the date by which the civil penalty must be paid;

(viii) a signed statement by a duly authorized agent of the Department that, based on inspection of surveillance images, the motor vehicle was being used by an individual who was committing a violation of the State litter control law or a local law or ordinance relating to the unlawful disposal of litter;

(ix) a statement that surveillance images are evidence of a violation of the State litter control law or a local law or ordinance relating to the unlawful disposal of litter;

(x) information advising the person alleged to be liable under this section of the manner and time in which liability as alleged in the citation may be contested in the District Court; and

(xi) information advising the person alleged to be liable under this section that failure to pay the civil penalty or to contest liability in a timely manner:

1. is an admission of liability;

2. may result in the refusal by the Motor Vehicle Administration to register the motor vehicle; and

3. may result in the suspension of the motor vehicle registration.

(2) The Department may mail a warning notice instead of a citation to the owner liable under subsection (d) of this section.

(3) Except as provided in subsection (g)(4) of this section, the Department may not mail a citation to a person who is not an owner.

(4) Except as provided in subsection (g)(4) of this section, a citation issued under this section shall be mailed no later than 2 weeks after the alleged violation.

(5) A person who receives a citation under paragraph (1) of this subsection may:

(i) pay the civil penalty, in accordance with the instructions on the citation, directly to Baltimore City; or

(ii) elect to stand trial in the District Court for the alleged violation.

(f) *Evidence.* — (1) A certificate alleging that a violation of the State litter control law or a local law or ordinance relating to the unlawful disposal of litter occurred, sworn to or affirmed by a duly authorized agent of the Department, based on inspection of surveillance images produced by a surveillance system, shall be evidence of the facts contained in the certificate and shall be admissible in a proceeding alleging a violation under this section.

(2) Adjudication of liability shall be based on a preponderance of the evidence.

(g) *Defenses.* — (1) The District Court may consider in defense of a violation:

(i) subject to paragraph (2) of this subsection, that:

1. the motor vehicle was stolen before the violation occurred and was not under the control or possession of the owner at the time of the violation; or

2. the registration plates of the motor vehicle were stolen before the violation occurred and were not under the control or possession of the owner at the time of the violation;

(ii) subject to paragraph (3) of this subsection, evidence that the person named in the citation was not the person in the surveillance image committing the violation of the State litter control law or a local law or ordinance relating to the unlawful disposal of litter; and

(iii) any other issues and evidence that the District Court deems pertinent.

(2) In order to assert a defense under paragraph (1)(i) of this subsection, the owner shall submit proof that a police report regarding the stolen motor vehicle or registration plates was filed in a timely manner.

(3) In order to satisfy the evidentiary burden under paragraph (1)(ii) of this subsection, the person named in the citation shall provide to the District Court evidence to the satisfaction of the court of the identity of the person in the surveillance image who was actually committing the violation, including, at a minimum, the person's name and current address.

(4) (i) If the District Court finds that the person named in the citation did not commit the violation or receives evidence under paragraph (3) of this subsection identifying the person who committed the violation, the clerk of the court shall provide the Department with a copy of any evidence substantiating who was operating the vehicle at the time of the violation.

(ii) On receipt of substantiating evidence from the District Court under subparagraph (i) of this paragraph, the Department may issue a citation as provided in subsection (e) of this section to the person that the evidence indicates committed the violation.

(iii) A citation issued under subparagraph (ii) of this paragraph shall be mailed no later than 2 weeks after the receipt of the evidence from the District Court.

(h) *Sanctions on failure to pay civil penalty.* — If the person named in the citation does not pay the civil penalty and does not contest the violation, the Motor Vehicle Administration may:

(1) refuse to register the motor vehicle cited in the violation; or

(2) suspend the registration of the motor vehicle cited in the violation.

(i) *Effects of civil penalty.* — A violation for which a civil penalty is imposed under this section:

(1) may not be recorded by the Motor Vehicle Administration on the driving record of the owner or the driver of the motor vehicle; and

(2) may be treated as a parking violation for purposes of § 26-305 of the Transportation Article.

(j) *Establishment of procedures in District Court.* — In consultation with the Department, the Chief Judge of the District Court shall adopt procedures for the issuance of citations, the trial of civil violations, and the collection of civil penalties under this section. (2006, chs. 13, 16; ch. 44, § 6.)

University of Baltimore Law Review. — For a 2010 development, "Limiting Death: Maryland's New Death Penalty Law," see 70 U. Md. L. Rev. 272 (2010).

Part II. Alcoholic Beverages Violations.

§ 10-113. Misrepresentation of age.

An individual may not knowingly and willfully make a misrepresentation or false statement as to the age of that individual or another to any person licensed to sell alcoholic beverages or engaged in the sale of alcoholic beverages, for the purpose of unlawfully obtaining, procuring, or having unlawfully furnished an alcoholic beverage to an individual. (An. Code 1957, art. 27, § 400; 2002, ch. 26, § 4; ch. 213, § 1; 2009, ch. 499.)

SPECIAL REVISOR'S NOTE

This Special Revisor's note comprises information related to the revision by Acts 2002, ch. 26 and other chapters amending this section from the 2002 Legislative Session.

Chapter 26, Acts of 2002, enacted this section as Art. 2B, § 22-101, which was new language derived without substantive change from former Art. 27, § 400. However, Chs. 108 and 109, Acts of 2002, each added §§ 10-113 through 10-117 under a new part "Part II. Alcoholic Beverage Consumption or Possession of Open Container in Passenger Area of Motor Vehicle". Also, Ch. 213, § 1, transferred Article 2B, §§ 22-101 through 22-108, as enacted by Ch. 26, § 4, to be §§ 10-113 through 10-120, under the new part "Part II. Alcoholic Beverages Vio-

lations". Precedence in numbering has been given to Ch. 213 as the later enactment. *See* Art. 1, § 17. Accordingly, this section appears as § 10-113 under Part II.

The references to an "individual" were substituted by Ch. 26 for the former references to a "person" because only an individual may make a misrepresentation about the age of the individual or may be furnished with an alcoholic beverage.

The former reference to "inducing to unlawfully furnish" an alcoholic beverage to a person was deleted by Ch. 26 as included in the reference to "procuring" the beverage.

Defined term:
"Person"   § 1-101

Effect of amendments. — Chapter 499, Acts 2009, effective October 1, 2009, reenacted the section without change.

Editor's note. — Section 1, ch. 213, Acts 2002, effective Oct. 1, 2002, redesignated §§ 22-101 through 22-108 of Article 2B of the Code, as enacted by ch. 26, § 4, Acts 2002, effective Oct. 1, 2002, to be §§ 10-113 through

10-120 of this subtitle under the part heading, "Alcoholic Beverages Violations."

Section 1, chs. 108 and 109, Acts 2002, both effective Sept. 30, 2002, also enacted a Part II of this subtitle, "Alcoholic Beverage Consumption or Possession of Open Container in Passenger Area of Motor Vehicle," which has been redesignated as Part III of this subtitle, and the sections thereunder have been redesignated as §§ 10-123 through 10-127.

Jury instructions deemed erroneous. — In an insured's action seeking additional underinsured payments from his insurer, a trial judge erred in including a jury instruction regarding the age misrepresentation statute, contained in this section, where the insurer had failed to show how the insured's use of his false identification was a proximate cause of his injuries; neither the insured's nor anyone else's testimony supported the insurer's contention that the insured purchased alcoholic beverages for the driver. Maurer v. Pa. Nat'l Mut. Cas. Ins. Co., 404 Md. 60, 945 A.2d 629 (2007).

§ 10-114. Underage possession.

(a) *Prohibition.* — Except as provided in subsection (b)(1) of this section, and subject to subsection (b)(2) of this section, an individual under the age of 21 years may not:

(1) possess or have under the individual's charge or control an alcoholic beverage unless the individual is a bona fide employee of the license holder as defined in Article 2B, § 1-102 of the Code and the alcoholic beverage is in the possession or under the charge or control of the individual in the course of the individual's employment and during regular working hours; or

(2) consume an alcoholic beverage.

(b) *Exception.* — (1) The prohibitions set forth in subsection (a)(1) and (2) of this section do not apply if:

(i) 1. an adult furnishes the alcoholic beverage to the individual or allows the individual to possess or consume the alcoholic beverage;

2. the individual possessing or consuming the alcoholic beverage and the adult who furnished the alcoholic beverage to the individual or allowed the individual to possess or consume the alcoholic beverage are members of the same immediate family; and

3. the alcoholic beverage is furnished and consumed in a private residence of the adult or within the curtilage of the residence; or

(ii) the individual consumes the alcoholic beverage as a participant in a religious ceremony.

(2) An individual may not be stopped on suspicion of a violation of subsection (a)(2) of this section or charged with a violation of subsection (a)(2) of this section unless the individual is observed in possession of an alcoholic beverage. (An. Code 1957, art. 27, § 400A; 2002, ch. 26, §§ 4, 12; ch. 213, § 1; 2003, ch. 21, § 1; 2009, ch. 499.)

SPECIAL REVISOR'S NOTE

This Special Revisor's note comprises information related to the revision by Acts 2002, ch. 26 and other chapters amending this section from the 2002 Legislative Session.

Chapter 26, Acts of 2002, enacted this section as Art. 2B, § 22-102, which was new language derived without substantive change from former Art. 27, § 400A. However, Chs. 108 and 109, Acts of 2002, each added §§ 10-113 through 10-117 under a new part "Part II. Alcoholic Beverage Consumption or Possession of Open Container in Passenger Area of Motor Vehicle". Also, Ch. 213, § 1, transferred Article 2B, §§ 22-101 through 22-108, as enacted by Ch. 26, § 4, to be §§ 10-113 through 10-120, under the new part "Part II. Alcoholic Beverages Violations". Precedence in numbering has been given to Ch. 213 as the later enactment. *See* Art. 1, § 17. Accordingly, this section appears as § 10-114.

The references to an "individual" were substituted by Ch. 26 for the former references to a "person" because only an individual may be under the age of 21 years and have possession, charge, or control of an alcoholic beverage.

The former reference to a license holder "as defined in Article 2B" was deleted by Ch. 26 as surplusage. However, because of the recodification of this section in the Criminal Law Article by Ch. 213, the reference to a license holder "as defined in Article 2B, § 1-102 of the Code" was added under the authority of Ch. 26, § 12.

Effect of amendments. — Chapter 499, Acts 2009, effective October 1, 2009, added the (a) and (a)(1) designations; in the introductory language of (a) added the exception; added (a)(2) and (b); and made related and stylistic changes.

Search and seizure. — Where a lost and intoxicated boy was bitten by a police dog used by an officer to find the boy in cold weather, the boy was seized because the officer specifically used the dog to locate and stop the boy and there was an element of criminality involved due to the possibility that the boy had engaged in underage drinking; however, the officer was entitled to qualified immunity as to the parent's Fourth Amendment claims. Melgar v. Greene, 593 F.3d 348 (4th Cir. 2010).

§ 10-115. False documentation.

An individual under the age of 21 years may not possess a card or document that falsely identifies the age of the individual under circumstances that reasonably indicate an intention to violate the provisions of this part. (An. Code 1957, art. 27, § 400B; 2002, ch. 26, §§ 4, 12; ch. 213, § 1; 2003, ch. 21, § 1; 2009, ch. 499.)

SPECIAL REVISOR'S NOTE

This Special Revisor's note comprises information related to the revision by Acts 2002, ch. 26 and other chapters amending this section from the 2002 Legislative Session.

Chapter 26, § 4, Acts of 2002, enacted this section as Art. 2B, § 22-103, which formerly was Art. 27, § 400B. However, Chs. 108 and 109, Acts of 2002, each added §§ 10-113 through 10-117 under a new part "Part II. Alcoholic Beverage Consumption or Possession of Open Container in Passenger Area of Motor Vehicle". Also, Ch. 213, § 1, transferred Article 2B, §§ 22-101 through 22-108, as enacted by Ch. 26, § 4, to be §§ 10-113 through 10-120, under the new part "Part II. Alcoholic Bever-

ages Violations". Precedence in numbering has been given to Ch. 213 as the later enactment. *See* Art. 1, § 17. Accordingly, this section appears as § 10-115.

The reference to this "subtitle" was substituted by Ch. 26 for the former reference to this "subheading" to reflect the reorganization of material derived from the former "Alcoholic Beverages Offenses and Misrepresentation of Age" subheading of Article 27 in this subtitle. However, because of the recodification of this section in the Criminal Law Article by Ch. 213, the reference to this "part" was substituted for the reference to this "subtitle" enacted by Ch. 26, § 4, under the authority of Ch. 26, § 12.

No other changes were made by Ch. 26.

Effect of amendments. — Chapter 499, Acts 2009, effective October 1, 2009, reenacted the section without change.

§ 10-116. Obtaining for underage consumption.

An individual may not obtain, or attempt to obtain by purchase or otherwise, an alcoholic beverage from any person licensed to sell alcoholic beverages for consumption by another who the individual obtaining or attempting to obtain the beverage knows is under the age of 21 years. (An. Code 1957, art. 27, § 401; 2002, ch. 26, § 4; ch. 213, § 1; 2009, ch. 499.)

This Special Revisor's note comprises information related to the revision by Acts 2002, ch. 26 and other chapters amending this section from the 2002 Legislative Session.

Chapter 26, Acts of 2002, enacted this section as Art. 2B, § 22-104, which was new language derived without substantive change from former Art. 27, § 401. However, Chs. 108 and 109, Acts of 2002, each added §§ 10-113 through 10-117 under a new part "Part II. Alcoholic Beverage Consumption or Possession of Open Container in Passenger Area of Motor Vehicle".

Also, Ch. 213, § 1, transferred Article 2B, §§ 22-101 through 22-108, as enacted by Ch. 26, § 4, to be §§ 10-113 through 10-120, under the new part "Part II. Alcoholic Beverages Violations". Precedence in numbering has been given to Ch. 213 as the later enactment. *See* Art. 1, § 17. Accordingly, this section appears as § 10-116.

The references to an "individual" were substituted by Ch. 26 for the former references to a "person" because only an individual may be under the age of 21 years and consume an alcoholic beverage.

Effect of amendments. — Chapter 499, Acts 2009, effective October 1, 2009, added "or attempt to obtain by purchase or otherwise" and "or attempting to obtain."

§ 10-117. Furnishing for or allowing underage consumption.

(a) *Furnishing alcohol.* — Except as provided in subsection (c) of this section, a person may not furnish an alcoholic beverage to an individual if:

(1) the person furnishing the alcoholic beverage knows that the individual is under the age of 21 years; and

(2) the alcoholic beverage is furnished for the purpose of consumption by the individual under the age of 21 years.

(b) *Allowing possession or consumption of alcohol.* — Except as provided in subsection (c) of this section, an adult may not knowingly and willfully allow an individual under the age of 21 years actually to possess or consume an alcoholic beverage at a residence, or within the curtilage of a residence that the adult owns or leases and in which the adult resides.

(c) *Exceptions.* — (1) The prohibition set forth in subsection (a) of this section does not apply if the person furnishing the alcoholic beverage and the individual to whom the alcoholic beverage is furnished:

(i) are members of the same immediate family, and the alcoholic beverage is furnished and consumed in a private residence or within the curtilage of the residence; or

(ii) are participants in a religious ceremony.

(2) The prohibition set forth in subsection (b) of this section does not apply if the adult allowing the possession or consumption of the alcoholic beverage and the individual under the age of 21 years who possesses or consumes the alcoholic beverage:

(i) are members of the same immediate family, and the alcoholic beverage is possessed and consumed in a private residence, or within the curtilage of the residence, of the adult; or

(ii) are participants in a religious ceremony. (An. Code 1957, art. 27, § 401A; 2002, ch. 26, § 4; ch. 213, § 1; 2005, ch. 268; 2008, chs. 565, 566; 2009, ch. 499.)

SPECIAL REVISOR'S NOTE

This Special Revisor's note comprises information related to the revision by Acts 2002, ch. 26 and other chapters amending this section from the 2002 Legislative Session.

Chapter 26, Acts of 2002, enacted this section as Art. 2B, § 22-105, which was new language derived without substantive change from former Art. 27, § 401A. However, Chs. 108 and 109, Acts of 2002, each added §§ 10-113 through 10-117 under a new part "Part II. Alcoholic Beverage Consumption or Possession of Open Container in Passenger Area of Motor Vehicle". Also, Ch. 213, § 1, transferred Article 2B, §§ 22-101 through 22-108, as enacted by

Ch. 26, § 4, to be §§ 10-113 through 10-120, under the new part "Part II. Alcoholic Beverages Violations". Precedence in numbering has been given to Ch. 213 as the later enactment. *See* Art. 1, § 17. Accordingly, this section appears as § 10-117.

In subsections (a) and (c)(1) of this section, the references to an "individual" were substituted by Ch. 26 for the former references to a "person" because only an individual may be under the age of 21 years and be furnished an alcoholic beverage.

Defined term:
"Person"　　　　　　　　　　§ 1-101

Effect of amendments. — Chapter 499, Acts 2009, effective October 1, 2009, reenacted the section without change.

Search and seizure. — Where a lost and intoxicated boy was bitten by a police dog used by an officer to find the boy in cold weather, the boy was seized because the officer specifically

used the dog to locate and stop the boy and there was an element of criminality involved due to the possibility that the boy had engaged in underage drinking; however, the officer was entitled to qualified immunity as to the parent's Fourth Amendment claims. Melgar v. Greene, 593 F.3d 348 (4th Cir. 2010).

§ 10-118. Unregistered keg.

(a) *Possession; altering registration form.* — Except for a person licensed as an alcoholic beverages licensee under Article 2B of the Code who possesses a keg in the course of that person's business, a person may not knowingly:

(1) possess a keg that has not been registered under or does not have a registration form affixed to it as required by Article 2B, § 21-106 of the Code; or

(2) remove, alter, or obliterate, or allow to be removed, altered, or obliterated, a registration form that is affixed to a keg.

(b) *Allowing underage consumption.* — A person may not allow an individual under the age of 21 years to consume any of the contents of a keg purchased by that person. (An. Code 1957, art. 27, § 401B; 2002, ch. 26, §§ 4, 12; ch. 213, § 1; 2009, ch. 499.)

SPECIAL REVISOR'S NOTE

This Special Revisor's note comprises information related to the revision by Acts 2002, ch. 26 and other chapters amending this section from the 2002 Legislative Session.

Chapter 26, § 4, Acts of 2002, enacted this section as Art. 2B, § 22-106, which was new language derived without substantive change from former Art. 27, § 401B. However, Chs. 108 and 109, Acts of 2002, each added §§ 10-113 through 10-117 under a new part "Part II. Alcoholic Beverage Consumption or Possession of Open Container in Passenger Area of Motor Vehicle". Also, Ch. 213, § 1, transferred Article

2B, §§ 22-101 through 22-108, as enacted by Ch. 26, § 4, to be §§ 10-113 through 10-120, under the new part "Part II. Alcoholic Beverages Violations". Precedence in numbering has been given to Ch. 213 as the later enactment. *See* Art. 1, § 17. Accordingly, this section appears as § 10-118.

In the introductory language of subsection (a) of this section, the reference to "this article" was substituted by Ch. 26 for the former reference to "Article 2B of the Code" to reflect the reorganization of material derived from the former "Alcoholic Beverages Offenses and Misrepresentation of Age" subheading of Article 27 in Article 2B. Similarly, in subsection (a)(1) of this section, the reference to "§ 21-106 of this article" was substituted by Ch. 26 for the former reference to "Article 2B, § 21-106 of the Code". However, because of the recodification of this section in the Criminal Law Article by Ch.

213, these references have been restored under the authority of Ch. 26, § 12.

Defined term:
"Person" § 1-101

Effect of amendments. — Chapter 499, Acts 2009, effective October 1, 2009, reenacted the section without change.

§ **10-119. Citation.**

(a) *In general.* — (1) A person who violates §§ 10-113 through 10-115 or § 10-118 of this part shall be issued a citation under this section.

(2) A minor who violates § 10-116 or § 10-117(a) of this part shall be issued a citation under this section.

(b) *Who may issue.* — A citation for a violation of §§ 10-113 through 10-115 or a violation of § 10-118 of this part may be issued by:

(1) a police officer authorized to make arrests;

(2) in State forestry reservations, State parks, historic monuments, and recreation areas, a forest or park warden under § 5-206(a) or (b) of the Natural Resources Article; and

(3) in Anne Arundel County, Frederick County, Harford County, Montgomery County, and Prince George's County, and only in the inspector's jurisdiction, an alcoholic beverages inspector who investigates license violations under Article 2B of the Code if the inspector:

(i) has successfully completed an appropriate program of training in the proper use of arrest authority and pertinent police procedures as required by the board of license commissioners; and

(ii) does not carry firearms in the performance of the inspector's duties.

(c) *Issuance on probably cause.* — A person authorized under this section to issue a citation shall issue it if the person has probable cause to believe that the person charged is committing or has committed a Code violation.

(d) *Form and contents.* — (1) Subject to paragraph (2) of this subsection, the form of citation issued to an adult shall be as prescribed by the District Court and shall be uniform throughout the State.

(2) The citation issued to an adult shall contain:

(i) the name and address of the person charged;

(ii) the statute allegedly violated;

(iii) the location, date, and time that the violation occurred;

(iv) the fine that may be imposed;

(v) a notice stating that prepayment of the fine is not allowed;

(vi) a notice that the District Court shall promptly send the person charged a summons to appear for trial;

(vii) the signature of the person issuing the citation; and

(viii) a space for the person charged to sign the citation.

(3) The form of citation issued to a minor shall:

(i) be prescribed by the State Court Administrator;

(ii) be uniform throughout the State; and

(iii) contain the information listed in § 3-8A-33(b) of the Courts Article.

(e) *Request for trial; scheduling.* — (1) Except for a citation subject to the jurisdiction of a circuit court, the issuing jurisdiction shall forward a copy of the citation and a request for trial to the District Court in the district having venue.

(2) (i) The District Court shall promptly schedule the case for trial and summon the defendant to appear.

(ii) Willful failure of the defendant to respond to the summons is contempt of court.

(f) *Code violation; disposition.* — (1) For purposes of this section, a violation of §§ 10-113 through 10-115 or a violation of § 10-118 of this part is a Code violation and is a civil offense.

(2) A person charged who is under the age of 18 years shall be subject to the procedures and dispositions provided in Title 3, Subtitle 8A of the Courts Article.

(3) A person charged who is at least 18 years old shall be subject to the provisions of this section.

(4) Adjudication of a Code violation is not a criminal conviction for any purpose, and it does not impose any of the civil disabilities ordinarily imposed by a criminal conviction.

(g) *Burden of proof; procedure.* — In any proceeding for a Code violation:

(1) the State has the burden to prove the guilt of the defendant to the same extent as is required by law in the trial of criminal causes, and in any such proceeding, the court shall apply the evidentiary standards as prescribed by law or rule for the trial of criminal causes;

(2) the court shall ensure that the defendant has received a copy of the charges against the defendant and that the defendant understands those charges;

(3) the defendant is entitled to cross-examine all witnesses who appear against the defendant, to produce evidence or witnesses on behalf of the defendant, or to testify on the defendant's own behalf, if the defendant chooses to do so;

(4) the defendant is entitled to be represented by counsel of the defendant's choice and at the expense of the defendant; and

(5) the defendant may enter a plea of guilty or not guilty, and the verdict of the court in the case shall be:

(i) guilty of a Code violation;

(ii) not guilty of a Code violation; or

(iii) before rendering judgment, the court may place the defendant on probation in the same manner and to the same extent as is allowed by law in the trial of a criminal case.

(h) *Amount of fine.* — (1) Except as provided in paragraph (2) of this subsection, if the District Court finds that a person has committed a Code violation, the court shall require the person to pay:

(i) a fine not exceeding $500; or

(ii) if the violation is a subsequent violation, a fine not exceeding $1,000.

(2) If the District Court finds that a person has committed a Code violation under § 10-117 of this subtitle, the court shall require the person to pay:

(i) a fine not exceeding $2,500; or

(ii) if the violation is a subsequent violation, a fine not exceeding $5,000.

(3) The Chief Judge of the District Court may not establish a schedule for the prepayment of fines for a Code violation under this part.

(i) *Suspension of fine; failure to pay.* — When a defendant has been found guilty of a Code violation and a fine has been imposed by the court:

(1) the court may direct that the payment of the fine be suspended or deferred under conditions that the court may establish; and

(2) if the defendant willfully fails to pay the fine imposed by the court, that willful failure may be treated as a criminal contempt of court, for which the defendant may be punished by the court as provided by law.

(j) *Costs; Criminal Injuries Compensation Fund.* — (1) The defendant is liable for the costs of the proceedings in the District Court and for payment to the Criminal Injuries Compensation Fund.

(2) The court costs in a Code violation case in which costs are imposed are $5.

(k) *Notice to Motor Vehicle Administration.* — (1) In this subsection, "driver's license" means a license or permit to drive a motor vehicle that is issued under the laws of this State or any other jurisdiction.

(2) This subsection applies only to:

(i) a person who is at least 18 but under 21 years of age; or

(ii) a minor if the minor is subject to the jurisdiction of the court.

(3) If a person is found guilty of a Code violation under § 10-113 of this part that involved the use of a driver's license or a document purporting to be a driver's license, the court shall notify the Motor Vehicle Administration of the violation.

(4) The Chief Judge of the District Court, in conjunction with the Motor Vehicle Administrator, shall establish uniform procedures for reporting Code violations described in this subsection.

(l) *Appeal.* — (1) A defendant who has been found guilty of a Code violation has the right to appeal or to file a motion for a new trial or a motion for a revision of a judgment provided by law in the trial of a criminal case.

(2) A motion shall be made in the same manner as provided in the trial of criminal cases, and the court, in ruling on the motion has the same authority provided in the trial of criminal cases.

(m) *Authority of State's Attorney.* — (1) The State's Attorney for any county may prosecute a Code violation in the same manner as prosecution of a violation of the criminal laws of this State.

(2) In a Code violation case the State's Attorney may:

(i) enter a nolle prosequi in or place the case on the stet docket; and

(ii) exercise authority in the same manner as prescribed by law for violation of the criminal laws of this State. (An. Code 1957, art. 27, §§ 402, 403; 2002, ch. 26, §§ 4, 12; ch. 213, §§ 1, 6; 2003, chs. 13, 155; 2005, ch. 268; 2008, chs. 565, 566; 2009, ch. 499.)

SPECIAL REVISOR'S NOTE

This Special Revisor's note comprises information related to the revision by Acts 2002, ch. 26 and other chapters amending this section from the 2002 Legislative Session.

Chapter 26, § 4, Acts of 2002, enacted this section as Art. 2B, § 22-107, which was new language derived without substantive change from former Art. 27, §§ 402 and 403. However, Chs. 108 and 109, Acts of 2002, each added §§ 10-113 through 10-117 under a new part "Part II. Alcoholic Beverage Consumption or Possession of Open Container in Passenger Area of Motor Vehicle". Also, Ch. 213, § 1, transferred Article 2B, §§ 22-101 through 22-108, as enacted by Ch. 26, § 4, to be §§ 10-113 through 10-120, under the new part "Part II. Alcoholic Beverages Violations". Precedence in numbering has been given to Ch. 213 as the later enactment. *See* Art. 1, § 17. Accordingly, this section appears as § 10-119. Also, Ch. 213, § 6, corrected cross-references to material in this part in subsections (a), (b), (f)(1), and (k)(3) of this section, added "or (b)" in subsection (b)(2) of this section, added "[w]illful" before "[f]ailure" in subsection (e)(2) of this section, and substituted "subsequent" for "repeat" in subsection (h)(1)(ii) of this section.

In subsections (a) and (b) of this section, the references to this "subtitle" were substituted by Ch. 26 for the former references to this "subheading" to reflect the reorganization of material derived from the former "Alcoholic Beverages Offenses and Misrepresentation of Age" subheading of Article 27 in this subtitle. Similarly, in subsection (b) of this section, the reference to "this section" was substituted by Ch. 26 for the former reference to "§ 403 of this subheading". However, Ch. 213, § 6 further corrected these cross-references.

In subsection (b)(2) of this section, the reference to the exercise of authority by a forest or park warden in State "reservations" was substituted by Ch. 26 for the former archaic reference to the exercise of that authority in State "preservations" for consistency with NR § 5-206, which established the authority and jurisdiction of State forest and park wardens.

In subsection (b)(3) of this section, the reference to "this article" was substituted by Ch. 26 for the former reference to "Article 2B of the Code" to reflect the reorganization of material derived from the former "Alcoholic Beverages Offenses and Misrepresentation of Age" subheading of Article 27 in this article. Although "this article" was defined in Art. 2B, § 1-102(a)(25) to include portions of the Tax - General Article derived from Article 2B, none of those provisions affected any provision revised in this subtitle. No substantive change was intended by Ch. 26. However, because of the recodification of this section in the Criminal Law Article by Ch. 213, the former reference was restored under the authority of Ch. 26, § 12.

In subsection (c) of this section, the references to a "person authorized under this section to issue a citation" and the "person" were substituted by Ch. 26 for the former references to a "law enforcement officer" and the "officer" for clarity and accuracy.

In subsection (e)(2) of this section, the reference to "[f]ailure of the defendant to appear" was substituted by Ch. 26 for the former reference to the "defendant's failure to respond to the summons" for clarity and accuracy.

In subsections (a), (b), and (f)(1) of this section, the references to "§§ 22-101 through 22-106 of this subtitle" were substituted by Ch. 26 for the former references to "this subheading" to reflect the reorganization of material derived from the former "Alcoholic Beverages Offenses and Misrepresentation of Age" subheading of Article 27 in this article. The references excluded a violation of § 22-108 of this subtitle (now § 10-120) as a Code violation rather than as a crime, because that section was expressly stated by Ch. 26 as a statutory misdemeanor rather than as a civil offense, and was charged as a crime rather than as a Code violation. No substantive change was intended by Ch. 26. However, Ch. 213 further corrected these cross-references.

For specific provisions on contempt of court, *see* Md. Rules 15-203 *et seq.*

The Criminal Law Article Review Committee noted, for the consideration of the General Assembly, that the jurisdiction of State forest and park wardens granted under NR § 5-206(b) extended to property beyond that described in subsection (b)(2) of this section, including but not limited to public and private property adjoining State property managed by the Department of Natural Resources, federal park property in the State, waters of the State within one mile of the shoreline of all properties owned by the Department, and any property in Maryland for the purpose of executing a warrant that has resulted from law enforcement activities on property on which a forest, park, and wildlife ranger may exercise law enforcement powers. The General Assembly was asked to consider addressing the disparity between the grant of jurisdiction to forest and park wardens under this subtitle and NR § 5-206(b). Chapter 213 addressed this concern.

The Criminal Law Article Review Committee noted, for the consideration of the General Assembly, that the contempt provision of subsection (e)(2) of this section appeared not to comport with the minimum legal standards for contempt. The provision treated as contempt the mere failure to respond to a summons, rather than a "willful" failure. Contempt generally requires a willful action in defiance of legal process, and some means of purging the contempt. The General Assembly was asked to consider addressing this deficiency. Chapter 213 addressed this concern.

The Criminal Law Article Review Committee noted, for the consideration of the General Assembly, that it was unclear whether the "repeat" violation in subsection (h)(2) of this section referred to a subsequent violation of the same section, or of this subtitle, or to any violation involving the use of alcoholic beverages. The General Assembly was asked to consider addressing the scope of repeat violations under this provision. Chapter 213 addressed this concern.

Defined term:
"Person"   § 1-101

Effect of amendments. — Chapter 499, Acts 2009, effective October 1, 2009, added the (a)(1), (e)(2)(i), and (e)(2)(ii) designations; in (a)(1) substituted "§§ 10-113 through 10-115 or § 10-118" for "§§ 10-113 through § 10-118"; added (a)(2); in the introductory language of (b) and in (f)(1) added "10-115 or a violation of"; in (e)(1) added the exception; in (h)(3) added "for a Code violation under this part"; and made a stylistic change.

Editor's note. — Section 2, ch. 13, Acts 2003, provides that "this Act may not be construed to prevent the use of any supplies of citation forms in existence on October 1, 2003."

§ 10-120. Failure to provide proof of age; jurisdiction.

(a) *Prohibited.* — A person being issued a citation under §§ 10-113 through 10-119 of this part or § 26-103 of the Education Article may not fail or refuse to furnish proof of identification and age on request of the person issuing the citation.

(b) *Penalty.* — A person who violates this section is guilty of a misdemeanor and on conviction is subject to a fine not exceeding $50.

(c) *Jurisdiction.* — (1) The juvenile court has jurisdiction over a minor who is within the age of juvenile court jurisdiction.

(2) If there is a waiver of juvenile jurisdiction with respect to a minor who is otherwise subject to juvenile court jurisdiction, the District Court has jurisdiction over the matter, notwithstanding any contrary provision of § 4-301 of the Courts Article. (An. Code 1957, art. 27, § 403A; 2002, ch. 26, § 4; ch. 213, §§ 1, 6; 2009, ch. 499.)

SPECIAL REVISOR'S NOTE

This Special Revisor's note comprises information related to the revision by Acts 2002, ch. 26 and other chapters amending this section from the 2002 Legislative Session.

Chapter 26, Acts of 2002, enacted this section as Art. 2B, § 22-108, which is new language derived without substantive change from former Art. 27, § 403A. However, Chs. 108 and 109, Acts of 2002, each added §§ 10-113 through 10-117 under a new part "Part II. Alcoholic Beverage Consumption or Possession of Open Container in Passenger Area of Motor Vehicle". Also, Ch. 213, § 1, transferred Article 2B, §§ 22-101 through 22-108, as enacted by Ch. 26, § 4, to be §§ 10-113 through 10-120, under the new part "Part II. Alcoholic Bever-

ages Violations". Precedence in numbering has been given to Ch. 213 as the later enactment. *See* Art. 1, § 17. Accordingly, this section appears as § 10-120. Also, Ch. 213, § 6, corrected the cross-references to material in this part in subsection (a) of this section.

In subsection (a) of this section, the reference to "§§ 22-101 through 22-107 of this subtitle" was substituted by Ch. 26 for the former reference to "§§ 400 through 403 of this article" to reflect the reorganization of material derived from the former "Alcoholic Beverages Offenses and Misrepresentation of Age" subheading of Article 27 in this subtitle. However, Ch. 213 corrected these cross-references.

Defined term:
"Person"   § 1-101

Effect of amendments. — Chapter 499, Acts 2009, effective October 1, 2009, reenacted the section without change.

Editor's note. — See Editor's note under § 10-113 of this article.

§ 10-121. Penalties for violation of § 10-116 or § 10-117.

(a) *Applicability.* — This section does not apply to a person who:

(1) was acting in the capacity of a licensee, or an employee of a licensee, under Article 2B of the Code; and

(2) has committed a violation of and is subject to the penalties under Article 2B, § 12-108 of the Code.

(b) *Penalties.* — An adult who violates § 10-116 or § 10-117 of this subtitle is guilty of a misdemeanor and on conviction is subject to:

(1) a fine not exceeding $2,500 for a first offense; or

(2) a fine not exceeding $5,000 for a second or subsequent offense. (2009, ch. 499.)

Editor's note. — Section 2, ch. 499, Acts 2009, provides that the act shall take effect October 1, 2009.

§ 10-122.

Reserved.

Part III. Alcoholic Beverage Consumption or Possession of Open Container in Passenger Area of Motor Vehicle.

§ 10-123. Definitions.

(a) *In general.* — In this part the following words have the meanings indicated.

(b) *Alcoholic beverage.* — "Alcoholic beverage" has the meaning stated in § 21-903 of the Transportation Article.

(c) *Bus.* — "Bus" has the meaning stated in § 11-105 of the Transportation Article.

(d) *Highway.* — "Highway" has the meaning stated in § 11-127 of the Transportation Article.

(e) *Limousine.* — "Limousine" has the meaning stated in § 11-129.1 of the Transportation Article.

(f) *Motor home.* — "Motor home" has the meaning stated in § 11-134.3 of the Transportation Article.

(g) *Motor vehicle.* — "Motor vehicle" has the meaning stated in § 11-135 of the Transportation Article.

(h) *Moving violation.* — "Moving violation" has the meaning stated in § 11-136.1 of the Transportation Article.

(i) *Open container.* — "Open container" means a bottle, can, or other receptacle:

(1) that is open;

(2) that has a broken seal; or

(3) from which the contents are partially removed.

(j) *Passenger area.* — "Passenger area" has the meaning stated in § 21-903 of the Transportation Article.

(k) *Taxicab.* — "Taxicab" has the meaning stated in § 11-165 of the Transportation Article. (2002, chs. 108, 109; 2003, ch. 21, § 1; 2006, ch. 127.)

SPECIAL REVISOR'S NOTE

This Special Revisor's note comprises information related to the revision by Acts 2002, ch. 26 and other chapters amending this section from the 2002 Legislative Session.

Chapters 108 and 109 each added this section as § 10-113 under a new part "Part II. Alcoholic Beverage Consumption or Possession of Open Container in Passenger Area of Motor Vehicle". However, Ch. 213, § 1, Acts of 2002, transferred Article 2B, §§ 22-101 through 22-108, as enacted by Ch. 26, § 4, Acts of 2002, to be §§ 10-113 through 10-120, under the new part "Part II. Alcoholic Beverages Violations". Precedence in numbering has been given to Ch. 213 as the later enactment. *See* Art. 1, § 17. Accordingly, this section appears as § 10-123 under Part III.

Editor's note. — Section 1, chs. 108 and 109, Acts 2002, both effective Sept. 30, 2002, originally enacted this part as Part II of this subtitle and the sections thereunder as §§ 10-113 through 10-117. However, § 1, ch 213, Acts 2002, effective Oct. 1, 2002, redesignated §§ 22-101 through 22-108 of Article 2B, as enacted by ch. 26, § 4, Acts 2002, effective Oct. 1, 2002, to be §§ 10-113 through 10-120 under Part II of this article. The part enacted by chs. 108 and 109 has therefore been redesignated as Part III of this subtitle and the sections thereunder have been redesignated as §§ 10-123 through 10-127.

Section 2, chs. 108 and 109, Acts 2002, provides that "this Act shall be construed to conform to the provisions of 23 U.S.C. § 154."

§ **10-124. Application of part.**

(a) *In general.* — This part applies to a motor vehicle that is driven, stopped, standing, or otherwise located on a highway.

(b) *Exception.* — This part does not affect the provisions of § 21-903 of the Transportation Article. (2002, chs. 108, 109.)

SPECIAL REVISOR'S NOTE

This Special Revisor's note comprises information related to the revision by Acts 2002, ch. 26 and other chapters amending this section from the 2002 Legislative Session.

Chapters 108 and 109 each added this section as § 10-114 under a new part "Part II. Alcoholic Beverage Consumption or Possession of Open Container in Passenger Area of Motor Vehicle". However, Ch. 213, § 1, Acts of 2002, transferred Article 2B, §§ 22-101 through 22-108, as enacted by Ch. 26, § 4, Acts of 2002, to be §§ 10-113 through 10-120, under the new part "Part II. Alcoholic Beverages Violations". Precedence in numbering has been given to Ch. 213 as the later enactment. *See* Art. 1, § 17. Accordingly, this section appears as § 10-124.

§ **10-125. Violations.**

(a) *Open container in passenger area.* — (1) Except as otherwise provided in subsection (c) of this section, an occupant of a motor vehicle may not possess an open container that contains any amount of an alcoholic beverage in a passenger area of a motor vehicle on a highway.

(2) A driver of a motor vehicle may not be subject to prosecution for a violation of this subsection based solely on possession of an open container that

contains any amount of an alcoholic beverage by another occupant of the motor vehicle.

(b) *Consumption in passenger area.* — (1) This subsection does not apply to the driver of a motor vehicle.

(2) Except as otherwise provided in subsection (c) of this section, an occupant of a motor vehicle may not consume an alcoholic beverage in a passenger area of a motor vehicle on a highway.

(c) *Exceptions.* — Subsections (a)(1) and (b)(2) of this section do not apply to an occupant, who is not the driver, in:

(1) a motor vehicle designed, maintained, and used primarily for the transportation of a person for compensation, including:

(i) a bus;

(ii) a taxicab; or

(iii) a limousine; or

(2) the living quarters of a motor home, motor coach, or recreational vehicle.

(d) *Statewide application.* — Notwithstanding Article 2B, Title 19 of the Code or any other provision of law, the prohibitions contained in this section apply throughout the State.

(e) *Classification of violation.* — A violation of this section is not:

(1) a moving violation for the purposes of § 16-402 of the Transportation Article; or

(2) a traffic violation for the purposes of the Maryland Vehicle Law. (2002, chs. 108, 109; 2006, ch. 127.)

SPECIAL REVISOR'S NOTE

This Special Revisor's note comprises information related to the revision by Acts 2002, ch. 26 and other chapters amending this section from the 2002 Legislative Session.

Chapters 108 and 109 each added this section as § 10-115 under a new part "Part II. Alcoholic Beverage Consumption or Possession of Open Container in Passenger Area of Motor Vehicle". However, Ch. 213, § 1, Acts of 2002, transferred Article 2B, §§ 22-101 through 22-108, as enacted by Ch. 26, § 4, Acts of 2002, to be §§ 10-113 through 10-120, under the new part "Part II. Alcoholic Beverages Violations". Precedence in numbering has been given to Ch. 213 as the later enactment. *See* Art. 1, § 17. Accordingly, this section appears as § 10-125.

§ 10-126. Citation; civil offense.

(a) *Issuance.* — A police officer may issue a citation to a person who the police officer has probable cause to believe has committed a violation under this part.

(b) *Civil offense.* — (1) A violation under this part is a civil offense.

(2) Adjudication of a violation under this part:

(i) is not a criminal conviction for any purpose; and

(ii) does not impose any of the civil disabilities that may result from a criminal conviction.

(c) *Contents.* — A citation issued under this part shall be signed by the police officer who issues the citation and shall contain:

(1) the name and address of the person charged;

(2) the statute allegedly violated;

(3) the date, location, and time that the violation occurred;

(4) the fine that may be imposed;

(5) a notice stating that prepayment of the fine is allowed; and

(6) a notice that states that the District Court shall promptly send the person a summons to appear for trial.

(d) *Form.* — The form of the citation shall be uniform throughout the State and shall be prescribed by the District Court.

(e) *Prepayment.* — The Chief Judge of the District Court shall establish a schedule for the prepayment of a fine.

(f) *Request for trial; scheduling.* — (1) The law enforcement agency of the police officer who issued the citation shall forward to the District Court having venue a copy of the citation and a request for trial.

(2) The District Court shall promptly schedule the case for trial and summon the defendant to appear.

(g) *Amount of fine.* — If a person is found to have committed a violation under this part, the person is subject to a fine not exceeding $25.

(h) *Costs.* — The court costs for a violation under this part are $5. (2002, chs. 108, 109.)

SPECIAL REVISOR'S NOTE

This Special Revisor's note comprises information related to the revision by Acts 2002, ch. 26 and other chapters amending this section from the 2002 Legislative Session.

Chapters 108 and 109 each added this section as § 10-116 under a new part "Part II. Alcoholic Beverage Consumption or Possession of Open Container in Passenger Area of Motor Vehicle". However, Ch. 213, § 1, Acts of 2002, transferred Article 2B, §§ 22-101 through 22-108, as enacted by Ch. 26, § 4, Acts of 2002, to be §§ 10-113 through 10-120, under the new part "Part II. Alcoholic Beverages Violations". Precedence in numbering has been given to Ch. 213 as the later enactment. *See* Art. 1, § 17. Accordingly, this section appears as § 10-126.

§ 10-127. Procedure.

(a) *In general.* — In a proceeding for a violation under this part:

(1) the State has the burden to prove the guilt of the defendant to the same extent as is required by law in the trial of a criminal case;

(2) the court shall apply the evidentiary standards as prescribed by law for the trial of a criminal case;

(3) the court shall ensure that the defendant has received a copy of the charges against the defendant and that the defendant understands those charges;

(4) the defendant is entitled to:

(i) cross-examine each witness who appears against the defendant;

(ii) produce evidence and witnesses on the defendant's own behalf;

(iii) testify on the defendant's own behalf if the defendant chooses to do so; and

(iv) be represented by counsel of the defendant's own selection and expense;

(5) the defendant may enter a plea of guilty or not guilty;

(6) the verdict shall be:

(i) guilty of a civil violation; or

(ii) not guilty of a civil violation; and

(7) before entering a judgment, a court may place the defendant on probation in the same manner and to the same extent as is permitted by law in a criminal case.

(b) *Suspension of fine.* — If a defendant is found guilty of a violation under this part and a fine is imposed, a court may direct that the payment of the fine be suspended or deferred under conditions determined by the court.

(c) *Failure to pay.* — A defendant's willful failure to pay a fine imposed under this part may be treated as a criminal contempt punishable as provided by law.

(d) *Appeal.* —A defendant who is found guilty of a violation under this part, as provided by law for a criminal case, may file:

(1) an appeal;

(2) a motion for a new trial; or

(3) a motion for a revision of a judgment.

(e) *Authority of State's Attorney.* — The State's Attorney for each county may:

(1) prosecute a violation under this part in the same manner as a prosecution of a criminal case, including entering a nolle prosequi or placing the case on violation on a stet docket; and

(2) exercise authority in the same manner prescribed by law for a violation of the criminal laws of the State. (2002, chs. 108, 109.)

SPECIAL REVISOR'S NOTE

This Special Revisor's note comprises information related to the revision by Acts 2002, ch. 26 and other chapters amending this section from the 2002 Legislative Session.

Chapters 108 and 109 each added this section as § 10-117 under a new part "Part II. Alcoholic Beverage Consumption or Possession of Open Container in Passenger Area of Motor Vehicle". However, Ch. 213, § 1, Acts of 2002, transferred Article 2B, §§ 22-101 through 22-108, as enacted by Ch. 26, § 4, Acts of 2002, to be §§ 10-113 through 10-120, under the new part "Part II. Alcoholic Beverages Violations". Precedence in numbering has been given to Ch. 213 as the later enactment. *See* Art. 1, § 17. Accordingly, this section appears as § 10-127.

Editor's note. — See Editor's note under § 10-123 of this article.

§§ 10-128, 10-129.

Reserved.

Part IV. Salvia Divinorum.

§ 10-130. In general.

(a) *"Salvia divinorum" defined.* — In this part, "Salvia divinorum" includes Salvinorin A and any material, compound, mixture, preparation, or product that contains Salvia divinorum or Salvinorin A.

(b) *Use for research in accredited academic or medical institution or research facility permitted.* — Nothing in this part shall prohibit an accredited academic or medical institution or research facility from conducting research on Salvia divinorum or Salvinorin A or a derivative of Salvia divinorum or Salvinorin A.

(c) *Local or municipal regulation not preempted.* — This part does not preempt any local or municipal law regulating the use, possession, or distribution of Salvia divinorum or Salvinorin A. (2010, chs. 200, 201.)

Editor's note. — Section 3, chs. 200 and 201, Acts 2010, provides that the acts shall take effect June 1, 2010.

§ 10-131. Violations; defenses; penalties.

(a) *Distribution to persons under 21 years of age prohibited.* — A person may not distribute Salvia divinorum to an individual under the age of 21 years.

(b) *Defenses.* — In a prosecution for a violation of this section, it is a defense that the defendant examined the purchaser's or recipient's driver's license or other valid identification issued by an employer, a government unit, or an institution of higher education that positively identified the purchaser or recipient as at least 21 years of age.

(c) *Penalties.* — A person who violates this section is guilty of a misdemeanor and on conviction is subject to a fine not exceeding:

(1) $1,000 for a first violation;

(2) $2,000 for a second violation occurring within 2 years after the first violation; and

(3) $6,000 for each subsequent violation occurring within 2 years after the preceding violation.

(d) *Separate violations.* — For purposes of this section, each separate incident at a different time and occasion is a separate violation. (2010, chs. 200, 201; 2011, ch. 392.)

Effect of amendments. — Chapter 392, Acts 2011, effective October 1, 2011, substituted "$1,000" for "$300" in (c)(1); in (c)(2) substituted "$2,000" for "$1,000"; and in (c)(3) substituted "$6,000" for "$3,000."

§ 10-132. Possession by person under 21 years of age prohibited.

An individual under the age of 21 years may not possess Salvia divinorum. (2010, chs. 200, 201.)

§ 10-133. Citations.

(a) *In general.* — A person who violates § 10-132 of this part shall be issued a citation under this section.

(b) *Who may issue.* — A citation for a violation of § 10-132 of this part may be issued by:

(1) a police officer authorized to make arrests; and

(2) in State forestry reservations, State parks, historic monuments, and recreation areas, a forest or park warden under § 5-206(a) of the Natural Resources Article.

(c) *Issuance on probable cause of violation.* — A person authorized under this section to issue a citation shall issue the citation if the person has probable cause to believe that the person charged is committing or has committed a violation of § 10-132 of this part.

(d) *Form and contents.* — (1) Subject to paragraph (2) of this subsection, the form of citation issued to an adult for a violation of § 10-132 of this part shall be as prescribed by the District Court and shall be uniform throughout the State.

(2) The citation issued to an adult shall contain:

(i) the name and address of the person charged;

(ii) the statute allegedly violated;

(iii) the location, date, and time that the violation occurred;

(iv) the fine that may be imposed;

(v) a notice stating that prepayment of the fine is not allowed;

(vi) a notice that the District Court shall promptly send to the person charged a summons to appear for trial;

(vii) the signature of the person issuing the citation; and

(viii) a space for the person charged to sign the citation.

(3) The form of citation issued to a minor shall:

(i) be prescribed by the State Court Administrator;

(ii) be uniform throughout the State; and

(iii) contain the information listed in § 3-8A-33(b) of the Courts Article.

(e) *Copy to be forwarded to the District Court.* — (1) The issuing jurisdiction shall forward a copy of the citation and a request for trial to the District Court in the district having venue.

(2) The District Court shall promptly schedule the case for trial and summon the defendant to appear.

(3) Willful failure of the defendant to respond to a summons described in paragraph (2) of this subsection is contempt of court.

(f) *Nature of offense; disposition.* — (1) For purposes of this section, a violation of § 10-132 of this part is a Code violation and is a civil offense.

(2) A person charged who is under the age of 18 years shall be subject to the procedures and dispositions provided in Title 3, Subtitle 8A of the Courts Article.

(3) A person charged who is at least 18 years old shall be subject to the provisions of this section.

(4) Adjudication of a Code violation under § 10-132 of this part is not a criminal conviction for any purpose and does not impose any of the civil disabilities ordinarily imposed by a criminal conviction.

(g) *Procedure.* — In any proceeding for a Code violation under § 10-132 of this part:

(1) the State has the burden to prove the guilt of the defendant to the same extent as is required by law in the trial of criminal causes;

(2) the court shall apply the evidentiary standards as prescribed by law or rule for the trial of criminal causes;

(3) the court shall ensure that the defendant has received a copy of the charges against the defendant and that the defendant understands those charges;

(4) the defendant is entitled to cross-examine all witnesses who appear against the defendant, to produce evidence or witnesses on behalf of the defendant, or to testify on the defendant's own behalf, if the defendant chooses to do so;

(5) the defendant is entitled to be represented by counsel of the defendant's choice and at the expense of the defendant; and

(6) the defendant may enter a plea of guilty or not guilty, and the verdict of the court in the case shall be:

(i) guilty of a Code violation;

(ii) not guilty of a Code violation; or

(iii) probation before judgment, imposed by the court in the same manner and to the same extent as is allowed by law in the trial of a criminal case.

(h) *Fines.* — (1) If the District Court finds that a person has committed a Code violation, the court shall require the person to pay:

(i) for a first violation, a fine not exceeding $500; or

(ii) for a second or subsequent violation, a fine not exceeding $1,000.

(2) The Chief Judge of the District Court may not establish a schedule for the prepayment of fines for a violation under § 10-132 of this part.

(i) *Fines — Payment.* — When a defendant has been found guilty of a Code violation and a fine has been imposed by the court:

(1) the court may direct that the payment of the fine be suspended or deferred under conditions that the court may establish; and

(2) if the defendant willfully fails to pay the fine imposed by the court, that willful failure may be treated as a criminal contempt of court, for which the defendant may be punished by the court as provided by law.

(j) *Costs.* — (1) The defendant is liable for the costs of the proceedings in the District Court and for payment to the Criminal Injuries Compensation Fund.

(2) The court costs in a Code violation case under § 10-132 of this part in which costs are imposed are $5.

(k) *Appeals.* — (1) A defendant who has been found guilty of a Code violation under § 10-132 of this part has the right to appeal or to file a motion for a new trial or a motion for a revision of a judgment provided by law in the trial of a criminal case.

(2) A motion shall be made in the same manner as provided in the trial of criminal cases, and the court, in ruling on the motion, has the same authority provided in the trial of criminal cases.

(l) *Nature of prosecution.* — (1) The State's Attorney for any county may prosecute a Code violation under § 10-132 of this part in the same manner as prosecution of a violation of the criminal laws of the State.

(2) In a Code violation case under § 10-132 of this part, the State's Attorney may:

(i) enter a nolle prosequi in or place the case on the stet docket; and

(ii) exercise authority in the same manner as prescribed by law for violation of the criminal laws of the State. (2010, chs. 200, 201.)

Editor's note. — See note to § 10-130 of this article.

Subtitle 2. Disturbing the Peace, Disorderly Conduct, and Related Crimes.

§ 10-201. Disturbing the public peace and disorderly conduct.

(a) *Definitions.* — (1) In this section the following words have the meanings indicated.

(2) (i) "Public conveyance" means a conveyance to which the public or a portion of the public has access to and a right to use for transportation.

(ii) "Public conveyance" includes an airplane, vessel, bus, railway car, school vehicle, and subway car.

(3) (i) "Public place" means a place to which the public or a portion of the public has access and a right to resort for business, dwelling, entertainment, or other lawful purpose.

(ii) "Public place" includes:

1. a restaurant, shop, shopping center, store, tavern, or other place of business;

2. a public building;

3. a public parking lot;

4. a public street, sidewalk, or right-of-way;

5. a public park or other public grounds;

6. the common areas of a building containing four or more separate dwelling units, including a corridor, elevator, lobby, and stairwell;

7. a hotel or motel;

8. a place used for public resort or amusement, including an amusement park, golf course, race track, sports arena, swimming pool, and theater;

9. an institution of elementary, secondary, or higher education;

10. a place of public worship;

11. a place or building used for entering or exiting a public conveyance, including an airport terminal, bus station, dock, railway station, subway station, and wharf; and

12. the parking areas, sidewalks, and other grounds and structures that are part of a public place.

(b) *Construction of section.* — For purposes of a prosecution under this section, a public conveyance or a public place need not be devoted solely to public use.

(c) *Prohibited.* — (1) A person may not willfully and without lawful purpose obstruct or hinder the free passage of another in a public place or on a public conveyance.

(2) A person may not willfully act in a disorderly manner that disturbs the public peace.

(3) A person may not willfully fail to obey a reasonable and lawful order that a law enforcement officer makes to prevent a disturbance to the public peace.

(4) A person who enters the land or premises of another, whether an owner or lessee, or a beach adjacent to residential riparian property, may not willfully:

(i) disturb the peace of persons on the land, premises, or beach by making an unreasonably loud noise; or

(ii) act in a disorderly manner.

(5) A person from any location may not, by making an unreasonably loud noise, willfully disturb the peace of another:

(i) on the other's land or premises;

(ii) in a public place; or

(iii) on a public conveyance.

(6) In Worcester County, a person may not build a bonfire or allow a bonfire to burn on a beach or other property between 1 a.m. and 5 a.m.

(d) *Penalty.* — A person who violates this section is guilty of a misdemeanor and on conviction is subject to imprisonment not exceeding 60 days or a fine not exceeding $500 or both. (An. Code 1957, art. 27, § 121; 2002, ch. 26, § 2.)

REVISOR'S NOTE

This Revisor's note comprises information related to the revision by Acts 2002, ch. 26.

This section is new language derived without substantive change from former Art. 27, § 121.

Subsection (b) of this section is revised as a construction provision for clarity.

In subsection (a)(2)(i) and (3)(i) of this section, the former references to the "general" public are deleted as unnecessary.

In subsection (a)(2)(ii) of this section, the former reference to a "boat" is deleted as included in the comprehensive reference to a "vessel".

Also in subsection (a)(2)(ii) of this section, the former reference to a "school bus" is deleted in light of the comprehensive reference to a "school vehicle".

In subsection (a)(3)(ii)12 of this section, the former reference to parking "lots" is deleted as included in the reference to "parking areas".

In subsection (c)(5) of this section, the former phrase "in a place of business" is deleted as included in the definition of "public place".

Defined term:
"Person"   § 1-101

University of Baltimore Law Review. — For note, "Constitutional Law — First Amendment Freedom of Speech — Statute Prohibiting 'Loud and Unseemly' Noises Is a Content-Neutral Regulation of Protected Speech," 20 U. Balt. L. Rev. 507 (1991).

Constitutionality. — The proscription of a prior similar version of this section, which makes it unlawful for anyone to willfully disturb any neighborhood in any Maryland city, town or county by loud and unseemly noises is constitutional when used by the State to limit the volume level of speech protected by the First Amendment to the United States Constitution. Eanes v. State, 318 Md. 436, 569 A.2d 604 (1990), cert. denied, 496 U.S. 938, 110 S. Ct. 3218, 110 L. Ed. 2d 665 (1990).

This section is content neutral, narrowly tailored to serve a significant State interest, and does not inhibit the use of various alternative channels of communication. Eanes v. State, 318 Md. 436, 569 A.2d 604 (1990), cert. denied, 496 U.S. 938, 110 S. Ct. 3218, 110 L. Ed. 2d 665 (1990).

Prohibitions embrace only unprotected speech. — Language prohibitions of this section embrace only unprotected speech; and they do not apply to protected expression. In re Nawrocki, 15 Md. App. 252, 289 A.2d 846, cert. denied, 266 Md. 741 (1972).

The statutes punish spoken words, but they cannot apply to speech, although vulgar or offensive, that is protected by the First and Fourteenth Amendments. In re Nawrocki, 15 Md. App. 252, 289 A.2d 846, cert. denied, 266 Md. 741 (1972).

Whether the "loud and unseemly noise" (now "an unreasonably loud noise") prohibitions of the statutes are within the ambit of protected expression depends on the nature and content of them, a question to be determined on the facts of the particular case. In re Nawrocki, 15 Md. App. 252, 289 A.2d 846, cert. denied, 266 Md. 741 (1972).

Construction. — A prior similar statute proscribed two general courses of conduct on or about any public place: the first, acting in a disorderly manner to the disturbance of the public peace may be committed silently as by one indecently exposing his person, explicitly prohibited, or by failing to obey a lawful order of the police, such as a command to move on, when not to do so may endanger the public peace; the second contemplated noises made, either loud and unseemly, or by profanely cursing, swearing or using obscene language. In re Nawrocki, 15 Md. App. 252, 289 A.2d 846, cert. denied, 266 Md. 741 (1972).

When determining whether § 18-325(b)(1) of the Health - General Article, criminalizing behaving in a disorderly manner at a placement for tuberculosis treatment, was unconstitutionally vague, the phrase "disorderly manner" had to be analyzed in the context of a treatment facility for tuberculosis because while disorderly conduct offenses generally, such as under (c)(2) of this section, were concerned with maintaining public peace and order, behaving in a disorderly manner in a tuberculosis treatment facility required consideration of (1) the purpose of the statute, which was to prevent and control the spread of tuberculosis, (2) the purpose of medical quarantine, which was to safeguard the public health, (3) the need to maintain peace and order within the treatment facility, and (4) the need to ensure the safety of medical professionals, staff members, other patients, visitors, and the public at large. Livingston v. State, 192 Md. App. 553, 995 A.2d 812 (2010).

Jurisdiction. — Cases charging violations of a prior version of this section, are within the exclusive original jurisdiction of the District Court because the offense charged is a statutory misdemeanor as to which the maximum penalty authorized for confinement is less than three years. Howard v. State, 32 Md. App. 75, 359 A.2d 568 (1976).

Arrest need not be made after first disobedience or at scene. — Officer did not have to arrest defendant immediately after defendant's first disobedience of the officer's lawful order, nor did the officer have to arrest defendant at the scene in order to initiate a prosecution for failure to obey a peace officer under (c)(3). Spry v. State, 396 Md. 682, 914 A.2d 1182 (2007).

Enforcement. — A prior similar version of this section does not invite arbitrary or discriminatory enforcement. It can be enforced to limit protected speech only to the extent the speaker's actions are willful, the volume clearly exceeds what is necessary to address passersby, and the noise is actually disruptive to the "captive" audience in the neighborhood. Eanes v. State, 318 Md. 436, 569 A.2d 604 (1990), cert.

denied, 496 U.S. 938, 110 S. Ct. 3218, 110 L. Ed. 2d 665 (1990).

"Curse" and "swear" are synonymous. — Within the contemplation of the statutes, "curse" and "swear" are synonymous — "to use profane oaths," "abuse profanely," "to invoke evil, calamity, or injury upon," "to damn." Although a synonym for "profane" is "blasphemous," it is better considered in its secular sense of being "abusive, vulgar, or irreverent language." In re Nawrocki, 15 Md. App. 252, 289 A.2d 846, cert. denied, 266 Md. 741 (1972).

Profanity per se would not amount to disorderly conduct. The words used by the accused would have to be "fighting" words to be punishable. In re Nawrocki, 15 Md. App. 252, 289 A.2d 846, cert. denied, 266 Md. 741 (1972).

"Fighting" words. — "Fighting" words have a direct tendency to cause acts of violence by the person to whom, individually, the remark is addressed. In re Nawrocki, 15 Md. App. 252, 289 A.2d 846, cert. denied, 266 Md. 741 (1972).

The State is free to ban the simple use, without a demonstration of additional justifying circumstances, of so-called fighting words, those personally abusive epithets which, when addressed to the ordinary citizen, are, as a matter of common knowledge, inherently likely to provoke violent reaction. In re Nawrocki, 15 Md. App. 252, 289 A.2d 846, cert. denied, 266 Md. 741 (1972).

The test is what men of common intelligence would understand would be words likely to cause an average addressee to fight. Derisive and annoying words can be taken as coming within the purview of the statute proscribing offensive, derisive and annoying words only when they have the characteristic of plainly tending to excite the addressee to a breach of the peace. In re Nawrocki, 15 Md. App. 252, 289 A.2d 846, cert. denied, 266 Md. 741 (1972).

"Loud". — "Loud" is characterized by high volume and intensity of sound — clamorous and insistent. In re Nawrocki, 15 Md. App. 252, 289 A.2d 846, cert. denied, 266 Md. 741 (1972).

"Obscene." — The State has the power to punish obscene expression, but to be obscene such expression must be, in some significant way, erotic so as to conjure up such psychic stimulation in anyone likely to be confronted with it. In re Nawrocki, 15 Md. App. 252, 289 A.2d 846, cert. denied, 266 Md. 741 (1972).

The "obscene language" prohibited by a prior similar provision means obscene in the constitutional sense. In re Nawrocki, 15 Md. App. 252, 289 A.2d 846, cert. denied, 266 Md. 741 (1972).

"Public peace". — Because this section makes it plain that the "public peace" is a central element of the crime, and since the public must be present for its peace to be threatened, neither party was entitled to sum-mary judgment on federal claims for false arrest, false imprisonment, and malicious prosecution where there was a genuine dispute as to the presence of a crowd. White v. State Transp. Auth., 151 F. Supp. 2d 651 (D. Md. 2001).

"Public place." — Doubt was expressed as to whether a prior similar version of this section applied to a location where there were 11 other homes nearby but there was no express evidence that it was in a town. Wanzer v. State, 202 Md. 601, 97 A.2d 914 (1953).

Prohibited conduct. — Applying normal meanings to words of common understanding leads to the conclusion that speech that is so unreasonably loud as to unreasonably intrude on the privacy of a captive audience may be punished; the words "loud and unseemly," in prior similar provision, give sufficient notice of what conduct was penalized; "unseemly" (now "unreasonably") modifies "loud" and means "unreasonably loud in the circumstances." Eanes v. State, 318 Md. 436, 569 A.2d 604 (1990), cert. denied, 496 U.S. 938, 110 S. Ct. 3218, 110 L. Ed. 2d 665 (1990).

Other persons must be within hearing of disturbing noises. — By the express provisions of a prior similar provision, other persons must be within hearing of the disturbing noises. So a person standing on a county highway making loud and unseemly noises and profanely cursing and swearing would not be committing the crime proscribed by a prior similar provision unless within the hearing of others passing by or along the highway. In re Nawrocki, 15 Md. App. 252, 289 A.2d 846, cert. denied, 266 Md. 741 (1972).

State not required to prove other persons heard noises. — It is not necessary that the State prove that other persons in fact heard the noises. It would be sufficient if they were passing by or along the highway so that reasonably they may have heard them. In re Nawrocki, 15 Md. App. 252, 289 A.2d 846, cert. denied, 266 Md. 741 (1972).

Conduct must be willful. — Failure to instruct jury that a defendant in a disorderly conduct case had to have acted "willfully" was plain error justifying reversal. Dziekonski v. State, 127 Md. App. 191, 732 A.2d 367 (1999).

There is no need that the action be for the purpose of disturbing the public peace. — Party charged need not act for the purpose of disturbing the public peace. The effect of the actor's conduct need only be that the peace was disturbed. Dziekonski v. State, 127 Md. App. 191, 732 A.2d 367 (1999).

Arrest need not be made after first disobedience or at scene. — Officer did not have to arrest defendant immediately after defendant's first disobedience of the officer's lawful order, nor did the officer have to arrest defendant at the scene in order to initiate a prosecution for failure to obey a police officer's reasonable and lawful order to prevent a disturbance to public peace under (c)(3). Spry v. State, 393 Md. 477, 903 A.2d 416 (2006).

Verbal protest. — Where a person is acting in a lawful manner and is the object of an unlawful police order, it is not usually a criminal violation for such person to verbally protest a police officer's insistence upon submission to such an order. Diehl v. State, 294 Md. 466, 451 A.2d 115 (1982), cert. denied, 460 U.S. 1098, 103 S. Ct. 1798, 76 L. Ed. 2d 363 (1983).

Person going beyond bounds of protest subject to arrest. — A prior similar provision is not intended to prevent a citizen, outraged by police misconduct toward him, from loudly protesting such misconduct. If the citizen goes beyond the bounds of the protest and seeks to enlist the crowd to interfere with the police officer and consequently precipitates public disorder amounting to a breach of the peace, the police officer may, under such circumstances, take steps to quell the disorder, even to the extent of arresting the citizen. Diehl v. State, 294 Md. 466, 451 A.2d 115 (1982), cert. denied, 460 U.S. 1098, 103 S. Ct. 1798, 76 L. Ed. 2d 363 (1983).

Complaint required. — Police may act under a prior similar version of this section only upon receipt of a complaint from an affected citizen upon the basis of which the officer reasonably believes that the section has been violated. Eanes v. State, 318 Md. 436, 569 A.2d 604 (1990), cert. denied, 496 U.S. 938, 110 S. Ct. 3218, 110 L. Ed. 2d 665 (1990).

Indictment. — Count in indictment which charged that defendants "unlawfully did conspire, combine, etc., riotously and tumultuously to assemble and gather together to disturb the peace," charged a common law offense, and would not be quashed as too vague. Winkler v. State, 194 Md. 1, 69 A.2d 674 (1949), cert. denied, 339 U.S. 919, 70 S. Ct. 621, 94 L. Ed. 1343 (1950).

Right to jury trial. — Defendants were not entitled to a jury trial in cases charging a violation of a prior similar provision, and could not deprive the District Court under § 4-302 (d) of the Courts Article, of its exclusive original jurisdiction over those cases by demanding a jury trial. Howard v. State, 32 Md. App. 75, 359 A.2d 568 (1976).

Evidence of profanity. — Officer's statement that the accused was "using profane language" was a conclusion and, in the absence of evidence setting out the language the officer concluded was profane, there was not enough for the trier of fact to determine that the language was "profane" within the ambit of a prior similar statute. In re Nawrocki, 15 Md. App. 252, 289 A.2d 846, cert. denied, 266 Md. 741 (1972).

Trier of fact ascertains profanity of language. — What the officer felt was "profane" may not have been profane within the contemplation of a prior similar statute. It was for the trier of fact, not the officer, to ascertain whether the language was profane vel non. A bald statement by the officer characterizing the language of the accused as profane is simply not sufficient in law. In re Nawrocki, 15 Md. App. 252, 289 A.2d 846, cert. denied, 266 Md. 741 (1972).

Sufficiency of evidence. — Jury acquittal on charges of assault and inciting to riot does not necessarily mean the jury concluded that there was no evidence legally sufficient to justify conviction under a prior similar provision. Hallengren v. State, 14 Md. App. 43, 286 A.2d 213 (1972).

There was no clear error in the fact finder's determination that defendant was arrested for disorderly conduct not because of foul language addressed to a hospital police officer, but because of the loudness of her voice, which defendant refused to lower; the definition of the offense struck a reasonable balance between free speech rights and privacy rights, which were entitled to special protection in a hospital setting. Polk v. State, 378 Md. 1, 835 A.2d 575 (2003), cert. denied, 541 U.S. 951, 124 S. Ct. 1691, 158 L. Ed. 2d 382 (2004).

Evidence establishing that a group of juveniles conspired to assault the victims, that the bus was rocking violently and that people thought there was a riot on the bus, and that the interior of the bus was damaged during the attack was sufficient to support appellants' convictions for disorderly conduct. In re Lavar D., 189 Md. App. 526, 985 A.2d 102 (2009).

Separate offenses. — Where persons were arrested and charged with a violation of a prior version of this section and acquitted, the acquittal was held not to bar a prosecution for assault and battery committed in resisting the arrest. Williams v. State, 204 Md. 55, 102 A.2d 714 (1954).

Merger of offenses. — A jury could have concluded from the evidence that in addition to making loud and unseemly noises and uttering obscene language within the hearing of persons passing on the street, defendant's conduct in urging the murder of police officers, his clenched-fist gestures in support of his exhortations, his refusal to obey reasonable police commands, and his stone and bottle throwing activity, constituted a violation of a prior version of § 3-803 of this article, and there would be no merger of offenses under that section into a conviction under a prior version of this section. Hallengren v. State, 14 Md. App. 43, 286 A.2d 213 (1972).

Applied in State v. Long, 405 Md. 527, 954 A.2d 1083 (2008).

Stated in Todd v. State, 161 Md. App. 332, 868 A.2d 944 (2005).

Cited in Smith v. State, 399 Md. 565, 924 A.2d 1175 (2007); Pinkney v. State, 200 Md. App. 563, 28 A.3d 118 (2011).

§ 10-202. Keeping disorderly house — Penalty.

A person who keeps a disorderly house is guilty of a misdemeanor and on conviction is subject to imprisonment not less than 10 days and not exceeding 6 months or a fine not less than $50 and not exceeding $300 or both. (An. Code 1957, art. 27, § 122; 2002, ch. 26, § 2.)

REVISOR'S NOTE

This Revisor's note comprises information related to the revision by Acts 2002, ch. 26.

This section is new language derived without substantive change from former Art. 27, § 122.

The reference to a person who keeps a disorderly house being "guilty of a misdemeanor" is added to state expressly that which was only implied in the former law. At common law, keeping a disorderly house was a misdemeanor, and former Art. 27, § 122 merely established the penalty for it. Ward v. State, 9 Md. App. 583 (1970); Beard v. State, 71 Md. 275 (1889). In this State, any crime that was not considered a felony at common law and has not been declared a felony by statute is considered a misdemeanor. See State v. Canova, 278 Md. 483, 490 (1976); Bowser v. State, 136 Md. 342, 354 (1920); Dutton v. State, 123 Md. 373, 378 (1914); and Williams v. State, 4 Md. App. 342, 347 (1968).

The former reference to imprisonment "in jail" is deleted for consistency within this article. Currently inmates are sentenced to the custody of a unit such as the Division of Correction and then are placed in a particular facility. See CS § 9-103.

Defined term:

"Person" § 1-101

Cross references. — For provisions relating to bawdyhouses, prostitution, and related crimes, see § 11-301 et seq. of this article.

Keeping disorderly house still common law crime. — Keeping a disorderly house is still a common law crime in Maryland, although the punishment for it has been fixed by an act of the General Assembly. Jackson v. State, 176 Md. 399, 5 A.2d 282 (1939).

Section deals only with punishment. — This section only deals with the punishment and not with definition of the common law offense. Lutz v. State, 167 Md. 12, 172 A. 354 (1934).

The offense of keeping a disorderly house is a common law misdemeanor in Maryland, although punishment for the offense is fixed by this section. Since the crime is not defined by statute, it must be afforded its common law meaning in this State. Ward v. State, 9 Md. App. 583, 267 A.2d 255 (1970).

Crime was nuisance at common law. — Crime was held nuisance at common law because it drew together dissolute persons engaged in unlawful and injurious practices, thereby to endanger the public peace and corrupt good morals. Ward v. State, 9 Md. App. 583, 267 A.2d 255 (1970).

The classification of a disorderly house as a nuisance was well established at common law. Ward v. State, 9 Md. App. 583, 267 A.2d 255 (1970).

A disorderly house is a kind of offensive nuisance. Ward v. State, 9 Md. App. 583, 267 A.2d 255 (1970).

"House" defined. — "House" means an edifice, apartment or place. It includes, among other places, a room, a place of business, a tent, a wagon or a boat. Curley v. State, 215 Md. 382, 137 A.2d 640 (1958).

"Bawdyhouse" or "house of ill fame" defined. — At common law a "bawdyhouse" or a "house of ill fame," in the popular sense of the terms, is a species of disorderly house. Speaks v. State, 3 Md. App. 371, 239 A.2d 600, cert. denied, 251 Md. 752 (1968).

"Disorderly house" defined. — A house may be disorderly either from the purpose for which it is appropriated, or from the mode in which it is kept. The charge does not respect ownership or proprietorship, but the conduct of the place. Curley v. State, 215 Md. 382, 137 A.2d 640 (1958).

A house is disorderly if kept as a place where acts prohibited by statute are habitually indulged in or permitted. Speaks v. State, 3 Md. App. 371, 239 A.2d 600, cert. denied, 251 Md. 752 (1968).

A house may be disorderly either from the purpose for which it is appropriated or from the mode in which it is kept. The offense is one respecting the conduct of the place, and not its ownership. Ward v. State, 9 Md. App. 583, 267 A.2d 255 (1970).

While a house is disorderly if kept as a place where acts prohibited by statute are habitually indulged in or permitted, this is but one species of a disorderly house. It is not required to constitute the offense that the acts constituting the nuisance be prohibited by statute. Ward v. State, 9 Md. App. 583, 267 A.2d 255 (1970).

A place may be a disorderly house though it is quietly kept, no conspicuous improprieties are permitted, and the activities are not open to public observation. Ward v. State, 9 Md. App. 583, 267 A.2d 255 (1970).

Elements of offense. — The crime consists in the keeping of the house as a place of habitual or common resort of people of evil name and fame, and of dishonest conversation, there to consort together, thus affording opportunities for and temptations to the indulgence of their bad habits and passions, to the evil example and scandal of the neighborhood. Ward v. State, 9 Md. App. 583, 267 A.2d 255 (1970).

Owning or managing business not prerequisites to "keeping." — The facts supported a finding that the defendant was keeping and maintaining the diner and cocktail lounge where his activities in violation of the gaming laws were carried on, though he had no ownership in it nor did he exercise any active participation in the management of the usual business conducted there. Curley v. State, 215 Md. 382, 137 A.2d 640 (1958).

Scienter. — In a conviction based upon a prior similar provision, the Court of Appeals assumed that scienter must be shown. Kolker v. State, 230 Md. 157, 186 A.2d 212 (1962).

Indictment. — An indictment for keeping a disorderly house was not bad for duplicity because it alleged unlawful possession and sale of alcoholic beverages at the disorderly house. Jackson v. State, 176 Md. 399, 5 A.2d 282 (1939).

The offense of keeping a disorderly house is that of a common nuisance, and it is necessary that the indictment should contain facts to show that a common nuisance has been created or permitted. This is done by allegation of such facts as show that the traverser maintains, promotes, or continues, what is noisome and offensive, or annoying and vexatious, or plainly hurtful to the public, or is a public outrage against common decency or common morality, or which tends plainly and directly to the corruption of the morals, honesty, and good habits of the people. Ward v. State, 9 Md. App. 583, 267 A.2d 255 (1970).

There can be no valid objection to an indictment for keeping a disorderly house merely because it contains averments which are explanatory of the elements of the disorder. Such an indictment may aver any of the acts which the State might establish in order to show the character of the house. Jackson v. State, 176 Md. 399, 5 A.2d 282 (1939).

Sufficient probable cause. — The admission of a policeman and policewoman into a house and the assignment of a room to them, without inquiry as to their marital status and without asking them to register, was sufficient probable cause for the officers to believe that the misdemeanor of keeping a disorderly house was being committed in their presence, and to justify the arrest without a warrant of the defendant, who had leased the house. As an incident of the lawful arrest, the officers had authority to search the premises within the use and under the control of the defendant, and to seize tangible evidence of the crime. Matthews v. State, 228 Md. 401, 179 A.2d 892 (1962).

Evidence held sufficient to convict. — See Matthews v. State, 228 Md. 401, 179 A.2d 892 (1962).

Where the State's evidence justified a finding that the defendant violated the gambling statutes by taking bets on horse races many times on the several days charged in the indictment, and that he was keeping and maintaining the place where the violations occurred in the eyes of the law, the trial judge was warranted in finding him guilty of keeping and maintaining a disorderly house. Curley v. State, 215 Md. 382, 137 A.2d 640 (1958).

Assistant State's Attorney signing petition for injunction. — Signing of petition for injunction by assistant State's Attorney is not a violation of this section. Marques v. State, 267 Md. 542, 298 A.2d 408 (1973).

§ 10-203. Interference with commercial athletic event.

(a) *Definitions.* — (1) In this section the following words have the meanings indicated.

(2) "Commercial athletic contest" means an athletic or sporting event held in a public arena, field, hall, or stadium for admission to which the general public must pay an admission charge.

(3) "Object" means an item that may cause injury to a participant in or observer of the commercial athletic contest.

(b) *Prohibited.* — A person may not disrupt or interfere with a commercial athletic contest by throwing or projecting an object on the playing field or seating area.

(c) *Penalty.* — A person who violates this section is guilty of a misdemeanor and on conviction is subject to imprisonment not exceeding 3 months or a fine not exceeding $250 or both. (An. Code 1957, art. 27, § 125 1/2; 2002, ch. 26, § 2.)

REVISOR'S NOTE

This Revisor's note comprises information related to the revision by Acts 2002, ch. 26.

This section is new language derived without substantive change from former Art. 27, § 125 ½.

In subsection (a)(2) of this section, the former phrase "of the State" is deleted as surplusage.

Also in subsection (a)(2) of this section, the references to the potential venues for a commercial athletic event are revised in light of Art. 1, § 8 which provides that the singular generally includes the plural.

The Criminal Law Article Review Committee notes, for the consideration of the General

Assembly, that in subsection (b) of this section the reference to the "playing field or seating area" may not include many areas that may need to be secured from disruption and interference in the course of a commercial athletic contest. For example, it is not clear that a bullpen, on-deck circle, dugout, or penalty box is part of the "playing field or seating area". The General Assembly may wish to explore the areas that may need to be included in order to secure a commercial athletic contest from interference.

Defined term:
"Person" § 1-101

§ 10-204. Interference with access to or egress from a medical facility.

(a) *Definitions.* — (1) In this section the following words have the meanings indicated.

(2) (i) "Medical facility" means:

1. a facility as defined in § 10-101 of the Health - General Article; or

2. a health care facility as defined in § 19-114 of the Health - General Article.

(ii) "Medical facility" includes an agency, clinic, or office operated under the direction of the local health officer or under the regulatory authority of the Department of Health and Mental Hygiene.

(b) *Scope of section.* — (1) This section does not apply to:

(i) the chief executive officer of the medical facility;

(ii) a designee of the chief executive officer of the medical facility;

(iii) an agent of the medical facility; or

(iv) a law enforcement officer.

(2) This section does not prohibit:

(i) speech; or

(ii) picketing in connection with a labor dispute as defined in § 4-301 of the Labor and Employment Article.

(c) *Prohibited.* — A person may not intentionally act, alone or with others, to prevent another from entering or exiting a medical facility by physically:

(1) detaining the other; or

(2) obstructing, impeding, or hindering the other's passage.

(d) *Penalty.* — A person who violates this section is guilty of a misdemeanor and on conviction is subject to imprisonment not exceeding 90 days or a fine not exceeding $1,000 or both. (An. Code 1957, art. 27, § 577B; 2002, ch. 26, § 2.)

REVISOR'S NOTE

This Revisor's note comprises information related to the revision by Acts 2002, ch. 26.

This section is new language derived without substantive change from former Art. 27, § 577B.

Subsection (b) of this section is revised as a scope provision for clarity.

In subsection (b)(2)(ii) of this section, the former reference to a picketing "assembly" is deleted for consistency with § 3-707 of this article.

Defined term:
"Person"   § 1-101

§ 10-205. Obstruction, etc., of entry to or exit from funeral, burial, memorial service, or funeral procession.

(a) *Scope.* — (1) This subsection does not apply to a person who conducts a funeral, burial, memorial service, or funeral procession.

(2) A person may not knowingly obstruct, hinder, impede, or block another person's entry to or exit from a funeral, burial, memorial service, or funeral procession.

(b) *Prohibited speech.* — A person may not address speech to a person attending a funeral, burial, memorial service, or funeral procession that is likely to incite or produce an imminent breach of the peace.

(c) *Prohibited picketing.* — A person may not engage in picketing activity within 500 feet of a funeral, burial, memorial service, or funeral procession that is targeted at one or more persons attending the funeral, burial, memorial service, or funeral procession.

(d) *Penalty.* — A person who violates this section is guilty of a misdemeanor and on conviction is subject to imprisonment not exceeding 90 days or a fine not exceeding $1,000 or both. (2006, ch. 357; 2011, ch. 570.)

Effect of amendments. — Chapter 570, Acts 2011, effective October 1, 2011, substituted "500 feet" for "100 feet" in (c).

Subtitle 3. Hate Crimes.

§ 10-301. Definitions.

(a) *In general.* — In this subtitle the following words have the meanings indicated.

(b) *Homeless.* — "Homeless" means:

(1) lacking a fixed, regular, and adequate nighttime residence; or

(2) having a primary nighttime residence that is:

(i) a supervised publicly or privately operated shelter designed to provide temporary living accommodations; or

(ii) a public or private place not designed for or ordinarily used as a regular sleeping accommodation for human beings.

(c) *Sexual orientation.* — "Sexual orientation" means the identification of an individual as to male or female homosexuality, heterosexuality, bisexuality, or gender-related identity. (2005, ch. 571; 2009, ch. 201.)

Effect of amendments. — Chapter 201, Acts 2009, effective October 1, 2009, added (a) and (b); added the (c) designation; in (c) deleted "In this subtitle" at the beginning; and made a stylistic change.

§ 10-302. Damaging property of religious entity.

A person may not deface, damage, or destroy, or attempt to deface, damage, or destroy, personal or real property that is owned, leased, or used by a religious entity or for any religious purpose including:

(1) a place of worship;

(2) a cemetery;

(3) a religious school, educational facility, or community center; and

(4) the grounds adjacent to them. (An. Code 1957, art. 27, § 470A(a)(1), (3), (b)(1); 2002, ch. 26, § 2; 2005, chs. 482, 571.)

This Revisor's note comprises information related to the revision by Acts 2002, ch. 26.

This section is new language derived without substantive change from former Art. 27, § 470A(a)(1) and (3) and (b)(1).

In this section, the term "religious real property" defined in former Art. 27, § 470A(a)(3) is incorporated into the substantive provision to which it applied.

In item (3) of this section, the former reference to a religious "structure, or other real property" is deleted as surplusage.

Defined term:
"Person" § 1-101

Maryland Law Review. — For note on 1995 decisions, see 54 Md. L. Rev. 670 (1995).

Constitutionality. — To the extent that the provisions of the former version of this section are directed at commission of crimes or damage to property they are constitutionally defensible because they are directed at conduct, not at speech. 77 Op. Att'y Gen. 23 (December 3, 1992).

§ 10-303. Obstructing exercise of religious belief.

A person may not, by force or threat of force, obstruct or attempt to obstruct another in the free exercise of that person's religious beliefs. (An. Code 1957, art. 27, § 470A(b)(2); 2002, ch. 26, § 2; 2005, chs. 482, 571.)

This Revisor's note comprises information related to the revision by Acts 2002, ch. 26.

This section is new language derived without substantive change from former Art. 27, § 470A(b)(2).

Defined term:
"Person" § 1-101

§ 10-304. Harassment; destruction of property.

Because of another's race, color, religious beliefs, sexual orientation, gender, disability, or national origin, or because another is homeless, a person may not:

(1) (i) commit a crime or attempt to commit a crime against that person;

(ii) damage the real or personal property of that person;

(iii) deface, damage, or destroy, or attempt to deface, damage, or destroy the real or personal property of that person; or

(iv) burn or attempt to burn an object on the real or personal property of that person; or

(2) commit a violation of item (1) of this section that:

(i) except as provided in item (ii) of this item, involves a separate crime that is a felony; or

(ii) results in the death of the victim. (An. Code 1957, art. 27, § 470A(b)(3)(i), (4)(i); 2002, ch. 26, § 2; 2005, chs. 482, 571; 2006, ch. 44; 2009, chs. 201, 402.)

This Revisor's note comprises information related to the revision by Acts 2002, ch. 26.

This section is new language derived without substantive change from former Art. 27, § 470A(b)(3)(i) and (4)(i).

Defined term:
"Person"   § 1-101

Effect of amendments. — Chapter 201, Acts 2009, effective October 1, 2009, in the introductory language added "gender" and "or because another is homeless"; and added "or attempt to commit a crime" in (1)(i).

Chapter 402, Acts 2009, effective October 1, 2009, in the introductory language added "disability"; and added "or attempt to commit a crime" in (1)(i).

Editor's note. — Chapters 201 and 402, Acts 2009, both amended this section. Neither of the chapters referred to the other, and the language in the introductory paragraph has been reconciled to give effect to both, and the chapters made identical amendments in (1)(i).

Standing to challenge constitutionality. — Defendant lacked standing to challenge a former version of this section facially, on the basis that the harassment prong is vague and overbroad, where he was neither charged nor convicted under that prong. Ayers v. State, 335 Md. 602, 645 A.2d 22 (1994), cert. denied, 513 U.S. 1130, 115 S. Ct. 942, 130 L. Ed. 2d 886 (1995).

Motive is essential element of offense. — In order to prove a case under former subsection (b)(3 (i) (now this section), the prosecution is required to show that a defendant has committed a crime based upon a person "because of that person's race"; thus, motive is an essential element of the crime. Ayers v. State, 335 Md. 602, 645 A.2d 22 (1994), cert. denied, 513 U.S. 1130, 115 S. Ct. 942, 130 L. Ed. 2d 886 (1995).

Evidence of motivation. — Under a former version of this section, only speech actually connected with the offense should be used as evidence of motivation. Ayers v. State, 335 Md. 602, 645 A.2d 22 (1994), cert. denied, 513 U.S. 1130, 115 S. Ct. 942, 130 L. Ed. 2d 886 (1995).

Sentence held not excessive or oppressive. — Sentence imposed by the trial court for kidnapping and racially motivated crimes was not so excessive and oppressive as to evidence an abuse of discretion and to constitute cruel and unusual punishment under the Eighth Amendment to the United States Constitution and articles 16 and 25 of the Maryland Declaration of Rights. Ayers v. State, 335 Md. 602, 645 A.2d 22 (1994), cert. denied, 513 U.S. 1130, 115 S. Ct. 942, 130 L. Ed. 2d 886 (1995).

§ 10-305. Damage to associated building.

A person may not deface, damage, or destroy, attempt to deface, damage, or destroy, burn or attempt to burn an object on, or damage the real or personal property connected to a building that is publicly or privately owned, leased, or used, including a cemetery, library, meeting hall, recreation center, or school:

(1) because a person or group of a particular race, color, religious belief, sexual orientation, gender, disability, or national origin, or because a person or group that is homeless, has contacts or is associated with the building; or

(2) if there is evidence that exhibits animosity against a person or group, because of the race, color, religious beliefs, sexual orientation, gender, disability, or national origin of that person or group or because that person or group is homeless. (An. Code 1957, art. 27, § 470A(a)(1), (2), (b)(3)(ii), (4)(ii); 2002, ch. 26, § 2; 2005, chs. 482, 571; 2009, chs. 201, 402.)

REVISOR'S NOTE

This Revisor's note comprises information related to the revision by Acts 2002, ch. 26.

This section is new language derived without substantive change from former Art. 27, § 470A(a)(1) and (2) and (b)(3)(ii) and (4)(ii).

In this section, the term "institution" defined in former Art. 27, § 470A(a)(2) is incorporated into the substantive provision to which it applied.

Defined term:
"Person"   § 1-101

Effect of amendments. — Chapter 201, Acts 2009, effective October 1, 2009, added "gender" and "or because a person or group that is homeless" or variant in (1) and (2).

Chapter 402, Acts 2009, effective October 1, 2009, added "disability" in (1) and (2).

Editor's note. — Chapters 201 and 402, Acts 2009, both amended this section. Neither of the chapters referred to the other, and the language in (1) and (2) has been reconciled to give effect to both.

See Editor's note under § 10-302 of this subtitle.

§ 10-306. Penalty.

(a) *For violation of subtitle.* — Except as provided in subsection (b) of this section, a person who violates this subtitle is guilty of a misdemeanor and on conviction is subject to imprisonment not exceeding 3 years or a fine not exceeding $5,000 or both.

(b) *For violation of § 10-304 of this subtitle.* — (1) A person who violates § 10-304(2)(i) of this subtitle is guilty of a felony and on conviction is subject to imprisonment not exceeding 10 years or a fine not exceeding $10,000 or both.

(2) A person who violates § 10-304(2)(ii) of this subtitle is guilty of a felony and on conviction is subject to imprisonment not exceeding 20 years or a fine not exceeding $20,000 or both. (An. Code 1957, art. 27, § 470A(c); 2002, ch. 26, § 2; 2005, ch. 25, § 12; chs. 482, 571; 2009, chs. 201, 402.)

REVISOR'S NOTE

This Revisor's note comprises information related to the revision by Acts 2002, ch. 26.

This section is new language derived without substantive change from former Art. 27, § 470A(c).

Defined term:
"Person" § 1-101

Effect of amendments. — Chapter 201, Acts 2009, effective October 1, 2009, reenacted the section without change.

Chapter 402, Acts 2009, effective October 1, 2009, reenacted the section without change.

Editor's note. — See Editor's note under § 10-302 of this subtitle.

§ 10-307. Sentencing.

A sentence imposed under this subtitle may be separate from and consecutive to or concurrent with a sentence for any crime based on the act establishing the violation of this subtitle. (2005, chs. 482, 571.)

Editor's note. — See Editor's note under § 10-302 of this subtitle.

§ 10-308. First Amendment rights protected.

Nothing in this subtitle may be construed to infringe on the speech of a religious leader or other individual during peaceable activity intended to express the leader's or individual's religious beliefs or convictions. (2005, ch. 571.)

Subtitle 4. Crimes Relating to Human Remains.

§ 10-401. Definitions.

(a) *In general.* — In this subtitle the following words have the meanings indicated.

REVISOR'S NOTE

This subsection is new language derived without substantive change from former Art. 27, § 265(a)(1) and the introductory language of former §§ 267(a)(1) and 267A(a)(1).

In this subsection, the reference to this "subtitle" is substituted for the former references to "subheading" and this "section" to reflect the reorganization of material derived from the former subheadings on the removal of human remains from burial sites, graveyard desecra-

tion, and trading in human remains and associated funerary objects. Although this substitution applies the defined term "permanent cemetery" in § 10-404(e), which is derived from former Art. 27, § 267(d), a provision to which it did not originally apply, the term is used in a manner consistent with the term "permanent cemetery" used in the former law. No substantive change is intended.

(b) *Associated funerary object.* — (1) "Associated funerary object" means an item of human manufacture or use that is intentionally placed:

(i) with human remains at the time of interment in a burial site; or

(ii) after interment, as a part of a death ceremony of a culture, religion, or group.

(2) "Associated funerary object" includes a gravestone, monument, tomb, or other structure in or directly associated with a burial site.

REVISOR'S NOTE

This subsection is new language substituted for former Art. 27, §§ 265(a)(2), 267(a), and 267A(a) as they defined "associated funerary object".

In this subsection and throughout this subtitle, the defined term "funerary object" is substi-

tuted for the former defined term "associated funerary object" for brevity.

In this subsection, the reference to placement "after interment" is substituted for the former reference to "later" placement for clarity.

(c) *Burial site.* — (1) "Burial site" means a natural or prepared physical location, whether originally located below, on, or above the surface of the earth, into which human remains or associated funerary objects are deposited as a part of a death ceremony of a culture, religion, or group.

(2) "Burial site" includes the human remains and associated funerary objects that result from a shipwreck or accident and are left intentionally to remain at the site.

REVISOR'S NOTE

This subsection is new language substituted for former Art. 27, § 265(a)(3).

In this subsection and throughout this subtitle, the former references to a death "rite" are

deleted as included in the references to a death "ceremony".

(d) *Permanent cemetery.* — "Permanent cemetery" means a cemetery that is owned by:

(1) a cemetery company regulated under Title 5 of the Business Regulation Article;

(2) a nonprofit organization; or

(3) the State.

(An. Code 1957, art. 27, §§ 265(a), 267(a), 267A(a); 2002, ch. 26, § 2; 2003, ch. 21, § 1; 2009, ch. 675.)

§ 10-402. Removing human remains without authority.

(a) *Prohibited.* — Except as provided in subsections (b) and (f) of this section, a person may not remove or attempt to remove human remains from a burial site.

(b) *Exception.* — Subject to subsection (c) of this section, the State's Attorney for a county may authorize in writing the removal of human remains from a burial site in the State's Attorney's jurisdiction:

(1) to ascertain the cause of death of the person whose remains are to be removed;

(2) to determine whether the human remains were interred erroneously;

(3) for the purpose of reburial; or

(4) for medical or scientific examination or study allowed by law.

(c) *Exception — Notice.* — (1) Except as provided in paragraph (4) of this subsection, the State's Attorney for a county shall require a person who requests authorization to relocate permanently human remains from a burial site to publish a notice of the proposed relocation in a newspaper of general circulation in the county where the burial site is located.

(2) The notice shall be published in the newspaper one time.

(3) The notice shall contain:

(i) a statement that authorization from the State's Attorney is being requested to remove human remains from a burial site;

(ii) the purpose for which the authorization is being requested;

(iii) the location of the burial site, including the tax map and parcel number or liber and folio number; and

(iv) all known pertinent information concerning the burial site, including the names of the persons whose human remains are interred in the burial site, if known.

(4) (i) The State's Attorney may authorize the temporary relocation of human remains from a burial site for good cause, notwithstanding the notice requirements of this subsection.

(ii) If the person requesting the authorization subsequently intends to relocate the remains permanently, the person promptly shall publish notice as required under this subsection.

(5) The person requesting the authorization from the State's Attorney shall pay the cost of publishing the notice.

(6) The State's Attorney may authorize the removal of the human remains from the burial site after:

(i) receiving proof of the publication required under paragraph (1) of this subsection; and

(ii) 15 days after the date of publication.

(7) This subsection may not be construed to delay, prohibit, or otherwise limit the State's Attorney's authorization for the removal of human remains from a burial site.

(8) For a known, but not necessarily documented, unmarked burial site, the person requesting authorization for the removal of human remains from the burial site has the burden of proving by archaeological excavation or another acceptable method the precise location and boundaries of the burial site.

(d) *Exception — Reinterment.* — (1) Any human remains that are removed from a burial site under this section shall be reinterred in:

(i) 1. a permanent cemetery that provides perpetual care; or

2. a place other than a permanent cemetery with the agreement of a person in interest as defined under § 14-121(a)(4) of the Real Property Article; and

(ii) in the presence of:

1. a mortician, professional cemeterian, or other individual qualified in the interment of human remains;

2. a minister, priest, or other religious leader; or

3. a trained anthropologist or archaeologist.

(2) The location of the final disposition and treatment of human remains that are removed from a burial site under this section shall be entered into the local burial sites inventory or, if no local burial sites inventory exists, into a record or inventory deemed appropriate by the State's Attorney or the Maryland Historical Trust.

(e) *Construction of section.* — This section may not be construed to:

(1) preempt the need for a permit required by the Department of Health and Mental Hygiene under § 4-215 of the Health - General Article to remove human remains from a burial site; or

(2) interfere with the normal operation and maintenance of a cemetery, as long as the operation and maintenance of the cemetery are performed in accordance with State law.

(f) *Reinterment of human remains or remains after cremation.* — (1) Subject to paragraphs (2) and (3) of this subsection, human remains or the remains of a decedent after cremation, as defined in § 5-508 of the Health - General

Article, may be removed from a burial site within a permanent cemetery and reinterred in:

(i) the same burial site; or

(ii) another burial site within the boundary of the same permanent cemetery.

(2) The following persons, in the order of priority stated, may arrange for a reinterment of remains under paragraph (1) of this section:

(i) the surviving spouse or domestic partner of the decedent;

(ii) an adult child of the decedent;

(iii) a parent of the decedent;

(iv) an adult brother or sister of the decedent;

(v) a person acting as a representative of the decedent under a signed authorization of the decedent; or

(vi) the guardian of the person of the decedent at the time of the decedent's death, if one has been appointed

(3) (i) The reinterment under paragraph (1) of this subsection may be done without the need for obtaining the authorization of the State's Attorney under subsection (b) of this section or providing the notice required under subsection (c) of this section.

(ii) 1. A person who arranges for the reinterment of remains within a permanent cemetery under paragraph (1)(ii) of this subsection, within 30 days after the reinterment, shall publish a notice of the reinterment in a newspaper of general circulation in the county where the permanent cemetery is located.

2. The notice shall be published in the newspaper one time.

3. The notice shall contain:

A. a statement that the reinterment took place;

B. the reason for the reinterment;

C. the location of the burial site from which remains have been removed, including the tax map and parcel number or liber and folio number;

D. the location of the burial site in which the remains have been reinterred, including the tax map and parcel number or liber and folio number; and

E. all known pertinent information concerning the burial sites, including the names of the persons whose cremated remains or human remains are interred in the burial sites, if known.

(iii) Within 45 days after the reinterment, a person who arranges for a reinterment of remains under paragraph (1)(ii) of this subsection shall provide a copy of the notice required under this paragraph to the Office of Cemetery Oversight.

(4) The location of a reinterment of remains under paragraph (1) of this subsection shall be entered into the inventory of the local burial sites or, if no inventory exists, into a record or inventory deemed appropriate by the Maryland Historical Trust.

(g) *Penalty.* — A person who violates this section is guilty of a misdemeanor and on conviction is subject to imprisonment not exceeding 5 years or a fine not exceeding $10,000 or both.

(h) *Statute of limitations and in banc review.* — A person who violates this section is subject to § 5-106(b) of the Courts Article. (An. Code 1957, art. 27, § 265(b)-(g); 2002, ch. 26, § 2; 2009, ch. 675.)

REVISOR'S NOTE

This Revisor's note comprises information related to the revision by Acts 2002, ch. 26.

This section is new language derived without substantive change from former Art. 27, § 265(b) through (g).

In subsection (a) of this section, the former reference to "the State" is deleted as unnecessary.

In the introductory language of subsection (b) of this section and throughout this section, the former references to "the provisions of" specified law are deleted as surplusage.

Also in the introductory language of subsection (b) of this section and throughout this section, the former references to "Baltimore City" are deleted in light of the defined term "county".

In subsection (b)(1) and (2) of this section, the references to authorization "to ascertain [or determine]" certain facts are substituted for the former references to authorization "for the purpose of ascertaining [or determining]" certain facts for clarity and brevity.

In subsection (b)(4) of this section, the reference to examination or study "allowed" by law is substituted for the former reference to examination or study "as permitted" by law for clarity.

In subsection (c)(4)(ii) of this section, the reference to a person "subsequently" intending certain action is substituted for the former reference to a person "thereafter" intending certain action for clarity.

In subsection (c)(6)(ii) of this section, the reference to 15 days "after" publication is substituted for the former reference to 15 days "having expired after" publication for clarity and brevity.

Also in subsection (c)(6)(ii) of this section, the former redundant reference to publication "of the required notice" is deleted as unnecessary.

In the introductory language of subsection (d)(1) of this section and throughout this section, the reference to removal "under" certain law is substituted for the former reference to removal "in accordance with" certain law for brevity.

In subsection (d)(1)(i)2 of this section, the former reference to reinterment in a certain place "at the request of" a person in interest is deleted as included in the reference to reinterment in a certain place "with the agreement of" a person in interest.

In subsection (d)(2) of this section, the reference to "a" record is substituted for the former reference to "whatever" record for clarity and consistency.

In subsection (e)(2) of this section, the former reference to a "public or private" cemetery is deleted as surplusage.

Defined terms:

"Burial site"	§ 10-401
"County"	§ 1-101
"Permanent cemetery"	§ 10-401
"Person"	§ 1-101

Effect of amendments. — Chapter 675, Acts 2009, effective October 1, 2009, substituted "subsections (b) and (f)" for "subsection (b)" in (a); added (f); and redesignated accordingly.

Application. — Prior version of this section does not apply to the Historic St. Mary's City Commission because the Commission is an agency of the State and the word "person" in a statute does not include the State or its agencies. 82 Op. Att'y Gen. 8 (June 30, 1997).

Developers' discovery of abandoned cemetery on lot. — When the developers discovered the abandoned cemetery on Lot 20, as alleged, they were prohibited by law from removing the gravestones and could have faced misdemeanor charges and, upon conviction, prison time and/or a fine for doing so; they could have accomplished their goal of developing Lot 20 but only with the authorization of the State's Attorney for Howard County and by taking the measures required by statute to remove and rebury any human remains. It was implicit in the allegations in the first amended complaint that they sought to circumvent that process, and the expenses they would incur, by engaging in criminal acts to cover up the cemetery's existence. Rhee v. Highland Dev. Corp., 182 Md. App. 516, 958 A.2d 385 (2008).

§ 10-403. Removal of human remains or funerary object.

(a) *Scope of section.* — This section does not apply to:

(1) a person acting in the course of medical, archaeological, educational, or scientific study;

(2) a licensed mortician or other professional who transports human remains in the course of carrying out professional duties; or

(3) a person acting under the authority of:

(i) § 10-402 of this subtitle; or

(ii) § 4-215 or § 5-408 of the Health - General Article.

(b) *Prohibited.* — A person may not knowingly sell, buy, or transport for sale or profit, or offer to buy, sell, or transport for sale or profit:

(1) unlawfully removed human remains; or

(2) an associated funerary object obtained in violation of § 10-404 of this subtitle.

(c) *Penalty.* — A person who violates this section is guilty of a misdemeanor and on conviction is subject to imprisonment not exceeding 1 year or a fine not exceeding $5,000 or both.

(d) *Appropriation and disposition.* — The Maryland Historical Trust may appropriate all human remains and associated funerary objects obtained in violation of this subtitle for management, care, and administration until a determination of final disposition as provided by law.

(e) *Construction of section.* — This section may not be construed to interfere with the normal operation and maintenance of a cemetery including:

(1) correction of improper burial siting; and

(2) moving the human remains within a cemetery with the consent of a person who qualifies as an heir as defined in § 1-101 of the Estates and Trusts Article. (An. Code 1957, art. 27, § 267A(b)-(d); 2002, ch. 26, § 2; 2003, ch. 21, § 1.)

REVISOR'S NOTE

This Revisor's note comprises information related to the revision by Acts 2002, ch. 26.

This section is new language derived without substantive change from former Art. 27, § 267A(b) through (d).

In subsection (a)(2) of this section, the former reference to "responsibilities" is deleted as surplusage.

In subsections (b) and (d) of this section, the former references to the "State" are deleted as unnecessary.

In subsection (d) of this section, the reference to this "subtitle" is substituted for the former

reference to "this subheading or of Article 27, §§ 265 and 267 of the Code" to reflect the reorganization of material derived from the former subheading on graveyard desecration.

In subsection (e) of this section, the reference to an heir as defined in "§ 1-101 of" the Estates and Trusts Article is added for clarity.

Also in subsection (e) of this section, the former references to a "public or private" cemetery are deleted as surplusage.

Defined terms:
"Funerary object"	§ 10-401
"Person"	§ 1-101

§ 10-404. Cemetery — Destroying funerary objects; indecent conduct.

(a) *Prohibited — Destruction of funerary object; exception for repair or replacement.* — (1) Subject to the provisions of paragraph (2) of this subsection, a person may not willfully destroy, damage, deface, or remove:

(i) an associated funerary object or another structure placed in a cemetery; or

(ii) a building, wall, fence, railing, or other work, for the use, protection, or ornamentation of a cemetery.

(2) The provisions of paragraph (1) of this subsection do not prohibit the removal of a funerary object or a building, wall, fence, railing, or other object installed for the use, protection, or ornamentation of a cemetery or burial site, for the purpose of repair or replacement, either at the request of or with the permission of heirs or descendants of the deceased or the owner or manager of the cemetery or burial site.

(b) *Prohibited — Destruction of foliage; exception for routine care and maintenance.* — (1) Subject to the provisions of paragraph (2) of this subsection, a person may not willfully destroy, damage, or remove a tree, plant, or shrub in a cemetery.

(2) The provisions of paragraph (1) of this subsection do not prohibit normal maintenance of a cemetery or burial site, including trimming of trees and shrubs, removal of weeds or noxious growths, grass cutting, or other routine care and maintenance.

(c) *Prohibited — Indecent or disorderly conduct.* — A person may not engage in indecent or disorderly conduct in a cemetery.

(d) *Penalty.* — A person who violates this section is guilty of a misdemeanor and on conviction is subject to:

(1) for a violation of subsection (a) of this section, imprisonment not exceeding 5 years or a fine not exceeding $10,000 or both; and

(2) for a violation of subsection (b) or (c) of this section, imprisonment not exceeding 2 years or a fine not exceeding $500 or both.

(e) *Penalty — Payment for restoration.* — A person who violates this section shall pay for the restoration of any damaged or defaced real or personal property in a cemetery to the owner of the property or the owner of the cemetery.

(f) *Construction of section.* — This section does not prohibit the removal of human remains or a funerary object from an abandoned cemetery if:

(1) the removal is authorized in writing by the State's Attorney of the county in which the cemetery containing the human remains or funerary object is located; and

(2) the human remains or funerary object are placed in an accessible place in a permanent cemetery. (An. Code 1957, art. 27, § 267(b)-(d); 2002, ch. 26, § 2; 2003, ch. 21, § 1; 2005, ch. 208; 2006, ch. 38; 2008, ch. 268.)

REVISOR'S NOTE

This Revisor's note comprises information related to the revision by Acts 2002, ch. 26.

This section is new language derived without substantive change from former Art. 27, § 267(b) through (d).

In subsections (a) and (b) of this section, the former references to "this State" are deleted as unnecessary.

In subsection (a) of this section, the former references to a person who "mutilates" or "injures" are deleted as included in the reference to a person who "destroy[s], damage[s], [or] deface[s]".

In subsection (b) of this section, the word "damage" is substituted for the former reference to "cuts [and] breaks" for clarity and brevity.

In subsection (e) of this section, the words "human remains" are substituted for the former reference to "remains of any human body" for clarity and uniformity within this subtitle.

In subsection (e)(1) of this section, the former reference to "Baltimore City" is deleted in light of the defined term "county".

The Criminal Law Article Review Committee notes, for the consideration of the General Assembly, that a literal reading of subsection (b) of this section, prohibiting the willful de-struction, damage, and removal of a plant in a cemetery, would prohibit normal horticultural maintenance, including trimming of trees and shrubs and even lawn cutting.

Defined terms:

"County"	§ 1-101
"Funerary object"	§ 10-401
"Permanent cemetery"	§ 10-401
"Person"	§ 1-101

When developers discovered abandoned cemetery. — When the developers discovered the cemetery on Lot 20, as alleged, they were prohibited by law from removing the grave-stones and could have faced misdemeanor charges and, upon conviction, prison time and/or a fine for doing so; they could have accomplished their goal of developing Lot 20 but only with the authorization of the State's Attorney for Howard County and by taking the measures required by statute to remove and rebury any human remains. It was implicit in the allegations in the first amended complaint that they sought to circumvent that process, and the expenses they would incur, by engaging in criminal acts to cover up the cemetery's existence. Rhee v. Highland Dev. Corp., 182 Md. App. 516, 958 A.2d 385 (2008).

Subtitle 5. Crimes Against Marriage.

§ 10-501. Adultery.

(a) *Prohibited.* — A person may not commit adultery.

(b) *Penalty.* — A person who violates this section is guilty of a misdemeanor and on conviction shall be fined $10. (An. Code 1957, art. 27, § 3; 2002, ch. 26, § 2.)

REVISOR'S NOTE

This Revisor's note comprises information related to the revision by Acts 2002, ch. 26.

This section is new language derived without substantive change from former Art. 27, § 3.

This section is revised in standard language used to describe a statutory crime. Adultery was not a crime at common law, although it did have consequences relating to marriage and divorce. *See Cole v. State,* 126 Md. 239, 94 A. 913 (1915).

In subsection (b) of this section, the reference to being "guilty of a misdemeanor" is added to state expressly that which only was implied in the former law by the reference to a "conviction". In this State, any crime that was not a felony at common law and has not been de-clared a felony by statute, is considered to be a misdemeanor. *See State v. Canova,* 278 Md. 483, 490 (1976), *Bowser v. State,* 136 Md. 342, 345 (1920), *Dutton v. State,* 123 Md. 373, 378 (1914), and *Williams v. State,* 4 Md. App. 342, 347 (1968).

The former phrase "in any of the circuit courts for counties in this State" is deleted in light of CJ § 4-301, which provides that the District Court generally has exclusive original jurisdiction of common-law and statutory mis-demeanors, unless the potential penalty includes confinement for at least 3 years or a fine of at least $2,500. The Criminal Law Article Review Committee brings this substitution to the attention of the General Assembly.

Defined term:

"Person"	§ 1-101

Maryland Law Review. — For note discussing fault considerations in the determination of alimony awards, see 41 Md. L. Rev. 539 (1982).

University of Baltimore Law Review. — For article, "A Diagnosis, Dissection, and Prognosis of Maryland's New Wiretap and Electronic Surveillance Law," see 8 U. Balt. L. Rev. 183 (1979).

History of section. — See Evans v. Murff, 135 F. Supp. 907 (D. Md. 1955).

Common law. — Adultery was not an offense at common law. Cole v. State, 126 Md. 239, 94 A. 913 (1915).

At common law, the test was whether the woman was married. The essence of adultery at common law, and under the statute passed during the Commonwealth in England, was criminal intercourse with a married woman. Evans v. Murff, 135 F. Supp. 907 (D. Md. 1955).

It has been held that when this section was passed the General Assembly intended "adultery" to carry its common law meaning, the test being whether the woman was married. Hughes v. State, 14 Md. App. 497, 287 A.2d 299, cert. denied, 409 U.S. 1025, 93 S. Ct. 469, 34 L. Ed. 2d 317 (1972).

"Adultery." — Chapter 27, Laws of 1715, from which this section derives, was passed at a time when anticlerical feeling was high, and it therefore seems probable that the General Assembly intended the word "adultery" to carry its common law meaning rather than its meaning in ecclesiastical law. Evans v. Murff, 135 F. Supp. 907 (D. Md. 1955).

Neither the Court of Appeals nor the Court of Special Appeals has ever decided whether the crime of adultery in violation of this section embraces the common law or canon law definition. Consequently, the Maryland law with respect to adultery is unclear, and a prosecution for the crime might be instituted without regard to the marital status of the woman involved. Payne v. Payne, 33 Md. App. 707, 366 A.2d 405 (1976), cert. denied, 280 Md. 733 (1977).

Charging one with adultery not slander per se. — Since the penalty prescribed by this section is a pecuniary fine, charging a person with adultery does not amount per se to slander. Wagaman v. Byers, 17 Md. 183 (1861).

Costs of prosecution. — The costs of prosecution in an adultery case may be imposed upon the defendant under the provisions of Article 38, § 1 (see now § 7-502 of the Courts Article). The costs to be included, however, are only those of the prosecution and it was error to assess as costs the appearance fee of the defendant's attorney. Cole v. State, 126 Md. 239, 94 A. 913 (1915).

§ 10-502. Bigamy.

(a) *Scope of section.* — This section does not apply to a person if:

(1) the person's previous lawful spouse has been absent from the person for a continuous period of 7 years; and

(2) the person does not know whether the person's previous lawful spouse is living at the time of the subsequent marriage ceremony.

(b) *Prohibited.* — While lawfully married to a living person, a person may not enter into a marriage ceremony with another.

(c) *Penalty.* — A person who violates this section is guilty of the felony of bigamy and on conviction is subject to imprisonment not exceeding 9 years.

(d) *Charging document.* — An indictment or warrant for bigamy is sufficient if it substantially states:

"(name of defendant) on (date), in (county), having a living spouse, feloniously entered into a marriage ceremony with (name of subsequent spouse), in violation of § 10-502 of the Criminal Law Article, against the peace, government, and dignity of the State.". (An. Code 1957, art. 27, §§ 18, 19; 2002, ch. 26, § 2.)

REVISOR'S NOTE

This Revisor's note comprises information related to the revision by Acts 2002, ch. 26.

This section is new language derived without substantive change from former Art. 27, §§ 18 and 19.

In subsection (c) of this section, the reference to being "guilty of the felony" is added to state expressly that which only was implied in the former law by the reference to a "conviction". At common law, the crime of bigamy is classified as a felony. *See Barber v. State*, 50 Md. 161, 170 (1878).

In subsection (d) of this section, the reference to "§ 10-502 of the Criminal Law Article" is substituted for the former archaic phrase "contrary to the form of the Act of Assembly . . . and

provided" for clarity and consistency within this article.

In subsection (d) of this section, the reference to "enter[ing] into a marriage ceremony with" a subsequent spouse is substituted for the former reference to "marr[ying]" a subsequent spouse for consistency within this section.

Defined terms:
"County"   § 1-101
"Person"   § 1-101

Cross references. — As to marriages generally, see § 2-101 et seq. of the Family Law Article.

Maryland Law Review. — For article discussing the mens rea in bigamy in Maryland, see 23 Md. L. Rev. 224 (1963).

History of section. — See Braun v. State, 230 Md. 82, 185 A.2d 905 (1962).

Bigamy is felony. — Bigamy is a felony. Barber v. State, 50 Md. 161 (1878); Oliver v. Oliver, 185 F.2d 429 (D.C.C. 1950).

Criminal intent unnecessary. — The crime of bigamy is considered to be on a par with various police regulations where criminal intent is unnecessary. Braun v. State, 230 Md. 82, 185 A.2d 905 (1962).

Elements of offense. — A valid first marriage must be proved in order to establish the second as bigamous. Braun v. State, 230 Md. 82, 185 A.2d 905 (1962).

Burden of proof. — In prosecution for bigamy, burden is on State to prove that first marriage was valid and the first spouse was living at time of second marriage. Wright v. State, 198 Md. 163, 81 A.2d 602 (1951).

Where defendant proves that he and his wife had lived apart for seven years preceding the second marriage, prosecution must show that during the time he knew of her existence. Barber v. State, 50 Md. 161 (1878).

Where the first marriage and the continuance of the life of the first wife are proved, the burden is cast upon the accused to show that a divorce was granted before the second marriage was performed. Braun v. State, 230 Md. 82, 185 A.2d 905 (1962).

Presumed divorce no defense. — Even if the defendant in a bigamy case had entertained a bona fide belief that his first wife had divorced him before his second marriage, and even if this erroneous belief were to be regarded as a mistake of fact and not of law (which the Court of Appeals did not decide), this would not constitute a defense to a charge under this section. Braun v. State, 230 Md. 82, 185 A.2d 905 (1962).

Absent spouse does not mean second marriage valid. — Although the proviso to this section exempts from the operation of the statute a husband who marries another woman after his first wife has been absent and not heard of for the period of seven years, the second marriage in such a case is nevertheless void if the first wife is still alive and undivorced. Townsend v. Morgan, 192 Md. 168, 63 A.2d 743 (1949).

Marriage before divorce final. — Marriage in Maryland held bigamous when one of parties was subject to a District of Columbia divorce decree which was not yet absolute and final. Oliver v. Oliver, 185 F.2d 429 (D.C.C. 1950).

Marriage after out-of-state divorce. — A man who goes to Nevada to obtain a divorce assumes the risk that Maryland might justifiably find that he had not been domiciled in Nevada; if the divorce obtained in Nevada had no legal validity in Maryland and his Maryland wife was still alive and he marries another woman, he subjects himself to prosecution for bigamous cohabitation under Maryland law. Slansky v. State, 192 Md. 94, 63 A.2d 599 (1949).

In prosecution for bigamy, the jury found that accused had not acquired domicile in Nevada and, therefore, divorce was not valid. Slansky v. State, 192 Md. 94, 63 A.2d 599 (1949).

Admissibility of evidence. — See Pontier v. State, 107 Md. 384, 68 A. 1059 (1908); Braun v. State, 230 Md. 82, 185 A.2d 905 (1962).

Conviction of bigamy was ground for divorce. — The clause of former Article 16, § 24 (see now § 7-103 of the Family Law Article), "secondly, for any cause which by the laws of this State, render a marriage null and void ab initio," clearly covered the case of bigamy and established another prevenient ground of divorce, as distinguished from annulment under Maryland Rules, Rule S76. Clayton v. Clayton, 231 Md. 74, 188 A.2d 550 (1963).

Cited in Aleem v. Aleem, 175 Md. App. 663, 931 A.2d 1123 (2007), cert. granted, 402 Md. 355, 936 A.2d 852 (2007), aff'd, 404 Md. 404, 947 A.2d 489 (2008).

Subtitle 6. Crimes Relating to Animals.

§ 10-601. Definitions.

(a) *In general.* — In this subtitle the following words have the meanings indicated.

REVISOR'S NOTE

This subsection is new language added as the standard introductory language to a definition section.

(b) *Animal.* — "Animal" means a living creature except a human being.

REVISOR'S NOTE

This subsection is new language derived without substantive change from former Art. 27, § 62, as it defined "animal".

(c) *Cruelty.* — (1) "Cruelty" means the unnecessary or unjustifiable physical pain or suffering caused or allowed by an act, omission, or neglect.

(2) "Cruelty" includes torture and torment.

REVISOR'S NOTE

This subsection is new language derived without substantive change from former Art. 27, § 62, as it defined "cruelty".

(d) *Humane society.* — "Humane society" means a society or association incorporated in Maryland for the prevention of cruelty to animals.

REVISOR'S NOTE

This subsection is new language derived without substantive change from former Art. 27, §§ 60B and 63, as they related to humane societies.

(An. Code 1957, art. 27, §§ 60B, 62, 63; 2002, ch. 26, § 2; 2008, ch. 697.)

REVISOR'S NOTE TO SECTION

The Revisor's notes in this section comprise information related to the revision by Acts 2002, ch. 26.

Maryland Law Review. — For article, "Survey of Developments in Maryland Law, 1983-84," see 44 Md. L. Rev. 534 (1985).

University of Baltimore Law Forum. — For an article, "Protecting the Family Pet: The New Face of Maryland Domestic Violence Protective Orders," see 40 U. Balt. L. F. 81 (2010).

Constitutionality. — The 1975 amendment to former Art. 27, § 59 cured the consti-

tutional defect perceived by the Attorney General in 58 Op. Att'y Gen. 80 (1973). 65 Op. Att'y Gen. 174 (1980).

Former Art. 27, § 59 (see now this subtitle) was not unconstitutionally vague. In re William G., 52 Md. App. 131, 447 A.2d 493 (1982).

Dog "cruelly" killed. — It could be inferred that defendant "cruelly" killed the second dog and that the second dog suffered pain in between the first shot, which crippled him, and the fatal third shot. Hurd v. State, 190 Md. App. 479, 988 A.2d 1143 (2010), cert. denied, 415 Md. 40, 997 Md. 790 (2010).

§ 10-602. Legislative intent.

It is the intent of the General Assembly that each animal in the State be protected from intentional cruelty, including animals that are:

(1) privately owned;

(2) strays;

(3) domesticated;

(4) feral;

(5) farm animals;

(6) corporately or institutionally owned; or

(7) used in privately, locally, State, or federally funded scientific or medical activities. (An. Code 1957, art. 27, § 59(a); 2002, ch. 26, § 2.)

REVISOR'S NOTE

This Revisor's note comprises information related to the revision by Acts 2002, ch. 26.

This section is new language derived without substantive change from former Art. 27, § 59(a).

In the introductory language of this section, the word "including" is substituted for the former word "if" for clarity.

Defined terms:	
"Animal"	§ 10-601
"Cruelty"	§ 10-601

University of Baltimore Law Forum. — For an article, "Protecting the Family Pet: The New Face of Maryland Domestic Violence Protective Orders," see 40 U. Balt. L. F. 81 (2010).

Original intent. — The General Assembly in adopting the general act (Acts 1890, ch. 198), from which former Art. 27, § 59 [and now this subtitle] was derived, intended to adopt an entirely new and comprehensive law on the subject of cruelty to animals, one that operates equally throughout the whole State, and superseded all provisions of law, whether general or local, on the same subject. State v. Falkenham, 73 Md. 463, 21 A. 370 (1891).

§ 10-603. Application of §§ 10-601 through 10-608.

Sections 10-601 through 10-608 of this subtitle do not apply to:

(1) customary and normal veterinary and agricultural husbandry practices including dehorning, castration, tail docking, and limit feeding;

(2) research conducted in accordance with protocols approved by an animal care and use committee, as required under the federal Animal Welfare Act or the federal Health Research Extension Act;

(3) an activity that may cause unavoidable physical pain to an animal, including food processing, pest elimination, animal training, and hunting, if the person performing the activity uses the most humane method reasonably available; or

(4) normal human activities in which the infliction of pain to an animal is purely incidental and unavoidable. (An. Code 1957, art. 27, § 59(d); 2002, ch. 26, § 2.)

This Revisor's note comprises information related to the revision by Acts 2002, ch. 26.

This section is new language derived without substantive change from former Art. 27, § 59(d).

In the introductory language of this section, the reference to "[s]ections 10-601 through 10-608 of this subtitle" is substituted for the former reference to "[t]his section" to reflect the reorganization of material derived from former Art. 27, § 59.

In item (1) of this section, the former phrase "but not limited to" is deleted in light of Art. 1, § 30, which provides that "[t]he words 'includes' or 'including' mean, unless the context requires otherwise, includes or including by way of illustration and not by way of limitation".

Item (3) of this section is revised as an exclusion from the application of animal cruelty provisions, rather than a definition of "cruelty" for clarity. Similarly, item (4) of this section is revised as an exclusion from the application of animal cruelty provisions, rather than as a provision granting an immunity from criminal prosecution, for clarity and consistency within this article.

For provisions relating to humane methods of slaughtering livestock, see AG § 4-123.1.

Defined term:
"Animal"   § 1-101

University of Baltimore Law Forum. — For an article, "Protecting the Family Pet: The New Face of Maryland Domestic Violence Protective Orders," see 40 U. Balt. L. F. 81 (2010).

Research facility. — Former Art. 27, § 59 (see now this subtitle) was not applicable to a research institute conducting medical and scientific research pursuant to a federal program. Taub v. State, 296 Md. 439, 463 A.2d 819 (1983).

§ 10-604. Abuse or neglect of animal.

(a) *Prohibited.* — A person may not:

(1) overdrive or overload an animal;

(2) deprive an animal of necessary sustenance;

(3) inflict unnecessary suffering or pain on an animal;

(4) cause, procure, or authorize an act prohibited under item (1), (2), or (3) of this subsection; or

(5) if the person has charge or custody of an animal, as owner or otherwise, unnecessarily fail to provide the animal with nutritious food in sufficient quantity, necessary veterinary care, proper drink, air, space, shelter, or protection from the weather.

(b) *Penalty.* — (1) A person who violates this section is guilty of a misdemeanor and on conviction is subject to imprisonment not exceeding 90 days or a fine not exceeding $1,000 or both.

(2) As a condition of sentencing, the court may order a defendant convicted of violating this section to participate in and pay for psychological counseling.

(3) As a condition of probation, the court may prohibit a defendant from owning, possessing, or residing with an animal. (An. Code 1957, art. 27, § 59(b)(1)(i)-(iv), (2); 2002, ch. 26, § 2; 2006, ch. 448; 2011, chs. 26, 27.)

This Revisor's note comprises information related to the revision by Acts 2002, ch. 26.

This section is new language derived without substantive change from former Art. 27, § 59(b)(1)(i) through (iv) and (2).

| Defined terms: | | "Person" | § 1-101 |
| "Animal" | § 10-601 | | |

Effect of amendments. — Chapters 26 and 27, Acts 2011, effective October 1, 2011, made identical changes. Each added (b)(3).

Editor's note. — Section 2, ch. 448, Acts 2006, provides that "this Act may not be construed to apply to lawful hunting or lawful trapping."

University of Baltimore Law Forum. — For an article, "Protecting the Family Pet: The New Face of Maryland Domestic Violence Protective Orders," see 40 U. Balt. L. F. 81 (2010).

Mousetraps. — Use of glueboards to kill rodents did not necessarily violate former Article 27, § 59 (see now this subtitle). 71 Op. Att'y Gen. 102 (1986).

Indictment. — An indictment following the language of former Art. 27, § 59 (see now this section) was sufficient. State v. Falkenham, 73 Md. 463, 21 A. 370 (1891).

Cited in Coroneos v. Montgomery County, 161 Md. App. 411, 869 A.2d 410 (2005); Silver v. State, 420 Md. 415, 23 A.3d 867 (2011).

§ 10-605. Attending dogfights or cockfights.

(a) *Dogfighting.* — A person may not knowingly attend a deliberately conducted dogfight as a spectator.

(b) *Cockfighting.* — A person may not knowingly attend as a spectator a deliberately conducted event that uses a fowl, cock, or other bird to fight with another fowl, cock, or other bird.

(c) *Penalty.* — (1) A person who violates this section is guilty of a misdemeanor and on conviction is subject to imprisonment not exceeding 1 year or a fine not exceeding $2,500 or both.

(2) As a condition of sentencing, the court may order a defendant convicted of violating this section to participate in and pay for psychological counseling. (An. Code 1957, art. 27, § 59(b)(1)(v), (2); 2002, ch. 26, § 2; 2004, chs. 120, 121; 2008, chs. 350, 351.)

REVISOR'S NOTE

This Revisor's note comprises information related to the revision by Acts 2002, ch. 26.

This section is new language derived without substantive change from former Art. 27, § 59(b)(1)(v) and (2).

Defined term:
"Person" § 1-101

University of Baltimore Law Forum. — For an article, "Protecting the Family Pet: The New Face of Maryland Domestic Violence Protective Orders," see 40 U. Balt. L. F. 81 (2010).

§ 10-606. Aggravated cruelty to animals — In general.

(a) *Prohibited.* — A person may not:

(1) intentionally mutilate, torture, cruelly beat, or cruelly kill an animal;

(2) cause, procure, or authorize an act prohibited under item (1) of this subsection; or

(3) except in the case of self-defense, intentionally inflict bodily harm, permanent disability, or death on an animal owned or used by a law enforcement unit.

(b) *Penalty.* — (1) A person who violates this section is guilty of the felony of aggravated cruelty to animals and on conviction is subject to imprisonment not exceeding 3 years or a fine not exceeding $5,000 or both.

(2) As a condition of sentencing, the court may order a defendant convicted of violating this section to participate in and pay for psychological counseling.

(3) As a condition of probation, the court may prohibit a defendant from owning, possessing, or residing with an animal. (An. Code 1957, art. 27, § 59(c)(1)(i), (ii), (v), (2); 2002, ch. 26, § 2; 2011, chs. 26, 27.)

REVISOR'S NOTE

This Revisor's note comprises information related to the revision by Acts 2002, ch. 26.

This section is new language derived without substantive change from former Art. 27, § 59(c)(1)(i), (ii), and (v) and (2).

Defined terms:

"Animal"	§ 10-601
"Cruelty"	§ 10-601
"Person"	§ 1-101

Effect of amendments. — Chapters 26 and 27, Acts 2011, effective October 1, 2011, made identical changes. Each added (b)(3).

University of Baltimore Law Forum. — For an article, "Protecting the Family Pet: The New Face of Maryland Domestic Violence Protective Orders," see 40 U. Balt. L. F. 81 (2010).

Dog "cruelly" killed. — Conviction for cruelty to animals as to defendant's shooting of the second dog survived, as it could be inferred that defendant "cruelly" killed the second dog and that the second dog suffered pain in between the first shot, which crippled him, and the fatal third shot. Hurd v. State, 190 Md. App. 479, 988 A.2d 1143 (2010), cert. denied, 415 Md. 40, 997 Md. 790 (2010).

§ 10-607. Aggravated cruelty to animals — Certain activities related to dogfights prohibited.

(a) *Prohibited activities.* — A person may not:

(1) use or allow a dog to be used in a dogfight;

(2) arrange or conduct a dogfight;

(3) possess, own, sell, transport, or train a dog with the intent to use the dog in a dogfight; or

(4) knowingly allow premises under the person's ownership, charge, or control to be used to conduct a dogfight.

(b) *Penalty.* — (1) A person who violates this section is guilty of the felony of aggravated cruelty to animals and on conviction is subject to imprisonment not exceeding 3 years or a fine not exceeding $5,000 or both.

(2) As a condition of sentencing, the court may order a defendant convicted of violating this section to participate in and pay for psychological counseling. (An. Code 1957, art. 27, § 59(c)(1)(iii), (2); 2002, ch. 26, § 2; 2004, chs. 120, 121.)

REVISOR'S NOTE

**This Revisor's note comprises informa-
tion related to the revision by Acts 2002,
ch. 26.**

This section is new language derived without
substantive change from former Art. 27,
§ 59(c)(1)(iii) and (2).

Defined terms:
"Animal"	§ 10-601
"Cruelty"	§ 10-601
"Person"	§ 1-101

§ 10-608. Aggravated cruelty to animals — Certain activities related to cockfights prohibited.

(a) *"Implement of cockfighting" defined.* — (1) In this section, "implement of cockfighting" means any implement or device intended or designed:

(i) to enhance the fighting ability of a fowl, cock, or other bird; or

(ii) for use in a deliberately conducted event that uses a fowl, cock, or other bird to fight with another fowl, cock, or other bird.

(2) "Implement of cockfighting" includes:

(i) a gaff;

(ii) a slasher;

(iii) a postiza;

(iv) a sparring muff; and

(v) any other sharp implement designed to be attached in place of the natural spur of a gamecock or other fighting bird.

(b) *Prohibited acts.* — A person may not:

(1) use or allow the use of a fowl, cock, or other bird to fight with another animal;

(2) possess, with the intent to unlawfully use, an implement of cockfighting;

(3) arrange or conduct a fight in which a fowl, cock, or other bird fights with another fowl, cock, or other bird;

(4) possess, own, sell, transport, or train a fowl, cock, or other bird with the intent to use the fowl, cock, or other bird in a cockfight; or

(5) knowingly allow premises under the person's ownership, charge, or control to be used to conduct a fight in which a fowl, cock, or other bird fights with another fowl, cock, or other bird.

(c) *Penalty.* — (1) A person who violates this section is guilty of the felony of aggravated cruelty to animals and on conviction is subject to imprisonment not exceeding 3 years or a fine not exceeding $5,000 or both.

(2) As a condition of sentencing, the court may order a defendant convicted of violating this section to participate in and pay for psychological counseling. (An. Code 1957, art. 27, § 59(c)(1)(iv), (2); 2002, ch. 26, § 2; 2004, chs. 120, 121.)

REVISOR'S NOTE

**This Revisor's note comprises informa-
tion related to the revision by Acts 2002,
ch. 26.**

This section is new language derived without
substantive change from former Art. 27,
§ 59(c)(1)(iv) and (2).

In subsection (a) of this section, the former phrase "commonly known as cockfighting" is deleted as unnecessary.

"Cruelty"　　§ 10-601
"Person"　　§ 1-101

Defined terms:
"Animal"　　§ 10-601

§ 10-609. Arrest by humane society officer.

(a) *In general.* — Except as provided in subsections (b) and (c) of this section, if an officer of a humane society sees a person committing a misdemeanor that involves cruelty to an animal, the officer shall arrest and bring before the District Court the person committing the misdemeanor.

(b) *Local enforcement — Calvert County.* — In Calvert County, if an officer of a humane society or an animal control officer appointed by the County Commissioners or the County Commissioners' designee sees a person committing a misdemeanor that involves cruelty to an animal, the officer shall arrest and bring before the District Court the person committing the misdemeanor.

(c) *Local enforcement — Baltimore County.* — In Baltimore County, the Baltimore County Department of Health, Division of Animal Control shall enforce this section. (An. Code 1957, art. 27, § 63; 2002, ch. 26, § 2; 2008, ch. 309.)

REVISOR'S NOTE

This Revisor's note comprises information related to the revision by Acts 2002, ch. 26.

This section is new language derived without substantive change from former Art. 27, § 63.

In subsection (a) of this section, the former reference to a "commissioner" is deleted as included in the reference to the "District Court".

In subsection (b) of this section, the reference to the Baltimore County "Department of Health, Division of Animal Control" is substituted for the former obsolete reference to the "Bureau of Animal Control" for accuracy.

Defined terms:

"Animal"	§ 10-601
"Cruelty"	§ 10-601
"Humane society"	§ 10-601
"Person"	§ 1-101

University of Baltimore Law Forum. — For an article, "Protecting the Family Pet: The New Face of Maryland Domestic Violence Protective Orders," see 40 U. Balt. L. F. 81 (2010).

§ 10-610. Animal as prize.

(a) *Scope of section.* — This section does not apply to a person giving away an animal:

(1) as an agricultural project;

(2) for conservation purposes; or

(3) that is intended for slaughter.

(b) *Prohibited.* — Without the approval of the Secretary of Agriculture, a person may not give away a live animal as:

(1) a prize for, or inducement to enter, a contest, game, or other competition;

(2) an inducement to enter a place of amusement; or

(3) an incentive to make a business agreement if the offer is to attract trade.

(c) *Penalty.* — A person who violates this section is guilty of a misdemeanor and on conviction is subject to a fine not exceeding $500. (An. Code 1957, art. 27, § 60A; 2002, ch. 26, § 2.)

REVISOR'S NOTE

This Revisor's note comprises information related to the revision by Acts 2002, ch. 26.

This section is new language derived without substantive change from former Art. 27, § 60A.

In the introductory language of subsection (b) of this section, the former reference to a live "equine, or bird" is deleted as included in the comprehensive reference to a live "animal".

The Criminal Law Article Review Committee notes, for the consideration of the General Assembly, that the purpose paragraph of Ch.

480, Acts of 1978, which enacted former Art. 27, § 60A, described the animals the offer of which is regulated by this section as "vertebrate" animals. No bill review letter, nor any other advice of the Attorney General, noted the discrepancy between the term "vertebrate animal" used in the title of the bill and the term "animal" used in the body of the bill.

Defined terms:
"Animal"   § 10-601
"Person"   § 1-101

Cross references. — As to sale, coloring, etc., of baby chickens, etc., see § 10-614 of this article.

§ 10-611. Killing of dog or cat — Prohibited means.

(a) *Prohibited.* — A person may not kill or allow a dog or cat to be killed by use of:

(1) a decompression chamber;

(2) carbon monoxide gas; or

(3) curariform drugs.

(b) *Penalty.* — A person who violates this section is guilty of a misdemeanor and on conviction is subject to a fine not exceeding $500. (An. Code 1957, art. 27, § 59A; 2002, ch. 26, § 2.)

REVISOR'S NOTE

This Revisor's note comprises information related to the revision by Acts 2002, ch. 26.

This section is new language derived without substantive change from former Art. 27, § 59A.

In subsection (a)(1) of this section, the former reference to the description of a decompression

chamber as a "high-altitude, low-pressure chamber" is deleted as surplusage.

Defined term:
"Person"   § 1-101

Curariform drugs. — The General Assembly intended to adopt the technical and narrower meaning of "curariform drugs" in the context of a prior similar version of this section. 67 Op. Att'y Gen. 110 (1982).

T-61 Euthanasia Solution. — T-61 Euthanasia Solution is not a "curariform drug" and its

use is consonant with the underlying policy of a prior similar provision which is the humane killing of dogs and cats. 67 Op. Att'y Gen. 110 (1982).

§ 10-612. Abandoning domestic animal.

(a) *Prohibited.* — A person who owns, possesses, or has custody of a domestic animal may not drop or leave the animal on a road, in a public place, or on private property with the intent to abandon the animal.

(b) *Penalty.* — A person who violates this section is guilty of a misdemeanor and on conviction is subject to a fine not exceeding $100. (An. Code 1957, art. 27, § 60; 2002, ch. 26, § 2.)

REVISOR'S NOTE

This Revisor's note comprises information related to the revision by Acts 2002, ch. 26.

This section is new language derived without substantive change from former Art. 27, § 60.

In subsection (a) of this section, the former reference to a "partnership or corporation" is deleted as included in the reference to the defined term "person".

Also in subsection (a) of this section, the former references to a "dog" and a "cat" are deleted as included in the reference to a "domestic animal".

Defined terms:
"Animal"	§ 10-601
"Person"	§ 1-101

§ 10-613. Sale of puppy or kitten.

(a) *Scope of section.* — This section does not apply to:

(1) a biomedical facility that is licensed by the United States Department of Agriculture; or

(2) an animal that is accompanied by a signed statement from a licensed veterinarian stating that the animal's dam is incapacitated for humane or medical reasons and cannot care for the animal.

(b) *Prohibited.* — (1) Except as provided in paragraph (2) of this subsection, a person may not sell or distribute in the State or bring into the State for the purpose of sale or distribution a domestic dog or cat less than 8 weeks of age unless accompanied by its dam.

(2) A person may give an unaccompanied dog or cat to:

(i) an animal shelter or pound that is operated or supported by a government; or

(ii) a humane society.

(c) *Penalty.* — (1) A person who violates this section is guilty of a misdemeanor and on conviction is subject to a fine not exceeding $500.

(2) For purposes of humane disposal, a court may seize an animal brought into this State in violation of this section. (An. Code 1957, art. 27, § 60B; 2002, ch. 26, § 2.)

REVISOR'S NOTE

This Revisor's note comprises information related to the revision by Acts 2002, ch. 26.

This section is new language derived without substantive change from former Art. 27, § 60B.

In subsection (b) of this section, the former parenthetical references to "Canis familiaris" and "Felis catus" are deleted as surplusage.

Defined terms:
"Animal"	§ 10-601
"Humane society"	§ 10-601
"Person"	§ 1-101

§ 10-614. Transfer or coloring of chick.

(a) *"Chick" defined.* — In this section, "chick" means a chicken, duckling, or other fowl under the age of 3 weeks.

(b) *Exception.* — This section does not prohibit the sale or display of a chick in proper facilities by a breeder or store engaged in the business of selling chicks for commercial breeding and raising.

(c) *Prohibited.* — A person may not:

(1) sell, offer for sale, barter, or give away a chick as a pet, toy, premium, or novelty; or

(2) color, dye, stain, or otherwise change the natural color of a chick.

(d) *Penalty.* — A person who violates this section is guilty of a misdemeanor and on conviction is subject to a fine not exceeding $25. (An. Code 1957, CL § 11-904; 2002, ch. 26, § 2.)

REVISOR'S NOTE

This Revisor's note comprises information related to the revision by Acts 2002, ch. 26.

This section is new language derived without substantive change from former CL § 11-904.

Defined term:
"Person"   § 1-101

§ 10-615. Care of mistreated animal.

(a) *Court-ordered removal.* — If an owner or custodian of an animal is convicted of an act of animal cruelty, the court may order the removal of the animal or any other animal at the time of conviction for the protection of the animal.

(b) *Seizure.* — (1) An officer or authorized agent of a humane society, or a police officer or other public official required to protect animals may seize an animal if necessary to protect the animal from cruelty.

(2) (i) An animal that a medical and scientific research facility possesses may be removed under this subsection only after review by and a recommendation from the Department of Health and Mental Hygiene, Center for Veterinary Public Health.

(ii) The Department of Health and Mental Hygiene shall:

1. conduct an investigation within 24 hours after receiving a complaint; and

2. within 24 hours after completing the investigation, report to the State's Attorney for the county in which the facility is situated.

(c) *Impounded animal.* — (1) If an animal is impounded, yarded, or confined without necessary food, water, or proper attention, is subject to cruelty, or is neglected, an officer or authorized agent of a humane society, a police officer, another public official required to protect animals, or any invited and accompanying veterinarian licensed in the State, may:

(i) enter the place where the animal is located and supply the animal with necessary food, water, and attention; or

(ii) remove the animal if removal is necessary for the health of the animal.

(2) A person who enters a place under paragraph (1) of this subsection is not liable because of the entry.

(d) *Notification to owner.* — (1) A person who removes an animal under subsection (c) of this section shall notify the animal's owner or custodian of:

(i) the removal; and

(ii) any administrative remedies that may be available to the owner or custodian.

(2) If an administrative remedy is not available, the owner or custodian may file a petition for the return of the animal in the District Court of the county in which the removal occurred within 10 days after the removal.

(e) *Stray.* — An animal is considered a stray if:

(1) an owner or custodian of the animal was notified under subsection (d) of this section and failed to file a petition within 10 days after removal; or

(2) the owner or custodian of the animal is unknown and cannot be ascertained by reasonable effort for 20 days to determine the owner or custodian.

(f) *Limitations.* — This section does not allow:

(1) entry into a private dwelling; or

(2) removal of a farm animal without the prior recommendation of a veterinarian licensed in the State.

(g) *Local enforcement — Baltimore County.* — In Baltimore County, the Baltimore County Department of Health, Division of Animal Control or an organization that the Baltimore County government approves shall enforce this section. (An. Code 1957, art. 27, § 67; 2002, ch. 26, § 2; 2004, ch. 25.)

REVISOR'S NOTE

This Revisor's note comprises information related to the revision by Acts 2002, ch. 26.

This section is new language derived without substantive change from former Art. 27, § 67.

The Criminal Law Article Review Committee notes, for the consideration of the General Assembly, that in subsection (a) of this section, the reference to removal of "the animal or any other animal" is substituted for the former reference to removal of "that animal or animals" for clarity and accuracy.

In subsections (c)(1) and (f)(2) of this section, the references to a "veterinarian licensed in the State" are substituted for the former references to a "licensed veterinarian of the State" for clarity.

The Criminal Law Article Review Committee notes, for the consideration of the General Assembly, that in subsection (c)(1) of this section, the former reference to an animal "continu[ing]" without necessary food, water, or proper attention is deleted as implicit in the reference to "confine[ment]" of the animal.

In subsection (d) of this section, the former phrase "[i]n all cases" is deleted as redundant.

In subsection (e) of this section, the reference to being "considered a stray" is substituted for the former phrase "held to be an estray" for clarity.

In subsection (f)(2) of this section, the reference to "removal" is substituted for the former reference to "taking" for clarity.

In subsection (g) of this section, the reference to the Baltimore County "Department of Health, Division of Animal Control" is substituted for the former obsolete reference to the "Bureau of Animal Control" for accuracy.

For other provisions on stray animals, *see* AG Title 3, Subtitle 6.

Defined terms:

"Animal"	§ 10-601
"County"	§ 1-101
"Cruelty"	§ 10-601
"Humane society"	§ 10-601
"Person"	§ 1-101

University of Baltimore Law Forum. — For an article, "Protecting the Family Pet: The New Face of Maryland Domestic Violence Protective Orders," see 40 U. Balt. L. F. 81 (2010).

§ 10-616. Kennel inspection.

(a) *Scope of section.* — This section does not apply to premises:

(1) where dogs are kept or bred solely for medical or related research or laboratory tests;

(2) operated by a licensed and regularly practicing veterinarian; or

(3) where hunting dogs are housed, if the buying, selling, trading, or breeding is incidental to the main purposes of housing, keeping, and using dogs.

(b) *Authority to inspect.* — (1) To determine if dogs are being treated inhumanely in violation of this subtitle or other law, an authorized director of a humane society, accompanied by a sheriff or a deputy sheriff, may inspect a premises:

(i) where a person is engaged in the business of buying, selling, trading, or breeding dogs; or

(ii) of a kennel where 25 or more dogs are kept.

(2) A person who inspects premises under paragraph (1) of this subsection shall give prior written notice of the time and date of the inspection to the owner or occupant of the premises.

(c) *Local enforcement.* — (1) In Baltimore City, the Baltimore City Health Department shall enforce this section.

(2) In Baltimore County, the Baltimore County Department of Health, Division of Animal Control or an organization that the Baltimore County government approves shall enforce this section. (An. Code 1957, art. 27, § 67A; 2002, ch. 26, § 2.)

REVISOR'S NOTE

This Revisor's note comprises information related to the revision by Acts 2002, ch. 26.

This section is new language derived without substantive change from former Art. 27, § 67A.

In subsection (b)(1) of this section, the former reference to "applicable law" is deleted as implicit in the reference to "other law".

Also in subsection (b)(1) of this section, the former reference to a "State-chartered" humane society is deleted as implicit in the definition of "humane society" in § 10-601 of this subtitle.

Also in subsection (b)(1) of this section, the former reference to "visit[ing]" is deleted as implicit in the reference to "inspect[ing]".

In subsection (c)(2) of this section, the reference to the Baltimore County "Department of Health, Division of Animal Control" is substituted for the former obsolete reference to the "Bureau of Animal Control" for accuracy.

Defined terms:
"Humane society" § 10-601
"Person" § 1-101

§ 10-617. Disposal of domestic animal.

(a) *"Animal control unit" defined.* — In this section, "animal control unit" means the local organization or governmental unit that the appropriate local governmental body designates to house, care for, and control domestic animals of unknown ownership.

(b) *In general.* — An animal control unit shall dispose of an unclaimed dog or cat only by:

(1) placing the animal in a suitable home;

(2) retaining the animal in the animal control unit; or

(3) humanely destroying the animal.

(c) *Waiting period.* — A domestic animal that is impounded by an animal control unit may not be sold, placed, or destroyed until the animal has been carefully inspected for a tag, tattoo, or other identification to ascertain the owner and:

(1) 72 hours have elapsed after notice has been given to the owner;

(2) if the owner cannot be notified, 72 hours have elapsed after the animal is impounded;

(3) the animal is seriously diseased or severely injured; or

(4) the animal is under 3 months of age.

(d) *Liability of owner and new owner.* — (1) An owner who retrieves an animal from an animal control unit shall pay all fees, costs, and expenses incurred by the animal control unit.

(2) The necessary expenses for food and attention given to an animal under this section may be collected from the owner, and the animal is not exempt from levy and sale on execution of a judgment for the expenses.

(3) A new owner with whom an animal is placed under subsection (b)(1) of this section may be charged an adoption fee.

(e) *Penalty.* — A person who violates this section is guilty of a misdemeanor and on conviction is subject to a fine not exceeding $500. (An. Code 1957, art. 27, §§ 67B, 68; 2002, ch. 26, § 2.)

REVISOR'S NOTE

This Revisor's note comprises information related to the revision by Acts 2002, ch. 26.

This section is new language derived without substantive change from former Art. 27, §§ 67B and 68.

Throughout this section, the references to an animal control "unit" are substituted for the former references to an animal control "agency" for consistency within this article. *See* General Revisor's Note to article.

In subsection (b)(1) of this section, the former reference to "adoption" is deleted as implicit in the reference to "placing ... in a suitable home".

In subsection (b)(2) of this section, the reference to retaining an animal "in the animal control unit" is substituted for the former reference to retention "by the shelter" for consistency within this section.

In subsection (c)(4) of this section, the former reference to a "litter" is deleted as unnecessary since an individual animal is treated the same whether or not part of a litter.

Defined terms:

"Animal"	§ 10-601
"Person"	§ 1-101

§ 10-618. Poisoning dog.

(a) *Prohibited.* — A person may not willfully and maliciously give poison or ground glass to a dog, or expose poison or ground glass, with the intent that a dog ingest it.

(b) *Penalty.* — A person who violates this section is guilty of a misdemeanor and on conviction is subject to a fine not exceeding $100 for each violation. (An. Code 1957, art. 27, § 69; 2002, ch. 26, § 2.)

REVISOR'S NOTE

This Revisor's note comprises information related to the revision by Acts 2002, ch. 26.

This section is new language derived without substantive change from former Art. 27, § 69.

In subsection (a) of this section, the former phrase "on his own lands or the lands of another" is deleted as surplusage.

Defined term:
"Person"   § 1-101

University of Baltimore Law Forum. — For an article, "Protecting the Family Pet: The New Face of Maryland Domestic Violence Protective Orders," see 40 U. Balt. L. F. 81 (2010).

§ 10-619. Dangerous dog.

(a) *Definitions.* — (1) In this section the following words have the meanings indicated.

(2) "Dangerous dog" means a dog that:

(i) without provocation has killed or inflicted severe injury on a person; or

(ii) is determined by the appropriate unit of a county or municipal corporation under subsection (c) of this section to be a potentially dangerous dog and, after the determination is made:

1. bites a person;

2. when not on its owner's real property, kills or inflicts severe injury on a domestic animal; or

3. attacks without provocation.

(3) (i) "Owner's real property" means real property owned or leased by the owner of a dog.

(ii) "Owner's real property" does not include a public right-of-way or a common area of a condominium, apartment complex, or townhouse development.

(4) "Severe injury" means a physical injury that results in broken bones or disfiguring lacerations requiring multiple sutures or cosmetic surgery.

(b) *Exception.* — This section does not apply to a dog owned by and working for a governmental or law enforcement unit.

(c) *Determination of potentially dangerous dog.* — An appropriate unit of a county or municipal corporation may determine that a dog is potentially dangerous if the unit:

(1) finds that the dog:

(i) has inflicted a bite on a person while on public or private real property;

(ii) when not on its owner's real property, has killed or inflicted severe injury on a domestic animal; or

(iii) has attacked without provocation; and

(2) notifies the dog owner in writing of the reasons for this determination.

(d) *Prohibited.* — A dog owner may not:

(1) leave a dangerous dog unattended on the owner's real property unless the dog is:

(i) confined indoors;

(ii) in a securely enclosed and locked pen; or

(iii) in another structure designed to restrain the dog; or

(2) allow a dangerous dog to leave the owner's real property unless the dog is leashed and muzzled, or is otherwise securely restrained and muzzled.

(e) *Required notice.* — An owner of a dangerous dog or potentially dangerous dog who sells or gives the dog to another shall notify in writing:

(1) the authority that made the determination under subsection (c) of this section, of the name and address of the new owner of the dog; and

(2) the person taking possession of the dog, of the dangerous behavior or potentially dangerous behavior of the dog.

(f) *Penalty.* — A person who violates this section is guilty of a misdemeanor and on conviction is subject to a fine not exceeding $2,500. (An. Code 1957, art. 27, § 70E(a)(1), (2), (4), (5), (b)-(f); 2002, ch. 26, § 2.)

REVISOR'S NOTE

This Revisor's note comprises information related to the revision by Acts 2002, ch. 26.

This section is new language derived without substantive change from former Art. 27, § 70E(a)(1), (2), (4), (5), and (b) through (f).

In subsections (a)(2) and (c) of this section, the references to a "unit" of a county or municipal corporation are substituted for the former references to a county or municipal "authority" for consistency within this article. *See* General Revisor's Note to article. Similarly, in subsection (c) of this section, the reference to a governmental or law enforcement "unit" is substituted for the former reference to a governmental or law enforcement "agency".

In subsection (a)(3) of this section, the defined term "owner's real property" is substituted for the former defined term "real property" for clarity and accuracy.

In subsections (c)(2) and (d) of this section, the references to the "dog owner" are substituted for the former references to the "owner" for clarity.

In subsection (d) of this section, the reference to a "municipal corporation" is substituted for the former reference to a "municipality" for consistency with Md. Constitution, Art. XI-E.

In subsection (e) of this section, the defined term "person" is substituted for the former word "owner" for consistency within this article.

Former Art. 27, § 70E (a)(3) which defined "owner" to mean "any person or local entity that has a possessory right in a dog" is deleted as surplusage.

Defined terms:

"Animal"	§ 10-601
"County"	§ 1-101
"Person"	§ 1-101

Editor's note. — Section 2, ch. 364, Acts 1988, which enacted a prior similar provision, provides that "this act may not be applied or construed to limit the authority of a county or municipal authority to enact legislation that regulates to a greater extent the ownership or possession of dangerous dogs."

University of Baltimore Law Forum. — For an article, "Protecting the Family Pet: The New Face of Maryland Domestic Violence Protective Orders," see 40 U. Balt. L. F. 81 (2010).

§ 10-620. Interference with race horse.

(a) *Prohibited.* — A person may not:

(1) willfully and maliciously interfere with, injure, destroy, or tamper with a horse used for racing or breeding or for a competitive exhibition of skill, breed, or stamina;

(2) willfully start, instigate, engage in, or further an act that interferes with, injures, destroys, or tampers with a horse used for racing or breeding or for a competitive exhibition of skill, breed, or stamina; or

(3) commit an act that tends to interfere with, injure, destroy, or tamper with a horse used for racing or breeding or for a competitive exhibition of skill, breed, or stamina.

(b) *Penalty.* — A person who violates this section is guilty of a felony and on conviction is subject to imprisonment of not less than 1 year and not exceeding 3 years. (An. Code 1957, art. 27, § 61; 2002, ch. 26, § 2.)

REVISOR'S NOTE

This Revisor's note comprises information related to the revision by Acts 2002, ch. 26.

This section is new language derived without substantive change from former Art. 27, § 61.

In subsection (a) of this section, the former phrase "whether such horse be the property of himself or another," is deleted as unnecessary in light of the unqualified references to inter-fering with, injuring, destroying, or tampering with "a" horse.

In subsection (a)(2) of this section, the reference to "start[ing]" a horse is substituted for the former reference to "set[ting] [a horse] on foot" for clarity.

Defined term:
"Person" § 1-101

University of Baltimore Law Forum. — For an article, "Protecting the Family Pet: The New Face of Maryland Domestic Violence Protective Orders," see 40 U. Balt. L. F. 81 (2010).

§ 10-621. Import, offer, or transfer of dangerous animal.

(a) *Scope of section.* — (1) This section does not apply to:

(i) a research facility or federal research facility licensed under the federal Animal Welfare Act;

(ii) an exhibitor licensed under the federal Animal Welfare Act that displays the animals specified in subsection (b) of this section in a public setting as the exhibitor's primary function;

(iii) a person who possesses a valid license or permit issued by the Department of Natural Resources to import, sell, trade, barter, possess, breed, or exchange an animal specified in subsection (b) of this section;

(iv) an animal sanctuary that:

1. is a nonprofit organization qualified under § 501(c)(3) of the Internal Revenue Code;

2. operates a place of refuge for abused, neglected, impounded, abandoned, orphaned, or displaced wildlife;

3. does not conduct commercial activity with respect to any animal of which the organization is an owner; and

4. does not buy, sell, trade, lease, or breed any animal except as an integral part of the species survival plan of the American Zoo and Aquarium Association;

(v) an animal control officer under the jurisdiction of the State or a local governing authority, a law enforcement officer acting under the authority of this subtitle, or a private contractor of a county or municipal corporation that is responsible for animal control operations;

    (vi) a person who holds a valid license to practice veterinary medicine in the State and treats the animal specified in subsection (b) of this section in accordance with customary and normal veterinary practices; and

    (vii) a person who is not a resident of the State and is in the State for 10 days or less for the purpose of traveling between locations outside of the State.

    (2) (i) This section does not prohibit a person who had lawful possession of an animal specified in subsection (b) of this section on or before May 31, 2006, from continuing to possess that animal if the person provides written notification to the local animal control authority on or before August 1, 2006.

    (ii) The notification shall include:

        1. the person's name, address, and telephone number;

        2. the number and type of animals being kept; and

        3. a photograph of the animal or a description of a tattoo or microchip identification of the animal.

    (3) This section does not prohibit a person who has a disability that severely limits mobility from possessing an animal specified in subsection (b) of this section if that animal is:

    (i) trained to perform tasks for the owner by an organization described in section 501(c) of the Internal Revenue Code; and

    (ii) dedicated to improving the quality of life of a person who has a disability that severely limits mobility.

(b) *Prohibited.* — A person may not import into the State, offer for sale, trade, barter, possess, breed, or exchange a live:

    (1) fox, skunk, raccoon, or bear;

    (2) caiman, alligator, or crocodile;

    (3) member of the cat family other than the domestic cat;

    (4) hybrid of a member of the cat family and a domestic cat if the hybrid weighs over 30 pounds;

    (5) member of the dog family other than the domestic dog;

    (6) hybrid of a member of the dog family and a domestic dog;

    (7) nonhuman primate, including a lemur, monkey, chimpanzee, gorilla, orangutan, marmoset, loris, or tamarin; or

    (8) poisonous snake in the family groups of Hydrophidae, Elapidae, Viperidae, or Crotolidae.

(c) *Penalty.* — (1) A person who violates this section is guilty of a misdemeanor and on conviction is subject to:

    (i) if an individual, a fine not exceeding $1,000; or

    (ii) if not an individual, a fine not exceeding $10,000.

    (2) The provisions of this section may be enforced by:

    (i) any State or local law enforcement officer; or

    (ii) the local animal control authority for the jurisdiction where the violation occurs.

(d) *Seizure of animal.* — (1) An animal specified in subsection (b) of this section may be immediately seized if:

(i) there is probable cause to believe that the possession of the animal is in violation of this section; or

(ii) the animal poses a risk to public health or public safety.

(2) An animal specified in subsection (b) of this section that is seized may be returned to the person who had possession of the animal at the time the animal was seized only if it is established that:

(i) possession of the animal by the person is not a violation of this section; and

(ii) the return of the animal does not pose a risk to public health or public safety.

(3) (i) Notice that the animal was seized shall be served on the person who had possession of the animal at the time the animal was seized by:

1. posting a copy of the notice at the place where the animal was seized;

2. regular and certified mail, return receipt requested; or

3. delivering the notice to a person residing on the property from which the animal was seized.

(ii) The notice shall include:

1. a description of the animal seized;

2. the authority for and the purpose of the seizure;

3. the time, place, and circumstances of the seizure;

4. a contact person and telephone number;

5. a statement that the person from whom the animal was seized may:

A. post security to prevent disposition of the animal; and

B. request a hearing concerning the seizure;

6. a statement that failure to post security or request a hearing within 10 days of the date of the notice will result in the disposition of the animal; and

7. a statement that, unless a court finds that the seizure of the animal was not justified, the actual costs of the care, keeping, and disposal of the animal are the responsibility of the person from whom the animal was seized.

(4) (i) Before a seizure under paragraph (1) of this subsection occurs, the person in possession of the animal to be seized may request that the animal remain in the person's physical custody for 30 days after the date the animal was to be seized.

(ii) During the 30 days provided in subparagraph (i) of this paragraph, the person shall take all necessary actions to comply with this section.

(iii) At any reasonable time during the 30-day period, the local animal control authority may inspect the premises where the animal is being kept.

(5) (i) If a person who retains possession of an animal under paragraph (4) of this subsection is not in compliance with this section after the 30-day period has expired, the local animal control authority shall seize the animal and place it in a holding facility that is appropriate for the species.

(ii) The authority seizing an animal under this paragraph shall provide notice of the seizure in the same manner as provided in paragraph (3) of this subsection.

(6) (i) A person from whom an animal was seized may request a hearing in the District Court within 10 days of the seizure.

(ii) A hearing shall be held as soon as practicable to determine the validity of the seizure and the disposition of the animal.

(7) (i) Unless the court finds that the seizure of the animal was not justified by law, a person from whom the animal specified in subsection (b) of this section is seized is liable for all actual costs of care, keeping, and disposal of the animal.

(ii) The costs required under this paragraph shall be paid in full unless a mutually satisfactory agreement is made between the local animal control authority and the person claiming an interest in the animal.

(8) (i) If there is no request for a hearing within 10 days of the notice or if the court orders a permanent and final disposition of the animal, the local animal control authority may take steps to find long-term placement of the animal with another appropriate facility that is equipped for the continued care of the particular species of the animal.

(ii) If there is no entity that is suitable for the care of the animal, the animal may be euthanized.

(e) *Regulations.* — This section does not limit a county or municipality from enacting laws or adopting regulations that are more restrictive pertaining to any potentially dangerous animals, including those specified in subsection (b) of this section.

(f) *Death of owner of animal.* — If the owner of an animal specified in subsection (b) of this section dies without making arrangements for the transfer of custody of the animal to another person, the animal may be turned over to one of the organizations specified in subsection (a)(1) of this section or euthanized if no suitable location can be found in a reasonable amount of time. (An. Code 1957, art. 27, § 70D; 2002, ch. 26, § 2; 2006, ch. 468.)

REVISOR'S NOTE

This Revisor's note comprises information related to the revision by Acts 2002, ch. 26.

This section is new language derived without substantive change from former Art. 27, § 70D.

Defined terms:
"Animal"	§ 10-601
"Person"	§ 1-101

Seizure of animal. — Fact that a wolf may have been lawfully possessed did not mean that the lawfulness of its possession had to be verified as a prerequisite to its seizure when that seizure was necessary to protect the public safety or otherwise; because the court could not say that it would have been apparent to a reasonable officer in defendant animal control officer's position that her actions violated the Fourth Amendment, she was entitled to qualified immunity. Walker v. Prince George's County, 575 F.3d 426 (4th Cir. 2009).

§ 10-622. Injuring or trapping carrier pigeon.

(a) *Killing or maiming.* — A person may not shoot, kill, or maim a carrier pigeon.

(b) *Trapping or detaining.* — A person may not entrap, catch, or detain a carrier pigeon that has:

(1) the owner's name stamped on the carrier pigeon's wing or tail; or

(2) a leg band that includes the owner's initials, name, or number.

(c) *Penalty.* — A person who violates this section is guilty of a misdemeanor and on conviction is subject to a fine not exceeding $10 for each violation. (An. Code 1957, art. 27, §§ 64-66; 2002, ch. 26, § 2.)

REVISOR'S NOTE

This Revisor's note comprises information related to the revision by Acts 2002, ch. 26.

This section is new language derived without substantive change from former Art. 27, §§ 64, 65, and 66.

In subsection (a) of this section, the term "carrier pigeon" is substituted for the former reference to "Antwerp or homing" pigeons for brevity.

Also in subsection (a) of this section, the former reference to "persons" is deleted in light of Art. 1, § 8, which states that the singular generally includes the plural.

Also in subsection (a) of this section, the former reference to a carrier pigeon "either while in flight or at rest" is deleted as unnecessary in light of the unqualified reference to shooting, killing, or maiming "a" carrier pigeon.

In subsection (c) of this section, the reference to "each violation" is substituted for the former reference to "every such offense" for consistency within this article. *See* General Revisor's Note to article.

Defined term:
"Person" § 1-101

§ 10-623. Leaving dogs outside and unattended by use of restraints.

(a) *Definitions.* — (1) In this section the following words have the meanings indicated.

(2) "Collar" means a device constructed of nylon, leather, or similar material specifically designed to be used around the neck of a dog.

(3) "Restraint" means a chain, rope, tether, leash, cable, or other device that attaches a dog to a stationary object or trolley system.

(b) *Prohibited.* — A person may not leave a dog outside and unattended by use of a restraint:

(1) that unreasonably limits the movement of the dog;

(2) that uses a collar that:

(i) is made primarily of metal; or

(ii) is not at least as large as the circumference of the dog's neck plus 1 inch;

(3) that restricts the access of the dog to suitable and sufficient clean water or appropriate shelter;

(4) in unsafe or unsanitary conditions; or

(5) that causes injury to the dog.

(c) *Penalties.* — A person who violates this section is guilty of a misdemeanor and on conviction is subject to imprisonment not exceeding 90 days or a fine not exceeding $1,000 or both. (2007, ch. 570.)

Editor's note. — Section 2, ch. 570, Acts 2007, provides that the act shall take effect October 1, 2007.

University of Baltimore Law Forum. — For an article, "Protecting the Family Pet: The New Face of Maryland Domestic Violence Protective Orders," see 40 U. Balt. L. F. 81 (2010).

Former Art. 27, § 70, which prohibited the owner of a dog in heat in Cecil, Dorchester, Frederick, Talbot, and Wicomico counties from allowing the dog to run at large, is revised in Art. 24, § 11-512.

Former Art. 27, § 70A, which prohibited the owner of a dog in heat in Harford County from allowing the dog outdoors loose or on a leash, is revised in Art. 24, § 11-513.

Former Art. 27, § 70B, which required the owner of a dog in heat in Howard and St. Mary's counties to confine and protect the dog from other dogs, is revised in Art. 24, § 11-514.

Former Art. 27, § 70C, which required an owner of a dog kept out-of-doors in Frederick County to provide shelter for it, is revised in § 1-5-26 of the Public Local Laws of Frederick County.

Subtitle 7. Maryland Uniform Flag Law.

§ 10-701. "Flag" defined.

In this subtitle, "flag" includes any size flag, standard, color, ensign, or shield made of any substance or represented or produced on any substance, that purports to be a flag, standard, color, ensign, or shield of the United States or of this State. (An. Code 1957, art. 27, § 81; 2002, ch. 26, § 2.)

REVISOR'S NOTE

This Revisor's note comprises information related to the revision by Acts 2002, ch. 26.

This section is new language derived without substantive change from former Art. 27, § 81.

The phrase "on any substance" is added for clarity.

Throughout this subtitle, the former reference to a "standard, color, ensign or shield" is deleted as included in the defined term "flag".

§ 10-702. Scope of subtitle.

This subtitle does not apply to:

(1) an act allowed by the statutes of the United States or of this State, or by the regulations of the armed forces of the United States; or

(2) a document or product, stationery, ornament, picture, apparel, or jewelry that depicts a flag without a design or words on the flag and that is not connected with an advertisement. (An. Code 1957, art. 27, § 84; 2002, ch. 26, § 2; ch. 213, § 6.)

SPECIAL REVISOR'S NOTE

This Special Revisor's note comprises information related to the revision by Acts 2002, ch. 26 and other chapters amending this section from the 2002 Legislative Session.

As enacted by Ch. 26, Acts of 2002, this section was new language derived without substantive change from former Art. 27, § 84. However, Ch. 213, Acts of 2002, substituted the phrase "armed forces of the United States" for the former phrase "United States Army or Navy" enacted by Ch. 26 in item (1) of this section.

In item (2) of this section, the former reference to "printed or written" was deleted by Ch. 26 as implicit in the word "document".

The Criminal Law Article Review Committee noted, for the consideration of the General Assembly, that item (1) of this section referred to regulations of the "United States Army or Navy", and not of the "Air Force". At the time of enactment of the former law, there was not yet a separate United States Air Force. American military air operations in the World War were being conducted by the recently formed Air Service of the United States Army in the American Expeditionary Force. *See* Ch. 281, Acts of 1918. Chapter 213 addressed this concern.

Defined term:
"Flag"   § 10-701

§ 10-703. Marked flag and merchandise.

(a) *Scope of section.* — This section applies to a flag of the United States or of this State, or a flag that is authorized by law of the United States or of this State.

(b) *Prohibited — Advertising marking.* — For exhibition or display, a person may not place or cause to be placed a word, figure, mark, picture, design, or advertisement of any nature on a flag.

(c) *Prohibited — Public display of marked flag.* — A person may not publicly exhibit a flag with a word, figure, mark, picture, design, or advertisement printed, painted, or produced on or attached to the flag.

(d) *Prohibited — Merchandise marked with flag.* — A person may not publicly display for sale, manufacture, or otherwise, or sell, give, or possess for sale or for use as a gift or for any other purpose, an article of merchandise or receptacle on which a flag is produced or attached to advertise, decorate, or mark the merchandise.

(e) *Penalty.* — A person who violates this section is guilty of a misdemeanor and on conviction is subject to a fine not exceeding $500. (An. Code 1957, art. 27, §§ 82, 85; 2002, ch. 26, § 2.)

REVISOR'S NOTE

This Revisor's note comprises information related to the revision by Acts 2002, ch. 26.

This section is new language derived without substantive change from former Art. 27, § 82 and the first sentence of § 85.

In subsections (b) and (c) of this section, the former references to a "drawing" are deleted as included in the references to a "figure".

In subsection (b) of this section, the former reference to placing any word, etc. "in any manner" is deleted as surplusage.

In subsection (c) of this section, the former reference to being "appended, affixed or annexed" is deleted as included in the reference to being "attached".

Also in subsection (c) of this section, the former reference to "[e]xpos[ing] to public view" is deleted as included in the reference to "ex-

hibit[ing]". Similarly, in subsection (d) of this section, the former reference "for exhibition or display [e]xpos[ing] to public view" is deleted as included in the reference to "display[ing]".

In subsection (d) of this section, the former reference to "any substance" is deleted as included in the reference to "an article".

Also in subsection (d) of this section, the former reference to a "thing for holding or carrying merchandise" is deleted as included in the reference to a "receptacle".

Also in subsection (d) of this section, the former references to "call[ing] attention to" and "distinguish[ing]" an article are deleted as included in the references to "advertis[ing]" and "mark[ing]" the merchandise.

Defined terms:

"Flag"	§ 10-701
"Person"	§ 1-101

§ 10-704. Mutilation.

(a) *Prohibited.* — A person may not intentionally mutilate, deface, destroy, burn, trample, or use a flag:

(1) in a manner intended to incite or produce an imminent breach of the peace; and

(2) under circumstances likely to incite or produce an imminent breach of the peace.

(b) *Penalty.* — A person who violates this section is guilty of a misdemeanor and on conviction is subject to imprisonment not exceeding 1 year or a fine not exceeding $1,000 or both. (An. Code 1957, art. 27, §§ 83, 85; 2002, ch. 26, § 2.)

REVISOR'S NOTE

This Revisor's note comprises information related to the revision by Acts 2002, ch. 26.

This section is new language derived without substantive change from former Art. 27, § 83 and the second sentence of § 85.

In subsection (b) of this section, the phrase "is guilty of a misdemeanor" is added to state expressly that which was only implied in the former law by reference to a "punishable" violation. In this State, any crime that was not a felony at common law and has not been declared a felony by statute is considered to be a misdemeanor. *See State v. Canova*, 278 Md. 483, 490 (1976), *Bowser v. State*, 136 Md. 342, 345 (1920), *Dutton v. State*, 123 Md. 373, 378 (1914), and *Williams v. State*, 4 Md. App. 342, 347 (1968).

Also in subsection (b) of this section, the former phrase "in the discretion of the court" is deleted as implicit in the establishment of maximum penalties.

Defined terms:

"Flag"	§ 10-701
"Person"	§ 1-101

Maryland Law Review. — For comment discussing flag desecration statutes and the right to free speech, see 30 Md. L. Rev. 332 (1970).

Constitutionality. — Unlike the federal Flag Protection Act (18 U.S.C. § 700), the prior version of this section is a breach of the peace statute, and as such, it seeks to regulate non-speech activities and is justified by a sufficiently important governmental interest unrelated to the suppression of free expression, and even if it were aimed at expression, it would pass muster under the First Amendment because it expressly proscribes only unlawful conduct not protected by the Constitution, specifically, flag destruction intended to incite imminent lawless action and likely to produce that action. 75 Op. Att'y Gen. 147 (November 14, 1990).

Former version of this section could not be constitutionally applied to curtail freedom of expression as such. Korn v. Elkins, 317 F. Supp. 138 (D. Md. 1970).

Pictorial representations. — Former version of this section could not be applied by officials of the University of Maryland to prohibit publication of issues of a student magazine which pictured a burning flag on the cover and to prohibit publication of future issues containing the same type of material. Korn v. Elkins, 317 F. Supp. 138 (D. Md. 1970).

§ 10-705. Construction of subtitle.

This subtitle shall be construed to carry out its general purpose and to make uniform the laws of the states that enact it. (An. Code 1957, art. 27, § 86; 2002, ch. 26, § 2.)

REVISOR'S NOTE

This Revisor's note comprises information related to the revision by Acts 2002, ch. 26.

This section is new language derived without substantive change from former Art. 27, § 86.

Defined term:

"State"	§ 1-101

§ 10-706. Short title.

This subtitle may be cited as the Maryland Uniform Flag Law. (An. Code 1957, art. 27, § 87; 2002, ch. 26, § 2.)

REVISOR'S NOTE

This Revisor's note comprises information related to the revision by Acts 2002, ch. 26.

This section is new language derived without substantive change from former Art. 27, § 87.

The reference to the "Maryland" Uniform Flag Law is added to reflect changes made to this subtitle that were not reflected in the former uniform law recommended by the National Conference of Commissioners on Uniform State Laws.

Defined term:
"Flag" § 10-701

GENERAL REVISOR'S NOTE TO SUBTITLE

The National Conference of Commissioners on Uniform State Laws originally promulgated and recommended the Uniform Flag Law in 1917. It remained a recommended uniform law until 1966, when the National Conference withdrew the uniform law as obsolete. During its history as a uniform law, the Uniform Flag Law was adopted by 17 states, four of which substantially modified it. Only three other states still style their statutes as the "Uniform Flag Law" and retain language on uniform construction among the adopting states. They are Maine, Vermont, and Virginia.

The Criminal Law Article Review Committee notes, for the consideration of the General Assembly, that §§ 10-703 and 10-704 of this subtitle present constitutional issues relating to freedom of expression under the First Amendment to the U.S. Constitution and Md. Decl. of Rights, Art. 40. In particular, former Art. 27, § 82, which prohibits marking and merchandising involving a flag and is revised as § 10-703 of this subtitle, has been limited to apply only to the flag and Great Seal of the State, not to representations of either. Former Art. 27, § 83, which prohibits mutilation of a flag and is revised as § 10-704 of this subtitle, constitutionally may reach only commercial actions, not political expression. The General Assembly may wish to address these concerns in substantive legislation. *See* Letter of Advice from Attorney General J. Joseph Curran, Jr. to Judge Alan M. Wilner, pp. 3-7 (October 17, 2000).

TITLE 11.

INDECENCY AND OBSCENITY.

Subtitle 1. Adult Sexual Displays and Related Crimes.

§ 11-101. Definitions.

(a) *In general.* — In this subtitle the following words have the meanings indicated.

REVISOR'S NOTE

This subsection is new language derived without substantive change from the introductory language of former Art. 27, § 416A.

The reference to "this subtitle" is substituted for the former reference to "this subheading". Although this subtitle contains material on "indecent exposure" derived from material outside of the former "Nudity and Sexual Displays" subheading of Article 27, the terms defined in this section are only used in revised material that is derived from that former subheading; thus no substantive change results.

(b) *Advertising purposes.* — "Advertising purposes" means the purpose of propagandizing in connection with the commercial:

(1) sale of a product;

(2) offering of a service; or

(3) exhibition of entertainment.

REVISOR'S NOTE

This subsection is new language derived without substantive change from former Art. 27, § 416A(a).

In item (1) of this subsection, the former reference to "products" is deleted in light of Art.

1, § 8, which provides that the singular generally includes the plural.

(c) *Sadomasochistic abuse.* — "Sadomasochistic abuse" means:

(1) flagellation or torture committed by or inflicted on an individual who is:

(i) nude;

(ii) wearing only undergarments; or

(iii) wearing a revealing or bizarre costume; or

(2) binding, fettering, or otherwise physically restraining an individual who is:

(i) nude;

(ii) wearing only undergarments; or

(iii) wearing a revealing or bizarre costume.

REVISOR'S NOTE

This subsection is new language derived without substantive change from former Art. 27, § 416A(c).

In item (2) of this subsection, the former phrase "or so clothed" is deleted for brevity.

(d) *Sexual conduct.* — "Sexual conduct" means:

(1) human masturbation;

(2) sexual intercourse; or

(3) whether alone or with another individual or animal, any touching of or contact with:

(i) the genitals, buttocks, or pubic areas of an individual; or

(ii) breasts of a female individual.

REVISOR'S NOTE

This subsection is new language derived without substantive change from former Art. 27, § 416A(d).

In item (3) of this subsection, the reference to conduct "with another individual" is substituted for the former reference to conduct "between members of the same or opposite sex" for brevity and clarity.

Also in item (3) of this subsection, the reference to buttocks "of an individual" is substituted for the former reference to buttocks "of the human male or female" for brevity and clarity.

(e) *Sexual excitement.* — "Sexual excitement" means:

(1) the condition of the human genitals when in a state of sexual stimulation;

250

(2) the condition of the human female breasts when in a state of sexual stimulation; or

(3) the sensual experiences of individuals engaging in or witnessing sexual conduct or nudity.

REVISOR'S NOTE

This subsection is new language derived without substantive change from former Art. 27, § 416A(e).

In item (1) of this subsection, the former reference to "male or female" genitals is deleted as included in the reference to "human" genitals.

(An. Code 1957, art. 27, § 416A, 416A(a), (c)-(e); 2002, ch. 26, § 2.)

REVISOR'S NOTE TO SECTION

The Revisor's notes in this section comprise information related to the revision by Acts 2002, ch. 26.

Former Art. 27, § 416A(b), which defined "minor", is revised in § 1-101 of this article.

Definitions not unconstitutionally vague and overbroad. — The definitions in (c), (d) and (e) of a former version of this section are directed against obscene displays and are not unconstitutionally vague and overbroad. State v. Randall Book Corp., 53 Md. App. 30, 452 A.2d 187 (1982), cert. denied, 295 Md. 441, cert. denied, 464 U.S. 919, 104 S. Ct. 286, 78 L. Ed. 2d 263 (1983).

"Sexual conduct." — The child pornography statute contains a scienter element — knowledge of the nature and character of the materials — because a defendant photographer must have knowledge that he or she is taking pictures of sexual conduct as defined in this section. Outmezguine v. State, 335 Md. 20, 641 A.2d 870 (1994).

§ 11-102. Adult sexual displays — Selling or offering to sell to minor.

(a) *Prohibited.* — A person may not knowingly sell or offer to sell to a minor:

(1) a picture, photograph, drawing, sculpture, motion picture, film, or other visual representation or image of an individual or portion of the human body that depicts sadomasochistic abuse, sexual conduct, or sexual excitement;

(2) a book, magazine, paperback, pamphlet, or other written or printed matter however reproduced, that contains:

(i) any matter enumerated in item (1) of this section;

(ii) obscene material; or

(iii) explicit verbal descriptions or narrative accounts of sadomasochistic abuse, sexual conduct, or sexual excitement; or

(3) a sound recording that contains:

(i) obscene material; or

(ii) explicit verbal descriptions or narrative accounts of sadomasochistic abuse, sexual conduct, or sexual excitement.

(b) *Penalty.* — A person who violates this section is guilty of a misdemeanor and on conviction is subject to imprisonment not exceeding 6 months or a fine not exceeding $1,000 or both. (An. Code 1957, art. 27, §§ 416B, 416G; 2002, ch. 26, § 2; ch. 45; 2004, ch. 444.)

This Special Revisor's note comprises information related to the revision by Acts 2002, ch. 26 and other chapters amending this section from the 2002 Legislative Session.

As enacted by Ch. 26, Acts of 2002, this section was new language derived without substantive change from former Art. 27, §§ 416B and 416G. However, Ch. 45, Acts of 2002, added "or both" following "$1,000" in subsection (b) of this section.

In subsection (a)(2)(ii) and (3)(i) of this section and throughout this subtitle, the references to "obscene material" were substituted by Ch. 26 for the former reference to "obscenities" for clarity. *See* Letter of Advice from Attorney General J. Joseph Curran, Jr. to Judge Alan M. Wilner, pp. 3-4 (May 21, 2001).

In subsection (a)(3) of this section, the former reference to "any matter enumerated in subsection (a) [picture, photograph, . . .]" was deleted by Ch. 26 because sound recordings cannot contain "visual representations".

The Criminal Law Article Review Committee notes, for the consideration of the General Assembly, that in this section and throughout this subtitle, the standard for determining whether material is "obscene" appears to follow that established by Supreme Court precedent. This applies equally to prohibitions on obscene material relating to minors, §§ 11-102 through 11-104 of this subtitle, derived from former Art. 27, §§ 416B, 416C, and 416E, and to the prohibition on obscene material in advertising, § 11-105, derived from former Art. 27, § 416D. *See* Letter of Advice from Attorney General J. Joseph Curran to Judge Alan M. Wilner, pp. 1-3 (May 21, 2001), citing *Smiley v. State*, 294 Md. 461 (1982). *See, also, State v. Randall Book Corp.*, 53 Md. App. 30 (1982), *cert. denied*, 295 Md. 441, *cert. denied*, 464 U.S. 919 (1983); and *cf. Ginsberg v. New York*, 390 U.S. 629 (1968).

As to the penalty provided in subsection (b) of this section, *see* General Revisor's Note to subtitle.

Defined terms:

"Minor"	§ 1-101
"Person"	§ 1-101
"Sadomasochistic abuse"	§ 11-101
"Sexual conduct"	§ 11-101
"Sexual excitement"	§ 11-101

§ 11-103. Adult sexual displays — Exhibition to minors.

(a) *Scope of section.* — This section applies to a motion picture show or other presentation, whether animated or live, that wholly or partly:

(1) depicts or reveals:

(i) sadomasochistic abuse;

(ii) sexual conduct; or

(iii) sexual excitement; or

(2) includes obscene material or explicit verbal descriptions or narrative accounts of sexual conduct.

(b) *Prohibited.* — For monetary consideration or other valuable commodity or service, a person may not knowingly:

(1) exhibit to a minor without the presence of the minor's parent or guardian a motion picture show or other presentation described in subsection (a) of this section;

(2) sell to a minor an admission ticket or other means to gain entrance to a motion picture show or other presentation described in subsection (a) of this section; or

(3) admit a minor without the presence of the minor's parent or guardian to premises where a motion picture show or other presentation described in subsection (a) of this section is exhibited.

(c) *Penalty.* — A person who violates this section is guilty of a misdemeanor and on conviction is subject to imprisonment not exceeding 6 months or a fine not exceeding $1,000 or both. (An. Code 1957, art. 27, §§ 416C, 416G; 2002, ch. 26, § 2; ch. 45; 2004, ch. 444.)

This Special Revisor's note comprises information related to the revision by Acts 2002, ch. 26 and other chapters amending this section from the 2002 Legislative Session.

As enacted by Ch. 26, Acts of 2002, this section was new language derived without substantive change from former Art. 27, §§ 416C and 416G. However, Ch. 45, Acts of 2002, added "or both" following "$1,000" in subsection (c) of this section.

In subsection (a)(2) of this section, the reference to "obscene material" was substituted by Ch. 26 for the former reference to "obscenities" for clarity.

In subsection (b)(1) and (3) of this section, the phrase "without the presence of the minor's parent or guardian" was substituted by Ch. 26 for the former phrase "unaccompanied by his parent or guardian" for style.

As to the penalty provided in subsection (c) of this section, *see* General Revisor's Note to subtitle.

Defined terms:

"Minor"	§ 1-101
"Person"	§ 1-101
"Sadomasochistic abuse"	§ 11-101
"Sexual conduct"	§ 11-101
"Sexual excitement"	§ 11-101

§ 11-104. Adult sexual displays — Allowing minors to enter or remain on premises.

(a) *Prohibited.* — A person who operates or is employed in a sales, cashier, or managerial capacity in a retail establishment may not knowingly allow a minor without the presence of the minor's parent or guardian to enter or remain on any premises where an item or activity detailed in § 11-102(a) of this subtitle is shown, displayed, or depicted.

(b) *Penalty.* — A person who violates this section is guilty of a misdemeanor and on conviction is subject to imprisonment not exceeding 6 months or a fine not exceeding $1,000 or both. (An. Code 1957, art. 27, §§ 416E, 416G; 2002, ch. 26, § 2; ch. 45.)

This Special Revisor's note comprises information related to the revision by Acts 2002, ch. 26 and other chapters amending this section from the 2002 Legislative Session.

As enacted by Ch. 26, Acts of 2002, this section was new language derived without substantive change from former Art. 27, §§ 416E and 416G. However, Ch. 45, Acts of 2002, added "or both" following "$1,000" in subsection (b) of this section.

In subsection (a) of this section, the phrase "without the presence of the minor's parent or guardian" was substituted by Ch. 26 for the former phrase "unaccompanied by his parent or guardian" for style.

As to the penalty provided in subsection (b) of this section, *see* General Revisor's Note to subtitle.

Defined terms:

"Minor"	§ 1-101
"Person"	§ 1-101

§ 11-104.1. Adult sexual displays — Allowing minors to enter or remain on premises — Bookstores and entertainment venues.

(a) *Harford and Cecil counties.* — In Harford County and Cecil County, a person who operates a bookstore or entertainment venue in which an item or activity described in § 11-102 or § 11-103 of this subtitle is shown, displayed, or depicted and constitutes a majority of the items or activities offered for sale or rental by the bookstore or entertainment venue:

(1) shall require each individual upon entering the premises to display a driver's license or an identification card that substantiates the individual's age; and

(2) may not knowingly allow a minor to remain on the premises.

(b) *Penalties.* — A person who violates this section is guilty of a misdemeanor and on conviction is subject to imprisonment not exceeding 6 months or a fine not exceeding $1,000 or both. (2004, ch. 444.)

§ 11-105. Adult sexual displays — Displaying or allowing display for advertising purposes.

(a) *Prohibited — Display.* — A person may not knowingly display for advertising purposes a picture, photograph, drawing, sculpture, or other visual representation or image of an individual or portion of a human body that:

(1) depicts sadomasochistic abuse;

(2) depicts sexual conduct;

(3) depicts sexual excitement; or

(4) contains a verbal description or narrative account of sadomasochistic abuse, sexual conduct, or sexual excitement.

(b) *Prohibited — Allowing display.* — A person may not knowingly allow a display described in subsection (a) of this section on premises that the person owns, rents, or manages.

(c) *Penalty.* — A person who violates this section is guilty of a misdemeanor and on conviction is subject to imprisonment not exceeding 6 months or a fine not exceeding $1,000 or both. (An. Code 1957, art. 27, §§ 416D, 416G; 2002, ch. 26, § 2; ch. 45; 2003, ch. 21, § 1.)

SPECIAL REVISOR'S NOTE

This Special Revisor's note comprises information related to the revision by Acts 2002, ch. 26 and other chapters amending this section from the 2002 Legislative Session.

As enacted by Ch. 26, Acts of 2002, this section was new language derived without substantive change from former Art. 27, §§ 416D and 416G. However, Ch. 45, Acts of 2002, added "or both" following "$1,000" in subsection (c) of this section.

In subsection (a)(4) of this section, the reference to "sadomasochistic abuse, sexual conduct, or sexual excitement" was substituted by Ch. 26 for the former reference to "these activities or items" for clarity.

As to the penalty provided in subsection (c) of this section, *see* General Revisor's Note to subtitle.

Defined terms:

"Advertising purposes"	§ 11-101
"Person"	§ 1-101
"Sadomasochistic abuse"	§ 11-101
"Sexual conduct"	§ 11-101
"Sexual excitement"	§ 11-101

§ 11-106. Adult sexual displays — Presumptions.

For purposes of §§ 11-101 through 11-105 of this subtitle, an employee of a person who operates premises where a public display violates this subtitle is presumed to have been the operator of the premises when the violation occurred if the employee was on the premises at the time of the violation. (An. Code 1957, art. 27, § 416F; 2002, ch. 26, § 2.)

This Revisor's note comprises information related to the revision by Acts 2002, ch. 26.

This section is new language derived without substantive change from former Art. 27, § 416F.

This section applies only to §§ 11-101 through 11-105 of this subtitle to reflect the reorganization of the former Nudity and Sexual Displays subheading. The crime of "indecent exposure" was not included in the former subheading and is not subject to the presumption outlined in this section.

Defined term:
"Person"   § 1-101

§ 11-107. Indecent exposure.

A person convicted of indecent exposure is guilty of a misdemeanor and is subject to imprisonment not exceeding 3 years or a fine not exceeding $1,000 or both. (An. Code 1957, art. 27, § 335A; 2002, ch. 26, § 2.)

This Revisor's note comprises information related to the revision by Acts 2002, ch. 26.

This section is new language derived without substantive change from former Art. 27, § 335A.

Defined term:
"Person"   § 1-101

Language clear and unambiguous. — Language of section is clear and unambiguous. Neal v. State, 45 Md. App. 549, 413 A.2d 1386, cert. denied, 288 Md. 740 (1980).

Preemption of common law. — When determining whether the enactment of § 8-803 of the Correctional Services Article was intended to preempt the field concerning indecent exposure by inmates in a correctional facility, the fact that the penalties for a statutory violation, under § 8-803(c) of the Correctional Services Article, and the penalty for a common law violation, under this section, were the same did not mean the statute preempted the field because the sameness of the penalties was not determinative. Genies v. State, 196 Md. App. 590, 10 A.3d 854 (2010).

Preamble not operative portion of law. — Preamble to section is not an operative portion of the law, notwithstanding that it may be resorted to as a statutory construction aid. Neal v. State, 45 Md. App. 549, 413 A.2d 1386, cert. denied, 288 Md. 740 (1980).

Indecent exposure not infamous crime. — The wide spectrum of conduct and degrees of depravity associated with indecent exposure make it clear that it does not conform with those offenses regarded as infamous. Whatever else it may be, indecent exposure is not an infamous crime. Ricketts v. State, 291 Md. 701, 436 A.2d 906 (1981).

Indecent exposure is not crime of moral turpitude for purposes of assessing defen-dant's credibility. — Indecent exposure is a general intent crime that includes within its scope an innumerable variety of offenses, including acts that are reckless or negligent. As such its meaning is entirely too unspecific to warrant the appellation of a crime of moral turpitude, at least in the context of determining whether conviction for indecent exposure was relevant to assessment of the credibility of a criminal defendant. Ricketts v. State, 291 Md. 701, 436 A.2d 906 (1981).

Conviction under this section inadmissible for impeachment of defendant's credibility. — Indecent exposure is a lesser crime for which the proscribed conduct includes such a wide variety of behavior that the factfinder would be unable to make a reasoned judgment as to whether the offense affects the defendant's credibility; it is inadmissible for purposes of impeachment. Ricketts v. State, 291 Md. 701, 436 A.2d 906 (1981).

Indecent exposure not sexual in nature. — Defendant was not required to register pursuant to § 11-704 of the Criminal Procedure Article as an "offender" under § 11-701(h)(7) of the Criminal Procedure Article because the crime of indecent exposure was not sexual in nature; the lewdness element incorporated conduct that was not sexual in addition to that which could be sexual. State v. Duran, 407 Md. 532, 967 A.2d 184 (2009).

Quoted in Wisneski v. State, 398 Md. 578, 921 A.2d 273 (2007).

Cited in Ellis v. State, 185 Md. App. 522, 971 A.2d 379 (2009); Md. State Police v. McLean, 197 Md. App. 430, 14 A.3d 658 (2011).

GENERAL REVISOR'S NOTE TO SUBTITLE

The former Nudity and Sexual Displays subheading of Article 27 contained a general penalty provision, Art. 27, § 416G, that applied to all violations of the subheading. In *Randall Book Corp. v. State*, 316 Md. 315, 329 (1989), the Court of Appeals concluded that "the legislature [in Art. 27, § 416D] intended the knowing display of each separate obscene magazine to constitute a separate offense, separately punishable". As each crime is separately punishable, for clarity, the former penalty provision is repeated in each section to which the penalty applies.

The Criminal Law Article Review Committee noted, for the consideration of the General Assembly, that, in §§ 11-102 through 11-105 of this subtitle, a violator was subject to either imprisonment or a fine, but not both. In almost every other criminal statute that allows punishment by imprisonment or a fine, a violator may be sentenced to both imprisonment and fine. Chapter 45, Acts of 2002, addressed this concern.

Subtitle 2. Obscene Matter.

§ 11-201. Definitions.

(a) *In general.* — In this subtitle the following words have the meanings indicated.

REVISOR'S NOTE

This subsection is new language derived without substantive change from the introductory language of former Art. 27, § 417.

(b) *Distribute.* — "Distribute" means to transfer possession.

REVISOR'S NOTE

This subsection is new language derived without substantive change from former Art. 27, § 417(3).

The former phrase "whether with or without consideration" is deleted because it does not limit the transfers that are included in the scope of the definition.

(c) *Knowingly.* — "Knowingly" means having knowledge of the character and content of the matter.

REVISOR'S NOTE

This subsection is new language derived without substantive change from former Art. 27, § 417(4).

(d) *Matter.* — "Matter" means:

(1) a book, magazine, newspaper, or other printed or written material;

(2) a picture, drawing, photograph, motion picture, or other pictorial representation;

(3) a statue or other figure;

(4) a recording, transcription, or mechanical, chemical, or electrical reproduction; or

(5) any other article, equipment, machine, or material.

REVISOR'S NOTE

This subsection is new language derived without substantive change from former Art. 27, § 417(1).

(e) *Sadomasochistic abuse.* — "Sadomasochistic abuse" has the meaning stated in § 11-101 of this title.

REVISOR'S NOTE

This subsection is new language derived without substantive change from the references in former Art. 27, §§ 419A(b), (c), (d), (e), and (g) and 419B(a) to the definitions in former Art. 27, § 416A — now § 11-101 of this title — to avoid repetition of the phrase "as defined in § 11-101 of this title".

(f) *Sexual conduct.* — "Sexual conduct" has the meaning stated in § 11-101 of this title.

REVISOR'S NOTE

This subsection is new language derived without substantive change from the references in former Art. 27, §§ 419A(b), (c), (d), (e), and (g) and 419B(a) to the definitions in former § 416A — now § 11-101 of this title — to avoid repetition of the phrase "as defined in § 11-101 of this title".

(g) *Sexual excitement.* — "Sexual excitement" has the meaning stated in § 11-101 of this title.

REVISOR'S NOTE

This subsection is new language derived without substantive change from former Art. 27, § 419B(a) as it related to a definition of "sexual excitement".

(An. Code 1957, art. 27, §§ 417(1), (3), (4), 419A(b)-(e), (g), 419B(a); 2002, ch. 26, § 2; 2009, chs. 510, 511.)

REVISOR'S NOTE TO SECTION

The Revisor's notes in this section comprise information related to the revision by Acts 2002, ch. 26.

Former Art. 27, §§ 417(2) and 419A(a), which defined "person" and "minor", respectively, are revised in § 1-101 of this article.

Effect of amendments. — Chapters 510 and 511, Acts 2009, effective October 1, 2009, made identical changes. Each reenacted (f) without change.

State has power to regulate obscenity. — A state has the power to regulate obscenity. Adler v. Pomerleau, 313 F. Supp. 277 (D. Md. 1970).

§ 11-202. Obscene matter — Distribution, exhibition, importation, and publication.

(a) *Prohibited.* — A person may not:

(1) knowingly send or cause to be sent any obscene matter into the State for sale or distribution;

(2) knowingly bring or cause to be brought any obscene matter into the State for sale or distribution;

(3) in the State prepare, publish, print, exhibit, distribute, or offer to distribute any obscene matter; or

(4) possess any obscene matter in the State with the intent to distribute, offer to distribute, or exhibit.

(b) *Penalty.* — A person who violates this section is guilty of a misdemeanor and on conviction is subject to:

(1) for a first violation, imprisonment not exceeding 1 year or a fine not exceeding $1,000 or both; and

(2) for each subsequent violation, imprisonment not exceeding 3 years or a fine not exceeding $5,000 or both.

(c) *Injunction.* — (1) The State's Attorney may maintain an action for an injunction in the circuit court against a person to prevent the sale, further sale, distribution, further distribution, acquisition, publication, or possession within the State of any book, magazine, pamphlet, newspaper, story paper, writing paper, picture, card, drawing, photograph, motion picture film or showing, or any article, item, or instrument the use of which is obscene.

(2) The circuit court may enjoin the sale or distribution of a book, magazine, motion picture film or showing, or other publication or item that is prohibited under this section from sale or distribution.

(3) After being served a summons and complaint in an action by the State's Attorney under this section, a person who sells, distributes, or acquires the enjoined material is chargeable with knowledge of the contents of the materials described in this section.

(4) The defendant is entitled to a trial of the issues within 1 day after joinder of issue.

(5) The court shall render a decision within 2 days after the conclusion of the trial.

(6) If an order or judgment is entered in favor of the State's Attorney, the final order or judgment shall contain provisions:

(i) directing the person to surrender the obscene matter to the peace officer designated by the court or the county sheriff; and

(ii) directing the peace officer or county sheriff to seize and destroy the obscene matter.

(7) In an action brought under this section, the State's Attorney is not:

(i) required to file a bond before an injunction order is issued;

(ii) liable for costs; or

(iii) liable for damages sustained because of the injunction order if judgment is rendered in favor of the defendant. (An. Code 1957, art. 27, §§ 418, 418A, 424; 2002, ch. 26, § 2; ch. 213, § 6.)

SPECIAL REVISOR'S NOTE

This Special Revisor's note comprises information related to the revision by Acts 2002, ch. 26 and other chapters amending this section from the 2002 Legislative Session.

As enacted by Ch. 26, Acts of 2002, this section was new language derived without substantive change from former Art. 27, §§ 418, 418A, and 424. However, Ch. 213, Acts of 2002, added the reference to an "item" the use of which is obscene in subsection (c)(1) of this section.

As to the penalty provided in subsection (b) of this section, *see* General Revisor's Note to subtitle.

In subsection (b) of this section, the former phrase "unless otherwise provided" was deleted by Ch. 26 because there are no alternative penalties provided for a violation of this section.

In subsection (b)(1) of this section, the qualification "[f]or a first violation" was added by Ch. 26 for clarity.

In subsection (c)(1) of this section, the former reference to the circuit courts "of the counties" was deleted by Ch. 26 as implicit in the reference to the "circuit court".

Also in subsection (c)(1) of this section, the phrase "under this section", was substituted by Ch. 26 for the former phrase "as hereinafter specified" for clarity.

In subsection (c)(2) of this section, the former reference to "the counties in which a person . . . sells . . . any book . . . which is obscene" was deleted by Ch. 26 because it described the person to be enjoined, not the action which the State's Attorney sought to enjoin.

In subsection (c)(4) and (7)(iii) of this section, the references to the "defendant" were substituted by Ch. 26 for the former references to the "person sought to be enjoined" for brevity and clarity.

In subsection (c)(6) of this section, the former phrase "against the person . . . sought to be enjoined" was deleted by Ch. 26 as implicit in the reference to an order or judgment in favor of the State's Attorney, which, by definition, must be against the person sought to be enjoined.

Also in subsection (c)(6) of this section, the word "materials" was substituted by Ch. 26 for the former reference to "matter" because "matter" was a defined term and its use here would be inconsistent with that definition.

In subsection (c)(7) of this section, the former phrase "provided for by this section" was deleted by Ch. 26 in light of the scope of the paragraph being limited to an "action brought under this section".

The Criminal Law Article Review Committee noted, for the consideration of the General Assembly, that the list of material that may be enjoined did not appear to include some of the newer materials that may contain obscene matter, such as videodiscs, computer software, and interactive CD-ROM or DVD discs.

The Criminal Law Article Review Committee also notes, for the attention of the General Assembly, that in subsection (c)(1) and (3) of this section, the defined term "matter" could not be used because the list of items contained in (c)(2) differed in several particulars from the items listed in the defined term. This section, derived from former Art. 27, § 418A, which was enacted by Ch. 382, Acts of 1961, contains a list based on former Art. 27, § 418, which prohibited the preparation, distribution, and importation of lewd, obscene, or indecent books and materials, and which was completely rewritten under Ch. 394 of the Acts of 1967. The one substantive amendment to the § 418A list was the inclusion of "a motion picture film or showing" under Ch. 619, Acts of 1968. The list of "matter" in former Art. 27, § 417, enacted by Ch. 394 of the Acts of 1967, had never been amended. In order to treat the various forms of obscene material in a consistent manner, the General Assembly may wish to reconcile the different lists of obscene material in this subtitle in substantive legislation.

Defined terms:

"Distribute"	§ 11-201
"Knowingly"	§ 11-201
"Matter"	§ 11-201
"Person"	§ 1-101

I. GENERAL CONSIDERATION.

A. In General.

Cross references. — See § 11-201 of this article.

Maryland Law Review. — For article, "Survey of Developments in Maryland Law, 1984-85," see 45 Md. L. Rev. 634 (1986).

Separate offenses. — This statute creates separate offenses. Ayre v. State, 21 Md. App. 61, 318 A.2d 828 (1974).

Effect of severability clause. — The severability clause enacted by § 2, Chapter 394, 1967 Laws of Maryland, does not save a former version of this section in terms of a constitutional challenge. Wheeler v. State, 281 Md. 593, 380 A.2d 1052 (1977), cert. denied, 435 U.S. 997, 98 S. Ct. 1650, 56 L. Ed. 2d 86 (1978).

Legislative purpose. — Reading this section together with the definition of "person" (see § 1-101 of this article), the legislative purpose is clear — to deter the dissemination of obscene matter by making designated acts a crime punishable by imprisonment and fine. Wheeler v. State, 281 Md. 593, 380 A.2d 1052 (1977), cert. denied, 435 U.S. 997, 98 S. Ct. 1650, 56 L. Ed. 2d 86 (1978).

Historical development of obscenity law. — See 400 E. Baltimore St., Inc. v. State, 49 Md. App. 147, 431 A.2d 682 (1981), cert. denied, 455 U.S. 940, 102 S. Ct. 1431, 71 L. Ed. 2d 650 (1982).

Obscenity not protected speech and press. — Obscenity is not within the area of constitutionally protected speech and press. Monfred v. State, 226 Md. 312, 173 A.2d 173 (1961), cert. denied, 368 U.S. 953, 82 S. Ct. 395, 7 L. Ed. 2d 386 (1962); Donnenberg v. State, 1 Md. App. 591, 232 A.2d 264 (1967).

Obscenity is beyond the pale of First Amendment protection. Marques v. State, 267 Md. 542, 298 A.2d 408 (1973).

Test for obscenity. — Test of obscenity is whether to the average person, applying contemporary community standards, the dominant theme of the material taken as a whole appeals to prurient interest. Monfred v. State, 226 Md. 312, 173 A.2d 173 (1961), cert. denied, 368 U.S. 953, 82 S. Ct. 395, 7 L. Ed. 2d 386 (1962); Yudkin v. State, 229 Md. 223, 182 A.2d 798 (1962).

Material having a prurient interest is defined as material having a tendency to excite lustful thoughts. Monfred v. State, 226 Md. 312, 173 A.2d 173 (1961), cert. denied, 368 U.S. 953, 82 S. Ct. 395, 7 L. Ed. 2d 386 (1962).

When each of certain magazines were taken as a whole, that is, when the pictures reproduced therein were examined in conjunction with a perusal of the textual material, it was apparent that all of the publications were obscene within the meaning of a former version of

this section. Monfred v. State, 226 Md. 312, 173 A.2d 173 (1961), cert. denied, 368 U.S. 953, 82 S. Ct. 395, 7 L. Ed. 2d 386 (1962).

Two of the elements set forth under the Roth-Alberts test of obscenity, as stated in Roth v. United States, 354 U.S. 476, 77 S. Ct. 1304, 1 L. Ed. 2d 1498 (1957), and summarized in the "Fanny Hill" decision, 383 U.S. 413, 86 S. Ct. 975, 16 L. Ed. 2d 1 (1966), are: The dominant theme of the material taken as a whole appeals to a prurient interest in sex, and the material is patently offensive because it affronts contemporary community standards relating to the description or representation of sexual matters. Levin v. State, 1 Md. App. 139, 228 A.2d 487 (1967), cert. denied, 247 Md. 740 (1967), cert. denied, 389 U.S. 1048, 88 S. Ct. 767, 19 L. Ed. 2d 840 (1968).

It is understood that the Roth-Alberts definition of obscenity — "whether to the average person, applying contemporary community standards, the dominant theme of the material taken as a whole appeals to the prurient interest" — as reiterated in Jacobellis v. Ohio, 378 U.S. 184, 84 S. Ct. 1676, 12 L. Ed. 2d 793 (1964), elaborated in Ginzburg v. United States, 383 U.S. 463, 86 S. Ct. 942, 969, 16 L. Ed. 2d 31 (1966), adjusted in Mishkin v. New York, 383 U.S. 502, 86 S. Ct. 958, 16 L. Ed. 2d 56 (1966), and summarized in A Book Named "John Cleland's Memoirs of a Woman of Pleasure" v. Attorney General (the Fanny Hill decision), 383 U.S. 413, 86 S. Ct. 975, 16 L. Ed. 2d 1 (1966), establishes the following test for obscenity: Three elements must coalesce; it must be established that: (1) The dominant theme of the material taken as a whole appeals to a prurient interest in sex [where the material is designed for and primarily disseminated to clearly defined deviant sexual group, rather than the public at large, the prurient-appeal requirement is satisfied if the dominant theme of the material taken as a whole appeals to the prurient interest in sex of the members of that group]. (2) The material is patently offensive because it affronts contemporary community standards relating to the description or representation of sexual matters. (3) The material is utterly without redeeming social value. Each of the above three federal constitutional criteria must be applied independently and neither be weighed against nor canceled by any of the others. Dillingham v. State, 9 Md. App. 669, 267 A.2d 777 (1970), cert. denied, 259 Md. 731, 259 Md. 736 (1970).

The test for obscenity, as set forth in the Roth decision is: (1) The dominant theme of the material taken as a whole appeals to a prurient interest in sex; (2) the material is patently offensive because it affronts contemporary community standards relating to the description or representation of sexual matters; and (3) the material is utterly without redeeming social value. Donnenberg v. State, 1 Md. App. 591, 232 A.2d 264 (1967).

Under the Roth-Alberts definition of obscenity, three elements must coalesce; it must be established that: (1) The dominant theme of the material taken as a whole appeals to a prurient interest in sex; (2) the material is patently offensive because it affronts contemporary community standards relating to the description or representation of sexual matters; and (3) the material is utterly without redeeming social value. Lancaster v. State, 7 Md. App. 602, 256 A.2d 716 (1969).

To come within the definition of obscenity, three elements must coalesce; it must be established that: (1) The dominant theme of the material taken as a whole appeals to a prurient interest in sex. (2) The material is patently offensive because it affronts contemporary community standards relating to the description or representation of sexual matters. (3) The material is utterly without redeeming social value. Each of the above three federal constitutional criteria must be applied independently and neither be weighed against nor canceled by any of the others. Woodruff v. State, 11 Md. App. 202, 273 A.2d 436, cert. denied, 262 Md. 750, 262 Md. 751 (1971).

The definition of obscenity originally announced by the Supreme Court of the United States in Roth v. United States, 354 U.S. 476, 77 S. Ct. 1304, 1 L. Ed. 2d 1498 (1957), was significantly refined by the plurality opinion in Memoirs v. Massachusetts, 383 U.S. 413, 86 S. Ct. 975, 16 L. Ed. 2d 1 (1966). Recognizing that the Memoirs plurality test for the determination of obscenity vel non had represented a sharp break with the test announced in Roth, the Court reformulated the test in Miller v. California, 413 U.S. 15, 93 S. Ct. 2607, 37 L. Ed. 2d 419 (1973). Village Books, Inc. v. State, 22 Md. App. 274, 323 A.2d 698, cert. denied, 273 Md. 723 (1974).

The guidelines for determining obscenity are: (a) Whether the average person, applying contemporary community standards, would find that the work, taken as a whole, appeals to the prurient interest; (b) whether the work depicts or describes, in a patently offensive way, sexual conduct specifically defined by the applicable state law; and (c) whether the work, taken as a whole, lacks serious literary, artistic, political, or scientific value. Village Books, Inc. v. State, 22 Md. App. 274, 323 A.2d 698, cert. denied, 273 Md. 723 (1974); 400 E. Baltimore St., Inc. v. State, 49 Md. App. 147, 431 A.2d 682 (1981), cert. denied, 291 Md. 774 (1981), cert. denied, 455 U.S. 940, 102 S. Ct. 1431, 71 L. Ed. 2d 650 (1982).

A thing is obscene if, considered as a whole, its predominant appeal is to prurient interest, i.e., a shameful or morbid interest in nudity, sex, or excretion, and if it goes substantially beyond customary limits of candor in description or representation of such matters. Little Store, Inc. v. State, 295 Md. 158, 453 A.2d 1215 (1983).

First establish dominant theme. — It is first necessary to establish what the dominant theme of the material is before it can be determined whether that theme would appeal to the prurient interest of anyone. Woodruff v. State, 11 Md. App. 202, 273 A.2d 436, cert. denied, 262 Md. 750, 262 Md. 751 (1971).

Unpopular political views socially valuable. — Where virtually every page of an underground newspaper containing allegedly obscene matter was packed with political comment and with vigorously urged political views, and many, if not most, of the views were unpopular, and were, to many persons, outrageous, they were, therefore, socially valuable — not despite their unpopularity but by virtue of that unpopularity. Woodruff v. State, 11 Md. App. 202, 273 A.2d 436, cert. denied, 262 Md. 750, 262 Md. 751 (1971).

Mere nudity not obscene. — Mere nudity, in and of itself, is not obscene. Levin v. State, 1 Md. App. 139, 228 A.2d 487 (1967), cert. denied, 247 Md. 740 (1967), cert. denied, 389 U.S. 1048, 88 S. Ct. 767, 19 L. Ed. 2d 840 (1968); Donnenberg v. State, 1 Md. App. 591, 232 A.2d 264 (1967).

Sex and obscenity not synonymous. — Sex and obscenity are not synonymous. Levin v. State, 1 Md. App. 139, 228 A.2d 487 (1967), cert. denied, 247 Md. 740 (1967), cert. denied, 389 U.S. 1048, 88 S. Ct. 767, 19 L. Ed. 2d 840 (1968); Donnenberg v. State, 1 Md. App. 591, 232 A.2d 264 (1967).

Exemption does not render proscription nugatory. — Exemption from criminality in no way renders general proscription of this section nugatory, nor does it eradicate or annul the concept or definition of obscenity or the State's power to regulate that obscenity. 400 E. Baltimore St., Inc. v. State, 49 Md. App. 147, 431 A.2d 682 (1981), cert. denied, 291 Md. 774, 291 Md. 782 (1981), cert. denied, 455 U.S. 940, 102 S. Ct. 1431, 71 L. Ed. 2d 650 (1982).

Intent that section be exclusively civil. — General Assembly intended this section to be exclusively civil in nature and, by necessary implication, that it may not be subverted to uses ancillary to a criminal proceeding. Marques v. State, 267 Md. 542, 298 A.2d 408 (1973).

Proceeding under this section was civil. Village Books, Inc. v. State, 22 Md. App. 274, 323 A.2d 698, cert. denied, 273 Md. 723 (1974).

B. Definitions.

"Obscene" defined. — The term "obscene," though not precise, when applied according to the standards set forth in the Roth case and summarized in the "Fanny Hill" decision, was held to give adequate warning of the conduct proscribed and to mark boundaries sufficiently distinct for judges and juries fairly to administer the law. Levin v. State, 1 Md. App. 139, 228 A.2d 487 (1967), cert. denied, 247 Md. 740 (1967), cert. denied, 389 U.S. 1048, 88 S. Ct. 767, 19 L. Ed. 2d 840 (1968).

The General Assembly intended, by its use of the word "obscene," what the word means in prevailing leading legal thought. Levin v. State, 1 Md. App. 139, 228 A.2d 487 (1967), cert. denied, 389 U.S. 1048, 88 S. Ct. 767, 19 L. Ed. 2d 840 (1968); Woodruff v. State, 11 Md. App. 202, 273 A.2d 436, cert. denied, 262 Md. 750, 262 Md. 751 (1971).

The term "obscene," applied according to prevailing leading legal thought, gives adequate warning of the conduct proscribed and marks boundaries sufficiently distinct for judges and juries fairly to administer the law. Donnenberg v. State, 1 Md. App. 591, 232 A.2d 264 (1967); B & A Co. v. State, 24 Md. App. 367, 330 A.2d 701 (1975).

"Lewd" and "indecent" defined. — Words "lewd" and "indecent" have been absorbed into the word "obscene" and have no independent vitality of their own. Woodruff v. State, 11 Md. App. 202, 273 A.2d 436, cert. denied, 262 Md. 750, 262 Md. 751 (1971).

Supreme Court's definition of obscenity is binding. — The courts, trial and appellate, of this State are bound by the definition of obscenity as enunciated by the Supreme Court of the United States. Woodruff v. State, 11 Md. App. 202, 273 A.2d 436, cert. denied, 262 Md. 750, 262 Md. 751 (1971).

With regard to this section, courts are to follow the dictates of the United States Supreme Court as to the basic guidelines under the reformulated test for the determination of obscenity announced in Miller v. California, 413 U.S. 15, 93 S. Ct. 2607, 37 L. Ed. 2d 419 (1973). Village Books, Inc. v. State, 22 Md. App. 274, 323 A.2d 698, cert. denied, 273 Md. 723 (1974).

In enacting its obscenity law, the State of Maryland chose not to define "obscene" but to permit courts to apply whatever definition the United States Supreme Court supplied from time to time to describe that which is proscribed. B & A Co. v. State, 24 Md. App. 367, 330 A.2d 701 (1975), cert. denied, 274 Md. 725 (1975).

Although the Supreme Court's definition of obscenity in Miller v. California, 413 U.S. 15, 93 S. Ct. 2607, 37 L. Ed. 2d 419 (1973), controls the scope of a former version of this section, it has no direct impact on former Art. 27, § 423 (see now § 11-210 of this article), nor does it reintroduce the concept of variable obscenity. 400 E. Baltimore St., Inc. v. State, 49 Md. App. 147, 431 A.2d 682 (1981), cert. denied, 291 Md. 774

(1981), cert. denied, 455 U.S. 940, 102 S. Ct. 1431, 71 L. Ed. 2d 650 (1982).

Extent to which other definitions of obscenity may be adopted. — States are free to adopt other definitions of obscenity only to the extent that those adopted stay within the bounds set by the constitutional criteria of the definition set forth in Roth v. United States, 354 U.S. 476, 77 S. Ct. 1304, 1 L. Ed. 2d 1498 (1957), which criteria restrict the regulation of the publication and sale of books to that traditionally and universally tolerated in our society. Donnenberg v. State, 1 Md. App. 591, 232 A.2d 264 (1967).

A state legislature's or state court's definition of "obscene" may not be broader than that constitutionally permitted by the First and Fourteenth Amendments. Woodruff v. State, 11 Md. App. 202, 273 A.2d 436, cert. denied, 262 Md. 750, 262 Md. 751 (1971).

A state may choose to define an obscenity offense in terms of "contemporary community standards" without further specification, or it may choose to define the standards in more precise geographic terms. Village Books, Inc. v. State, 22 Md. App. 274, 323 A.2d 698, cert. denied, 273 Md. 723 (1974).

"Prurient interest" defined. — Principal definition of prurient interest in sex for legal purposes comes from Roth v. United States, 354 U.S. 476, 77 S. Ct. 1304, 1 L. Ed. 2d 1498 (1957), wherein the Supreme Court defines it as "a tendency to excite lustful thoughts . . . itching; longing; uneasy with desire or longing; . . . morbid . . . ." The basic definition of a prurient interest in sex remains the same although subsequent cases have broadened the scope of inquiry in determining whether an appeal is made to prurient interest. Dillingham v. State, 9 Md. App. 669, 267 A.2d 777 (1970), cert. denied, 259 Md. 731, 259 Md. 736 (1970).

Juries' discretion in determining "patently offensive" not unbridled. — Even though questions of appeal to the "prurient interest" or of patent offensiveness are essentially questions of fact, juries do not have unbridled discretion in determining what is "patently offensive." Village Books, Inc. v. State, 22 Md. App. 274, 323 A.2d 698, cert. denied, 273 Md. 723 (1974).

"Community" not specified. — This section is construed as permitting the trier of fact to determine obscenity vel non by applying community standards without specifying what community. Village Books, Inc. v. State, 22 Md. App. 274, 323 A.2d 698, cert. denied, 273 Md. 723 (1974).

Hard-core pornography. — Hard-core pornography, which is difficult to define, has been described as commercially produced material in obvious violation of present law, wherein there is no desire to portray the material in pseudoscientific or "arty" terms. Levin v. State, 1 Md. App. 139, 228 A.2d 487 (1967), cert. denied, 247 Md. 740 (1967), cert. denied, 389 U.S. 1048, 88 S. Ct. 767, 19 L. Ed. 2d 840 (1968).

Hard-core pornography is material which focuses predominantly upon what is sexually morbid, grossly perverse, and bizarre without any artistic or scientific purpose or justification. Levin v. State, 1 Md. App. 139, 228 A.2d 487 (1967), cert. denied, 247 Md. 740 (1967), cert. denied, 389 U.S. 1048, 88 S. Ct. 767, 19 L. Ed. 2d 840 (1968); Donnenberg v. State, 1 Md. App. 591, 232 A.2d 264 (1967); Lancaster v. State, 7 Md. App. 602, 256 A.2d 716 (1969).

Explicitly illustrated incidents of sexual activity, normal or perverted, involving some "act," are not necessary to constitute hard-core pornography. Levin v. State, 1 Md. App. 139, 228 A.2d 487 (1967), cert. denied, 247 Md. 740 (1967), cert. denied, 389 U.S. 1048, 88 S. Ct. 767, 19 L. Ed. 2d 840 (1968).

Photographs sold by accused, depicting young nude males were held to have gone substantially beyond customary limits of candor, deviating from society's standards of decency in the representation of the matters with which they dealt, and were found to constitute hard-core pornography. Levin v. State, 1 Md. App. 139, 228 A.2d 487 (1967), cert. denied, 247 Md. 740 (1967), cert. denied, 389 U.S. 1048, 88 S. Ct. 767, 19 L. Ed. 2d 840 (1968).

An 8 mm. motion picture "stag" film, which contained no audio or textual portion and depicted a man and woman engaged in various nude poses and participating in several acts of conventional and unconventional sexual intercourse, constituted hard-core pornography. Lancaster v. State, 7 Md. App. 602, 256 A.2d 716 (1969).

II. PROCEDURAL MATTERS.

A. In General.

Failure to allege knowing violation renders indictment defective. — Charging documents failing to allege that defendants "knowingly" violated this section are defective. Fitzsimmons v. State, 48 Md. App. 193, 426 A.2d 4, cert. denied, 291 Md. 774, 291 Md. 782 (1981).

Warrant alleging violation fatally defective. — Warrant alleging violation of a former version of this section was fatally defective because it lumped all the offenses in one charge rather than having a separate charge for each offense. Ayre v. State, 21 Md. App. 61, 318 A.2d 828 (1974).

A charging document which does not allege directly that the matter is obscene and fails to allege that the violation was committed knowingly is defective. Ayre v. State, 291 Md. 155, 433 A.2d 1150 (1981).

Materials should be designated specifically. — It is the better practice for charging document to designate the materials involved in an alleged violation of this section with more specificity than is afforded by the generic term "matter," so all encompassing even within the express definition of the statute. Ayre v. State, 21 Md. App. 61, 318 A.2d 828 (1974).

Indictment. — An indictment was sufficient where each count laid the charge substantially in the language of this statute, and also specified the alleged obscene publications. State v. Monfred, 183 Md. 303, 37 A.2d 912 (1944).

Where two persons jointly sell an obscene publication, they may be charged together in one indictment; but where the sales of such publications by two or more persons are separate and distinct, as where booksellers who are not partners sell the publications at their respective stores, they may be charged only in separate indictments. State v. Monfred, 183 Md. 303, 37 A.2d 912 (1944).

State juries need not apply federal standards. — State juries need not be instructed to apply national standards. Village Books, Inc. v. State, 22 Md. App. 274, 323 A.2d 698, cert. denied, 273 Md. 723 (1974).

State juries need not apply standards of hypothetical statewide community. — The Constitution does not require that juries be instructed in State obscenity cases to apply the standards of a hypothetical statewide community. Village Books, Inc. v. State, 22 Md. App. 274, 323 A.2d 698, cert. denied, 273 Md. 723 (1974).

Hearing is prerequisite to seizure of materials. — A prior adversary hearing is a constitutional prerequisite to seizure of materials for violation of obscenity laws. Adler v. Pomerleau, 313 F. Supp. 277 (D. Md. 1970).

Purpose of pre-seizure hearing. — The purpose of pre-seizure hearing is to safeguard against governmental suppression of nonobscene expression. Adler v. Pomerleau, 313 F. Supp. 277 (D. Md. 1970).

Nature of pre-seizure hearing. — While the Constitution requires an adversary hearing to determine obscenity before seizure of a movie, the hearing need not be a fully matured action at law. Adler v. Pomerleau, 313 F. Supp. 277 (D. Md. 1970).

Pre-seizure hearing not precluded. — Former Art. 27, § 551 (see now § 1-203 of the Criminal Procedure Article), concerning search warrants, does not preclude an adversary hearing. Adler v. Pomerleau, 313 F. Supp. 277 (D. Md. 1970).

Return of materials where no pre-seizure hearing. — Where no adversary hearing takes place before issuance and execution of warrants pursuant to which allegedly obscene material is seized, the material seized pursuant to those warrants must be returned. Adler v. Pomerleau, 313 F. Supp. 277 (D. Md. 1970).

Pre-seizure hearing not required before arrest. — Although several recent cases have enunciated the general proposition that an adversary hearing on the issue of obscenity of the materials in question must be held before arrest, this is not an entirely proper view. Adler v. Pomerleau, 313 F. Supp. 277 (D. Md. 1970).

Adequate protection of First Amendment rights. — The requirement of an adversary hearing prior to seizure, in combination with the traditional safeguards inherent in a criminal prosecution, will adequately protect First Amendment rights. Adler v. Pomerleau, 313 F. Supp. 277 (D. Md. 1970).

Scope of review. — The reviewing court has the obligation to make an independent, reflective constitutional judgment on the facts. Woodruff v. State, 11 Md. App. 202, 273 A.2d 436, cert. denied, 262 Md. 750, 262 Md. 751 (1971).

Appellate courts have the power to review independently the constitutional fact of obscenity. Village Books, Inc. v. State, 22 Md. App. 274, 323 A.2d 698, cert. denied, 273 Md. 723 (1974).

Reviewing court must view material as a whole. — In fulfilling its obligation to make an independent review of and judgment on the material in question, the reviewing court must view that material as a whole and not look narrowly at isolated fragments of it. Woodruff v. State, 11 Md. App. 202, 273 A.2d 436, cert. denied, 262 Md. 750, 262 Md. 751 (1971).

Scope of equity court. — The General Assembly obviously intended that the equity court, once it obtained jurisdiction over the parties, could prevent the distribution of obscene material by the parties any place within the State. Mangum v. State's Att'y, 275 Md. 450, 341 A.2d 786 (1975).

B. Evidence; witnesses.

Matter in issue must be specifically found to be obscene. — In a nonjury trial for allegedly violating a former version of this section, the court must specifically find that the matter in issue is obscene; obscenity may not be assumed. 400 E. Baltimore St., Inc. v. State, 49 Md. App. 147, 431 A.2d 682 (1981), cert. denied, 291 Md. 774 (1981), cert. denied, 455 U.S. 940, 102 S. Ct. 1431, 71 L. Ed. 2d 650 (1982).

Appeal measured in terms of audience. — Prurient appeal of theme must be measured in terms of particular audience. Woodruff v. State, 11 Md. App. 202, 273 A.2d 436, cert. denied, 262 Md. 750, 262 Md. 751 (1971).

Average person as audience. — Where there is no evidence to indicate that the material was designed for or primarily disseminated to a clearly defined deviant sexual group, prurience must be measured in terms of its appeal to the average person. Woodruff v. State, 11 Md. App. 202, 273 A.2d 436, cert. denied, 262 Md. 750, 262 Md. 751 (1971).

Member of deviant sexual group as audience. — Where the material is designed for and primarily disseminated to a clearly defined deviant sexual group, rather than the public at large, the prurient-appeal requirement is satisfied if the dominant theme of the material taken as a whole appeals to the prurient interest in sex of the members of that group. Woodruff v. State, 11 Md. App. 202, 273 A.2d 436, cert. denied, 262 Md. 750, 262 Md. 751 (1971).

Setting in which material was presented may be considered. — As an aid to determining the questions of obscenity, the setting in which the material was presented may be considered. Dillingham v. State, 9 Md. App. 669, 267 A.2d 777 (1970), cert. denied, 259 Md. 731, 259 Md. 736 (1970); Woodruff v. State, 11 Md. App. 202, 273 A.2d 436, cert. denied, 262 Md. 750, 262 Md. 751 (1971).

Evidence of pandering is relevant. — Evidence of pandering (the business of purveying textual or graphic matter openly advertised to appeal to the erotic interest) is relevant, and where a purveyor's sole emphasis is on the sexually provocative aspects of his publications, a court could accept his evaluation on its face value. Dillingham v. State, 9 Md. App. 669, 267 A.2d 777 (1970), cert. denied, 259 Md. 731, 259 Md. 736 (1970); Woodruff v. State, 11 Md. App. 202, 273 A.2d 436, cert. denied, 262 Md. 750, 262 Md. 751 (1971).

Evidence without which pandering not a factor. — Where there was no evidence that the accused advertised the allegedly obscene material in any fashion, nor was there evidence that he displayed it or presented it to the customer in such a manner as to place emphasis on the sexually provocative aspects of the publication, pandering was no factor in the case. Woodruff v. State, 11 Md. App. 202, 273 A.2d 436, cert. denied, 262 Md. 750, 262 Md. 751 (1971).

Obscene matter not intended to serve evidentiary purpose before destruction. — The General Assembly did not intend for the obscene matter surrendered to serve an evidentiary purpose before its destruction. Marques v. State, 267 Md. 542, 298 A.2d 408 (1973).

Expert testimony required to prove elements of Roth test. — Expert testimony is required, except in cases involving hard-core pornography, to prove the elements of the Roth test for obscenity. Donnenberg v. State, 1 Md. App. 591, 232 A.2d 264 (1967).

The judge would not ordinarily be qualified to determine whether a film exceeded constitutional standards or tests without enlightening testimony. Woodruff v. State, 11 Md. App. 202, 273 A.2d 436, cert. denied, 262 Md. 750, 262 Md. 751 (1971).

The uncontradicted opinion of two men learned in the arts was helpful in making an evaluation of the redeeming social value of the questioned cartoon. Woodruff v. State, 11 Md. App. 202, 273 A.2d 436, cert. denied, 262 Md. 750, 262 Md. 751 (1971).

Refusal to receive testimony is abuse of discretion. — The refusal of the trial court to receive the testimony of the two witnesses offered by the accused, who might have thrown some light on contemporary community standards, and its refusal to receive exhibits of other newspapers and magazines then circulating freely in the area for comparison purposes on the subject of contemporary community standards were abuses of the court's discretion. Woodruff v. State, 11 Md. App. 202, 273 A.2d 436, cert. denied, 262 Md. 750, 262 Md. 751 (1971).

Expert testimony not necessary. — Expert testimony is not necessary to enable the trier of fact to judge the obscenity of material which has been placed into evidence. Village Books, Inc. v. State, 22 Md. App. 274, 323 A.2d 698, cert. denied, 273 Md. 723 (1974).

The ability of the juror in State obscenity cases to ascertain the sense of the "average person applying contemporary community standards" without the benefit of expert evidence is sufficient. Village Books, Inc. v. State, 22 Md. App. 274, 323 A.2d 698, cert. denied, 273 Md. 723 (1974).

Proof of obscenity. — No proof, other than the viewing of it, is required to determine if hard-core pornography is, in fact, obscene. Donnenberg v. State, 1 Md. App. 591, 232 A.2d 264 (1967); Lancaster v. State, 7 Md. App. 602, 256 A.2d 716 (1969).

Where the publication, taken as a whole, not only speaks for itself but screams for all to hear that it is obscene, no other proof of its obscenity is required. Donnenberg v. State, 1 Md. App. 591, 232 A.2d 264 (1967).

The State had the burden of proving (1) what the dominant theme of the work taken as a whole was, (2) whether that theme would appeal to a prurient interest in sex, (3) what contemporary community standards happen to be, (4) whether the questioned material was patently offensive in that it affronted those community standards, and (5) that the material was utterly devoid of all redeeming social value; and the enlightening testimony of experts on all of these questions is necessary. Woodruff v. State, 11 Md. App. 202, 273 A.2d 436, cert. denied, 262 Md. 750, 262 Md. 751 (1971).

Where the State did not prove what the contemporary standards are, the second element was not proved and this alone would be good reason to reverse the conviction. Woodruff v. State, 11 Md. App. 202, 273 A.2d 436, cert. denied, 262 Md. 750, 262 Md. 751 (1971).

The more traditional methods of proof by expert testimony may be dispensed with, where the questioned material is such hard-core pornography that it screams for all to hear as to its pornographic content. This evidentiary shortcut has been permitted, however, only in dealing with the most flagrant pornography. Woodruff v. State, 11 Md. App. 202, 273 A.2d 436, cert. denied, 262 Md. 750, 262 Md. 751 (1971).

"Hard-core pornography," which "screams for all to hear," relieves the State of its burden of producing some extrinsic evidence to establish the elements of obscenity. Woodruff v. State, 11 Md. App. 202, 273 A.2d 436, cert. denied, 262 Md. 750, 262 Md. 751 (1971).

A magazine of pictures of nude males aimed at the homosexual market and a magazine of pictures of heterosexual nudity aimed at the general market, were held to be not "hard-core pornography," and the convictions based upon that material could not be sustained in the absence of outside evidence as to all the necessary elements of obscenity. Woodruff v. State, 11 Md. App. 202, 273 A.2d 436, cert. denied, 262 Md. 750, 262 Md. 751 (1971).

Material not without redeeming social value. — Allegedly obscene material held not utterly without redeeming social value. See Dillingham v. State, 9 Md. App. 669, 267 A.2d 777 (1970), cert. denied, 259 Md. 731, 259 Md. 736 (1970).

Acts must be committed knowingly. — All the various acts described in this section are made criminal only if they are committed knowingly. Ayre v. State, 291 Md. 155, 433 A.2d 1150 (1981).

State must prove scienter. — The constitutionally mandated element of scienter would bar a conviction where the State's evidence failed to prove scienter. Woodruff v. State, 11 Md. App. 202, 273 A.2d 436, cert. denied, 262 Md. 750, 262 Md. 751 (1971).

Scienter or knowledge must be alleged and proven by the State. Fitzsimmons v. State, 48 Md. App. 193, 426 A.2d 4, cert. denied, 291 Md. 774, 291 Md. 782 (1981).

Proof of knowledge may be indirect. — Proof of knowledge on the part of an entrepreneur of the merchandise he carries may be indirect, as well as direct. Woodruff v. State, 11 Md. App. 202, 273 A.2d 436, cert. denied, 262 Md. 750, 262 Md. 751 (1971).

Knowledge may be general. — The knowledge may be general, as well as specific, but the constitutionally mandated requirement of scienter cannot be totally dispensed with. Woodruff v. State, 11 Md. App. 202, 273 A.2d 436, cert. denied, 262 Md. 750, 262 Md. 751 (1971).

Evidence which is admissible. — In prosecution for knowingly selling allegedly obscene book, all relevant evidence (if otherwise competent) concerning community standards and prurient interest, as well as evidence bearing on literary merit, was admissible to show either obscenity or the lack of it. Yudkin v. State, 229 Md. 223, 182 A.2d 798 (1962).

Admissible evidence includes contents of comparable books accepted by public. — Because the trier of the facts is required to apply "contemporary community standards" in determining what is and what is not obscene, it is essential that the jury or court, instead of being required to depend on what may well be a limited knowledge of the moral and literary standards of the community, has a right to read, or to be informed of, the contents of comparable books that have been generally accepted or tolerated by the public. Yudkin v. State, 229 Md. 223, 182 A.2d 798 (1962).

Critique of book admissible. — The trial court erred when it refused to admit as evidence a critique of the alleged obscene book, offered as evidence of its literary merit. Yudkin v. State, 229 Md. 223, 182 A.2d 798 (1962).

Admissible evidence includes post office's determination that book was mailable. — The trial court erred when it refused to permit introduction of evidence showing that the post office department had determined that the alleged obscene book was mailable. Yudkin v. State, 229 Md. 223, 182 A.2d 798 (1962).

Expert opinions admissible. — Where the conviction or acquittal of a defendant depended on whether or not the alleged obscene book was in fact obscene, the defendant was prejudiced by the refusal of the trial court to permit him to offer the testimony of expert witnesses, who, had they been allowed to do so, would have testified that the book had literary merit, that it fell within contemporary community standards and that it would not stimulate lustful thoughts in the average reader. The expert opinions were admissible and should have been received. Yudkin v. State, 229 Md. 223, 182 A.2d 798 (1962).

§ 11-203. Sale or display of obscene item to minor.

(a) *Definitions.* — (1) In this section the following words have the meanings indicated.

(2) "Distribute" includes to rent.

(3) "Illicit sex" means:

(i) human genitals in a state of sexual stimulation or arousal;

(ii) acts of human masturbation, sexual intercourse, or sodomy; or

(iii) fondling or other erotic touching of human genitals.

(4) "Item" means a:

(i) still picture or photograph;

(ii) book, pocket book, pamphlet, or magazine;

(iii) videodisc, videotape, video game, film, or computer disc; or

(iv) recorded telephone message.

(5) "Obscene" means:

(i) that the average adult applying contemporary community standards would find that the work, taken as a whole, appeals to the prurient interest;

(ii) that the work depicts sexual conduct specified in subsection (b) of this section in a way that is patently offensive to prevailing standards in the adult community as a whole with respect to what is suitable material; and

(iii) that the work, taken as a whole, lacks serious artistic, educational, literary, political, or scientific value.

(6) "Partially nude figure" means a figure with:

(i) less than completely and opaquely covered human genitals, pubic region, buttocks, or female breast below a point immediately above the top of the areola; or

(ii) human male genitals in a discernibly turgid state, even if completely and opaquely covered.

(b) *Prohibited.* — (1) A person may not willfully or knowingly display or exhibit to a minor an item:

(i) the cover or content of which is principally made up of an obscene description or depiction of illicit sex; or

(ii) that consists of an obscene picture of a nude or partially nude figure.

(2) A person may not willfully or knowingly engage in the business of displaying, exhibiting, selling, showing, advertising for sale, or distributing to a minor an item:

(i) the cover or content of which is principally made up of an obscene description or depiction of illicit sex; or

(ii) that consists of an obscene picture of a nude or partially nude figure.

(3) If a newsstand or other place of business is frequented by minors, the owner, operator, franchisee, manager, or an employee with managerial responsibility may not openly and knowingly display at the place of business an item whose sale, display, exhibition, showing, or advertising is prohibited by paragraph (2) of this subsection.

(c) *Exception.* — The provision of services or facilities by a telephone company under a tariff approved by the Public Service Commission is not a violation of subsection (b) of this section relating to recorded telephone messages.

(d) *Penalty.* — A person who violates this section is guilty of a misdemeanor and on conviction is subject to:

(1) for a first violation, imprisonment not exceeding 1 year or a fine not exceeding $1,000 or both; and

(2) for each subsequent violation, imprisonment not exceeding 3 years or a fine not exceeding $5,000 or both. (An. Code 1957, art. 27, §§ 419, 424; 2002, ch. 26, § 2; 2006, ch. 346.)

REVISOR'S NOTE

This Revisor's note comprises information related to the revision by Acts 2002, ch. 26.

This section is new language derived without substantive change from former Art. 27, §§ 419 and 424.

In subsection (a)(6) of this section, the term "partially nude figure" is substituted for the former term "nude and partially denuded figures" for accuracy and clarity. By definition, nude figures are not covered or clothed.

In subsection (b) of this section, the defined term "minor" is substituted for the former reference to any "person under the age of 18 years".

Also in subsection (b) of this section, the reference to the defined term "item" is substituted for the former reference to "any still picture . . . or recorded telephone messages" for consistency and brevity.

In subsection (b)(3) of this section, the reference to "the place of business" is substituted for the former reference to "the newsstand or other place of business" for brevity.

In subsection (d) of this section, the former phrase "unless otherwise provided" is deleted because there are no alternative penalties provided for a violation of this section.

As to the penalty provided in subsection (d) of this section, *see* General Revisor's Note to subtitle.

In subsection (d)(1) of this section, the qualification "for a first violation" is added for clarity.

Defined terms:

"Knowingly"	§ 11-201
"Minor"	§ 1-101
"Person"	§ 1-101

University of Baltimore Law Forum. — For 1994 developments, "Outmezguine v. State: Absence of Scienter Element Under State's Child Pornography Statute is Not Violative of the First Amendment," 25.1 U. Balt. Law Forum 61 (1994).

Cited in Ellis v. State, 185 Md. App. 522, 971 A.2d 379 (2009).

§ 11-204. Obscene performance in certain counties.

(a) *Scope of section.* — This section applies only in Allegany, Anne Arundel, Charles, Howard, Somerset, Wicomico, and Worcester counties.

(b) *Prohibited.* — (1) A person may not prepare, give, direct, present, perform or participate in an obscene performance, exhibition, drama, play, show, dancing exhibition, tableau, or other entertainment in which individuals perform or participate live in an obscene manner in the presence of individuals who have paid any kind of consideration to observe the exhibition or performance.

(2) An owner, lessee, or manager of a building, garden, place, room, structure, or theater may not knowingly allow or assent to the use of the premises for the types of exhibitions prohibited by paragraph (1) of this subsection.

(c) *Penalty.* — A person who violates this section is guilty of a misdemeanor and on conviction is subject to:

(1) for a first violation, imprisonment not exceeding 1 year or a fine not exceeding $1,000 or both; and

(2) for each subsequent violation, imprisonment not exceeding 3 years or a fine not exceeding $5,000 or both. (An. Code 1957, art. 27, §§ 418B, 424; 2002, ch. 26, § 2; ch. 218, § 2.)

SPECIAL REVISOR'S NOTE

This Special Revisor's note comprises information related to the revision by Acts 2002, ch. 26 and other chapters amending this section from the 2002 Legislative Session.

As enacted by Ch. 26, Acts of 2002, this section was new language derived without substantive change from former Art. 27, §§ 418B and 424. However, Ch. 218, Acts of 2002, added "Allegany" to the list of counties to which this section applies in subsection (a) of this section.

In subsection (b)(1) of this section, the former reference to a person "who as actor, dancer . . . or in any other capacity" performs specified acts was deleted by Ch. 26 in light of the absolute prohibition against the acts without regard to the title of the person.

In subsection (b)(2) of this section, the phrase "allow or assent to the use of the premises for the types of exhibitions prohibited by paragraph (1) of this subsection" was substituted by Ch. 26 for the former phrase "permits the same . . . for any such purpose" for clarity and brevity.

In subsection (c) of this section, the former phrase "unless otherwise provided" was deleted by Ch. 26 because there are no alternative penalties provided for a violation of this section.

As to the penalty provided in subsection (c) of this section, *see* General Revisor's Note to subtitle.

In subsection (c)(1) of this section, the qualification "for a first violation" was added by Ch. 26 for clarity.

Defined terms:

"Knowingly"	§ 11-201
"Person"	§ 1-101

§ 11-205. Obscene matter — Advertising.

(a) *Prohibited.* — A person may not knowingly:

(1) write or create advertising or otherwise promote the sale or distribution of matter the person represents or holds out to be obscene; or

(2) solicit the publication of advertising that promotes the sale or distribution of matter the person represents or holds out to be obscene.

(b) *Penalty.* — A person who violates this section is guilty of a misdemeanor and on conviction is subject to:

(1) for a first violation, imprisonment not exceeding 1 year or a fine not exceeding $1,000 or both; and

(2) for each subsequent violation, imprisonment not exceeding 3 years or a fine not exceeding $5,000 or both. (An. Code 1957, art. 27, §§ 421, 424; 2002, ch. 26, § 2.)

REVISOR'S NOTE

This Revisor's note comprises information related to the revision by Acts 2002, ch. 26.

This section is new language derived without substantive change from former Art. 27, §§ 421 and 424.

In subsection (b) of this section, the former phrase "unless otherwise provided" is deleted because there are no alternative penalties provided for a violation of this section.

As to the penalty provided in subsection (b) of this section, *see* General Revisor's Note to subtitle.

In subsection (b)(1) of this section, the qualification "for a first violation" is added for clarity.

Defined terms:

"Knowingly"	§ 11-201
"Matter"	§ 11-201
"Person"	§ 1-101

§ 11-206. Obscene matter — Requiring acceptance.

(a) *Prohibited.* — (1) A person may not knowingly require a purchaser or consignee to receive obscene matter as a condition to a sale, allocation, consignment, or delivery for resale of a paper, magazine, book, periodical, publication, or other merchandise.

(2) In response to a person's return of or failure to accept obscene matter, a person may not knowingly:

(i) deny or revoke a franchise;

(ii) threaten to deny or revoke a franchise; or

(iii) impose a financial or other penalty.

(b) *Penalty.* — A person who violates this section is guilty of a misdemeanor and on conviction is subject to:

(1) for a first violation, imprisonment not exceeding 1 year or a fine not exceeding $1,000 or both; and

(2) for each subsequent violation, imprisonment not exceeding 3 years or a fine not exceeding $5,000 or both. (An. Code 1957, art. 27, §§ 422, 424; 2002, ch. 26, § 2.)

REVISOR'S NOTE

This Revisor's note comprises information related to the revision by Acts 2002, ch. 26.

This section is new language derived without substantive change from former Art. 27, §§ 422 and 424.

In subsection (b) of this section, the former phrase "unless otherwise provided" is deleted because there are no alternative penalties provided for a violation of this section.

As to the penalty provided in subsection (b) of this section, *see* General Revisor's Note to subtitle.

In subsection (b)(1) of this section, the qualification "for a first violation" is added for clarity.

Defined terms:

"Knowingly"	§ 11-201
"Matter"	§ 11-201

§ 11-207. Child pornography.

(a) *Prohibited.* — A person may not:

(1) cause, induce, solicit, or knowingly allow a minor to engage as a subject in the production of obscene matter or a visual representation or performance that depicts a minor engaged as a subject in sadomasochistic abuse or sexual conduct;

(2) photograph or film a minor engaging in an obscene act, sadomasochistic abuse, or sexual conduct;

(3) use a computer to depict or describe a minor engaging in an obscene act, sadomasochistic abuse, or sexual conduct;

(4) knowingly promote, advertise, solicit, distribute, or possess with the intent to distribute any matter, visual representation, or performance:

(i) that depicts a minor engaged as a subject in sadomasochistic abuse or sexual conduct; or

(ii) in a manner that reflects the belief, or that is intended to cause another to believe, that the matter, visual representation, or performance depicts a minor engaged as a subject of sadomasochistic abuse or sexual conduct; or

(5) use a computer to knowingly compile, enter, transmit, make, print, publish, reproduce, cause, allow, buy, sell, receive, exchange, or disseminate any notice, statement, advertisement, or minor's name, telephone number, place of residence, physical characteristics, or other descriptive or identifying information for the purpose of engaging in, facilitating, encouraging, offering, or soliciting unlawful sadomasochistic abuse or sexual conduct of or with a minor.

(b) *Penalty.* — A person who violates this section is guilty of a felony and on conviction is subject to:

(1) for a first violation, imprisonment not exceeding 10 years or a fine not exceeding $25,000 or both; and

(2) for each subsequent violation, imprisonment not exceeding 20 years or a fine not exceeding $50,000 or both.

(c) *Evidence.* — (1) (i) This paragraph applies only if the minor's identity is unknown or the minor is outside the jurisdiction of the State.

(ii) In an action brought under this section, the State is not required to identify or produce testimony from the minor who is depicted in the obscene matter or in any visual representation or performance that depicts the minor engaged as a subject in sadomasochistic abuse or sexual conduct.

(2) The trier of fact may determine whether an individual who is depicted in an obscene matter, or any visual representation or performance as the subject in sadomasochistic abuse or sexual conduct, was a minor by:

(i) observation of the matter depicting the individual;

(ii) oral testimony by a witness to the production of the matter, representation, or performance;

(iii) expert medical testimony; or

(iv) any other method authorized by an applicable provision of law or rule of evidence. (An. Code 1957, art. 27, § 419A(b)-(g); 2002, ch. 26, § 2; 2003, ch. 21, § 1; 2004, ch. 539; 2010, ch. 454.)

REVISOR'S NOTE

This Revisor's note comprises information related to the revision by Acts 2002, ch. 26.

This section is new language derived without substantive change from former Art. 27, § 419A(b) through (g).

In subsection (a)(3) of this section, the phrase "use a computer" is substituted for the former reference "by means of a computer" for clarity.

In subsection (b) of this section, the former references to "the discretion of the court" are deleted as implicit in setting maximum penalties.

In subsection (b)(1) of this section, the qualification "for a first violation" is added for clarity.

Also in subsection (b)(1) of this section, the reference to being "subject to imprisonment" is substituted for the former phrase "shall be imprisoned" to reflect that the term of imprisonment for a first violation of this section is discretionary, in the same manner as the discretionary imprisonment for a subsequent violation under subsection (b)(2) of this section. *See* Letter of Advice from Attorney General J.

Joseph Curran, Jr. to Judge Alan M. Wilner, pp. 4-5 (May 21, 2001). The Criminal Law Article Review Committee calls this substitution to the attention of the General Assembly.

In subsection (c)(1)(ii) of this section, the reference to the "State" is substituted for the former reference to the "State's Attorney" for clarity and consistency within this article.

In subsection (c)(2) of this section, the reference to the "trier of fact" is substituted for the former reference to the "court or jury" for clarity.

In subsection (c)(2)(ii) of this section, the reference to a "representation, or performance" is added for consistency within this section.

Former Art. 27, § 419A(a), which defined "minor", is revised in § 1-101 of this article.

Defined terms:

"Distribute"	§ 11-201
"Knowingly"	§ 11-201
"Matter"	§ 11-201
"Minor"	§ 1-101
"Person"	§ 1-101
"Sadomasochistic abuse"	§ 11-201
"Sexual conduct"	§ 11-201

Effect of amendments. — Chapter 454, Acts 2010, effective October 1, 2010, added "advertise, solicit" in the introductory language of (a)(4); added the (a)(4)(i) designation; and added (a)(4)(ii).

Maryland Law Review. — For note, on 1995 decisions, 54 Md. L. Rev. 670 (1995).

University of Baltimore Law Review. — For note, "Maryland's Child Pornography Statute Holds Photographers Strictly Liable for the Use of Under-Age Subjects But Leaves Open the Possibility of the Mistake of Age Defense," see 25 U. Balt. L. Rev. 109 (1995).

University of Baltimore Law Forum. — For 2005 development, "Moore v. State: A Person Who Downloads Child Pornography Using a Computer, Absent Any Involvement in its Creation or Distribution, Does Not Commit a Felony in Violation of Section 11-207(A)(3) of the Criminal Law Article," see 36 U. Balt. L.F. 73 (2005).

Elements of offense. — The State is not required to prove knowledge of a child's age when the defendant "solicits, causes, or induces" a minor to engage in child pornography, but requires the State to prove scienter when the defendant is merely "permitting" a minor to

engage in child pornography. Outmezguine v. State, 335 Md. 20, 641 A.2d 870 (1994).

The State need not prove that defendant had knowledge that victim was under 18 when the photographs were taken, because the statute does not require knowledge as an element. Outmezguine v. State, 97 Md. App. 151, 627 A.2d 541 (1993), aff'd, 335 Md. 20, 641 A.2d 870 (1994).

Knowledge of the nature and character of the materials, is a scienter element because a defendant photographer must have knowledge that he or she is taking pictures of sexual conduct as defined in former Art. 27, § 416A (see now § 11-101 of this article). Outmezguine v. State, 335 Md. 20, 641 A.2d 870 (1994).

Knowledge of a minor's age is not an element of the offense of violating subsection (c) of a former version of this section (see now subsection (a)(2)), but mistake of age is a defense which may be raised by the defendant. Outmezguine v. State, 335 Md. 20, 641 A.2d 870 (1994).

"Depiction or description" of sex acts by a child using a computer properly referred to creation of child pornography, not to the mere act of merely downloading such materials created by someone else; therefore, defendant should have been convicted, not of the felony defined in this section, but of the misdemeanor defined at § 11-208 of this subtitle, which related to possession of such materials. Moore v. State, 388 Md. 446, 879 A.2d 1111 (2005).

Both the use of the term "minor" throughout the statute and criminal statutes generally and legislative history made it clear that the statute only criminalized computer contact to set up an illicit meeting with a real minor; defendant could not be convicted where all contact had been with an undercover police officer pretending to be a minor. Moore v. State, 388 Md. 623, 882 A.2d 256 (2005).

Elements of a distribution offense. — Distribution addresses distributors and consumers of child pornography, who enjoy greater First Amendment protection than photographers and filmmakers of child pornography; thus, a scienter requirement is appropriate. Outmezguine v. State, 335 Md. 20, 641 A.2d 870 (1994).

Defense of mistake of age. — It is constitutional to place the burden of production on a defendant to raise the issue of reasonable mistake of age; the mere shifting of the burden of production does not rise to a rebuttable presumption that the person involved was a minor, especially considering the fact that this subsection could have been drawn to provide strict criminal liability. Outmezguine v. State, 335 Md. 20, 641 A.2d 870 (1994).

Defendant's argument that he "did not know how old she was" was insufficient to generate the issue of reasonable mistake of age. Outmezguine v. State, 335 Md. 20, 641 A.2d 870 (1994).

Incriminating statements not made while in custody. — Trial court properly denied a defendant's motion to suppress the incriminating statements he made to a police officer executing a search warrant of the trailer wherein he resided with regard to the defendant's conviction on 47 counts of possession of child pornography, because the defendant was not in custody when he told the police officer of his prior trouble with child pornography and his usage of screen names. In support of the State's argument that the defendant was not in custody, the reviewing court found that the defendant was questioned near the trailer where he lived and that the duration of the questioning was short; only one police officer was present, who provided unrebutted testimony at trial that he was considerate toward the defendant in that he offered him a doughnut, told him that he was not under arrest, and also advised him that he did not have to speak with the officer; the defendant was not physically restrained; the doors in the officer's vehicle were not locked; there was no indication whatsoever of implied physical restraint, such as guns drawn or a guard at the door; the defendant walked to the police cruiser unrestrained; and the defendant was permitted to leave after the interview was concluded. McIntyre v. State, 168 Md. App. 504, 897 A.2d 296 (2006).

§ 11-208. Possession of visual representation of child under 16 engaged in certain sexual acts.

(a) *Prohibited.* — A person may not knowingly possess and intentionally retain a film, videotape, photograph, or other visual representation showing an actual child under the age of 16 years:

(1) engaged as a subject of sadomasochistic abuse;

(2) engaged in sexual conduct; or

(3) in a state of sexual excitement.

(b) *Penalty.* — (1) Except as provided in paragraph (2) of this subsection, a person who violates this section is guilty of a misdemeanor and on conviction is subject to imprisonment not exceeding 5 years or a fine not exceeding $2,500 or both.

(2) A person who violates this section, having previously been convicted under this section, is guilty of a felony and on conviction is subject to imprisonment not exceeding 10 years or a fine not exceeding $10,000 or both.

(c) *Exemption.* — Nothing in this section may be construed to prohibit a parent from possessing visual representations of the parent's own child in the nude unless the visual representations show the child engaged:

(1) as a subject of sadomasochistic abuse; or

(2) in sexual conduct and in a state of sexual excitement.

(d) *Affirmative defense.* — It is an affirmative defense to a charge of violating this section that the person promptly and in good faith:

(1) took reasonable steps to destroy each visual representation; or

(2) reported the matter to a law enforcement agency. (An. Code 1957, art. 27, § 419B; 2002, ch. 26, § 2; 2004, ch. 539; 2007, ch. 596; 2009, chs. 510, 511.)

REVISOR'S NOTE

This Revisor's note comprises information related to the revision by Acts 2002, ch. 26.

This section is new language derived without substantive change from former Art. 27, § 419B.

In subsection (b) of this section, the references to a "violation" are substituted for the former references to an "offense" for consistency within this article. *See* General Revisor's Note to article.

In subsection (b)(2) of this section, the reference to "each" violation is substituted for the former reference to "a second or" subsequent offense for consistency within this article.

Defined terms:

"Knowingly"	§ 11-201
"Person"	§ 1-101
"Sadomasochistic abuse"	§ 11-201
"Sexual conduct"	§ 11-201
"Sexual excitement"	§ 11-201

Effect of amendments. — Chapters 510 and 511, Acts 2009, effective October 1, 2009, made identical changes. Each rewrote (b).

Elements of offense. — "Depiction or description" of sex acts by a child using a computer properly referred to creation of child pornography, not to the mere act of merely downloading such materials created by someone else; therefore, defendant should have been convicted, not of the felony defined at § 11-207 of this subtitle, but of the misdemeanor defined in this section, which related to possession of such materials. Moore v. State, 388 Md. 446, 879 A.2d 1111 (2005).

Incriminating statements not made while in custody. — Trial court properly denied a defendant's motion to suppress the incriminating statements he made to a police officer executing a search warrant of the trailer wherein he resided with regard to the defendant's conviction on 47 counts of possession of child pornography, because the defendant was not in custody when he told the police officer of his prior trouble with child pornography and his usage of screen names. In support of the State's argument that the defendant was not in custody, the reviewing court found that the defendant was questioned near the trailer where he lived and that the duration of the questioning was short; only one police officer was present, who provided unrebutted testimony at trial that he was considerate toward the defendant in that he offered him a donut, told him that he was not under arrest, and also advised him that he did not have to speak with the officer; the defendant was not physically restrained; the doors in the officer's vehicle were not locked; there was no indication whatsoever of implied physical restraint, such as guns drawn or a guard at the door; the defendant walked to the police cruiser unrestrained; and the defendant was permitted to leave after the interview was concluded. McIntyre v. State, 168 Md. App. 504, 897 A.2d 296 (2006).

§ 11-208.1. Removal of child pornography from Internet.

(a) *Definitions.* — (1) In this section the following words have the meanings indicated.

(2) "Child pornography" means any electronic image or visual depiction that is unlawful under § 11-207 or § 11-208 of this subtitle.

(3) "Controlled or owned", with respect to a server or other storage device, means to be entirely owned by an interactive computer service provider or to be subject to exclusive management by an interactive computer service provider by agreement or otherwise.

(4) "Interactive computer service provider" means an entity that provides a service that provides or enables computer access via the Internet by multiple

users to a computer server or similar device used for the storage of graphics, video, or images.

(b) *Duties of investigative or law enforcement officer upon receiving information of alleged child pornography.* — An investigative or law enforcement officer who receives information that an item of alleged child pornography resides on a server or other storage device controlled or owned by an interactive computer service provider shall:

(1) contact the interactive computer service provider that controls or owns the server or other storage device where the item of alleged child pornography is located;

(2) inform the interactive computer service provider of the provisions of this section; and

(3) request that the interactive computer service provider voluntarily comply with this section and remove the item of alleged child pornography from its server or other storage device, if practicable, within 5 business days.

(c) *Application for court order upon noncompliance by interactive computer service provider.* — (1) If the interactive computer service provider does not voluntarily remove the item of alleged child pornography within the time period established in subsection (b) of this section, the investigative or law enforcement officer shall apply for a court order of authorization to remove the item of alleged child pornography in accordance with Title 10, Subtitle 4 of the Courts Article.

(2) The application for a court order shall:

(i) identify the item of alleged child pornography discovered on the server or other storage device controlled or owned by an interactive computer service provider;

(ii) provide its location on the server or other storage device in the form of an Internet protocol (IP) address or uniform resource locator (URL);

(iii) state the grounds for the issuance of the order;

(iv) verify that the item of alleged child pornography resides on the server or other storage device controlled or owned by the interactive computer service provider;

(v) describe the steps taken to obtain voluntary compliance of the interactive computer service provider with this section;

(vi) inform the interactive computer service provider of its right to request a hearing on the application; and

(vii) state the name and title of the affiant.

(3) The investigative or law enforcement officer shall serve the application on the interactive computer service provider.

(4) The interactive computer service provider has the right to request a hearing before the court imposes any penalty under this section.

(d) *Contents of court order.* — The court shall review the application and testimony, if offered, and, upon a finding of probable cause, issue an order that:

(1) an item of child pornography resides on a server or other storage device controlled or owned by the interactive computer service provider or is accessible to persons located in the State;

(2) there is probable cause to believe that the item violates § 11-207 or § 11-208 of this subtitle;

(3) the interactive computer service provider shall remove the item residing on a server or other storage device controlled or owned by the interactive computer service provider within 5 business days after receiving the order, if practicable;

(4) failure of the interactive computer service provider to comply with the court's order is a violation of this section;

(5) the removal of the item on the server or other storage device controlled or owned by the interactive computer service provider may not unreasonably interfere with a request by a law enforcement agency to preserve records or other evidence;

(6) the process of removal shall be conducted in a manner that prevents the removal of images, information, or data not otherwise subject to removal under this section; and

(7) provides the interactive computer service provider notice and opportunity for a hearing before the court imposes any penalty under this section.

(e) *Service and notification.* — (1) The Office of the State's Attorney shall serve the court's order on the interactive computer service provider.

(2) The order shall be accompanied by:

(i) the application made under subsection (c) of this section;

(ii) notification requiring the interactive computer service provider to remove the item residing on a server or other storage device controlled or owned by the interactive computer service provider, if practicable, within 5 business days after receiving the order;

(iii) notification of the criminal penalties for failure to remove the item of child pornography;

(iv) notification of the right to appeal the court's order; and

(v) contact information for the Office of the State's Attorney.

(f) *Time frame for removal of child pornography.* — An interactive computer service provider who is served with a court order under subsection (e) of this section shall remove the item of child pornography that is the subject of the order within 5 business days after receiving the court order, if practicable.

(g) *Relief for cause from court order.* — (1) An interactive computer service provider may petition the court for relief for cause from an order issued under subsection (d) of this section.

(2) The petition may be based on considerations of:

(i) the cost or technical feasibility of compliance with the order; or

(ii) the inability of the interactive computer service provider to comply with the order without also removing data, images, or information that are not subject to this section.

(h) *Report of child pornography by service provider.* — (1) (i) Subject to subparagraph (ii) of this paragraph, an interactive computer service provider shall report the location of an item of child pornography to the State Police if the item of child pornography:

1. resides on a server or other storage device that is:

A. controlled or owned by the interactive computer service provider; and

B. located in the State; or

    2. based on information apparent to the provider at the time of the report or discovery of an item of child pornography, pertains to a subscriber or user of the interactive computer service who resides in the State.

    (ii) Subparagraph (i) of this paragraph does not apply to an interactive computer service provider if:

    1. federal law expressly provides for or permits the referral of a report of an item of child pornography to a State or local law enforcement agency; and

    2. the interactive computer service provider complies with the federal law.

    (2) An interactive computer service provider who knowingly and willfully fails to report the information required under paragraph (1) of this subsection is guilty of a misdemeanor and on conviction is subject to:

    (i) for a first violation, a fine not exceeding $5,000;

    (ii) for a second violation, a fine not exceeding $20,000; and

    (iii) for each subsequent violation, a fine not exceeding $30,000.

    (i) *Penalty for violation of subsection (f).* — An interactive computer service provider who willfully violates subsection (f) of this section is guilty of a misdemeanor and on conviction is subject to:

    (1) for a first violation, a fine not exceeding $5,000;

    (2) for a second violation, a fine not exceeding $20,000; and

    (3) for each subsequent violation, a fine not exceeding $30,000.

    (j) *Penalty for violation of subsection (f) or (h).* — An interactive computer service provider who willfully violates subsection (f) or (h) of this section may be prosecuted, indicted, tried, and convicted in any county in or through which:

    (1) the interactive computer service provider provides access to the Internet;

    (2) any communication from the interactive computer service provider traveled; or

    (3) the communication from the interactive computer service provider originated or terminated.

    (k) *No duty by service provider to actively monitor its service.* — (1) This section does not impose a duty on an interactive computer service provider actively to monitor its service or affirmatively to seek evidence of an item of child pornography on its service.

    (2) This section does not apply to the interactive computer service provider's transmission or routing of, or intermediate temporary storage or caching of, an image, information, or data that otherwise is subject to this section.

    (l) *Good faith action to comply.* — An interactive computer service provider may not be held liable for any action taken in good faith to comply with this section. (2004, ch. 539.)

§ 11-209. Hiring minor for prohibited purpose.

    (a) *Prohibited.* — A person may not hire, employ, or use an individual, if the person knows, or possesses facts under which the person should reasonably know, that the individual is a minor, to do or assist in doing an act described in § 11-203 of this subtitle.

(b) *Penalty.* — A person who violates this section is guilty of a misdemeanor and on conviction is subject to:

(1) for a first violation, imprisonment not exceeding 1 year or a fine not exceeding $1,000 or both; and

(2) for each subsequent violation, imprisonment not exceeding 3 years or a fine not exceeding $5,000 or both. (An. Code 1957, art. 27, §§ 420, 424; 2002, ch. 26, § 2; ch. 45.)

SPECIAL REVISOR'S NOTE

This Special Revisor's note comprises information related to the revision by Acts 2002, ch. 26 and other chapters amending this section from the 2002 Legislative Session.
As enacted by Ch. 26, Acts of 2002, this section was new language derived without substantive change from former Art. 27, §§ 420 and 424. However, Ch. 45, Acts of 2002, substituted "or" for "and" in relation to possessing actual knowledge or a reasonable basis for knowledge.
The Criminal Law Article Review Committee noted, for the consideration of the General Assembly, that in subsection (a) of this section, the reference to a person who "knows, *and* possesses facts under which the person should reasonably know, that the individual is a minor" required both actual knowledge and a reasonable basis for knowledge that an em-

ployee was a minor. The General Assembly was asked to consider whether requiring actual knowledge "or" a reasonable basis for knowledge was more appropriate. Chapter 45 addressed this concern.
In subsection (b) of this section, the former phrase "unless otherwise provided" was deleted by Ch. 26 because there are no alternative penalties provided for a violation of this section.
As to the penalty provided in subsection (b) of this section, *see* General Revisor's Note to subtitle.
In subsection (b)(1) of this section, the qualification "for a first violation" was added by Ch. 26 for clarity.

Defined terms:
"Minor"	§ 1-101
"Person"	§ 1-101

§ 11-210. Exemption from subtitle.

(a) *Bona fide justification.* — (1) A person having a bona fide scientific, educational, governmental, artistic, news, or other similar justification for possessing or distributing prohibited matter is not subject to the prohibitions and penalties imposed by this subtitle.

(2) A distribution made in accordance with a bona fide scientific, educational, governmental, artistic, news, or other similar justification is not subject to the prohibitions and penalties imposed by this subtitle.

(b) *Exception to justification.* — A justification is not bona fide under this section if a reasonable person would find that a dominant purpose of the depiction of an individual under the age of 16 years engaging in sexual conduct is to arouse or gratify sexual desire in either the violator, the individual under the age of 16 years, or the viewer. (An. Code 1957, art. 27, § 423; 2002, ch. 26, § 2.)

SPECIAL REVISOR'S NOTE

This Special Revisor's note comprises information related to the revision by Acts 2002, ch. 26 and other chapters amending this section from the 2002 Legislative Session.
This section is new language derived without substantive change from former Art. 27, § 423.

In subsection (a) of this section, the phrase "is not subject" is substituted for the former phrase "shall not extend" for consistency within this article.
In subsection (b) of this section, the reference to a "violator" is substituted for the former reference to a "perpetrator" for consistency

§ 11-211. Destruction of obscene matter under court order.

When the conviction of a person for a violation of this subtitle becomes final, the court may order the destruction of any matter or advertisement that was the basis of the person's conviction and that remains in the possession or under the control of the court, the State, or a law enforcement unit. (An. Code 1957, art. 27, § 425; 2002, ch. 26, § 2.)

REVISOR'S NOTE

This Revisor's note comprises information related to the revision by Acts 2002, ch. 26.

This section is new language derived without substantive change from former Art. 27, § 425.

The former phrase "[u]pon the conviction of the accused" is deleted in light of the reference to a conviction "becom[ing] final".

The reference to "a violation of this subtitle" is added for clarity.

The reference to the "State" is substituted for the former reference to the "State's Attorney" for clarity and consistency within this article.

The reference to a law enforcement "unit" is substituted for the former reference to a law enforcement "agency" for consistency within this article. *See* General Revisor's Note to article.

Defined terms:
  "Matter"   § 11-201
  "Person"   § 1-101

GENERAL REVISOR'S NOTE TO SUBTITLE

The former Obscene Matter subtitle contained a general penalty provision, former Art. 27, § 424, that applied to all violations of the subtitle that did not have a separate penalty provision. As each crime without its own penalty provision is separately punishable, the former penalty is repeated in each section to which the penalty applies for clarity.

Subtitle 3. Prostitution and Related Crimes.

§ 11-301. Definitions.

(a) *In general.* — In this subtitle the following words have the meanings indicated.

REVISOR'S NOTE

This subsection formerly was Art. 27, § 426(a).

No changes are made.

(b) *Assignation.* — "Assignation" means the making of an appointment or engagement for prostitution or any act in furtherance of the appointment or engagement.

REVISOR'S NOTE

This subsection formerly was Art. 27, § 426(b). The only changes are in style.

(c) *Prostitution.* — "Prostitution" means the performance of a sexual act, sexual contact, or vaginal intercourse for hire.

REVISOR'S NOTE

This subsection formerly was Art. 27, § 426(c). No changes are made.

(d) *Sexual act.* — "Sexual act" has the meaning stated in § 3-301 of this article.

REVISOR'S NOTE

This subsection is new language derived without substantive change from former Art. 27, § 426(d), as it defined "sexual act".

(e) *Sexual contact.* — "Sexual contact" has the meaning stated in § 3-301 of this article.

REVISOR'S NOTE

This subsection is new language derived without substantive change from former Art. 27, § 426(d), as it defined "sexual contact".

(f) *Sexually explicit performance.* — "Sexually explicit performance" means a public or private, live, photographed, recorded, or videotaped act or show in which the performer is wholly or partially nude, and which is intended to sexually arouse or appeal to the prurient interest of patrons or viewers.

(g) *Solicit.* — "Solicit" means urging, advising, inducing, encouraging, requesting, or commanding another.

REVISOR'S NOTE

This subsection formerly was Art. 27, § 426(e). No other changes are made.

The former reference to another "person" is deleted for consistency within this article.

(h) *Vaginal intercourse.* — "Vaginal intercourse" has the meaning stated in § 3-301 of this article.

REVISOR'S NOTE

This subsection is new language derived without substantive change from former Art. 27, § 426(d), as it defined "vaginal intercourse".

(An. Code 1957, art. 27, § 426; 2002, ch. 26, § 2; 2010, chs. 289, 529, 530.)

Effect of amendments. — Chapter 289, Acts 2010, effective October 1, 2010, reenacted (c) without change.

Chapters 529 and 530, Acts 2010, effective October 1, 2010, made identical changes. Each added (f) and redesignated accordingly.

Attorney discipline. — In an attorney disciplinary proceeding, it was not error for a hearing judge to find that an attorney's conduct constituted an assignation, under (b), when the attorney exchanged Vicodin for oral sex, because a telephone conversation between the attorney and the other person made it clear that the oral sex was accepted in exchange for a controlled dangerous substance, which was an item of value, so the encounter between the two was an assignation. Att'y Griev. Comm'n v. Marcalus, 414 Md. 501, 996 A.2d 350 (2010).

Quoted in In re Areal B., 177 Md. App. 708, 938 A.2d 43 (2007).

§ 11-302. Effect of subtitle on other laws.

A person charged with a crime under this subtitle may also be prosecuted and sentenced for violating any other applicable law. (An. Code 1957, art. 27, § 427; 2002, ch. 26, § 2.)

§ 11-303. Human trafficking.

(a) *Prohibited — In general.* — (1) A person may not knowingly:

(i) take or cause another to be taken to any place for prostitution;

(ii) place, cause to be placed, or harbor another in any place for prostitution;

(iii) persuade, induce, entice, or encourage another to be taken to or placed in any place for prostitution;

(iv) receive consideration to procure for or place in a house of prostitution or elsewhere another with the intent of causing the other to engage in prostitution or assignation;

(v) engage in a device, scheme, or continuing course of conduct intended to cause another to believe that if the other did not take part in a sexually explicit performance, the other or a third person would suffer physical restraint or serious physical harm; or

(vi) destroy, conceal, remove, confiscate, or possess an actual or purported passport, immigration document, or government identification document of another while otherwise violating or attempting to violate this subsection.

(2) A parent, guardian, or person who has permanent or temporary care or custody or responsibility for supervision of another may not consent to the taking or detention of the other for prostitution.

(b) *Prohibited — Minor.* — (1) A person may not violate subsection (a) of this section involving a victim who is a minor.

(2) A person may not knowingly take or detain another with the intent to use force, threat, coercion, or fraud to compel the other to marry the person or a third person or perform a sexual act, sexual contact, or vaginal intercourse.

(c) *Penalty.* — (1) (i) Except as provided in paragraph (2) of this subsection, a person who violates subsection (a) of this section is guilty of the misdemeanor of human trafficking and on conviction is subject to imprisonment not exceeding 10 years or a fine not exceeding $5,000 or both.

(ii) A person who violates subsection (a) of this section is subject to § 5-106(b) of the Courts Article.

(2) A person who violates subsection (b) of this section is guilty of the felony of human trafficking and on conviction is subject to imprisonment not exceeding 25 years or a fine not exceeding $15,000 or both.

(d) *Venue.* — A person who violates this section may be charged, tried, and sentenced in any county in or through which the person transported or attempted to transport the other.

(e) *Same penalties for person benefiting or aider and abetter.* — (1) A person who knowingly benefits financially or by receiving anything of value from participation in a venture that includes an act described in subsection (a) or (b) of this section is subject to the same penalties that would apply if the person had violated that subsection.

(2) A person who knowingly aids, abets, or conspires with one or more other persons to violate any subsection of this section is subject to the same penalties that apply for a violation of that subsection. (An. Code 1957, art. 27, § 428; 2002, ch. 26, § 2; 2007, chs. 340, 341; 2009, ch. 143; 2010, chs. 529, 530; 2011, ch. 218.)

REVISOR'S NOTE

This Revisor's note comprises information related to the revision by Acts 2002, ch. 26.

This section formerly was Art. 27, § 428.

Throughout this section, the references to another "person" and the other "person" are deleted for consistency within this article.

In subsection (d) of this section, the reference to a violation being "subject to § 5-106(b) of the Courts Article" is substituted for the former reference to the violation subjecting the defendant to imprisonment "in the penitentiary" for clarity and consistency within this article. *See* General Revisor's Note to article.

No other changes are made.

Defined terms:

"Assignation"	§ 11-301
"Person"	§ 1-101
"Prostitution"	§ 11-301
"Sexual act"	§ 11-301
"Sexual contact"	§ 11-301
"Vaginal intercourse"	§ 11-301

Effect of amendments. — Chapter 143, Acts 2009, effective October 1, 2009, substituted "persuade, induce, entice, or encourage" for "persuade or encourage by threat or promise" in (a)(1)(iii).

Chapters 529 and 530, Acts 2010, effective October 1, 2010, made identical changes. Each deleted (a)(1)(iv) and redesignated accordingly; added (a)(1)(v), (a)(1)(vi), (b)(2), and (e); and made related changes.

Chapter 218, Acts 2011, effective October 1, 2011, reenacted the section without change.

University of Baltimore Law Forum. — For an article, "The Crime Next Door: An Examination of the Sex Trafficking Epidemic in the United States and How Maryland Is Addressing the Problem," see 41 U. Balt. L. F. 43 (2010).

§ 11-304. Receiving earnings of prostitute.

(a) *Prohibited.* — A person may not receive or acquire money or proceeds from the earnings of a person engaged in prostitution with the intent to:

(1) promote a crime under this subtitle;

(2) profit from a crime under this subtitle; or

(3) conceal or disguise the nature, location, source, ownership, or control of money or proceeds of a crime under this subtitle.

(b) *Penalty.* — A person who violates this section is guilty of a misdemeanor and on conviction is subject to imprisonment not exceeding 10 years or a fine not exceeding $10,000 or both.

(c) *Statute of limitations and in banc review.* — A person who violates this section is subject to § 5-106(b) of the Courts Article. (An. Code 1957, art. 27, § 429; 2002, ch. 26, § 2.)

REVISOR'S NOTE

This Revisor's note comprises information related to the revision by Acts 2002, ch. 26.

This section formerly was Art. 27, § 429.

In subsection (c) of this section, the reference to a violation being "subject to § 5-106(b) of the Courts Article" is substituted for the former reference to the violation subjecting the defendant to imprisonment "in the penitentiary" for clarity and consistency within this article. *See* General Revisor's Note to article.

No other changes are made.

Defined terms:

"Person"	§ 1-101
"Prostitution"	§ 11-301

University of Baltimore Law Forum. — For an article, "The Crime Next Door: An Examination of the Sex Trafficking Epidemic in the United States and How Maryland Is Addressing the Problem," see 41 U. Balt. L. F. 43 (2010).

§ 11-305. Abduction of child under 16.

(a) *Prohibited.* — For purposes of prostitution or committing a crime under Title 3, Subtitle 3 of this article, a person may not:

(1) persuade or entice or aid in the persuasion or enticement of an individual under the age of 16 years from the individual's home or from the custody of the individual's parent or guardian; or

(2) knowingly secrete or harbor or aid in the secreting or harboring of an individual under the age of 16 years who has been persuaded or enticed in the manner described in item (1) of this subsection.

(b) *Penalty.* — A person who violates this section is guilty of a misdemeanor and on conviction is subject to imprisonment not exceeding 10 years or a fine not exceeding $5,000 or both.

(c) *Statute of limitations and in banc review.* — A person who violates this section is subject to § 5-106(b) of the Courts Article. (An. Code 1957, art. 27, § 430; 2002, ch. 26, § 2.)

This Revisor's note comprises information related to the revision by Acts 2002, ch. 26.

This section formerly was Art. 27, § 430.

In subsection (a) of this section, the reference to "Title 3, Subtitle 3 of this article" is substituted for the former reference to "the sexual offenses subheading of this article" to reflect the reorganization of material on rape and other sexual crimes in this article.

Also in subsection (a) of this section, the references to "an individual" and "the individual's" are substituted for the former references to "a person" and "the person's" because only a human being, and not the other entities included in the defined term "person", may be persuaded or enticed.

In subsection (c) of this section, the reference to a violation being "subject to § 5-106(b) of the Courts Article" is substituted for the former reference to the violation subjecting the defendant to imprisonment "in the penitentiary" for clarity and consistency within this article. *See* General Revisor's Note to article.

No other changes are made.

Defined terms:

"Person"	§ 1-101
"Prostitution"	§ 11-301

University of Baltimore Law Forum. — For an article, "The Crime Next Door: An Examination of the Sex Trafficking Epidemic in the United States and How Maryland Is Addressing the Problem," see 41 U. Balt. L. F. 43 (2010).

§ 11-306. House of prostitution.

(a) *Prohibited.* — A person may not knowingly:

(1) engage in prostitution or assignation by any means;

(2) keep, set up, occupy, maintain, or operate a building, structure, or conveyance for prostitution or assignation;

(3) allow a building, structure, or conveyance owned or under the person's control to be used for prostitution or assignation;

(4) allow or agree to allow a person into a building, structure, or conveyance for prostitution or assignation; or

(5) procure or solicit or offer to procure or solicit for prostitution or assignation.

(b) *Penalty.* — A person who violates this section is guilty of a misdemeanor and on conviction is subject to imprisonment not exceeding 1 year or a fine not exceeding $500 or both. (An. Code 1957, art. 27, § 431; 2002, ch. 26, § 2.)

This Revisor's note comprises information related to the revision by Acts 2002, ch. 26.

This section formerly was Art. 27, § 431. No changes are made.

Defined terms:

"Assignation"	§ 11-301
"Person"	§ 1-101
"Prostitution"	§ 11-301

University of Baltimore Law Forum. — For an article, "The Crime Next Door: An Examination of the Sex Trafficking Epidemic in the United States and How Maryland Is Addressing the Problem," see 41 U. Balt. L. F. 43 (2010).

Charging instrument. — Charging defendant, a juvenile, in a petition with engaging in prostitution did not expressly charge the act of solicitation for prostitution, and a general reference in the petition to this section did not enlarge the scope of the charge to include a charge of solicitation. Furthermore, because solicitation for prostitution was not a lesser included offense of engaging in prostitution, the State did not charge defendant with solicitation for prostitution merely by charging her with engaging in prostitution. In re Areal B., 177 Md. App. 708, 938 A.2d 43 (2007).

When defendant, a juvenile, had been charged with engaging in prostitution under (a), it violated due process under the Fourteenth Amendment and art. 21 of the Declaration of Rights to allow the State, after it rested its case, to amend the petition under Rule 11-108(a) to allege solicitation. The amendment, after which defendant was immediately adjudicated delinquent based on the solicitation charge, deprived the defense of notice as to what she was called upon to defend and of the opportunity to properly prepare for the hearing. In re Areal B., 177 Md. App. 708, 938 A.2d 43 (2007).

Lesser included offenses. — Solicitation for prostitution is not a lesser included offense of prostitution. In re Areal B., 177 Md. App. 708, 938 A.2d 43 (2007).

Cited in Att'y Griev. Comm'n v. Marcalus, 414 Md. 501, 996 A.2d 350 (2010).

TITLE 12.

GAMING — STATEWIDE PROVISIONS.

Subtitle 1. General Provisions.

§ 12-101. Definitions.

(a) *In general.* — In this subtitle the following words have the meanings indicated.

REVISOR'S NOTE

This subsection is new language derived without substantive change from former Art. 27, § 261E(a)(1).

The reference to this "subtitle" is substituted for the former reference to this "section", which referred only to Art. 27, § 261E. Although this subtitle is derived, in part, from provisions outside of former Art. 27, § 261E, substituting the reference to this "subtitle" does not constitute a substantive change because the terms used in the newly covered sections are used as defined in this section.

(b) *Candidate.* — "Candidate" has the meaning stated in § 1-101 of the Election Law Article.

SPECIAL REVISOR'S NOTE

This section is new language added for clarity and consistency with usage in Article 33 of the Code. However, Ch. 213, § 7, Acts of 2002, substituted the reference to "§ 1-101 of the Election Law Article" for the reference to "Article 33, § 1-101 of the Code" enacted by Ch. 26. Chapter 213, § 8, provided that § 7 would take effect January 1, 2003, to reflect the delayed

effective date of the Election Law Article enacted by Ch. 291, Acts of 2002.

(c) *Credit.* — (1) "Credit" means payment by a credit card or promissory
note.

(2) "Credit" includes selling or pledging personal property in exchange for
cash or tokens.

REVISOR'S NOTE

This subsection is new language derived
without substantive change from former Art.
27, § 261E(a)(2).

(d) *Gaming device.* — (1) "Gaming device" means:

(i) a gaming table, except a billiard table, at which a game of chance is
played for money or any other thing or consideration of value; or

(ii) a game or device at which money or any other thing or consideration
of value is bet, wagered, or gambled.

(2) "Gaming device" includes a paddle wheel, wheel of fortune, chance
book, and bingo.

REVISOR'S NOTE

This subsection is new language derived
without substantive change from former Art.
27, §§ 238, 244, and 261E(a)(3).

In the introductory language of paragraph (1)
of this subsection, the term "[g]aming device" is
substituted for the former term "gaming table"
in light of former Art. 27, § 244, which deemed
a gaming table to be "[a]ll games, devices and
contrivances at which money or any other thing
shall be bet or wagered . . .".

In paragraph (1)(i) and (ii) of this subsection,
the reference to "consideration of value" is
added for consistency with § 12-102 of this
subtitle.

In paragraph (1)(i) of this subsection, the
word "table" is substituted for the former specific references to a "faro table, E. O. table,
equality, or any other kind of gaming table" for
brevity and in light of the comprehensive reference to any table "at which a game of chance is
played".

In paragraph (1)(ii) of this subsection, the
former reference to "contrivances" is deleted in
light of the references to a "game" and a "device".

Also in paragraph (1)(ii) of this subsection,
the word "gambled" is added for consistency
with § 12-102 of this subtitle.

Also in paragraph (1)(ii) of this subsection,
the former reference to a gaming table "within
the meaning of §§ 237, 238, 239, 241 and 242"
is deleted in light of subsection (a) of this
section.

Also in paragraph (1)(ii) of this subsection,
the former specific reference to a "paddle wheel,
wheel of fortune, chance book, [or] bingo" is
deleted as included in the comprehensive reference to a "game or device at which money or
any other thing or consideration of value is bet,
wagered, or gambled".

(e) *Gaming event.* — "Gaming event" means:

(1) a bingo game;

(2) a carnival;

(3) a bazaar;

(4) a raffle;

(5) a benefit performance; or

(6) any other event at which a gaming device is operated.

REVISOR'S NOTE

This subsection is new language derived without substantive change from former Art. 27, § 261E(a)(4).

(f) *Organization.* — "Organization" includes:

(1) a fraternal, religious, civic, patriotic, educational, or charitable organization;

(2) a volunteer fire company, rescue squad, or auxiliary unit;

(3) a veterans' organization or club;

(4) a bona fide nonprofit organization that is raising money for an exclusively charitable, athletic, or educational purpose; or

(5) any organization that is authorized to conduct a gaming event under Subtitle 1 or 2 of this title or Title 13 of this article.

REVISOR'S NOTE

This subsection is new language derived without substantive change from former Art. 27, § 261E(a)(5).

In item (1) of this subsection, the former reference to a "corporation" is deleted as included in the reference to an "organization" for consistency within this article.

In item (5) of this subsection, the reference to "Subtitle 1 or 2 or Title 13 of this article" is substituted for the former erroneous reference to "this subtitle" to reflect the reorganization of material derived from the former "Gaming" subheading of Article 27.

(g) *Political committee.* — "Political committee" has the meaning stated in § 1-101 of the Election Law Article.

SPECIAL REVISOR'S NOTE

This subsection is new language derived without substantive change from former Art. 27, § 261D(a), as it related to political committees. However, Ch. 213, § 7, Acts of 2002, substituted the reference to '§ 1-101 of the Election Law Article' for the reference to 'Article 33, § 1-101 of the Code' enacted by Ch. 26. Chapter 213, § 8, provided that § 7 would take effect January 1, 2003, to reflect the delayed effective date of the Election Law Article enacted by Ch. 291, Acts of 2002.

REVISOR'S NOTE

In this subsection, the former reference to a "bona fide" political committee is deleted as surplusage.

(h) *Token.* — "Token" means a poker chip, bingo chip, or other device commonly used instead of money in the playing of a gaming device.

REVISOR'S NOTE

This subsection is new language derived without substantive change from former Art. 27, § 261E(a)(6).

In this section, the term "money" is substituted for the former term "cash" for consistency with § 12-102 of this subtitle.

(An. Code 1957, art. 27, §§ 238, 244, 261D(a), 261E(a); 2002, ch. 26, § 2; ch. 213, § 7.)

The Revisor's notes in this section comprise information related to the revision by Acts 2002, ch. 26.

University of Baltimore Law Forum. — For a 2006 development, "F.A.C.E. Trading v. Todd: Games of Chance Bundled With the Purchase of Consumer Products, Where the Nature of the Product Is Incidental to the Playing of the Game, Constitute Illegal Gaming," see 37 U. Balt. L.F. 52 (2006).

Machine dispensing discount coupons and chance to win cash prohibited gambling device. — Machine which dispensed coupons, for cash, offering discounts on merchandise and a chance to win cash was an illegal gaming device, under (d)(1)(ii) because it contained all the elements of gambling, which were the payment of consideration for a chance to win a prize or reward, so its operation was punishable as a misdemeanor, under § 12-104 of this subtitle. F.A.C.E. Trading, Inc. v. Todd, 393 Md. 364, 903 A.2d 348 (2006).

§ 12-102. Betting, wagering, gambling, etc.

(a) *Prohibited.* — A person may not:

(1) bet, wager, or gamble;

(2) make or sell a book or pool on the result of a race, contest, or contingency;

(3) establish, keep, rent, use, or occupy, or knowingly allow to be established, kept, rented, used, or occupied, all or a part of a building, vessel, or place, on land or water, within the State, for the purpose of:

(i) betting, wagering, or gambling; or

(ii) making, selling, or buying books or pools on the result of a race, contest, or contingency; or

(4) receive, become the depository of, record, register, or forward, or propose, agree, or pretend to forward, money or any other thing or consideration of value, to be bet, wagered, or gambled on the result of a race, contest, or contingency.

(b) *Penalty.* — A person who violates this section is guilty of a misdemeanor and on conviction is subject to imprisonment for not less than 6 months and not exceeding 1 year or a fine of not less than $200 and not exceeding $1,000 or both.

(c) *Applicability.* — (1) The provisions of this subsection apply only in Baltimore City.

(2) A person who violates this section may be charged by a citation.

(3) A citation for a violation of this section may be issued to a person by a police officer authorized to make arrests in Baltimore City if there is probable cause to believe that the person is committing or has committed a violation of this section.

(4) A citation issued under this subsection shall contain:

(i) the name and address of the person charged;

(ii) the statute allegedly violated;

(iii) the location, date, and time that the violation occurred;

(iv) the fine or term of imprisonment that may be imposed;

(v) a notice stating that prepayment of a fine is not allowed;

(vi) a notice that the court shall promptly send the person charged a summons to appear for trial; and

(vii) the signature of the police officer issuing the citation.

(5) (i) The police officer who issued the citation shall forward to the appropriate court a copy of the citation.

(ii) The court shall promptly schedule the case for trial and summon the defendant to appear.

(iii) Willful failure of the defendant to respond to the summons is contempt of court. (An. Code 1957, art. 27, § 240; 2002, ch. 26, § 2; 2004, ch. 123.)

REVISOR'S NOTE

This Revisor's note comprises information related to the revision by Acts 2002, ch. 26.

This section is new language derived without substantive change from former Art. 27, § 240.

In the introductory language of subsection (a) of this section, the former reference to "persons, or association of persons, or . . . any corporation within the State of Maryland" is deleted in light of Art. 1, § 8, which provides that the singular generally includes the plural, and Art. 1, § 15 and § 1-101 of this article, which provide that the term "person" includes a corporation and other specified entities.

In subsection (a)(1) of this section, the former phrase "in any manner, or by any means," is deleted as surplusage.

In subsection (a)(2) of this section, the former phrase "any trotting, pacing or running race of horses or other beasts," is deleted as surplusage.

Also in subsection (a)(2) of this section, the former reference to a race, contest, or contingency "of any kind" is deleted as surplusage.

In subsection (a)(3) of this section, the word "established" is added for consistency with the word "establish" in that subsection and with § 12-105 of this subtitle.

Also in subsection (a)(3) of this section, the former reference to a "house" is deleted in light of the reference to a "building".

Also in subsection (a)(3) of this section, the former reference to "grounds" is deleted in light of the reference to a "place".

In subsection (a)(3)(i) of this section, the former phrases "in any manner, or by any means," and "by any means or devices whatsoever" are deleted as surplusage.

In subsection (a)(4) of this section, the word "agree" is substituted for the former word "argue" to correct a publishing error by the Michie Company, which occurred in the publication of the 1992 Replacement Volume of Article 27.

Also in subsection (a)(4) of this section, the reference to "propos[ing]" to forward is substituted for the former reference to "purpos[ing]" to forward for clarity.

Also in subsection (a)(4) of this section, the former references to "bet" and "wager", used as nouns, are deleted for consistency with § 12-101(d)(1) and (2) of this subtitle.

Also in subsection (a)(4) of this section, the former reference to money bet "in any manner" is deleted as surplusage.

In subsection (b) of this section, the former phrase "in the discretion of the court" is deleted as implicit in the establishment of minimum and maximum penalties.

The Criminal Law Article Review Committee notes, for consideration of the General Assembly, that the specific reference to establishing a place for making, selling, or "buying" books or pools contained in subsection (a)(3)(ii) of this section is not reflected in the specific prohibition against "making or selling" books or pools in subsection (a)(2) of this section, although it is covered by the general prohibition against "bet-[ting], wager[ing], or gambl[ing]" in subsection (a)(1) of this section. The General Assembly may wish to add a specific prohibition against "buying" books or pools in subsection (a)(2) of this section, in order to ensure that the outright prohibitions against books and pools in subsection (a)(2) of this section reflect the prohibitions against establishing a place for books and pools in subsection (a)(3)(ii) of this section.

The Criminal Law Article Review Committee also notes, for the consideration of the General Assembly, that in subsection (b) of this section, the former reference to "one half of said fine to go to the informer", enacted by Ch. 285, Acts of 1890, is deleted in light of Art. 38, § 3, enacted by Ch. 37, Acts of 1931, which provides that no portion of any fine, penalty, or forfeiture shall be paid to any informer.

Defined term:
"Person"   § 1-101

Poker tournaments. — Poker tournaments do not involve illegal gambling so long as the participants do not pay any money or other valuable consideration, directly or indirectly, in order to participate in the tournaments at any level. 91 Op. Att'y Gen. 64 (Mar. 2, 2006).

"Instant Racing" wagering prohibited. — Wagering on video replays of historic (previously held) horse races, by means of a product known as "Instant Racing," is not authorized at race tracks and satellite simulcast betting facilities in Maryland under current law, since it does not constitute pari-mutuel betting, as authorized by the Maryland Horse Racing Act, at those locations. 94 Op. Att'y Gen. 32 (March 17, 2009).

§ 12-103. Playing certain games.

(a) *Prohibited.* — For money or any other thing or consideration of value, a person may not play:

(1) the game called "thimbles";

(2) the game called "little joker";

(3) dice or the game commonly called "craps"; or

(4) any other gaming device or fraudulent trick.

(b) *Penalty.* — A person who violates this section is guilty of a misdemeanor and on conviction is subject to imprisonment for not less than 6 months and not exceeding 2 years or a fine not exceeding $100 or both. (An. Code 1957, art. 27, § 245; 2002, ch. 26, § 2; 2003, ch. 21, § 1.)

REVISOR'S NOTE

This Revisor's note comprises information related to the revision by Acts 2002, ch. 26.

This section is new language derived without substantive change from former Art. 27, § 245.

In the introductory language of subsection (a) of this section, the phrase "or consideration of value" is added for consistency with § 12-102 of this subtitle.

In subsection (a)(4) of this section, the defined term "gaming device" is substituted for the former term "device" for consistency with § 12-101(d) of this subtitle.

In subsection (b) of this section, the reference to being "guilty of a misdemeanor" is added to state expressly that which was only implied in the former law. In this State, any crime that was not a felony at common law and has not been declared a felony by statute, is considered to be a misdemeanor. *See State v. Canova*, 278 Md. 483, 490 (1976); *Bowser v. State*, 136 Md. 342, 345 (1920); *Dutton v. State*, 123 Md. 373, 378 (1914); and *Williams v. State*, 4 Md. App. 342, 347 (1968).

Also in subsection (b) of this section, the reference to a sentence to "imprisonment" is substituted for the former reference to a sentence to being "imprisoned. . . in the Maryland House of Correction" for consistency within this article. Currently, inmates are sentenced to the custody of a unit such as the Division of Correction and then are placed in a particular facility. *See* CS § 9-103.

Also in subsection (b) of this section, the former phrase "in the discretion of the court" is deleted as implicit in the establishment of minimum and maximum penalties.

Defined terms:

"Gaming device"	§ 12-101
"Person"	§ 1-101

§ 12-104. Gaming device, or building, vessel, or place for gambling.

(a) *Prohibited.* — A person may not:

(1) keep a gaming device, or all or a part of a building, vessel, or place, on land or water within the State for the purpose of gambling;

(2) own, rent, or occupy all or a part of a building, vessel, or place and knowingly allow a gaming device to be kept in the building, vessel, or place;

(3) lease or rent all or a part of a building, vessel, or place to be used for the purpose of gambling;

(4) deal at a gaming device or in a building, vessel, or place for gambling;

(5) manage a gaming device or a building, vessel, or place for gambling; or

(6) have an interest in a gaming device or the profits of a gaming device.

(b) *Penalty.* — A person who violates this section is guilty of a misdemeanor and on conviction is subject to imprisonment for not less than 6 months and not exceeding 1 year or a fine not exceeding $500 or both. (An. Code 1957, art. 27, §§ 237, 239, 241, 242; 2002, ch. 26, § 2.)

REVISOR'S NOTE

This Revisor's note comprises information related to the revision by Acts 2002, ch. 26.

This section is new language derived without substantive change from former Art. 27, §§ 237, 239, 241, and 242.

In this section, the defined term "gaming device" is substituted for the former term "gaming table" for consistency with § 12-101(d) of this subtitle.

In subsection (a)(1) of this section, the phrase "within the State" is added for consistency with §§ 12-102(a)(3) and 12-105(a)(1) of this subtitle.

Also in subsection (a)(1) of this section, the term "building" is substituted for the former term "house" for consistency with § 12-102(a) of this subtitle.

Also in subsection (a)(1) of this section, the phrase "all or a part of a building, vessel, or place" is added for consistency with § 12-102(a) of this subtitle.

In subsection (a)(2) of this section, the former reference to a "house" is deleted in light of the reference to a "building" and for consistency with subsection (a)(1) of this section and § 12-102(a) of this subtitle.

In subsection (a)(3) of this section, the phrase "all or a part of a building, vessel, or place" is added for consistency with item (a)(1) of this section and § 12-102(a)(3) of this subtitle.

In subsection (a)(4) and (5) of this section, the phrase "building, vessel, or place" is substituted for the former phrase "other place" for consistency with subsection (a)(1) of this section and § 12-102(a) of this subtitle.

In subsection (b) of this section, the former phrase "in the discretion of the court" is deleted as implicit in the establishment of minimum and maximum penalties.

The Criminal Law Article Review Committee notes, for the consideration of the General Assembly, that in subsection (b) of this section, the former reference to "one half to go to the informer", enacted by Ch. 285, Acts of 1890, is deleted in light of Art. 38, § 3, enacted by Ch. 37, Acts of 1931, which provides that no portion of any fine, penalty, or forfeiture shall be paid to any informer.

Defined terms:
"Gaming device" § 12-101
"Person" § 1-101

Cross references. — As to lotteries, see § 12-201 et seq. of this article.

As to indictments for gambling, see § 12-112 of this article.

As to when pool or billiard tables are deemed gambling tables, see § 17-504 of the Business Regulation Article.

As to horse racing generally, see § 11-101 et seq. of the Business Regulation Article.

As to abolition of informers' fees, see § 7-506 of the Courts Article.

University of Baltimore Law Forum. — For a 2006 development "Trading v. Todd: Games of Chance Bundled With the Purchase of Consumer Products, Where the Nature of the Product Is Incidental to the Playing of the Game, Constitute Illegal Gaming," see 37 U. Balt. L.F. 52 (2006).

History. — In essentially the same form as they now are, the "Gaming" laws and the "Lottery" laws have been on the books since long before the first Code, that of 1860. Bender v. Arundel Arena, Inc., 248 Md. 181, 236 A.2d 7 (1967).

Offenses against the gambling laws involving machines or mechanical devices have always been prosecuted by Maryland State's Attorneys under the gaming and not the lottery laws. Bender v. Arundel Arena, Inc., 248 Md. 181, 236 A.2d 7 (1967).

Common law. — Gambling, unless it became a public nuisance, and gaming contracts were lawful at common law. Bender v. Arundel Arena, Inc., 248 Md. 181, 236 A.2d 7 (1967).

Scope of lottery and gaming laws. — Officials and courts in Maryland appear to have considered (a) that the lottery laws covered schemes for awarding a prize by lot or chance in which the only direct or personal participation by the seeker of the prize is his purchase of a ticket or its equivalent; and (b) that the gaming laws covered gambling by games of chance or gaming tables, as broadly defined (even though skill plays no part), in which the player participates personally and directly and is present when the game ends and the result becomes known and would seem always to have drawn a definitive distinction between games of chance and schemes of lottery. Bender v. Arundel Arena, Inc., 248 Md. 181, 236 A.2d 7 (1967).

Construing the statutes liberally, there is no reason to confine the application of a prior version of this section to those devices that depend upon chance, as distinguished from skill. In its broader aspects, playing any game for money is gaming. Brown v. State, 210 Md. 301, 123 A.2d 324 (1956).

Lottery Agency is prohibited from operating video lottery machines. — Video lottery machines, in addition to being devices for gambling, are slot machines, and the Lottery Agency is prohibited from operating them under a prior version of this section and former § 264B of former Article 27. 77 Op. Att'y Gen. 82 (November 13, 1992).

Gaming device. — It is playing of a game of chance which makes a gaming table criminal. James v. State, 63 Md. 242 (1885).

Pinball machines held to be capable of use for gambling purposes in violation of prior versions of §§ 12-101 et seq. Becraft v. Shipley, Daily Record, May 5, 1939, (Cir. Ct. for Carroll County).

If a pinball machine is not a gambling device per se, it may become one when it is shown that it is in fact put to such use. Brown v. State, 210 Md. 301, 123 A.2d 324 (1956).

The insertion of the money and the operation of a pinball machine by the player in the hope of winning a monetary reward in varying amounts constitutes a bet or wager, regardless of the element of skill. Brown v. State, 210 Md. 301, 123 A.2d 324 (1956).

Football pool tickets held not to constitute gaming table under prior versions of §§ 12-101 et seq. State v. Asner & Dolgoff, Daily Record, Nov. 8, 1939, (Crim. Ct. of Baltimore).

A vending machine discharging a cylinder of mint wafers on deposit of nickel and also frequently, but not invariably, metal discs the size of a nickel, varying in number from 2 to 20, was held to be gambling device. Gaither v. Cate, 156 Md. 254, 144 A. 239 (1929).

Machine which dispensed coupons, for cash, offering discounts on merchandise and a chance to win cash was an illegal gaming device, under § 12-101(d)(1)(ii) of this subtitle because it contained all the elements of gambling, which were the payment of consideration for a chance to win a prize or reward, so its operation was punishable as a misdemeanor, under this section. F.A.C.E. Trading, Inc. v. Todd, 393 Md. 364, 903 A.2d 348 (2006).

Sale of pools. — Keeping of rooms for the sale of pools on horse races and the selling of such pools or tickets is not indictable under prior versions of §§ 12-101 et seq. of this article. James v. State, 63 Md. 242 (1885).

Indictment. — Indictment for operating slot machine which paid out only in tokens or metal discs, on the ground that it was violation of prior versions of §§ 12-101 et seq. of this article, was sustained although it was stipulated that State could not prove that the tokens or metal discs were redeemed. State v. DiGiovanni, Daily Record, Jan. 2, 1947, (Cir. Ct. for Cecil County).

Counts under prior versions of §§ 12-101 et seq., and counts for keeping such a common gambling house as constituted a nuisance at common law, may be joined in one indictment. An indictment may include separate offenses in separate counts where offenses are of same general character, differing only in degree. If indictment contains one good count, a general demurrer will not prevent a judgment upon such count. An indictment was held sufficient under a prior version of this section. Wheeler v. State, 42 Md. 563 (1875).

Evidence. — In prosecution for maintaining pinball machine for gambling purposes, evidence as previous payments for free games was held admissible as tending to show guilt of such offense. Hunter v. State, 193 Md. 596, 69 A.2d 505 (1949).

Effect of conviction. — Conviction of operating gambling place held not to warrant revocation of billiard license, as that was not a cause provided in ordinance for revocation. Burley v. City of Annapolis, 182 Md. 307, 34 A.2d 603 (1943).

Conviction upheld. — Conviction for violation of prior versions of §§ 12-101 et seq. of this article on evidence secured by search warrant upheld. Frankel v. State, 178 Md. 553, 16 A.2d 93 (1940).

Gambling in Anne Arundel County. — The General Assembly has always considered the forms of gambling it permitted to be made legal in Anne Arundel County to be gambling games or in the nature of a gambling table, within the purview of the proscriptions of the provisions of statutory law relating to "Gaming," and has never considered those forms of gambling to be schemes in the nature of a lottery prohibited by or within the purview of the provisions of statutory law relating to "Lotteries." Bender v. Arundel Arena, Inc., 248 Md. 181, 236 A.2d 7 (1967).

The General Assembly has repeatedly shown recognition that coin-operated gambling machines and commercial bingo have been legalized in Anne Arundel County. Bender v. Arundel Arena, Inc., 248 Md. 181, 236 A.2d 7 (1967).

County Commissioners of Allegany County authorized to impose tax on gambling. — Except as provided in Article XI-F,

§ 9, of the Maryland Constitution the General Assembly is not prohibited from authorizing the County Commissioners of Allegany County to impose a tax on gambling activities. 64 Op. Att'y Gen. 296 (1979).

§ 12-105. Gambling on vessel or building or other structure on or over water within the State.

(a) *Construction of section.* — This section:

(1) applies notwithstanding the issuance of a license or permit through or by a county, municipal corporation, or other political subdivision of the State; and

(2) does not authorize an act that is otherwise prohibited by law.

(b) *Prohibited — Gaming device on or over waters of the State.* — A person may not bet, wager, or gamble or keep, conduct, maintain, or operate a gaming device on:

(1) a vessel or a part of a vessel on water within the State, except as provided in § 6-209 of the Transportation Article; or

(2) all or a part of a building or other structure that is built on or over water within the State, if the building or other structure cannot be entered from the shore of the State by a person on foot.

(c) *Prohibited — Keeping vessel or structure for gaming device.* — To conduct, maintain, or operate a gaming device, a person may not establish, keep, rent, use, or occupy, or knowingly allow to be established, kept, rented, used, or occupied:

(1) a vessel on water within the State; or

(2) a building or other structure that is built on or over water within the State, if the building or other structure cannot be entered from the shore of the State by a person on foot.

(d) *Penalty.* — A person who violates this section is guilty of a misdemeanor and on conviction is subject to imprisonment not exceeding 1 year or a fine of not less than $200 and not exceeding $1,000 or both for each violation. (An. Code 1957, art. 27, § 246A; 2002, ch. 26, § 2.)

REVISOR'S NOTE

This Revisor's note comprises information related to the revision by Acts 2002, ch. 26.

This section is new language derived without substantive change from former Art. 27, § 246A.

In the introductory language of subsections (b) and (c) and in subsection (d) of this section, the former phrase "firm, association or corporation" is deleted in light of Art. 1, § 15 and § 1-101 of this article, which provide that the defined term "person" includes a corporation and other specified entities.

In the introductory language of subsection (b) of this section, the defined term "gaming device" is substituted for the former phrase "game of chance, gaming table or coin-operated gambling machine or device" for brevity in light of

the definition of "gaming device" in § 12-101(d) of this subtitle. Similarly, in subsections (b) and (c) of this section, the defined term "gaming device" is substituted for the former term "gaming table". *See* § 12-101(d) of this subtitle.

In subsection (b)(1) of this section, the former phrase "except as provided in § 6-209 of the Transportation Article" is revised to apply only to the prohibition on gambling on a vessel on waters within the State because TR § 6-209 allows gambling under specified circumstances only on a vessel.

Also in subsection (b)(1) of this section, the reference to "a part of a vessel" is added for consistency with § 12-102(a)(3) of this subtitle.

In subsection (b)(2) of this section, the former references to a "pier" and a "wharf" are deleted in light of the reference to an "other structure".

Also in subsection (b)(2) of this section, the reference to "part of a building" is added for consistency with § 12-102(a)(3) of this subtitle.

In subsection (d) of this section, the former phrase "in the discretion of the court" is deleted as implicit in the establishment of maximum penalties.

Defined terms:

"County"	§ 1-101
"Gaming device"	§ 12-101
"Person"	§ 1-101

Constitutionality. — Prior version of this section was validly enacted under, Article III, § 15 of the Maryland Constitution because it was "legislation in the general public welfare," which may, by the terms of Article III, § 15, be considered at an even-year session of the General Assembly. Miedzinski v. Landman, 218 Md. 3, 145 A.2d 220 (1958), appeal dismissed, 358 U.S. 644, 79 S. Ct. 537, 3 L. Ed. 2d 567 (1959).

(decision prior to amendment of Art. III, § 15 of the Maryland Constitution by ch. 161, Acts 1964).

Prior version of this section does not violate the equal protection clause of the Fourteenth Amendment to the federal Constitution. Miedzinski v. Landman, 218 Md. 3, 145 A.2d 220 (1958), appeal dismissed, 358 U.S. 644, 79 S. Ct. 537, 3 L. Ed. 2d 567 (1959).

§ 12-106. Raffles [Amendment subject to contingency; amended version follows this section].

(a) *Charitable organization.* — (1) Notwithstanding any other provision of this subtitle, Subtitle 2 of this title, or Title 13 of this article and except as otherwise provided in this subsection, a bona fide charitable organization in this State may conduct a raffle for the exclusive benefit of the charitable organization if the prize awarded is real property:

(i) to which the charitable organization holds title; or

(ii) for which the charitable organization has the ability to convey title.

(2) A charitable organization may not conduct more than two raffles of real property in a calendar year.

(3) The Secretary of State may adopt regulations governing a raffle of real property by a charitable organization under this subsection.

(b) *Political committee or candidate for public office.* — (1) Notwithstanding any other provision of this article and except as otherwise provided in this subsection, a political committee or candidate for public office may conduct a raffle if the prizes awarded are money or merchandise.

(2) (i) The cost of a raffle ticket under this subsection may not exceed $5.

(ii) An individual may not purchase more than $50 worth of tickets.

(3) This subsection does not relieve a political committee or candidate from the reporting and record keeping requirements under the Election Law Article. (An. Code 1957, art. 27, §§ 236, 261D; 2002, ch. 26, § 2; ch. 213, § 7.)

SPECIAL REVISOR'S NOTE

This Special Revisor's note comprises information related to the revision by Acts 2002, ch. 26 and other chapters amending this section from the 2002 Legislative Session.

As enacted by Ch. 26, Acts of 2002, this section was new language derived without substantive change from former Art. 27, §§ 236 and 261D. However, Ch. 213, § 7, Acts of 2002, substituted the reference to "the Election Law

Article" for the reference to "Article 33 of the Code" enacted by Ch. 26 in subsection (b)(3) of this section. Chapter 213, § 8, provided that § 7 would take effect January 1, 2003, to reflect the delayed effective date of the Election Law Article enacted by Ch. 291, Acts of 2002.

In subsection (a)(1) of this section, the phrase "[n]otwithstanding any other provision of this subtitle, Subtitle 2 of this title, or Title 13 of this article" was substituted by Ch. 26 for the former phrase "[t]his subtitle may not be construed to make it unlawful" to clarify that the other provisions of this subtitle, Subtitle 2 of this title, and Title 13 of this article did not prohibit a raffle authorized under subsection (a)(1) of this section.

In subsection (a)(1)(i) and (ii) and (2) of this section, the term "charitable organization" was substituted by Ch. 26 for the former term "organization" for consistency with the introductory language of subsection (a)(1) of this section and to distinguish between a charitable organization and an "organization" defined in § 12-101(f) of this subtitle.

In subsection (b)(1) of this section, the former phrase "bona fide" was deleted by Ch. 26 as surplusage.

Also in subsection (b)(1) of this section, the reference to "money" was substituted by Ch. 26 for the former reference to "cash" for consistency within this title.

Also in subsection (b)(1) of this section, the former phrase "as defined in Article 33, § 1-101 of the Code", which referred to the term "political committee", was deleted by Ch. 26 in light of the definition of "political committee" in § 12-101(g) of this subtitle.

Defined terms:

"Candidate"	§ 12-101
"Organization"	§ 12-101
"Political committee"	§ 12-101

Issues and ramifications of prior version of (a). — For discussion of special problems, issues, and ramifications of a prior version of (a), see 67 Op. Att'y Gen. 125 (1982).

Record keeping. — With respect to the raffles permitted under a prior version of this section, the record keeping requirements in Article 33, § 26-7 (a) [now § 13-240 of the Election Law Article] must be complied with. 71 Op. Att'y Gen. 120 (1986).

(Amendment effective October 1, 2010, subject to contingency.)

§ 12-106. Raffles.

(a) Charitable organization. — (1) Notwithstanding any other provision of this subtitle, Subtitle 2 of this title, or Title 13 of this article and except as otherwise provided in this subsection, a bona fide charitable organization in this State may conduct a raffle for the exclusive benefit of the charitable organization if the prize awarded is real property:

(i) to which the charitable organization holds title; or

(ii) for which the charitable organization has the ability to convey title.

(2) A charitable organization may not conduct more than two raffles of real property in a calendar year.

(3) The Secretary of State may adopt regulations governing a raffle of real property by a charitable organization under this subsection.

(b) Political committee or candidate for public office. — (1) Notwithstanding any other provision of this article and except as otherwise provided in this subsection, a political committee or candidate for public office may conduct a raffle if the prizes awarded are money or merchandise.

(2) (i) The cost of a raffle ticket under this subsection may not exceed $5.

(ii) An individual may not purchase more than $50 worth of tickets.

(3) This subsection does not relieve a political committee or candidate from the reporting and record keeping requirements under the Election Law Article.

(c) Savings promotion raffle by credit unions or depository institution. — (1) Notwithstanding any other provision of this article, a credit union organized under Title 6 of the Financial Institutions Article may conduct a savings promotion raffle under § 6-716 of the Financial Institutions Article.

(2) Notwithstanding any other provision of this article, a depository institution, as defined in § 1-211 of the Financial Institutions Article, may conduct a savings promotion raffle under § 1-211 of the Financial Institutions Article.
(2010, chs. 627, 628.)

Amendment effective October 1, 2010, subject to contingency. — Chapters 627 and 628, Acts 2010, effective October 1, 2010, made identical changes. Each added (c).

Editor's note. — Section 2, chs. 627 and 628, Acts 2010, provides that "this Act shall take effect October 1, 2010, contingent on depository institutions that are subject to regulation by the Office of the Comptroller of the Currency, the Office of Thrift Supervision, the Federal Deposit Insurance Corporation, or the Federal Reserve Board being allowed to provide prize-linked savings products such as a savings promotion raffle authorized by this Act. The Commissioner of Financial Regulation shall monitor federal regulatory and legislative action relating to the authorization of depository institutions to provide prize-linked savings products such as savings promotion raffles, and shall notify the Department of Legislative Services within 30 days after learning that federal action has been taken to allow depository institutions to provide prize-linked products such as a savings promotion raffle authorized by this Act. If notice from the Commissioner is not received by the Department on or before October 1, 2014, this Act shall be null and void without the necessity of further action by the General Assembly."

Bill review letter. — Chapters 627 and 628, Acts 2010, (Senate Bill 886 and House Bill 990) were approved for constitutionality and legal sufficiency as the raffles authorized do not constitute a lottery grant within the meaning of Article III, § 36 of the Maryland Constitution, and are not subject to the referendum requirement of Article XIX of the Maryland Constitution. (Letter of the Attorney General dated May 18, 2010.)

§ 12-107. Pari-mutuel betting.

(a) *Construction of section.* — (1) The prohibition in subsection (b) of this section applies notwithstanding a license or permit granted through or by a county, municipal corporation, or other political subdivision of this State.

(2) This section does not apply to:

(i) pari-mutuel betting conducted under the Maryland Horse Racing Act;

(ii) bingo, carnivals, raffles, bazaars, or similar games of entertainment; or

(iii) mechanical or electrical devices, commonly known as slot machines, that are authorized in the State and that require the insertion of a coin or token.

(b) *Prohibited.* — A person may not conduct or operate with pari-mutuel betting, or with any similar form of betting, wagering, or gambling:

(1) the game, contest, or event commonly known as "jai alai"; or

(2) any other game, contest, or event.

(c) *Penalty.* — A person who violates this section is guilty of a misdemeanor and on conviction is subject to a fine of not less than $200 and not exceeding $1,000 for each violation. (An. Code 1957, art. 27, § 264A; 2002, ch. 26, § 2.)

REVISOR'S NOTE

This Revisor's note comprises information related to the revision by Acts 2002, ch. 26.

This section is new language derived without substantive change from former Art. 27, § 264A.

In subsection (a)(2) of this section, the defined term "gaming device" is substituted for the former term "device" for consistency with § 12-101(c) of this subtitle.

Also in subsection (a)(2) of this section, the former reference to being "legalized" is deleted in light of the reference to being "authorized in the State".

In subsections (b) and (c) of this section, the former phrase "firm, association or corporation" is deleted in light of Art. 1, § 15 and § 1-101 of this article, which provide that the defined term "person" includes a corporation and other specified entities.

In subsection (b) of this section, the term "gambling" is added for consistency with § 12-102(a) of this subtitle.

In subsection (b)(2) of this section, the former reference to any "similar" game is deleted as unnecessary in light of the comprehensive reference to any "other game".

Defined terms:

"County"	§ 1-101
"Person"	§ 1-101
"Token"	§ 12-101

Cross references. — As to Maryland Horse Racing Act, see § 11-101 et seq. of the Business Regulation Article.

"Instant Racing" wagering prohibited. — Wagering on video replays of historic (previously held) horse races, by means of a product known as "Instant Racing," is not authorized at race tracks and satellite simulcast betting facilities in Maryland under current law, since it does not constitute pari-mutuel betting, as authorized by the Maryland Horse Racing Act, at those locations. 94 Op. Att'y Gen. 32 (March 17, 2009).

§ 12-108. Gaming event — Acceptance of credit.

(a) *Prohibited.* — An organization that operates a gaming event authorized under this subtitle, Subtitle 2 of this title, or Title 13 of this article may not accept credit from a person to allow that person to play a gaming device at the gaming event.

(b) *Use of token allowed.* — Subsection (a) of this section does not prohibit an organization from accepting a token instead of money from a person who has paid the organization money for the use of the token.

(c) *Penalty.* — An organization that violates this section is guilty of a misdemeanor and on conviction is subject to a fine not exceeding $1,000 or loss of privileges to conduct a gaming event not exceeding 60 days or both. (An. Code 1957, art. 27, § 261E(b)-(d); 2002, ch. 26, § 2.)

REVISOR'S NOTE

This Revisor's note comprises information related to the revision by Acts 2002, ch. 26.

This section is new language derived without substantive change from former Art. 27, § 261E(b), (c), and (d).

In subsection (a) of this section, the reference to "this subtitle, Subtitle 2 of this title, or Title 13 of this article" is substituted for the former erroneous reference to "this subtitle" to reflect the reorganization of material derived from the former "Gaming" subheading of Article 27.

In subsection (b) of this section, the references to "money" are substituted for the former references to "cash" for consistency within this title.

Defined terms:

"Credit"	§ 12-101
"Gaming device"	§ 12-101
"Gaming event"	§ 12-101
"Organization"	§ 12-101
"Person"	§ 1-101
"Token"	§ 12-101

§ 12-109. Prearrangement or predetermination of horse race results.

(a) *Prohibited.* — A person may not willfully, knowingly, and unlawfully cause or attempt to cause the prearrangement or predetermination of the results of a horse race.

(b) *Penalty.* — A person who violates this section is guilty of a misdemeanor and on conviction is subject to imprisonment not exceeding 3 years or a fine not exceeding $5,000 or both. (An. Code 1957, art. 27, § 240A; 2002, ch. 26, § 2.)

REVISOR'S NOTE

This Revisor's note comprises information related to the revision by Acts 2002, ch. 26.

This section is new language derived without substantive change from former Art. 27, § 240A.

Defined term:
  "Person"   § 1-101

§ 12-110. Recovery of gambling loss.

(a) *In general.* — A person who loses money at a gaming device that is prohibited by this subtitle, Subtitle 2 of this title, or Title 13 of this article:

    (1) may recover the money as if it were a common debt; and

    (2) is a competent witness to prove the loss.

(b) *Limitation.* — Notwithstanding subsection (a) of this section, a person may not recover money or any other thing that the person won by betting at a gaming device prohibited by this subtitle, Subtitle 2 of this title, or Title 13 of this article. (An. Code 1957, art. 27, § 243; 2002, ch. 26, § 2.)

REVISOR'S NOTE

This Revisor's note comprises information related to the revision by Acts 2002, ch. 26.

This section is new language derived without substantive change from former Art. 27, § 243.

In subsections (a) and (b) of this section, the references to a gaming device that is "prohibited by this subtitle, Subtitle 2 of this title, or Title 13 of this article" are added for clarity and to make explicit that civil recovery of a gambling loss is allowed under this section only when the gambling that produced the loss was illegal. *See Bender v. Arundel Arena, Inc.*, 248 Md. 181, 236 A.2d 7 (1967).

In subsection (a) of this section, the defined term "gaming device" is substituted for the former term "gaming table". *See* § 12-101(c) of this subtitle.

Defined terms:
  "Gaming device"   § 12-101
  "Person"   § 1-101

§ 12-111. Duty of law enforcement officer.

If a law enforcement officer has a reason to suspect a gaming device is kept unlawfully at a place, the law enforcement officer shall:

    (1) visit the place; and

    (2) charge all persons who violate a law that prohibits gambling. (An. Code 1957, art. 27, § 263; 2002, ch. 26, § 2.)

This Revisor's note comprises information related to the revision by Acts 2002, ch. 26.

This section is new language derived without substantive change from former Art. 27, § 263.

In the introductory language of this section, the reference to a "law enforcement officer" is substituted for the former reference to "[a]ll constables and police officers" for clarity and consistency within this article.

Also in the introductory language of this section, the defined term "gaming device" is substituted for the former term "gaming table". *See* § 12-101(c) of this subtitle.

Also in the introductory language of this section, the term "unlawfully" is added for clarity to make explicit that the duty to visit a place where a gaming device is kept applies to a place where a gaming device is kept unlawfully.

Defined terms:

"Gaming device"	§ 12-101
"Person"	§ 1-101

§ 12-112. Charging document for gaming.

(a) *Contents.* — (1) An indictment for violating the prohibition against gaming is sufficient if it states that the defendant kept a gaming device.

(2) The indictment need not state the particular kind of gaming or gaming device involved in the alleged violation.

(b) *Bill of particulars.* — A defendant, on timely request, may obtain a bill of particulars. (An. Code 1957, art. 27, § 610; 2002, ch. 26, § 2.)

This Revisor's note comprises information related to the revision by Acts 2002, ch. 26.

This section is new language derived without substantive change from former Art. 27, § 610, as it related to gaming and gaming devices.

In subsection (a)(1) and (2) of this section, the defined term "gaming device" is substituted for the former term "gaming table". *See* § 12-101(c) of this subtitle.

In subsection (a)(1) of this section, the former phrase "as the case may be" is deleted as unnecessary.

In subsection (a)(2) of this section, the reference to a kind of gaming or gaming device "involved in the alleged violation" is added for clarity.

In subsection (b) of this section, the reference to a "timely request" is added for consistency within this article and with Md. Rule 4-241, which governs the request for a bill of particulars in the circuit court.

Also in subsection (b) of this section, the former inaccurate reference to an "application to the State's Attorney" is deleted in light of the requirement to file a request for a bill of particulars with the circuit court, rather than the State's Attorney, in a criminal cause that is in the circuit court. *See* Md. Rule 4-241.

Also in subsection (b) of this section, the former reference to the offense intended to be proved "under such indictment" is deleted as unnecessary.

Defined term:

"Gaming device"	§ 12-101

Cross references. — As to gaming generally, see § 12-101 et seq. of this article.

As to lotteries generally, see § 12-201 et seq. of this article.

Indictments held sufficient. — See Hubin v. State, 180 Md. 279, 23 A.2d 706, cert. denied, 316 U.S. 680, 62 S. Ct. 1107, 86 L. Ed. 1753 (1942); Shelton v. State, 198 Md. 405, 84 A.2d 76 (1951).

§ 12-113. Construction of title.

A court shall construe liberally this title relating to gambling and betting to prevent the activities prohibited. (An. Code 1957, art. 27, § 246; 2002, ch. 26, § 2.)

REVISOR'S NOTE

This Revisor's note comprises information related to the revision by Acts 2002, ch. 26.

This section is new language derived without substantive change from former Art. 27, § 246.

The reference to "this title" is substituted for the former reference to "the preceding sections" in light of the construction that this section applies to all statutes to prevent gambling, including those enacted after passage of this section. *Gaither v. Cate*, 156 Md. 254 (1929); *State v. Crescent Cities Jaycees Found., Inc.*, 330 Md. 460 (1993).

The reference to "activities prohibited" is substituted for the former reference to "mischiefs intended to be provided against" for brevity.

Application. — Prior version of this section applies to all statutes to prevent gambling, including those enacted after its passage. Gaither v. Cate, 156 Md. 254, 144 A. 239 (1929); State v. Crescent Cities Jaycees Found., Inc., 330 Md. 460, 624 A.2d 955 (1993).

Construction. — General Assembly has reversed usual presumption in favor of strict construction of criminal statutes. Allen v. State, 18 Md. App. 459, 307 A.2d 493 (1973).

When considering whether a machine which dispensed coupons, for cash, offering discounts on merchandise and a chance to win cash, was an illegal gambling device, this section mandated that the prohibition against gambling was to be broadly construed. F.A.C.E. Trading, Inc. v. Todd, 393 Md. 364, 903 A.2d 348 (2006).

Subtitle 2. Lotteries.

§ 12-201. "Lottery device" defined.

In this subtitle, "lottery device" means a policy, certificate, or other thing by which a person promises or guarantees that a number, character, ticket, or certificate will, when an event or contingency occurs, entitle the purchaser or holder to receive money, property, or evidence of debt. (An. Code 1957, art. 27, §§ 356, 359, 360, 362; 2002, ch. 26, § 2.)

REVISOR'S NOTE

This Revisor's note comprises information related to the revision by Acts 2002, ch. 26.

This section is new language derived without substantive change from former Art. 27, §§ 356, 359, 360, and 362, as they related to the characteristics of a lottery device.

The reference to an "other thing" is substituted for the former references to "anything", "other device", and "any other thing" for brevity and clarity.

The former references to "the vendor" are deleted as included in the reference to "a person".

The former references to a "particular" number, character, ticket, or certificate are deleted as surplusage.

The reference to "when an event or contingency occurs" is substituted for the former reference to "in any event, or on the happening of a contingency" for brevity.

The former references to a contingency "in the nature of a lottery" are deleted as surplusage.

Defined term:
"Person"   § 1-101

Price constant throughout promotion. — Where the price for the purchase of the product is constant before, during and at the termination of the promotion, the fact that some of its purchasers (or nonpurchasers) may receive a prize awarded on the basis of chance does not violate the provisions of the Constitution or of this section. Mid-Atlantic Coca-Cola Bottling Co. v. Chen, Walsh & Tecler, 296 Md. 99, 460 A.2d 44 (1983).

Legislative intent. — The General Assembly unequivocally intended that gambling activities exempted under former versions of §§ 12-201 and 12-204 of this article not be considered or held to be lotteries within the scope of this subheading even though they possess elements of a lottery. American Legion, Clopper Michael Post No. 10 v. State, 294 Md. 1, 447 A.2d 842 (1982).

Gambling activities of American Legion Post not a lottery within scope of section. — Gambling activities, conducted by an American Legion Post, utilizing chance books in the form of packs of tickets and the gaming device of a jar or bowl from which those chance books were drawn were held not to be a lottery within the scope of this section. American Legion, Clopper Michael Post No. 10 v. State, 294 Md. 1, 447 A.2d 842 (1982).

Lottery defined. — See Ballock v. State, 73 Md. 1, 20 A. 184 (1890); Long v. State, 74 Md. 565, 22 A. 4 (1891).

Sale of out-of-state tickets. — Sale in Maryland of out-of-state lottery tickets clearly constitutes violation of this section. 57 Op. Att'y Gen. 346 (1972).

The maintenance of a computer entry order device in Maryland to permit the electronic purchase of out-of-state lottery tickets is unlawful. 77 Op. Att'y Gen. 78 (January 22, 1992).

Legality in other state irrelevant. — It makes no difference that lottery in question may be legal under laws of a sister state. 57 Op. Att'y Gen. 346 (1972).

Elements of lottery. — A lottery is a species of gaming, the classic elements of which are consideration, chance, and prize. Silbert v. State, 12 Md. App. 516, 280 A.2d 55, cert. denied, 263 Md. 720 (1971).

The fundamental point of a lottery is that in each case there is the offering of a prize, the giving of a consideration for an opportunity to win the prize, and the awarding of the prize by chance. Silbert v. State, 12 Md. App. 516, 280 A.2d 55, cert. denied, 263 Md. 720 (1971).

A "lottery" contains each of three classic elements — consideration, prize and chance. 62 Op. Att'y Gen. 561 (1977).

The essential elements of lottery are consideration, chance and price; the element of consideration requires the payment of money or other thing of value by the purchaser to the lottery sponsor for the opportunity to win a prize awarded by chance. Mid-Atlantic Coca-Cola Bottling Co. v. Chen, Walsh & Tecler, 296 Md. 99, 460 A.2d 44 (1983).

It was conceded that a machine which dispensed coupons, for cash, offering discounts on merchandise and a chance to win cash did not fall within the illegal lottery prohibition in this section, because lotteries were viewed in a separate category from other forms of gaming due to considerations under art. III, § 36 of the Maryland Constitution and "lottery" had a narrow meaning in Maryland. F.A.C.E. Trading, Inc. v. Todd, 393 Md. 364, 903 A.2d 348 (2006).

"Lottery ticket." — In the sense used in this section, requiring liberal interpretation under a prior version of present § 12-208 of this article, a "lottery ticket" represents anything, tangible or intangible, by which the sale of a chance or share in a lottery is manifested. Silbert v. State, 12 Md. App. 516, 280 A.2d 55, cert. denied, 263 Md. 720 (1971).

A "lottery ticket" [now "lottery device"], within the contemplation of the Maryland statutory scheme prohibiting the sale thereof, is not necessarily limited to a physical object. Silbert v. State, 12 Md. App. 516, 280 A.2d 55.

Advertising promotion. — Advertising promotionwhich awards prizes on the basis of chance to persons who purchase the company's products and which also provides methods for entering the promotion without purchasing the company's products is not an illegal lottery under this subheading. Mid-Atlantic Coca-Cola Bottling Co. v. Chen, Walsh & Tecler, 296 Md. 99, 460 A.2d 44 (1983).

Offense resides in substantive acts, not method or form. — The offenses of drawing a lottery or selling a lottery ticket reside not in the method by which the lottery is drawn, or in the form in which the lottery ticket is sold, or in the manner in which the sales transaction is concluded, but rather in the substantive acts showing, without regard to method or form, that a lottery is being conducted and chances sold in furtherance of the lottery scheme. Silbert v. State, 12 Md. App. 516, 280 A.2d 55, cert. denied, 263 Md. 720 (1971).

Whether bets comitted to paper irrelevant. — It makes no difference whether the bets are committed to paper or not. Where it is shown by legally sufficient evidence that a lottery operator has by any method sold a chance on a lottery, he has under this section in effect sold a "lottery ticket" [now "lottery device"]. Silbert v. State, 12 Md. App. 516, 280 A.2d 55, cert. denied, 263 Md. 720 (1971).

Ticket may constitute exchange of words. Lottery ticket may constitute mere exchange of words between the lottery operator and the bettor by which they agree upon the terms under which a chance or share in the lottery is being acquired. Silbert v. State, 12

Md. App. 516, 280 A.2d 55, cert. denied, 263 Md. 720 (1971).

Tickets are evidence of sales. — Lottery tickets themselves are evidence of prior sales and the trier of the facts may draw a permissible inference that an automobile in which the tickets were found was used for the purpose of consummating such sales. Gatewood v. State, 244 Md. 609, 224 A.2d 677 (1966).

Austrian bond. — Austrian bond held to be a lottery ticket within the meaning of this and the following sections. The prohibition of the sale of such bonds was held not to violate treaty stipulations or constitutional provisions. Ballock v. State, 73 Md. 1, 20 A. 184 (1890).

Football pool tickets. — Football pool tickets held not to be lottery tickets within this and the following sections. State v. Asner & Dolgoff, Daily Record, Nov. 8, 1939, (Crim. Ct. of Baltimore).

Unlawful search. — Where arrest without warrant was not lawful, neither was search of defendant's automobile after arrest, and lottery tickets and paraphernalia found by the search were not admissible in evidence. Robinson v. State, 229 Md. 503, 184 A.2d 814 (1962).

Warrants held reasonable. — Commands of the warrants to search certain described persons, to arrest all persons participating in "said criminal activities" (violations of the lottery laws), to seize all paraphernalia used in or incident to the operation and conduct of said criminal activities, and any evidence that pertains thereto were reasonable and proper directives. They describe with reasonable particularity and certainty the property to be searched for and seized, so as to satisfy both the Maryland and federal Constitutions. Griffin v. State, 232 Md. 389, 194 A.2d 80 (1963).

Objection to testimony as to what slips meant waived. — In prosecution for violation of lottery laws permitting police sergeant as an expert to testify as to significance of slips of papers which were found on appellant after a legal arrest was not prejudicial where the only objection was to the admissibility of the slips themselves, following sergeant's explanation of their meaning, and there was no objection to the explanation of what they meant, because this being so appellant must be deemed to have waived his right to object to the testimony as inadmissible. Gatewood v. State, 207 Md. 374, 114 A.2d 619 (1955).

Verdict found not erroneous. — Verdict of the trial court, sitting without a jury, finding appellant guilty of violating the lottery law, held not clearly erroneous. Shipley v. State, 207 Md. 63, 112 A.2d 911 (1955).

Duplicity. — Two counts, one charging unlawful possession of a book of lottery tickets, the other, the unlawful possession of tickets and other lottery paraphernalia are duplicitous and separate sentences under each would be improper. Gatewood v. State, 244 Md. 609, 224 A.2d 677 (1966).

§ 12-202. Scope of subtitle.

(a) *In general.* — Except as provided in subsection (b) of this section, this subtitle applies to all lotteries, including those authorized by any other state or foreign country.

(b) *Exception.* — This subtitle does not apply to the State lottery established under Title 9, Subtitle 1 of the State Government Article. (An. Code 1957, art. 27, §§ 367, 371A; 2002, ch. 26, § 2.)

REVISOR'S NOTE

This Revisor's note comprises information related to the revision by Acts 2002, ch. 26.

This section is new language derived without substantive change from former Art. 27, § 371A and the first clause of § 367.

In subsection (a) of this section, the reference to "this subtitle" is substituted for the former reference to "[t]he preceding sections" to reflect the reorganization of material derived from former Art. 27, §§ 356 through 371A, which comprised the former "Lotteries" subheading of Article 27. Similarly, in subsection (b) of this section, the reference to this "subtitle" is substituted for the former reference to this "subheading" to the same effect.

Also in subsection (a) of this section, the former reference to any other "district or territory" is deleted as included in the defined term "state". *See* § 1-101 of this article.

In subsection (b) of this section, the former references to provisions "relating to lotteries" and to the State lottery "system" are deleted as surplusage.

Defined term:
  "State"   § 1-101

Austrian bond. — Austrian bond held to be violative of the lottery laws. Ballock v. State, 73 Md. 1, 20 A. 184 (1890).

§ 12-203. Sales and draw of lottery devices.

(a) *Prohibited.* — A person may not:

(1) hold a lottery in this State; or

(2) sell a lottery device in the State for a lottery drawn in this State or elsewhere.

(b) *Penalty.* — A person who violates this section is guilty of a misdemeanor and on conviction shall be sentenced to imprisonment for not less than 3 months and not exceeding 12 months or a fine of not less than $200 and not exceeding $1,000 or both for each violation.

(c) *Civil recovery.* — In addition to the penalty provided under subsection (b) of this section, a person who gives money or any other thing to purchase or obtain a lottery device, for each lottery device purchased or obtained, may recover $50 from:

(1) the person to whom the money or other thing was given; or

(2) any person who aided or abetted that person. (An. Code 1957, art. 27, §§ 356-359, 367; 2002, ch. 26, § 2.)

REVISOR'S NOTE

This Revisor's note comprises information related to the revision by Acts 2002, ch. 26.

This section is new language derived without substantive change from former Art. 27, §§ 356, 357, 358, 359, and the second clause of 367.

In subsection (a)(1) of this section, the reference to "hold[ing]" a lottery is substituted for the former reference to "draw[ing]" a lottery to eliminate an archaic construction.

In subsection (a)(2) of this section and throughout this subtitle, the references to the defined term "lottery device" are substituted for the former references to a "lottery ticket", "policies, certificates or anything by which the vendor or other person promises or guarantees that any particular number, character, ticket or certificate shall in any event or on the happening of contingency entitle the purchaser or holder to receive money, property or evidence of debt", and a "contrivance" for brevity. Similarly, in subsection (c) of this section, the defined term "lottery device" is substituted for the former phrase "certificate, or any other device, by which the vendor promises that he or any other person will pay or deliver to the purchaser any money, property or evidence of debt, on the happening of any contingency in the nature of a lottery" for brevity.

In subsection (b) of this section, the former reference to a person's "aiders and abettors" is deleted because the distinctions among principals and accessories before the fact have been abrogated. *See* General Revisor's Note to article and CP § 4-204.

Also in subsection (b) of this section, the former phrase "in the discretion of the court" is deleted as implicit in the establishment of minimum and maximum penalties.

Also in subsection (c) of this section, the reference to a "lottery device purchased or obtained" is substituted for the former phrase "every lottery ticket, certificate or other device in the nature thereof so purchased or obtained by him" for brevity.

Defined terms:

"Lottery device"	§ 12-201
"Person"	§ 1-101

Cross references. — As to the abolishment of informers' fees, see § 7-506 of the Courts Article.

As to indictments for lotteries, see § 12-211 of this article.

Purpose. — By its enactment of this section, making it unlawful for any person to "draw any lottery" or to "sell any lottery ticket," it was the obvious intention and unmistakable purpose of the General Assembly to broadly inhibit the creation, sponsorship, promotion, conduct, and operation of lotteries. Silbert v. State, 12 Md. App. 516, 280 A.2d 55, cert. denied, 263 Md. 720 (1971).

Warrantless arrest not lawful. — Arrest without warrant was not lawful where there was no sale at or immediately prior to the arrest and, hence, no misdemeanor committed in the presence of officers. Robinson v. State, 229 Md. 503, 184 A.2d 814 (1962).

An alleged conspiracy to violate the lottery laws involving a writer and a player fell within the concert of action rule, even though only the seller would be guilty of an offense. Robinson v. State, 229 Md. 503, 184 A.2d 814 (1962).

An indictment charging conspiracy "to violate the lottery laws of the State" sufficiently charges the crime of conspiracy to participate in a lottery. Scarlett v. State, 201 Md. 310, 93 A.2d 753, cert. denied, 345 U.S. 955, 73 S. Ct. 937, 97 L. Ed. 1377 (1953).

Conspiracy to violate lottery law. — Where a conspiracy contemplates bringing to pass a continuous result that will not continue without the continuous cooperation of the conspirators to keep it up (in this case the conduct of a lottery), such continuous cooperation is a single conspiracy rather than a series of distinct conspiracies, and although the original unlawful agreement was reached more than two years before the indictment, the crime is not then exhausted in the sense that the statute cannot be tolled by the commission of a subsequent overt act. Scarlett v. State, 201 Md. 310, 93 A.2d 753, cert. denied, 345 U.S. 955, 73 S. Ct. 937, 97 L. Ed. 1377 (1953).

Computerized order device for purchase of out-of-state lottery tickets unlaw-

ful. — The maintenance of a computer entry order device in Maryland to permit the electronic purchase of out-of-state lottery tickets is unlawful. 77 Op. Att'y Gen. 78 (January 22, 1992).

No application to Anne Arundel County. — This section has no application to the present legalized gambling in Anne Arundel County. Bender v. Arundel Arena, Inc., 248 Md. 181, 236 A.2d 7 (1968).

Advertising promotion. — Advertising promotion which awards prizes on the basis of chance to persons who purchase the company's products and which also provides methods for entering the promition without purchasing the company's products is not an illegal lottery under this subheading. Mid-Atlantic Coca-Cola Bottling Co. v. Chen, Walsh & Tecler, 296 Md. 99, 460 A.2d 44 (1983).

Consideration absent when no money or thing of value given or required to be given. — The words "sell any lottery ticket [now "lottery device"]" and "give money or any other thing for any lottery ticket" in this section compel the conclusion that lottery's essential element of consideration is absent when there is no money or other thing of value given or required to be given for the opportunity to receive an award determined by chance. Mid-Atlantic Coca-Cola Bottling Co. v. Chen, Walsh & Tecler, 296 Md. 99, 460 A.2d 44 (1983).

Maximum sentence for first conviction. — Under this section the maximum imprisonment which can be imposed for a first conviction under the lottery laws is a year. Gatewood v. State, 244 Md. 609, 224 A.2d 677 (1966).

§ 12-204. Location of sales or barter of lottery devices.

(a) *Prohibited.* — A person may not:

(1) keep a house, office, or other place for the purpose of selling or bartering a lottery device in violation of § 12-203 of this subtitle; or

(2) allow a house or office that the person owns to be used for the purpose of selling or bartering a lottery device in violation of § 12-203 of this subtitle.

(b) *Presumption.* — A person who knows that the person's house or office is being used for the purpose of selling or bartering a lottery device in violation of § 12-203 of this subtitle is deemed to be allowing the house or office to be used for those purposes.

(c) *Penalty.* — A person who violates this section is guilty of a misdemeanor and on conviction is subject to imprisonment not exceeding 1 year or a fine not exceeding $1,000 or both. (An. Code 1957, art. 27, §§ 360, 361; 2002, ch. 26, § 2.)

REVISOR'S NOTE

This Revisor's note comprises information related to the revision by Acts 2002, ch. 26.

This section is new language derived without substantive change from former Art. 27, §§ 360 and 361.

In subsection (a) of this section, the former references to being liable or subject to "indictment" for keeping or allowing a house or office to be used for selling or bartering lottery tickets or devices are deleted as implicit in the prohibition on conducting these activities and on conviction, being subject to imprisonment and fine. The former references are construed to mean simply that a person "may be charged" with violating this section, rather than requiring an "indictment", as opposed to any other form of criminal charging document to be used to charge the person. The Criminal Law Article Review Committee brings this deletion to the attention of the General Assembly.

In subsection (a)(1) of this section, the former reference to a "policy, certificate or any other thing by which the vendor or other person promises or guarantees that any particular number, character, ticket, or certificate shall, in any event or on the happening of any contin-gency in the nature of a lottery, entitle the purchaser or holder to receive money, property or evidence of debt" is deleted as included in the defined term "lottery device".

In subsection (a)(2) of this section, the reference to "bartering" is substituted for the former reference to "any of the things in the nature thereof mentioned in § 360 of this article" for brevity.

In subsection (c) of this section, the reference to being "guilty of a misdemeanor" is added to state expressly that which was only implied in the former law. In this State, any crime that was not a felony at common law and has not been declared a felony by statute, is considered to be a misdemeanor. *See State v. Canova*, 278 Md. 483, 490 (1976); *Bowser v. State*, 136 Md. 342, 345 (1920); *Dutton v. State*, 123 Md. 373, 378 (1914); and *Williams v. State*, 4 Md. App. 342, 347 (1968).

Also in subsection (c) of this section, the former phrases "in the discretion of the court" are deleted as implicit in the establishment of maximum penalties.

Defined terms:

"Lottery device"	§ 12-201
"Person"	§ 1-101

Exemptions. — The General Assembly unequivocally intended that gambling activities exempted under former Art. 27, § 255 (b) (now see title 13 of this article) not be considered or held to be lotteries within the scope of this subheading even though they possess elements of a lottery. American Legion, Clopper Michael Post No. 10 v. State, 294 Md. 1, 447 A.2d 842 (1982).

Knowledge required. — On their face this section and former Art. 27, § 240 (now see § 12-102 of this article) require that to be guilty a person must know that his premises are being used for illegal purposes. Propst v. State, 5 Md. App. 36, 245 A.2d 88 (1968), cert. denied, 252 Md. 731, 252 Md. 732 (1969).

"Owner of any house or office" construed. — "Owner of any house or office" within the meaning of this section includes a person vested with title of property in fee or has title to the leasehold interest under a 99-year lease. Williams v. State, 7 Md. App. 5, 252 A.2d 880 (1969).

Occupancy of house is not ownership. — Mere occupancy of or presence in a house or office does not satisfy the requirement of ownership; there must be some proprietary interest. Williams v. State, 7 Md. App. 5, 252 A.2d 880 (1969).

Lease constitutes sufficient ownership. — Interest in property as lessee is suffi-cient ownership. Williams v. State, 7 Md. App. 5, 252 A.2d 880 (1969).

"House or office" construed. — "House or office" includes an automobile. Williams v. State, 7 Md. App. 5, 252 A.2d 880 (1969).

Ownership not element of crime. — Ownership is not an element of the crime proscribed by former section. Williams v. State, 7 Md. App. 5, 252 A.2d 880 (1969).

Permitting automobile to be used for sale of lottery tickets. — See Moore v. State, 199 Md. 676, 87 A.2d 577 (1952); Robinson v. State, 229 Md. 503, 184 A.2d 814 (1962).

Using home or office for sale of out-of-state lottery tickets. — Using home or office in Maryland as place for sale of out-of-state lottery tickets violates section. 57 Op. Att'y Gen. 346 (1972).

Keeping place in Maryland for sale or barter of out-of-state lottery tickets is violation of former version of this section. 57 Op. Att'y Gen. 348 (1972).

Legality in other state irrelevant. — It makes no difference that lottery in question may be legal under laws of a sister state. 57 Op. Att'y Gen. 346 (1972).

Probable cause to believe former section violated. — See Henderson v. State, 243 Md. 342, 221 A.2d 76 (1966).

Evidence sufficient to sustain conviction. — There was sufficient evidence to sustain defendants' convictions for unlawfully maintaining premises for the purpose of selling lottery tickets and (in the case of one defendant) for unlawfully gambling on the results of horse races, where police officers, upon executing a warrant authorizing the search of defendants' premises, discovered defendants in an upstairs bedroom with an adding machine and also found on the premises two telephones with separate numbers, two pads of water-soluble paper beside the telephones, an intercom device, assorted scratch sheets, and approximately $3,600 in United States currency. Dawson v. State, 11 Md. App. 694, 276 A.2d 680, cert. denied, 263 Md. 711, 263 Md. 712 (1971).

§ 12-205. Possession of lottery devices and records.

(a) *Scope of section.* — This section does not apply to a person who possesses:

(1) an item that is prohibited under this section that was obtained to procure or furnish evidence of a violation of this subtitle; or

(2) a lottery ticket or slip issued by this State or another government.

(b) *Prohibited.* — A person may not:

(1) bring a lottery device into the State; or

(2) possess a book, list, slip, or record of:

(i) the numbers drawn in a lottery in this State or another state or country;

(ii) a lottery device; or

(iii) money received or to be received from the sale of a lottery device.

(c) *Penalty.* — A person who violates this section is guilty of a misdemeanor and on conviction is subject to imprisonment not exceeding 1 year or a fine not exceeding $1,000 or both. (An. Code 1957, art. 27, § 362; 2002, ch. 26, § 2.)

REVISOR'S NOTE

This Revisor's note comprises information related to the revision by Acts 2002, ch. 26.

This section is new language derived without substantive change from former Art. 27, § 362.

In subsection (b) of this section, the former references to a "lottery ticket" and a "policy, certificate, or any other thing by which the vendor or other person promises or guarantees that any particular number, character, ticket, or certificate shall, in any event or on the happening of any contingency in the nature of a lottery, entitle the purchaser or holder to receive money, property or evidence of debt" are deleted as included within the defined term "lottery device".

Also in subsection (b) of this section, the reference to "another state or country" is substituted for the former reference to "elsewhere" for clarity and consistency with § 12-202(a) of this subtitle.

In subsection (c) of this section, the reference to being "guilty of a misdemeanor" is added to state expressly that which was only implied in the former law. In this State, any crime that was not a felony at common law and has not been declared a felony by statute, is considered to be a misdemeanor. *See State v. Canova,* 278 Md. 483, 490 (1976); *Bowser v. State,* 136 Md. 342, 345 (1920); *Dutton v. State,* 123 Md. 373, 378 (1914); and *Williams v. State,* 4 Md. App. 342, 347 (1968).

Also in subsection (c) of this section, the former phrase "in the discretion of the court" is deleted as implicit in the establishment of maximum penalties.

Defined terms:
"Lottery device"	§ 12-201
"Person"	§ 1-101
"State"	§ 1-101

Constitutionality. — Former version of this section was constitutional and valid. Ford v. State, 85 Md. 465, 37 A. 172 (1897).

Language of section plain. — The language of the former version of this section was too plain to admit of any discussion as to its meaning. Williams v. State, 7 Md. App. 5, 252 A.2d 880 (1969).

Intent not required. — The mere possession of a lottery slip is an indictable offense; it is not necessary to allege or prove the scienter. Williams v. State, 7 Md. App. 5, 252 A.2d 880 (1969).

Lack of knowledge not defense. — That defendant did not know that tickets in his possession were lottery tickets, or that the law prohibited them, is no defense to indictment under this section. Ford v. State, 85 Md. 465, 37 A. 172 (1897).

Mere possession is unlawful. — Mere possession of lottery tickets is unlawful. Ford v. State, 85 Md. 465, 37 A. 172 (1897); Rucker v. State, 196 Md. 334, 76 A.2d 572 (1950).

This section makes unlawful the mere possession of a lottery slip irrespective of the purpose for which it may be held. Williams v. State, 7 Md. App. 5, 252 A.2d 880 (1969).

Receipt or possession is unlawful. — Receipt or possession in this State of out-of-state lottery ticket is violation of this section. 57 Op. Att'y Gen. 346 (1972).

Legality in other state irrelevant. — It makes no difference that lottery in question may be legal under laws of a sister state. 57 Op. Att'y Gen. 346 (1972).

"Possession" defined. — "Possession" is the act or condition of having in or taking into one's control or holding at one's disposal. Williams v. State, 7 Md. App. 5, 252 A.2d 880 (1969); Gatewood v. State, 15 Md. App. 450, 291 A.2d 688, cert. denied, 266 Md. 737 (1972).

What constitutes possession within the meaning of this section is the same as that which constitutes possession within the meaning of the narcotic laws of this State. Williams v. State, 7 Md. App. 5, 252 A.2d 880 (1969).

When the proscribed articles are found on the person of the traverser, possession by him is clear. He may also possess them by having them in his immediate control. Williams v. State, 7 Md. App. 5, 252 A.2d 880 (1969).

Sole possession not required. — Sole possession is not required. There may be joint possession in several persons. Williams v. State, 7 Md. App. 5, 252 A.2d 880 (1969).

Actual, immediate, and direct possession not required. — There need not be actual physical possession. It is not necessary that the possession be immediate and direct. Williams v. State, 7 Md. App. 5, 252 A.2d 880 (1969).

Constructive possession. — There may be constructive possession. Williams v. State, 7 Md. App. 5, 252 A.2d 880 (1969).

Duration and quantity not material. — The duration of the possession and the quantity possessed are not material. Williams v. State, 7 Md. App. 5, 252 A.2d 880 (1969).

Not necessary to prove ownership. — It is not necessary to prove ownership in sense of title. Williams v. State, 7 Md. App. 5, 252 A.2d 880 (1969).

Probable cause to believe section violated. — See Henderson v. State, 243 Md. 342, 221 A.2d 76 (1966).

There was probable cause for accused's arrest by an experienced vice squad detective who observed accused in a poolroom, writing, on a brown paper bag, a sequence of three-digit numbers of the kind used in conventional lottery operations. Johnson v. State, 8 Md. App. 187, 259 A.2d 97 (1969), cert. denied, 257 Md. 734 (1970).

Expertise of arresting officer. — Expertise of arresting officer in lottery cases is an important factor in assessing the existence of probable cause. Johnson v. State, 8 Md. App. 187, 259 A.2d 97 (1969), cert. denied, 257 Md. 734 (1970).

Right of police officer to give testimony. — The right of a police officer, experienced in such matters, to give testimony as to the meaning of figures, words, etc., appearing on alleged gambling paraphernalia has been clearly established by decisions of the Court of Appeals. Spriggs v. State, 226 Md. 50, 171 A.2d 715 (1961); Silbert v. State, 12 Md. App. 516, 280 A.2d 55, cert. denied, 263 Md. 720 (1971).

Observations of law enforcement officer, given in evidence, of the conduct of a lottery operation on dates other than those charged in the indictment were properly to be considered by way of background in assessing the character and meaning of the objects possessed by the defendant on the dates charged in the indictment. Silbert v. State, 12 Md. App. 516, 280 A.2d 55, cert. denied, 263 Md. 720 (1971).

One admitting possession may be arrested without warrant. — One admitting, when accosted by police officer, that he had lottery tickets in his possession, could be arrested without warrant. Blager v. State, 162 Md. 664, 161 A. 1 (1932).

Warrantless arrest authorized. — Arrest without warrant for possession of lottery paraphernalia authorized by circumstances. Franklin v. State, 208 Md. 628, 119 A.2d 439 (1956).

Where defendant dropped an envelope containing lottery slips in officers' presence, the commission of the crime of having lottery material in his possession was disclosed to the view of the officers and his arrest by the officers was justified. Brown v. State, 207 Md. 282, 113 A.2d 916 (1955).

Admissibility of slip representing lottery wagers. — There was no error in the admission of a slip of paper representing lottery wagers into evidence, as the Court of Appeals has repeatedly held that a probability of connection of proffered evidence with a crime is enough to make it admissible, its weight being for the trier of fact to evaluate. Spriggs v. State, 226 Md. 50, 171 A.2d 715 (1961).

Actual production of gambling paraphernalia not required. — There is no merit in the contention that one cannot be convicted under this section unless the State actually produces the physical gambling paraphernalia in evidence. Silbert v. State, 12 Md. App. 516, 280 A.2d 55, cert. denied, 263 Md. 720 (1971).

§ 12-206. Publication of accounts of lotteries and lottery prizes.

(a) *Scope of section.* — This section does not apply to a lottery conducted by a government.

(b) *Prohibited.* — A person may not print, write, or publish an account of a lottery that describes:

(1) when or where the lottery is to be drawn;

(2) any prize available in the lottery;

(3) the price of a lottery ticket or share of a lottery ticket; or

(4) where a lottery ticket may be obtained.

(c) *Penalty.* — A person who violates this section is guilty of a misdemeanor and on conviction is subject to imprisonment not exceeding 60 days or a fine not exceeding $100 or both. (An. Code 1957, art. 27, § 363; 2002, ch. 26, § 2.)

REVISOR'S NOTE

This Revisor's note comprises information related to the revision by Acts 2002, ch. 26.

This section is new language derived without substantive change from former Art. 27, § 363.

In subsection (a) of this section, the phrase "does not apply" is substituted for the former phrase "may not be construed or interpreted as being applicable" for brevity.

In subsection (b) of this section, the former reference to a person's "in any way aiding or assisting in the same" is deleted because the distinctions among principals and accessories before the fact have been abrogated. *See* General Revisor's Note to article and CP § 4-204.

Also in subsection (b) of this section, the former reference to "the prizes therein, or any of them" is deleted as included in the reference to "any prize available in the lottery" for clarity.

In subsection (c) of this section, the former phrase "at the discretion of the court" is deleted as implicit in the establishment of maximum penalties.

Defined term:
"Person"   § 1-101

Publishing account of out-of-state lottery. — Publishing in Maryland account of out-of-state lottery is a violation of this section. 57 Op. Att'y Gen. 346 (1972).

Legality of out-of-state lottery irrelevant. — It makes no difference that lottery in question may be legal under laws of a sister state. 57 Op. Att'y Gen. 346 (1972).

§ 12-207. Lottery insurance.

(a) *Prohibited.* — A person may not:

(1) insure or receive consideration for insuring for or against the drawing of a lottery ticket or part of a lottery ticket;

(2) receive money, property, or evidence of debt in consideration of an agreement to repay or deliver the money, property, or evidence of debt, if a lottery ticket or a part of a lottery ticket is drawn or not drawn on a particular day or in a particular order;

(3) if contingent on the results of a lottery, and whether or not consideration is paid, promise or agree to:

(i) pay or deliver money, property, or evidence of debt; or

(ii) refuse to do anything for the benefit of another; or

(4) publish a notice of an intent to perform or notice of a proposal to perform items (1) through (3) of this subsection.

(b) *Penalty.* — A person who violates this section is guilty of a misdemeanor and on conviction is subject to imprisonment of not less than 3 months and not exceeding 6 months or a fine of not less than $100 and not exceeding $1,000 or both. (An. Code 1957, art. 27, § 364; 2002, ch. 26, § 2.)

REVISOR'S NOTE

This Revisor's note comprises information related to the revision by Acts 2002, ch. 26.

This section is new language derived without substantive change from former Art. 27, § 364.

In subsection (a)(1) and (2) of this section, the former references to a "policy or certificate" are deleted as included in the reference to a "lottery ticket".

In subsection (a)(2) of this section, the former phrase "shall prove fortunate or unfortunate" is deleted as included in the phrase "is drawn or not drawn".

In subsection (a)(4) of this section, the reference to "a notice of an intent to perform or a notice of a proposal to perform items (1) through (3) of this subsection" is substituted for the former reference to a "notice or proposal for the purposes aforesaid" for clarity.

In subsection (b) of this section, the reference to being "guilty of a misdemeanor" is added to state expressly that which was only implied in the former law. In this State, any crime that was not a felony at common law and has not been declared a felony by statute, is considered to be a misdemeanor. *See State v. Canova*, 278 Md. 483, 490 (1976); *Bowser v. State*, 136 Md. 342, 345 (1920); *Dutton v. State*, 123 Md. 373, 378 (1914); and *Williams v. State*, 4 Md. App. 342, 347 (1968).

Also in subsection (b) of this section, the former phrase "in the discretion of the court" is deleted as implicit in the establishment of maximum penalties.

Defined term:
"Person" § 1-101

§ 12-208. Construction of lottery provisions.

A court shall interpret §§ 12-201 through 12-207 of this subtitle liberally to treat as a lottery ticket any ticket, part of a ticket, or lottery device by which money is paid or another item is delivered when, in the nature of a lottery, an event or contingency occurs. (An. Code 1957, art. 27, § 368; 2002, ch. 26, § 2.)

REVISOR'S NOTE

This Revisor's note comprises information related to the revision by Acts 2002, ch. 26.

This section is new language derived without substantive change from former Art. 27, § 368.

The phrase "[a] court shall interpret" is substituted for the former phrase "[t]he courts shall construe the foregoing provisions" for brevity.

The defined term "lottery device" is substituted for the former reference "certificates, or any other device" for clarity.

The phrase "when, in the nature of a lottery, an event or contingency occurs" is substituted for the former phrase "on the happening of any event or contingency, in the nature of a lottery" for clarity.

Defined term:
"Lottery device" § 12-201

"Lottery ticket." — Any device whatsoever, by which money or any other thing is to be paid or delivered on the happening of any event or contingency in the nature of a lottery, is a lottery ticket. Silbert v. State, 12 Md. App. 516, 280 A.2d 55, cert. denied, 263 Md. 720 (1971).

§ 12-209. Conveyance void.

A grant, bargain, or transfer of real estate, goods, a right of action, or personal property is void if it occurs while engaging in, or aiding or assisting in a lottery. (An. Code 1957, art. 27, § 365; 2002, ch. 26, § 2.)

REVISOR'S NOTE

This Revisor's note comprises information related to the revision by Acts 2002, ch. 26.

This section is new language derived without substantive change from former Art. 27, § 365.

The former phrase "and of no effect" is deleted as included in the word "void".

The reference to "engaging in" a lottery is substituted for the former reference to being "in pursuance of" a lottery for clarity.

The former reference to a "sale [or] conveyance" of real estate is deleted as included in the reference to "transfer" of real estate.

The former reference to "chattels" is deleted as included in the reference to "personal property".

§ 12-210. Sentencing — Repeat lottery violation.

(a) *Construction of section.* — Any recovery of a penalty for a violation of any of the provisions of this subtitle relating to a lottery, whether by indictment or action of debt, or before a justice of the peace before July 5, 1971, or before any court of competent jurisdiction, is considered a first conviction under this section.

(b) *Enhanced penalty.* — A person convicted a second or subsequent time of a violation of any of the provisions of this subtitle relating to a lottery is subject to imprisonment not exceeding 5 years or a fine not exceeding $5,000 or both. (An. Code 1957, art. 27, § 366; 2002, ch. 26, § 2.)

REVISOR'S NOTE

This Revisor's note comprises information related to the revision by Acts 2002, ch. 26.

This section is new language derived without substantive change from former Art. 27, § 366.

In this section, the references to a violation of this "subtitle" relating to a lottery are substituted for the former references to a violation of this "article" relating to lotteries to reflect the reorganization of all material relating to lotteries in this subtitle.

Also in this section, the references to a violation "relating to [a] lotter[y]" are retained in light of § 12-212 of this subtitle, relating to gift enterprises.

In subsection (a) of this section, the reference to "July 5, 1971" is substituted for the former reference to "the first Monday of July, 1971" for clarity.

Defined term:
"Person"   § 1-101

"Second" defined. — Word "second" in this section means "another, additional to that which has already taken place." Gatewood v. State, 244 Md. 609, 224 A.2d 677 (1966).

"Time" defined. — Word "time" in this section may properly be taken as meaning "time or times." Gatewood v. State, 244 Md. 609, 224 A.2d 677 (1966).

The word "time" as used in this section is to be construed in the light of Article 1, § 8, which provides as one of the rules of interpretation of

the Code that "the singular always includes the plural, and vice versa, except where such construction would be unreasonable." Gatewood v. State, 244 Md. 609, 224 A.2d 677 (1966).

Maximum sentence given for later convictions. — Maximum five-year sentence may be given if person is convicted another time or times of any lottery offense. Gatewood v. State, 244 Md. 609, 224 A.2d 677 (1966).

This section contains no gradation. Distinction between convictions after first is therefore unnecessary. Gatewood v. State, 244 Md. 609, 224 A.2d 677 (1966).

Use of prior conviction for enhancement without counsel forbidden. — Use of prior conviction without counsel against person to enhance punishment is forbidden by Gatewood v. State, 15 Md. App. 450, 291 A.2d 688, cert. denied, 266 Md. 737 (1972).

Right to fair trial not prejudiced. — Defendant's right to fair trial before court without jury was not prejudiced because the judge was made aware, before trial, that there was a subsequent offender addendum attached to the indictment. Gatewood v. State, 15 Md. App. 450, 291 A.2d 688, cert. denied, 266 Md. 737 (1972).

§ 12-211. Charging document for lottery indictment.

(a) *Contents.* — (1) An indictment for violating the prohibition against the drawing of lotteries or the selling of lottery devices is sufficient if it states that the defendant drew a lottery or sold a lottery device.

(2) The indictment need not state the particular kind of lottery scheme involved in the alleged violation.

(b) *Bill of particulars.* — The defendant, on timely request, is entitled to a bill of particulars. (An. Code 1957, art. 27, § 610; 2002, ch. 26, § 2.)

REVISOR'S NOTE

This Revisor's note comprises information related to the revision by Acts 2002, ch. 26.

This section is new language derived without substantive change from former Art. 27, § 610, as it related to lotteries.

In subsection (a)(1) of this section, the defined term "lottery device" is substituted for the former reference to a "lottery ticket" for consistency within this subtitle.

Also in subsection (a)(1) of this section, the former phrase "as the case may be" is deleted as unnecessary.

In subsection (a)(2) of this section, the reference to a kind of lottery scheme "involved in the alleged violation" is added for clarity.

In subsection (b) of this section, the reference to a "timely request" is added for consistency within this article and with Md. Rule 4-241, which governs the request for a bill of particulars in the circuit court.

Also in subsection (b) of this section, the former inaccurate reference to an "application to the State's Attorney" is deleted in light of the requirement to file a request for a bill of particulars with the circuit court, rather than the State's Attorney, in a criminal cause that is in the circuit court. *See* Md. Rule 4-241.

Also in subsection (b) of this section, the former reference to the offense intended to be proved "under such indictment" is deleted as unnecessary.

Defined term:
"Lottery device"   § 12-201

§ 12-212. Barter, sale, or trade of gift enterprise.

(a) *Prohibited.* — A person may not directly or indirectly barter, sell, or trade or offer by publication or in any other manner to barter, sell, or trade goods or merchandise, in a package or in bulk, in exchange for a scheme or device constituting a gift enterprise.

(b) *Penalty.* — A person who violates this section is guilty of a misdemeanor and on conviction shall be sentenced to a fine of not less than $50 for each violation. (An. Code 1957, art. 27, §§ 369, 370; 2002, ch. 26, § 2.)

REVISOR'S NOTE

This Revisor's note comprises information related to the revision by Acts 2002, ch. 26.

This section is new language derived without substantive change from former Art. 27, §§ 369 and 370.

In subsection (a) of this section, the former phrase "by agent or otherwise" is deleted as included in the phrase "directly or indirectly".

Also in subsection (a) of this section, the former reference to "wares" is deleted as included in the reference to "goods or merchandise".

Also in subsection (a) of this section, the former phrase "of any description" is deleted as surplusage.

Also in subsection (a) of this section, the phrase "in exchange for" a scheme or device is substituted for the former phrase "holding out as an inducement for any such" scheme or device for brevity.

Also in subsection (a) of this section, the former reference to an enterprise "of any kind or character whatsoever" is deleted as surplusage.

In subsection (b) of this section, the former archaic reference to a "body corporate" is deleted as included in the defined term "person".

Also in subsection (b) of this section, the former reference to conviction "thereof before any court of competent jurisdiction in this State" is deleted as implicit.

The Criminal Law Article Review Committee notes, for the consideration of the General Assembly, that in subsection (b) of this section, no maximum penalty is provided.

Defined term:
"Person"   § 1-101

Section invalid as to gift enterprises not involving chance. — The provisions of this section by reason of its general terms have been construed as including all gift enterprises, those including the elements of chance as well as those that do not. Insofar as it prohibits gifts, not involving the element of chance, to purchasers of goods as an inducement to make the purchases, it is unconstitutional and void. Long v. State, 74 Md. 565, 22 A. 4 (1891).

Scheme was "gift enterprise". — Scheme held to be a "gift enterprise" within the meaning of this section. Long v. State, 73 Md. 527, 21 A. 683 (1891).

Subtitle 3. Slot Machines.

§ 12-301. "Slot machine" defined.

In this subtitle:

(1) "slot machine" means a machine, apparatus, or device that:

(i) operates or can be made to operate by inserting, depositing, or placing with another person money, a token, or another object; and

(ii) through the element of chance, the reading of a game of chance, the delivery of a game of chance, or any other outcome unpredictable by the user, awards the user:

1. money, a token, or other object that represents or that can be converted into money; or

2. the right to receive money, a token, or another object that represents and can be converted into money;

(2) "slot machine" includes:

(i) a machine, apparatus, or device described in item (1) of this section that also sells, delivers, or awards merchandise, money, or some other tangible thing of value; and

(ii) a pinball machine or console machine that pays off in merchandise; and

(3) "slot machine" does not include a machine, apparatus, or device that:

(i) awards the user only free additional games or plays;

(ii) awards the user only noncash merchandise or noncash prizes of minimal value;

(iii) dispenses paper pull tab tip jar tickets or paper pull tab instant bingo tickets that must be opened manually by the user provided that the machine, apparatus, or device does not:

1. read the tickets electronically;

2. alert the user to a winning or losing ticket; or

3. tabulate a player's winnings and losses;

(iv) 1. displays facsimiles of bingo cards that users mark and monitor according to numbers called on the premises by an individual where the user is operating the machine; and

2. does not permit a user to play more than 54 bingo cards at the same time;

(v) is used by the State Lottery Commission under Title 9 of the State Government Article; or

(vi) if legislation takes effect authorizing the operation of video lottery terminals, is a video lottery terminal as defined in and licensed under that legislation. (An. Code 1957, art. 27, § 264B; 2002, ch. 26, § 2; 2008, ch. 474; 2009, ch. 661.)

REVISOR'S NOTE

This Revisor's note comprises information related to the revision by Acts 2002, ch. 26.

This section is new language derived without substantive change from the introductory paragraph of former Art. 27, § 264B, as it defined a slot machine.

The introductory language of this section is revised in standard language used to introduce a definition section.

Throughout this section, the term "money" is substituted for the former terms "coin" and "piece of money" for brevity and consistency within this article.

The former reference to a machine "that is adapted for use in such a way" is deleted as surplusage.

In item (1)(ii)1 of this section, the phrase "that represents or that can be converted into money" is substituted for the former phrase "representative of and convertible into money" to reflect the construction of the latter phrase of former Art. 27, § 264B by the Court of Appeals in *Clerk of Circuit Court for Calvert County v. Chesapeake Beach Park, Inc.*, 251 Md. 657 (1968).

In item (1)(ii)2 of this section, the reference to an object "that represents" money is substituted for the former reference to an object that is "representative of" money for clarity.

Also in item (1)(ii)2 of this section, the reference to an object that "can be converted" into money is substituted for the former reference to an object "convertible" into money for clarity.

In item (2)(i) of this section, the reference to "awards" is substituted for the former reference to a "present" for clarity.

The Criminal Law Article Review Committee notes, for the consideration of the General Assembly, that in item (2)(ii) of this section, the reference to a "pinball machine or console machine that pays off in merchandise" is added to reflect the holdings of the Court of Appeals in *Clerk of Circuit Court for Calvert County v. Chesapeake Beach Park, Inc.*, 251 Md. 657 (1968) and in *Board of County Commissioners of Charles County et al. v. Conner t/a Southern Trails Reno*, 251 Md. 670 (1968), that such devices are slot machines prohibited under former Art. 27, § 264B.

The Criminal Law Article Review Committee also notes, for the consideration of the General Assembly, that the Court of Appeals, in *Clerk of the Circuit Court for Calvert County v. Chesapeake Beach Park, Inc.*, 251 Md. 657 (1968) and in *State v. One Hundred Fifty-Eight Gaming Devices*, 304 Md. 404 (1985), held that a machine that pays off only in free plays that are not redeemable for any other item, is not a slot machine. On the other hand, the Court, in *One Hundred Fifty-Eight Gaming Devices*, held that a machine that involves an element of chance and is equipped with odds mechanisms or a meter for recording the number of free plays released, "established indicia of a gambling device", is an illegal slot machine. The General Assembly may wish to consider substantive legislation to clarify this section in light of these decisions.

Defined term:
"Person"   § 1-101

Effect of amendments. — Chapter 661, Acts 2009, effective June 1, 2009, reenacted the section without change.

Editor's note. — Section 2, ch. 474, Acts 2008, as amended by ch. 661, Acts 2009, provides that "notwithstanding the provisions of Section 1 of this Act, an entity licensed to offer instant bingo under a commercial bingo license as of July 1, 2007, or by a qualified organization as defined in § 13-201 of this article on the premises of the qualified organization may continue to operate a game of instant bingo in the same manner using electronic machines until July 1, 2012, provided that:

"(a)(1) the machines have been in operation for a 1-year period ending December 31, 2007; or

"(2) the machines were in operation under a commercial bingo license as of December 31, 2007;

"(b) the entity does not operate more than the number of electronic machines operated as of February 28, 2008; and

" (c) the conduct of the gaming and operation of the machines is consistent with all other provisions of the Criminal Law Article."

Section 4, ch. 474, Acts 2008, provides that "notwithstanding any other provision of law, if any action is brought for declaratory, injunctive, or other relief to challenge the legality of any provision of this Act or any amendment made by this Act, the enforcement and implementation of this Act may not be stayed pending the disposition of the action."

Section 2, ch. 661, Acts 2009, provides that "on or before July 1, 2012, a county may not impose a fee or tax on electronic bingo in addition to any tax or fee imposed by the county as of January 1, 2009."

Section 3, ch. 661, Acts 2009, provides that "notwithstanding any other law, an action for declaratory, injunctive, or other relief to challenge the legality of any provision of this Act or any amendment made by this Act:

"(1) may be brought only in the circuit court for Anne Arundel County; and

"(2) does not stay the enforcement and implementation of this Act pending the disposition of the action"

Section 4, ch. 661, Acts 2009, provides that "notwithstanding any provision of this Act, it is the intent of the General Assembly that the proliferation of gaming in the State be reduced by limiting the use of gaming machines that are similar in appearance and operation to video lottery terminals and that, in authorizing the temporary continuation of gaming activity with such machines by commercial and charitable entities that have operated such machines over a long period of time, this Act be construed not as approval of an expansion of such gaming, but as enacting a mechanism to provide additional funding required to address the State's important fiscal needs on a temporary basis while the State video lottery terminal program is being implemented."

Maryland Law Review. — For note, "The Maryland Survey: 2000-2001: Recent Decisions; B. Defining Slot Machines: The Court of Appeals Refuses to Expand Section 264B to Include Pull-Tab Dispensers," see 61 Md. L. Rev. 1027 (2002).

University of Baltimore Law Forum. — For a 2001 development, "Chesapeake Amusements v. Riddle: A Dispensing Slot Machine with Player Enhancement Features that Signal When a Winning Ticket is Being Dispensed Does Not Violate Maryland's Statutory Provision Prohibiting Illegal Slot Machines," see 32 U. Balt. Law Forum 39 (2001).

Application. — Inoperable slot machines and machines or parts adaptable for slot machines are not slot machines under the law; however, partially dismantled slot machines are illegal devices. State v. One Hundred & Fifty-Eight Gaming Devices, 59 Md. App. 44, 474 A.2d 545 (1984), modified on other grounds, 304 Md. 404, 499 A.2d 940 (1985).

Machine which itself does not pay off is lawful in Baltimore City and thus exempt from confiscation under § 1177 of Title 15 of the United States Code. United States v. One Bally Bounty In-Line Pinball Mach., 261 F. Supp. 187 (D. Md. 1966).

Any machine that could be licensed under the predecessor to § 17-401 et seq. of the Business Regulation Article is not outlawed by the prior version of this section. United States v. One Bally Bounty In-Line Pinball Mach., 261 F. Supp. 187 (D. Md. 1966).

Machine which dispensed coupons, for cash, offering discounts on merchandise and a chance to win cash was found by a trial court not to be an illegal slot machine, under this section, because the element of chance was in the coupons dispensed and not in the machine. F.A.C.E. Trading, Inc. v. Todd, 393 Md. 364, 903 A.2d 348 (2006).

Free-play devices. — Free-play devices not adapted for gambling, which award automatic replays only, and which contain nothing more than a knockoff switch, are not slot machines under the statutory definition. State v. One Hundred & Fifty-Eight Gaming Devices, 304 Md. 404, 499 A.2d 940 (1985).

Console and pinball machines. — Console and pinball machines that pay off in merchandise are slot machines within the definition of the prior version of this section. Board of County Comm'rs v. Conner, 251 Md. 670, 248 A.2d 486 (1968).

Video lottery machines. — Video lottery machines, in addition to being devices for gambling, are slot machines, and the Lottery Agency is prohibited from operating them under prior versions of this section and § 12-104. 77 Op. Att'y Gen. 82 (November 13, 1992).

Pull-tab bingo machine. — An amusement corporation's pull-tab bingo machine was not an illegal slot machine under a prior version of this section, because the machine dispensed the pull-tabs non-randomly and in sequence, so that the element of chance was in the pull-tabs themselves, and not in the operation of the machine. Chesapeake Amusements, Inc. v. Riddle, 363 Md. 16, 766 A.2d 1036 (2001).

Construction. — The phrase "representative of and convertible into money" must be read to mean representative of or convertible into money. Clerk of Circuit Court v. Chesapeake Beach Park, 251 Md. 657, 248 A.2d 479 (1968).

"Become entitled to receive" construed. — "Become entitled to receive" means "become entitled to receive" from the machine and not "become entitled to receive" as a result of playing the machine. United States v. One Bally Bounty In-Line Pinball Mach., 261 F. Supp. 187 (D. Md. 1966).

Source of reward. — The phraseology of the prior version of this section leads to the conclusion that evidence of the reward or the material reward itself may, without distinction and with the same consequences, come directly from the machine or from an attendant of the machine, and in every instance of material reward by chance the machine would be a slot machine. Clerk of Circuit Court v. Chesapeake Beach Park, 251 Md. 657, 248 A.2d 479 (1968).

Aggregate value of free plays. — If the phrase defining the material reward of the winner is read as money, coin, token or other object "representative of or convertible into money," as it should be, it is apparent that not only the tokens which fall to a winner in the cup of the one-arm bandit but the aggregate value of the free plays won on the console or pinball machine, whether evidenced by a receipt or not, are alike "representative of" money in that under the evidence they can be used to purchase beverages, food or merchandise of a specified dollar value. The predecessor of this section proscribes machines or devices through the operation of which this result can occur by chance. Clerk of Circuit Court v. Chesapeake Beach Park, 251 Md. 657, 248 A.2d 479 (1968).

When a device contains an odds mechanism, a method of releasing free plays, and a knock-off meter, the potential for valuating aggregate free plays exists and the machine is illegal under the prior version of this section. State v. One Hundred & Fifty-Eight Gaming Devices, 59 Md. App. 44, 474 A.2d 545 (1984), modified on other grounds, 304 Md. 404, 499 A.2d 940 (1985).

The registration of a free play upon a machine adapted as a gambling device, without more, is an "object" within the ambit of the prior version of this section which is representative of or convertible into money. State v. One Hundred & Fifty-Eight Gaming Devices, 304 Md. 404, 499 A.2d 940 (1985).

Sufficiency of evidence. — The evidence in case was not sufficient to have permitted the trial court to conclude that either of the two apparatuses seized from the appellant was a device which "is adopted" for use as a slot machine. Allen v. State, 18 Md. App. 459, 307 A.2d 493 (1973).

§ 12-302. Possession or operation of slot machine.

(a) *Prohibited.* — Except as allowed under §§ 12-304 through 12-306 of this subtitle, a person may not locate, possess, keep, or operate a slot machine in the State as an owner, lessor, lessee, licensor, licensee, or in any other capacity.

(b) *Penalty.* — A person who violates this section is guilty of a misdemeanor and on conviction is subject to imprisonment not exceeding 1 year or a fine of $1,000 or both for each violation. (An. Code 1957, art. 27, § 264B I, III; 2002, ch. 26, § 2; 2008, ch. 474.)

REVISOR'S NOTE

This Revisor's note comprises information related to the revision by Acts 2002, ch. 26.

This section is new language derived without substantive change from former Art. 27, § 264B I and III.

In this section, the defined term "person" is substituted for the former references to a "person, firm or corporation" and "firm, person or corporation". *See* § 1-101 of this article.

In subsection (a) of this section, the former reference to "maintain[ing]" a slot machine is deleted as included in the reference to "keep[ing]" a slot machine.

Defined terms:

"Person"	§ 1-101
"Slot machine"	§ 12-301

Constitutionality. — The prior version of slot machine prohibitions is constitutional. Mills v. Agnew, 286 F. Supp. 107 (D. Md. 1968).

Legislative intent. — The legislative history of the enactment of the prior version of this statute permits the inference that the more restrictive language which the General Assembly used was not an accidental decision. Allen v. State, 18 Md. App. 459, 307 A.2d 493 (1973).

General Assembly was aiming to outlaw payouts by the machine in its enactment of the prior version of this section. United States v. One Bally Bounty In-Line Pinball Mach., 261 F. Supp. 187 (D. Md. 1966).

Construction. — The prior version of the slot machine prohibitions speaks narrowly. Allen v. State, 18 Md. App. 459, 307 A.2d 493 (1973).

And it covers only devices which are fit, or adjusted, for use as slot machines. Allen v. State, 18 Md. App. 459, 307 A.2d 493 (1973).

Licensing provisions for amusement devices in predecessor to § 17-401 et seq. of the Business Regulation Article must be read in pari materia with the provisions in the prior version of this section relating to slot machines. State v. One Hundred & Fifty-Eight Gaming Devices, 304 Md. 404, 499 A.2d 940 (1985).

Forfeiture as contraband. — Prior version of this statute does not authorize forfeiture of gaming devices, however, the State has a common law right to require forfeiture of slot machines as contraband. State v. One Hundred & Fifty-Eight Gaming Devices, 59 Md. App. 44, 474 A.2d 545 (1984), modified on other grounds, 304 Md. 404, 499 A.2d 940 (1985).

Devices which award a successful player, directly or indirectly with money or merchandise, including the so-called antique slot machines, are clearly forfeitable as contraband per se. State v. One Hundred Fifty-Eight Gaming Devices, 304 Md. 404, 499 A.2d 940 (1985).

Referral to electorate. — Referral of prior version of slot machine prohibitions to electorate properly refused. Abell v. Secretary of State, 251 Md. 319, 247 A.2d 258 (1968).

§ 12-303. Antique slot machine — Defense.

(a) *"Antique slot machine" defined.* — In this section, "antique slot machine" means a slot machine that was manufactured at least 25 years before the date on which the machine is seized.

(b) *In general.* — A person may not be convicted under § 12-302 of this subtitle if the person shows by a preponderance of the evidence that the slot machine:

(1) is an antique slot machine; and

(2) was not operated for gambling purposes while in the person's possession.

(c) *Destruction or alteration prohibited pending determination of status.* — If the defense is offered that a seized slot machine is an antique slot machine, the slot machine may not be destroyed or otherwise altered until after a final judicial determination, including review on appeal, that the defense does not apply.

(d) *Return of slot machine determined to be antique.* — If the defense applies, the person who seized the slot machine shall return the slot machine in accordance with applicable provisions of law for the return of property. (An. Code 1957, art. 27, § 264B V; 2002, ch. 26, § 2.)

REVISOR'S NOTE

This Revisor's note comprises information related to the revision by Acts 2002, ch. 26.

This section is new language derived without substantive change from former Art. 27, § 264B V.

In subsection (b) of this section, the phrase "[a] person may not be convicted" is substituted for the former phrase "[i]t shall be a defense to any prosecution" for brevity.

Also in subsection (b) of this section, the references to a "person" are substituted for the former references to a "defendant" for consistency within this article.

In subsection (c) of this section, the reference to "a final judicial determination" is substituted for the former reference to "a final court determination including review upon appeal, if any" for brevity.

Defined terms:
"Person" § 1-101
"Slot machine" § 12-301

Application of antique exemption. — Provision exempting antique slot machines from prohibition against illegal gaming devices applies to those cases in which forfeiture action was instituted on or after effective date, irrespective of when devices were seized. State v. One Hundred & Fifty-Eight Gaming Devices, 59 Md. App. 44, 474 A.2d 545 (1984), modified on other grounds, 304 Md. 404, 499 A.2d 940 (1985).

"Antique" slot machines which appear to have been of the conventional "one-arm" bandit variety, with a coin chute to facilitate direct monetary payment, are contraband per se if not excepted from seizure under the provisions of prior version of this section. State v. One Hundred & Fifty-Eight Gaming Devices, 304 Md. 404, 499 A.2d 940 (1985).

§ 12-304. Exception — Eligible organization in specified counties.

(a) *"Eligible organization" defined.* — In this section, "eligible organization" means:

(1) a nonprofit organization that:

(i) has been located in a county listed in subsection (b) of this section for at least 5 years before the organization applies for a license under subsection (e) of this section; and

(ii) is a bona fide:

1. fraternal organization;

2. religious organization; or

3. war veterans' organization; or

(2) a nonprofit organization that has been affiliated with a national fraternal organization for less than 5 years and has been located in a county listed in subsection (b) of this section for at least 50 years before the nonprofit organization applies for a license under subsection (e) of this section.

(b) *Scope of section.* — This section applies in:

(1) Caroline County;

(2) Cecil County;

(3) Dorchester County;

(4) Kent County;

(5) Queen Anne's County;

(6) Somerset County;

(7) Talbot County;

(8) Wicomico County; and

(9) Worcester County.

(c) *Ownership and operation by eligible organization allowed.* — (1) In this subsection, a console or set of affixed slot machines is not an individual slot machine.

(2) Notwithstanding any other provision of this subtitle, an eligible organization may own and operate a slot machine if the eligible organization:

(i) obtains a license under subsection (e) of this section for each slot machine;

(ii) owns each slot machine that the eligible organization operates;

(iii) owns not more than five slot machines;

(iv) locates and operates its slot machines at its principal meeting hall in the county in which the eligible organization is located;

(v) does not locate or operate its slot machines in a private commercial facility;

(vi) uses:

1. at least one-half of the gross proceeds from its slot machines for the benefit of a charity; and

2. the remainder of the proceeds from its slot machines to further the purposes of the eligible organization;

(vii) does not use any of the proceeds of the slot machine for the financial benefit of an individual; and

(viii) reports annually under affidavit to the State Comptroller:

1. the income of each slot machine; and

2. the disposition of the income from each slot machine.

(d) *Requirements for eligible use and operation.* — An eligible organization may not use or operate a slot machine unless:

(1) the slot machine is equipped with a tamperproof meter or counter that accurately records gross receipts; and

(2) the eligible organization keeps an accurate record of the gross receipts and payoffs of the slot machine.

(e) *Regulations; audits; license required.* — (1) (i) The State Comptroller shall regulate the operation of slot machines under this section.

(ii) The State Comptroller may adopt regulations to implement the requirements of this section, including requiring audits of the annual reports submitted to the State Comptroller under subsection (c)(2)(viii) of this section.

(2) Before an eligible organization may operate a slot machine under this section, the eligible organization shall obtain a license for the slot machine from the State Comptroller.

(3) (i) The State Comptroller shall:

1. charge an annual fee for each license for a machine; and

2. issue a license sticker to the applicant.

(ii) The applicant shall place the sticker on the slot machine.

(iii) The State Comptroller shall set the amount of the annual fee so that the total proceeds of the annual fee equal an amount directly related to administrative costs of the State Comptroller to regulate the operation of slot machines under this section.

(4) In the application to the State Comptroller for a license, one of the principal officers of the eligible organization shall certify under affidavit that the organization:

(i) is an eligible organization; and

(ii) will comply with this section.

(f) *Misrepresentation — Penalty.* — (1) A principal officer of the eligible organization may not intentionally misrepresent a statement of fact on the application.

(2) A person who violates this subsection is guilty of perjury and on conviction is subject to the penalty provided under Title 9, Subtitle 1 of this article.

(g) *No license for eligible organization in area of Ocean City.* — The Comptroller may not issue a license for a slot machine to an eligible organization located in Ocean City that is located east of South and North Baltimore Avenues. (An. Code 1957, art. 27, § 264B VI; 2002, ch. 26, § 2; 2003, ch. 21, § 1; 2007, ch. 645; 2011, ch. 65, § 5; ch. 315.)

REVISOR'S NOTE

This Revisor's note comprises information related to the revision by Acts 2002, ch. 26.

This section is new language derived without substantive change from former Art. 27, § 264B VI.

In subsection (c)(1) of this section, the former phrase "a console or set of affixed slot machines is not an individual slot machine" is revised to apply to the entire subsection for clarity.

In subsection (d)(2) of this section, the reference to "keep[ing]" is substituted for the former reference to "tak[ing] and maintain[ing]" for clarity and brevity.

In subsection (e)(3) of this section, the former reference to "the issuance of the license" is deleted as included in the reference to an application.

Defined terms:

"County"	§ 1-101
"Person"	§ 1-101
"Slot machine"	§ 12-301

Effect of amendments. — Chapter 315, Acts 2011, effective June 1, 2011, added (b)(9), (e)(1) and (g) and redesignated accordingly; in (c)(2)(vi)1 added "gross"; in (e)(2) substituted "State Comptroller" for "sheriff of the county in which the eligible organization plans to locate the slot machine"; in the introductory language of (e)(3)(i) substituted "State Comptroller" for "county"; in (e)(3)(i)1 deleted "of $50" after "annual fee"; rewrote (e)(3)(iii); in the introductory language of (e)(4) substituted "State Comptroller" for "sheriff"; and made related changes.

Editor's note. — Pursuant to § 5, ch. 65, Acts 2011, (e)(3) was redesignated as (e)(4) following the addition of (e)(3) by ch. 315, Acts 2011.

Section 2 ch. 361, Acts 2011, provides that "the Comptroller may not initiate any audit or reporting requirements, as authorized under § 12-304(e)(1)(ii) of the Criminal Law Article as enacted by this Act, until July 1, 2012."

§ **12-305. Exception — Distributor.**

(a) *In general.* — A person may take delivery of, possess, or transport a slot machine to demonstrate or sell the slot machine to a prospective customer who is allowed to purchase a slot machine if the person:

(1) operates with or under a distributorship contract with a manufacturer of slot machines;

(2) is registered with the United States Department of Justice as a distributor of slot machines; and

(3) has provided the Secretary of State Police with a copy of the person's current federal registration.

(b) *Violation — Penalty.* — A person who violates this section is guilty of a misdemeanor and on conviction is subject to imprisonment not exceeding 1 year or a fine of $1,000 or both for each violation. (An. Code 1957, art. 27, § 264B III, VII; 2002, ch. 26, § 2; 2010, ch. 72, § 5.)

REVISOR'S NOTE

This Revisor's note comprises information related to the revision by Acts 2002, ch. 26.

This section is new language derived without substantive change from former Art. 27, § 264B III and VII.

In the introductory language of subsection (a) of this section, the reference to "a prospective customer who is allowed" to purchase a slot machine is substituted for the former reference to "an entity lawfully permitted" to buy slot machines for clarity.

Defined terms:

"Person"	§ 1-101
"Slot machine"	§ 12-301

Editor's note. — Pursuant to § 5, ch. 72, Acts 2010, "Secretary of State Police" was substituted for "Secretary of the State Police" in (a)(3).

§ 12-306. Exception — Certain counties and municipal corporations.

(a) *"Premises" defined.* — In this section, "premises" means an improved or unimproved parcel or tract of land that is owned by:

   (1) a person; or

   (2) persons associated in a joint or common venture.

(b) *Registration and storage.* — (1) Except as provided in paragraph (2) of this subsection, in a county or municipal corporation where, before July 1, 1963, county or municipal officials licensed slot machines for operation, a person may not, as an owner, lessor, lessee, licensor, licensee, or in any other capacity, keep or operate a slot machine for any purpose in any place of business or building or on any premises.

   (2) Before disposing of a slot machine, the county commissioners or county executive of a county where a slot machine is located may require the slot machine to be:

      (i) registered in a manner appropriate to the office of county executive or county commissioners; and

      (ii) sealed against use, stored, and kept under the supervision and control of the county commissioners or county executive. (An. Code 1957, art. 27, § 264B II(B), (C); 2002, ch. 26, § 2.)

REVISOR'S NOTE

This Revisor's note comprises information related to the revision by Acts 2002, ch. 26.

This section is new language derived without substantive change from former Art. 27, § 264B II(B) and (C).

In subsection (b)(1) of this section, the phrase "county or municipal officials" is substituted for the former reference to "county commissioners or municipal authorities thereof" for brevity and consistency.

Also in subsection (b)(1) of this section, the former references to "possess[ing]" and "maintain[ing]" are deleted as included in the reference to "keep[ing]".

In subsection (b)(2) of this section, the word "require" is substituted for the former word "cause" for clarity.

In subsection (b)(2)(ii) of this section, the former reference to "possessed" is deleted as included in the reference to "kept".

Former Art. 27, § 264B II (A), which gradually phased out authorized slot machines in certain counties and municipal corporations between July 1, 1963 and June 30, 1968, is deleted as obsolete.

Defined terms:

"County"	§ 1-101
"Person"	§ 1-101
"Slot machine"	§ 12-301

§ 12-307. Change of location of slot machine.

(a) *In general.* — Because of an act of God, or condemnation or abandonment of the primary business by the owner of a business operating on the premises, a person may:

(1) remove a slot machine from any premises on which a slot machine is allowed to operate under law; and

(2) transfer the slot machine to another premises within the same county.

(b) *Restriction.* — A person who transfers a slot machine from one premises to another may not increase the total number of machines allowed by law. (An. Code 1957, art. 27, § 264C; 2002, ch. 26, § 2.)

REVISOR'S NOTE

This Revisor's note comprises information related to the revision by Acts 2002, ch. 26.

This section is new language derived without substantive change from former Art. 27, § 264C.

In subsection (a) of this section, the former phrase "as defined in § 264B of this article" is deleted as surplusage.

Also in subsection (a) of this section, the former phrase "in accordance with any existing public general or public local law" is deleted as included within the reference "under law".

Defined terms:

"County"	§ 1-101
"Person"	§ 1-101
"Slot machine"	§ 12-301

GENERAL REVISOR'S NOTE TO SUBTITLE

Former Art. 27, § 264B IV, which prohibited the charging of a license fee in certain counties until the date that a slot machine was removed, is deleted as obsolete.

TITLE 13.

GAMING — LOCAL PROVISIONS.

Subtitle 1. General Provisions.

§ 13-101. Scope of title.

(a) *Activities allowed.* — Activities conducted under this title are allowed notwithstanding the provisions of Title 12, Subtitles 1 and 2 of this article.

(b) *Issuance of commercial bingo license.* — A county may not issue a commercial bingo license under this title or under any public local law to an entity that was not licensed to conduct commercial bingo on or before June 30, 2008. (2002, ch. 26, § 2; 2004, ch. 25; 2008, ch. 474.)

REVISOR'S NOTE

This Revisor's note comprises information related to the revision by Acts 2002, ch. 26.

This section is new language added to state explicitly that which was only implicit in the former law, that the gambling activities included in this subtitle are allowed, notwithstanding the general prohibitions against gambling revised in Title 12 of this article. This title and the general provisions of Title 12, Subtitles 1 and 2 of this article are both derived from the former "Gaming" subheading of Article 27.

Editor's note. — Section 2, ch. 474, Acts 2008, as amended by ch. 661, Acts 2009, provides that "notwithstanding the provisions of Section 1 of this Act, an entity licensed to offer instant bingo under a commercial bingo license as of July 1, 2007, or by a qualified organization as defined in § 13-201 of this article on the premises of the qualified organization may continue to operate a game of instant bingo in the same manner using electronic machines until July 1, 2012, provided that:

"(a)(1) the machines have been in operation for a 1-year period ending December 31, 2007; or

"(2) the machines were in operation under a commercial bingo license as of December 31, 2007;

"(b) the entity does not operate more than the number of electronic machines operated as of February 28, 2008; and

" (c) the conduct of the gaming and operation of the machines is consistent with all other provisions of the Criminal Law Article."

Section 4, ch. 474, Acts 2008, provides that "notwithstanding any other provision of law, if any action is brought for declaratory, injunctive, or other relief to challenge the legality of any provision of this Act or any amendment made by this Act, the enforcement and implementation of this Act may not be stayed pending the disposition of the action."

Subtitle 2. Gaming events — Certain counties.

§ 13-201. Definitions.

(a) *In general.* — In this subtitle the following words have the meanings indicated.

REVISOR'S NOTE

This subsection is new language added as the standard introductory language to a definition section.

(b) *Gaming event.* — "Gaming event" means a carnival, bazaar, or raffle.

REVISOR'S NOTE

This subsection is new language added to avoid repetition.

It is based on the former references to a

"carnival, bazaar, or raffle" in former Art. 27, § 255(b)(1).

(c) *Qualified organization.* — "Qualified organization" means:
  (1) a volunteer fire company; or
  (2) a bona fide:
    (i) religious organization;
    (ii) fraternal organization;
    (iii) civic organization;
    (iv) war veterans' organization; or
    (v) charitable organization.

REVISOR'S NOTE

This subsection is new language added to avoid repetition. It is based on the former references to a "volunteer fire company or bona fide fraternal, civic, war veterans', religious or charitable organization or corporation" in former Art. 27, § 255(b)(1).

The former reference to a "corporation" is deleted as included in the references to an "organization".

(2002, ch. 26, § 2; 2003, ch. 21, § 1; ch. 462.)

REVISOR'S NOTE TO SECTION

The Revisor's notes in this section comprise information related to the revision by Acts 2002, ch. 26.

§ 13-202. Application of subtitle.

Except as otherwise provided in this title, this subtitle applies in the following counties:

(1) Allegany County;

(2) Anne Arundel County;

(3) Baltimore County;

(4) Calvert County;

(5) Caroline County;

(6) Carroll County;

(7) Dorchester County;

(8) Frederick County;

(9) Garrett County;

(10) Howard County;

(11) Prince George's County;

(12) St. Mary's County;

(13) Somerset County;

(14) Talbot County; and

(15) Washington County. (An. Code 1957, art. 27, § 255(a); 2002, ch. 26, § 2.)

REVISOR'S NOTE

This Revisor's note comprises information related to the revision by Acts 2002, ch. 26.

This section is new language derived without substantive change from former Art. 27, § 255(a).

The reference to "this subtitle" is substituted for the former reference to "this section", although this subtitle does not revise all of former Art. 27, § 255. The revision of this title separates local gaming provisions that apply in several counties from those that apply only in one county. This subtitle includes all the general provisions on local gaming events that were in former Art. 27, § 255. The other subtitles of this title include the remainder of former Art. 27, § 255, as well as provisions derived from other material on local gaming events.

The limitation "[e]xcept as otherwise provided in this title" is added to reflect the recodification of other, more specific material relating to individual counties derived from other provisions of former Art. 27, § 255 in other subtitles of this title, along with more specific material relating to individual counties derived from other provisions of the former "Gaming" subheading of Article 27. As a general rule of statutory construction, in the case of conflicting provisions, the more specific provision prevails over the more general provision. *See, e.g., Dejarnette v. Fed'l Kemper Ins. Co.*, 299 Md. 708 (1984); *Zellinger v. CDC Dev't Corp.*, 281 Md. 614 (1977).

Defined term:

"County"   § 1-101

Constitutionality. — Prior version of this section, providing exemptions from the gaming laws for certain organizations in certain counties of the State, including Washington County, does not violate equal protection. State v. Wyand, 304 Md. 721, 501 A.2d 43 (1985), cert. denied, 475 U.S. 1095, 106 S. Ct. 1492, 89 L. Ed. 2d 893 (1986).

County Commissioners of Allegany County authorized to impose tax on gambling. — Except as provided in Article XI-F, § 9 of the Maryland Constitution the General Assembly is not prohibited from authorizing the County Commissioners of Allegany County to impose a tax on gambling activities. 64 Op. Att'y Gen. 296 (1979).

§ 13-203. Gaming event without personal benefit — Allowed.

This title and Title 12 of this article do not prohibit a qualified organization from conducting a gaming event for the exclusive benefit of a qualified organization if an individual or group of individuals does not:

(1) benefit financially from the gaming event under this subtitle; or

(2) receive any of the proceeds from the gaming event under this subtitle for personal use or benefit. (An. Code 1957, art. 27, § 255(b)(1); 2002, ch. 26, § 2.)

REVISOR'S NOTE

This Revisor's note comprises information related to the revision by Acts 2002, ch. 26.

This section is new language derived without substantive change from former Art. 27, § 255(b)(1).

The reference to "[t]his title and Title 12 of this article" is substituted for the former reference to "this subtitle [sic]". Although Titles 12 and 13 of this article contain material derived, in part, from outside the former "Gaming" subheading of Article 27, the only other material contained in these titles is derived from the former "Slot Machines" subheading of Article 27. The organizations that may own and oper-ate a slot machine in specified counties are specifically set forth in Title 12, Subtitle 3 of this article and this section does not expand the class of qualified organizations that may own or operate a slot machine in any local jurisdiction. Therefore, no substantive change is made.

The references to a gaming event held "under this subtitle" are added for clarity.

In item (2) of this section, the former reference to being "paid" proceeds is deleted as included in the reference to "receiv[ing] proceeds".

Defined terms:
"Gaming event"	§ 13-201
"Qualified organization"	§ 13-201

Legislative intent. — The General Assembly unequivocally intended that gambling activities exempted under a prior version of this section not be considered or held to be lotteries within the scope of the "Lotteries" provisions of this article (see now Title 12, Subtitle 2), even though they possess elements of a lottery. American Legion, Clopper Michael Post No. 10 v. State, 294 Md. 1, 447 A.2d 842 (1982).

Prior version of this section and prior versions of §§ 13-1901 et seq. of this article were not intended to allow a profit-making entity to initiate and organize bingo games — i.e., to seek out nonprofit "sponsors" that would permit it to conduct bingo operations. 70 Op. Att'y Gen. 107 (1985).

Construction. — The exemptions in a prior version of this section from the anti-gambling statutes must be narrowly construed. 70 Op. Att'y Gen. 107 (1985).

Profit. — Any profit to a party other than the sponsoring organizations must solely derive from the reasonable and necessary expenses that the nonprofit organization incurs in operating its games. 70 Op. Att'y Gen. 107 (1985).

No personal use or benefit. — Dealers and attendants at nonprofit organizations' casino nights are not permitted to accept tips from patrons. 73 Op. Att'y Gen. 152 (1988).

Organizations that conduct casino nights in Prince George's County are not permitted to use part of the proceeds of those events to pay salaries or stipends to the organizations' officers or directors. 74 Op. Att'y Gen. 157 (1989).

Casino nights. — The statutory condition that no individual may benefit financially from gaming activity prohibits tipping of volunteer dealers and other workers, and this prohibition is applicable to casino night activities under prior versions of §§ 13-1901 et seq. of this article. State v. Crescent Cities Jaycees Found., Inc., 330 Md. 460, 624 A.2d 955 (1993).

Chance books. — Gambling activities, conducted by an American Legion Post, utilizing chance books in the form of packs of tickets and the gaming device of a jar or bowl from which those chance books were drawn were held to be within the scope of a prior version of this section. American Legion, Clopper Michael

Post No. 10 v. State, 294 Md. 1, 447 A.2d 842 (1982).

§ 13-204. Prizes and gaming devices allowed.

A qualified organization may award a prize in money or in merchandise at a gaming event using any gaming device, including:

(1) a paddle wheel;

(2) a wheel of fortune;

(3) a chance book; or

(4) bingo. (An. Code 1957, art. 27, § 255(b)(2); 2002, ch. 26, § 2.)

REVISOR'S NOTE

This Revisor's note comprises information related to the revision by Acts 2002, ch. 26.

This section is new language derived without substantive change from former Art. 27, § 255(b)(2).

The reference to "money" is substituted for the former reference to "cash" for consistency within this article.

The reference to a prize awarded "at a gaming event" is added for clarity.

The former reference to a gaming device "commonly designated as" a paddle wheel, wheel of fortune, chance book, or bingo is deleted in light of the comprehensive reference to "any gaming device".

Defined terms:
"Gaming event"   § 13-201
"Qualified organization"   § 13-201

§ 13-205. Management of gaming event.

A qualified organization that conducts a gaming event under this subtitle shall manage the gaming event personally through its members. (An. Code 1957, art. 27, § 255(b)(3); 2002, ch. 26, § 2.)

REVISOR'S NOTE

This Revisor's note comprises information related to the revision by Acts 2002, ch. 26.

This section is new language derived without substantive change from former Art. 27, § 255(b)(3).

The reference to a qualified organization that "conducts" a gaming event is added for consistency within this subtitle.

The reference to a gaming event "under this subtitle" is added for clarity.

Defined terms:
"Gaming event"   § 13-201
"Qualified organization"   § 13-201

Subtitle 3. Allegany County.

§ 13-301. Application of Subtitle 2.

Subtitle 2 of this title applies in Allegany County. (An. Code 1957, art. 27, § 255(a)(1); 2002, ch. 26, § 2; 2003, ch. 462.)

REVISOR'S NOTE

This Revisor's note comprises information related to the revision by Acts 2002, ch. 26.

This section is new language derived without substantive change from former Art. 27, § 255(a)(1).

The reference to "Subtitle 2 of this title" is substituted for the former reference to "this section" to reflect the reorganization of the general provisions on gaming events in specified counties contained in former Art. 27, § 255.

§ 13-302. Paper gaming.

(a) *"Paper gaming" defined.* — (1) In this section, "paper gaming" means a game of chance in which:

(i) prizes are awarded; and

(ii) the devices used to play the game are constructed out of paper or cardboard.

(2) "Paper gaming" includes tip jar and punchboard gaming.

(3) "Paper gaming" does not include bingo.

(b) *Applicability.* — This section applies only in Allegany County.

(c) *License requirements.* — (1) Subject to paragraphs (2) and (3) of this subsection, a person that is a for profit business or qualified organization may engage in paper gaming if the person obtains a paper gaming license that is issued by the Board of County Commissioners.

(2) If the person is a for profit business, the person shall also hold a Class A, C, or D retail alcoholic beverages license.

(3) Qualified organizations that do not have an alcoholic beverages license and fire and rescue departments may engage in paper gaming without obtaining a paper gaming license.

(d) *Sales of devices to licensees.* — A person may sell paper gaming devices to a paper gaming licensee if the person obtains a wholesale vendor's license issued by the Board of County Commissioners.

(e) *Annual fee.* — The Board of County Commissioners shall set annual fees for a paper gaming license and a wholesale vendor's license.

(f) *Quarterly lists.* — Monthly, wholesale vendor licensees shall provide a list to the Board of County Commissioners of all customers to whom they sell paper gaming products and the total number of products sold to each customer.

(g) *Gaming sticker to be displayed.* — A paper gaming licensee may not have on its premises a paper gaming device that does not display a gaming sticker.

(h) *Conformity of devices to bill of sale required.* — The Board of County Commissioners shall ensure that each retail alcoholic beverages licensee who holds a paper gaming license sells to the public the same serial-numbered paper gaming devices that are listed on the bill of sale from the wholesale vendor licensee.

(i) *Taxes.* — (1) The Board of County Commissioners may impose the following paper gaming taxes:

(i) on licensees that are qualified organizations, 10% of gross profits minus the costs of paper gaming products; and

(ii) on licensees that are for profit businesses, 40% of gross profits minus the costs of paper gaming products.

(2) The Board of County Commissioners may not impose a paper gaming tax on qualified organizations that do not have an alcoholic beverages license or fire and rescue departments that buy paper gaming devices from a licensed wholesale vendor.

(j) *Special Gaming Fund.* — (1) In this subsection, "Fund" means the Special Gaming Fund.

(2) The Board of County Commissioners may establish a Special Gaming Fund.

(3) The Fund is a special continuing, nonlapsing fund.

(4) The Fund may be used only to benefit fire and rescue departments and to pay for specified school costs.

(5) (i) The Fund consists of:

1. revenue derived from the taxation of gross profits from tip jar sales; and

2. subject to subparagraph (ii) of this paragraph, money received from other sources.

(ii) Money from the General Fund of the State or county, including any federal money, may not be transferred by budget amendment or otherwise to the Fund.

(6) The Fund shall be invested and reinvested in the same manner as other county funds.

(7) Annually the Board of County Commissioners shall:

(i) pay from the Fund all administrative costs of carrying out this section, including the hiring of additional necessary personnel; and

(ii) allocate the remaining money in the Fund as follows:

1. at least 25% but not more than 35% to fire and rescue departments; and

2. the balance to pay for school construction, school supplies, and other nonmaintenance of effort costs.

(k) *Rules and regulations.* — The Board of County Commissioners may adopt rules and regulations to administer and enforce this section.

(l) *Inspectors.* — The Board of County Commissioners may:

(1) hire one or more inspectors; and

(2) authorize each inspector to enter the premises of a licensee to ensure compliance with this section or a rule or regulation adopted under this section.

(m) *Violations; penalty.* — The Board of County Commissioners may adopt an ordinance or resolution declaring that a violation of this section or a rule or regulation adopted under this section is:

(1) a civil infraction under Article 25B, § 13C of the Code; or

(2) a misdemeanor punishable by a term of imprisonment not exceeding 30 days or a fine not exceeding $1,000 or both.

(n) *Suspension or revocation of license.* — After a hearing, if the Board of County Commissioners or a designee of the Board finds that a paper gaming licensee, a wholesale vendor licensee, or an agent of a licensee has violated this section or a rule or regulation adopted under this section, the Board may suspend or revoke the license in addition to any fine or penalty imposed under subsection (m) of this section. (2003, ch. 462; 2004, ch. 395.)

Subtitle 4. Anne Arundel County.

§ 13-401. Definitions.

(a) *In general.* — In this subtitle the following words have the meanings indicated.

REVISOR'S NOTE

This subsection is new language derived without substantive change from former Art. 27, § 255(h)(1)(i).

The reference to this "subtitle" is substituted for the former reference to this "subsection", although this subtitle is derived, in part, from material outside former Art. 27, § 255(h). Because the one term "casino event" that is both derived from that former subsection and is defined in this section is used only in material derived from former Art. 27, § 255(h), no substantive change results.

(b) *Casino event.* — (1) "Casino event" means any event that involves a card game, dice game, or roulette game.

(2) "Casino event" does not include a card game or dice game that is played for tokens for which no cash prize is offered or awarded.

REVISOR'S NOTE

This subsection is new language derived without substantive change from former Art. 27, § 255(h)(1)(iii).

(c) *Gaming event.* — "Gaming event" means a carnival, bazaar, raffle, or other organized gaming event.

REVISOR'S NOTE

This subsection is new language added to avoid repetition of the phrase "carnival, bazaar, raffle, or other organized gaming event" and for consistency within this title.

(An. Code 1957, art. 27, § 255(h)(1)(i), (iii); 2002, ch. 26, § 2.)

REVISOR'S NOTE TO SECTION

The Revisor's notes in this section comprise information related to the revision by Acts 2002, ch. 26.

§ 13-402. Scope and application of subtitle.

(a) *Scope of subtitle.* — This subtitle applies only in Anne Arundel County.

(b) *Application of Subtitle 2.* — Subtitle 2 of this title applies in Anne Arundel County. (An. Code 1957, art. 27, § 255(a)(2); 2002, ch. 26, § 2.)

REVISOR'S NOTE

This Revisor's note comprises information related to the revision by Acts 2002, ch. 26.

Subsection (a) of this section is new language added for clarity.

Subsection (b) of this section is new language

derived without substantive change from former Art. 27, § 255(a)(2).

§ 13-403. Gaming events.

(a) *"Qualified member" defined.* — "Qualified member" means a person who:

(1) obtained a membership in an organization in accordance with the charter and bylaws of the organization; and

(2) has been a member for at least 12 months immediately before the gaming event.

(b) *In general.* — A gaming device that is used at a gaming event shall be operated:

(1) by qualified members of the organization or qualified members of other organizations allowed to operate gaming devices under this section; and

(2) without the assistance of professional gaming device operators.

(c) *Compensation prohibited.* — (1) A person may not receive compensation from an organization for managing or operating a gaming device at a gaming event.

(2) Another organization that operates a gaming device under this subtitle may receive compensation from an organization for managing or operating a gaming device at a gaming event.

(d) *Accounting required.* — Each organization conducting a gaming event shall submit to the Department of Inspections and Permits, in a manner determined by the county, a report under oath for each gaming event that provides:

(1) an accounting of all funds received; and

(2) a listing of the names, addresses, ages, and dates of membership of each individual who managed or operated a gaming device at the gaming event, including a statement that the individual is a qualified member of the organization.

(e) *Scope of section.* — This section may not be construed to:

(1) limit or restrict the authority of the county to regulate, license, and designate the type of amusement or gaming devices that may be operated in the county; or

(2) amend or apply to the laws pertaining to raffles in the county under § 13-405 of this subtitle. (An. Code 1957, art. 27, § 255(h)(1)(ii), (2); 2002, ch. 26, § 2.)

REVISOR'S NOTE

This Revisor's note comprises information related to the revision by Acts 2002, ch. 26.

This section is new language derived without substantive change from former Art. 27, § 255(h)(1)(ii) and (2).

In subsection (b) of this section, the former phrase "[t]his subsection applies only in Anne Arundel County" is deleted in light of § 13-402(a) of this subtitle to the same effect.

In subsection (e) of this section, the former reference to "casino events" is deleted as obsolete. *See* Revisor's Note to § 13-404 of this subtitle.

Defined terms:

"Gaming event"	§ 13-401
"Person"	§ 1-101

§ 13-404. Casino events — Prohibited.

A person may not conduct a casino event in the county. (An. Code 1957, art. 27, § 255(h)(4); 2002, ch. 26, § 2.)

REVISOR'S NOTE

This Revisor's note comprises information related to the revision by Acts 2002, ch. 26.

This section is new language derived without substantive change from former Art. 27, § 255(h)(4).

Former Art. 27, § 255(h)(3), which established the requirements for an eligible organization to operate a casino night in Anne Arundel County before October 1, 1997, is deleted as obsolete.

Defined terms:
"Casino event"	§ 13-401
"Person"	§ 1-101

§ 13-405. Raffles.

(a) *In general.* — A bona fide fraternal, civic, war veterans', or charitable organization, or a volunteer fire company may conduct a raffle in the county for the benefit of charity if:

(1) the raffle is conducted to further the purposes of the organization; and

(2) no individual or group of individuals financially benefits from the holding of the raffle or receives any of the proceeds from the raffle for personal use.

(b) *Award of prizes.* — Prizes may be awarded by the use of paddle wheels, wheels of fortune, or chance books. (An. Code 1957, art. 27, § 248; 2002, ch. 26, § 2.)

REVISOR'S NOTE

This Revisor's note comprises information related to the revision by Acts 2002, ch. 26.

This section is new language derived without substantive change from former Art. 27, § 248.

Subsection (a) of this section is restated as an affirmative grant of authority to certain qualified organizations to conduct raffles for specified purposes for clarity.

In subsection (a) of this section, the former limitation "[n]othing in this subtitle [sic] shall be construed to make it unlawful" is deleted in light of § 13-101 of this title and the reorganization of material derived from the former

"Gaming" subheading of Article 27 in Titles 12 and 13 of this article.

Also in subsection (a) of this section, the former reference to a "corporation" is deleted as included in the reference to an "organization".

Also in subsection (a) of this section, the former reference to "hold[ing]" a raffle is deleted as included in the reference to "conduct[ing]" a raffle.

Also in subsection (a) of this section, the former reference to "be[ing] paid" any of the proceeds is deleted as included in the reference to "receiv[ing]" any of the proceeds.

Bingo not lottery. — Bingo is not a lottery. Bender v. Arundel Arena, Inc., 248 Md. 181, 236 A.2d 7 (1967).

§ 13-406. Political fundraisers — Paddle wheels.

(a) *In general.* — Notwithstanding any other provision of this article, a political committee, as defined in § 1-101 of the Election Law Article, may conduct a fundraiser at which prizes of merchandise or money are awarded in a game or spin using a paddle wheel or wheel of fortune.

(b) *Prizes.* — A political committee may award a merchandise or money prize under this section that does not exceed the amount otherwise allowed for a prize in the county. (An. Code 1957, art. 27, § 261C-1; 2002, ch. 26, § 2; ch. 213, § 7.)

SPECIAL REVISOR'S NOTE

This Special Revisor's note comprises information related to the revision by Acts 2002, ch. 26 and other chapters amending this section from the 2002 Legislative Session.

As enacted by Ch. 26, Acts of 2002, this section was new language derived without substantive change from former Art. 27, § 261C-1(b) and, as it related to political fundraisers in Anne Arundel County, (a). However, Ch. 213, § 7, Acts of 2002, substituted the reference to "§ 1-101 of the Election Law Article" for the reference to "Article 33, § 1-101 of the Code" enacted by Ch. 26 in subsection (a) of this

section. Chapter 213, § 8, provided that § 7 would take effect January 1, 2003, to reflect the delayed effective date of the Election Law Article enacted by Ch. 291, Acts of 2002.

In subsection (a) of this section, the former reference to a "bona fide" organization was deleted by Ch. 26 as surplusage.

Also in subsection (a) of this section, the reference to a "political committee, as defined in Article 33, § 1-101 of the Code" was substituted by Ch. 26 for the former reference to a "politically partisan organization or political committee as defined in Article 33 of the Code" for consistency with Article 33.

Record keeping. — The proceeds of gaming wheels are not excused from the record keeping requirements in Article 33, § 26-7(a) [now § 13-2240 of the Election Law Article]. However, those who have already held gaming events and who in good faith concluded that they were authorized to conduct the event in the traditional way — using cash, without individual records — should not be subject to penalty. 71 Op. Att'y Gen. 120 (1986).

§ 13-407. Bingo.

(a) *"Bingo" defined.* — In this section, "bingo" includes the game of instant bingo.

(b) *Qualified organizations authorized.* — A bona fide religious, fraternal, or charitable organization, or a volunteer fire company operating in a community that does not have a paid fire department, may conduct bingo in the county:

(1) for the benefit of charity in the county; or

(2) to further the purposes of the organization. (An. Code 1957, art. 27, § 247(a), (c); 2002, ch. 26, § 2.)

REVISOR'S NOTE

This Revisor's note comprises information related to the revision by Acts 2002, ch. 26.

This section is new language derived without substantive change from former Art. 27, § 247(c) and, as it related to bingo in Anne Arundel County, (a).

Subsection (b) of this section is restated as an affirmative grant of authority to certain qualified organizations to operate bingo for specified purposes for clarity.

In subsection (b) of this section, the former limitation "[n]othing in this subtitle [sic] shall

be construed to make it unlawful" is deleted in light of § 13-101 of this title and the reorganization of material derived from the former "Gaming" subheading of Article 27 in Titles 12 and 13 of this article.

Also in subsection (b) of this section, the former references to "corporations" are deleted as included in the references to an "organization".

Also in subsection (b) of this section, the former reference to "operat[ing]" bingo is deleted as included in the reference to "conduct[ing]" bingo.

Bingo not lottery. — Bingo is not a lottery.
Bender v. Arundel Arena, Inc., 248 Md. 181, 236
A.2d 7 (1967).

§ 13-408. Unauthorized gaming event.

(a) *Prohibited.* — A person may not knowingly operate or attempt to operate a gaming event in the county in violation of § 13-403 or § 13-404 of this subtitle.

(b) *Penalty.* — A person who violates this section is guilty of a misdemeanor and on conviction is subject to imprisonment not exceeding 6 months or a fine not exceeding $1,000 or both. (An. Code 1957, art. 27, § 255(h)(5); 2002, ch. 26, § 2.)

REVISOR'S NOTE

This Revisor's note comprises information related to the revision by Acts 2002, ch. 26.

This section is new language derived without substantive change from former Art. 27, § 255(h)(5).

In subsection (a) of this section, the reference to "§ 13-403 or § 13-404 of this subtitle" is substituted for the former reference to "this subsection" to reflect the reorganization of material derived from former Art. 27, § 255(h).

Also in subsection (a) of this section, the former reference to an "association, or corporation" is deleted as included in the defined term "person". *See* § 1-101 of this article.

Defined terms:
"Gaming event"	§ 13-401
"Person"	§ 1-101

Subtitle 5. Baltimore City.

§ 13-501. Definitions.

(a) *In general.* — In this subtitle the following words have the meanings indicated.

REVISOR'S NOTE

This subsection is new language added as the standard introductory language to a definition section.

(b) *Commissioner.* — "Commissioner" means the Baltimore City Police Commissioner.

REVISOR'S NOTE

This subsection is new language added for brevity in repeated references to the Baltimore City Police Commissioner.

(c) *Gaming event.* — "Gaming event" means a carnival, bazaar, or raffle.

REVISOR'S NOTE

This subsection is new language added to avoid repetition of the phrase "carnival, bazaar, or raffle" and for consistency within this title.

(d) *Raffle.* — "Raffle" means one or more drawings from a single series of chances sold from chance books.

REVISOR'S NOTE

This subsection is new language derived without substantive change from former Art. 27, § 257(a)(4).

Because the term "raffle" defined in this subsection is used only in the revision of material in which it originally appeared, its application to the entire subtitle does not constitute a substantive change.

The reference to chances sold "from" chance books is substituted for the former reference to chances sold "by means of" chance books for brevity and clarity.

(An. Code 1957, art. 27, § 257(a)(4); 2002, ch. 26, § 2.)

REVISOR'S NOTE TO SECTION

The Revisor's notes in this section comprise information related to the revision by Acts 2002, ch. 26.

§ 13-502. Scope of subtitle.

This subtitle applies only in Baltimore City. (2002, ch. 26, § 2.)

REVISOR'S NOTE

This Revisor's note comprises information related to the revision by Acts 2002, ch. 26.

This section is new language added to clarify the scope of this subtitle.

§ 13-503. Qualified organizations.

(a) *Permit required.* — Before an organization listed in subsection (b) of this section may operate a gaming event, the organization shall obtain a permit from the commissioner.

(b) *Qualifications.* — (1) An organization that meets the conditions of paragraph (2) of this subsection may conduct a gaming event for the benefit of any of the following listed organizations if the organization is a bona fide:

(i) religious organization;

(ii) fraternal organization;

(iii) civic organization;

(iv) veterans' hospital;

(v) amateur athletic organization in which all playing members are under the age of 18 years; or

(vi) charitable organization.

(2) An organization conducting a gaming event shall:

(i) be located in Baltimore City; and

(ii) spend a majority of the organization's funds in Baltimore City for:

1. fraternal purposes;

2. civic purposes;

3. purposes related to a veterans' hospital;

4. purposes related to amateur athletics; or

5. charitable purposes.

(c) *Application.* — (1) Before the commissioner may issue a permit, the commissioner shall review the character of the organization applying for the permit to ascertain that the organization meets the requirements of §§ 13-503 through 13-505 of this subtitle.

(2) The commissioner shall make any application for a permit and the action taken by the commissioner on that application a matter of public record.

(d) *Permit.* — (1) The permit shall state that the gaming event shall be managed and operated personally only by members of the organization obtaining the permit.

(2) The permit is not transferable.

(e) *Limitations.* — An organization conducting a gaming event in Baltimore City may not allow an individual or group of individuals to:

(1) benefit financially from the gaming event; or

(2) receive any of the proceeds of the gaming event for personal use or benefit. (An. Code 1957, art. 27, § 257(a)(1), (5), (6), (b); 2002, ch. 26, § 2.)

REVISOR'S NOTE

This Revisor's note comprises information related to the revision by Acts 2002, ch. 26.

This section is new language derived without substantive change from former Art. 27, § 257(a)(1), (5), and (6) and (b).

Subsection (b) of this section is restated as an affirmative grant of authority to certain qualified organizations to operate a gaming event for clarity.

In subsection (b) of this section, the former limitation "[n]othing in this subtitle [sic] shall be construed to make it unlawful" is deleted in light of § 13-101 of this title and the reorganization of material derived from the former "Gaming" subheading of Article 27 in Titles 12 and 13 of this article.

In subsection (b)(1)(vi) of this section, the former reference to a charitable "corporation" is deleted as included in the reference to a charitable "organization".

In subsection (c)(2) of this section, the reference to "[t]he commissioner" is added as implicit in the requirement that the application and the action taken by the commissioner on the application be made public.

In subsection (e) of this section, the former phrase "or be paid" is deleted as included in the reference to "receiv[ing]" proceeds.

The Criminal Law Article Review Committee notes, for the consideration of the General Assembly, that although subsection (b)(1)(i) of this section allows a "religious" organization to conduct a gaming event, the proceeds may be spent only on purposes, listed in subsection (b)(2)(ii) of this section, that do not explicitly include "religious" purposes.

The Criminal Law Article Review Committee also notes, for the consideration of the General Assembly, that in subsection (e) of this section, the scope of liability of an individual or organization that improperly receives proceeds of a gaming event is unclear.

Defined terms:
"Commissioner" § 13-501
"Gaming event" § 13-501

§ 13-504. Prizes allowed — Paddle wheels and filmed horse racing.

An organization conducting a gaming event may award a prize of money or merchandise to any individual in any amount in one game or spin using:

(1) a paddle wheel or wheel of fortune; or

(2) a film of a horse race. (An. Code 1957, art. 27, § 257(a)(2); 2002, ch. 26, § 2.)

REVISOR'S NOTE

This Revisor's note comprises informa-tion related to the revision by Acts 2002, ch. 26.

This section is new language derived without substantive change from former Art. 27, § 257(a)(2).

In this section and throughout this subtitle, the references to a prize of "money" are substi-tuted for the former references to a "cash" prize for consistency within this article.

The reference to an "organization" is added for clarity in light of the authority to perform the actions authorized under this section.

Defined term:
"Gaming event"   § 13-501

§ 13-505. Raffles.

(a) *Limitation on prizes.* — A permit holder may award prizes in merchan-dise and money in a raffle in any amount.

(b) *Limitation on number.* — A permit holder may not conduct more than 12 raffles in a calendar year. (An. Code 1957, art. 27, § 257(a)(3); 2002, ch. 26, § 2.)

REVISOR'S NOTE

This Revisor's note comprises informa-tion related to the revision by Acts 2002, ch. 26.

This section is new language derived without substantive change from former Art. 27, § 257(a)(3).

In subsection (a) of this section, the reference to a "permit holder" is added to clarify the object of the authorization.

In subsection (b) of this section, the reference to a "permit holder" is substituted for the for-mer reference to an "organization" for clarity.

Defined term:
"Raffle"   § 13-501

§ 13-506. Political fundraisers.

(a) *In general.* — Notwithstanding any other provisions of this title or Title 12 of this article, a political committee as defined in § 1-101 of the Election Law Article may conduct a fundraiser at which prizes of merchandise or money are awarded in a game or spin using a paddle wheel or wheel of fortune.

(b) *Prizes.* — A political committee may award a prize of merchandise or money at a fundraiser that does not exceed the amount otherwise allowed for a prize in Baltimore City. (An. Code 1957, art. 27, § 261C; 2002, ch. 26, § 2; ch. 213, § 7.)

SPECIAL REVISOR'S NOTE

This Special Revisor's note comprises information related to the revision by Acts 2002, ch. 26 and other chapters amending this section from the 2002 Legislative Ses-sion.

As enacted by Ch. 26, Acts of 2002, this section was new language derived without sub-stantive change from former Art. 27, § 261C. However, Ch. 213, § 7, Acts of 2002, substi-tuted the reference to "§ 1-101 of the Election Law Article" for the reference to "Article 33, § 1-101 of the Code" enacted by Ch. 26 in subsection (a) of this section. Chapter 213, § 8, provided that § 7 would take effect January 1, 2003, to reflect the delayed effective date of the Election Law Article enacted by Ch. 291, Acts of 2002.

In subsection (a) of this section, the reference to a "political committee" was substituted by Ch. 26 for the former reference to a "politically partisan organization" for consistency with current usage in Article 33 of the Code. Similarly, in subsection (b) of this section, the reference to a "political committee" was added by Ch. 26 for clarity.

Also in subsection (a) of this section, the former reference to a "bona fide" political organization was deleted by Ch. 26 as surplusage.

Also in subsection (a) of this section, the former phrase "by such devices commonly known as" was deleted by Ch. 26 as surplusage.

Also in subsection (a) of this section, the reference to "this title or Title 12 of this article" was substituted by Ch. 26 for the former reference to this "article" to reflect the reorganization of material relating to gambling and gaming derived from former Article 27 in this revision.

Record keeping. — The proceeds of gaming wheels are not excused from the record keeping requirements in Article 33, § 26-7(a) [now Article 33, § 13-240 of the Election Law Article]. However, those who have already held gaming events and who in good faith concluded that they were authorized to conduct the event in the traditional way — using cash, without individual records — should not be subject to penalty. 71 Op. Att'y Gen. 120 (1986).

§ 13-507. Bingo — In general.

(a) *Scope of section and § 13-509.* — This section and § 13-509 of this subtitle also apply to games of instant bingo.

(b) *Permit required.* — Before an organization listed in subsection (c) or (d) of this section may conduct bingo in Baltimore City, the organization shall obtain a permit to do so from the commissioner.

(c) *Qualified organizations.* — An organization that meets the conditions of subsection (i)(1) of this section may conduct bingo in Baltimore City if the organization is a bona fide:

(1) religious organization;

(2) fraternal organization;

(3) patriotic organization;

(4) educational organization; or

(5) charitable organization.

(d) *Qualified organizations — Alternative qualifications.* — An organization that meets the conditions of subsection (i)(2) of this section may conduct bingo in Baltimore City if the organization is:

(1) devoted exclusively to religious, charitable, or educational purposes;

(2) a service organization;

(3) a fraternal organization; or

(4) a veterans' organization.

(e) *Application.* — (1) Before the commissioner may issue a permit, the commissioner shall review the character of the organization applying for the permit to ascertain that the organization meets the requirements of this section.

(2) The organization applying for the permit shall pay the permit fee set in subsection (g) of this section.

(3) An application for a permit and the action taken by the commissioner on that application are public records.

(f) *Permit.* — The commissioner may issue a permit for:

(1) 1 day; or

(2) a period exceeding 1 day and not exceeding 12 months.

(g) *Permit fees.* — Except as allowed under subsection (h)(1) of this section, the commissioner shall collect from each permit holder, to cover the costs of administering the Baltimore City bingo laws, a permit fee not exceeding:

(1) $10 for each day on which bingo may be conducted;

(2) $750 for a 3-month period; or

(3) $3,000 for a 12-month period.

(h) *Special annual permit.* — (1) The commissioner may collect a special annual permit fee of $5 for a nonprofit organization or nonprofit corporation to conduct, over 1 year, a number of bingo games for which, for each game:

(i) the value of any prize of merchandise or money is not more than $5; and

(ii) not more than 100 individuals play.

(2) The commissioner may revoke a special annual permit for cause.

(i) *Limitations.* — (1) An organization conducting bingo in Baltimore City under subsection (c) of this section:

(i) except as provided in subsection (d) of this section, may not offer or award, in any game:

1. a money prize of more than $45; or

2. a prize of merchandise worth more than $45; and

(ii) after reimbursing any costs incurred in conducting bingo for personnel, supplies, equipment, and other expenses, shall use the entire proceeds for:

1. charitable purposes; or

2. to further the purposes of an organization listed in subsection (c) of this section.

(2) An organization conducting bingo in Baltimore City under subsection (d) of this section:

(i) may not use the net proceeds to benefit a stockholder or member of the organization;

(ii) after reimbursing any costs incurred in conducting bingo for personnel, supplies, equipment, and other expenses, shall use the net proceeds:

1. solely for charitable purposes; or

2. to further the purposes of an organization listed in subsection (d) of this section; and

(iii) shall limit prizes of money or merchandise to a value not exceeding:

1. $5,000 for the total of all prizes;

2. $75 for the total of all door prizes;

3. $45 for each of not more than five early bird games;

4. $75 for each of not more than 19 regular games;

5. $150 for the starting prize of one regular game with a jackpot, with nightly increases not exceeding $75 and a consolation prize not exceeding $75;

6. $150 for each of not more than four regular special games;

7. 50% of the proceeds for each of not more than four split-the-pot games;

8. 100% of the proceeds for not more than one winner-take-all game;

9. $3,000 for a jackpot game which starts at 50 numbers and adds one number every second night;

10. if the jackpot is not won, $375 for a consolation prize for any jackpot game;

11. $300 for the first jackpot game in a buildup jackpot game which starts at $300 and 50 numbers and adds one number and $75 each night; and

12. if the jackpot is not won, $225 for the consolation prize for any buildup jackpot game.

(3) A bingo permit holder issued a permit under either subsection (c) or (d) of this section may not conduct bingo:

(i) in a restaurant or tavern where alcoholic beverages are sold;

(ii) in a permanent place of amusement or entertainment; or

(iii) on Sunday, except by a bona fide religious organization that conducts bingo on property owned or leased by the organization. (An. Code 1957, art. 27, § 260; 2002, ch. 26, § 2; ch. 572; 2003, ch. 21, § 1.)

SPECIAL REVISOR'S NOTE

This Special Revisor's note comprises information related to the revision by Acts 2002, ch. 26 and other chapters amending this section from the 2002 Legislative Session.

As enacted by Ch. 26, Acts of 2002, this section was new language derived without substantive change from former Art. 27, § 260(a), (b), and (c)(2) and the first through sixth sentences of (1). However, Ch. 572, Acts of 2002, amended subsection (i)(2)(iii)1 of this section by increasing the total prize limit to "$5,000" from the original limit of "$4,000".

Throughout this section, the former references to a "corporation" were deleted by Ch. 26 as included in the references to an "organization".

In subsection (a) of this section, the reference to "[t]his section and § 13-509 of this subtitle" was substituted by Ch. 26 for the former reference to "this section" to reflect the reorganization of material relating to bingo in this revision.

In subsections (c) and (d) of this section, the former references to "operat[ing]" were deleted

by Ch. 26 as included in the reference "conduct-[ing]".

In subsection (h)(1)(ii) of this section, the reference to "individuals play[ing]" was substituted by Ch. 26 for the former reference to "participants" for clarity, since arguably the individuals conducting the bingo game also participate in the game in some capacity.

In subsection (i)(2) of this section, the reference to "net proceeds" was substituted by Ch. 26 for the former references to "net earnings" and "entire proceeds, excluding costs incurred for" for clarity, brevity, and consistency.

In subsection (i)(2)(iii) of this section, the reference to "a value not exceeding" a specified amount was added by Ch. 26 for clarity, since prizes of merchandise may be awarded.

In subsection (i)(3)(i) of this section, the word "regular", which formerly modified the phrase "restaurant or tavern", was deleted by Ch. 26 as surplusage.

Defined term:
"Commissioner" § 13-501

Bingo not lottery. — Bingo is not a lottery. Bender v. Arundel Arena, Inc., 248 Md. 181, 236 A.2d 7 (1967).

§ 13-508. Bingo — Social club.

Notwithstanding § 13-507 of this subtitle, an organization may conduct bingo if:

(1) the membership of the organization consists only of individuals who are at least 60 years old;

(2) the organization was formed primarily for social purposes;

(3) all proceeds of the games of bingo are used only to further the purposes of the organization; and

(4) the organization complies with the permit procedures and conditions imposed under § 13-507 of this subtitle. (An. Code 1957, art. 27, § 260A; 2002, ch. 26, § 2.)

REVISOR'S NOTE

This Revisor's note comprises information related to the revision by Acts 2002, ch. 26.

This section is new language derived without substantive change from former Art. 27, § 260A.

In item (3) of this section, the word "all" is substituted for the former phrase "the entire".

The second sentence of former Art. 27, § 260A(b), which provided that nothing in the provisions of the former "Gaming" subheading of Article 27 may be construed to defeat the intent of former § 260A, is deleted as surplusage.

The Criminal Law Article Review Committee notes, for the consideration of the General Assembly, that this section raises constitutional concerns under the federal and State constitutions regarding equal protection, in that it establishes a class of organizations based on the age of membership. The rational basis for this classification is unclear.

§ 13-509. Bingo — Regulations.

The commissioner may adopt regulations reasonably necessary to administer § 13-507 of this subtitle. (An. Code 1957, art. 27, § 260(c)(1); 2002, ch. 26, § 2.)

REVISOR'S NOTE

This Revisor's note comprises information related to the revision by Acts 2002, ch. 26.

This section is new language derived without substantive change from the seventh sentence of former Art. 27, § 260(c)(1).

Defined term:
"Commissioner"   § 13-501

§ 13-510. Unauthorized bazaar or raffle.

(a) *Prohibited.* — A person may not knowingly conduct or attempt to conduct a bazaar or raffle in violation of §§ 13-503 through 13-505 of this subtitle.

(b) *Penalty.* — A person who violates this section is guilty of a misdemeanor and on conviction is subject to imprisonment not exceeding 1 year or a fine not exceeding $1,000 or both. (An. Code 1957, art. 27, § 257(c); 2002, ch. 26, § 2.)

REVISOR'S NOTE

This Revisor's note comprises information related to the revision by Acts 2002, ch. 26.

This section is new language derived without substantive change from former Art. 27, § 257(c).

In subsection (a) of this section, the reference to "conduct[ing]" a bazaar or raffle is substituted for the former reference to "operat[ing]" for consistency within this subtitle.

In subsection (b) of this section, the reference to being "guilty of a misdemeanor" is added to state expressly that which was only implied in the former law. In this State, any crime that was not a felony at common law and has not been declared a felony by statute, is considered to be a misdemeanor. *See State v. Canova*, 278 Md. 483, 490 (1976); *Bowser v. State*, 136 Md. 342, 345 (1920); *Dutton v. State*, 123 Md. 373, 378 (1914); and *Williams v. State*, 4 Md. App. 342, 347 (1968).

Also in subsection (b) of this section, the former phrase "in the discretion of the court" is deleted as implicit in the establishment of maximum penalties.

Defined terms:
"Person"   § 1-101
"Raffle"   § 13-501

Subtitle 6. Baltimore County.

§ 13-601. "Gaming event" defined.

In this subtitle, "gaming event" means a carnival, bazaar, or raffle. (2002, ch. 26, § 2.)

REVISOR'S NOTE

This Revisor's note comprises information related to the revision by Acts 2002, ch. 26.

This section is new language added to avoid repetition of the phrase "carnival, bazaar, or raffle" and for consistency within this title.

§ 13-602. Scope and application of subtitle.

(a) *Scope of subtitle.* — This subtitle applies only in Baltimore County.

(b) *Application of Subtitle 2.* — Subtitle 2 of this title applies in Baltimore County to:

(1) except as provided in § 13-606 of this subtitle, bingo;

(2) instant bingo;

(3) a bona fide amateur athletic organization in which all playing members are under the age of 18 years;

(4) a bona fide veterans' hospital; and

(5) a bona fide veterans' organization. (An. Code 1957, art. 27, § 255(a)(3), (f)(2), (3); 2002, ch. 26, § 2; 2006, ch. 616.)

REVISOR'S NOTE

This Revisor's note comprises information related to the revision by Acts 2002, ch. 26.

Subsection (a) of this section is new language added for clarity.

Subsection (b) of this section is new language derived without substantive change from former Art. 27, § 255(f)(2) and (3) and (a)(3).

Former Art. 27, § 252(m), which provided for the regulation of instant bingo in Baltimore County, is deleted in light of the reorganization of material in this revision.

§ 13-603. Gaming events and casino events — In general.

(a) *Permit required.* — Before an organization listed in subsection (b) of this section may operate a gaming event or casino event, the organization shall obtain a permit from the Department of Permits and Development Management.

(b) *Qualified organizations.* — (1) An organization that meets the conditions of paragraph (2) of this subsection may conduct a gaming event or casino event if the organization is a bona fide:

(i) religious organization;

(ii) fraternal organization;

(iii) civic organization, including:

1. a hunting organization;

2. a social organization; or

3. a sporting organization;

    (iv) volunteer fire organization;

    (v) veterans' organization;

    (vi) veterans' hospital;

    (vii) amateur athletic organization; or

    (viii) charitable organization.

    (2) An organization that conducts a gaming event or casino event under this section shall spend a majority of the net proceeds from the gaming event or casino event for the following in the county:

    (i) purposes that benefit religious purposes;

    (ii) fraternal purposes;

    (iii) civic purposes;

    (iv) volunteer fire operations;

    (v) purposes that benefit veterans;

    (vi) purposes that benefit a veterans' hospital;

    (vii) purposes related to amateur athletics; or

    (viii) charitable purposes.

    (c) *Permit terms.* — (1) A permit to conduct a gaming event or casino event shall provide that only the members of the permit holder may manage the gaming event or casino event.

    (2) A permit is not transferable.

    (d) *Conditions and limitations.* — (1) An organization that obtains a permit may award a prize of money or merchandise using:

    (i) a paddle wheel;

    (ii) a wheel of fortune;

    (iii) a chance book;

    (iv) bingo; or

    (v) any other gaming device except:

      1. a card game;

      2. a dice game; or

      3. roulette.

    (2) Except as provided in § 13-604 of this subtitle, a person may not:

    (i) operate a card game, a dice game, or roulette; or

    (ii) conduct a casino event.

    (3) An organization that obtains a permit shall ensure that:

    (i) an individual or group of individuals does not benefit financially from the holding of the gaming event;

    (ii) an individual or group of individuals does not receive any of the proceeds of the gaming event for personal use or benefit; and

    (iii) the gaming event is managed personally by the members of the permit holder. (An. Code 1957, art. 27, § 255(b)(1), (3), (f)(1), (4), (5)(i); 2002, ch. 26, § 2; 2003, ch. 21, § 1.)

REVISOR'S NOTE

This Revisor's note comprises information related to the revision by Acts 2002, ch. 26.

This section is new language derived without substantive change from former Art. 27,

§ 255(b)(3), (f)(1), (4), and (5)(i) and the second sentence of (b)(1) as it related to limits and conditions of permits.

    In subsection (a) of this section, the phrase "from the Department of Permits and Development Management" is added to indicate the source of the permit.

In subsections (b) and (d) of this section, the former references to a "corporation" are deleted as included in the comprehensive references to an "organization".

In subsection (b)(2) of this section, the reference to "conduct[ing]" an event is substituted for the former reference to "operating" for consistency throughout this subtitle.

In subsection (c) of this section, the former reference to "personally" managing an event is deleted as implicit in the restriction to operations by the listed individuals.

In subsection (d)(1) and (2) of this section, the former references to "Baltimore County" are deleted in light of the scope provision of § 13-602(a) of this subtitle.

In subsection (d)(1) of this section, the reference to "money" is substituted for the former reference to "cash" for consistency within this article.

Also in subsection (d)(1) of this section, the former phrase "notwithstanding the provisions of subsection (b) of this section" is deleted as included in the reference to the application of "Subtitle 2 of this title" in § 13-602(b) of this subtitle.

Also in subsection (d)(1) of this section, the former reference to "paragraph (4) of this subsection" is deleted in light of the reorganization of material in this revision.

Also in subsection (d)(1) of this section, the former reference to events "commonly designated" as casino events is deleted as surplusage.

In subsection (d)(2) of this section, the reference to a "person" is added to indicate who must comply with the prohibition.

Also in subsection (d)(2) of this section, the reference to a "casino event" is substituted for the former reference to "casino nights" for consistency within this subtitle.

Defined terms:

| "Gaming event" | § 13-601 |
| "Person" | § 1-101 |

§ 13-604. Casino events.

(a) *In general.* — Subject to subsections (b) and (c) of this section, an organization may conduct:

(1) one casino event that includes a card game during each calendar month; and

(2) one casino event that includes roulette during each calendar year.

(b) *Qualifications.* — To conduct a casino event under subsection (a) of this section, an organization shall be a bona fide:

(1) religious organization;

(2) fraternal organization;

(3) civic organization, including:

(i) a hunting organization;

(ii) a social organization; or

(iii) a sporting organization;

(4) volunteer fire company;

(5) war veterans' organization; or

(6) charitable organization.

(c) *Conditions and limitations.* — (1) A permit holder for a casino event that includes a card game or roulette shall ensure that:

(i) the event is conducted in accordance with § 13-603(d)(3) of this subtitle;

(ii) a parent, subsidiary, or affiliate of the organization sponsoring the event has not sponsored a casino event within the calendar month; and

(iii) the casino event is conducted between 4 p.m. and 1 a.m.

(2) A person that holds a casino event that includes a card game or roulette may not:

(i) offer or award a money prize to a player of the card game or roulette game;

(ii) allow a player to bet more than $10 in any one game within the calendar month;

(iii) exchange tokens used in wagering for an item of merchandise that is worth more than $1,000; or

(iv) exchange merchandise that was received for tokens that were used in wagering for:

    1. money; or

    2. an item of merchandise having a value that is different from the fair retail market value of the item of merchandise that was received for the tokens.

(3) (i) Within 60 days after holding a casino event that includes a card game or roulette, the holder of the permit for the event shall submit to the Department of Permits and Development Management a financial report that lists the receipts and expenditures for the casino event.

(ii) Before the permit holder submits the report to the Department of Permits and Development Management, the permit holder shall submit the report to the county police department for review.

(d) *Regulations.* — (1) The Department of Permits and Development Management shall adopt regulations to govern:

(i) the issuing of a permit to conduct a casino event; and

(ii) the conduct and management of a casino event in a manner designed to prevent fraud and protect the public.

(2) The regulations shall require that a separate permit be issued for each casino event to be conducted. (An. Code 1957, art. 27, § 255(f)(1), (5)(ii), (iii); 2002, ch. 26, § 2; 2006, ch. 616.)

REVISOR'S NOTE

This Revisor's note comprises information related to the revision by Acts 2002, ch. 26.

This section is new language derived without substantive change from former Art. 27, § 255(f)(1) and (5)(ii) and (iii).

In subsection (b)(1)(ii) of this section, the former reference to a "corporation" is deleted as included in the reference to an "organization".

In subsection (b)(2) of this section, the restriction on allowing "a player to bet more than $10 in any one game" is substituted for the former phrase "[n]o game exceeds a $10 limit" for clarity.

In subsection (b)(2)(i) of this section, the reference to a "money" prize is substituted for the former reference to a "cash" prize for consistency within this article.

In subsections (b)(3) and (c) of this section and throughout this subtitle, the references to the "Department of Permits and Development Management" are substituted for the former references to the "County Department of Permits and Licenses" to reflect the abolition of the former Baltimore County Department of Permits and Licenses and the transfer of its functions to the Baltimore County Department of Permits and Development Management. *See* County Bill No. 69-95, effective July 1, 1995.

In subsection (b)(3)(ii) of this section, the former reference to review of the report "by the county police department" is deleted as implicit in the submission of the report to the county police department.

Defined term:
    "Person"   § 1-101

§ 13-605. Political fundraisers — Paddle wheels.

(a) *In general.* — Notwithstanding any other provision of this article, a political committee, as defined in § 1-101 of the Election Law Article, may conduct a fundraiser at which prizes of money or merchandise are awarded in a game or spin using a paddle wheel or wheel of fortune.

(b) *Prizes.* — A political committee may award a money or merchandise prize under this section if the prize does not exceed the amount otherwise allowed for a prize in the county. (An. Code 1957, art. 27, § 261C-1; 2002, ch. 26, § 2; ch. 213, § 7.)

SPECIAL REVISOR'S NOTE

This Special Revisor's note comprises information related to the revision by Acts 2002, ch. 26 and other chapters amending this section from the 2002 Legislative Session.

As enacted by Ch. 26, Acts of 2002, this section was new language derived without substantive change from former Art. 27, § 261C-1(b) and, as it related to political fundraisers in Baltimore County, (a). However, Ch. 213, § 7, Acts of 2002, substituted the reference to "§ 1-101 of the Election Law Article" for the reference to "Article 33, § 1-101 of the Code" en-

acted by Ch. 26 in subsection (a) of this section. Chapter 213, § 8, provided that § 7 would take effect January 1, 2003, to reflect the delayed effective date of the Election Law Article enacted by Ch. 291, Acts of 2002.

In subsection (a) of this section, the reference to a "political committee, as defined in Article 33, § 1-101 of the Code" was substituted by Ch. 26 for the former reference to a "politically partisan organization or political committee as defined in Article 33 of the Code" for consistency with current usage in Article 33 of the Code.

§ 13-606. Bingo.

(a) *License required.* — Before an organization may conduct bingo in the county, the organization shall obtain a bingo license from the Department of Permits and Development Management.

(b) *Qualified organizations.* — An organization may conduct bingo to benefit charity in the county or to further its purposes if the organization is:

(1) a tax-supported volunteer fire company or an auxiliary unit whose members are directly associated with a tax-supported volunteer fire company;

(2) a nationally chartered veterans' organization or an auxiliary unit whose members are directly associated with a nationally chartered veterans' organization;

(3) a bona fide religious group that has conducted religious services at a fixed location in the county for at least 3 years before applying for a bingo license;

(4) the Maryland State Fair and Agricultural Society;

(5) a bona fide fraternal organization;

(6) a bona fide patriotic organization; or

(7) a bona fide charitable organization that has been located at a fixed location in the county for 3 years before applying for a bingo license.

(c) *Application.* — (1) An applicant for a bingo license shall apply for a license on the application form that the Department of Permits and Development Management provides.

(2) The application shall include:

(i) the name of the applicant;

(ii) the name and address of each officer and director of the applicant;

(iii) a complete statement of the purposes of the applicant;

(iv) a statement of the purpose for which the proceeds of the bingo operation will be used;

(v) an affidavit that an agreement does not exist to divide any part of the proceeds of the bingo operation with any other person that is made by:

    1. the president;

    2. the treasurer;

    3. the chief executive; or

    4. a fiscal officer;

(vi) an affidavit that only the applicant or a member of the applicant will receive any of the proceeds of the bingo operation except to further the purposes of the applicant organization; and

(vii) any other information the Department of Permits and Development Management requires.

(d) *License.* — (1) (i) An annual bingo license issued by the Department of Permits and Development Management authorizes the license holder to conduct bingo at the fixed location stated on the license:

    1. at any time during the year for which the license is issued; but

    2. not more often than twice each week in the year for which the license is issued.

(ii) An applicant for an annual license shall pay the fee that the Department of Permits and Development Management sets.

(2) (i) A temporary license issued by the Department of Permits and Development Management authorizes the license holder to conduct bingo at the fixed location stated on the license for not more than 10 days in the year for which the license is issued.

(ii) An applicant for a temporary license shall pay the fee that the administrative officer of the county sets.

(3) (i) A 1-day license issued by the Department of Permits and Development Management authorizes the license holder to conduct bingo at a fixed location stated on the license for not more than 1 day in the year for which the license is issued.

(ii) An applicant for a 1-day license shall pay a fee that the administrative officer of the county sets.

(iii) The Department of Permits and Development Management may not grant an applicant more than three 1-day licenses in any calendar year.

(e) *Conditions and limitations.* — (1) The Department of Permits and Development Management may require the holder of a bingo license to produce its financial records for inspection so that the Department may ensure that the license holder and the members of the license holder have complied with subsection (c)(2)(v) and (vi) of this section.

(2) A person may not conduct bingo on Sunday.

(f) *Proceeds of license.* — The Department of Permits and Development Management shall deposit the fees paid for bingo licenses issued under this section in the county Widows' Pension Fund.

(g) *Revocation of license.* — After a public hearing, the Department of Permits and Development Management may revoke the license of a license holder that fails to comply with this section or the regulations that the Department adopts under this section.

(h) *Regulations.* — The Department of Permits and Development Management may adopt regulations to govern:

(1) the conduct of bingo;

(2) the amounts of the prizes that may be awarded in a game of bingo;

(3) the method of awarding prizes;

(4) the hours that bingo may be conducted; and

(5) any other matters related to the proper conduct of bingo.

(i) *Prohibited acts; penalty.* — (1) (i) A person may not divert or pay any proceeds of bingo conducted under a bingo license to:

    1. any other person, except to a member of the license holder; or

    2. any other partnership or corporation, except to further the purposes of the license holder.

(ii) A person who is not a member of a license holder may not receive any of the proceeds of bingo conducted under a bingo license except to further the purposes of the license holder.

(iii) A person may not violate a regulation that the Department of Permits and Development Management adopts under subsection (h) of this section.

(2) A person who violates this subsection is guilty of a misdemeanor and on conviction is subject to imprisonment not exceeding 2 years or a fine not exceeding $1,000 or both. (An. Code 1957, art. 27, § 252(a)-(l); 2002, ch. 26, § 2.)

REVISOR'S NOTE

This Revisor's note comprises information related to the revision by Acts 2002, ch. 26.

This section is new language derived without substantive change from former Art. 27, § 252(a) through (l).

Throughout this section, the references to the "Department of Permits and Development Management" are substituted for the former references to the "County Department of Permits and Licenses" to reflect the abolition of the former Baltimore County Department of Permits and Licenses and the transfer of its functions to the Baltimore County Department of Permits and Development Management. *See* County Bill No. 69-95, effective July 1, 1995.

In the introductory language of subsection (b) of this section, the former reference to "operat-[ing]" is deleted as included in the reference to "conduct[ing]" bingo.

In subsection (b)(7) of this section, the former reference to organizations "which have been in existence" is deleted as included within the reference to an organization that "has been located at a fixed location" for a specified period.

In subsection (c)(2)(iii) of this section, the former reference to "objects" of an organization is deleted as included in the reference to its "purposes".

Also in subsection (c)(2)(iii) of this section, the former reference to a "full" statement is deleted in light of the reference to a "complete" statement.

In subsection (d)(1), (2), and (3)(i) of this section, the reference to "the year for which the license is issued" is added for clarity and consistency.

In subsection (e) of this section, the former reference to the "authorized agents" of the department is deleted as implicit in the reference to the "Department of Permits and Development Management".

In subsection (f) of this section, the reference to the "county Widows' Pension Fund" is substituted for the former reference to the "special fund for surviving spouses and other dependents of the Baltimore County police and fire bureaus, known as the 'Widows' Pension Fund'" for brevity.

Also in subsection (f) of this section, the reference to "fees paid for bingo licenses" is substituted for the former reference to "[t]he proceeds from the issuance of the license" for clarity and brevity.

Also in subsection (f) of this section, the reference to "[t]he Department of Permits and Development Management" is added to clarify who has the responsibility for depositing the license fees.

In subsection (h) of this section, the former reference to bingo "in Baltimore County" is deleted in light of § 13-602 of this subtitle.

Also in subsection (h) of this section, the former reference to regulations "as ... [the department] may deem necessary" is deleted as implicit in the authority to adopt regulations.

<table>
<tr><td>In subsection (i) of this section, the former references to penalties imposed "in the discretion of the court" are deleted as implicit in the reference to being "subject to imprisonment . . . or a fine . . . or both".</td><td>Defined term:
"Person"</td><td>§ 1-101</td></tr>
</table>

Bingo not lottery. — Bingo is not a lottery. Bender v. Arundel Arena, Inc., 248 Md. 181, 236 A.2d 7 (1967).

§ 13-607. Unauthorized gaming event or casino event.

(a) *Prohibited.* — A person may not knowingly conduct or attempt to conduct a gaming event or casino event in violation of §§ 13-603 through 13-605 of this subtitle.

(b) *Penalty.* — A person who violates this section is guilty of a misdemeanor and on conviction is subject to imprisonment not exceeding 1 year or a fine not exceeding $1,000 or both. (An. Code 1957, art. 27, § 255(f)(6); 2002, ch. 26, § 2.)

REVISOR'S NOTE

This Revisor's note comprises information related to the revision by Acts 2002, ch. 26.

This section is new language derived without substantive change from former Art. 27, § 255(f)(6).

In subsection (a) of this section, the former reference to "Baltimore County" is deleted in light of § 13-602 of this subtitle.

Also in subsection (a) of this section, the reference to "conduct[ing]" an event is substituted for the former reference to "operat[ing]" an event for consistency within this subtitle.

In subsection (b) of this section, the reference to being "guilty of a misdemeanor" is added to

state expressly that which was only implied in the former law. In this State, any crime that was not a felony at common law and has not been declared a felony by statute, is considered to be a misdemeanor. *See State v. Canova*, 278 Md. 483, 490 (1976); *Bowser v. State*, 136 Md. 342, 345 (1920); *Dutton v. State*, 123 Md. 373, 378 (1914); and *Williams v. State*, 4 Md. App. 342, 347 (1968).

Defined terms:

"Gaming event"	§ 13-601
"Person"	§ 1-101

Subtitle 7. Calvert County.

§ 13-701. Definitions.

(a) *In general.* — In this subtitle the following words have the meanings indicated.

REVISOR'S NOTE

This subsection is new language added as the standard introductory language to a definition section.

(b) *Committee.* — "Committee" means the Gambling Permit Review Committee appointed by the county commissioners under § 13-704 of this subtitle.

This subsection is new language added to avoid repetition of the phrase "Gambling Permit Review Committee".

(c) *County commissioners.* — "County commissioners" means the Board of County Commissioners of Calvert County.

This subsection is new language added to avoid repetition of the phrase "Board of County Commissioners of Calvert County".

(d) *Gaming event.* — "Gaming event" includes a carnival and a bazaar.

This subsection is new language added to avoid repetition of the phrase "carnival, bazaar, or other gaming event".

(2002, ch. 26, § 2.)

REVISOR'S NOTE TO SECTION

The Revisor's notes in this section comprise information related to the revision by Acts 2002, ch. 26.

§ 13-702. Scope and application of subtitle.

(a) *Scope of subtitle.* — This subtitle applies only in Calvert County.

(b) *Application of Subtitle 2.* — Subtitle 2 of this title applies in Calvert County. (An. Code 1957, art. 27, § 255(a)(4); 2002, ch. 26, § 2.)

This Revisor's note comprises information related to the revision by Acts 2002, ch. 26.

Subsection (a) of this section is new language added to clarify the scope of the subtitle.

Subsection (b) of this section is new language derived without substantive change from former Art. 27, § 255(a)(4).

§ 13-703. Gaming events.

(a) *Permit required.* — Before an organization may conduct a gaming event, the organization shall obtain a permit from the county commissioners.

(b) *Qualified organizations.* — An organization may conduct a gaming event in the county if the organization is:

(1) a volunteer fire company; or

(2) a bona fide:

(i) religious organization;

(ii) fraternal organization;

(iii) civic organization;

(iv) war veterans' organization; or

(v) charitable organization.

(c) *Permit.* — (1) The permit shall state:

(i) the nature of any gaming device to be operated at the gaming event; and

(ii) the frequency with which the gaming event will be conducted.

(2) The county commissioners may charge a reasonable fee for a permit. (An. Code 1957, art. 27, § 255(i)(1), (7); 2002, ch. 26, § 2.)

REVISOR'S NOTE

This Revisor's note comprises information related to the revision by Acts 2002, ch. 26.

This section is new language derived without substantive change from former Art. 27, § 255(i)(1) and (7).

In subsection (a) of this section, the reference to an "organization" is added for clarity.

In the introductory language of subsection (b) of this section, the former word "hold" is deleted as redundant of the word "conduct".

In subsection (b)(2) of this section, the former references to a "corporation" are deleted as included in the references to an "organization".

In subsection (c)(2) of this section, the former phrase "for the issuance of" is deleted as surplusage.

Defined terms:
"County commissioners"	§ 13-701
"Gaming event"	§ 13-701

§ 13-704. Gambling Permit Review Committee.

(a) *In general.* — (1) The county commissioners shall appoint a Gambling Permit Review Committee.

(2) The committee consists of five regular members and two alternate members.

(3) A quorum of the committee consists of:

(i) three regular members; or

(ii) if fewer than three regular members are present at a meeting, enough alternate members designated by the chairperson to act as regular members to create a quorum.

(4) An alternate member of the committee may serve only as provided under paragraph (3) of this subsection.

(b) *Duties.* — Subject to the approval of the county commissioners, the committee shall adopt regulations to govern gambling activities and the issuance of permits under § 13-703 of this subtitle. (An. Code 1957, art. 27, § 255(i)(2)-(6); 2002, ch. 26, § 2.)

REVISOR'S NOTE

This Revisor's note comprises information related to the revision by Acts 2002, ch. 26.

This section is new language derived without substantive change from former Art. 27, § 255(i)(2) through (6).

In subsection (a)(3)(ii) of this section, the reference to the "chairperson" is substituted for the former reference to the "chairman" because SG § 2-1238 requires the use of words that are neutral as to gender to the extent practicable.

Defined terms:
"Committee"	§ 13-701
"County commissioners"	§ 13-701

§ 13-705. Bingo — Commercial.

(a) *Instant bingo.* — For purposes of this section, a game of instant bingo conducted under a Class NG beach license is considered to be bingo.

(b) *License required.* — Before a person may conduct bingo in the county, the person shall obtain a license from the county commissioners.

(c) *Qualifications.* — Notwithstanding any other provision of this article, a person who complies with this section may conduct bingo in the county.

(d) *Application.* — (1) (i) The county commissioners may not issue a license unless the application was filed at least 30 days before the date of issuance.

(ii) An applicant for a license shall:

1. file an application on a form that the county commissioners provide; and

2. sign the application under oath.

(iii) The application shall include:

1. the name of the applicant;

2. the address of the applicant;

3. any trade name of the applicant;

4. if the applicant is a partnership, the name and address of each partner;

5. if the applicant is a corporation, the name and address of each officer of the corporation;

6. if a resident agent is required under paragraph (3) of this subsection, the name and address of the applicant's resident agent;

7. the name and address of any person having a financial interest in the operation of the proposed bingo; and

8. the signatures of all of the individuals listed in items 1 through 7 of this subparagraph indicating consent to individual liability for any unlawful operation of licensed bingo.

(iv) 1. The county commissioners may refuse to issue a license based on the facts disclosed on an application.

2. Subparagraph (i) of this paragraph does not require the county commissioners to investigate an applicant's statements on the application before issuing a license.

(2) Each applicant for a license shall present evidence to the county commissioners that the applicant has obtained a public liability insurance policy that:

(i) covers the period covered by the proposed license;

(ii) provides coverage for personal injury to:

1. any bingo patron in an amount not less than $100,000; and

2. more than one bingo patron in an amount not less than $500,000.

(3) (i) Each nonresident applicant for a license shall designate a resident agent.

(ii) A resident agent must be:

1. a voter in the county;

2. a taxpayer of the county; and

3. an owner of property in the county assessed at not less than $25,000.

(e) *License.* — (1) The county commissioners may issue the following licenses:

(i) a Class NA license, for bingo that does not exceed a seating or player capacity of 750 individuals;

(ii) a Class NB license, for bingo that does not exceed a seating or player capacity of 500 individuals;

(iii) a Class NC license, for bingo that does not exceed a seating or player capacity of 1,000 individuals;

(iv) a Class ND beach license, for bingo that:

    1. does not exceed a seating or player capacity of 500 individuals;

    2. may be operated within the town limits of North Beach or Chesapeake Beach; and

    3. may be operated between May 1 and September 30;

(v) a Class NE beach license, for bingo that:

    1. does not exceed a seating or player capacity of 1,000 individuals;

    2. may be operated within the town limits of North Beach or Chesapeake Beach; and

    3. may be operated between May 1 and September 30;

(vi) a Class NF beach license, for bingo that:

    1. does not exceed a seating or player capacity of 500 individuals;

    2. may be operated within the town limits of North Beach or Chesapeake Beach; and

    3. may be operated throughout the year; or

(vii) a Class NG beach license, for bingo that:

    1. does not have a limitation on seating or player capacity;

    2. may be operated within the town limits of North Beach or Chesapeake Beach; and

    3. may be operated throughout the year.

(2) The county commissioners shall:

(i) retain a copy of each license issued;

(ii) issue a copy of the license to the license holder; and

(iii) forward a copy of the license to the State Comptroller.

(3) A license is not transferable.

(f) *Fees.* — The county commissioners shall assess the following annual license fees:

(1) $3,500 for a Class NA license;

(2) $3,000 for a Class NB license;

(3) $4,000 for a Class NC license;

(4) $500 for a Class ND beach license;

(5) $1,000 for a Class NE beach license;

(6) $3,000 for a Class NF beach license; and

(7) $5,000 for a Class NG beach license.

(g) *Limitations.* — (1) The county commissioners may not issue a license if the conduct of bingo would:

(i) unduly disturb the peace of the neighborhood in which the applicant proposes to conduct bingo;

(ii) create a nuisance; or

(iii) be detrimental to the health or welfare of the community.

(2) (i) The county commissioners may not issue a license to conduct bingo in a building that is not permanent and covered by a roof.

(ii) This paragraph does not apply to a person who is not required to obtain a license to conduct bingo.

(3) (i) The following licenses may not allow the conduct of bingo on Sunday:

    1. a Class NA license;

    2. a Class NB license; or

    3. a Class NC license.

(ii) The following licenses may not allow the conduct of bingo before 1 p.m. on Sunday:

    1. a Class ND beach license;

    2. a Class NE beach license; or

    3. a Class NF beach license.

(iii) A Class NG beach license may not allow the conduct of bingo between 2 a.m. and 1 p.m. on Sunday. (An. Code 1957, art. 27, § 259A(a), (b)(1)-(8), (11); 2002, ch. 26, § 2.)

REVISOR'S NOTE

This Revisor's note comprises information related to the revision by Acts 2002, ch. 26.

This section is new language derived without substantive change from former Art. 27, § 259A(a) and (b)(1), (3) through (8), the first sentence of (2), and the first sentence and the first clause of the second sentence of (11).

The Criminal Law Article Review Committee notes, for the consideration of the General Assembly, that only under a Class NG beach license is instant bingo "considered to be bingo". *See* subsection (a) of this section.

In subsections (b) and (c) of this section, the former references to "operating" and "operate" are deleted as included in the references to "conduct[ing]".

In subsection (d)(1)(ii)1 of this section, the reference to the "county commissioners" is added to clarify who must provide the required form. Similarly, in subsection (g)(1) and (2) of this section, the reference to the "county commissioners" is added to clarify who may not issue licenses for bingo to be conducted under certain conditions.

In subsection (d)(1)(iii)8 of this section, the reference "individuals" is substituted for the former reference to "persons" because only an individual, and not any other entity included in the defined term "person", has a signature.

Also in subsection (d)(1)(iii)8 of this section, the term "unlawful" is substituted for the former phrase "any violation of the laws" for brevity.

In subsection (d)(1)(iv)2 of this section, the reference to "an applicant's statements" is added to clarify the subject of the county commissioners' investigation.

In subsection (e)(2) of this section, the former reference to preparing a license "in triplicate" is deleted as implicit in the enumeration of three separate required copies of the license: one to the holder, one to the State Comptroller, and one for the records of the county commissioners.

In subsection (g)(1)(i) of this section, the former reference to "quiet" is deleted as included in the reference to "peace".

Defined terms:

"County commissioners"	§ 13-701
"Person"	§ 1-101

Bingo-styled game not authorized. — The MegaMania online bingo game, which is operated by an entity outside of Calvert County and which would involve the simultaneous participation of players within and without of the County, is not currently authorized by an earlier version of this section. 84 Op. Att'y Gen. 127 (Mar. 1, 1999).

§ 13-706. Bingo — Exempt organizations.

The following organizations are not required to obtain a license under § 13-705 of this subtitle to conduct bingo:

    (1) a religious organization;

    (2) a patriotic organization;

    (3) an educational organization;

    (4) a charitable or benevolent organization;

    (5) a civic organization;

    (6) a volunteer fire company; or

    (7) any other organization that is authorized under § 13-703 of this subtitle and Subtitle 2 of this title to conduct bingo in the county. (An. Code 1957, art. 27, § 259A(b)(10); 2002, ch. 26, § 2.)

REVISOR'S NOTE

This Revisor's note comprises information related to the revision by Acts 2002, ch. 26.

This section is new language derived without substantive change from former Art. 27, § 259A(b)(10).

The former specific references to the kinds of licenses that may be required are deleted in light of the reference to a "license under § 13-705 of this subtitle".

In item (7) of this section, the reference to an "organization" is substituted for the former reference to an "agency" for clarity.

Also in item (7) of this section, the reference to an organization authorized "under § 13-703 of this subtitle and Subtitle 2 of this title to conduct bingo in the county" is substituted for the former reference to one "authorized by law to operate any such game" for clarity.

§ 13-707. Bingo — Prizes.

(a) *Form.* — A license holder may issue as a prize or award to the patron of licensed bingo:

    (1) merchandise;

    (2) money;

    (3) a token or ticket redeemable for money or merchandise; or

    (4) any other thing of value.

(b) *Limitations.* — (1) Except as provided under paragraphs (2) and (3) of this subsection, a license holder may not issue for one game a prize or award with a value exceeding $100.

    (2) A holder of a Class NG beach license may issue for one game a prize with a value exceeding $100.

    (3) A license holder may issue once each day:

      (i) a grand prize not exceeding $1,500; and

      (ii) a grand prize not exceeding $3,000 in retail value. (An. Code 1957, art. 27, § 259A(b)(2); 2002, ch. 26, § 2; 2003, ch. 21, § 1.)

REVISOR'S NOTE

This Revisor's note comprises information related to the revision by Acts 2002, ch. 26.

This section is new language derived without substantive change from the second and third sentences of former Art. 27, § 259A(b)(2).

In subsection (a)(2) of this section, the reference to a "money" prize is substituted for the former references to a prize of "coins" or "currency" for consistency within this title.

§ 13-708. Bingo — Revocation of license.

In addition to any other penalty provided by law, the county commissioners may revoke a bingo license forthwith if:

(1) the county commissioners determine after an investigation that:

(i) the license holder made a false statement in the application for the license; or

(ii) the conduct of licensed bingo at the premises named in the license would:

1. disturb the peace of the neighborhood;

2. create a nuisance; or

3. be detrimental to the morals, health, or welfare of the community;

or

(2) the license holder is convicted of:

(i) violating §§ 13-705 through 13-707 of this subtitle; or

(ii) a felony. (An. Code 1957, art. 27, § 259A(b)(9), (11); 2002, ch. 26, § 2.)

REVISOR'S NOTE

This Revisor's note comprises information related to the revision by Acts 2002, ch. 26.

This section is new language derived without substantive change from former Art. 27, § 259A(b)(9) and the second clause of the second sentence of (11).

In the introductory language of this section, the phrase "[i]n addition to any other penalty provided by law" is substituted for the former phrase "the applicant shall be subject to all the penalties provided by law" for consistency within this article.

In item (1)(ii)1 of this section, the former reference to "quiet" is deleted as included in the reference to "peace".

The Criminal Law Article Review Committee notes, for the consideration of the General Assembly, that item (1)(ii)3 of this section varies from an analogous provision in § 13-705(g)(1)(iii) of this subtitle. Only in this section may the county commissioners revoke a license for conduct that would be detrimental to the "morals" of the community.

In item (2) of this section, the phrase "convicted of" is substituted for the former phrase "found guilty . . . of" for consistency within this article.

Also in item (2) of this section, the former reference to conviction "by a court of competent jurisdiction" is deleted as surplusage.

Defined term:
"County commissioners"   § 13-701

§ 13-709. Regulations.

(a) *In general.* — The county commissioners may adopt regulations to govern:

(1) the conduct or play of bingo;

(2) the issuance of bingo licenses;

(3) the setting of fees for bingo licenses; and

(4) the determination of the election districts and precincts in which bingo may be conducted.

(b) *Uniform application.* — In adopting regulations, the county commissioners shall ensure uniform application as to:

(1) the determination of the districts and precincts in which bingo may be conducted; and

(2) the setting of fees. (An. Code 1957, art. 27, § 259A(c), (d); 2002, ch. 26, § 2.)

REVISOR'S NOTE

This Revisor's note comprises information related to the revision by Acts 2002, ch. 26.

This section is new language derived without substantive change from former Art. 27, § 259A(c) and (d).

Defined term:
"County commissioners"   § 13-701

Subtitle 8. Caroline County.

§ 13-801. Application of Subtitle 2.

Subtitle 2 of this title applies in Caroline County. (An. Code 1957, art. 27, § 255(a)(5); 2002, ch. 26, § 2.)

REVISOR'S NOTE

This Revisor's note comprises information related to the revision by Acts 2002, ch. 26.

This section is new language derived without substantive change from former Art. 27, § 255(a)(5).

The reference to "Subtitle 2 of this title" is substituted for the former reference to "this section" to reflect the reorganization of the general provisions on gaming events in specified counties contained in former Art. 27, § 255.

Subtitle 9. Carroll County.

§ 13-901. Definitions.

(a) *In general.* — In this subtitle the following words have the meanings indicated.

REVISOR'S NOTE

This subsection is new language added as the standard introductory language to a definition section.

(b) *County commissioners.* — "County commissioners" means the Board of County Commissioners of Carroll County.

REVISOR'S NOTE

This subsection is new language added to avoid repetition of the phrase "Board of County Commissioners of Carroll County" and for consistency within this title.

(c) *Gaming event.* — "Gaming event" means a carnival, bazaar, raffle, or other game of entertainment.

This subsection is new language added to avoid repetition of the phrase "carnival, bazaar, raffle, or other game of entertainment" and for consistency within this title.

(2002, ch. 26, § 2; 2007, ch. 273.)

The Revisor's notes in this section comprise information related to the revision by Acts 2002, ch. 26.

§ 13-902. Scope and application of subtitle.

(a) *Scope of subtitle.* — This subtitle applies only in Carroll County.

(b) *Application of Subtitle 2.* — Subject to this subtitle, Subtitle 2 of this title applies in Carroll County. (An. Code 1957, art. 27, § 255(a)(6), (b)(4); 2002, ch. 26, § 2; 2004, ch. 404; 2006, ch. 196; 2007, ch. 273.)

This Revisor's note comprises information related to the revision by Acts 2002, ch. 26.

Subsection (a) of this section is new language added to clarify the scope of this subtitle.

Subsection (b) of this section is new language derived without substantive change from former Art. 27, § 255(a)(6) and (b)(4).

In subsection (b) of this section, the reference to "this subtitle" is substituted for the former reference to "§ 258 of this article", although this subtitle is derived in part from material outside former § 258. Because former § 255(b)(4) subjected all gaming in Carroll County to former § 258, including bingo under former § 248A and gaming events under former § 255, no substantive change results.

§ 13-903. Gaming events — In general.

(a) *Permit required.* — Before an organization may conduct a gaming event, the organization shall obtain a permit from the county commissioners.

(b) *Qualified organizations.* — To conduct bingo or a gaming event an organization must be a bona fide:

(1) religious organization;

(2) fraternal organization;

(3) civic organization;

(4) war veterans' organization;

(5) hospital;

(6) amateur athletic organization;

(7) charitable organization; or

(8) volunteer fire company.

(c) *Application.* — (1) Before the county commissioners issue a permit, they shall determine whether the organization applying for the permit qualifies under this subtitle and the conditions of this subtitle are met.

(2) An application for a permit and the action taken by the county commissioners on that application are public records.

(d) *Permit.* — (1) The permit shall state that the gaming event shall be managed and operated only by members of the organization holding the permit.

(2) A permit is not transferable.

(e) *Limitations.* — (1) A gaming event conducted under this section shall be conducted for the benefit of an organization listed in subsection (b) of this section.

(2) An individual or group of individuals may not benefit financially, or receive proceeds for personal use or benefit, from a gaming event conducted under this section.

(3) A permit may not authorize the operation of a gaming event after 1 a.m. on Sunday.

(4) (i) Except as provided in subparagraphs (ii) and (iv) of this paragraph, an organization conducting a gaming event may award a money prize not exceeding $100 or merchandise not exceeding $100 of value to any individual in any one game.

(ii) The maximum amount of a prize awarded in a raffle is governed by § 13-904(c) of this subtitle.

(iii) The maximum amount of a prize awarded in a paddle wheel or wheel of fortune game is governed by § 13-905(a) of this subtitle.

(iv) The maximum amount of a prize awarded in bingo is governed by § 13-908 of this subtitle. (An. Code 1957, art. 27, § 258(a)(1), (2)(v), (c); 2002, ch. 26, § 2; 2003, ch. 21, § 1; 2004, ch. 404; 2007, ch. 273.)

REVISOR'S NOTE

This Revisor's note comprises information related to the revision by Acts 2002, ch. 26.

Subsections (a) through (e)(4)(i) of this section are new language derived without substantive change from former Art. 27, § 258(c) and (a)(1) and (2)(v).

Subsection (e)(4)(ii) through (iv) of this section is new language added for clarity.

In subsection (b) of this section, the former reference to "hold[ing]" an event is deleted as included in the reference to "conduct[ing]" the event.

In subsection (c) of this section, the reference to "determin[ing] whether the organization applying for the permit qualifies under this sub-

title" is substituted for the former reference to "ascertain[ing] the character of the organization on whose behalf the application is made" for clarity.

In subsection (e)(2) of this section, the former reference to "be[ing] paid" is deleted as redundant of the reference to "receiv[ing]".

In subsection (e)(4)(i) of this section, the phrase "[e]xcept as provided in subparagraphs (ii) and (iv) of this paragraph," is added to acknowledge that money prizes exceeding $100 may be awarded to players of special bingo games and to winners of raffles and jackpots.

Defined terms:
"County commissioners"	§ 13-901
"Gaming event"	§ 13-901

Maryland Law Review. — For article, "Survey of Developments in Maryland Law, 1986-87," see 47 Md. L. Rev. 739 (1988).

§ 13-904. Raffles.

(a) *Definitions.* — (1) In this section the following words have the meanings indicated.

(2) "Multi-drawing raffle" means a raffle for which the drawings are held on more than 1 day.

(3) "Raffle" means one or more drawings using a single series of chances sold in chance books or similar devices, at which one or more prizes are awarded.

(4) "Single-drawing raffle" means a raffle for which the drawings are held on a single day.

(b) *Chance books.* — At a gaming event, the holder of a raffle may award a prize of money or merchandise using a chance book.

(c) *Prizes.* — (1) A single-drawing raffle may have only one major prize.

(2) During a year, an organization listed in § 13-903 of this subtitle may hold not more than:

(i) six single-drawing raffles in which the major prize is worth $2,500 or more; or

(ii) ten single-drawing raffles in which the major prize is worth less than $2,500.

(3) An organization listed in § 13-903 of this subtitle may not hold:

(i) more than 30 weekly drawings in a multi-drawing raffle;

(ii) more than two multi-drawing raffles during a year; or

(iii) a multi-drawing raffle in which the major prize is worth more than $1,100. (An. Code 1957, art. 27, § 258(a)(2)(i)-(iv); 2002, ch. 26, § 2; 2004, ch. 404.)

REVISOR'S NOTE

This Revisor's note comprises information related to the revision by Acts 2002, ch. 26.

This section is new language derived without substantive change from former Art. 27, § 258(a)(2)(i) through (iv).

In subsection (b) of this section, the reference to "the holder of a raffle" is added to clarify who is authorized to award a prize.

Also in subsection (b) of this section, the former reference to a "raffle" is deleted as included in the defined term "gaming event". See § 13-901 of this subtitle.

In subsection (c)(2) and (3) of this section, the references to an organization "listed in § 13-903 of this subtitle" are added for clarity.

In subsection (c)(3) of this section, the conjunction "or" is added to the list of prohibited activities for clarity.

Defined term:
"Gaming event" § 13-901

§ 13-905. Prizes — Paddle wheels and other gaming devices.

(a) *Paddle wheels or wheels of fortune.* — (1) Notwithstanding § 13-903 of this subtitle, an organization listed in § 13-903 of this subtitle that operates a paddle wheel or wheel of fortune game at a gaming event may not award a prize to a person in any one game or spin of the wheel of:

(i) money that exceeds $10; or

(ii) merchandise with a value that exceeds $250.

(2) An organization listed in § 13-903 of this subtitle may not hold more than 10 days of paddle-wheel games in a calendar year.

(b) *Other gaming devices.* — An organization listed in § 13-903 or § 13-907 of this subtitle may award a prize of money or merchandise using a gaming device other than a card game, dice game, or roulette. (An. Code 1957, art. 27, § 258(b)(2), (e); 2002, ch. 26, § 2; 2006, ch. 196.)

REVISOR'S NOTE

This Revisor's note comprises information related to the revision by Acts 2002, ch. 26.

This section is new language derived without substantive change from former Art. 27, § 258(e) and (b)(2).

In subsection (a)(1) of this section, the reference to "§ 13-903 of this subtitle" is substituted for the former reference to "any provision of this section" for accuracy and clarity.

Also in subsection (a)(1) of this section, the former reference to a carnival, bazaar, or raffle "authorized by this section" is deleted in light of the term "gaming event" defined in § 13-901 of this subtitle and the reorganization of material

on gaming events derived from former Art. 27, § 258 in this subtitle.

In subsection (a)(1)(ii) of this section, the reference to not awarding "merchandise with a value that exceeds" is substituted for the former reference to awarding "merchandise totaling up to" for clarity.

In subsections (a)(1)(i) and (b) of this section, the references to a "money" prize are substituted for the former references to a "cash" prize for consistency within this title.

Defined terms:
"Gaming event"   § 13-901
"Person"   § 1-101

§ 13-905.1. Prizes — Billiard games.

(a) *In general.* — A senior center site council may conduct billiards in a senior center 5 days per week, excluding Sunday.

(b) *Prize limits.* — A senior center site council may not award a prize of money to a winner exceeding $5 in each session.

(c) *Tournaments.* — (1) A senior center site council may conduct a billiards tournament with a maximum entry fee of $2 for each participant.

(2) Prizes of money may be awarded to first, second, and third place winners from the entry fee money collected.

(3) All money that remains after prizes are awarded shall be distributed to the senior center site council. (2006, ch. 196.)

§ 13-906. Card games, dice games, roulette, and casino nights — Prohibited; exceptions.

(a) *In general.* — Notwithstanding § 13-903 of this subtitle, a person may not conduct a card game, dice game, roulette, or casino night unless the person is a senior center site council that conducts a card game under subsection (b) of this section.

(b) *Senior citizen site council games.* — (1) A senior center site council may conduct a card game in a senior center 5 days per week, excluding Sunday.

(2) A senior center site council may not:

(i) award a prize of money exceeding $5 to a winner in each session; and

(ii) charge a participant more than $1 to play one session.

(3) All money that remains after prizes are awarded shall be distributed to the senior center site council. (An. Code 1957, art. 27, § 258(b)(1); 2002, ch. 26, § 2; 2006, ch. 196.)

REVISOR'S NOTE

**This Revisor's note comprises informa-
tion related to the revision by Acts 2002,
ch. 26.**

This section is new language derived without
substantive change from former Art. 27,
§ 258(b)(1).

The former phrase "events commonly known
as" is deleted as surplusage.

Defined term:
"Person"   § 1-101

§ 13-907. Bingo.

(a) *Permit required.* — Before an organization may conduct bingo under
this subtitle, the organization shall obtain a permit from the county commissioners.

(b) *Qualified organizations.* — (1) In this subsection, "qualified organization" means a bona fide:

    (i) religious organization;

    (ii) fraternal organization;

    (iii) patriotic organization;

    (iv) educational organization;

    (v) charitable organization;

    (vi) volunteer fire company; or

    (vii) senior center site council.

(2) A qualified organization may conduct bingo in the county to benefit
charity or to further the purpose of the qualified organization.

(c) *Senior citizen site council games.* — (1) A senior center site council may
obtain a permit to conduct bingo in a senior center 5 days per week, excluding
Sunday.

(2) A senior center site council may not:

    (i) award a prize of money to a winner exceeding $50 in each session; or

    (ii) charge more than 5 cents for each bingo card.

(3) All money that remains after prizes are awarded shall be distributed
to the senior center site council.

(d) *Permit.* — (1) An applicant for a permit shall pay the fee that the
county commissioners set.

(2) The county commissioners shall set the permit fee at a level sufficient
to cover the costs of issuing the permit.

(e) *Limitations.* — (1) Only the holder of a permit issued under this section
may conduct bingo authorized by the permit.

(2) The holder of a permit issued under this section may not transfer or
assign the right to conduct bingo to another person. (An. Code 1957, art. 27,
§ 248A(a)-(c); 2002, ch. 26, § 2; 2006, ch. 196; 2007, ch. 273.)

REVISOR'S NOTE

**This Revisor's note comprises informa-
tion related to the revision by Acts 2002,
ch. 26.**

This section is new language derived without
substantive change from former Art. 27,
§ 248A(a) through (c).

In subsections (a) and (b)(1) of this section,
the former references to a "corporation" are
deleted as included in the references to an
"organization". Similarly, in subsection (d) of
this section, the former references to a "firm, or
corporation" are deleted as included in the

defined term "person". *See* § 1-101 of this article.

In subsection (b) of this section, the former reference to "operat[ing]" is deleted in light of the reference to "conduct[ing]". Similarly, in subsections (a) and (d) of this section, the former references to "operate" and "operated" are deleted.

In subsection (d) of this section, the reference to the "holder of a permit issued under this section" is substituted for the former reference to an "organization, corporation or volunteer fire company securing the permit therefor" for brevity.

Defined terms:

"County commissioners"	§ 13-901
"Person"	§ 1-101

§ 13-908. Bingo — Prizes.

(a) *Money prizes.* — Except as provided in subsection (b) of this section and § 13-907(c)(2)(i) of this subtitle, a permit holder may not award a money prize greater than:

(1) $100 to a player of a regular bingo game; or

(2) $250 to a player of a special bingo game, such as a build-up or progressive pot game, split-the-pot game, or winner-take-all game.

(b) *Jackpots.* — A permit holder may award a jackpot not exceeding $1,000 if the jackpot is directly connected with the playing of bingo. (An. Code 1957, art. 27, § 248A(d); 2002, ch. 26, § 2; 2006, ch. 196.)

REVISOR'S NOTE

This Revisor's note comprises information related to the revision by Acts 2002, ch. 26.

This section is new language derived without substantive change from former Art. 27, § 248A(d).

Throughout this section, the references to a "permit holder" are added to clarify who must comply with this section.

In subsection (a) of this section, the reference to a "money" prize is substituted for the former reference to a "cash" prize for consistency within this title.

In subsection (b) of this section, the former reference to "games" is deleted as surplusage.

§ 13-909. Prohibited act; penalty.

(a) *Prohibited.* — A person may not knowingly operate or attempt to operate a gaming event in violation of this subtitle.

(b) *Penalty.* — A person who violates this section is guilty of a misdemeanor and on conviction is subject to imprisonment not exceeding 1 year or a fine not exceeding $1,000 or both. (An. Code 1957, art. 27, § 258(d); 2002, ch. 26, § 2.)

REVISOR'S NOTE

This Revisor's note comprises information related to the revision by Acts 2002, ch. 26.

This section is new language derived without substantive change from former Art. 27, § 258(d).

In subsection (a) of this section, the former references to an "association" and a "corporation" are deleted as included in the reference to the defined term "person". *See* § 1-101 of this article.

Also in subsection (a) of this section, the reference to violating "this subtitle" is substituted for the former references to violating "this section [former Art. 27, § 258]" although this subtitle is derived in part from material outside former § 258. Specifically, the remaining provisions are derived from former Art. 27, § 248A, revised as §§ 13-907 and 13-908 of this subtitle, which governed bingo conducted in Carroll County by certain charitable and similar organizations, and from § 255(a)(6) and (b), which generally covered gaming events in the State. Because former § 255(b), revised as Subtitle 2 of this title, applied in Carroll County, and in particular because former § 255(b)(4) provided that "*any* bazaar, carnival, raffle, or game of bingo" in Carroll County was subject to former § 258 (emphasis added), the penalties of this section apply to a violation of §§ 13-907 and 13-908. Thus, no substantive change results.

In subsection (b) of this section, the reference to being "guilty of a misdemeanor" is added to state expressly that which was only implied in the former law. In this State, any crime that was not a felony at common law and has not been declared a felony by statute, is considered to be a misdemeanor. *See State v. Canova*, 278 Md. 483, 490 (1976); *Bowser v. State*, 136 Md. 342, 345 (1920); *Dutton v. State*, 123 Md. 373, 378 (1914); and *Williams v. State*, 4 Md. App. 342, 347 (1968).

Also in subsection (b) of this section, the former phrase "in the discretion of the court" is deleted as implicit in the establishment of maximum penalties.

Defined terms:

"Gaming event"	§ 13-901
"Person"	§ 1-101

Subtitle 10. Cecil County.

§ 13-1001. Definitions.

(a) *In general.* — In this subtitle the following terms have the meanings indicated.

REVISOR'S NOTE

This subsection is new language used as the standard introductory language to a definition section.

(b) *Bingo.* — "Bingo" includes instant bingo.

REVISOR'S NOTE

This subsection is new language derived without substantive change from former Art. 27, § 261(a).

(c) *Gaming event.* — "Gaming event" means a carnival, bazaar, raffle, or other game of entertainment.

REVISOR'S NOTE

This subsection is new language added to avoid repetition of the phrase "carnival, bazaar, raffle, or other game of entertainment" and for consistency within this title.

(d) *Qualified organization.* — "Qualified organization" means:
  (1) a volunteer fire company; or
  (2) a bona fide:
    (i) religious organization;
    (ii) fraternal organization;
    (iii) civic organization;
    (iv) war veterans' organization; or
    (v) charitable organization.

REVISOR'S NOTE

This subsection is new language derived without substantive change from former Art. 27, § 261(b), as it related to the types of organizations that are allowed to conduct gaming events and bingo in Cecil County.

The former references to a "corporation" are deleted as included in the reference to an "organization".

(An. Code 1957, art. 27, § 261(a), (b); 2002, ch. 26, § 2.)

REVISOR'S NOTE TO SECTION

The Revisor's notes in this section comprise information related to the revision by Acts 2002, ch. 26.

§ 13-1002. Application of subtitle.

This subtitle applies only in Cecil County. (2002, ch. 26, § 2.)

REVISOR'S NOTE

This Revisor's note comprises information related to the revision by Acts 2002, ch. 26.
This section is new language added to state expressly that which was only implied in former Art. 27, § 261 by the former reference to qualified organizations "in Cecil County".

§ 13-1003. Gaming events and bingo.

A qualified organization may conduct bingo or a gaming event for the exclusive benefit of any qualified organization if an individual or group of individuals does not:

(1) benefit financially; or

(2) receive proceeds of the bingo or gaming event for personal use or benefit. (An. Code 1957, art. 27, § 261(b); 2002, ch. 26, § 2.)

REVISOR'S NOTE

This Revisor's note comprises information related to the revision by Acts 2002, ch. 26.
This section is new language derived without substantive change from the first sentence of former Art. 27, § 261(b).

This section is restated as a qualified permission to conduct a bingo or a gaming event for clarity and consistency within this title.

The former reference to "hold[ing]" a carnival is deleted as included in the reference to "conduct[ing]" a gaming event.

The former reference to benefiting financially "from the holding of any . . . game of bingo" and the former reference to "games of entertainment" are deleted as implicit in the reference to "conduct[ing] bingo or a gaming event".

In item (2) of this section, the former reference to "be[ing] paid" proceeds is deleted as included in the reference to "receiv[ing]" proceeds.

The Criminal Law Article Review Committee notes, for the consideration of the General Assembly, that this section allows a qualified organization to conduct a gaming event for the exclusive benefit of "any" qualified organization, not only the qualified organization conducting the gaming event.

Defined terms:

"Bingo"	§ 13-1001
"Gaming event"	§ 13-1001
"Qualified organization"	§ 13-1001

Bingo not lottery. — Bingo is not a lottery.
Bender v. Arundel Arena, Inc., 248 Md. 181, 236
A.2d 7 (1967).

§ 13-1004. Devices for awarding prizes at carnivals, etc.

A qualified organization may award a prize of money or merchandise at bingo or a gaming event through a paddle wheel, wheel of fortune, chance book, or bingo. (An. Code 1957, art. 27, § 261(b); 2002, ch. 26, § 2.)

REVISOR'S NOTE

This Revisor's note comprises information related to the revision by Acts 2002, ch. 26.
This section is new language derived without substantive change from the first clause of the second sentence of former Art. 27, § 261(b).

The reference to a "money" prize is substituted for the former reference to a "cash" prize for consistency within this title.

Defined terms:
"Bingo"	§ 13-1001
"Gaming event"	§ 13-1001
"Qualified organization"	§ 13-1001

§ 13-1005. Management of gaming event or bingo.

The bingo or gaming event shall be managed personally by members of the qualified organization conducting the event. (An. Code 1957, art. 27, § 261(b); 2002, ch. 26, § 2.)

REVISOR'S NOTE

This Revisor's note comprises information related to the revision by Acts 2002, ch. 26.
This section is new language derived without substantive change from the second clause of the second sentence of former Art. 27, § 261(b).

Defined terms:
"Bingo"	§ 13-1001
"Gaming event"	§ 13-1001
"Qualified organization"	§ 13-1001

Subtitle 11. Charles County.

§ 13-1101. Definitions.

(a) *In general.* — In this subtitle the following words have the meanings indicated.

REVISOR'S NOTE

This subsection is new language derived without substantive change from former Art. 27, § 253A(a)(1).

Throughout this subtitle, the references to "this subtitle" are substituted for the former references to "this section" to reflect the reorganization of material derived from former Art. 27, § 253A, relating to gaming in Charles County, in this subtitle.

(b) *Board.* — "Board" means the Charles County Gaming Permit Review Board.

This subsection formerly was Art. 27, § 253A(a)(2).   No changes are made.

(c) *County commissioners.* — "County commissioners" means the Board of County Commissioners of Charles County.

This subsection is new language added to avoid repetition of the phrase "Board of County   Commissioners" and for consistency with other subtitles in this title.

(d) *Fundraising organization.* — "Fundraising organization" means an incorporated or unincorporated bona fide:
(1) religious organization;
(2) fraternal organization;
(3) civic organization;
(4) war veterans' organization;
(5) charitable organization;
(6) volunteer fire company;
(7) rescue squad; or
(8) ambulance company.

This subsection is new language derived without substantive change from former Art. 27, § 253A(a)(4).

(e) *Gaming device.* — (1) "Gaming device" means a mechanism for playing a game of chance.
(2) "Gaming device" includes a paddle wheel, wheel of fortune, and chance book.
(3) "Gaming device" does not include bingo, a slot machine, or other gaming device that is otherwise regulated by State law.

This subsection is new language derived without substantive change from former Art. 27, § 253A(a)(5).

(f) *Gaming event.* — (1) "Gaming event" means an event involving a game of chance.
(2) "Gaming event" includes:
(i) a carnival;
(ii) a bazaar; and
(iii) a raffle involving prizes of cash exceeding $1,000 or merchandise with a cash equivalent exceeding $1,000.
(3) "Gaming event" does not include bingo.

REVISOR'S NOTE

This subsection is new language derived without substantive change from former Art. 27, § 253A(a)(6).

(g) *Gaming permit.* — "Gaming permit" means a permit to operate a gaming device at a gaming event that the county commissioners issue under this subtitle.

REVISOR'S NOTE

This subsection is new language derived without substantive change from former Art. 27, § 253A(a)(7).

(h) *Person.* — "Person" includes a joint interest held by two or more persons.

REVISOR'S NOTE

This subsection is new language derived without substantive change from former Art. 27, § 253A(a)(8).

The portion of former Art. 27, § 253A(a)(8) that is not included in the article-wide defined term "person" appears in this subsection. *See* § 1-101 of this article for the balance of the definition.

Defined term:
"Person"   § 1-101

(i) *Representative.* — "Representative" means a person who has been a bona fide member of a fundraising organization or educational organization for at least 1 year before the date of a gaming permit application by the fundraising organization or educational organization.

REVISOR'S NOTE

This subsection is new language derived without substantive change from former Art. 27, § 253A(a)(9).

The reference to an application "by the fundraising organization" is added to clarify that a representative may only represent the particular fundraising organization that applies for the gaming permit application for purposes of that application, and not another fundraising organization.

The references to an "educational organization" are added to reflect the exclusive use of representatives of such an organization to manage or conduct bingo under § 13-1110 of this subtitle.

Defined term:
"Person"   § 1-101

(An. Code 1957, art. 27, § 253A(a)(1), (2), (4)-(9); 2002, ch. 26, § 2; 2003, ch. 21, § 1.)

REVISOR'S NOTE TO SECTION

The Revisor's notes in this section comprise information related to the revision by Acts 2002, ch. 26.

§ 13-1102. Scope of subtitle.

This subtitle applies to bingo and gaming events in Charles County. (An. Code 1957, art. 27, § 253A(a)(3), (b); 2002, ch. 26, § 2.)

REVISOR'S NOTE

This Revisor's note comprises information related to the revision by Acts 2002, ch. 26.

This section is new language derived without substantive change from former Art. 27, § 253A(a)(3) and (b).

The former term "county", which was defined in Art. 27, § 253A(a)(3) as Charles County, is incorporated into this section to avoid confusion with the general term "county" defined in § 1-101 of this article.

Defined term:
"Gaming event"   § 13-1101

§ 13-1103. Authority of county commissioners.

The county commissioners may:

(1) designate the types of gaming devices that may be operated in the county;

(2) set fees for gaming permits issued under this subtitle;

(3) set salaries and funding for the board and the board's clerk, legal counsel, and support staff;

(4) approve or deny gaming permit applications;

(5) investigate persons involved in gaming events and examine records of fundraising organizations with respect to gaming events;

(6) delegate its powers and duties under this subtitle to the board; and

(7) adopt regulations to carry out this subtitle. (An. Code 1957, art. 27, § 253A(c); 2002, ch. 26, § 2.)

REVISOR'S NOTE

This Revisor's note comprises information related to the revision by Acts 2002, ch. 26.

This section is new language derived without substantive change from former Art. 27, § 253A(c).

In item (3) of this section, the reference to "the board's clerk" is added for consistency with § 13-1104(f) of this subtitle.

The former phrase "[i]n addition to any powers conferred by State law" is deleted as implicit in the grant of authority to the county commissioners in this section.

Defined terms:
"Board"	§ 13-1101
"County commissioners"	§ 13-1101
"Fundraising organization"	§ 13-1101
"Gaming device"	§ 13-1101
"Gaming event"	§ 13-1101
"Gaming permit"	§ 13-1101
"Person"	§§ 1-101, 13-1101

§ 13-1104. Gaming Permit Review Board.

(a) *Established.* — There is a Charles County Gaming Permit Review Board.

(b) *Membership.* — (1) The board consists of seven members.

(2) Of the seven members of the board:

(i) one shall be a member of the county sheriff's office;

(ii) one shall be a member of the Department of State Police;

(iii) one shall be a member of a fundraising organization in the county;

(iv) one shall be an individual with background and experience in finance; and

(v) three shall be members at large.

(3) Each member at large:

(i) shall be a member of the general public;

(ii) may not be a member of a fundraising organization or otherwise be subject to regulation by the board;

(iii) may not, within 1 year before appointment, have had a financial interest in or have received compensation from a person regulated by the board; and

(iv) may not, while a member of the board, have a financial interest in or receive compensation from a person regulated by the board.

(4) Each member of the board shall be a resident of the county.

(5) The board shall select a chairperson from among its members, to serve the term that the board sets.

(c) *Term.* — (1) The term of a member is 4 years.

(2) The terms of members are staggered as required by the terms provided for members of the board on October 1, 2002.

(3) At the end of a term, a member continues to serve until a successor is appointed and qualifies.

(4) A member who is appointed after a term has begun serves only for the rest of the term and until a successor is appointed and qualifies.

(d) *Recommendations.* — The board may recommend to the county commissioners:

(1) the types of gaming devices that may be operated in the county;

(2) approval or denial of a gaming permit; and

(3) modifications of the county gaming regulations and procedures.

(e) *Duties.* — The board shall:

(1) review at least quarterly gaming permit applications;

(2) review gaming regulations and permit procedures;

(3) keep a list of all approved lessors of gaming devices and premises for gaming events;

(4) keep a record of the gaming permits that the board has reviewed; and

(5) undertake the other duties regarding gaming regulation that the county commissioners delegate.

(f) *Support and funding.* — As the county commissioners consider appropriate, the county commissioners shall provide for the board a clerk, legal counsel, supplies, and funding.

(g) *Salary.* — The county commissioners may pay salaries to the members of the board. (An. Code 1957, art. 27, § 253A(d); 2002, ch. 26, § 2; ch. 499.)

SPECIAL REVISOR'S NOTE

This Special Revisor's note comprises information related to the revision by Acts 2002, ch. 26 and other chapters amending this section from the 2002 Legislative Session.

As enacted by Ch. 26, Acts of 2002, this section was new language derived without sub-stantive change from former Art. 27, § 253A(d). However, Ch. 499, Acts of 2002, deleted subsection (b)(2)(iii) of this section as enacted by Ch. 26, removing the required member of the clergy from the board, renumbered the following items accordingly, and adding an additional member at large to the board in renumbered subsection (b)(2)(v) of this section.

In subsection (b)(5) of this section, the reference to a "chairperson" was substituted by Ch. 26 for the former reference to a "chairman" because SG § 2-1238 requires the use of words that are neutral as to gender to the extent practicable.

In subsection (c)(2) of this section, the reference to "October 1, 2002" was substituted by Ch. 26 for the former reference to "July 1, 1989" to reflect the effective date of this article.

In the introductory language of subsection (d) of this section, the former phrase "[i]n addition to any powers set forth elsewhere" was deleted by Ch. 26 as implicit in the grant of powers to the board under subsection (d) of this section. Similarly, in the introductory language of subsection (e) of this section, the former phrase "[i]n addition to any duties set forth elsewhere" was deleted by Ch. 26 as implicit in the imposition of duties on the board under subsection (e) of this section.

The Criminal Law Article Review Committee noted, for the consideration of the General Assembly, that in subsection (b)(2)(iii) of this section as enacted by Ch. 26, the requirement to have a member of the clergy on a body created by State law appeared to violate both the federal and State constitutions. The involvement of religion in a regulatory body appeared to violate the First Amendment to the U.S. Constitution. In addition, the requirement appeared to violate Md. Decl. of Rights, Art. 37, in that it required a governmental body to use religion as a qualification of office. *See* Letter of Advice from Attorney General J. Joseph Curran, Jr. to Judge Alan M. Wilner, pp. 6-7 (May 21, 2001). Chapter 499 addressed this concern.

Defined terms:

"Board"	§ 13-1101
"County commissioners"	§ 13-1101
"Fundraising organization"	§ 13-1101
"Gaming device"	§ 13-1101
"Gaming event"	§ 13-1101
"Gaming permit"	§ 13-1101
"Person"	§§ 1-101, 13-1101

§ 13-1105. Bingo and gaming events generally prohibited.

Except as otherwise provided in this subtitle, a person may not conduct bingo or a gaming event in the county. (An. Code 1957, art. 27, § 253A(e); 2002, ch. 26, § 2.)

REVISOR'S NOTE

This Revisor's note comprises information related to the revision by Acts 2002, ch. 26.

This section is new language derived without substantive change from former Art. 27, § 253A(e).

Defined terms:

"Gaming event"	§ 13-1101
"Person"	§§ 1-101, 13-1101

§ 13-1106. Gaming event — In general.

(a) *Qualified organization.* — A gaming event may be conducted only by a fundraising organization that has been located in the county for at least 5 years before applying for a gaming permit.

(b) *Gaming permit required.* — A fundraising organization shall obtain a gaming permit for each gaming event that the fundraising organization conducts.

(c) *Application submission.* — (1) At least 30 days before the first day of the calendar quarter in which the gaming event is to be conducted, a fundraising organization seeking a gaming permit shall submit to the board an application and the application fee.

(2) The application shall contain the following:

(i) the name of the fundraising organization;

(ii) a statement that the fundraising organization qualifies to conduct a gaming event under this subtitle;

(iii) the dates, times, and location of the gaming event;

(iv) the name, address, and telephone number of the representative responsible for the gaming event;

(v) a roster of the current membership of the fundraising organization that includes names, ages, and addresses;

(vi) a statement that:

1. an agreement does not exist for sharing the proceeds of the gaming event with any other person; and

2. no person other than the fundraising organization or its representative may receive any proceeds of the gaming event except to further the purposes of the fundraising organization; and

(vii) any other information that the board considers necessary or helpful.

(3) A principal officer of the fundraising organization shall sign and verify the application under the penalties of perjury.

(d) *Application fee.* — The county commissioners may set a reasonable application fee for a gaming permit.

(e) *Review of application.* — (1) The board shall:

(i) review the gaming permit applications for a calendar quarter within 10 days after the application deadline set in subsection (c)(1) of this section;

(ii) recommend approval or denial of each application; and

(iii) promptly forward the applications and recommendations to the county commissioners.

(2) The county commissioners shall:

(i) review the applications and recommendations;

(ii) approve or disapprove each application within 15 days after the application deadline set in subsection (c) (1) of this section;

(iii) promptly notify each applicant of the county commissioners' action on the application; and

(iv) issue a gaming permit for each approved application.

(3) This section does not prevent the board or the county commissioners from reviewing gaming permit applications more frequently or earlier than required by this subsection. (An. Code 1957, art. 27, § 253A(h)(1), (2), (3)(i)-(vi), (viii); 2002, ch. 26, § 2.)

REVISOR'S NOTE

This Revisor's note comprises information related to the revision by Acts 2002, ch. 26.

This section is new language derived without substantive change from former Art. 27, § 253A(h)(1), (2), and (3)(i) through (vi) and (viii).

In subsection (a) of this section, the former reference to a fundraising organization located in the county "[p]rior to January 1, 1988" is deleted as obsolete.

Subsection (b) of this section is revised as an affirmative requirement to obtain a gaming permit for each gaming event for clarity and to avoid overlap with the gaming permit application procedure of subsection (c)(1) of this section.

In subsection (e)(3) of this section, the reference to this "section" is substituted for the former reference to this "paragraph", although this section is derived, in part, from material outside former Art. 27, § 253A(h)(3)(viii). Because no other portion of this section affects the timing of gaming permit application review by the board or the county commissioners, no substantive change results.

Defined terms:

"Board"	§ 13-1101
"County commissioners"	§ 13-1101
"Fundraising organization"	§ 13-1101

| "Gaming event" | § 13-1101 | "Person" | §§ 1-101, 13-1101 |
| "Gaming permit" | § 13-1101 | "Representative" | § 13-1101 |

Bingo not lottery. — Bingo is not a lottery. Bender v. Arundel Arena, Inc., 248 Md. 181, 236 A.2d 7 (1967).

No limitation that games be conducted on nonrecurring basis. — Predecessor to this section does not include limitation that the conducting of bingo games or raffles in Charles County be on a nonrecurring basis. 61 Op. Att'y Gen. 315 (1976).

§ 13-1107. Gaming event — Permit.

The gaming permit shall include:

    (1) the name of the fundraising organization;

    (2) the nature of the approved gaming event;

    (3) the dates, times, and location of the approved gaming event;

    (4) the gaming devices to be operated at the gaming event; and

    (5) the name of the representative responsible for the approved gaming event. (An. Code 1957, art. 27, § 253A(h)(3)(vii); 2002, ch. 26, § 2.)

REVISOR'S NOTE

This Revisor's note comprises information related to the revision by Acts 2002, ch. 26.

This section is new language derived without substantive change from former Art. 27, § 253A(h)(3)(vii).

Defined terms:

"Fundraising organization"	§ 13-1101
"Gaming device"	§ 13-1101
"Gaming event"	§ 13-1101
"Gaming permit"	§ 13-1101
"Representative"	§ 13-1101

§ 13-1108. Gaming event — Conduct.

(a) *In general.* — (1) A gaming event may be conducted only in accordance with this subtitle.

(2) A gaming device may only be managed or operated by a representative of the fundraising organization named in the gaming permit for the gaming event.

(3) A professional gaming operator may not manage, operate, or assist in the management or operation of a gaming device.

(4) A person may not receive any commission, salary, reward, tip, or other compensation for managing or operating a gaming device at a gaming event.

(5) A minor may not participate in a gaming event.

(6) A fundraising organization may lease gaming devices or premises for a gaming event only from a fundraising organization that the board approves.

(7) (i) A lease agreement of gaming devices or premises for a gaming event shall be priced on the basis of fair market value of the equipment or premises.

    (ii) A lease agreement may not include a provision for sharing profit from a gaming event with a lessor or a provision that reasonably may be interpreted to provide for sharing profit from a gaming event.

(8) A fundraising organization may not conduct more than three gaming events during a calendar quarter.

(9) (i) A fundraising organization may not conduct a gaming event under a single gaming permit for a period greater than 48 hours.

(ii) The actual gaming time may not exceed 24 hours in that 48-hour period, which may be divided into not more than two separate gaming periods.

(iii) Notwithstanding subparagraph (i) of this paragraph, a fundraising organization that conducts a gaming event at the Charles County Fair in conjunction with the Charles County Fair Board may conduct the gaming event under a single gaming permit for more than 48 hours, subject to regulations that the county commissioners adopt on recommendation of the board.

(b) *Report.* — (1) A fundraising organization that has conducted a gaming event shall submit a report to the board within 30 days after the end of the calendar quarter in which the gaming event was conducted.

(2) The report shall contain:

(i) the name of the fundraising organization;

(ii) the number of the gaming permit;

(iii) the date of the gaming event;

(iv) the date, amount, nature, source, and recipient of each receipt and expenditure associated with the gaming event, in the format that the board prescribes;

(v) a separate list of the date, amount, and recipient of each charitable donation from the proceeds;

(vi) the name, age, address, and date of membership of each representative who managed, operated, or assisted in the operation or management of a gaming device at the gaming event;

(vii) a statement that each listed representative qualified as a representative under § 13-1101(i) of this subtitle at the time of the gaming event;

(viii) a statement that:

1. an agreement does not exist and has not existed for sharing the proceeds of a gaming event with any other person; and

2. only the fundraising organization or its representative has received or will receive any proceeds of the gaming event, except to further the purposes of the fundraising organization; and

(ix) any other information that the board considers necessary or helpful.

(3) A principal officer of the fundraising organization shall sign and verify the report under the penalties of perjury.

(c) *Record keeping and availability.* — A fundraising organization that conducts a gaming event shall maintain accurate records of each transaction concerning the gaming event, and shall keep the records available for examination by the board and the county commissioners for 3 years after the gaming event. (An. Code 1957, art. 27, § 253A(h)(4)-(6); 2002, ch. 26, § 2.)

REVISOR'S NOTE

This Revisor's note comprises information related to the revision by Acts 2002, ch. 26.

This section is new language derived without substantive change from former Art. 27, § 253A(h)(4) through (6).

In subsection (a)(3) of this section, the reference to management "or" operation is added for clarity.

In subsection (b)(2)(vi) of this section, the reference to "manage[ment]" of a gaming device is added for consistency with subsection (a)(2) and (3) of this section.

Defined terms:
"Board"   § 13-1101

"County commissioners"	§ 13-1101
"Fundraising organization"	§ 13-1101
"Gaming device"	§ 13-1101
"Gaming event"	§ 13-1101
"Gaming permit"	§ 13-1101
"Minor"	§ 1-101
"Person"	§§ 1-101, 13-1101
"Representative"	§ 13-1101

§ 13-1109. Bingo.

(a) *In general.* — A fundraising organization or educational organization may conduct bingo either for the benefit of charity in the county or to further the purposes of the organization.

(b) *Form of prize.* — Subject to subsection (c) of this section, a fundraising organization or educational organization may award money or merchandise as a prize in a bingo game.

(c) *Prize limits.* — (1) A fundraising organization or educational organization may not award a money prize exceeding $5,000 to any player in a bingo game.

(2) A fundraising organization or educational organization may not award more than $10,000 in total money prizes in a single day.

(d) *Time limits.* — A fundraising organization or educational organization may not conduct bingo at one location for more than 4 hours per day for:

(1) 4 days in a 7-day period; or

(2) 3 consecutive days. (An. Code 1957, art. 27, § 253A(g); 2002, ch. 26, § 2; 2003, ch. 21, § 1; ch. 438.)

REVISOR'S NOTE

This Revisor's note comprises information related to the revision by Acts 2002, ch. 26.

This section is new language derived without substantive change from former Art. 27, § 253A(g).

In subsections (b) and (c) of this section, the references to a "money" prize are substituted for the former references to a "cash" prize for consistency within this title.

In subsections (c)(2) and (d) of this section, the references to a "fundraising organization or educational organization" are added to clarify the entities that may conduct bingo under this section.

Defined term:
"Fundraising organization"   § 13-1101

§ 13-1110. Management of bingo and gaming events.

A fundraising organization or educational organization may only allow its representatives to manage or operate bingo or gaming devices at its bingo or gaming event. (An. Code 1957, art. 27, § 253A(i); 2002, ch. 26, § 2.)

REVISOR'S NOTE

This Revisor's note comprises information related to the revision by Acts 2002, ch. 26.

This section is new language derived without substantive change from former Art. 27, § 253A(i).

The reference to an "educational organization" is added to state explicitly that which was only implied in the former law, that any organization, including an educational organization, that conducts bingo under this subtitle may allow only its representatives to manage or operate bingo.

The reference to managing or operating "bingo", which is excluded from the term "gaming device" defined in § 13-1101 of this subtitle, is added for clarity.

Defined terms:

"Fundraising organization"	§ 13-1101
"Gaming device"	§ 13-1101
"Gaming event"	§ 13-1101
"Representative"	§ 13-1101

§ 13-1111. Use of proceeds.

Proceeds of bingo or a gaming event may not:

(1) benefit a person other than the fundraising organization or educational organization that conducts the bingo or gaming event; or

(2) be shared with a person other than the fundraising organization or educational organization, except to further the purposes of the fundraising organization or educational organization. (An. Code 1957, art. 27, § 253A(j); 2002, ch. 26, § 2.)

REVISOR'S NOTE

This Revisor's note comprises information related to the revision by Acts 2002, ch. 26.

This section is new language derived without substantive change from former Art. 27, § 253A(j).

The former reference to a "portion" of the proceeds of a bingo or gaming event is deleted as included in the reference to the "[p]roceeds" themselves.

Defined terms:

"Fundraising organization"	§ 13-1101
"Gaming event"	§ 13-1101
"Person"	§§ 1-101, 13-1101

§ 13-1112. Donation to Fair Board allowed.

Notwithstanding any other provision of this subtitle, a fundraising organization or educational organization may donate part of the proceeds of bingo or a gaming event at the Charles County Fair to the Charles County Fair Board. (An. Code 1957, art. 27, § 253A(k); 2002, ch. 26, § 2.)

REVISOR'S NOTE

This Revisor's note comprises information related to the revision by Acts 2002, ch. 26.

This section is new language derived without substantive change from former Art. 27, § 253A(k).

Defined terms:

"Fundraising organization"	§ 13-1101
"Gaming event"	§ 13-1101

§ 13-1113. Penalty.

A person who violates this subtitle is guilty of a misdemeanor and on conviction is subject to imprisonment not exceeding 1 year or a fine not exceeding $1,000 or both. (An. Code 1957, art. 27, § 253A(l); 2002, ch. 26, § 2.)

§ 13-1114. Disqualification after violation.

In addition to any other penalty, a person who violates this subtitle is ineligible to obtain a gaming permit for 3 years after the date of the violation. (An. Code 1957, art. 27, § 253A(m); 2002, ch. 26, § 2.)

§ 13-1115. Effect of other law.

This subtitle does not restrict the authority of the county commissioners to adopt regulations on amusements and entertainments under Chapter 4 of the Code of Public Local Laws of Charles County or other State law. (An. Code 1957, art. 27, § 253A(f); 2002, ch. 26, § 2.)

Subtitle 12. Dorchester County.

§ 13-1201. "Gaming event" defined.

In this subtitle, "gaming event" means a carnival, bazaar, or raffle. (2002, ch. 26, § 2.)

§ 13-1202. Scope and application of subtitle.

(a) *Scope of subtitle.* — This subtitle applies only in Dorchester County.

(b) *Application of Subtitle 2.* — Subtitle 2 of this title applies in Dorchester County. (An. Code 1957, art. 27, § 255(a)(7); 2002, ch. 26, § 2.)

REVISOR'S NOTE

This Revisor's note comprises information related to the revision by Acts 2002, ch. 26.

Subsection (a) of this section is new language added to clarify that this subtitle applies only to Dorchester County.

Subsection (b) of this section is new language derived without substantive change from former Art. 27, § 255(a)(7).

§ **13-1203. Bingo.**

(a) *License required.* — A person must have a license for each day that the person conducts bingo unless the bingo is conducted in a licensed gaming event.

(b) *Issued by clerk.* — Notwithstanding any other provision of this subtitle or Subtitle 2 of this title, in addition to bingo conducted in connection with a gaming event under Subtitle 2 of this title, the clerk of the circuit court of the county may issue a license to conduct bingo.

(c) *Qualified organizations.* — To qualify for a license to conduct bingo, an applicant shall be a:

(1) bona fide religious group that has conducted religious services at a fixed location in the county for at least 3 years before applying for a license;

(2) tax-supported volunteer fire company or an auxiliary unit whose members are directly associated with the fire company;

(3) nationally chartered veterans' organization or an auxiliary unit whose members are directly associated with the organization; or

(4) nonprofit organization that:

(i) intends to raise money for an exclusively charitable, athletic, or educational purpose that is described in the application for a license; and

(ii) has operated in the county for at least 3 years before applying for a license.

(d) *Application for license.* — An application for a license to conduct bingo shall contain a certification, by a principal officer of the applicant, stating:

(1) the time and place of the activities for which the license is sought;

(2) that the bingo will be conducted and managed solely and personally by the regular members of the applicant without the assistance of gaming professionals; and

(3) that no compensation or reward will be paid to any person for conducting or assisting in the conducting of the bingo. (An. Code 1957, art. 27, § 255A(a)-(c); 2002, ch. 26, § 2.)

REVISOR'S NOTE

This Revisor's note comprises information related to the revision by Acts 2002, ch. 26.

This section is new language derived without substantive change from former Art. 27, § 255A(a), (b), and the fourth sentence of (c).

In subsection (a) of this section, the reference to a "gaming event" is substituted for the former reference to a "carnival" for clarity and consistency with subsection (b) of this section. The Criminal Law Article Review Committee calls this substitution to the attention of the General Assembly.

Also in subsection (a) of this section, the former reference to a "duly" licensed gaming event is deleted as surplusage.

In subsection (b) of this section, the reference to a gaming event "under Subtitle 2 of this title" is added for clarity.

Also in subsection (b) of this section, the reference to the clerk of the "circuit" court is added for clarity.

In subsection (c)(4)(i) of this section, the reference to "intend[ing]" to raise money is substituted for the former reference to "desiring" to raise money for consistency within this title.

Also in subsection (c)(4)(i) of this section, the former reference to a purpose that is "specifically" described in an application is deleted as surplusage.

In subsection (d)(2) of this section, the reference to a "gaming" professional is added for clarity.

In subsection (d)(3) of this section, the former reference to a "commission, salary. . . or recompense" is deleted in light of the comprehensive reference to a "compensation or reward".

Also in subsection (d)(3) of this section, the former reference to "operat[ing]" bingo is deleted as included in the reference to "conducting" bingo.

Defined terms:

"Gaming event"	§ 13-1201
"Person"	§ 1-101

§ 13-1204. Prohibited acts.

(a) *Sunday gaming.* — A license issued under this subtitle may not authorize a game or carnival on a Sunday.

(b) *Minors.* — An individual under the age of 16 years may not be allowed to play, conduct, or operate bingo. (An. Code 1957, art. 27, § 255A(c), (d); 2002, ch. 26, § 2.)

REVISOR'S NOTE

This Revisor's note comprises information related to the revision by Acts 2002, ch. 26.

This section is new language derived without substantive change from former Art. 27, § 255A(d) and the third sentence of (c).

The Criminal Law Article Review Committee notes, for the consideration of the General Assembly, that in subsection (a) of this section, the reference to "a game or carnival" may be too narrow to cover all gaming activities.

In subsection (b) of this section, the reference to an age limit for playing bingo under a "permit . . . issued under this section" is deleted in light of § 13-1203(a) of this subtitle, which requires a license to conduct bingo.

§ 13-1205. Coin or slot machines.

This subtitle does not authorize the use of a slot machine or coin machine for gambling purposes. (An. Code 1957, art. 27, § 255A(e); 2002, ch. 26, § 2.)

REVISOR'S NOTE

This Revisor's note comprises information related to the revision by Acts 2002, ch. 26.

This section is new language derived without substantive change from former Art. 27, § 255A(e).

The former reference to "any type of" coin machine is deleted as surplusage.

§ 13-1206. Enforcement.

The bailiffs, municipal police officers, prosecuting officials, and other peace officers of the county shall enforce this subtitle. (An. Code 1957, art. 27, § 255A(f); 2002, ch. 26, § 2.)

REVISOR'S NOTE

This Revisor's note comprises information related to the revision by Acts 2002, ch. 26.

This section is new language derived without substantive change from former Art. 27, § 255A(f).

The former reference to being "strictly charged with" the enforcement of this subtitle is deleted as implicit in the phrase "shall enforce".

§ 13-1207. License fees.

(a) *Raffle or carnival.* — The clerk of the circuit court of the county shall collect $5 for a license for a raffle or carnival.

(b) *Bingo.* — The clerk of the circuit court shall collect $25 from an applicant for an annual bingo license to conduct bingo and $1 for issuance of the license.

(c) *Daily bingo license.* — (1) Except as provided in paragraph (3) of this subsection, a 1-day bingo license is required for each day a bingo game is conducted.

(2) The clerk of the circuit court of the county shall collect $1 for a 1-day bingo license.

(3) A 1-day bingo license is not required for bingo conducted at a licensed carnival or under an annual bingo license. (An. Code 1957, art. 27, § 255A(c); 2002, ch. 26, § 2.)

REVISOR'S NOTE

This Revisor's note comprises information related to the revision by Acts 2002, ch. 26.

This section is new language derived without substantive change from the first, second, and fourth sentences of former Art. 27, § 255A(c).

In subsections (b) and (c)(2) of this section, the references to the clerk of the "circuit" court are added for clarity and consistency with § 13-1203(b) of this subtitle. Correspondingly, in subsection (a) of this section, the reference to the "clerk of the circuit court" is added.

The Criminal Law Article Review Committee notes, for the consideration of the General Assembly, that in subsection (a) of this section, the reference to a "raffle or carnival" may be too narrow to cover all gaming activities. The Committee also notes that, in practice, the clerk does not accept fees for raffles or carnivals nor will the clerk issue a license for a raffle or carnival.

Subtitle 13. Frederick County.

§ 13-1301. Definitions.

(a) *In general.* — In this subtitle the following words have the meanings indicated.

This subsection is new language derived without substantive change from the introductory language of former Art. 27, § 258A(a).

In this subsection, the reference to this "subtitle" is substituted for the former reference to this "section", although this subtitle is derived, in part, from material outside former Art. 27, § 258A. Because the term "gaming event" defined in this section is used only in provisions that are derived from former Art. 27, §§ 255 and 258A, and in light of § 13-1303 of this subtitle, no substantive change results.

(b) *County commissioners.* — "County commissioners" means the Board of County Commissioners of Frederick County.

This subsection is new language derived without substantive change from former Art. 27, § 258A(a)(1).

The defined term "county commissioners" is substituted for the former defined term "Board" for consistency within this title.

(c) *Gaming event.* — "Gaming event" includes a:
(1) bazaar;
(2) carnival;
(3) raffle;
(4) tip jar; and
(5) punchboard.

This subsection is new language derived without substantive change from former Art. 27, § 258A(a)(4).

The former reference to "other similar games of chance" is deleted in light of the use of the word "includes". *See* Art. 1, § 30.

(An. Code 1957, art. 27, § 258A, (a)(1), (4); 2002, ch. 26, § 2.)

The Revisor's notes in this section comprise information related to the revision by Acts 2002, ch. 26.

Former Art. 27, § 258A(a)(2), which defined "county" to mean Frederick County, is deleted as unnecessary in light of § 13-1302 of this subtitle.

§ 13-1302. Scope of subtitle.

This subtitle applies only in Frederick County. (2002, ch. 26, § 2; 2009, chs. 618, 619.)

This Revisor's note comprises information related to the revision by Acts 2002, ch. 26.

This section is new language added to clarify the scope of this subtitle.

Effect of amendments. — Chapters 618 and 619, Acts 2009, effective July 1, 2009, made identical changes. Each reenacted the section without change.

§ 13-1303. Application of Subtitle 2.

(a) *In general.* — Subtitle 2 of this title applies in Frederick County.

(b) *Application of Subtitle 2.* — A gaming event under Subtitle 2 of this title is subject to the requirements of this subtitle.

(c) *Additional qualified organizations.* — In addition to the qualified organizations listed in Subtitle 2 of this title, the following organizations and their auxiliaries may conduct activities governed by that subtitle:

(1) a volunteer fire company;

(2) a volunteer rescue company; and

(3) a volunteer ambulance company.

(d) *Additional activities regulated.* — Subtitle 2 of this title also regulates any gaming device, including a:

(1) chance book;

(2) tip jar;

(3) paddle wheel; and

(4) wheel of fortune. (An. Code 1957, art. 27, § 255(a)(8), (j); 2002, ch. 26, § 2.)

§ 13-1304. Gaming events.

(a) *Permit required.* — Before an organization listed in subsection (b) of this section may conduct a gaming event, the organization shall obtain a permit from the county agency that the county commissioners designate.

(b) *Qualified organizations.* — An organization may conduct a gaming event for its own benefit if the organization is:

(1) a bona fide:

(i) religious organization;

(ii) fraternal organization;

(iii) civic organization;

(iv) war veterans' organization;

(v) hospital;

(vi) amateur athletic organization;

(vii) patriotic organization;

(viii) educational organization; or

(ix) charitable organization;

(2) a Frederick County volunteer:

(i) fire company;

(ii) rescue company; or

(iii) ambulance company; or

(3) an auxiliary for a Frederick County volunteer:

(i) fire company;

(ii) rescue company; or

(iii) ambulance company.

(c) *Application.* — (1) Before the county agency may issue a gaming permit, the county agency shall determine whether the organization applying for the gaming permit meets the requirements of this section.

(2) An application and the action that the county agency takes on the application are public records.

(d) *Terms.* — (1) (i) A gaming permit is valid for 1 year after the date that it is issued.

(ii) A gaming permit may not be transferred.

(2) The county commissioners may charge a permit fee.

(e) *Limitations.* — (1) Only members of an organization that holds a gaming permit may conduct the gaming event.

(2) Except as allowed under § 13-1305 of this subtitle, an individual may not benefit financially from a gaming event.

(3) A gaming permit may not authorize a gaming event to be conducted on a Sunday before 1 p.m.

(f) *Prizes.* — (1) The holder of a gaming permit may award:

(i) prizes to individuals at a gaming event; and

(ii) only one major prize at each gaming event.

(2) During each calendar year, the holder of a gaming event, including a raffle for which the prize drawings are held on a single day, may not hold or receive the proceeds from:

(i) more than one gaming event in which the major prize has a value of more than $5,000; and

(ii) more than five raffles for which the prize drawings are held on a single day and in which the major prize has a value of $5,000 or less.

(3) During each calendar year, the holder of a gaming event may hold one raffle in which prize drawings are held on more than a single day if the major prize has a value of $5,000 or less.

(g) *Regulations.* — The county commissioners may adopt regulations to carry out this section and §§ 13-1305 and 13-1307 of this subtitle. (An. Code 1957, art. 27, § 258A(b)-(d); 2002, ch. 26, § 2; 2006, ch. 167.)

REVISOR'S NOTE

This Revisor's note comprises information related to the revision by Acts 2002, ch. 26.

This section is new language derived without substantive change from former Art. 27, § 258A(b) through (d).

In subsection (a) of this section, the reference to "conduct[ing]" a gaming event is substituted for the former reference to "operating" a gaming event for consistency throughout this subtitle.

In subsection (c)(1) of this section, the reference to "determin[ing]" whether the organization applying for the gaming permit" meets requirements is substituted for the former reference to "ascertain[ing] the character of the organization for whom the application is made to determine if the application meets" requirements for clarity.

In subsection (e)(1) of this section, the former reference to a "managed" gaming event is deleted as included in the reference to "conduct-[ing]" a gaming event.

In subsection (e)(3) of this section, the phrase "[a] gaming permit may not authorize a gaming event to be conducted on a Sunday before 1 p.m." is substituted for the former ambiguous phrase "[t]he permit authorizes the operation of a gaming event after 1 p.m. on Sunday" for clarity.

In subsection (g) of this section, the reference to "§§ 13-1305 and 13-1307 of this subtitle" is added to reflect the reorganization of material derived from former Art. 27, § 258A in this revision.

The Criminal Law Article Review Committee notes, for the consideration of the General Assembly, that the reference to a "major prize" in subsection (f)(1)(ii) is vague. Because a violation of that provision is a misdemeanor, the General Assembly may wish to clarify the reference.

§ 13-1305. Tip jars and punchboards.

(a) *Qualified operators.* — (1) To operate a tip jar or punchboard in the county, an establishment or proprietor must be licensed to serve food and alcoholic beverages for consumption on the premises.

(2) The operator of a tip jar shall display conspicuously a gaming permit issued to the beneficiary of the tip jar under § 13-1304 of this subtitle.

(3) The operator of a punchboard shall display within the establishment a gaming permit issued to the beneficiary of the punchboard under § 13-1304 of this subtitle.

(b) *Qualified beneficiaries.* — (1) A person may operate a tip jar or punchboard in the county only for the benefit of one of the following organizations located in the county:

    (i) a bona fide:

        1. religious organization;

        2. fraternal organization;

        3. civic organization;

        4. war veterans' organization;

        5. hospital;

        6. amateur athletic organization;

        7. patriotic organization;

        8. charitable organization; or

        9. educational organization;

    (ii) a Frederick County volunteer:

        1. fire company;

        2. rescue company; or

        3. ambulance company; or

    (iii) an auxiliary of a Frederick County volunteer:

        1. fire company;

        2. rescue company; or

        3. ambulance company.

(2) The beneficiary of a tip jar may not hold more than three permits to operate tip jars or punchboards outside of the beneficiary's premises.

(c) *Financial accounting.* — (1) The beneficiary of a tip jar or punchboard must receive at least 70% of the gross proceeds of the tip jar or punchboard after paying winning players and reimbursing the operator for operating expenses.

(2) For each tip jar or punchboard operated, the operator shall submit to the county agency that issued the gaming permit monthly reports detailing:

    (i) gross proceeds;

    (ii) prizes;

    (iii) expenses; and

    (iv) the amount paid to the beneficiary.

(d) *Licensed distributors.* — The tip jar or punchboard shall be purchased from a distributor that:

    (1) has an office in the State;

    (2) is licensed by the county agency that issues gaming event permits; and

    (3) keeps the records that the county commissioners require.

(e) *Records.* — A person who keeps records about tip jars or punchboards shall make those records available for inspection and copying by a law enforcement unit or by the county agency that issues the gaming event permit. (An. Code 1957, art. 27, § 258A(e); 2002, ch. 26, § 2; 2009, chs. 618, 619.)

REVISOR'S NOTE

This Revisor's note comprises information related to the revision by Acts 2002, ch. 26.

This section is new language derived without substantive change from former Art. 27, § 258A(e).

In subsection (a)(2) and (3) of this section, the phrase "issued to the beneficiary" is added because of the statement in former Art. 27, § 258A(e)(5) that permits are issued to the beneficiary organizations and, because former Art. 27, § 258A(e)(2) limits the operation of games to establishments or proprietors that are licensed to serve food and alcoholic beverages for consumption on the premises.

In subsections (b)(2) and (c)(1) of this section, the reference to a "beneficiary" is substituted for the former reference to an "organization" for clarity.

In subsection (c)(2)(ii) of this section, the reference to "prizes" is substituted for the former reference to "payouts for winnings" for brevity and clarity.

In subsection (e) of this section, the reference to a law enforcement "unit" is substituted for the former reference to a law enforcement "agency" for consistency within this article. *See* General Revisor's Note to article.

Defined terms:

"County commissioners"	§ 13-1301
"Gaming event"	§ 13-1301
"Person"	§ 1-101

Effect of amendments. — Chapters 618 and 619, Acts 2009, effective July 1, 2009, made identical changes. Each reenacted (a)(1) without change and substituted "State" for "county" in (d)(1).

§ 13-1306. Bingo — Generally.

(a) *Permit required.* — A person authorized to conduct bingo under this subtitle shall obtain a bingo permit from the county agency designated by the county commissioners to issue a bingo permit.

(b) *Qualified organizations.* — Any of the following organizations, if a legal resident of the county, may conduct bingo to benefit charity in the county or to further the purposes of one of the following organizations:

    (1) a bona fide:

        (i) religious organization;

        (ii) fraternal organization;

        (iii) patriotic organization;

        (iv) educational organization;

(v) civic organization;

(vi) war veterans' organization;

(vii) hospital;

(viii) amateur athletic organization; or

(ix) charitable organization;

(2) a volunteer:

(i) fire company;

(ii) rescue company; or

(iii) ambulance company; or

(3) an auxiliary for a volunteer:

(i) fire company;

(ii) rescue company; or

(iii) ambulance company.

(c) *Unqualified persons.* — (1) A person who is not a legal resident of Frederick County may not conduct bingo.

(2) Notwithstanding paragraph (1) of this subsection, each year the Frederick County Agricultural Association may sell or lease a right or concession to any person to conduct bingo at the Frederick County Fair.

(d) *Application.* — (1) To qualify for a bingo permit, a person shall meet the requirements set by the county commissioners.

(2) The county commissioners may require an applicant for a bingo permit to pay a permit fee set by the county commissioners.

(e) *Prize limitations.* — A person who conducts bingo may not offer or award:

(1) a prize or award with a fair market value exceeding $5,000; or

(2) a money prize exceeding $5,000.

(f) *Regulations.* — The county commissioners may adopt regulations to carry out this section. (An. Code 1957, art. 27, § 249; 2002, ch. 26, § 2.)

REVISOR'S NOTE

This Revisor's note comprises information related to the revision by Acts 2002, ch. 26.

This section is new language derived without substantive change from former Art. 27, § 249.

In subsections (a) and (d) of this section, the references to a "bingo" permit are added for clarity.

In subsection (a) of this section, the reference to "conduct[ing]" bingo is substituted for the former reference to "operat[ing]" bingo for consistency with other provisions of this subtitle. Similarly, in subsection (b) of this section, the former reference to "operat[ing]" bingo is deleted as included in the reference to "conduct[ing]" bingo.

In the introductory language of subsection (b) of this section, the phrase "if a legal resident of the county," is added for clarity and consistency with subsection (c) of this section.

In subsection (b)(9) of this section, the former reference to "corporations" is deleted in light of the reference to an "organization".

In subsection (c) of this section, the former phrase "regardless of the residence of the purchaser or lessee" is deleted as surplusage.

Also in subsection (c) of this section, the former reference to a "copartnership, firm, group, corporation or organization" is deleted as included in the defined term "person". *See* § 1-101 of this article.

In subsection (e) of this section, the former references to offering a prize or award "to any player" and to "no such player" are deleted as surplusage.

Defined terms:

"County commissioners" § 13-1301

"Person" § 1-101

Bingo not lottery. — Bingo is not a lottery.
Bender v. Arundel Arena, Inc., 248 Md. 181, 236
A.2d 7 (1967).

§ 13-1307. Prohibited acts; penalty.

(a) *Prohibited.* — A person may not knowingly violate § 13-1304 or § 13-1305 of this subtitle.

(b) *Penalty.* — A person who violates this section is guilty of a misdemeanor and on conviction is subject to imprisonment not exceeding 1 year or a fine not exceeding $1,000 or both. (An. Code 1957, art. 27, § 258A(f); 2002, ch. 26, § 2.)

REVISOR'S NOTE

This Revisor's note comprises information related to the revision by Acts 2002, ch. 26.

This section is new language derived without substantive change from former Art. 27, § 258A(f).

Defined term:
"Person"   § 1-101

Subtitle 14. Garrett County.

§ 13-1401. Definitions.

(a) *In general.* — In this subtitle the following words have the meanings indicated.

(b) *County Commissioners.* — "County Commissioners" means the Board of County Commissioners of Garrett County.

(c) *Gaming event.* — "Gaming event" includes a bazaar, carnival, raffle, tip jar, punchboard, and any other event at which a gaming device is operated.

(d) *Gaming device.* — (1) "Gaming device" means:

(i) except for a billiard table, a gaming table at which a game of chance is played for money or any other thing or consideration of value; or

(ii) a game or device at which money or any other thing or consideration of value is bet, wagered, or gambled.

(2) "Gaming device" includes a paddle wheel, wheel of fortune, and chance book. (2005, ch. 234.)

§ 13-1402. Applicability.

(a) *Subtitle 14.* — This subtitle applies only in Garrett County.

(b) *Subtitle 2.* — Subtitle 2 of this title applies in Garrett County. (2005, ch. 234; 2006, ch. 297.)

§ 13-1403. Gaming events.

(a) *Permit required.* — Before an organization listed in subsection (b) of this section may conduct a gaming event, the organization shall obtain a permit from the county agency that the County Commissioners designate.

(b) *Qualifying organizations.* — An organization may conduct a gaming event for its own benefit if the organization is:

(1) a bona fide:

 (i) religious organization;

 (ii) fraternal organization;

 (iii) civic organization;

 (iv) war veterans' organization;

 (v) hospital;

 (vi) amateur athletic organization;

 (vii) patriotic organization;

 (viii) educational organization; or

 (ix) charitable organization;

(2) a county volunteer fire department or rescue squad; or

(3) an auxiliary for a county volunteer fire department or rescue squad.

(c) *Determination of qualification.* — (1) Before the county agency may issue a gaming permit, the county agency shall determine whether the organization applying for the gaming permit meets the requirements of this section.

(2) An application and the action that the county agency takes on the application are public records.

(d) *Annual permit nontransferable; fee.* — (1) (i) A gaming permit is valid for 1 year after the date that it is issued.

 (ii) A gaming permit may not be transferred.

(2) The County Commissioners may charge a permit fee.

(e) *Limitations.* — (1) Only members of an organization that holds a gaming permit may conduct a gaming event.

(2) Except as allowed under § 13-1405 of this subtitle, an individual may not benefit financially from a gaming event.

(3) A gaming permit may not authorize a gaming event to be conducted on a Sunday before 1 p.m.

(f) *Prizes.* — The holder of a gaming permit may award:

(1) prizes to individuals at a gaming event; and

(2) only one major prize at each gaming event. (2005, ch. 234; 2006, ch. 297.)

§ 13-1404. Paper gaming.

(a) *"Paper gaming" defined.* — (1) In this section, "paper gaming" means a game of chance in which:

 (i) prizes are awarded; and

 (ii) the devices used to play the game are constructed out of paper or cardboard.

(2) "Paper gaming" includes tip jar and punchboard gaming.

(3) "Paper gaming" does not include bingo.

(b) *Requirements.* — (1) Subject to paragraphs (2) and (3) of this subsection, a person that is a for profit business or an organization listed under § 13-1403(b) of this subtitle may engage in paper gaming if the person obtains a paper gaming license that is issued by the County Commissioners.

(2) If the person is a for profit business, the person:

(i) shall also hold a Class A, B, C, or D retail alcoholic beverages license; and

(ii) may engage in paper gaming only on the premises of the for profit business.

(3) Subject to paragraph (4) of this subsection, an organization may engage in paper gaming if the organization:

(i) is listed under § 13-1403(b) of this subtitle and does not have an alcoholic beverages license; or

(ii) is a county volunteer fire department or rescue squad and has an alcoholic beverages license.

(4) An organization under paragraph (3) of this subsection may engage in paper gaming only on its premises.

(c) *Wholesaler's license.* — A person may sell paper gaming devices to a paper gaming licensee if the person obtains a wholesale vendor's license issued by the County Commissioners.

(d) *Annual license fees.* — The County Commissioners shall set annual fees for a paper gaming license and a wholesale vendor's license.

(e) *Monthly wholesaler's reports.* — Not later than the fifteenth of each month, wholesale vendor licensees shall provide to the County Commissioners a list for the previous month of all customers to whom they sold paper gaming products and the total number of products sold to each customer.

(f) *Gaming sticker required.* — A paper gaming licensee may not have on its premises a paper gaming device that does not display a gaming sticker issued by the county.

(g) *Devices required to conform to bill of sale.* — The County Commissioners shall ensure that each licensee who conducts paper gaming under a paper gaming license sells to the public the same serial-numbered paper gaming devices that are listed on the bill of sale from the wholesale vendor licensee.

(h) *Taxes.* — The County Commissioners may impose the following paper gaming taxes:

(1) on licensees that are qualified organizations, 10% of gross profits minus the costs of paper gaming products; and

(2) on licensees that are for profit businesses, 40% of gross profits minus the costs of paper gaming products.

(i) *Special Gaming Fund.* — (1) In this subsection, "Fund" means the Special Gaming Fund.

(2) The County Commissioners shall establish a Special Gaming Fund.

(3) The Fund is a special continuing, nonlapsing fund.

(4) The Fund shall be used only to benefit fire and rescue services.

(5) (i) The Fund consists of:

1. revenue derived from the taxation of gross profits from tip jar sales; and

2. subject to subparagraph (ii) of this paragraph, money received from other sources.

(ii) Money from the General Fund of the State or the county, including any federal money, may not be transferred by budget amendment or otherwise to the Fund.

(6) The Fund shall be invested and reinvested in the same manner as other county funds.

(7) Annually the County Commissioners shall:

(i) pay from the Fund all administrative costs of carrying out this section, including the hiring of additional necessary personnel; and

(ii) allocate the remaining money in the Fund to fire and rescue services.

(j) *Rules and regulations.* — The County Commissioners may adopt rules and regulations to administer and enforce this section.

(k) *Inspectors.* — The County Commissioners may:

(1) hire or designate one or more inspectors; and

(2) authorize each inspector to enter the premises of a licensee to ensure compliance with this section or a rule or regulation adopted under this section.

(l) *Violations; penalties.* — The County Commissioners may adopt an ordinance or resolution declaring that:

(1) a violation of this section or a rule or regulation adopted under this section is a misdemeanor punishable by a term of imprisonment not exceeding 30 days or a fine not exceeding $1,000 or both; and

(2) each day that a violation continues is a separate offense.

(m) *Suspension or revocation of license.* — After a hearing, if the County Commissioners or a designee of the Board finds that a paper gaming licensee, a wholesale vendor licensee, or an agent of a licensee has violated this section or a rule or regulation adopted under this section, the Board may suspend or revoke the license in addition to any fine or penalty imposed under this subsection. (2005, ch. 25, § 13; ch. 234; 2006, ch. 297.)

§ 13-1405. Bingo.

(a) *Permits required.* — A person authorized to conduct bingo under subsection (b) of this section shall obtain a bingo permit from the county agency designated by the County Commissioners to issue a bingo permit.

(b) *Requirements.* — An organization may conduct bingo for its own benefit or to benefit charity in the county if the organization is a legal resident of the county and is:

(1) a bona fide:

(i) religious organization;

(ii) fraternal organization;

(iii) civic organization;

(iv) war veterans' organization;

(v) hospital;

(vi) amateur athletic organization;

(vii) patriotic organization;

(viii) educational organization; or

(ix) charitable organization;

(2) a county volunteer fire department or rescue squad; or

(3) an auxiliary for a county volunteer fire department or rescue squad.

(c) *Nonresidents prohibited from conducting.* — A person who is not a legal resident of the county may not conduct bingo.

(d) *Qualification.* — To qualify for a bingo permit, a person shall meet the requirements set by the county.

(e) *Operation by qualifying organization only.* — Only members of an organization listed under subsection (b) of this section may conduct and operate bingo games. (2005, ch. 234; 2006, ch. 297.)

§ 13-1406. Political fundraisers — Paddle wheels.

The County Commissioners may adopt regulations to carry out this subtitle, including age restrictions for participants in any activity involving a gaming event or bingo. (2005, ch. 234; 2006, ch. 44, § 6; ch. 297; 2007, ch. 5.)

Subtitle 15. Harford County.

§ 13-1501. Definitions.

(a) *In general.* — In this subtitle the following words have the meanings indicated.

REVISOR'S NOTE

This subsection formerly was Art. 27, § 254(a)(1).

In this section and throughout this subtitle, the references to this "subtitle" are substituted for the former references to this "section" to reflect the reorganization of material derived from former Art. 27, § 254 in this subtitle.

No other changes are made.

(b) *Bingo.* — "Bingo":
(1) includes instant bingo; but
(2) does not include members-only instant bingo.

REVISOR'S NOTE

This subsection is new language derived without substantive change from former Art. 27, § 254(a)(2).

(c) *50/50.* — "50/50" means a drawing from a finite number of chances in which the proceeds from the sale of chances are split evenly between the winner and the organization conducting the game.

REVISOR'S NOTE

This subsection is new language derived without substantive change from former Art. 27, § 254(e)(1).

The former phrase "[f]or the purposes of this subsection" is deleted in light of the reorganization of material derived from former Art. 27, § 254(e) in this subtitle.

(d) *Gaming event.* — "Gaming event" means bingo, members-only instant bingo, a raffle, or a paddle wheel.

REVISOR'S NOTE

This subsection is new language added to reflect the gaming activities authorized under this subtitle and for consistency within this title.

(e) *Members-only instant bingo.* — "Members-only instant bingo" means an instant bingo game that is limited to members and guests of an organization listed in § 13-1503(b) of this subtitle.

REVISOR'S NOTE

This subsection is new language derived without substantive change from former Art. 27, § 254(a)(3).

(f) *Sheriff.* — "Sheriff" means the Sheriff of Harford County.

REVISOR'S NOTE

This subsection is new language added to avoid repetition of the full title "Sheriff of Harford County".

(An. Code 1957, art. 27, § 254(a), (e)(1); 2002, ch. 26, § 2; 2007, ch. 281; 2009, ch. 374.)

REVISOR'S NOTE TO SECTION

The Revisor's notes in this section comprise information related to the revision by Acts 2002, ch. 26.

Effect of amendments. — Chapter 374, Acts 2009, effective July 1, 2009, reenacted (a), (c), and (f) without change.

§ 13-1502. Scope of subtitle.

(a) *Application of subtitle.* — This subtitle applies only in Harford County.

(b) *Slot machines and coin machines not authorized.* — This subtitle does not authorize the use of a slot machine or any type of coin machine for gambling purposes. (An. Code 1957, art. 27, § 254(h); 2002, ch. 26, § 2; 2007, ch. 281; 2009, ch. 374.)

REVISOR'S NOTE

This Revisor's note comprises information related to the revision by Acts 2002, ch. 26.

Subsection (a) of this section is new language added to state expressly that which was only implied in former Art. 27, § 254, *i.e.*, that this subtitle applies only in Harford County.

Subsection (b) of this section is new language derived without substantive change from former Art. 27, § 254(h).

Effect of amendments. — Chapter 374, Acts 2009, effective July 1, 2009, reenacted (a) without change.

§ 13-1503. Gaming events.

(a) *License required.* — Before an organization conducts a gaming event under this subtitle, the organization shall obtain a license from the sheriff.

(b) *Qualified organizations.* — The following organizations may obtain a license to conduct a gaming event:

(1) a bona fide religious group that has conducted religious services at a fixed location in the county for at least 3 years before applying for a license;

(2) a State-chartered organization authorized by a nationally chartered veterans organization;

(3) a tax-supported volunteer fire company; or

(4) a nonprofit organization that intends to raise money for an exclusively charitable, athletic, or educational purpose which is specifically described in the application for a license.

(c) *Application.* — An application for a license shall contain a certification by a principal officer of the organization that states:

(1) the scheduled time and place of the gaming event and the date of any raffle drawing;

(2) that the licensed activities will be managed and conducted solely and personally by the regular members of the organization without the assistance of gaming professionals;

(3) that all money prizes offered will comply with the limits listed in this subtitle;

(4) that the organization, by one of its principal officers, shall, within 15 days after the last day named in the application for conducting the licensed activities, file a report under penalties of perjury containing the information required by § 13-1509 of this subtitle; and

(5) if the organization is a nonprofit organization that intends to raise money for an exclusively charitable, athletic, or educational purpose, a specific description of the purpose.

(d) *Fees.* — The sheriff shall charge the following license fees:

(1) $5 for a bingo license;

(2) $10 for a paddle wheel license;

(3) $10 for a raffle license;

(4) $10 for a 50/50 license; and

(5) $15 for a members-only instant bingo license.

(e) *Professional involvement prohibited.* — An activity for which a license is issued under this subtitle must be conducted and managed solely and personally by regular members of the organization:

(1) who do not regularly conduct gaming activities for any other organization; and

(2) without the assistance of gaming professionals. (An. Code 1957, art. 27, § 254(b), (c), (d)(1); 2002, ch. 26, § 2; 2009, ch. 374.)

REVISOR'S NOTE

This Revisor's note comprises information related to the revision by Acts 2002, ch. 26.

This section is new language derived without substantive change from former Art. 27, § 254(b), (c), and, as it related to license fees, (d)(1).

In subsection (b)(4) of this section, the reference to "intend[ing]" to raise money is substituted for the former reference to "desiring" to raise money for consistency within this title.

In subsection (c)(1) of this section, the term "scheduled" is added for clarity.

In subsection (c)(2) of this section, the former reference to "operat[ing]" is deleted as included in the reference to "conduct[ing]".

In subsection (c) of this section, the reference to "all money prizes offered ... comply[ing] with the limits listed in this subtitle" is substituted for the former specific limits, which are revised in §§ 13-1504 through 13-1508 of this subtitle, for brevity.

Subsection (e) of this section is revised as a substantive prohibition on certain types of gaming involvement, rather than as a mere certification of intent in a license application, for clarity.

Defined terms:

"Bingo"	§ 13-1501
"Gaming event"	§ 13-1501
"Members-only instant bingo"	§ 13-1501
"Sheriff"	§ 13-1501

Effect of amendments. — Chapter 374, Acts 2009, effective July 1, 2009, reenacted (b) without change; added (d)(4) and redesignated accordingly; and made related changes.

§ 13-1504. Bingo.

(a) *Limitations.* — (1) The sheriff may not issue to a single organization in 1 calendar year more than 52 bingo licenses.

(2) Except as provided in paragraph (3) of this subsection, not more than one bingo license may be issued to a single organization in a single calendar week.

(3) A license to conduct bingo is valid:

(i) for 24 consecutive hours; or

(ii) if the license is issued for use in conjunction with and at a carnival, during carnival hours, and for the shorter of the duration of the carnival or 14 consecutive days.

(b) *Prize.* — A money prize for a bingo game may not exceed:

(1) $500; or

(2) $1,000 for a jackpot.

(c) *Instant bingo — Location.* — An instant bingo game may be sold and played only at the location listed on the license.

(d) *Prize — Minors prohibited.* — A minor may not sell or play instant bingo.

(e) *Paddle wheel license as authorization to conduct bingo.* — A license to operate a paddle wheel shall also operate as a license to conduct bingo, if authorized by the sheriff on request. (An. Code 1957, art. 27, § 254(c)(3)(i), (d)(2), (3)(i), (ii), (4), (f)(1), (2); 2002, ch. 26, § 2; 2009, ch. 374.)

REVISOR'S NOTE

This Revisor's note comprises information related to the revision by Acts 2002, ch. 26.

This section is new language derived without substantive change from former Art. 27, § 254(d)(2), (3)(i), (ii), (4), (f)(2), (c)(3)(i) as it related to bingo, and (f)(1) as it related to instant bingo.

In subsection (c) of this section, the reference to "all money prizes offered ... comply[ing] with the limits listed in this subtitle" is substituted for the former specific limits, which are revised in §§ 13-1504 through 13-1508 of this subtitle, for brevity.

In subsection (d) of this section, the defined term "minor" is substituted for the former phrase "person under the age of 18 years" for brevity.

Defined terms:

"Bingo"	§ 13-1501
"Minor"	§ 1-101
"Sheriff"	§ 13-1501

Effect of amendments. — Chapter 374, Acts 2009, effective July 1, 2009, substituted "$500" for "$50" in (b)(1).

Bingo not lottery. — Bingo is not a lottery. Bender v. Arundel Arena, Inc., 248 Md. 181, 236 A.2d 7 (1967).

§ 13-1505. Members-only instant bingo.

(a) *Duration of license.* — A members-only instant bingo license is valid for 3 months.

(b) *Limitation.* — The sheriff may not issue to a single organization in 1 calendar year more than four licenses for members-only instant bingo.

(c) *Prize.* — A money prize for a members-only instant bingo game may not exceed $500.

(d) *Location.* — A members-only instant bingo game may be sold and played only at the location listed on the license. (An. Code 1957, art. 27, § 254(c)(3)(i), (d)(1), (3)(i), (f)(1); 2002, ch. 26, § 2; 2009, ch. 374.)

REVISOR'S NOTE

This Revisor's note comprises information related to the revision by Acts 2002, ch. 26.

This section is new language derived without substantive change from the second sentence of former Art. 27, § 254(d)(1) and, as they related to members-only instant bingo, (c)(3)(i), (d)(3)(i), and (f)(1).

Defined terms:

"Members-only instant bingo"	§ 13-1501
"Sheriff"	§ 13-1501

Effect of amendments. — Chapter 374, Acts 2009, effective July 1, 2009, substituted "$500" for "$50" in (c).

§ 13-1506. Raffles.

(a) *Limitations.* — (1) The sheriff may not issue to a single organization in 1 calendar year more than 12 raffle licenses, no more than one of which may be for a raffle with a money prize exceeding $1,000.

(2) All raffle drawings shall be conducted in 1 calendar day.

(3) A raffle license is valid until all raffles are drawn.

(4) A raffle license shall state the day for the drawing or drawings.

(b) *Prizes.* — A money prize for a raffle may not exceed:

(1) $10,000 if the sponsoring organization has not held a raffle for a money prize exceeding $1,000 in the current calendar year; or

(2) $1,000 if the sponsoring organization has held a raffle for a money prize exceeding $1,000 in the current calendar year.

(c) *Security required.* — An organization that intends to conduct a raffle for a money prize exceeding $1,000 shall:

(1) post a bond in the amount of the money prize; or

(2) obtain an irrevocable letter of credit from a bank in the amount of the money prize. (An. Code 1957, art. 27, § 254(c)(3)(i), (ii), (d)(3)(i), (5), (6); 2002, ch. 26, § 2.)

REVISOR'S NOTE

This Revisor's note comprises information related to the revision by Acts 2002, ch. 26.

This section is new language derived without substantive change from former Art. 27, § 254(c)(3)(ii), (d)(5) and (6), and, as they related to raffles, (c)(3)(i) and (d)(3)(i).

Throughout this section, the references to a "money" prize are substituted for the former references to a "cash" prize for consistency within this title.

In subsection (a)(3) of this section, the reference to a raffle license being valid until "all raffles are drawn" is substituted for the former references to being valid until "the time of the drawing or drawings" for clarity.

In the introductory language of subsection (c) of this section, the phrase "intends to" is added to clarify that an organization must post a bond or obtain an irrevocable letter of credit before conducting the raffle.

Defined term:
"Sheriff"   § 13-1501

§ 13-1507. Paddle wheels.

(a) *Limitations.* — (1) The sheriff may not issue to a single organization in 1 calendar year more than 12 licenses for paddle wheels.

(2) Except as provided in paragraph (3) of this subsection, not more than one paddle wheel license or bingo license may be issued to a single organization in a single calendar week.

(3) A license to operate paddle wheels is valid:

(i) for 24 consecutive hours; or

(ii) if the license is issued for use in conjunction with and at a carnival, during carnival hours, and for the shorter of the duration of the carnival or 14 consecutive days.

(b) *Prize.* — A money prize for a paddle wheel game may not exceed $10.

(c) *Authorization to conduct bingo.* — A license to operate a paddle wheel shall also operate as a license to conduct bingo, if authorized by the sheriff on request. (An. Code 1957, art. 27, § 254(c)(3)(i), (d)(2), (3), (4); 2002, ch. 26, § 2.)

REVISOR'S NOTE

This Revisor's note comprises information related to the revision by Acts 2002, ch. 26.

This section is new language derived without substantive change from former Art. 27, § 254(d)(2) and, as they related to paddle wheels, (c)(3)(i) and (d)(3) and (4).

In subsection (c) of this section, the reference to authorization "by the sheriff" is added for clarity.

Defined terms:
"Bingo"   § 13-1501
"Sheriff"   § 13-1501

§ 13-1508. 50/50.

(a) *License not required.* — An organization listed in § 13-1503(b) of this subtitle may conduct a game of 50/50:

(1) without a 50/50 license, at a meeting of the organization; or

(2) with a 50/50 license, at an event other than a meeting of the organization.

(b) *Prize.* — A money prize for a game of 50/50 may not exceed $500.

(c) *Minors prohibited.* — A minor may not participate in a game of 50/50. (An. Code 1957, art. 27, § 254(e)(2)-(5); 2002, ch. 26, § 2; 2009, ch. 374.)

REVISOR'S NOTE

This Revisor's note comprises information related to the revision by Acts 2002, ch. 26.

This section is new language derived without substantive change from former Art. 27, § 254(e)(2) through (5).

In subsection (c) of this section, the reference to a "money" prize is substituted for the former reference to a "cash" prize for consistency within this title.

Defined terms:

"50/50"	§ 13-1501
"Minor"	§ 1-101

Effect of amendments. — Chapter 374, Acts 2009, effective July 1, 2009, deleted "without a license" at the end of (a); deleted former (b), added the (a)(1) designation and (a)(2) and redesignated accordingly; in (a)(1) added "without a 50/50 license"; in (b) substituted "$500" for "$50"; and made related changes.

§ 13-1508.1. Exception for political committee fundraisers.

(a) *In general.* — Notwithstanding any other provision of this article, a political committee, as defined in § 1-101 of the Election Law Article, may conduct a fundraiser at which prizes of money or merchandise are awarded in a gaming event or 50/50.

(b) *Prize amount not to exceed prize limits for county.* — A political committee may award a money or merchandise prize under this section if the prize does not exceed the amount otherwise allowed for a prize in the county. (2007, ch. 281.)

§ 13-1509. Report.

Within 15 days after the last day of licensed activity named in the license application, one of the principal officers of the organization shall file a report under the penalties of perjury certifying:

(1) that the activities authorized by the license were conducted at the time and place stated in the application solely by the regular members of the organization without the assistance of gaming professionals, and that the members conducting the activities do not regularly conduct gaming activities for any other organization;

(2) that money prizes were not offered, except as authorized under this subtitle; and

(3) the amount and disposition of the cash proceeds of the activities authorized by the license. (An. Code 1957, art. 27, § 254(c)(4); 2002, ch. 26, § 2.)

REVISOR'S NOTE

This Revisor's note comprises information related to the revision by Acts 2002, ch. 26.

This section is new language derived without substantive change from former Art. 27, § 254(c)(4).

This section is revised as a substantive requirement to file a report with specified contents, rather than as a mere certification by an officer of an applicant organization that the organization will file the report, in light of the penalty for failing to file the report under § 13-1510(d) of this subtitle.

§ 13-1510. Requirements; penalty.

(a) *Unlicensed operation.* — An organization may not conduct a gaming event unless the organization has acquired the appropriate license.

(b) *Obeying license — Organization.* — An organization shall obey the terms of a license.

(c) *Obeying license — Person signing application.* — Each person who signed an application for a license shall obey the terms of the license.

(d) *Filing report.* — A person shall file the report required under § 13-1509 of this subtitle.

(e) *Penalty.* — A person who violates this section is guilty of a misdemeanor and on conviction is subject to imprisonment not exceeding 30 days or a fine not exceeding $1,000 or both.

(f) *Separate violation.* — Each day that a gaming event is operated without a license or in violation of any of the terms of the license is a separate violation. (An. Code 1957, art. 27, § 254(h); 2002, ch. 26, § 2.)

REVISOR'S NOTE

This Revisor's note comprises information related to the revision by Acts 2002, ch. 26.

This section is new language derived without substantive change from former Art. 27, § 254(h).

In subsection (d) of this section, the former reference to the "proper" report is deleted as surplusage.

In subsection (f) of this section, the reference to the "appropriate" license is substituted for the former reference to a "proper" license for clarity.

Defined terms:
"Gaming event"   § 13-1501
"Person"   § 1-101

§ 13-1511. Disqualification.

(a) *Failure to report.* — An organization that fails to file a report required by § 13-1509 of this subtitle is not entitled to a license under this subtitle until the later of:

(1) 1 year after the date the report is due; or

(2) the day the report is filed properly.

(b) *Conviction of gambling violation.* — An organization that is convicted of violating a gambling law of this State may not be issued a license under this subtitle until 1 month after the date of conviction. (An. Code 1957, art. 27, § 254(g), (i); 2002, ch. 26, § 2.)

§ 13-1512. Enforcement.

The sheriff, other peace officers of the county, and municipal police in the
county shall enforce this subtitle. (An. Code 1957, art. 27, § 254(j); 2002, ch.
26, § 2.)

Subtitle 16. Howard County.

§ 13-1601. Scope of subtitle.

(a) *In general.* — This subtitle applies only in Howard County.

(b) *Application of Subtitle 2 of this title.* — (1) Except as provided in
paragraph (2) of this subsection, Subtitle 2 of this title applies in Howard
County.

(2) Subtitle 2 of this title does not apply to bingo regulated under
§ 13-1602 of this subtitle. (An. Code 1957, art. 27, § 255(a)(10), (g)(1), (2);
2002, ch. 26, § 2.)

§ 13-1602. Bingo.

(a) *Qualified organizations.* — Any of the following organizations may
conduct bingo to benefit charity in the county or to further the purposes of the
organization:

(1) a bona fide:

(i) religious organization;

(ii) fraternal organization;

(iii) patriotic organization;

(iv) educational organization; or

(v) charitable organization; or

(2) a volunteer fire company.

(b) *Operation by county residents only.* — A person who is not a legal resident of the county may not conduct bingo in the county, even if the game is for the benefit of an organization listed in subsection (a) of this section. (An. Code 1957, art. 27, § 250; 2002, ch. 26, § 2.)

REVISOR'S NOTE

This Revisor's note comprises information related to the revision by Acts 2002, ch. 26.

This section is new language derived without substantive change from former Art. 27, § 250.

In subsection (a) of this section, the former references to "corporations" and a "corporation" are deleted as included in the references to an "organization".

Also in subsection (a) of this section, the former term "operate" is deleted as redundant of the term "conduct". Similarly, in subsection (b) of this section, the term "conduct" is substituted for the former term "operate" for consistency with other subtitles in this article.

Also in subsection (a) of this section, the former reference to a "game of" bingo is deleted for consistency within this title.

In subsection (b) of this section, the defined term "person" is substituted for the former reference to an "individual, partnership, corporation, group, or organization" for clarity. *See* § 1-101 of this article.

Defined term:
"Person"   § 1-101

§ 13-1603. Other gaming events.

A qualified organization under Subtitle 2 of this title may award prizes in money or merchandise using:

(1) a paddle wheel;

(2) a wheel of fortune;

(3) a chance book;

(4) bingo; or

(5) any other gaming device except:

(i) a card game;

(ii) a dice game; or

(iii) roulette. (An. Code 1957, art. 27, § 255(g)(3)(ii); 2002, ch. 26, § 2.)

REVISOR'S NOTE

This Revisor's note comprises information related to the revision by Acts 2002, ch. 26.

This section is new language derived without substantive change from former Art. 27, § 255(g)(3)(ii).

The reference to a "money" prize is substituted for the former reference to a "cash" prize for consistency within this title.

The former reference to devices "commonly designated as" the listed devices is deleted as surplusage.

§ 13-1604. Prohibited activities.

Notwithstanding Subtitle 2 of this title, a person may not conduct a casino night or operate any of the following gaming devices:

(1) a card game;

(2) a dice game; or

(3) roulette. (An. Code 1957, art. 27, § 255(g)(3)(i); 2002, ch. 26, § 2.)

This Revisor's note comprises information related to the revision by Acts 2002, ch. 26.

This section is new language derived without substantive change from former Art. 27, § 255(g)(3)(i).

The reference to a "person" is added to clarify who is prohibited from performing the specified activities.

The former reference to "any events commonly known as" casino nights is deleted as surplusage.

Defined term:
"Person"   § 1-101

Subtitle 17. Kent County.

§ 13-1701. Definitions.

(a) *In general.* — In this subtitle the following words have the meanings indicated.

REVISOR'S NOTE

This subsection is new language derived without substantive change from former Art. 27, § 253(a)(1)(i).

The reference to this "subtitle" is substituted for the former reference to this "section" although this subtitle is derived, in part, from material outside former Art. 27, § 253. Only § 13-1705 of this subtitle, which is derived from former Art. 27, § 247 as it related to Kent County, is also included in this subtitle, and it does not use any of the terms defined in this section. No substantive change results.

(b) *County commissioners.* — "County commissioners" means the Board of County Commissioners of Kent County.

REVISOR'S NOTE

This subsection is new language added to avoid repetition of the phrase "County Commissioners of Kent County" and for consistency within this title.

(c) *Permit.* — "Permit" means:

(1) a multiple gaming device permit issued under § 13-1703 of this subtitle; or

(2) a raffle permit issued under § 13-1704 of this subtitle.

REVISOR'S NOTE

This subsection is new language derived without substantive change from former Art. 27, § 253(a)(1)(ii).

(d) *Raffle.* — "Raffle" means a lottery in which a prize is won by a person who buys a paper chance.

REVISOR'S NOTE

This subsection is new language derived without substantive change from former Art. 27, § 253(a)(1)(iii)1.

The Criminal Law Article Review Committee notes, for the consideration of the General Assembly, that the reference to a "paper" chance may be overly specific.

Defined term:
"Person"   § 1-101

(An. Code 1957, art. 27, § 253(a)(1)(i), (ii), (iii)1; 2002, ch. 26, § 2.)

REVISOR'S NOTE TO SECTION

The Revisor's notes in this section comprise information related to the revision by Acts 2002, ch. 26.

§ 13-1702. Scope of subtitle.

(a) *Application of subtitle.* — This subtitle applies only in Kent County.

(b) *Slot machines.* — This subtitle does not authorize gambling using a slot machine or coin machine. (An. Code 1957, art. 27, § 253(a)(2), (6); 2002, ch. 26, § 2.)

REVISOR'S NOTE

This Revisor's note comprises information related to the revision by Acts 2002, ch. 26.

This section is new language derived without substantive change from former Art. 27, § 253(a)(2) and the first sentence of (6).

The second sentence of former Art. 27, § 253(a)(6), which stated that slot machines are regulated under [former] § 264B, is deleted as surplusage.

For current State provisions on slot machines, *see* Title 12, Subtitle 3 of this article.

§ 13-1703. Gaming — Eligible organizations.

(a) *Permit required.* — The county commissioners may issue a permit to an organization specified in subsection (c) of this section to use two or more of the following gaming devices in conducting a fundraiser at which a prize of merchandise or money may be awarded:

(1) a paddle wheel;

(2) a wheel of fortune;

(3) a chance book;

(4) a card game;

(5) a raffle; or

(6) any other gaming device.

(b) *Exception.* — Unless conducted at an event requiring a permit under subsection (a) of this section, a raffle is not a multiple gaming device regulated under this section.

(c) *Qualified organizations.* — (1) In this subsection, "charity" means an organization, institution, association, society, or corporation that is exempt from taxation under § 501(c)(3) of the Internal Revenue Code.

(2) The county commissioners may issue a permit to use multiple gaming devices to:

(i) a bona fide religious organization that has conducted religious services at the same location in the county for at least 3 years before applying for a permit;

(ii) a county-supported or municipally supported volunteer fire company or an auxiliary unit whose members are directly associated with the volunteer fire company or auxiliary unit;

(iii) a nationally chartered veterans' organization or an auxiliary unit whose members are directly associated with the veterans' organization;

405

(iv) for the purpose of conducting a fundraiser for the benefit of a charity located in the county, a bona fide:

    1. fraternal organization;

    2. educational organization;

    3. civic organization;

    4. patriotic organization; or

    5. charitable organization; or

(v) a bona fide nonprofit organization that:

    1. has operated on a nonprofit basis in the county for at least 3 years before applying for a permit; and

    2. intends to use the multiple gaming devices to raise money for an exclusively charitable, athletic, or educational purpose specifically described in the permit application.

(d) *Application.* — Before issuing a permit, the county commissioners shall determine that the organization seeking the permit:

    (1) is organized in and serves the residents of the county; and

    (2) meets the conditions of this subtitle.

(e) *Permit.* — (1) (i) Except as provided in subparagraph (ii) of this paragraph, a permit is valid for one event that does not last longer than 6 hours.

    (ii) The county commissioners may issue a permit for an event longer than 6 hours if the permit holder does not seek more than one permit in the same year.

    (2) The county commissioners may not approve a permit for gaming events to be held on premises that are licensed under a Class B or Class D alcoholic beverages license.

    (3) The county commissioners may not issue more than two permits to an organization in a single year.

    (4) The county commissioners may:

        (i) charge a fee set by resolution for each permit;

        (ii) set the number of permits that may be issued each year; and

        (iii) adopt regulations governing permit applications and the issuance of permits.

(f) *Limitations.* — (1) An organization that is issued a permit shall conduct its fundraiser in a:

    (i) structure that the organization owns, leases, or occupies;

    (ii) structure that any organization that would qualify for a permit owns, leases, or occupies; or

    (iii) public location that is:

        1. described in the permit application; and

        2. approved by the State's Attorney for the county.

    (2) (i) Unless the county commissioners grant a waiver, only a resident of the county may manage and operate a fundraiser for which a permit is issued on behalf of the permit holder.

    (ii) Each permit holder shall designate an individual to be responsible for compliance with the terms and conditions of this subtitle and a permit issued under this subtitle.

    (iii) A person may not be compensated for operating the gaming activity conducted under a permit.

(g) *Financial accounting.* — (1) The permit holder shall use at least one-half of the funds raised using the permit for civic, charitable, or educational purposes.

(2) Within 30 days after a fundraiser, the permit holder shall send to the county commissioners:

(i) an accounting of all funds received or pledged;

(ii) an accounting of all expenses paid or incurred; and

(iii) a statement under oath of the application of the net profits.

(h) *Disqualification.* — The county commissioners may deny a permit for not more than 3 years to an organization that violates this subtitle or regulations adopted under this subtitle. (An. Code 1957, art. 27, § 253(a)(1)(iii)2, (3)-(5), (b)-(g), (i); 2002, ch. 26, § 2.)

REVISOR'S NOTE

This Revisor's note comprises information related to the revision by Acts 2002, ch. 26.

This section is new language derived without substantive change from former Art. 27, § 253(a)(1)(iii)2 and (3) through (5), (b) through (g), and (i).

Subsection (c)(2) of this section is restated as an affirmative grant of authority to issue permits to certain organizations for clarity.

In subsection (c)(2) of this section, the former limitation "[n]otwithstanding any other provision of this article," is deleted in light of § 13-101 of this title and the reorganization of material derived from the former "Gaming" subheading of Article 27 in Titles 12 and 13 of this article.

In subsection (c)(2)(v)2 of this section, the phrase "intends to use two or more gaming devices" is added to clarify that the permit is for the use of multiple gaming devices.

Also in subsection (c)(2)(v)2 of this section, the phrase "multiple gaming devices" is added for clarity.

In subsection (e)(1)(ii) of this section, the reference to the "same" year is added for clarity.

In subsection (e)(2) of this section, the reference to "[t]he county commissioners" is added to clarify who is prohibited from issuing the permit.

In subsection (e)(3)(ii) of this section, the former reference to permits issued to "organizations" is deleted as surplusage.

In subsection (f)(1) of this section, the reference to an "organization that is issued a permit" is substituted for the former reference to "organization receiving the permit" for clarity and brevity.

In subsection (f)(2)(i) of this section, the reference to "a resident of" is substituted for the former reference to "individuals domiciled" for clarity.

In subsection (f)(2)(ii) of this section, the reference to "[e]ach permit holder" is substituted for the former reference to "[e]ach organization" for clarity.

In subsection (f)(2)(iii) of this section, the former reference to "management" of a gaming activity is deleted as included in the reference to "operating" a gaming activity.

In subsection (g)(1) of this section, the reference to "[t]he permit holder" is added to clarify which entity has the obligation imposed under this section.

Also in subsection (g)(1) of this section, the phrase "raised using the permit" is substituted for the former phrase "derived from a multiple gaming device fundraiser that permits the use of two or more gaming devices" for brevity.

In subsection (h) of this section, the former phrase "the provisions of" is deleted as surplusage.

Defined terms:

"County commissioners"	§ 13-1701
"Permit"	§ 13-1701
"Person"	§ 1-101
"Raffle"	§ 13-1701

§ 13-1704. Raffles.

(a) *In general.* — The county commissioners may issue a raffle permit to an organization that qualifies for a permit under this subtitle or under regulations that the county commissioners adopt.

(b) *Duration of permit.* — The holder of a raffle permit must award the last prize in the raffle within 1 year after the date that the permit for the raffle is issued.

(c) *Limitation on number.* — The county commissioners may regulate the number of raffle permits that an organization may be issued in 1 year. (An. Code 1957, art. 27, § 253(h); 2002, ch. 26, § 2.)

REVISOR'S NOTE

This Revisor's note comprises information related to the revision by Acts 2002, ch. 26.

This section is new language derived without substantive change from former Art. 27, § 253(h).

In subsection (b) of this section, the reference to "[t]he holder of a raffle permit" is added to clarify which entity has the obligation to award the prize within 1 year.

Defined terms:
"County commissioners"	§ 13-1701
"Permit"	§ 13-1701
"Raffle"	§ 13-1701

§ 13-1705. Bingo.

To benefit charity in the county or to further the purposes of an organization qualified to conduct bingo under this section, an organization may conduct bingo if the organization is a bona fide:

(1) religious organization;

(2) fraternal organization;

(3) war veterans' organization;

(4) charitable organization; or

(5) volunteer fire company operating in a community that does not have a paid fire department. (An. Code 1957, art. 27, § 247(a); 2002, ch. 26, § 2.)

REVISOR'S NOTE

This Revisor's note comprises information related to the revision by Acts 2002, ch. 26.

This section is new language derived without substantive change from former Art. 27, § 247(a), as it related to Kent County.

The former reference to "operat[ing]" bingo is deleted as included in the reference to "conduct[ing]" bingo.

In item (4) of this section, the former reference to charitable "corporations" is deleted as included in the reference to a charitable "organization".

Former Art. 27, § 247(b), which provided that nothing in former Article 27 prohibited bingo on Sunday in Kent County, is deleted as unnecessary in light of the reorganization of material on gaming in Kent County in this revision.

§ 13-1706. Prohibited act; penalty.

(a) *In general.* — A person who violates a provision of §§ 13-1702 through 13-1704 of this subtitle is guilty of a misdemeanor and on conviction is subject to imprisonment not exceeding 1 year or a fine not exceeding $1,000 or both.

(b) *Separate violation.* — Each day that a person is in violation under this section is a separate violation. (An. Code 1957, art. 27, § 253(j); 2002, ch. 26, § 2.)

This Revisor's note comprises information related to the revision by Acts 2002, ch. 26.

This section is new language derived without substantive change from former Art. 27, § 253(j).

In subsection (b) of this section, the reference to a separate "violation" is substituted for the former reference to a separate "offense" for consistency within this article. *See* General Revisor's Note to article.

Defined term:
"Person"   § 1-101

Subtitle 18. Montgomery County.

§ 13-1801. Definitions.

(a) *In general.* — In this subtitle the following words have the meanings indicated.

This subsection is new language added as the standard introductory language to a definition section.

(b) *Breakout ticket.* — "Breakout ticket" includes instant bingo, Nevada club, lucky seven, and similar games.

This subsection is new language derived without substantive change from former Art. 27, § 255B(b)(10).

(c) *Qualified organization.* — (1) "Qualified organization" means a bona fide nonprofit organization qualified under 26 U.S.C. § 501(c)(3), (4), (7), or (10).

(2) "Qualified organization" includes:

(i) a religious organization;

(ii) a volunteer fire company;

(iii) a volunteer rescue squad;

(iv) a fraternal organization;

(v) a patriotic organization;

(vi) an educational organization; and

(vii) a charitable organization.

This subsection is new language derived without substantive change from former Art. 27, § 255B(a)(1), as it related to organizations that are authorized to hold bingo games or raffles. It is revised as a definition for clarity and brevity.

In paragraph (2)(iv) and (vii) of this section, the former references to a "corporation" are deleted as included in the references to an "organization".

(An. Code 1957, art. 27, § 255B(a)(1), (b)(10); 2002, ch. 26, § 2.)

The Revisor's notes in this section comprise information related to the revision by Acts 2002, ch. 26.

§ 13-1802. Scope of subtitle.

This subtitle applies only in Montgomery County. (2002, ch. 26, § 2.)

REVISOR'S NOTE

This Revisor's note comprises information related to the revision by Acts 2002, ch. 26.

This section is new language added to clarify that this subtitle applies only in Montgomery County.

§ 13-1803. Bingo — In general.

(a) *Authorized.* — (1) A qualified organization may conduct bingo in the county to benefit charity or to further the purpose of the qualified organization.

(2) Bingo shall be conducted only by the qualified organization and not by a person who:

(i) retains a portion of the proceeds from the bingo game; or

(ii) is compensated by the qualified organization for which the bingo is held.

(3) A person may not receive a private profit from the proceeds of bingo.

(4) A qualified organization that conducts bingo shall:

(i) keep accurate records of all transactions that occur on behalf of the bingo game;

(ii) keep the records for 2 years after the bingo game; and

(iii) on request, make the records available for examination by:

   1. the State's Attorney for the county;

   2. the county sheriff;

   3. the county Department of Health and Human Services;

   4. the county attorney;

   5. the Department of State Police; or

   6. a designated officer or agent of any of those units.

(5) A person conducting bingo shall be a resident of the county and a member of the qualified organization.

(6) Alcoholic beverages may not be sold or consumed in the room in which bingo is conducted, either during a game or an intermission between games.

(7) Money prizes not exceeding $1,000 in each game may be awarded in bingo.

(8) The qualified organization may sell breakout tickets in the room in which bingo is conducted, either during a game or an intermission between games.

(b) *Montgomery County Fair.* — (1) Notwithstanding any other provision of this subtitle, a person may conduct bingo at the annual Montgomery County Fair for the benefit of the Montgomery County Agricultural Center, Inc.

(2) A person who conducts bingo under this subsection may award only noncash prizes. (An. Code 1957, art. 27, § 255B(a)(1), (3), (4), (b)(1), (6), (8), (10), (c); 2002, ch. 26, § 2; 2005, ch. 211.)

REVISOR'S NOTE

This Revisor's note comprises information related to the revision by Acts 2002, ch. 26.

This section is new language derived without substantive change from former Art. 27, § 255B(c), (a)(1), (3), and (4) as they related to the rights, privileges, and duties of a person who conducts a raffle, and (b)(1), (6), (8), and, as it related to breakout tickets, (10).

Subsection (a)(1) of this section is restated as an affirmative grant of authority to certain organizations to conduct bingo under this subtitle for clarity.

In this section and throughout this subtitle, the references to "conduct[ing] bingo" are substituted for the former references to "operat[ing] a bingo game" and "hold[ing] a bingo game" for consistency within this title.

In subsection (a)(1) of this section, the former limitation "[n]otwithstanding the provisions of this subtitle [sic]," is deleted in light of § 13-101 of this title and the reorganization of material derived from the former "Gaming" subheading of Article 27 in this revision in Titles 12 and 13 of this article.

In subsection (a)(3) of this section and throughout this subtitle, the defined term "person" is substituted for the former reference to a "person, or legal or business entity" for clarity and brevity. Similarly, in subsection (a)(5) of this section and throughout this subtitle, the reference to "person" is substituted for the former reference to "individual" for consistency within this subtitle. *See* § 1-101 of this article.

Also in subsection (a)(3) of this section and throughout this subtitle, the former redundant phrase "which operates the game" is deleted for brevity and clarity.

Also in subsection (a)(3) of this section, the former reference to "gain" is deleted as included in the reference to "profit".

In subsection (a)(4)(i) and (ii) of this section and throughout this subtitle, the former redundant reference to "books" is deleted as included in the reference to "records".

In subsection (a)(4)(ii) and throughout this subtitle, the former redundant reference to a record "that is recorded" is deleted for clarity and brevity.

In subsection (b)(1) of this section, the reference to "the benefit of" the Montgomery County Agricultural Center, Inc. is added for clarity.

Defined terms:

"Breakout ticket"	§ 13-1801
"Person"	§ 1-101
"Qualified organization"	§ 13-1801

§ 13-1804. Bingo — License required.

A qualified organization that conducts bingo in the county shall be licensed by the county under this subtitle. (An. Code 1957, art. 27, § 255B(a)(2)(ii); 2002, ch. 26, § 2.)

REVISOR'S NOTE

This Revisor's note comprises information related to the revision by Acts 2002, ch. 26.

This section is new language derived without substantive change from former Art. 27, § 255B(a)(2)(ii).

Throughout this subtitle, the phrase "under this subtitle" is added for clarity.

The former redundant phrase "[i]f operating the game of bingo" is deleted as surplusage.

Defined term:

"Qualified organization"	§ 13-1801

§ 13-1805. Bingo — Qualification of applicants.

A qualified organization that conducts bingo in the county shall be located in the county. (An. Code 1957, art. 27, § 255B(a)(2)(i); 2002, ch. 26, § 2.)

This Revisor's note comprises information related to the revision by Acts 2002, ch. 26.

This section is new language derived without substantive change from former Art. 27, § 255B(a)(2)(i).

Defined term:
"Qualified organization"   § 13-1801

§ 13-1806. Bingo — License application.

(a) *In general.* — A qualified organization that intends to conduct bingo shall submit a bingo license application on a form that the county provides.

(b) *Contents.* — A qualified organization shall disclose the following information on the license application:

(1) the name of the qualified organization, and the names and addresses of its officers and directors;

(2) a complete statement of the purposes and objectives of the qualified organization and the purposes for which the qualified organization will use the proceeds from the bingo;

(3) a statement under oath by the president and treasurer, or the chief executive and fiscal officer, of the qualified organization that:

(i) an agreement does not exist to divert any of the proceeds of the bingo to another person; and

(ii) another person will not receive any of the proceeds of the bingo except to further the purpose of the qualified organization; and

(4) any additional information that the county requires. (An. Code 1957, art. 27, § 255B(b)(2); 2002, ch. 26, § 2.)

This Revisor's note comprises information related to the revision by Acts 2002, ch. 26.

This section is new language derived without substantive change from former Art. 27, § 255B(b)(2).

The former redundant reference to the requirement that a qualified organization secure a license from the county is deleted in light of § 13-1804 of this subtitle, which requires a qualified organization to obtain a license to conduct bingo.

In subsection (a) of this section, the reference to "submit[ting]" an application is substituted for the former reference to "ma[king]" an application for clarity and consistency within this title.

In subsection (b) of this section, the former redundant phrase "with respect to the nonprofit organization" is deleted for brevity and clarity, as the concept is repeated in all of the relevant following paragraphs.

In subsection (b)(2) of this section, the former reference to a "full" statement is deleted as included in the reference to a "complete" statement.

Defined terms:
"Person"   § 1-101
"Qualified organization"   § 13-1801

§ 13-1807. Bingo — License issuance.

The county may issue an annual bingo license authorizing the holder to conduct bingo at a specified fixed location:

(1) at any time during the year for which the license is issued; but

(2) not to exceed twice in any 1 week. (An. Code 1957, art. 27, § 255B(b)(3); 2002, ch. 26, § 2.)

REVISOR'S NOTE

This Revisor's note comprises information related to the revision by Acts 2002, ch. 26.

This section is new language derived without substantive change from the first sentence of former Art. 27, § 255B(b)(3).

In this section, the introductory phrase "[t]he county may issue" is added to clarify the entity that issues the bingo license.

§ 13-1808. Bingo — Temporary license.

(a) *In general.* — The county may issue:

(1) one temporary 10-day bingo license to each applicant each calendar year at a fee determined by the county; or

(2) a 1-day bingo license at a fee determined by the county, not to exceed three 1-day licenses to each applicant each calendar year, authorizing the holder to conduct bingo at a specified fixed location for 1 day.

(b) *Limitation.* — A temporary 10-day bingo license authorizes the holder to conduct bingo at a specified fixed location for a maximum of 10 days in any 1 year. (An. Code 1957, art. 27, § 255B(b)(4), (5); 2002, ch. 26, § 2.)

REVISOR'S NOTE

This Revisor's note comprises information related to the revision by Acts 2002, ch. 26.

This section is new language derived without substantive change from the first and second sentences of former Art. 27, § 255B(b)(4) and the first and third sentences of (5).

In the introductory language of subsection (a) of this section, the phrase "[t]he county may issue" is added to clarify which entity issues the bingo license.

§ 13-1809. Bingo — Administrative provisions.

(a) *In general.* — The county shall:

(1) adopt regulations for the conduct of bingo;

(2) establish license fees, based on the administrative cost of regulating bingo and issuing each class of license; and

(3) establish the hours of operation for bingo.

(b) *Disqualification of licensee.* — After a public hearing, the county may revoke a bingo license for failure of the holder to comply with this subtitle or regulations adopted under this subtitle. (An. Code 1957, art. 27, § 255B(b)(7), (9); 2002, ch. 26, § 2.)

REVISOR'S NOTE

This Revisor's note comprises information related to the revision by Acts 2002, ch. 26.

This section is new language derived without substantive change from former Art. 27, § 255B(b)(7) and (9).

In this section, the former redundant phrase "additional regulations deemed necessary" is deleted for brevity.

The second sentence of former Art. 27, § 255B(b)(3), the third sentence of former Art. 27, § 255B(b)(4), and the second sentence of former Art. 27, § 255B(b)(5), which required payment of certain license fees, are deleted in light of subsection (a)(2) of this section.

§ 13-1810. Raffles — In general.

(a) *Authorized.* — A qualified organization may conduct a raffle in the county to benefit charity or to further the purpose of the qualified organization.

(b) *Conducted by qualified organization.* — A raffle shall be conducted by a qualified organization and not by a person who:

(1) retains a portion of the proceeds from the raffle; or

(2) is compensated by the qualified organization for which the raffle is held.

(c) *Private profit prohibited.* — A person may not receive a private profit from the proceeds of a raffle.

(d) *Record keeping.* — A qualified organization that conducts a raffle shall:

(1) keep accurate records of all transactions that occur on behalf of the raffle;

(2) keep the records for 2 years after the raffle; and

(3) on request, make the records available for examination by:

(i) the State's Attorney for the county;

(ii) the county sheriff;

(iii) the county Department of Health and Human Services;

(iv) the county attorney;

(v) the Department of State Police; or

(vi) a designated officer or agent of any of those units.

(e) *Residency requirement.* — A person operating a raffle shall be a resident of the county and a member of the qualified organization.

(f) *Prize — Money or merchandise.* — Prizes of money or merchandise may be awarded in a raffle conducted under this subtitle.

(g) *Prize — Real property.* — For a raffle of real property, the requirements of this section are in addition to the requirements of § 12-106(a) of this article.

(h) *Limitation on number of raffles yearly; exception.* — (1) Except as provided in paragraph (2) of this subsection, a qualified organization may not conduct more than 12 raffles each year.

(2) There is no limit to the number of 50/50 raffles that a qualified organization may conduct if the prize for each 50/50 raffle does not exceed $300. (An. Code 1957, art. 27, § 255B(a)(1), (3), (4), (d)(1), (3), (5), (6), (8); 2002, ch. 26, § 2.)

REVISOR'S NOTE

This Revisor's note comprises information related to the revision by Acts 2002, ch. 26.

This section is new language derived without substantive change from former Art. 27, § 255B(a)(1), (3), and (4), as they related to the rights, privileges, and duties of a person who conducts a raffle, and (d)(1), (3), (5), (6), and, as it related to the rights, privileges, and duties of a person who conducts a raffle, (8).

Subsection (a) of this section is revised as an affirmative grant of authority to certain qualified organizations to conduct raffles for clarity.

In subsection (a) of this section, the former limitation "[n]otwithstanding the provisions of this subtitle" [sic] is deleted in light of § 13-101 of this title and the reorganization of material derived from the former "Gaming" subheading of Article 27 in Titles 12 and 13 of this article.

In subsection (b) of this section, the former phrase "which operates the game" is deleted as implicit in the reference to "conduct[ing]" the raffle.

Also in subsection (b) of this section, the reference to proceeds derived "from the raffle" is added for clarity.

In subsection (f) of this section, the reference to a "money" prize is substituted for the former reference to a "cash" prize for consistency within this title.

In subsection (h)(1) of this section, the phrase "[e]xcept as provided in paragraph (2) of this subsection" is added for clarity.

Defined term:
"Qualified organization"   § 13-1801

§ 13-1811. Raffles — Permit required; exception.

(a) *Permit required.* — Except as provided in subsection (b) of this section, a qualified organization that intends to conduct a raffle in the county shall obtain a permit from the county.

(b) *Exception.* — A permit is not required to conduct a 50/50 raffle. (An. Code 1957, art. 27, § 255B(d)(2), (8); 2002, ch. 26, § 2.)

REVISOR'S NOTE

This Revisor's note comprises information related to the revision by Acts 2002, ch. 26.

This section is new language derived without substantive change from former Art. 27, § 255B(d)(8), as it related to permit exception and the first sentence of (2).

The Criminal Law Article Review Committee notes, for the consideration of the General Assembly, that subsection (b) of this section is not limited to raffles with small prizes.

Defined term:
"Qualified organization"   § 13-1801

§ 13-1812. Raffles — Qualification of applicants.

A qualified organization that conducts a raffle in the county shall be located in the county. (An. Code 1957, art. 27, § 255B(a)(2)(i); 2002, ch. 26, § 2.)

REVISOR'S NOTE

This Revisor's note comprises information related to the revision by Acts 2002, ch. 26.

This section is new language derived without substantive change from former Art. 27, § 255B(a)(2)(i), as it related to raffles.

Defined term:
"Qualified organization"   § 13-1801

§ 13-1813. Raffles — Permit application.

(a) *In general.* — A qualified organization shall apply for a raffle permit on a form that the county provides.

(b) *Contents.* — A qualified organization shall disclose the following information on the permit application:

(1) the name of the qualified organization, and the names and addresses of its officers and directors;

(2) a complete statement of the purposes and objectives of the qualified organization, and the purposes for which the qualified organization will use the proceeds from the raffle;

(3) a statement under oath by the president and treasurer, or the chief executive and fiscal officer, of the qualified organization that:

(i) an agreement does not exist to divert any of the proceeds of the raffle to another; and

(ii) another person will not receive any of the proceeds of the raffle except to further the purpose of the qualified organization;

(4) in the case of a raffle of real property, under § 12-106(a) of this article, a copy of the disclosure statement filed with the Secretary of State; and

(5) any additional information that the county requires. (An. Code 1957, art. 27, § 255B(d)(2); 2002, ch. 26, § 2.)

REVISOR'S NOTE

This Revisor's note comprises information related to the revision by Acts 2002, ch. 26.

This section is new language derived without substantive change from former Art. 27, § 255B(d)(2), as it related to the content of a raffle permit application.

In the introductory language of subsection (b) of this section, the former redundant phrase "with respect to the nonprofit organization" is deleted for brevity and clarity, as the concept is repeated in all of the relevant following paragraphs.

In subsection (b)(2) of this section, the former reference to a "full" statement is deleted as included in the reference to a "complete" statement.

Defined terms:

"Person"	§ 1-101
"Qualified organization"	§ 13-1801

§ 13-1814. Raffles — Administrative provisions.

The county:

(1) may adopt regulations necessary for the conduct of a raffle; and

(2) after a public hearing, may revoke the permit of a holder for failure to comply with this subtitle or regulations adopted under this subtitle. (An. Code 1957, art. 27, § 255B(d)(4), (7); 2002, ch. 26, § 2; 2003, ch. 21, § 1.)

REVISOR'S NOTE

This Revisor's note comprises information related to the revision by Acts 2002, ch. 26.

This section is new language derived without substantive change from former Art. 27, § 255B(d)(4) and (7).

§ 13-1815. Prohibited act; penalty.

A person who violates this subtitle or a regulation adopted by the county under this subtitle is guilty of a misdemeanor and on conviction is subject to imprisonment not exceeding 1 year or a fine of $1,000 or both. (An. Code 1957, art. 27, § 255B(e); 2002, ch. 26, § 2.)

REVISOR'S NOTE

This Revisor's note comprises information related to the revision by Acts 2002, ch. 26.

This section is new language derived without substantive change from former Art. 27, § 255B(e).

The former references to "any of the provisions of", "adopted by Montgomery County", and "under the authority granted under this section" are deleted as surplusage.

Defined term:

"Person"	§ 1-101

Subtitle 19. Prince George's County.

§ 13-1901. Definitions.

(a) *In general.* — In this subtitle the following words have the meanings indicated.

REVISOR'S NOTE

This subsection is new language added as the standard introductory language to a definition section.

(b) *Benefit performance.* — "Benefit performance" includes an outdoor carnival, indoor carnival, fair, picnic, dance, card party, bingo party, bazaar, concert, contest, exhibition, lecture, barbecue, or dinner.

REVISOR'S NOTE

This subsection is new language derived without substantive change from former Art. 27, § 258B(a), as it related to the type of event that qualifies as a benefit performance, to clarify the meaning of "benefit performance," and to avoid repetition of the phrase "outdoor carnival, indoor carnival, fair, picnic, dance, card party, bingo party, bazaar, concert, contest, exhibition, lecture, barbecue, or dinner".

(c) *Qualified organization.* — (1) "Qualified organization" means an organization of a group of citizens of the county or a company, association, or corporation that is organized in good faith in the county to promote the purposes of a volunteer fire department or of a charitable, benevolent, patriotic, fraternal, educational, religious, or civic object.

(2) "Qualified organization" does not include a group organized for the private profit or gain of any member of the group, company, association, or corporation.

REVISOR'S NOTE

This subsection is new language derived without substantive change from former Art. 27, § 258B(a) and (b) as they related to organizations that may conduct benefit performances and raffles.

The defined term "qualified organization" is added to avoid repetition of the phrase "[a]ny group of citizens of Prince George's County, or any company, association or body corporate, bona fide organized within Prince George's County for the promotion of the purposes of a volunteer fire department, or of any charitable, benevolent, patriotic, fraternal, educational, religious or civic object, and not organized for the private profit or gain of any member of such group, company, association or body corporate".

(An. Code 1957, art. 27, § 258B(a), (b); 2002, ch. 26, § 2.)

REVISOR'S NOTE TO SECTION

The Revisor's notes in this section comprise information related to the revision by Acts 2002, ch. 26.

§ 13-1902. Scope and application of subtitle.

(a) *Scope of subtitle.* — This subtitle applies only in Prince George's County.

(b) *Application of Subtitle 2.* — Subtitle 2 of this title applies in Prince George's County. (An. Code 1957, art. 27, § 255(a)(11); 2002, ch. 26, § 2.)

REVISOR'S NOTE

This Revisor's note comprises information related to the revision by Acts 2002, ch. 26.

Subsection (a) of this section is new language added to clarify that this subtitle applies only in Prince George's County.

Subsection (b) of this section is new language derived without substantive change from former Art. 27, § 255(a)(11).

§ 13-1903. Benefit performances.

(a) *Authorized.* — Subject to subsection (b) of this section, a qualified organization may conduct a benefit performance to which the public is invited or admitted with or without charge.

(b) *Use of proceeds.* — The net proceeds of the benefit performance:

(1) shall benefit the qualified organization;

(2) shall be used for the purposes of the qualified organization; and

(3) may not benefit the private gain of a member of the qualified organization. (An. Code 1957, art. 27, § 258B(a); 2002, ch. 26, § 2.)

REVISOR'S NOTE

This Revisor's note comprises information related to the revision by Acts 2002, ch. 26.

This section is new language derived without substantive change from the first sentence of former Art. 27, § 258B(a).

In subsection (a) of this section, the limitation "[s]ubject to subsection (b) of this section" is added to qualify the circumstances under which a qualified organization may conduct a benefit performance.

Also in subsection (a) of this section, the former reference to "operat[ing]" a benefit performance is deleted as included in the reference to "conduct[ing]" a benefit performance.

In subsection (b) of this section, the more common term "benefit" is substituted for the former archaic term "inure" for clarity.

Also in subsection (b) of this section, the phrase "be used for the purposes of the qualified organization" is substituted for the former phrase "for the promotion of, and to be used for, one or more of the objects hereinbefore set forth" for clarity because the "objects" to which the former phrase refers are no longer listed in the same section, but are referred to in § 13-1901 as a part of the definition of a "qualified organization".

Defined terms:

"Benefit performance"	§ 13-1901
"Qualified organization"	§ 13-1901

Legislative intent. — An earlier version of this section was not intended to allow a profit-making entity to initiate and organize bingo games — i.e., to seek out nonprofit "sponsors" that would permit it to conduct bingo operations. 70 Op. Att'y Gen. 107 (1985).

Construction. — The exemptions in an earlier version of this section from the anti-gambling statutes must be narrowly construed. 70 Op. Att'y Gen. 107 (1985).

"Net proceeds" defined. — The statutory reference to "net proceeds" was intended to recognize that the conduct of a fundraising event may entail some expenditures and to authorize the organizations to pay those expenses out of the proceeds of the fundraisers. 74 Op. Att'y Gen. 157 (1989).

Profit. — Any profit to a party other than the sponsoring organizations must solely derive from reasonable and necessary expenses that the nonprofit organization incurs in operating its games. 70 Op. Att'y Gen. 107 (1985).

No personal use or benefit. — Dealers and attendants at nonprofit organizations' casino nights are not permitted to accept tips from patrons. 73 Op. Att'y Gen. 152 (1988).

Organizations that conduct casino nights in Prince George's County are not permitted to use part of the proceeds of those events to pay salaries or stipends to the organizations' officers or directors. 74 Op. Att'y Gen. 157 (1989).

The statutory condition that no individual may benefit financially from gaming activity prohibits tipping of volunteer dealers and other workers, and this prohibition is applicable to casino night activities under a prior version of this section. State v. Crescent Cities Jaycees Found., Inc., 330 Md. 460, 624 A.2d 955 (1993).

§ 13-1904. Benefit performances — Operation.

(a) *Requirements.* — A benefit performance shall be personally managed and conducted only by members of the qualified organization that sponsors the benefit performance.

(b) *Activities authorized.* — (1) At a benefit performance, a qualified organization may:

(i) conduct games of skill; or

(ii) dispose of merchandise and other things of value by auction, voting, or using a mechanical device such as a paddle wheel, wheel of fortune, bingo, or similar device.

(2) The activities allowed under this subsection may be conducted with or without an entrance or participation fee. (An. Code 1957, art. 27, § 258B(a); 2002, ch. 26, § 2.)

REVISOR'S NOTE

This Revisor's note comprises information related to the revision by Acts 2002, ch. 26.

This section is new language derived without substantive change from the second and fifth sentences of former Art. 27, § 258B(a).

In subsection (b) of this section, the former phrase "conducted under the conditions herein prescribed" is deleted in light of the defined term "benefit performance". *See* § 13-1901 of this subtitle.

Also in subsection (b) of this section, the former reference to a participation "charge" is deleted in light of the reference to a participation "fee".

Defined terms:
"Benefit performance"	§ 13-1901
"Qualified organization"	§ 13-1901

§ 13-1905. Benefit performances — Permit required.

A qualified organization shall obtain a written permit from the governing body of the county or its designee before conducting a benefit performance. (An. Code 1957, art. 27, § 258B(a); 2002, ch. 26, § 2.)

REVISOR'S NOTE

This Revisor's note comprises information related to the revision by Acts 2002, ch. 26.

This section is new language derived without substantive change from the fourth sentence of former Art. 27, § 258B(a).

Defined terms:
"Benefit performance"   § 13-1901
"Qualified organization"   § 13-1901

§ 13-1906. Benefit performances — Form of prizes.

At a benefit performance, a qualified organization may award:

(1) a merchandise prize; or

(2) a money prize of not more than $1,000 per prize. (An. Code 1957, art. 27, § 258B(a); 2002, ch. 26, § 2.)

REVISOR'S NOTE

This Revisor's note comprises information related to the revision by Acts 2002, ch. 26.

This section is new language derived without substantive change from the third sentence of former Art. 27, § 258B(a), and the second sentence, as it related to the form of prizes allowed at a benefit performance.

In item (2) of this section, the reference to a "money" prize is substituted for the former reference to a "cash" prize for consistency within this title.

Defined terms:
"Benefit performance"   § 13-1901
"Qualified organization"   § 13-1901

§ 13-1907. Benefit performances — Prohibited act; penalty.

A person who conducts or attempts to conduct a benefit performance in violation of this subtitle is guilty of a misdemeanor and on conviction is subject to imprisonment not exceeding 1 year or a fine not exceeding $1,000 or both. (An. Code 1957, art. 27, § 258B(a); 2002, ch. 26, § 2.)

REVISOR'S NOTE

This Revisor's note comprises information related to the revision by Acts 2002, ch. 26.

This section is new language derived without substantive change from the sixth sentence of former Art. 27, § 258B(a).

The former phrase "[e]xcept as otherwise provided in this section" is deleted as unnecessary as there are no other provisions in the former section relating to the penalties for operating or attempting to operate a benefit performance.

The term "person" is substituted for the former phrase "person, company, association or corporation" in light of § 1-101 of this article which defines the term "person" to include business entities.

The former phrases "in jail" and "in the discretion of the court" are deleted as implicit in setting a maximum penalty.

The reference to being "guilty of a misdemeanor" is added to state expressly that which was only implied in the former law. In this State, any crime that was not a felony at common law and has not been declared a felony by statute, is considered to be a misdemeanor. *See State v. Canova*, 278 Md. 483, 490 (1976); *Bowser v. State*, 136 Md. 342, 345 (1920); *Dutton v. State*, 123 Md. 373, 378 (1914); and *Williams v. State*, 4 Md. App. 342, 347 (1968).

The Criminal Law Article Review Committee notes, for the consideration of the General Assembly, that it is unclear whether this section applies to raffles conducted under this subtitle because there is no separate penalty for unauthorized raffles.

Defined terms:
"Person"   § 1-101
"Qualified organization"   § 13-1901

§ 13-1908. Raffles.

(a) *Authorized.* — Subject to subsection (b) of this section, a qualified organization may conduct a raffle.

(b) *Use of proceeds.* — (1) The proceeds of a raffle:

(i) shall benefit the qualified organization; and

(ii) shall be used for the purposes of the qualified organization.

(2) Except for a bona fide raffle winner, an individual or group may not:

(i) benefit financially from the holding of a raffle; or

(ii) receive or be paid any proceeds from a raffle for personal use or benefit. (An. Code 1957, art. 27, § 258B(b); 2002, ch. 26, § 2.)

REVISOR'S NOTE

This Revisor's note comprises information related to the revision by Acts 2002, ch. 26.

This section is new language derived without substantive change from the first and second sentences of former Art. 27, § 258B(b).

In subsection (a) of this section, the limitation "[s]ubject to subsection (b) of this section" is added to clarify the circumstances under which a qualified organization may conduct a raffle.

Also in subsection (a) of this section, the former reference to "operat[ing]" a raffle is deleted as included in the reference to "conduct[ing]" a raffle.

In subsection (b)(1)(i) of this section, the more common term "benefit" is substituted for the former archaic term "inure" for clarity.

In subsection (b)(1)(ii) of this section, the phrase "be used for the purposes of the qualified organization" is substituted for the former phrase "for the promotion of, and to be used for, one or more of the objects hereinbefore set forth" for clarity because the "objects" referred to in the former phrase are no longer listed in the same section, but are referred to in § 13-1901 as a part of the definition of a "qualified organization".

Defined term:
"Qualified organization"   § 13-1901

§ 13-1909. Raffles — Operation.

A raffle shall be personally conducted and managed only by regular members of the qualified organization. (An. Code 1957, art. 27, § 258B(b); 2002, ch. 26, § 2.)

REVISOR'S NOTE

This Revisor's note comprises information related to the revision by Acts 2002, ch. 26.

This section is new language derived without substantive change from the third sentence of former Art. 27, § 258B(b).

Defined term:
"Qualified organization"   § 13-1901

§ 13-1910. Raffles — Permit required.

(a) *In general.* — A qualified organization shall obtain a written permit from the Department of Environmental Resources before conducting a raffle if the total cash value of the prize exceeds $200.

(b) *Qualifications.* — (1) Before issuing a permit, the Department of Environmental Resources shall ascertain the character of the qualified organization applying for a permit under this section to determine if the application complies with this subtitle.

(2) A permit issued to a qualified organization to conduct a raffle may not be transferred.

(c) *Fee.* — The permit fee for each raffle is $15. (An. Code 1957, art. 27, § 258B(b); 2002, ch. 26, § 2.)

421

REVISOR'S NOTE

This Revisor's note comprises information related to the revision by Acts 2002, ch. 26.

This section is new language derived without substantive change from the fifth, sixth, and seventh sentences of former Art. 27, § 258B(b).

Defined term:

"Qualified organization" § 13-1901

§ 13-1911. Raffles — Form of prizes.

A qualified organization conducting a raffle may award prizes in money not exceeding a total of $5,000 and in merchandise in any amount or the merchandise cash equivalent. (An. Code 1957, art. 27, § 258B(b); 2002, ch. 26, § 2.)

REVISOR'S NOTE

This Revisor's note comprises information related to the revision by Acts 2002, ch. 26.

This section is new language derived without substantive change from the fourth sentence of former Art. 27, § 258B(b).

The reference to "[a] qualified organization conducting a raffle" awarding prizes is added for clarity.

The reference to a "money" prize is substituted for the former reference to a "cash" prize for consistency within this title.

The Criminal Law Article Review Committee notes, for the consideration of the General Assembly, that the Prince George's Department of Environmental Resources, which issues raffle permits, interprets the limits of this section to mean a combination of merchandise and cash not exceeding $5,000.

Defined term:

"Qualified organization" § 13-1901

§ 13-1912. Casino night.

(a) *"Casino night".* — In this section:

(1) "casino night" means a benefit performance at which:

(i) a card game, wheel of chance, or roulette is played; and

(ii) money winnings or tokens redeemable in money are awarded as prizes; but

(2) "casino night" does not include a benefit performance at which the only form of gaming is a wheel of fortune, big wheel, or other wheel of chance.

(b) *Prohibited.* — (1) This subtitle and Subtitle 2 of this title do not authorize casino nights in the county.

(2) A person may not conduct a casino night in the county.

(c) *Penalty.* — A person who violates this section or a county ordinance enacted under this section is guilty of a misdemeanor and on conviction is subject to imprisonment not exceeding 3 years or a fine not exceeding $5,000 or both. (An. Code 1957, art. 27, § 258B(c); 2002, ch. 26, § 2.)

REVISOR'S NOTE

This Revisor's note comprises information related to the revision by Acts 2002, ch. 26.

This section is new language derived without substantive change from former Art. 27, § 258B(c).

In subsection (b)(1) of this section, the phrase "[t]his subtitle" is substituted for the former phrase "[s]ubsection (a) or subsection (b) of this section or § 255 of this subheading" to reflect the reorganization of former §§ 255(a)(11) and 258B in this subtitle.

Subsection (b)(2) of this section is new language added to state that which was only implied in the former law: because casino nights are not authorized, they are prohibited and subject to a specific penalty under this section.

In subsection (c) of this section, the references to this "section" are substituted for the former references to this "subsection" to reflect the reorganization of material related to casino nights in this revision.

Defined terms:

"Benefit performance"	§ 13-1901
"Person"	§ 1-101

Subtitle 20. Queen Anne's County.

§ 13-2001. Definitions.

(a) *In general.* — In this subtitle the following words have the meanings indicated.

REVISOR'S NOTE

This subsection is new language derived without substantive change from former Art. 27, § 251C(a)(1)(i).

In this subsection and throughout this subtitle, the references to this "subtitle" are substituted for the former references to this "section", although portions of this subtitle are derived, in part, from material outside of former Art. 27, § 251C. The terms defined in this section do not appear in, or do not differ in substance from, the terms used in material derived from outside of former Art. 27, § 251C. No substantive change is intended.

(b) *County commissioners.* — "County commissioners" means the Board of County Commissioners of Queen Anne's County.

REVISOR'S NOTE

This subsection is new language added to avoid repetition of the phrase "Board of County Commissioners" and for consistency within this title and brevity.

(c) *Permit.* — "Permit" means:

(1) a multiple gaming device permit issued under § 13-2003 of this subtitle; or

(2) a raffle permit issued under § 13-2004 of this subtitle.

REVISOR'S NOTE

This subsection is new language derived without substantive change from former Art. 27, § 251C(a)(1)(ii).

(d) *Raffle.* — (1) "Raffle" means a lottery in which a prize is won by a person who buys a paper chance.

(2) A "raffle" is not a multiple gaming device regulated under § 13-2003 of this subtitle unless run in conjunction with an event that requires a multiple gaming device permit.

This subsection is new language derived without substantive change from former Art. 27, § 251C(a)(1)(iii).

The Criminal Law Article Review Committee notes, for the consideration of the General Assembly, that the reference to a "paper"

chance in paragraph (1) of this subsection may be overly specific.

Defined term:
"Person"   § 1-101

(An. Code 1957, art. 27, § 251C(a)(1); 2002, ch. 26, § 2.)

REVISOR'S NOTE TO SECTION

The Revisor's notes in this section comprise information related to the revision by Acts 2002, ch. 26.

§ 13-2002. Scope of subtitle.

(a) *Application.* — This subtitle applies only in Queen Anne's County.

(b) *Slot machines.* — This subtitle does not authorize gambling using a slot machine or coin machine. (An. Code 1957, art. 27, § 251C(a)(2), (6); 2002, ch. 26, § 2.)

REVISOR'S NOTE

This Revisor's note comprises information related to the revision by Acts 2002, ch. 26.

This section is new language derived without substantive change from former Art. 27, § 251C(a)(2) and the first sentence of (6).

In subsection (a) of this section, the reference to this "subtitle" is substituted for the former reference to this "section", although portions of this subtitle are derived from material outside former Art. 27, § 251C. Because the portions of those other provisions revised in this subtitle only apply to Queen Anne's County, no substan-

tive change results. Similarly, in subsection (b) of this section, the reference to this "subtitle" is substituted for the former reference to this "section". Because the portions of those other provisions revised in this subtitle do not authorize a slot machine or coin machine, no substantive change results.

The second sentence of former Art. 27, § 251C(a)(6), which stated that slot machines are regulated under [former] § 264B, is deleted as surplusage.

For current provisions on slot machines, *see* Title 12, Subtitle 3 of this article.

§ 13-2003. Gaming event — Multiple devices.

(a) *Permit required.* — An organization listed in subsection (b) of this section shall obtain a permit from the county commissioners before the organization may use two or more of the following gaming devices in conducting a fundraiser at which prizes of merchandise or money may be awarded:

(1) a paddle wheel;

(2) a wheel of fortune;

(3) a chance book;

(4) a card game;

(5) a raffle; or

(6) any other gaming device.

(b) *Qualified organization.* — (1) In this subsection, "charity" means an organization, institution, association, society, or corporation that is exempt from taxation under § 501(c)(3) of the Internal Revenue Code.

(2) Notwithstanding any other provision of this subtitle, the county commissioners may issue a permit to use multiple gaming devices to an organization if the organization is:

(i) a bona fide religious organization that has conducted religious services at the same location in the county for at least 3 years before applying for a permit;

(ii) a county-supported or municipally supported volunteer fire company or an auxiliary unit of the volunteer fire company whose members are directly associated with the volunteer fire company or auxiliary unit;

(iii) a nationally chartered veterans' organization or an auxiliary unit of the veterans' organization whose members are directly associated with the veterans' organization;

(iv) if the organization intends to use two or more gaming devices to conduct a fundraiser for the benefit of a charity located in the county, an organization that is a bona fide:

1. fraternal organization;
2. educational organization;
3. civic organization;
4. patriotic organization; or
5. charitable organization; or

(v) a bona fide nonprofit organization that:

1. has operated on a nonprofit basis in the county for at least 3 years before applying for a permit; and

2. intends to use the multiple gaming devices to raise money for an exclusively charitable, athletic, or educational purpose specifically described in the permit application.

(c) *Application review.* — Before issuing a permit, the county commissioners shall determine that the organization seeking the permit:

(1) is organized in and serves the residents of the county; and

(2) meets the conditions of this section.

(d) *Permit terms and administration.* — (1) (i) Except as provided in subparagraph (ii) of this paragraph, a permit is valid for one event that does not last longer than 6 hours.

(ii) The county commissioners may issue a permit for an event longer than 6 hours if the permit holder does not seek more than one permit in the same year.

(2) The county commissioners may not approve a permit for gaming events to be held on premises that are licensed under a Class B or Class D alcoholic beverages license.

(3) The county commissioners may not issue more than two permits to an organization in a single year.

(4) The county commissioners may:

(i) charge a fee set by resolution for each permit;

(ii) set the number of permits that may be issued each year; and

(iii) adopt regulations governing permit applications and the issuance of permits.

(e) *Operational requirements.* — (1) An organization that is issued a permit shall conduct its fundraiser in:

(i) a structure that the organization owns, leases, or occupies;

(ii) a structure that any organization that would qualify for a permit owns, leases, or occupies; or

(iii) a public location that is:

1. described in the permit application; and

2. approved by the State's Attorney for the county.

(2) (i) Unless the county commissioners grant a waiver, a fundraiser for which a permit is issued shall be managed and operated only by individuals who reside in the county and on behalf of the permit holder.

(ii) Each permit holder shall designate an individual to be responsible for compliance with the terms and conditions of this subtitle and a permit issued under this subtitle.

(iii) A person may not be compensated for operating the gaming activity conducted under a permit.

(f) *Financial accounting.* — (1) The permit holder shall use at least one-half of the funds raised using the permit for civic, charitable, or educational purposes.

(2) Within 30 days after a fundraiser, the permit holder shall send to the county commissioners:

(i) an accounting of all funds received or pledged;

(ii) an accounting of all expenses paid or incurred; and

(iii) a statement under oath of the application of the net profits.

(g) *Disqualification.* — The county commissioners may deny a permit for not more than 3 years to an organization that violates this subtitle or regulations adopted under this subtitle. (An. Code 1957, art. 27, § 251C(a)(3)-(5), (b)-(g), (i); 2002, ch. 26, § 2.)

REVISOR'S NOTE

This Revisor's note comprises information related to the revision by Acts 2002, ch. 26.

This section is new language derived without substantive change from former Art. 27, § 251C(a)(3) through (5), (b) through (g), and (i).

In subsection (b)(2) of this section, the reference to "subtitle" is substituted for the former reference to "article" because, under this revision, all Queen Anne's County gambling provisions are compiled within this subtitle.

In subsection (b)(2)(iv) of this section, the phrase "intends to use two or more gaming devices" is added to clarify that the permit is for the use of multiple gaming devices.

In subsection (b)(2)(v)2 of this section, the phrase "multiple gaming devices" is added for clarity.

In subsection (d)(1)(ii) of this section, the reference to the "same" year is added for clarity.

In subsection (d)(2) of this section, the reference to "[t]he county commissioners" is added to clarify who is prohibited from approving the permit.

In subsection (d)(4)(ii) of this section, the former phrase "to organizations" is deleted as surplusage.

In subsection (e)(2)(i) of this section, the reference to individuals "who reside" is substituted for the former reference to "individuals domiciled" for clarity.

In subsection (e)(2)(ii) of this section, the reference to each "permit holder" is substituted for the former reference to each "organization" for clarity.

In subsection (e)(2)(iii) of this section, the former reference to "management" of a gaming activity is deleted as included in the reference to "operating" a gaming activity.

In subsection (f) of this section, the reference to the "permit holder" is added to clarify which entity has the obligation imposed under this section.

In subsection (f)(1) of this section, the phrase "raised using the permit" is substituted for the former phrase "derived from a multiple gaming device fund-raiser that permits the use of two or more gaming devices" for brevity.

In subsection (g) of this section, the former reference to "the provisions of" is deleted as surplusage.

"Permit"	§ 13-2001
"Person"	§ 1-101
"Raffle"	§ 13-2001

Defined terms:

"County commissioners"	§ 13-2001

§ 13-2004. Raffles.

(a) *In general.* — The county commissioners may issue a raffle permit to an organization that qualifies for a permit under § 13-2003 of this subtitle or under regulations that the county commissioners adopt.

(b) *Duration of permit.* — The holder of a raffle permit must award the last prize in the raffle within 1 year after the date that the permit for the raffle is issued.

(c) *Limitation on number.* — The county commissioners may regulate the number of raffle permits that an organization may be issued in 1 year. (An. Code 1957, art. 27, § 251C(h); 2002, ch. 26, § 2.)

REVISOR'S NOTE

This Revisor's note comprises information related to the revision by Acts 2002, ch. 26.

This section is new language derived without substantive change from former Art. 27, § 251C(h).

In subsection (b) of this section, the reference to "[t]he holder of a raffle permit" is added to clarify which entity has the obligation to award the prize within 1 year.

Defined terms:

"County commissioners"	§ 13-2001
"Permit"	§ 13-2001
"Raffle"	§ 13-2001

§ 13-2005. Bingo.

To benefit charity in the county or to further its purposes, an entity may conduct bingo if the entity is a bona fide:

(1) religious organization;

(2) fraternal organization;

(3) charitable organization; or

(4) volunteer fire company operating in a community that does not have a paid fire department. (An. Code 1957, art. 27, § 247(a); 2002, ch. 26, § 2.)

REVISOR'S NOTE

This Revisor's note comprises information related to the revision by Acts 2002, ch. 26.

This section is new language derived without substantive change from former Art. 27, § 247(a), as it related to Queen Anne's County.

This section is restated as an affirmative grant of authority to certain qualified organizations to conduct bingo for clarity.

In the introductory language of this section, the former limitation "[n]othing in this subtitle [sic] shall be construed to make it unlawful" is deleted in light of § 13-101 of this title and the reorganization of material derived from the former "Gaming" subheading of Article 27 in Titles 12 and 13 of this article.

Also in the introductory language of this section, the former reference to the authority to "operate" bingo is deleted as included in the reference to the authority to "conduct" bingo.

In item (3) of this section, the former reference to "corporations" is deleted as included in the reference to an "organization".

§ 13-2006. Prohibited act; penalty.

(a) *In general.* — A person who violates a provision of § 13-2002, § 13-2003, or § 13-2004 of this subtitle is guilty of a misdemeanor and on conviction is subject to imprisonment not exceeding 1 year or a fine not exceeding $1,000 or both.

(b) *Separate violation.* — Each day that a person violates this section is a separate violation. (An. Code 1957, art. 27, § 251C(j); 2002, ch. 26, § 2.)

REVISOR'S NOTE

This Revisor's note comprises information related to the revision by Acts 2002, ch. 26.

This section is new language derived without substantive change from former Art. 27, § 251C(j).

In subsection (a) of this section, the reference to "§ 13-2002, § 13-2003, or § 13-2004 of this subtitle" is substituted for the former reference to this "section" to reflect the reorganization of substantive material derived from former Art. 27, § 251C.

In subsection (b) of this section, the reference to a separate "violation" is substituted for the former reference to a separate "offense" for consistency within this article. *See* General Revisor's Note to article.

Defined term:
"Person"   § 1-101

Subtitle 21. St. Mary's County.

§ 13-2101. Definitions.

(a) *In general.* — In this subtitle the following words have the meanings indicated.

REVISOR'S NOTE

This subsection is new language used as the standard introductory language to a definition section.

(b) *County commissioners.* — "County commissioners" means the Board of County Commissioners of St. Mary's County.

REVISOR'S NOTE

This subsection is new language added to avoid repetition of the phrase "Board of County Commissioners of St. Mary's County" and for consistency within this title.

(c) *Gaming device.* — (1) "Gaming device" includes a paddle wheel, wheel of fortune, chance book, bingo, Nevada card, and a stamp machine.

(2) "Gaming device" does not include a slot machine, as defined in § 12-301 of this article.

REVISOR'S NOTE

This subsection is new language added to avoid repetition of the phrase "paddle wheels, wheels of fortune, chance books, bingo, Nevada cards, stamp machines, or any other gaming device" found in former Art. 27, § 255(d).

(d) *Gaming event.* — "Gaming event" means a carnival, bazaar, or raffle.

REVISOR'S NOTE

This subsection is new language added for consistency within this title.

(e) *Qualified organization.* — "Qualified organization" means:
  (1) a volunteer fire company; or
  (2) a bona fide:
    (i) religious organization;
    (ii) fraternal organization;
    (iii) civic organization;
    (iv) war veterans' organization; or
    (v) charitable organization.

REVISOR'S NOTE

This subsection is new language added to avoid repetition of the phrase "a volunteer fire company or bona fide fraternal, civic, war veterans', religious, or charitable organization or corporation".

The former reference to a "corporation" is deleted as implicit in the references to an "organization".

(f) *Sheriff.* — "Sheriff" means the Sheriff of St. Mary's County.

REVISOR'S NOTE

This subsection is new language added to avoid repetition of the phrase "Sheriff of St. Mary's County" and for consistency within this title.

(2002, ch. 26, § 2.)

REVISOR'S NOTE TO SECTION

The Revisor's notes in this section comprise information related to the revision by Acts 2002, ch. 26.

§ 13-2102. Scope and application of subtitle.

(a) *Scope of subtitle.* — This subtitle applies only in St. Mary's County.
(b) *Application of Subtitle 2.* — Subtitle 2 of this title applies in St. Mary's County. (An. Code 1957, art. 27, § 255(a)(12), (d); 2002, ch. 26, § 2.)

REVISOR'S NOTE

This Revisor's note comprises information related to the revision by Acts 2002, ch. 26.
Subsection (a) of this section is new language added to clarify that this subtitle applies only in St. Mary's County.

Subsection (b) of this section is new language derived without substantive change from former Art. 27, § 255(a)(12) and the first sentence of (d), as it related to its application to St. Mary's County.

§ 13-2103. Bingo — License required.

A qualified organization must have a bingo license whenever the qualified organization conducts bingo. (An. Code 1957, art. 27, § 251(a); 2002, ch. 26, § 2.)

REVISOR'S NOTE

This Revisor's note comprises information related to the revision by Acts 2002, ch. 26.

This section is new language derived without substantive change from former Art. 27, § 251(a), as it related to the requirement of a qualified organization to conduct bingo.

The references to a "qualified" organization are substituted for the former reference to an "eligible" organization for consistency within this title.

Defined term:
"Qualified organization"   § 13-2101

§ 13-2104. Bingo — Qualified organizations.

To be eligible for a bingo license, an organization must be:

(1) a bona fide religious group that has conducted religious services at a fixed location in the county for at least 3 years before the application date;

(2) a volunteer fire company or volunteer rescue squad, regardless of whether the company or squad is supported by tax revenues, or an auxiliary unit whose members are associated directly with the company or squad;

(3) a nationally chartered veterans' organization, or an auxiliary unit whose members are associated directly with the organization; or

(4) a nonprofit organization that:

(i) has operated in the county for at least 3 years before the application date; and

(ii) intends to raise money for an exclusively charitable, athletic, or educational purpose specifically described in the application. (An. Code 1957, art. 27, § 251(b); 2002, ch. 26, § 2; 2003, ch. 21, § 1.)

REVISOR'S NOTE

This Revisor's note comprises information related to the revision by Acts 2002, ch. 26.

This section is new language derived without substantive change from former Art. 27, § 251(b).

In item (1) of this section, the former reference to "all types of licenses under this section" is deleted as unnecessary.

In items (3) and (4) of this section, the former references regarding submission of an application for a bingo license "to the Sheriff" are deleted in light of § 13-2105(a) of this subtitle.

§ 13-2105. Bingo — License application.

(a) *Submission to sheriff.* — An organization shall submit an application for a bingo license to the sheriff.

(b) *Contents.* — A principal officer of the organization shall certify in the application for a bingo license:

(1) the name and address of the organization;

(2) the name and address of the officer seeking the license for the organization;

(3) that the officer is authorized by the organization to file the application;

(4) the time and place of bingo;

(5) that, within 15 days after the last day named in the application for the license to conduct bingo, a principal officer of the organization will file under penalties of perjury the report required by § 13-2109 of this subtitle;

(6) that bingo will be conducted solely and personally by the regular members of the organization, without the assistance of gaming professionals; and

(7) that no compensation or reward will be paid to a person for conducting or assisting in conducting bingo. (An. Code 1957, art. 27, § 251(c); 2002, ch. 26, § 2.)

REVISOR'S NOTE

This Revisor's note comprises information related to the revision by Acts 2002, ch. 26.

Subsection (a) of this section is new language added to state expressly that which was only implied in the former references to submission of an application for a bingo license "to the Sheriff" in former Art. 27, § 251(b) and (c).

In subsection (a) of this section, the reference to "[a]n organization" submitting an application for a license is added to state expressly that which was only implied in the former reference to the ability of an organization to receive a license under former Art. 27, § 251(c).

Subsection (b) of this section is new language derived without substantive change from former Art. 27, § 251(c).

In the introductory language of subsection (b) of this section, the former reference to submission of an application "to the Sheriff" is deleted as unnecessary in light of subsection (a) of this section.

Also in the introductory language of subsection (b) of this section, the former reference to the "issuance of" a license is deleted as unnecessary.

In subsection (b)(1), (2), and (3) of this section, the former references to an "eligible" organization are deleted to clarify that an organization may submit an application, and is only considered "eligible" (now "qualified"), after consideration of the application by the sheriff.

In subsection (b)(2) of this section, the reference to a "license" is substituted for the former incorrect reference to a "permit" for consistency within this part.

In subsection (b)(3) of this section, the former phrase, "[t]he certification of the officer seeking the permit", is deleted for brevity.

In subsection (b)(5) of this section, the references to "bingo" are substituted for the former references to "activities for which the license is sought" for brevity and clarity.

In subsection (b)(6) of this section, the reference to "gaming" professionals is added for clarity.

In subsection (b)(7) of this section, the former references to "commission, salary" and "recompense" are deleted as included in the comprehensive reference to "compensation or reward".

Also in subsection (b)(7) of this section, the former references to "operating" and "holding" bingo are deleted as included in the references to "conducting" bingo.

Defined terms:

"Person"	§ 1-101
"Sheriff"	§ 13-2101

§ 13-2106. Bingo — License fee.

(a) *Established by county commissioners.* — By resolution, the county commissioners may establish a bingo license fee schedule based on criteria that the county commissioners consider appropriate.

(b) *Charged by sheriff.* — The sheriff shall charge for each license the annual license fee that the county commissioners set by resolution.

(c) *Deposit.* — A resolution adopted under subsection (a) of this section shall specify the fund in which the license fees are to be deposited. (An. Code 1957, art. 27, § 251(d); 2002, ch. 26, § 2.)

REVISOR'S NOTE

This Revisor's note comprises information related to the revision by Acts 2002, ch. 26.

This section is new language derived without substantive change from former Art. 27, § 251(d).

In subsections (a) and (b) of this section, the former references to a "bingo" license are deleted for consistency and clarity.

In subsection (b) of this section, the former reference to the "issuance of" a license is deleted as unnecessary.

Defined terms:
"County commissioners"   § 13-2101
"Sheriff"   § 13-2101

§ 13-2107. Bingo — Right to license.

The sheriff shall issue a numbered license to an organization that meets the requirements of §§ 13-2103 through 13-2110 of this subtitle to conduct bingo and award prizes. (An. Code 1957, art. 27, § 251(a); 2002, ch. 26, § 2.)

REVISOR'S NOTE

This Revisor's note comprises information related to the revision by Acts 2002, ch. 26.

This section is new language derived without substantive change from former Art. 27, § 251(a), as it related to the right of eligible organizations to bingo licenses.

The former phrase "[n]otwithstanding any other provisions of this subtitle [sic]" is deleted

as implicit in the reorganization of material derived from the former "Gaming" subheading of Article 27.

The defined term "sheriff" is substituted for the former reference to the "Sheriff of St. Mary's County" for brevity.

Defined term:
"Sheriff"   § 13-2101

Bingo not lottery. — Bingo is not a lottery. Bender v. Arundel Arena, Inc., 248 Md. 181, 236 A.2d 7 (1967).

§ 13-2108. Bingo — License term.

A license issued under this subtitle is valid for 1 year. (An. Code 1957, art. 27, § 251(a); 2002, ch. 26, § 2.)

REVISOR'S NOTE

This Revisor's note comprises information related to the revision by Acts 2002, ch. 26.

This section is new language derived without substantive change from former Art. 27,

§ 251(a), as it related to the term of a bingo license, and is revised for consistency with similar provisions elsewhere in the Code.

§ 13-2109. Bingo — Report.

Within 15 days after the last day authorized for bingo in the license, a principal officer of the organization shall file a report under penalties of perjury that certifies:

(1) that the regular members of the organization personally conducted bingo at the time and place stated in the application without the assistance of gaming professionals;

(2) the disposition of the cash proceeds of the bingo; and

(3) that the organization did not pay a premises rental fee to:

(i) itself;

(ii) its trustees;

(iii) a committee of the organization; or

(iv) any organization whose members are the same, or substantially the same, as the licensed organization. (An. Code 1957, art. 27, § 251(c)(7); 2002, ch. 26, § 2.)

REVISOR'S NOTE

This Revisor's note comprises information related to the revision by Acts 2002, ch. 26.

This section is new language derived without substantive change from former Art. 27, § 251(c)(7).

This section is revised as an affirmative requirement to file a report on bingo activities rather than as a mere promise to file a report contained in a license application under § 13-2105 of this subtitle, to reflect the duty to file

implicit in that promise and the sanction for failure to file the report under § 13-2110 of this subtitle.

In item (1) of this section, the reference to "gaming" professionals is added for clarity and consistency within this title.

In item (3)(iii) of this section, the reference to an "organization" is substituted for the former reference to a "licensee" for consistency.

In item (3)(iv) of this section, the reference to a "licensed" organization is added for clarity.

§ 13-2110. Bingo — Disqualification.

An organization is disqualified from obtaining a license under this subtitle for 1 year if the organization fails to:

(1) file the report required under § 13-2109 of this subtitle; or

(2) comply with §§ 13-2103 through 13-2110 of this subtitle. (An. Code 1957, art. 27, § 251(e); 2002, ch. 26, § 2.)

REVISOR'S NOTE

This Revisor's note comprises information related to the revision by Acts 2002, ch. 26.

This section is new language derived without substantive change from former Art. 27, § 251(e).

The reference to "[being] disqualified from obtaining" a license is substituted for the former reference to "forfeit[ing] its right to the issuance of" any license for clarity.

The reference to an organization that "fails" to file is substituted for the former reference to an organization "refusing" to file for consistency.

In item (2) of this section, the reference to "§§ 13-2103 through 13-2110 of this subtitle" is substituted for the former reference to this "section" to reflect the reorganization of material derived from former Art. 27, § 251.

§ 13-2111. Gaming events and gaming devices.

A qualified organization may hold a gaming event and may operate a gaming device if an individual or group of individuals does not:

(1) benefit financially from the operation of the gaming device; or

(2) receive from the operation of the gaming device any proceeds for personal use or benefit. (An. Code 1957, art. 27, § 255(d); 2002, ch. 26, § 2.)

REVISOR'S NOTE

This Revisor's note comprises information related to the revision by Acts 2002, ch. 26.

This section is new language derived without substantive change from the first sentence of former Art. 27, § 255(d).

The former reference to "St. Mary's County" is deleted in light of § 13-2101 of this subtitle.

The former reference to "conduct[ing]" a gaming event is deleted as included in the reference to "hold[ing]" a gaming event.

In item (2) of this section, the former reference to being "paid" proceeds from the operation of a gaming device is deleted as included in "receiv[ing]" the proceeds.

Defined terms:
"Gaming device"	§ 13-2101
"Gaming event"	§ 13-2101
"Qualified organization"	§ 13-2101

§ 13-2112. Gaming events and gaming devices — Management of operation.

Members of the qualified organization shall personally manage the operation of the gaming device. (An. Code 1957, art. 27, § 255(d); 2002, ch. 26, § 2.)

REVISOR'S NOTE

This Revisor's note comprises information related to the revision by Acts 2002, ch. 26.

This section is new language derived without substantive change from the fifth sentence of former Art. 27, § 255(d).

Defined terms:
"Gaming device"	§ 13-2101
"Qualified organization"	§ 13-2101

§ 13-2113. Gaming events and gaming devices — Daily use limitation.

If a qualified organization uses a gaming device on a daily basis:

(1) the qualified organization may not operate more than five gaming devices; and

(2) the premises in which the qualified organization operates the gaming device may not contain more than five gaming devices. (An. Code 1957, art. 27, § 255(d); 2002, ch. 26, § 2.)

REVISOR'S NOTE

This Revisor's note comprises information related to the revision by Acts 2002, ch. 26.

This section is new language derived without substantive change from the second sentence of former Art. 27, § 255(d).

In the introductory language of this section, the reference to "a qualified organization [that] uses a gaming device" on a daily basis is new language added to state expressly that which was only implied by the context of former Art. 27, § 255(d).

In items (1) and (2) of this section, the former reference to a "corporation" operating gaming devices is deleted as included in the reference to an "organization" operating gaming devices.

Defined terms:
"Gaming device"	§ 13-2101
"Qualified organization"	§ 13-2101

§ 13-2114. Gaming events and gaming devices — Proceeds.

(a) *Allowed uses.* — All proceeds from a gaming device shall be used solely for the legitimate charitable, benevolent, or tax-exempt purposes of the qualified organization.

(b) *Personal benefit prohibited.* — Proceeds from the operation of a gaming device may not be used to benefit personally any member of the qualified organization. (An. Code 1957, art. 27, § 255(d); 2002, ch. 26, § 2.)

REVISOR'S NOTE

This Revisor's note comprises information related to the revision by Acts 2002, ch. 26.

This section is new language derived without substantive change from the third sentence of former Art. 27, § 255(d).

In subsection (a) of this section, the reference to "tax-exempt" purposes is substituted for the former reference to "exempt" purposes for clarity. The Criminal Law Article Review Committee calls this substitution to the attention of the General Assembly.

In subsection (b) of this section, the reference to "[p]roceeds from the operation of a gaming device" is added for clarity.

Defined terms:
"Gaming device"	§ 13-2101
"Qualified organization"	§ 13-2101

§ 13-2115. Gaming events and gaming devices — Record keeping.

(a) *Required.* — A qualified organization shall keep accurate records of proceeds and expenditures involving gaming devices.

(b) *Inspection.* — On request, a qualified organization shall allow the State's Attorney for the county, a State Police officer, and the sheriff or deputy sheriff to examine the records required under subsection (a) of this section. (An. Code 1957, art. 27, § 255(d); 2002, ch. 26, § 2.)

REVISOR'S NOTE

This Revisor's note comprises information related to the revision by Acts 2002, ch. 26.

This section is new language derived without substantive change from the fourth sentence of former Art. 27, § 255(d).

In this section, the former reference to "books" is deleted as included in the term "records".

Defined terms:
"Gaming device"	§ 13-2101
"Qualified organization"	§ 13-2101
"Sheriff"	§ 13-2101

Subtitle 22. Somerset County.

§ 13-2201. Scope and application of subtitle.

(a) *Scope of subtitle.* — This subtitle applies only in Somerset County.

(b) *Application of Subtitle 2.* — Subtitle 2 of this title applies in Somerset County. (An. Code 1957, art. 27, § 255(a)(13); 2002, ch. 26, § 2.)

REVISOR'S NOTE

This Revisor's note comprises information related to the revision by Acts 2002, ch. 26.

Subsection (a) of this section is new language added to clarify that this subtitle applies only to Somerset County.

Subsection (b) of this section is new language derived without substantive change from former Art. 27, § 255(a)(13).

§ 13-2202. Bingo.

To benefit charity in the county or to further the purposes of an organization qualified to conduct bingo under this section, an organization may conduct bingo if the organization is a bona fide:

(1) religious organization;

(2) fraternal organization;

(3) war veterans' organization;

(4) charitable organization; or

(5) volunteer fire company operating in a community that does not have a paid fire department. (An. Code 1957, art. 27, § 247(a); 2002, ch. 26, § 2.)

REVISOR'S NOTE

This Revisor's note comprises information related to the revision by Acts 2002, ch. 26.

This section is new language derived without substantive change from former Art. 27, § 247(a), as it related to Somerset County.

This section is restated as an affirmative grant of authority to certain qualified organizations to conduct bingo for clarity.

The former limitation "[n]othing in this subtitle [sic] shall be construed to make it unlawful" is deleted in light of § 13-101 of this article and the reorganization of material derived from the former "Gaming" subheading of Article 27 in Titles 12 and 13 of this article.

The former reference to "operat[ing]" bingo is deleted as included in the reference to "conduct[ing]" bingo.

In item (5) of this section, the former reference to a charitable "corporation" is deleted as included in the reference to a charitable "organization".

Subtitle 23. Talbot County.

§ 13-2301. Application of Subtitle 2.

Subtitle 2 of this title applies in Talbot County. (An. Code 1957, art. 27, § 255(a)(14); 2002, ch. 26, § 2.)

REVISOR'S NOTE

This Revisor's note comprises information related to the revision by Acts 2002, ch. 26.

This section is new language derived without substantive change from former Art. 27, § 255(a)(14).

The reference to "Subtitle 2 of this title" is substituted for the former reference to "this section" to reflect the reorganization of the general provisions on gaming events in specified counties contained in former Art. 27, § 255.

Subtitle 24. Washington County.

Part I. General Provisions.

§ 13-2401. "County commissioners" defined.

In this subtitle, "county commissioners" means the Board of County Commissioners of Washington County. (An. Code 1957, art. 27, § 255C(a)(2); 2002, ch. 26, § 2.)

REVISOR'S NOTE

This Revisor's note comprises information related to the revision by Acts 2002, ch. 26.

This section is new language derived without substantive change from former Art. 27, § 255C(a)(2).

The term "county commissioners" is defined in place of the former definition of "Board" to avoid potential confusion with other public entities such as the Board of License Commissioners to which § 13-2437 of this subtitle refers.

Although the former provision defined "Board" of County Commissioners solely for purposes of Art. 27, § 255C — now Part III of this subtitle — it is redefined for purposes of this subtitle to avoid the need to repeat the full title of the Board of County Commissioners of Washington County in other provisions of this subtitle.

§ 13-2402. Scope of subtitle.

This subtitle applies only in Washington County. (2002, ch. 26, § 2.)

REVISOR'S NOTE

This Revisor's note comprises information related to the revision by Acts 2002, ch. 26.

This section is new language added to clarify the application of this subtitle and for consistency within this title.

§ 13-2403. Application of Subtitle 2.

Except as otherwise provided in this subtitle, Subtitle 2 of this title applies in Washington County. (An. Code 1957, art. 27, § 255(a)(15); 2002, ch. 26, § 2.)

REVISOR'S NOTE

This Revisor's note comprises information related to the revision by Acts 2002, ch. 26.

This section is new language derived without substantive change from former Art. 27, § 255(a)(15).

The introductory clause is added to indicate that exceptions exist.

§ 13-2404. General provisions.

(a) *Volunteer rescue companies.* — A volunteer rescue company shall be treated as a volunteer fire company for purposes of Subtitle 2 of this title.

(b) *Limitation on gaming activities in bingo halls.* — A person may not operate a chance book, paddle wheel, tip jar, wheel of fortune, or other gaming device, other than a bingo game, on premises that are owned by, leased to, or used as a place of business by a person that conducts a bingo game for purposes of making a profit.

(c) *Tip jars.* — (1) Subtitle 2 of this title does not apply to the operation of tip jars.

(2) Tip jars are regulated under Part III of this subtitle. (An. Code 1957, art. 27, § 255(c); 2002, ch. 26, § 2.)

REVISOR'S NOTE

This Revisor's note comprises information related to the revision by Acts 2002, ch. 26.

This section is new language derived without substantive change from former Art. 27, § 255(c).

Throughout this section, the former references to "Washington County" are deleted in light of § 13-2402 of this subtitle, which limits the application of this subtitle to Washington County.

In subsection (b) of this section, the reference to a "person" is substituted for the former references to an "individual, corporation, organization, or other entity" for brevity. *See* § 1-101 of this article.

Defined term:
"Person"　　　　　　　　　　§ 1-101

§§ 13-2405, 13-2406.

Reserved.

Part II. Bingo.

§ 13-2407. Effect of part.

Bingo may be conducted in accordance with Part II of this subtitle. (An. Code 1957, art. 27, § 259(a); 2002, ch. 26, § 2.)

REVISOR'S NOTE

This Revisor's note comprises information related to the revision by Acts 2002, ch. 26.

This section is new language derived without substantive change from former Art. 27, § 259(a).

This section is rewritten as an authorization to conduct bingo, rather than as an exception to the general prohibition against gambling under Title 12 of this article, in light of § 13-101 of this title, which casts the entire title as an

exception to the prohibitions contained in Title 12 of this article, and for consistency within this title.

The former reference to "Washington County" is deleted in light of § 13-2402 of this subtitle, which limits the application of this subtitle to Washington County.

The former reference to "operat[ing]" a bingo "game" is deleted in light of the reference to bingo "conducted" under this part.

Bingo not lottery. — Bingo is not a lottery. Bender v. Arundel Arena, Inc., 248 Md. 181, 236 A.2d 7 (1967).

§ 13-2408. Bingo — In general.

(a) *Permit required.* — Before a person may conduct bingo, the person shall obtain a bingo permit from the county commissioners.

(b) *Review by county commissioners.* — (1) Before issuing a bingo permit, the county commissioners shall ascertain:

(i) the purpose of the bingo game; and

(ii) the intended use of receipts from bingo.

(2) The county commissioners may not issue a new bingo permit for bingo that is to be conducted for profit. (An. Code 1957, art. 27, § 259(c)(1), (2), (4); 2002, ch. 26, § 2.)

REVISOR'S NOTE

This Revisor's note comprises information related to the revision by Acts 2002, ch. 26.

This section is new language derived without substantive change from former Art. 27, § 259(c)(1), (2), and (4).

In subsection (a) of this section, the former reference to "operat[ing]" a bingo game is deleted in light of the reference to "conduct[ing]" bingo.

In subsection (b)(1)(ii) of this section, the reference to the "intended" use of receipts is added to state expressly what was implied in the former law.

In subsection (b)(2) of this section, the former reference to "January 12, 1995," is deleted as obsolete.

As to subsection (b) of this section, Ch. 585, Acts of 1995, § 2, provides that this section does not "affect the right of any person . . . that is authorized to conduct the game of bingo in Washington County for profit on January 11, 1995 . . . and the person . . . may continue to operate . . . as permitted by the County Commissioners . . . but the authorization . . . may not be transferred".

Defined terms:
"County commissioners"	§ 13-2401
"Person"	§ 1-101

§ 13-2409. Permit fee.

(a) *Scope of section.* — This section does not apply to a nonprofit organization seeking a bingo permit.

(b) *Fee.* — The county commissioners may charge an annual fee not exceeding $5,000 for a bingo permit. (An. Code 1957, art. 27, § 259(c)(3); 2002, ch. 26, § 2.)

REVISOR'S NOTE

This Revisor's note comprises information related to the revision by Acts 2002, ch. 26.

This section is new language derived without substantive change from former Art. 27, § 259(c)(3).

Defined term:
"County commissioners"	§ 13-2401

§ 13-2410. Prize limitation.

A person may not give or offer in a single bingo game:

(1) a money prize exceeding $1,000;

(2) a merchandise prize exceeding a value of $1,000; or

(3) a prize of money and merchandise with a combined value exceeding $1,000. (An. Code 1957, art. 27, § 259(b); 2002, ch. 26, § 2.)

This Revisor's note comprises information related to the revision by Acts 2002, ch. 26.

This section is new language derived without substantive change from former Art. 27, § 259(b).

In item (1) of this section, the reference to a "money" prize is added for clarity and consistency within this title.

Defined term:
"Person"   § 1-101

§ 13-2411. Prohibited act; penalty.

(a) *In general.* — A person may not conduct bingo in violation of Part II of this subtitle.

(b) *Penalty.* — A person who violates this section is guilty of a misdemeanor and on conviction is subject to imprisonment not exceeding 1 year or a fine not exceeding $1,000 or both.

(c) *Separate violation.* — Each day that a violation occurs is a separate violation. (An. Code 1957, art. 27, § 259(d); 2002, ch. 26, § 2.)

This Revisor's note comprises information related to the revision by Acts 2002, ch. 26.

This section is new language derived without substantive change from former Art. 27, § 259(d).

In subsection (a) of this section, the former reference to "operat[ing]" a bingo game is de-

leted in light of the reference to "conduct[ing]" bingo.

Defined term:
"Person"   § 1-101

§§ 13-2412, 13-2413.

Reserved.

Part III. Tip Jars.

§ 13-2414. Definitions.

(a) *In general.* — In Part III of this subtitle the following words have the meanings indicated.

This subsection is new language derived without substantive change from former Art. 27, § 255C(a)(1).

(b) *Agency.* — "Agency" means the county agency that the county commissioners designate to administer Part III of this subtitle.

This subsection is new language derived without substantive change from former Art. 27, § 255C(a)(5).

Defined term:
"County commissioners"   § 13-2401

(c) *Fund.* — "Fund" means the Washington County Gaming Fund.

This subsection formerly was Art. 27, § 255C(a)(6).

No changes are made.

(d) *Gaming commission.* — "Gaming commission" means the Washington County Gaming Commission.

This subsection is new language derived without substantive change from former Art. 27, § 255C(a)(3).

The term "gaming commission" is substituted for the former term "Commission" to avoid potential confusion with the defined term "county commissioners".

(e) *Tip jar.* — "Tip jar" means:

(1) a gaming device from which for consideration a number, series of numbers, or other symbol is obtained by selection of a sealed piece of paper that may entitle the purchaser to a payoff in money or otherwise, either on receipt or as the result of a subsequent announcement of a winning number, series of numbers, or other symbol; or

(2) any other device commonly recognized as a tip jar.

This subsection is new language derived without substantive change from former Art. 27, § 255C(a)(8).

In item (1) of this subsection, the former reference to the purchaser "of the number or numbers or other symbol" is deleted as implicit.

(f) *Tip jar license.* — "Tip jar license" means a license that the agency issues to operate a tip jar.

This subsection is new language derived without substantive change from former Art. 27, § 255C(a)(10).

The former phrase "in the County" is deleted in light of § 13-2402 of this subtitle, which limits the application of this subtitle to Washington County.

Occasionally, the term "tip jar licensee" is used in this subtitle as a synonym for a "person who holds a tip jar license". Since "tip jar license" is defined, "tip jar licensee" need not be defined separately.

(g) *Tip jar packet.* — "Tip jar packet" means a package of numbers, series of numbers, or symbols on folded or sealed pieces of paper that is designed to be sold through a tip jar and that is sufficient for a single tip jar game.

This subsection is new language derived without substantive change from former Art. 27, § 255C(a)(9).

The reference to "numbers, series of numbers, or symbols on folded or sealed pieces of paper" is substituted for the former reference to "tips" for consistency with the definition of "tip jar". *See* subsection (e) of this section.

(h) *Wholesaler's license.* — "Wholesaler's license" means a license that the agency issues to sell or wholesale tip jar packets for profit.

REVISOR'S NOTE

This subsection is new language derived without substantive change from former Art. 27, § 255C(a)(11).

The former phrase "in the County" is deleted in light of § 13-2402 of this subtitle, which limits the application of this subtitle to Washington County.

(An. Code 1957, art. 27, § 255C(a)(1), (3), (5), (6), (8)-(11); 2002, ch. 26, § 2.)

REVISOR'S NOTE TO SECTION

The Revisor's notes in this section comprise information related to the revision by Acts 2002, ch. 26.

§ 13-2415. Gaming commission — Established.

There is a Washington County Gaming Commission. (An. Code 1957, art. 27, § 255C(b); 2002, ch. 26, § 2.)

REVISOR'S NOTE

This Revisor's note comprises information related to the revision by Acts 2002, ch. 26.

This section formerly was Art. 27, § 255C(b).

It is set forth as a separate section for emphasis.

No changes are made.

§ 13-2416. Gaming commission — Membership.

(a) *Composition; appointment of members.* — (1) The gaming commission consists of seven members.

(2) Of the seven members of the gaming commission:

(i) three shall be appointed by the county commissioners;

(ii) one shall be appointed by the State Senators whose districts are in or include part of the county;

(iii) one shall be appointed by the chairperson of the county delegation to the House of Delegates, with the concurrence of that delegation;

(iv) one shall be from the Washington County Clubs Association, appointed by the county Senate and House delegations; and

(v) one shall be a representative of the alcoholic beverages, restaurant, and tavern industries in the county, appointed by the county Senate and House delegations.

(b) *Qualifications for members.* — Each member of the gaming commission shall be a resident of the county.

(c) *Restrictions on select members.* — (1) A member appointed to the gaming commission under subsection (a)(2)(i), (ii), or (iii) of this section may not:

(i) hold a tip jar license or wholesaler's license or be employed by a person who holds a tip jar license or wholesaler's license; or

(ii) hold an ownership interest in or receive a direct benefit from a person who holds a tip jar license or wholesaler's license.

(2) If a member of the gaming commission serves on the board of directors or as an officer of an organization and that organization applies for funds from the gaming commission, the member shall cease immediately to serve on the gaming commission.

(d) *Tenure; vacancies.* — (1) The term of a member of the gaming commission is 2 years and begins on March 1 or October 1, according to the staggered schedule required by the terms provided for members of the gaming commission on October 1, 2002.

(2) At the end of a term, a member continues to serve until a successor is appointed.

(3) A member who is appointed after a term has begun serves only for the rest of the term and until a successor is appointed.

(e) *Term limit.* — A member who completes two full terms on the gaming commission may not be reappointed within the 5 years after the end of the second term. (An. Code 1957, art. 27, § 255C(c)(1), (2)(i)-(iii), (3)-(9); 2002, ch. 26, § 2.)

REVISOR'S NOTE

This Revisor's note comprises information related to the revision by Acts 2002, ch. 26.

This section is new language derived without substantive change from former Art. 27, § 255C(c)(1), (2)(i), (ii), and (iii), and (3) through (9).

In subsection (a)(2)(iii) of this section, the reference to the "chairperson" is substituted for the former reference to the "[c]hairman" because SG § 2-1238 requires the use of words that are neutral as to gender to the extent practicable.

In subsection (a)(2)(v) of this section, the former requirement that the representative of the alcoholic beverage, restaurant, and tavern industries be "from Washington County" is deleted in light of subsection (b) of this section, which requires that each member of the gaming commission be a county resident.

In subsection (c)(2) of this section, the former phrase "and a new member shall be appointed to complete the term" is deleted in light of subsection (d)(3) of this section, which implies that a vacancy requires the appointment of a replacement member for the duration of the term.

Also in subsection (c)(2) of this section, the former phrase "during the member's term" is deleted as surplusage. In subsection (d)(2) of

this section, the reference to "October 1, 2002" is substituted for the former reference to "October 1, 2000" and the former obsolete reference to "July 1, 1995". This substitution reflects the date that this revision becomes effective and is not intended to alter the term of any member of the gaming commission. *See* Chapter 26, § 8, Acts of 2002.

In subsection (e) of this section, the limitation that a member who completes "two full terms. . . may not be reappointed during the 5 years after the end of the second term" is substituted for the former phrase "within 5 years after completion of two 2-year terms" for clarity.

Former Art. 27, § 255C(c)(2)(iv), which prohibited select members of the gaming commission from serving on the board of directors or as officers of an organization that applies for funds from the gaming commission, is deleted in light of subsection (f) of this section, which provides for the removal of members who hold certain positions in organizations that apply to the gaming commission for funds.

Defined terms:

"County commissioners"	§ 13-2401
"Gaming commission"	§ 13-2414
"Person"	§ 1-101
"Tip jar license"	§ 13-2414
"Wholesaler's license"	§ 13-2414

§ 13-2417. Gaming commission — Chairperson.

(a) *In general.* — Each year the gaming commission shall elect a chairperson from among its members.

(b) *Election.* — The manner of election of a chairperson shall be as the gaming commission determines. (An. Code 1957, art. 27, § 255C(d)(1); 2002, ch. 26, § 2.)

REVISOR'S NOTE

This Revisor's note comprises information related to the revision by Acts 2002, ch. 26.

Subsection (a) of this section is new language derived without substantive change from former Art. 27, § 255C(d)(1).

Subsection (b) of this section is standard language added to clarify the manner of election for the chairperson of the gaming commission.

In subsections (a) and (b) of this section, the references to a "chairperson" are substituted for the former references to a "chairman" because SG § 2-1238 requires the use of words that are neutral as to gender to the extent practicable.

In subsection (a) of this section, the reference to "elect[ion]" of a chairperson is substituted for the former reference to "choos[ing]" to clarify the manner in which the chairperson is selected.

Defined term:
"Gaming commission"   § 13-2414

§ 13-2418. Gaming commission — Meetings; compensation; staff.

(a) *Reimbursement for expenses.* — A member of the gaming commission:

(1) may not receive compensation; but

(2) is entitled to reimbursement for expenses, in accordance with a policy of the county commissioners.

(b) *Staff.* — The county commissioners shall assign appropriate professional staff to the gaming commission for the gaming commission's meetings. (An. Code 1957, art. 27, § 255C(c)(10), (d)(2); 2002, ch. 26, § 2.)

REVISOR'S NOTE

This Revisor's note comprises information related to the revision by Acts 2002, ch. 26.

This section is new language derived without substantive change from former Art. 27, § 255C(c)(10) and (d)(2).

Defined terms:
"County commissioners"   § 13-2401
"Gaming commission"   § 13-2414

§ 13-2419. Gaming commission — Miscellaneous powers and duties.

(a) *Regulations.* — (1) The county commissioners shall adopt regulations to carry out Part III of this subtitle.

(2) The agency may recommend to the county commissioners regulations or guidelines concerning the administration of Part III of this subtitle.

(b) *Public access to reports.* — The county commissioners shall make available for public inspection:

(1) audit reports completed under § 13-2432(a) of this subtitle; and

(2) in accordance with regulations of the county commissioners, tip jar reports submitted under § 13-2424 of this subtitle.

(c) *Criminal history records checks.* — By regulation, the county commissioners may require:

(1) an applicant for a tip jar license or wholesaler's license or an individual involved in the operation of a tip jar to be fingerprinted for purposes of a criminal history records check; and

(2) the agency to obtain a criminal history records check in accordance with subsection (d) of this section.

(d) *Criminal history records checks — Implementation.* — (1) If the county commissioners direct the agency to obtain criminal history records checks, the agency shall apply to the Criminal Justice Information System Central Repository of the Department of Public Safety and Correctional Services for a State criminal history records check for each:

(i) applicant for a tip jar license or wholesaler's license; and

(ii) individual involved in the operation of a tip jar.

(2) As part of the application for a criminal history records check, the agency shall submit to the Criminal Justice Information System Central Repository:

(i) a complete set of the applicant's or individual's legible fingerprints on forms approved by the director of the Criminal Justice Information System Central Repository; and

(ii) the fee authorized under § 10-221(b) (7) of the Criminal Procedure Article.

(3) The Criminal Justice Information System Central Repository shall provide the requested information in accordance with Title 10, Subtitle 2 of the Criminal Procedure Article. (An. Code 1957, art. 27, § 255C(e)(1)-(4), (j)(2)(iii), (r)(6); 2002, ch. 26, § 2.)

REVISOR'S NOTE

This Revisor's note comprises information related to the revision by Acts 2002, ch. 26.

This section is new language derived without substantive change from former Art. 27, § 255C(e)(1) through (4), (j)(2)(iii), and (r)(6).

In subsection (c)(1) of this section, the phrase "for purposes of a criminal history records check" is added for clarity. Although subsection (c)(1) of this section authorizes the county commissioners to require an "applicant" or an "individual involved in the operation of a tip jar" to be fingerprinted, by regulation, the county commissioners have addressed fingerprinting requirements applicable to various entities. For example, all officers of a corporation may be required to be fingerprinted. Fingerprinting is to be done at the direction or under the supervision of the agency. (Washington County Rules and Regulations Relating to Gaming, Regulation 1-104(a)(5)).

In subsection (c)(2) of this section, the phrase "in accordance with subsection (d) of this section" is substituted for the former phrase "from the Criminal Justice Information System Central Repository of the Department of Public Safety and Correctional Services" for brevity.

In subsection (d)(2)(i) of this section, the reference to an "applicant's or individual's ... fingerprints" is substituted for the former reference to an "employee's ... fingerprints" for accuracy and consistency with subsection (d)(1) of this section.

In subsection (d) of this section, the former phrase "for access to Maryland criminal history records" is deleted as surplusage.

Defined terms:

"Agency"	§ 13-2414
"County commissioners"	§ 13-2401
"Tip jar"	§ 13-2414
"Tip jar license"	§ 13-2414
"Wholesaler's license"	§ 13-2414

§ 13-2420. Tip jar operations — License required.

(a) *In general.* — A person shall be licensed by the agency before operating a tip jar.

(b) *Eligibility.* — To be eligible for a license to operate a tip jar, an applicant shall be a:

(1) religious organization;

(2) civic organization;

(3) fraternal organization;

(4) veterans' organization;

(5) bona fide charitable organization;

(6) sportsmen's association that is tax exempt under § 501(c) of the Internal Revenue Code and that is approved by the county commissioners;

(7) holder of a Class A beer, wine and liquor license;

(8) restaurant with an alcoholic beverages license;

(9) tavern with an alcoholic beverages license;

(10) volunteer fire company; or

(11) volunteer rescue company.

(c) *Restrictions.* — (1) A person may not receive a tip jar license if the person:

(i) owes taxes to the State, the county, or a municipal corporation in the county;

(ii) unless authorized under paragraph (2) of this subsection, holds a wholesaler's license; or

(iii) has been convicted of a:

1. felony; or

2. misdemeanor involving a violation of a gambling or gaming law of the State.

(2) A volunteer fire company or volunteer rescue company may hold both a tip jar license and wholesaler's license. (An. Code 1957, art. 27, § 255C(f), (p); 2002, ch. 26, § 2.)

REVISOR'S NOTE

This Revisor's note comprises information related to the revision by Acts 2002, ch. 26.

This section is new language derived without substantive change from former Art. 27, § 255C(f) and (p).

In subsection (a) of this section, the former phrase "in the County" is deleted in light of § 13-2402 of this subtitle, which limits the application of this subtitle to Washington County.

In subsection (c)(1) of this section, the former prohibition on operating a tip jar under certain circumstances is revised as a restriction on receiving a license to operate a tip jar for clarity.

Subsection (c)(2) of this section repeats § 13-2427(c)(2) of this subtitle for clarity.

Defined terms:

"Agency"	§ 13-2414
"County commissioners"	§ 13-2401
"Person"	§ 1-101
"Tip jar"	§ 13-2414
"Tip jar license"	§ 13-2414
"Wholesaler's license"	§ 13-2414

§ 13-2421. Tip jar operations — Application.

(a) *In general.* — (1) An applicant for a tip jar license shall:

(i) submit to the agency an application on the form that the agency provides; and

(ii) subject to paragraph (2) of this subsection, pay an annual fee of $250 to the county.

(2) The county commissioners may waive or reduce the annual fee for an organization that qualifies for a license under § 13-2420(b)(1) through (6), (10), or (11) of this subtitle.

(b) *Disposition of license fees.* — The county shall credit license fees collected under subsection (a)(1)(ii) of this section to the general fund of the county. (An. Code 1957, art. 27, § 255C(g); 2002, ch. 26, § 2.)

REVISOR'S NOTE

This Revisor's note comprises information related to the revision by Acts 2002, ch. 26.

Subsection (a)(1)(i) of this section is standard language added to state expressly that which was only implied in the former law — *i.e.*, applications must be made on the form that the agency provides.

Subsections (a)(1)(ii) and (2) and (c) of this section are new language derived without substantive change from former Art. 27, § 255C(g)(2) and (3) and, as it related to the application fee for a license, (1).

In subsection (a)(1)(ii) of this section, the reference to "the county" is added for clarity.

This addition is supported by regulations adopted by the county commissioners. Similarly, in subsection (b) of this section, the reference to "the county" is added.

Criminal history records checks of applicants are obtained in accordance with § 13-2419(d) of this subtitle.

Defined terms:

"Agency"	§ 13-2414
"County commissioners"	§ 13-2401
"Tip jar license"	§ 13-2414

§ 13-2422. Tip jar operations — Issuance.

The agency may issue a tip jar license to each applicant that meets the requirements of Part III of this subtitle. (An. Code 1957, art. 27, § 255C(g)(1); 2002, ch. 26, § 2.)

REVISOR'S NOTE

This Revisor's note comprises information related to the revision by Acts 2002, ch. 26.

This section is new language derived without substantive change from former Art. 27, § 255C(g)(1), as it related to issuance of a license.

Defined terms:

"Agency"	§ 13-2414
"Tip jar license"	§ 13-2414

§ 13-2423. Tip jar operations — Licensed operations.

(a) *Location — Hours of operations.* — Unless otherwise authorized by the county commissioners, a tip jar licensee may operate a tip jar game only:

(1) during normal business hours; and

(2) on the tip jar licensee's premises.

(b) *Prizes.* — A tip jar licensee may award prizes in money or merchandise for a tip jar game.

(c) *Inspection of premises.* — The agency periodically shall send an agent to inspect the premises of each tip jar licensee to ensure compliance with Part III of this subtitle. (An. Code 1957, art. 27, § 255C(h), (j)(1); 2002, ch. 26, § 2.)

REVISOR'S NOTE

This Revisor's note comprises information related to the revision by Acts 2002, ch. 26.

This section is new language derived without substantive change from former Art. 27, § 255C(h) and (j)(1).

In subsection (b) of this section, the reference to a "money" prize is substituted for the former reference to a "cash" prize for consistency within this title.

Also in subsection (b) of this section, the phrase "for a tip jar game" is added for clarity.

Defined terms:

"Agency"	§ 13-2414
"County commissioners"	§ 13-2401

§ 13-2424. Tip jar operations — Reporting requirements.

(a) *Reports required.* — At least three times a year, a tip jar licensee shall submit to the county commissioners a report concerning the tip jars the person operates.

(b) *Contents — In general.* — Each report shall:

(1) identify gaming stickers used;

(2) indicate the number of tip jars in operation;

(3) indicate the number of tip jar packets purchased; and

(4) include any additional information that the county commissioners require.

(c) *Contents — For-profit establishments.* — (1) This subsection only applies to a person who qualifies for a tip jar license under § 13-2420(b)(7), (8), or (9) of this subtitle.

(2) In accordance with regulations of the county commissioners, a person subject to this subsection shall include in each report an accounting of receipts and disbursements made in connection with tip jars for the reporting period.

(d) *Contents — Certification of contents.* — Each report shall include a written statement, signed by the individual making the report, in which the individual affirms under the penalties of Part III of this subtitle and under the penalty of perjury that the contents of the report are true to the best of the individual's knowledge, information, and belief.

(e) *Contents — Select nonprofit organizations.* — (1) This subsection only applies to an organization that qualifies for a tip jar license under § 13-2420(b)(1) through (6) of this subtitle.

(2) Each report for an organization that is subject to this subsection:

(i) shall be filed by an officer of the organization; and

(ii) in accordance with regulations of the county commissioners, shall include for the reporting period an accounting of:

1. all receipts in connection with the operation of a tip jar; and

2. the disbursements made in compliance with § 13-2435(e) of this subtitle.

(3) In filing a report under this subsection, the officer of the organization may not:

(i) fraudulently use a false or fictitious name;

(ii) knowingly conceal a material fact;

(iii) knowingly make a false statement; or

(iv) otherwise commit fraud.

(4) A person who violates paragraph (3) of this subsection is guilty of a misdemeanor and on conviction is subject to imprisonment not exceeding 90 days or a fine not exceeding $1,000 or both. (An. Code 1957, art. 27, § 255C(r)(1)-(5); 2002, ch. 26, § 2.)

REVISOR'S NOTE

This Revisor's note comprises information related to the revision by Acts 2002, ch. 26.

This section is new language derived without substantive change from former Art. 27, § 255C(r)(1) through (5).

In subsection (d) of this section, the former reference to swearing "solemnly" is deleted as surplusage.

In subsection (e)(1) of this section, the reference to "§ 13-2420(b)(1) through (6) of this subtitle", pertaining to certain nonprofit organizations that qualify to operate tip jars, is substituted for the former reference to "an organization . . . subject to [§ 13-2435(e) of this subtitle]" for clarity and consistency with the scope provision in subsection (c) of this section.

In subsection (e)(3) of this section, the specific reference to "the officer of the organization" is substituted for the former vague reference to "an individual" who files a report for clarity and consistency with subsection (e)(2)(i) of this section.

Defined terms:

"County commissioners"	§ 13-2401
"Person"	§ 1-101
"Tip jar"	§ 13-2414
"Tip jar license"	§ 13-2414
"Tip jar packet"	§ 13-2414

§ **13-2425. Tip jar operations — Term; transfer prohibited.**

(a) *Term of license.* — A tip jar license expires on the first July 1 after its effective date.

(b) *License nontransferable.* — A tip jar license is not transferable. (An. Code 1957, art. 27, § 255C(i); 2002, ch. 26, § 2.)

REVISOR'S NOTE

This Revisor's note comprises information related to the revision by Acts 2002, ch. 26.

This section is new language derived without substantive change from former Art. 27, § 255C(i).

Defined term:

"Tip jar license"	§ 13-2414

§ **13-2426. Temporary license.**

(a) *Authorized.* — By regulation, the county commissioners may establish a temporary tip jar license for a nonprofit organization that desires to raise money solely for an athletic, charitable, or educational purpose that:

(1) meets the requirements for a charitable contribution under § 170(c) of the Internal Revenue Code; and

(2) does not benefit a:

(i) law enforcement agency;

(ii) law enforcement fraternal organization;

(iii) political club, political committee, or political party; or

(iv) unit of the State government or of a political subdivision of the State other than:

1. an ambulance, fire fighting, or rescue squad; or

2. a primary or secondary school or an institution of higher education.

(b) *Regulations.* — If the county commissioners establish a temporary tip jar license, by regulation, the county commissioners shall:

(1) set the fee for a temporary tip jar license;

(2) set the term of a temporary tip jar license;

(3) prescribe which provisions of Part III of this subtitle apply to the issuance of a temporary tip jar license and the operation of a tip jar under a temporary tip jar license; and

(4) establish any additional requirements that the county commissioners consider appropriate concerning operation of a tip jar under a temporary tip jar license.

(c) *Organization subject to audit.* — An organization that receives a temporary tip jar license is subject to audit by the gaming commission.

(d) *Personal profit prohibited.* — An individual involved in the operation of a tip jar under a temporary tip jar license may not personally benefit financially from the operation of the tip jar.

(e) *Final disposition of proceeds.* — If an organization that has operated a tip jar under a temporary tip jar license disbands, the organization shall transfer any remaining proceeds from the operation of a tip jar to the fund. (An. Code 1957, art. 27, § 255C(k); 2002, ch. 26, § 2.)

REVISOR'S NOTE

This Revisor's note comprises information related to the revision by Acts 2002, ch. 26.

This section is new language derived without substantive change from former Art. 27, § 255C(k).

In subsection (a)(2)(iv) of this section, the word "unit" is substituted for the former word "agency". *See* General Revisor's Note to article.

In subsection (a)(2)(iv)2 of this section, the reference to an "institution of higher education" is substituted for the former reference to a "college" for consistency with ED Division III.

In subsection (b) of this section, the introductory clause "[i]f the county commissioners establish a temporary tip jar license," is added for clarity.

Defined terms:

"County commissioners"	§ 13-2401
"Fund"	§ 13-2414
"Gaming commission"	§ 13-2414
"Tip jar"	§ 13-2414
"Tip jar license"	§ 13-2414

§ 13-2427. Wholesaler operations — License required.

(a) *In general.* — A person shall be licensed by the agency as a wholesaler before the person may sell a tip jar packet for profit.

(b) *Eligibility.* — (1) A person is eligible for a license under this section to sell or wholesale for profit a tip jar packet if the person:

(i) is of good moral character;

(ii) except for a volunteer fire company or volunteer rescue company, has had an established place of business in the county for at least 3 years, as evidenced by the filing of personal property tax returns;

(iii) in the case of a volunteer fire company or volunteer rescue company, has been established in the county for at least 1 year;

(iv) does not owe taxes to the State, the county, or a municipal corporation in the county;

(v) unless authorized under paragraph (2) of this subsection, does not hold a tip jar license;

(vi) has not been convicted of a:

1. felony; or

2. misdemeanor involving a violation of a gambling or gaming law of the State;

(vii) except for a volunteer fire company or volunteer rescue company, does not hold a tip jar license or own or have in any way an interest in an entity that holds a tip jar license;

(viii) except for a volunteer fire company or volunteer rescue company, is not an immediate family member of a person who holds a tip jar license or owns or has in any way an interest in an entity that holds a tip jar license; and

(ix) is not a corporation, limited liability company, or unincorporated association in which at least one stockholder or member is a holder of a tip jar license.

(2) A volunteer fire company or volunteer rescue company may hold both a tip jar license and a wholesaler's license. (An. Code 1957, art. 27, § 255C(l), (p); 2002, ch. 26, § 2; 2004, ch. 215.)

REVISOR'S NOTE

This Revisor's note comprises information related to the revision by Acts 2002, ch. 26.

This section is new language derived without substantive change from former Art. 27, § 255C(l) and (p).

In subsection (a) of this section, the former phrase "in the County" is deleted in light of § 13-2402 of this subtitle, which limits the application of this subtitle to Washington County.

Subsection (b)(2) of this section repeats § 13-2420(c)(2) for clarity.

Defined terms:

"Agency"	§ 13-2414
"Person"	§ 1-101
"Tip jar license"	§ 13-2414
"Tip jar packet"	§ 13-2414

Editor's note. — Section 2, ch. 215, Acts 2004, provides that "this Act shall be construed to apply to and interpreted to affect persons who apply for or hold a tip jar license or wholesaler's license issued by the Washington County agency that administers tip jar gaming."

§ 13-2428. Wholesaler operations — Application.

(a) *In general.* — (1) An applicant for a wholesaler's license shall:

(i) submit to the agency an application on the form that the agency provides; and

(ii) subject to paragraph (2) of this subsection, pay to the agency an annual fee of $500.

(2) The county commissioners shall waive the annual fee for a volunteer fire company or a volunteer rescue company.

(b) *Disposition of license fees.* — The agency shall credit license fees collected under subsection (a)(1)(ii) of this section to the general fund of the county. (An. Code 1957, art. 27, § 255C(m); 2002, ch. 26, § 2.)

REVISOR'S NOTE

This Revisor's note comprises information related to the revision by Acts 2002, ch. 26.

Subsection (a)(1)(i) of this section is standard language added to state expressly that which was only implied in the former law — *i.e.,* applications must be made on the form the agency requires.

Subsections (a)(1)(ii) and (2) and (c) of this section are new language derived without substantive change from former Art. 27, § 255C(m)(2) and (3) and, as it related to the application and fee for a wholesaler's license, (1).

In subsection (a)(1)(ii) of this section, the reference to an "annual" fee is added for clarity.

This addition is supported by the reference to an annual fee in former Art. 27, § 255C(m)(2) — now subsection (a)(2) of this section.

Subsection (b) of this section is revised to clarify that the agency is responsible for crediting license fees it collects to the county general fund.

Criminal history records checks of applicants are obtained in accordance with § 13-2419(d) of this subtitle.

Defined terms:
"Agency"	§ 13-2414
"County commissioners"	§ 13-2401
"Wholesaler's license"	§ 13-2414

§ 13-2429. Wholesaler operations — Issuance.

The agency may issue a wholesaler's license to each applicant that meets the requirements of Part III of this subtitle. (An. Code 1957, art. 27, § 255C(m)(1); 2002, ch. 26, § 2.)

REVISOR'S NOTE

This Revisor's note comprises information related to the revision by Acts 2002, ch. 26.

This section is new language derived without substantive change from former Art. 27, § 255C(m)(1), as it related to issuance of a wholesaler's license.

Defined terms:
"Agency"	§ 13-2414
"Wholesaler's license"	§ 13-2414

§ 13-2430. Wholesaler operations — Licensed operations.

(a) *Sales restricted.* — A holder of a wholesaler's license may not sell a tip jar packet to a person who does not have a tip jar license.

(b) *Required gaming sticker.* — Before selling a tip jar packet, a holder of a wholesaler's license shall:

(1) obtain a gaming sticker from the agency; and

(2) affix the gaming sticker to the tip jar packet in the manner the county commissioners require. (An. Code 1957, art. 27, § 255C(o); 2002, ch. 26, §§ 2, 3; 2003, ch. 21, § 2.)

REVISOR'S NOTE

This Revisor's note comprises information related to the revision by Acts 2002, ch. 26.

This section is new language derived without substantive change from former Art. 27,

§ 255C(o), as abrogated under Ch. 479, § 4, Acts of 2000.

Former subsection (c) of this section, which prohibited a person with a wholesaler's license from charging a fee to a volunteer fire company or a volunteer rescue company, is abrogated.

Defined terms:

"Agency"	§ 13-2414
"County commissioners"	§ 13-2401
"Person"	§ 1-101
"Tip jar license"	§ 13-2414
"Tip jar packet"	§ 13-2414
"Wholesaler's license"	§ 13-2414

§ 13-2431. Wholesaler operations — Term; transfer prohibited.

(a) *Term of license.* — A wholesaler's license expires on the first July 1 after its effective date.

(b) *License nontransferable.* — A wholesaler's license is not transferable. (An. Code 1957, art. 27, § 255C(n); 2002, ch. 26, § 2.)

REVISOR'S NOTE

This Revisor's note comprises information related to the revision by Acts 2002, ch. 26.

This section is new language derived without substantive change from former Art. 27, § 255C(n).

Defined term:

"Wholesaler's license"	§ 13-2414

§ 13-2432. Licensees subject to audit.

(a) *In general.* — The county commissioners may audit records relating to tip jars of a holder of a tip jar license or wholesaler's license.

(b) *Access to records.* — In accordance with regulations of the county commissioners, a holder of a tip jar license or a wholesaler's license shall make available to an auditor designated by the county commissioners the records that are required for an audit.

(c) *Record retention.* — A holder of a tip jar license or a wholesaler's license shall retain for at least 5 years the records that are required by the county commissioners by regulation. (An. Code 1957, art. 27, § 255C(j)(2)(i), (ii), (3); 2002, ch. 26, § 2.)

REVISOR'S NOTE

This Revisor's note comprises information related to the revision by Acts 2002, ch. 26.

This section is new language derived without substantive change from former Art. 27, § 255C(j)(2)(i) and (ii) and (3).

Defined terms:

"County commissioners"	§ 13-2401
"Person"	§ 1-101
"Tip jar"	§ 13-2414
"Tip jar license"	§ 13-2414
"Wholesaler's license"	§ 13-2414

§ 13-2433. Denials, reprimands, suspensions, revocations.

(a) *In general.* — Subject to the hearing provisions of § 13-2434 of this subtitle, the agency may:

(1) deny a tip jar license or a wholesaler's license to an applicant; or

(2) in accordance with § 13-2437 of this subtitle, discipline a holder of a tip jar license or wholesaler's license.

(b) *Effect of license revocation.* — The agency shall deny a license to an applicant whose tip jar license or wholesaler's license has been revoked.

(c) *Affiliated organizations.* — If the license of a holder of a tip jar license or wholesaler's license is revoked for two separate civil violations under § 13-2437 of this subtitle or a criminal violation under § 13-2424(e) or § 13-2438(a) of this subtitle, the agency may deny a tip jar license or wholesaler's license to:

(1) a corporate or limited liability entity applicant if 50% or more of the capital stock is owned by an individual, or an immediate family member of an individual, whose license was revoked; or

(2) a partnership applicant if the partnership includes as a partner an individual whose license was revoked. (An. Code 1957, art. 27, § 255C(s)(1), (t); 2002, ch. 26, § 2.)

REVISOR'S NOTE

This Revisor's note comprises information related to the revision by Acts 2002, ch. 26.

This section is new language derived without substantive change from former Art. 27, § 255C(s)(1) and (t).

Subsection (b) of this section has been revised to clarify that it is the obligation of the agency to deny a license to an applicant who previously had a tip jar license or wholesaler's license revoked.

Defined terms:

"Agency"	§ 13-2414
"Person"	§ 1-101
"Tip jar license"	§ 13-2414
"Wholesaler's license"	§ 13-2414

§ 13-2434. Denials, reprimands, suspensions, revocations — Hearings.

(a) *Right to hearing.* — Before the agency takes action under § 13-2433(a) of this subtitle, it shall give the person against whom the action is contemplated the opportunity for a hearing.

(b) *Hearing process.* — If a hearing is requested, the county commissioners shall:

(1) give notice and hold the hearing in accordance with Title 10, Subtitle 2 of the State Government Article; or

(2) delegate to the Office of Administrative Hearings the authority to hold the hearing.

(c) *Hearings by county commissioners — Oaths.* — If the county commissioners hold the hearing, the county commissioners may administer oaths in connection with the hearing.

(d) *Hearings by OAH.* — (1) If the Office of Administrative Hearings holds the hearing:

(i) the administrative law judge shall state on the record the conclusions of law and findings of fact; and

(ii) subject to paragraph (2) of this subsection, the determination of the administrative law judge is a final decision for purposes of judicial review in the same manner as a final decision in a contested case under § 10-222 of the State Government Article.

(2) In an appeal of a decision of the administrative law judge:

(i) if the civil penalty is less than $5,000, judicial review of disputed issues of fact shall be confined to the record; or

(ii) if the civil penalty is $5,000 or more, judicial review shall be de novo.

(e) *Failure to request hearing or appear.* — After notice, if the person against whom the action is contemplated:

(1) fails or refuses to appear, nevertheless the county commissioners may hear and determine the matter; or

(2) does not request a hearing, the county commissioners may impose a civil penalty without a hearing. (An. Code 1957, art. 27, § 255C(u); 2002, ch. 26, § 2.)

REVISOR'S NOTE

This Revisor's note comprises information related to the revision by Acts 2002, ch. 26.

This section is new language derived without substantive change from former Art. 27, § 255C(u).

In subsection (a) of this section, the reference to "§ 13-2433(a) of this subtitle" is substituted for the reference to former Art. 27, § 255C(s). Although the revised reference incorporates only former Art. 27, § 255C(s)(1), it was only that part of the former provision that addressed actions taken, subject to the interested party's right to an administrative hearing.

Also in subsection (a) of this section, the former reference to a hearing "before the Board" is deleted in light of subsection (b) of this section, which authorizes the county commissioners to delegate responsibility for a hearing to the Office of Administrative Hearings.

In subsection (c) of this section, the phrase "in connection with the proceeding" is added for clarity.

In subsection (d) of this section, the former phrase "[i]f the Board delegates the authority to hold a hearing" is deleted in light of subsection (b)(2) of this section.

In subsection (d)(1)(ii) of this section, the phrase "subject to paragraph (2) of this subsection" is added to reflect an exemption to the normal review process following a final decision in an administrative proceeding.

In subsection (e)(2) of this section, the reference to "a civil penalty" is substituted for the former reference to a "fine" for clarity.

Also in subsection (e)(2) of this section, the phrase "without a hearing" is substituted for the former phrase "may deem that the matter has been heard" to avoid the legal fiction that a hearing takes place.

Defined terms:

"Agency"	§ 13-2414
"County commissioners"	§ 13-2401
"Person"	§ 1-101

§ 13-2435. Washington County Gaming Fund.

(a) *"Gross profits" defined.* — In this section, "gross profits" means the total proceeds from the operation of a tip jar less the amount of money winnings or value of prizes distributed.

(b) *Fund established.* — There is a Washington County Gaming Fund.

(c) *Administration.* — (1) The county commissioners shall establish:

(i) the method and time of deposits to the fund; and

(ii) other procedures necessary to carry out subsections (d) and (e) of this section.

(2) In accordance with a written agreement between the county commissioners and the gaming commission, the gaming commission may use money from the fund to reimburse the county commissioners for the costs to the county for administering Part III of this subtitle.

(d) *Assessments — Business establishments.* — (1) This subsection applies only to a person who holds a tip jar license under § 13-2420(b)(7), (8), or (9) of this subtitle.

(2) Subject to paragraph (3) of this subsection, a person subject to this subsection shall deposit with a financial institution designated by the gaming

commission, to the credit of the fund, the gross profits from each tip jar that the person operates.

(3) To offset the costs of operating a tip jar, a person with a tip jar license may retain the lesser of $45 or 50% of the gross profits from each tip jar game.

(e) *Assessments — Nonprofit organizations; clubs.* — (1) This subsection applies only to a person who holds a tip jar license under § 13-2420(b)(1) through (6) of this subtitle.

(2) A person subject to this subsection shall deposit with a financial institution designated by the gaming commission, to the credit of the fund, 15% of the gross profits earned through the operation of tip jars during the 12-month period ending June 30.

(3) If a person fails to contribute the full amount required under paragraph (2) of this subsection, the person shall deposit the balance required during the next year.

(f) *Disbursement.* — After the reimbursement under subsection (c)(2) of this section, each year the gaming commission shall distribute:

(1) 50% of the money deposited in the fund to the Washington County Volunteer Fire and Rescue Association; and

(2) subject to any restriction that the county commissioners adopt by regulation, 50% of the money deposited in the fund to bona fide charitable organizations in the county. (An. Code 1957, art. 27, § 255C(q)(1)-(8), (10); 2002, ch. 26, §§ 2, 3; 2003, ch. 21, § 2; ch. 473, §§ 1, 2; 2004, ch. 25, § 5; ch. 215; 2005, ch. 25, § 1.)

REVISOR'S NOTE

This Revisor's note comprises information related to the revision by Acts 2002, ch. 26.

This section is new language derived without substantive change from former Art. 27, § 255C(q), as abrogated under Ch. 479, § 4, Acts of 2000.

Former subsection (f)(1)(i) of this section required 50% of the moneys deposited in the fund to be distributed to the Washington County Volunteer Fire and Rescue Association. Similarly, former subsection (f)(1)(ii) of this section required 50% of the moneys deposited in the

fund to be distributed to charitable organizations in the county.

Former subsection (f)(2) of this section prohibited the gaming commission from distributing more than $50,000 to a single applicant based on one application.

Former subsection (g) of this section required the gaming commission to report every 6 months to the Washington County delegation on how recipients of moneys from the fund were affected by the 50-50 formula for distributing moneys.

Editor's note. — Section 2, ch. 215, Acts 2004, provides that "this Act shall be construed to apply to and interpreted to affect persons who apply for or hold a tip jar license or

wholesaler's license issued by the Washington County agency that administers tip jar gaming."

§ 13-2436. Prohibited acts.

(a) *Operation of tip jar.* — Unless licensed to operate a tip jar by the agency, a person may not offer to another a chance from a tip jar or otherwise operate a tip jar.

(b) *Player, location restrictions.* — A holder of a tip jar license may not:

(1) allow a minor to play a tip jar; or

(2) operate a tip jar on property owned by the Board of Education of Washington County.

(c) *Sale of tip jar packets.* — Unless licensed as a wholesaler to sell tip jar packets by the agency, a person may not sell or wholesale a tip jar packet for profit. (An. Code 1957, art. 27, § 255C(v)(1)-(3); 2002, ch. 26, § 2.)

REVISOR'S NOTE

This Revisor's note comprises information related to the revision by Acts 2002, ch. 26.

This section is new language derived without substantive change from former Art. 27, § 255C(v)(1) through (3).

In subsection (b)(1) of this section, the defined term "minor" is substituted for the former reference to an "individual under the age of 18 years" for brevity. *See* § 1-101 of this article.

In subsection (b)(2) of this section, the reference to the "Board of Education of Washington County" is substituted for the former reference to the "Washington County School Board" for accuracy.

In subsection (c) of this section, the phrase "as a wholesaler" is added for clarity.

Defined terms:

"Agency"	§ 13-2414
"Minor"	§ 1-101
"Person"	§ 1-101
"Tip jar"	§ 13-2414
"Tip jar packet"	§ 13-2414

§ 13-2437. Administrative and civil penalties.

(a) *In general.* — If a person violates Part III of this subtitle, the person is subject to:

(1) for a first violation, suspension of the person's tip jar license or wholesaler's license and a civil penalty not exceeding $1,500; or

(2) for each subsequent violation, revocation of the person's tip jar license or wholesaler's license and a civil penalty not exceeding $5,000.

(b) *Action against liquor license.* — In addition to the penalties under subsection (a)(2) of this section, if the person has a liquor license, the agency may recommend to the Board of License Commissioners for Washington County that the Board suspend the person's liquor license for not less than 15 days for a subsequent violation.

(c) *Disposition of civil penalties.* — Civil penalties collected under subsection (a) of this section shall be credited to the general fund of the county. (An. Code 1957, art. 27, § 255C(s)(2)·(4); 2002, ch. 26, § 2; 2003, ch. 21, § 1.)

REVISOR'S NOTE

This section is new language derived without substantive change from former Art. 27, § 255C(s)(2) through (4).

In subsections (a) and (c) of this section, the references to a "civil penalt[y]" are substituted for the former references to a "civil fine" and "[f]ines" for accuracy.

In the introductory language of subsection (a) of this section, the former phrase "[i]f the County agency finds" is deleted for accuracy in light of § 13-2434 of this subtitle, which specifies that a final decision is made by the county commissioners or an administrative law judge.

In subsection (a)(1) and (2) of this section, the references to a "violation" are substituted for the former references to an "offense" for consis-

tency within this article. *See* General Revisor's Note to article.

In subsection (a)(1) of this section, the former reference to "denial" of a license is deleted as unnecessary in light of § 13-2433(a) of this subtitle, as it relates to applicants, and as inaccurate, as it relates to persons currently in possession of a license.

In subsection (a)(2) of this section, the reference to "each" subsequent violation is substituted for the former reference to "a second or" subsequent offense for consistency within this article.

In subsection (b) of this section, the reference to the Board of License Commissioners "for Washington County" is added for clarity.

Defined terms:

"Agency"   § 13-2414

"Person"   § 1-101

"Tip jar license"   § 13-2414

"Wholesaler's license" § 13-2414

This Revisor's note comprises information related to the revision by Acts 2002, ch. 26.

In general. — The General Assembly has implicitly imposed both criminal and civil sanctions for the same act or omission in violation of a prior version of this section. Long v. American Legion Potomac Post 202, Inc., 117 Md. App. 18, 699 A.2d 456 (1997).

The fines that could be imposed under an earlier version of this section were civil rather than criminal fines and did not come under the purview of Article 38, § 1 (see now § 7-501 et seq. of the Courts Article), and the District Court did not have original and exclusive jurisdiction over charges involving a violation of the earlier version. Long v. American Legion Potomac Post 202, Inc., 117 Md. App. 18, 699 A.2d 456 (1997).

§ 13-2438. Criminal penalty.

(a) *In general.* — (1) A person who violates § 13-2436 of this subtitle is guilty of a misdemeanor and on conviction is subject to a fine not exceeding:

 (i) for a first violation, $5,000; or

 (ii) for each subsequent violation, $10,000.

 (2) Each sale or offer of a chance from a tip jar is a separate violation.

(b) *Action against liquor license.* — If a person convicted under this section has a liquor license, the agency shall recommend to the Board of License Commissioners for Washington County that the Board suspend the person's liquor license for not less than 15 days. (An. Code 1957, art. 27, § 255C(v)(4)-(6); 2002, ch. 26, § 2.)

REVISOR'S NOTE

This Revisor's note comprises information related to the revision by Acts 2002, ch. 26.

This section is new language derived without substantive change from former Art. 27, § 255C(v)(4) through (6).

In subsection (a) of this section, the references to a "violation" are substituted for the former references to an "offense" for consistency within this article. *See* General Revisor's Note to article.

In subsection (a)(1)(ii) of this section, the reference to "each" subsequent violation is substituted for the former reference to "a" subsequent offense for consistency within this article.

In subsection (b) of this section, the reference to the Board of License Commissioners "for Washington County" is added for clarity.

Defined terms:

"Agency"   § 13-2414

"Person"   § 1-101

"Tip jar"   § 13-2414

§ 13-2439. Reports.

On or before February 1 of each year, the Gaming Commission shall submit a report to the Comptroller that includes:

 (1) the total amount of revenue received by the Gaming Commission for the previous calendar year as a result of the operation of tip jars in Washington County;

 (2) a detailed listing of the total distributions made by the Gaming Commission during the previous calendar year with regard to revenue received from the operation of tip jars in Washington County; and

(3) any additional information that the Comptroller may require. (2004, ch. 215.)

GENERAL REVISOR'S NOTE TO SUBTITLE

Former Art. 27, § 255C(a)(4), which defined "county" to mean Washington County, is deleted in light of § 13-2402 of this subtitle, which limits application of this subtitle to Washington County.

Former Art. 27, § 255C(a)(7), which defined "gaming sticker", is deleted in light of § 13-2430(b) of this subtitle, which requires that a person with a wholesaler's license obtain a gaming sticker and affix the sticker to a tip jar packet in the manner that the county commissioners require. The former reference to a bar code is deleted as unnecessary since the type of sticker required is left to the discretion of the county commissioners.

Former Art. 27, § 255C(q)(9), which prohibited the county commissioners from reducing appropriations to nonprofit organizations in the County below the amount budgeted in fiscal year 1996, was recodified as § 1-108(e) of the Public Local Laws of Washington County as part of the enactment of this article. *See* Chapter 26, § 4, Acts of 2002. This provision was initially enacted in 1996 as part of legislation concerning the regulation of tip jars. However, because it did not directly relate to the regulation of tip jars, the Criminal Law Article Review Committee determined that it would be more appropriately codified in the Public Local Laws rather than in this subtitle.

Portions of §§ 13-2430 and 13-2435, which are derived from former Art. 27, § 255C(o) and (q), respectively, are subject to abrogation on June 30, 2003, in accordance with Ch. 479, Acts of 2000.

Subtitle 25. Wicomico County.

§ 13-2501. Definitions.

(a) *In general.* — In this subtitle the following words have the meanings indicated.

REVISOR'S NOTE

This subsection is new language added as the standard introductory language to a definition section.

(b) *Committee.* — "Committee" means the Gaming Advisory Committee established under § 13-2505 of this subtitle.

REVISOR'S NOTE

This subsection is new language added to avoid repetition of the phrase "Gaming Advisory Committee" and for consistency within this subtitle.

(c) *Sheriff.* — "Sheriff" means the Sheriff of Wicomico County.

REVISOR'S NOTE

This subsection is new language added for brevity and consistency within this subtitle.

(2002, ch. 26, § 2.)

REVISOR'S NOTE TO SECTION

The Revisor's notes in this section comprise information related to the revision by Acts 2002, ch. 26.

§ 13-2502. Scope of subtitle.

(a) *Application.* — This subtitle applies only in Wicomico County.

(b) *Slot machines.* — This subtitle does not authorize gambling using a slot machine or a coin machine. (An. Code 1957, art. 27, § 256(g); 2002, ch. 26, § 2.)

REVISOR'S NOTE

This Revisor's note comprises information related to the revision by Acts 2002, ch. 26.

Subsection (a) of this section is new language added to clarify the scope of this subtitle.

Subsection (b) of this section is new language derived without substantive change from former Art. 27, § 256(g).

In subsection (b) of this section, the former reference to a "type of" machine is deleted as surplusage.

§ 13-2503. Gaming — In general.

(a) *License required.* — The sheriff may issue a license to an organization listed in subsection (b) of this section to conduct a game that uses any of the following devices to award prizes of merchandise or money:

(1) a paddle wheel;

(2) a wheel of fortune;

(3) a chance book;

(4) bingo;

(5) a raffle; or

(6) any other gaming device.

(b) *Qualified organization.* — To qualify for a license under this subtitle, an organization shall be:

(1) a bona fide religious organization that has conducted religious services at a fixed location in the county for at least 5 years before the organization applies for a license;

(2) a tax-supported volunteer fire company or an auxiliary unit whose members are directly associated with the fire company;

(3) an organization that has been located in the county for at least 5 years before it applies for a license and is:

(i) a nationally chartered veterans' organization or an auxiliary unit whose members are directly associated with the veterans' organization;

(ii) a nonprofit organization that is exempt from taxation under § 501(c)(3) or (4) of the Internal Revenue Code;

(iii) a nonprofit fraternal organization that is exempt from taxation under § 501(c)(10) of the Internal Revenue Code; or

(iv) a nonprofit organization that:

    1. intends to use the gaming license to raise money for an exclusively charitable, athletic, or educational purpose that meets the conditions of subsection (c) of this section; and

    2. states the charitable, athletic, or educational purpose in the application to the sheriff.

  (c) *Charitable purpose.* — For the purposes of subsection (b)(3)(iv) of this section, a purpose is considered a charitable, athletic, or educational purpose if the purpose:

    (1) meets the requirements for a charitable contribution under § 170(c) of the Internal Revenue Code; and

    (2) does not benefit a:

      (i) law enforcement unit;

      (ii) fraternal organization for a law enforcement unit;

      (iii) political club;

      (iv) political committee;

      (v) political party; or

      (vi) unit of State government or a political subdivision of the State other than:

        1. an ambulance company;

        2. a fire fighting company;

        3. a rescue company;

        4. a primary school;

        5. a secondary school; or

        6. an institution of higher education.

  (d) *Application.* — (1) An applicant for a license shall submit an application to the sheriff.

    (2) The application shall contain:

      (i) a copy of the tax-exempt verification of the organization;

      (ii) a copy of the applicant's charter, if applicable; and

      (iii) a certification by a principal officer of the applicant stating:

        1. the dates for which the license is sought;

        2. the place at which the game will be conducted;

        3. the type of game for which the license is sought;

        4. that only the regular members of the applicant will conduct the games and operate the gaming device for which the license is sought;

        5. that the applicant will not use the assistance of gaming professionals in conducting games or operating gaming devices;

        6. that persons conducting the games and operating the gaming devices or assisting in conducting the games and operating the gaming devices will not receive compensation or reward; and

        7. that all proceeds obtained under the license will be used to further the purposes of the organization.

    (3) The sheriff shall retain the copies of the applicant's verification of tax exemption and charter.

  (e) *License.* — (1) The sheriff may issue a license:

    (i) for one or more specific dates; or

    (ii) for a period not exceeding 1 year.

(2) The licensing year shall run from July 1 through the following June 30.

(3) The license shall state:

(i) the dates that the game will be conducted;

(ii) the place that the game will be conducted; and

(iii) the type of game authorized.

(f) *Limitations.* — (1) Except as provided under paragraph (2) of this subsection, a licensee may not conduct a game on Sunday.

(2) (i) A licensee may operate a raffle on Sunday.

(ii) A raffle is considered to be operated on the day that the licensee selects the raffle winner.

(iii) The sheriff shall license a 50/50 game operated for a period of more than 1 day as a raffle.

(3) A licensee may not allow a child who is under the age of 16 years to:

(i) operate a game or gaming device for which a license is issued under this subtitle;

(ii) conduct a game in which a gaming device is operated; or

(iii) play or participate in a game in which a gaming device is operated.

(4) The licensee may not pay a fee for the rental of the premises on which a game is conducted to:

(i) itself;

(ii) a trustee of the licensee;

(iii) a committee of the licensee; or

(iv) an organization with the same members or substantially the same members as the licensee.

(g) *Fees.* — The sheriff shall charge each applicant:

(1) a license fee of $1 for each day for which a license is issued; and

(2) the following additional amounts:

(i) except as provided in items (ii) through (v) of this item, $1 for each gaming device to be operated each day;

(ii) $1 for each day that a pull tab or instant bingo device is to be sold;

(iii) $1 for each day that a bingo event is to be conducted;

(iv) $1 for each day that a bingo special event is to be conducted; and

(v) $1 for each raffle to be conducted. (An. Code 1957, art. 27, § 256(a)-(c), (d)(1)(iii), (e), (f); 2002, ch. 26, § 2; 2003, ch. 21, § 1; 2011, ch, 65, § 5.)

REVISOR'S NOTE

This Revisor's note comprises information related to the revision by Acts 2002, ch. 26.

This section is new language derived without substantive change from former Art. 27, § 256(a), (b), (c), (d)(1)(iii), (e), and (f).

In subsection (a) of this section, the former limitation "[n]otwithstanding any other provisions of this subtitle [sic]," is deleted in light of § 13-101 of this title and the reorganization of material derived from the former "Gaming" subheading of Article 27 in Titles 12 and 13 of this article.

Also in subsection (a) of this section, the reference to a "money" prize is substituted for the former reference to a "cash" prize for consistency within this title.

In subsection (c)(2)(i) of this section, the reference to a "law enforcement unit" is substituted for the former reference to a "law enforcement agency" for consistency within this article.

In subsection (c)(2)(vi)1 through 3 of this section, the reference to a "company" is substituted for the former reference to a "squad" for consistency within this article.

In subsection (c)(2)(vi)6 of this section, the reference to an "institution of higher education" is substituted for the former reference to a "college" for accuracy and consistency with ED Division III.

In subsections (d)(2)(iii)1 and (e)(3) of this section, the former references to a "date" are deleted as included in the references to "dates". *See* Art. 1, § 8.

In subsection (d)(2)(iii)4 of this section, the word "only" is substituted for the former phrase "solely and personally" for brevity.

In subsection (d)(2)(iii)6 of this section, the former reference to "commission, salary [or] recompense" is deleted as included in the reference to "compensation or reward".

In subsection (e)(1)(i) of this section, the phrase "for one or more specific dates" is substituted for the former phrase "[o]n a daily basis for specific dates" for clarity.

In subsection (e)(3)(iii) of this section, the reference "the type of game" is substituted for the former reference "games" for clarity.

In subsection (f)(2)(ii) of this section, the reference to "the licensee" is added to clarify who selects the winner of the raffle.

In subsection (f)(2)(iii) of this section, the reference to the "sheriff" is added to clarify who has the authority to license the 50/50 game as a raffle.

In subsection (f)(3) of this section, the reference to "[a] licensee" is added to clarify who has the obligation to limit and control the actions of a minor.

In subsection (g)(2)(i) of this section, the introductory language "except as provided in items (ii) through (v) of this item" is added for clarity.

Defined terms:
"Person"	§ 1-101
"Sheriff"	§ 13-2501

Editor's note. — Pursuant to § 5, ch. 65, Acts 2011, "tax-exempt" was substituted for "tax exempt" in (d)(2)(i).

Bingo not lottery. — Bingo is not a lottery. Bender v. Arundel Arena, Inc., 248 Md. 181, 236 A.2d 7 (1967).

§ 13-2504. Reports.

(a) *Schedule.* — (1) In accordance with paragraph (2) of this subsection, a principal officer of a licensee shall file a report under oath with the sheriff on the form that the sheriff provides.

(2) (i) A licensee that is issued a license for a period of less than 1 year shall file the report within 15 days after the date that the license expires.

(ii) A licensee that is issued a license for a period of 1 year shall file:

1. a semiannual report on or before January 31 of the licensing year; and

2. an annual report within 30 days after the date that the license expires.

(3) (i) A licensee also shall keep a weekly report in the form that the sheriff requires.

(ii) The weekly report shall be completed under oath.

(iii) The weekly report is subject to audit at a reasonable hour by:

1. the sheriff;

2. the State's Attorney for the county; or

3. a representative of the sheriff or the State's Attorney.

(b) *Contents.* — The report that a licensee submits to the sheriff shall:

(1) state whether the authorized activities were conducted:

(i) on the dates and at the location stated in the application; and

(ii) by the regular members of the licensee without the assistance of gaming professionals;

(2) report the amount of the proceeds obtained from the licensed activities;

(3) report the disbursements made in connection with the licensed activities; and

(4) state that the licensee has not paid a fee for the rental of premises on which the game was conducted to:

    (i) itself;

    (ii) a trustee of the licensee;

    (iii) a committee of the licensee; or

    (iv) any organization with the same members or substantially the same members as the licensee. (An. Code 1957, art. 27, § 256(d); 2002, ch. 26, § 2.)

REVISOR'S NOTE

This Revisor's note comprises information related to the revision by Acts 2002, ch. 26.

This section is new language derived without substantive change from former Art. 27, § 256(d).

In subsections (a) and (b) of this section, the reference to a "licensee" is substituted for the former reference to an "applicant", because the required reports must be made after the applicant becomes a licensee.

In subsection (a)(3)(i) of this section, the former reference to keeping records "on file" is deleted as included in the reference to "keep[ing]" the records.

In subsection (a)(3)(iii) of this section, the reference to "the sheriff . . . the State's Attorney for the county; or . . . a representative of the sheriff or the State's Attorney" is substituted for the former reference to "member of the Sheriff's office or the State's Attorney's office" for clarity and consistency within this article.

Also in subsection (a)(3)(iii) of this section, the reference to the State's Attorney "for the county" is added for clarity and accuracy.

In the introductory language of subsection (b)(1) of this section, the reference to stating "whether" authorized activities were conducted in a certain manner is substituted for the former reference to stating "that" they were so conducted for accuracy.

In subsection (b)(1) of this section, the former reference to "the date" is deleted as included in the reference to "the dates". *See* Art. 1, § 8.

In subsection (b)(4) of this section, the reference to the premises "on which the game was conducted" is added for clarity.

Defined term:
"Sheriff"   § 13-2501

§ 13-2505. Wicomico County Gaming Advisory Committee.

(a) *Established.* — (1) There is a Gaming Advisory Committee in the county.

(2) The members of the committee are appointed by, and serve at the pleasure of, the sheriff.

(3) The members of the committee may not receive compensation.

(b) *Duties.* — The committee shall:

(1) recommend to the sheriff standards for reporting requirements for licensees;

(2) examine the audits and reports required under § 13-2504 of this subtitle; and

(3) make any other recommendations to assist the sheriff in the administration of licensing and other duties of the sheriff under this subtitle. (An. Code 1957, art. 27, § 256A; 2002, ch. 26, § 2.)

REVISOR'S NOTE

This Revisor's note comprises information related to the revision by Acts 2002, ch. 26.

This section is new language derived without substantive change from former Art. 27, § 256A.

In subsection (a) of this section, the reference to the appointment of the members of the committee by the sheriff is substituted for the former reference to "[t]he Sheriff . . . shall establish a Gaming Advisory Committee" for clarity.

Defined terms:
"Committee"   § 13-2501
"Sheriff"   § 13-2501

§ 13-2506. Penalties.

(a) *Suspension.* — (1) The sheriff shall suspend a license if the licensee fails to comply with the reporting requirements of § 13-2504 of this subtitle.

(2) The suspension shall continue until the licensee meets the reporting requirements of § 13-2504 of this subtitle.

(b) *Disqualification.* — Except as provided in subsection (a) of this section and subject to the procedures provided in subsection (c) of this section, the sheriff may not issue a new license for 1 year to a licensee that:

(1) has refused to file a report required under § 13-2504 of this subtitle; or

(2) has failed to comply with this subtitle.

(c) *Procedures.* — (1) The sheriff shall notify the licensee or applicant for a license by registered mail of the sheriff's suspension or refusal to issue a license.

(2) The licensee or applicant may appeal the decision in writing to the sheriff within 30 days after receiving the notice from the sheriff. (An. Code 1957, art. 27, § 256(d)(5), (i)(1), (2)(i), (ii); 2002, ch. 26, § 2.)

REVISOR'S NOTE

This Revisor's note comprises information related to the revision by Acts 2002, ch. 26.

This section is new language derived without substantive change from former Art. 27, § 256(d)(5) and (i)(1) and (2)(i) and (ii).

In subsection (a) of this section, the reference to "[t]he sheriff" is added to clarify who has the obligation to suspend a license.

In subsection (c)(1) of this section, the former reference to "a declaration by the sheriff" is deleted as surplusage.

Defined term:
"Sheriff"   § 13-2501

§ 13-2507. Judicial review.

A party may seek judicial review of:

(1) the sheriff's suspension of a license under this subtitle; or

(2) the sheriff's refusal to issue a license under this subtitle. (An. Code 1957, art. 27, § 256(i)(2)(iii); 2002, ch. 26, § 2.)

REVISOR'S NOTE

This Revisor's note comprises information related to the revision by Acts 2002, ch. 26.

This section is new language derived without substantive change from former Art. 27, § 256(i)(2)(iii).

Defined term:
"Sheriff"   § 13-2501

§ 13-2508. Enforcement.

This subtitle shall be enforced by:

(1) the sheriff;

(2) any municipal police officer in the county;

(3) any other law enforcement officer of the county; and

(4) any prosecutor of the county. (An. Code 1957, art. 27, § 256(h); 2002, ch. 26, § 2.)

REVISOR'S NOTE

This Revisor's note comprises information related to the revision by Acts 2002, ch. 26.

This section is new language derived without substantive change from former Art. 27, § 256(h).

In the introductory language of this section, the former reference to officials being "strictly charged" to enforce is deleted as implicit in the requirement that this subtitle "shall" be enforced by the listed officials.

In item (2) of this section, the reference to municipal police officers "in" the county is substituted for the former reference to municipal police officers "of" the county for accuracy.

In item (3) of this section, the reference "law enforcement officer" is substituted for the former obsolete reference to a "peace officer".

In item (4) of this section, the reference to a "prosecutor" is substituted for the former reference to "prosecuting . . . officers" for clarity. *See* Art. 1, § 8.

Defined term:
"Sheriff"   § 13-2501

Subtitle 26. Worcester County.

Part I. Definitions; General Provisions.

§ 13-2601. "County commissioners" defined.

In this subtitle, "county commissioners" means the Board of County Commissioners of Worcester County. (2002, ch. 26, § 2.)

REVISOR'S NOTE

This Revisor's note comprises information related to the revision by Acts 2002, ch. 26.

This section is new language added to allow concise and consistent reference to the Board of County Commissioners of Worcester County.

§ 13-2602. Scope of subtitle.

This subtitle applies only in Worcester County. (2002, ch. 26, § 2; 2009, ch. 415.)

REVISOR'S NOTE

This Revisor's note comprises information related to the revision by Acts 2002, ch. 26.

This section is new language added to clarify the application of this subtitle.

Former Art. 27, § 251A(m), which provided that former Art. 27, § 251A (revised as Part II of this subtitle) applied throughout Worcester County, is deleted in light of this section.

Effect of amendments. — Chapter 415, Acts 2009, effective July 1, 2009, reenacted the section without change.

§§ 13-2603, 13-2604.

Reserved.

Part II. Bingo.

§ 13-2605. "Board" defined.

In this part, "board" means the Worcester County Bingo Board. (2002, ch. 26, § 2.)

REVISOR'S NOTE

This Revisor's note comprises information related to the revision by Acts 2002, ch. 26.

This section is new language added to avoid repetition of the full title of the board and references to the "Bingo Board".

§ 13-2606. Qualified organizations.

The following organizations may conduct bingo in accordance with this part:

(1) a bona fide religious organization that has conducted religious services at a fixed location in the county for at least 6 years before applying for a license under this part;

(2) a municipal corporation in the county;

(3) a volunteer fire company in the county;

(4) a local unit of a nationwide bona fide nonprofit organization or club that consists solely of members who served in the armed forces of the United States; or

(5) a nonprofit organization that:

(i) intends to raise money for an exclusively charitable or educational purpose that is specifically described in the license application filed with the board; and

(ii) has operated as a nonprofit organization in the county for at least 5 years before applying for a license under this part. (An. Code 1957, art. 27, § 251A(a); 2002, ch. 26, § 2.)

REVISOR'S NOTE

This Revisor's note comprises information related to the revision by Acts 2002, ch. 26.

This section is new language derived without substantive change from former Art. 27, § 251A(a).

The introductory language of this section is revised as authorization to certain qualified organizations to conduct bingo for clarity and consistency within this title.

In the introductory language of this section, the former limitation "[n]othing in this subtitle

[sic] shall be construed to make it unlawful" is deleted in light of § 13-101 of this title and the reorganization of material derived from the former "Gaming" subheading of Article 27 in Titles 12 and 13 of this article.

Also in the introductory language of this section, the former reference to "operat[ing]" bingo is deleted in light of the reference to "conduct[ing]" bingo.

In item (1) of this section, the former reference to a municipal corporation in the county that is "subject to the provisions of Article XI-E of the Constitution of Maryland" is deleted because all municipal corporations in Worcester County are subject to Md. Constitution, Art. XI-E.

In items (1) and (5)(ii) of this section, the reference to "applying for a license under this part" is substituted for the former reference to "the application to the Worcester County bingo board" for clarity.

In item (1) of this section, the reference to a religious "organization" is substituted for the former reference to a religious "group" for accu-

racy and consistency with § 13-2621(a)(3) of this subtitle.

In item (5)(i) of this section, the reference to a "license" application is added for clarity.

Also in item (5)(i) of this section, the reference to the license application "filed with" the board is substituted for the former reference to the license application "to" the board for accuracy and clarity.

Defined term:
    "Board"   § 13-2605

§ 13-2607. Worcester County Bingo Board.

(a) *Established.* — There is a Worcester County Bingo Board.

(b) *Composition.* — The board consists of three members appointed by the Governor with the advice and consent of the Senate.

(c) *Qualifications of members.* — Each member of the board shall:

(1) be a registered voter of the county; and

(2) be an owner of real property according to the assessment records of the county.

(d) *Salaries and expenses.* — (1) Each member of the board is entitled to:

(i) an annual salary of at least $1,000 as determined by the county commissioners; and

(ii) a reasonable travel and expense allowance.

(2) The county commissioners shall pay the cost of the payments made under paragraph (1) of this subsection and all administrative expenses of the board from the proceeds paid to the county commissioners under this part.

(e) *Tenure; vacancies.* — (1) The term of a member is 6 years and begins on June 1.

(2) The terms of members are staggered as required by the terms provided for members of the board on October 1, 2002.

(3) The Governor shall fill any vacancy on the board occurring during the term of an appointed member for the unexpired term with the advice and consent of the Senate. (An. Code 1957, art. 27, § 251A(b)-(d); 2002, ch. 26, § 2.)

REVISOR'S NOTE

This Revisor's note comprises information related to the revision by Acts 2002, ch. 26.

Subsection (a) of this section is standard language added to provide expressly for the establishment of the Worcester County Bingo Board.

Subsections (b), (c), and (d) of this section are new language derived without substantive change from former Art. 27, § 251A(c), (d), and the first sentence of (b).

Subsection (e)(1) of this section is new language derived without substantive change from the former reference to "terms . . . for six years" in the second sentence of former Art. 27, § 251A(b).

Subsection (e)(2) of this section is standard language substituted for the first, second, and third phrases of the second sentence of former Art. 27, § 251A(b), which provided for the terms of the initial members of the board and were obsolete. This substitution is not intended to alter the term of any member of the board. *See* Ch. 26, § 8, Acts of 2002. Accordingly, in subsection (e)(1) of this section, the specific reference to "June 1" is added to conform to the practice of the board. The terms of the members serving on October 1, 2002, end as follows: (1) one in 2003; (2) one in 2005; and (3) one in 2007.

Subsection (e)(3) of this section is new language derived without substantive change from the third sentence of former Art. 27, § 251A(b).

In subsection (b) of this section, the reference to the board "consist[ing] of three members appointed by the Governor" is substituted for the former requirement that "[t]he Governor shall appoint . . . three persons to be members of the" board to conform to similar provisions in other revised articles of the Code.

In the introductory language of subsection (c) of this section, the reference to each "member of" the board is substituted for the former reference to each "person appointed to" the board for consistency within this section.

In the introductory language of subsection (d)(1) of this section, the phrase "is entitled to" is substituted for the former phrase "shall be paid" to conform to similar provisions in other revised articles of the Code.

In subsection (d)(2) of this section, the reference to administrative "expenses" is substituted for the former reference to administrative "costs" for accuracy.

In subsection (e)(3) of this section, the reference to any vacancy "occurring during the term

of an appointed member" is added for clarity and to conform to similar provisions in other revised articles of the Code.

Also in subsection (e)(3) of this section, the former reference to filling a vacancy "for any reason" is deleted in light of the reference to filling "any" vacancy.

The Criminal Law Article Review Committee notes, for the consideration of the General Assembly, that in subsection (d)(2) of this section, it is unclear whether the term "proceeds" received by the county commissioners refers only to proceeds received under § 13-2614 of this subtitle, or also to license fees received under § 13-2610(c) of this subtitle. If the latter is intended, another term such as "amounts" may be preferred, perhaps with an explicit cross-reference to all covered sources of funds.

Defined terms:
"Board"   § 13-2605
"County commissioners"   § 13-2601

§ 13-2608. Regulations.

(a) *Authorized.* — The board may adopt reasonable regulations to administer and enforce this part.

(b) *Copy.* — A copy of the regulations adopted by the board shall be made available at a reasonable cost. (An. Code 1957, art. 27, § 251A(e); 2002, ch. 26, § 2.)

REVISOR'S NOTE

This Revisor's note comprises information related to the revision by Acts 2002, ch. 26.

This section is new language derived without substantive change from former Art. 27, § 251A(e).

In subsections (a) and (b) of this section, the former references to "rules" are deleted for consistency throughout this article. *See* General Revisor's Note to article.

In subsection (a) of this section, the former reference to the board "promulgat[ing]" regulations is deleted as implicit in the reference to the board "adopt[ing]" regulations.

Defined term:
"Board"   § 13-2605

§ 13-2609. Supervision; right of entry.

(a) *Duty to supervise.* — (1) The board shall exercise control and supervision over all games of bingo to ensure that the games are conducted fairly in accordance with the provisions of the licenses issued under § 13-2610 of this subtitle, the regulations adopted by the board, and this part.

(2) The board shall prevent bingo from being conducted for a commercial purpose, for private profit, or in any manner other than as provided in this part.

(b) *Right of entry.* — For purposes of inspection, the board, its officers, and its agents may enter at any time any place where:

(1) bingo is being or will be conducted; or

(2) any equipment that is being or will be used to conduct bingo is located. (An. Code 1957, art. 27, § 251A(h); 2002, ch. 26, § 2.)

REVISOR'S NOTE

This Revisor's note comprises information related to the revision by Acts 2002, ch. 26.

This section is new language derived without substantive change from the second, third, and fourth sentences of former Art. 27, § 251A(h).

In subsections (a)(1) and (2) and (b)(1) of this section, the references to "bingo" are substituted for the former references to "games" for clarity. Correspondingly, in subsection (b)(2) of this section, the reference to equipment used to conduct "bingo" is substituted for the former reference to equipment used in the conduct "thereof".

In subsection (a)(1) of this section, the reference to the license "issued under § 13-2610 of this subtitle" is added for clarity.

Also in subsection (a)(1) of this section, the phrase "to ensure that" is substituted for the former phrase "to the end that" for clarity.

Also in subsection (a)(1) of this section, the reference to regulations "adopted by" the board is substituted for the former reference to regulations "of" the board for consistency with § 13-2608 of this subtitle.

Also in subsection (a)(1) of this section, the former reference to "rules" is deleted for consistency throughout this article. *See* General Revisor's Note to article.

In subsection (b)(1) of this section, the reference to any place where "bingo ... will be conducted" is substituted for the former reference to any place where "it is intended that any such games shall be conducted" for brevity. Correspondingly, in subsection (b)(2) of this section, the reference to equipment that "will be used" is substituted for the former reference to equipment "intended to be used".

Defined term:
"Board"   § 13-2605

§ 13-2610. License to conduct bingo.

(a) *Required.* — An organization or municipal corporation described in § 13-2606 of this subtitle that intends to conduct bingo under this part must obtain:

(1) an annual license to conduct bingo for more than 15 days in a year; or

(2) a temporary license to conduct bingo for 15 days or fewer in a year.

(b) *Application.* — (1) An applicant for a license shall submit to the board an application on the form that the board by regulation requires.

(2) The application form shall require:

(i) the name of the applicant;

(ii) the name of each principal officer of the applicant; and

(iii) a certification that no person will conduct bingo except a person who:

1. is a salaried employee or bona fide member of the applicant; and

2. shall not receive any form of commission or bonus.

(c) *Fees.* — (1) An applicant shall pay to the board a license fee of:

(i) $100 for an annual license; or

(ii) $25 in addition to $5 for each day bingo is conducted for a temporary license.

(2) The board shall pay to the county commissioners all license fees collected under this part.

(d) *Issuance.* — The board shall issue a license to each applicant who meets the requirements of this part and the regulations adopted under this part.

(e) *Approval of lease required.* — If an applicant conducts bingo on premises that are leased by the applicant, the lease agreement must be approved by the board before a license may be issued.

(f) *Revocation or suspension.* — The board may deny a license to an applicant or suspend or revoke a license if the applicant or licensee has violated this part or any regulation adopted under this part. (An. Code 1957, art. 27, § 251A(f)-(h), (j); 2002, ch. 26, § 2; 2009, ch. 415.)

REVISOR'S NOTE

This Revisor's note comprises information related to the revision by Acts 2002, ch. 26.

This section is new language derived without substantive change from former Art. 27, § 251A(g), the first, second, third, and fifth sentences of (f), the first sentence of (h), and the second and eighth sentences of (j).

In subsections (a), (b)(2)(iii), and (f) of this section, the former references to "operat[ing]" a game of bingo are deleted as unnecessary in light of the references to "conduct[ing]" a game of bingo.

In the introductory language of subsection (a) of this section, the reference to an entity "described in § 13-2606 of this subtitle" is substituted for the former specific enumeration of entities for brevity.

In subsection (a)(1) of this section, the reference to conducting a game of bingo for "more" than 15 days in a year is substituted for the former reference to conducting a game of bingo for "longer" than 15 days in a year for clarity.

Also in subsection (a)(1) of this section, the former reference to an annual license "covering bingo games over a period of one year" is deleted in light of the reference to an annual license "to conduct a game of bingo for more than 15 days in a year".

In subsection (a)(2) of this section, the requirement that certain entities "must obtain . . . a temporary license" is added to state expressly that which was only implied in the former law.

In subsection (b)(1) of this section, the reference to "[a]n applicant for a license" is added for clarity.

Also in subsection (b)(1) of this section, the former requirement that the application be "in such detail as" the board requires is deleted as implicit in the requirement that the application be "on the form" the board requires.

In the introductory language of subsection (b)(2) of this section, the requirement that the application form "require" certain information is substituted for the former requirement that the application form "contain" certain information for accuracy.

In subsections (b)(2)(i) and (f) of this section, the references to an "applicant" are substituted for the former references to an "organization or municipal corporation" for brevity and consistency within this section. Correspondingly, in subsection (b)(2)(iii)1 of this section, the reference to the "applicant" is substituted for the former reference to the "organization or municipal corporation" and "said organization".

In subsection (b)(2)(ii) of this section, the reference to "the name of each principal officer of the applicant" is substituted for the former reference to "a list of its principal officers" for clarity.

In subsection (b)(2)(iii)1 of this section, the reference to a person who is a "salaried employee" of the applicant is substituted for the former reference to a person who is "employed by" the applicant "on a regular salary" for brevity.

In subsection (b)(2)(iii)2 of this section, the reference to "not receiv[ing]" any form of commission or bonus is substituted for the former reference to "not in any way [being] subject to the payment of" any form of commission or bonus for brevity.

In the introductory language of subsection (c)(1) of this section, the requirement that "[a]n applicant . . . pay to the board a license fee of" is added to state expressly that which was only implied in the former references to the "cost" of licenses.

In subsection (c)(1)(i) and (ii) of this section, the former references to the "cost" of an annual or temporary license are deleted in light of the reference to the "fee" payable for these licenses in the introductory language of subsection (c)(1) of this section.

In subsections (d) and (g) of this section, the former references to "rules" are deleted for consistency throughout this article. *See* General Revisor's Note to article.

In subsection (d) of this section, the requirement that the board issue a license "to each applicant who meets" certain requirements is substituted for the former requirement that the board issue a license "[i]f the bingo board ascertains that the application conforms to" certain requirements for accuracy and to conform to similar provisions in other revised articles of the Code.

Also in subsection (d) of this section, the reference to regulations "adopted under this part" is substituted for the former reference to regulations "issued thereunder by the board" for accuracy and consistency with § 13-2608 of this subtitle.

Also in subsection (d) of this section, the former reference to issuing a license "as applied for" is deleted as implicit.

In subsection (e) of this section, the former reference to an applicant "qualified under the provisions of this section" is deleted because the prohibition on the issuance of a license under subsection (e) applies whether or not an applicant is otherwise qualified for a license.

In subsection (f) of this section, the former reference to premises "rented" by the applicant is deleted in light of the reference to premises "leased" by the applicant. Correspondingly, the former reference to a "rental" agreement is deleted in light of the reference to a "lease" agreement.

Also in subsection (f) of this section, the former requirement that the lease agreement "first" be approved is deleted in light of the requirement that the lease agreement be approved "before" a license may be issued.

In subsection (g) of this section, the reference to "deny[ing] a license to an applicant" is substituted for the former reference to "revok[ing] any application for a license" for accuracy and to conform to similar provisions in other revised articles of the Code.

Also in subsection (g) of this section, the former reference to regulations "promulgated" under this part is deleted as implicit in the reference to regulations "adopted" under this part.

Defined terms:

"Board"	§ 13-2605
"County commissioners"	§ 13-2601
"Person"	§ 1-101

Effect of amendments. — Chapter 415, Acts 2009, effective July 1, 2009, substituted "$25 in addition to $5" for "$3" in (c)(1)(ii); deleted former (e), and redesignated accordingly.

Bingo not lottery. — Bingo is not a lottery. Bender v. Arundel Arena, Inc., 248 Md. 181, 236 A.2d 7 (1967).

§ 13-2611. Conditions and limitations.

(a) *Admission charge.* — The charge for admission to a place in order to participate in bingo conducted under this part may not exceed $5.

(b) *Prize.* — (1) Except as provided in paragraphs (2) and (3) of this subsection, the value of a prize in money, merchandise, or services for any one game of bingo conducted under this part may not exceed $200.

(2) Jackpot prizes may be offered in a maximum amount of $5,000.

(3) "Winner Take All" games may be offered without a prize limit.

(c) *Employees conducting bingo.* — A licensee's employees and the terms of their employment must be approved by the board before they may conduct bingo under this part.

(d) *Minors prohibited.* — A minor may not be allowed to participate in bingo conducted under this part.

(e) *Location.* — Bingo may not be conducted under this part in a room or area where alcoholic beverages are sold or served during the game.

(f) *Number of days.* — A licensee under this part may not conduct bingo on more than 125 days in a year. (An. Code 1957, art. 27, § 251A(f), (j); 2002, ch. 26, § 2; 2009, ch. 415.)

REVISOR'S NOTE

This Revisor's note comprises information related to the revision by Acts 2002, ch. 26.

This section is new language derived without substantive change from the fourth sentence of former Art. 27, § 251A(f) and the first and third through seventh sentences of (j).

In subsection (a) of this section, the reference to a game of bingo "conducted under this part" is added for clarity and consistency within this part. Correspondingly, in subsections (c), (e), and (f) of this section, the references to a game of bingo conducted "under this part" are added.

Also in subsection (a) of this section, the former reference to admission to "any premises in order to engage or participate in" bingo is deleted as implicit in the reference to admission to "bingo".

In subsections (b)(1), (c), and (d) of this section, the former references to bingo "operat[ed]" under this part are deleted in light of the references to bingo "conduct[ed]" under this part. Correspondingly, in subsection (e) of this section, the former reference to the "operation" of bingo is deleted in light of the reference to the "conduct" of bingo.

In subsection (b)(1) of this section, the reference to a "money" prize is substituted for the former reference to a "cash" prize for consistency within this title.

In subsection (c) of this section, the reference to "[a] licensee's employees" is substituted for the former reference to "[a]ll such employees" for clarity.

In subsection (d) of this section, the defined term "minor" is substituted for the former reference to a "person under 18 years of age" for consistency within this article. *See* § 1-101 of this article.

Also in subsection (d) of this section, the former reference to "engag[ing]" in bingo is deleted in light of the reference to "participat[ing]" in bingo.

Subsection (e) of this section is revised as a prohibition on the conduct of bingo rather than as a rule of construction for clarity.

In subsection (f) of this section, the reference to "bingo" is substituted for the former reference to "games" for clarity and consistency within this part.

Also in subsection (f) of this section, the former reference to alcoholic beverages being sold or served during "the progress of" the game is deleted as surplusage.

Defined terms:
"Board"	§ 13-2605
"Minor"	§ 1-101

Effect of amendments. — Chapter 415, Acts 2009, effective July 1, 2009, substituted "$5" for "$1" in (a); in (b)(1), substituted "paragraphs (2) and (3)" for "paragraph (2)" and "$200" for "$50"; in (b)(2) substituted "$5000" for "$1000"; added (b)(3); deleted former (e), and redesignated accordingly.

§ 13-2612. Bingo advertisements.

Unless otherwise prohibited by county or municipal law, all forms of advertising for bingo are allowed. (2009, ch. 415.)

Editor's note. — Chapter 415, Acts 2009, effective July 1, 2009, repealed former § 13-2612 and enacted a new section in lieu thereof.

§ 13-2613. Accounting.

(a) *Statement of receipts and expenses required.* — Each licensee under this part shall submit to the board, at monthly intervals or at any other interval that the board sets, a statement of its gross receipts and expenses.

(b) *Contents.* — For each game of bingo conducted by the licensee, the statement shall include:

(1) the amount of gross receipts derived from the game;

(2) each item of expense incurred in the conduct of the game;

(3) each item of expenditure made in connection with the game; and

(4) the net profit derived from the conduct of the game. (An. Code 1957, art. 27, § 251A(k); 2002, ch. 26, § 2.)

REVISOR'S NOTE

This Revisor's note comprises information related to the revision by Acts 2002, ch. 26.

This section is new language derived without substantive change from the first, third, and fourth sentences of former Art. 27, § 251A(k).

In subsection (a) of this section, the reference to "gross" receipts is added for consistency with subsection (b)(1) of this section.

Also in subsection (a) of this section, the reference to other "intervals" is substituted for the former reference to other "periods" for consistency with the reference to monthly "intervals" in this subsection.

In the introductory language of subsection (b) of this section, the phrase "[f]or each game of bingo conducted by the licensee" is added for clarity.

In subsection (b)(2) and (4) of this section, the references to the "conduct" of the game are substituted for the former references to the

"operation" of the game for consistency within this part.

In subsection (b)(3) of this section, the reference to each item of expenditure made "in connection with the game" is added for clarity.

In subsection (b)(4) of this section, the reference to net profit "derived" from the conduct of the game is added for clarity and consistency within this part.

The first sentence of former Art. 27, § 251A(i) is deleted as redundant of this section.

Defined term:
"Board"   § 13-2605

§ 13-2614. Distribution and use of proceeds.

(a) *Payment to county commissioners.* — (1) Each licensee shall pay to the county commissioners 3% of the gross receipts derived from bingo for each day that bingo is conducted by the licensee under this part.

(2) The licensee shall pay the money at the time the licensee submits to the board the statement required under § 13-2613 of this subtitle.

(b) *Nonprofit organizations.* — (1) An organization described in § 13-2606(5) of this subtitle may retain up to one-half of the proceeds derived from bingo conducted under this part for the benefit of the organization.

(2) The organization shall distribute any remaining proceeds for educational or charitable purposes.

(c) *Payment to municipal corporation.* — If bingo is conducted in a municipal corporation in the county, the county commissioners shall pay one-third of the 3% of the gross receipts received under subsection (a) of this section to the municipal corporation, to be used for its general purposes.

(d) *Use of proceeds by county commissioners.* — (1) From the percentage of the gross receipts retained by the county commissioners, the county commissioners shall first pay the expenses necessary to administer this part.

(2) All additional funds shall be credited by the county commissioners to the general funds of the county. (An. Code 1957, art. 27, § 251A(a-1), (i), (k); 2002, ch. 26, § 2.)

REVISOR'S NOTE

This Revisor's note comprises information related to the revision by Acts 2002, ch. 26.

This section is new language derived without substantive change from former Art. 27, § 251A(a-1), the second through fifth sentences of (i), and the second sentence of (k).

In subsections (a)(1) and (c) of this section, the former references to the "operation" of bingo and bingo being "operat[ed]" are deleted in light of the references to bingo being "conducted".

In subsection (a)(1) of this section, the reference to gross receipts "derived" from bingo is added for clarity and consistency within this part.

Also in subsection (a)(1) of this section, the reference to bingo conducted "under this part" is added for clarity and consistency within this part.

Also in subsection (a)(1) of this section, reference to gross receipts "for each day that bingo is" conducted under this part is substituted for the former reference to gross receipts "for every day such games are operated and conducted" for clarity.

In subsection (a)(2) of this section, the requirement that payment be made "at the time the licensee submits to the board the statement required under § 13-2613 of this subtitle" is substituted for the former requirement that payment be made "[a]t the same time" for clarity.

In subsection (b)(1) of this section, the reference to proceeds "derived from bingo conducted under this part" is added for clarity.

In subsection (c) of this section, the reference to gross receipts "received under subsection (a) of this section" is added for clarity.

Also in subsection (c) of this section, the former reference to "the corporate boundaries of" a municipal corporation is deleted as surplusage.

Also in subsection (c) of this section, the former reference to a municipal corporation in the county "which is subject to the provisions of Article XI-E of the Constitution" is deleted because all municipal corporations in Worcester County are subject to Md. Constitution, Art. XI-E.

Defined terms:
"Board"	§ 13-2605
"County commissioners"	§ 13-2601

§ 13-2615. Books and reports.

(a) *Licensees.* — Each licensee under this part shall maintain the books and reports that the board requires for the purposes of this part.

(b) *Board.* — The board shall submit to the county commissioners a detailed annual report of all statements submitted to the board. (An. Code 1957, art. 27, § 251A(k); 2002, ch. 26, § 2.)

REVISOR'S NOTE

This Revisor's note comprises information related to the revision by Acts 2002, ch. 26.

This section is new language derived without substantive change from the fifth and sixth sentences of former Art. 27, § 251A(k).

In subsection (a) of this section, the reference to each licensee "under this part" is added for clarity and consistency within this part.

Also in subsection (a) of this section, the former reference to "keep[ing]" books and reports is deleted as included in the reference to "maintain[ing]" them.

In subsection (b) of this section, the requirement to "submit" a report is substituted for the former requirement to "make" a report for accuracy.

Defined terms:
"Board"	§ 13-2605
"County commissioners"	§ 13-2601

§ 13-2616. Prohibited acts; penalty.

(a) *Violations by licensees.* — (1) A licensee may not:

(i) divert or pay out any of the proceeds of bingo conducted under this part in any manner other than as required by this part or by the regulations adopted under this part; or

(ii) violate any other provision of this part.

(2) A person who violates this subsection is guilty of a misdemeanor and on conviction is subject to a fine not exceeding $500 for each violation.

(b) *Wrongful receipt of proceeds.* — (1) A person may not receive any of the proceeds of bingo conducted under this part except for the purposes provided in this part.

(2) A person who violates this subsection is guilty of a misdemeanor and on conviction is subject to imprisonment not exceeding 90 days or a fine not exceeding $500 or both. (An. Code 1957, art. 27, § 251A(l); 2002, ch. 26, § 2.)

REVISOR'S NOTE

This Revisor's note comprises information related to the revision by Acts 2002, ch. 26.

This section is new language derived without substantive change from former Art. 27, § 251A(l).

In subsections (a)(1) and (b)(1) of this section, the former references to any "portion" of the proceeds are deleted as surplusage.

In subsection (a)(1) of this section, the former reference to "rules" is deleted for consistency within this article. *See* General Revisor's Note to article.

Also in subsection (a)(1) of this section, the former reference to "in any manner" violating any other provision of this part is deleted as surplusage.

In subsection (a)(2) of this section, the reference to each "violation" is substituted for the former reference to each "offense" for consistency within this article. *See* General Revisor's Note to article.

In subsection (b)(1) of this section, the reference to bingo "conducted under this part" is substituted for the former reference to "any such" bingo for clarity.

In subsection (b)(2) of this section, the reference to imprisonment "not exceeding" 90 days is substituted for the former reference to imprisonment "for" 90 days to conform to the apparent legislative intent, expressed in the former provision that "such . . . imprisonment [be] in the discretion of the court", to establish a maximum, and not a mandatory minimum, term of imprisonment.

Also in subsection (b)(2) of this section, the former phrase "such fine and imprisonment in the discretion of the court" is deleted as implicit in the establishment of maximum penalties.

Defined term:
"Person"   § 1-101

§§ 13-2617, 13-2618.

Reserved.

Part III. Gaming.

§ 13-2619. Definitions.

(a) *In general.* — In this part the following words have the meanings indicated.

REVISOR'S NOTE

This subsection is new language derived without substantive change from former Art. 27, § 251B(a)(1)(i).

(b) *Gaming device.* — (1) "Gaming device" means a paddle wheel, wheel of fortune, chance book, raffle, or any other mechanism for playing a game of chance.

(2) "Gaming device" does not include bingo.

REVISOR'S NOTE

Paragraph (1) of this subsection is new language derived without substantive change from the introductory language of former Art. 27, § 251B(a)(2), as it described gaming devices. Paragraph (1) is revised as a definition to provide an express definition of "gaming device".

Paragraph (2) of this subsection is new language added to clarify that bingo is not a "gaming device" regulated under this part. As to the provisions of law governing bingo in Worcester County, *see* Part II of this subtitle.

In paragraph (1) of this subsection, the phrase "any other mechanism for playing a game of chance" is substituted for the former phrase "by any other gaming device" for clarity.

(c) *Multiple gaming device permit.* — "Multiple gaming device permit" means a permit that allows the use of two or more gaming devices.

REVISOR'S NOTE

This subsection is new language derived without substantive change from former Art. 27, § 251B(a)(1)(ii).

The reference to allowing "the use of" two or more gaming devices is added for clarity and accuracy.

The reference to "gaming devices" is substituted for the former reference to "devices specified in paragraph (2) of this subsection" for brevity.

(d) *Raffle.* — "Raffle" means a lottery using paper chances in which prizes are won by persons who buy chances in the lottery.

REVISOR'S NOTE

This subsection formerly was Art. 27, § 251B(a)(1)(iii).

No changes are made.

The Criminal Law Article Review Committee notes, for the consideration of the General

Assembly, that the reference to "paper" chances may be overly specific.

Defined term:
"Person" § 1-101

(An. Code 1957, art. 27, § 251B(a)(1), (2); 2002, ch. 26, § 2.)

REVISOR'S NOTE TO SECTION

The Revisor's notes in this section comprise information related to the revision by Acts 2002, ch. 26.

§ 13-2620. Effect of part.

This part does not authorize gambling using a slot machine or coin machine. (An. Code 1957, art. 27, § 251B(l); 2002, ch. 26, § 2.)

REVISOR'S NOTE

This Revisor's note comprises information related to the revision by Acts 2002, ch. 26.

This section is new language derived without substantive change from former Art. 27, § 251B(l).

§ 13-2621. Gaming permits.

(a) *Qualified organizations.* — The county commissioners may issue a permit to any of the following organizations to conduct a fundraiser at which merchandise or money prizes may be awarded by gaming devices:

(1) a bona fide religious organization that has conducted religious services at the same location in the county for at least 3 years before applying for a permit;

(2) a volunteer fire company that is supported by the county or a municipal corporation in the county or an auxiliary unit whose members are directly associated with the volunteer fire company or auxiliary unit;

(3) a nationally chartered veterans' organization or an auxiliary unit whose members are directly associated with the veterans' organization;

(4) a bona fide nonprofit fraternal, educational, civic, patriotic, or charitable organization that intends to conduct a fundraiser for the benefit of a charity located in the county; or

(5) a bona fide nonprofit organization that:

(i) intends to raise money for an exclusively charitable, athletic, or educational purpose that is specifically described in the permit application; and

(ii) has operated as a nonprofit organization in the county for at least 3 years before applying for a permit.

(b) *Determination.* — The county commissioners shall determine whether an organization qualifies for a permit under this section.

(c) *Organization in county required.* — An organization must be organized in and serve the residents of the county to be eligible for a permit under this section.

(d) *Bona fide charity.* — An organization that is exempt from taxation under § 501(c)(3) of the Internal Revenue Code is a bona fide charity under this section. (An. Code 1957, art. 27, § 251B(a)(2)-(4); 2002, ch. 26, § 2.)

REVISOR'S NOTE

This Revisor's note comprises information related to the revision by Acts 2002, ch. 26.

This section is new language derived without substantive change from former Art. 27, § 251B(a)(2), (3), and (4).

Subsection (a) of this section is restated as an affirmative grant of authority to certain organizations to conduct a fundraiser for clarity and consistency within this title.

In the introductory language of subsection (a) of this section, the reference to a "fundraiser" is substituted for the former reference to a "fundraising affair" for consistency with the terminology used throughout this part.

Also in the introductory language of subsection (a) of this section, the reference to "gaming devices" is substituted for the former reference to "devices commonly known as paddle wheels, wheels of fortune, chance books, raffles, or . . . any other gaming device" for brevity.

Also in the introductory language of subsection (a) of this section, the former limitation "[n]otwithstanding any other provision of this article," is deleted in light of § 13-101 of this title and the reorganization of material derived from the former "Gaming" subheading of Article 27 in Titles 12 and 13 of this article.

In subsection (a)(2) of this section, the reference to a volunteer fire company unit "that is supported by the county or a municipal corporation in the county" is substituted for the former reference to a "county or municipally supported" volunteer fire company or auxiliary unit for clarity and accuracy.

In subsection (a)(3) of this section, the reference to members who are directly associated with the organization "or auxiliary unit" is added for consistency within this subsection.

In subsection (a)(5)(ii) of this section, the reference to operating "as a nonprofit organization" is substituted for the former reference to operating "on a nonprofit basis" for clarity and consistency with § 13-2606(5)(ii) of this subtitle.

In subsection (c) of this section, the former reference to an organization "under paragraph (2) of this subsection" is deleted as implicit.

In subsection (d) of this section, the former reference to an "institution, association, society, or corporation" is deleted as included in the comprehensive reference to an "organization".

Defined terms:

"County commissioners"	§ 13-2601
"Gaming device"	§ 13-2619

"Order of finish" sweepstakes. — The General Assembly authorized only those lotteries that present features characteristic of a raffle; thus, a proposed sweepstakes in which a racetrack would award a set payout based on a person's holding a ticket which correctly listed the finish positions of all the horses in a nine horse race was not authorized. 83 Op. Att'y Gen. 92 (Jan. 7, 1998).

§ 13-2622. Regulation by county commissioners.

The county commissioners may:

(1) adopt regulations concerning the permit application and the issuance of permits under this part;

(2) set a fee by resolution for each kind of permit issued under this part;

(3) regulate the number of permits issued to organizations each year; and

(4) deny a permit to an organization for up to 3 years if the organization violates this part or the regulations adopted under this part. (An. Code 1957, art. 27, § 251B(b); 2002, ch. 26, § 2.)

REVISOR'S NOTE

This Revisor's note comprises information related to the revision by Acts 2002, ch. 26.

This section is new language derived without substantive change from former Art. 27, § 251B(b).

In item (1) of this section, the reference to the issuance of permits "under this part" is added for clarity. Correspondingly, in item (2) of this section, the reference to each permit "issued under this part" is added.

In item (2) of this section, the reference to each "kind of" permit is added for clarity.

In item (3) of this section, the former reference to the number of permits "which may be" issued to organizations is deleted as surplusage.

Defined term:
"County commissioners" § 13-2601

§ 13-2623. Multiple gaming device permits — Limitations.

(a) *Number per year.* — The county commissioners may not issue more than two multiple gaming device permits to an organization in any 1 year.

(b) *Number per facility.* — The county commissioners may not issue:

(1) more than eight multiple gaming device permits for fundraisers to be held in any one facility in any 1 year; or

(2) more than three multiple gaming device permits for fundraisers to be held in any one facility in any 27-day period.

(c) *Duration.* — A multiple gaming device permit issued under this part is valid for only one fundraiser lasting not more than 6 hours.

(d) *Ocean City.* — The county commissioners may not issue a multiple gaming device permit for use in Ocean City or on real property that is owned by Ocean City and located in the county.

(e) *Class B or D alcoholic beverages licensed premises.* — The county commissioners may not issue a multiple gaming device permit to hold a fundraiser on premises that are licensed under a Class B or Class D alcoholic beverages license. (An. Code 1957, art. 27, § 251B(c), (d), (g), (h); 2002, ch. 26, § 2.)

REVISOR'S NOTE

This Revisor's note comprises information related to the revision by Acts 2002, ch. 26.

This section is new language derived without substantive change from former Art. 27, § 251B(c), (d), (g), and (h).

Subsections (b), (d), and (e) of this section are revised in the active voice to clarify that it is the county commissioners who are prohibited from issuing multiple gaming device permits under certain circumstances.

In subsection (b)(1) and (2) of this section, the references to multiple gaming device permits "for fundraisers" are added for clarity.

In subsection (c) of this section, the reference to a fundraiser lasting "not more than" 6 hours is added for clarity and accuracy.

Also in subsection (c) of this section, the reference to a "fundraiser" is substituted for the former reference to an "event" for consistency with the terminology used throughout this part.

Also in subsection (c) of this section, the former reference to a multiple gaming device permit issued "for a fund-raiser at which 2 or more gaming devices will be used" is deleted in light of the use of the defined term "multiple gaming device permit".

In subsection (d) of this section, the reference to use "on" real property is substituted for the former reference to use "within the boundaries of" real property for brevity.

Also in subsection (d) of this section, the former reference to use in "the corporate limits of" Ocean City is deleted as surplusage.

In subsection (e) of this section, the prohibition against "issu[ing]" a multiple gaming device permit is substituted for the former prohibition against "approv[ing]" a multiple gaming device permit for consistency with the terminology used throughout this part.

Defined terms:
"County commissioners"   § 13-2601
"Multiple gaming device permit" § 13-2619

§ 13-2624. Multiple gaming device permits — Use of funds.

At least one-half of the funds derived from a fundraiser for which a multiple gaming device permit has been issued under this part shall be used for a civic, charitable, or educational purpose. (An. Code 1957, art. 27, § 251B(f); 2002, ch. 26, § 2.)

REVISOR'S NOTE

This Revisor's note comprises information related to the revision by Acts 2002, ch. 26.

This section is new language derived without substantive change from former Art. 27, § 251B(f).

The reference to funds derived from a "fundraiser for which a multiple gaming device permit has been issued under this part" is substituted for the former reference to funds derived from a "multiple gaming device fund-raiser that permits the use of 2 or more gaming devices" for clarity.

Defined term:
"Multiple gaming device permit" § 13-2619

§ 13-2625. Raffles.

(a) *Duration.* — A raffle conducted under a permit issued under this part may not last more than 1 year from the date the permit is issued to the date the last prize is awarded.

(b) *Number of permits.* — The county commissioners may regulate the number of permits to conduct a raffle that an organization may receive in a year.

(c) *Not a multiple gaming device.* — A raffle is not a multiple gaming device. (An. Code 1957, art. 27, § 251B(a)(5), (j); 2002, ch. 26, § 2.)

REVISOR'S NOTE

This Revisor's note comprises information related to the revision by Acts 2002, ch. 26.

This section is new language derived without substantive change from former Art. 27, § 251B(a)(5) and (j).

In subsection (b) of this section, the reference to "permits to conduct a raffle" is substituted for the former reference to "raffle permits" for consistency with subsection (a) of this section.

Defined terms:

"County commissioners"	§ 13-2601
"Raffle"	§ 13-2619

§ 13-2626. Conduct of fundraisers.

(a) *In general.* — (1) (i) A fundraiser conducted under this part shall be managed and operated only by members of the organization that receives the permit for the fundraiser.

(ii) A person may not be compensated for the management or operation of any gaming activity authorized by the permit.

(2) Each organization that receives a permit for a fundraiser under this part shall designate an individual who is responsible for complying with the terms and conditions of the permit and this part.

(b) *Location.* — An organization that receives a permit for a fundraiser under this part shall conduct the fundraiser in:

(1) a structure that is owned, leased, or occupied by the organization;

(2) a structure that is owned, leased, or occupied by an organization that would qualify for a permit under § 13-2621 of this subtitle; or

(3) a public location that is described in the permit application and approved by the State's Attorney for the county. (An. Code 1957, art. 27, § 251B(e), (i); 2002, ch. 26, § 2.)

REVISOR'S NOTE

This Revisor's note comprises information related to the revision by Acts 2002, ch. 26.

This section is new language derived without substantive change from former Art. 27, § 251B(e) and (i).

In subsection (a)(1)(i) of this section, and the introductory language of subsection (b) of this section, the references to a permit "for the fundraiser" are added for clarity.

In subsection (a)(2) of this section, the reference to each organization "that receives a permit for a fundraiser under this part" is added for clarity.

In the introductory language of subsection (b) of this section, the reference to an organization that "receives" a permit is substituted for the former reference to an organization that "is issued" a permit for consistency within this section.

In subsection (b)(1) of this section, the former reference to the organization "receiving the permit" is deleted in light of the reference in the introductory language of subsection (b) to "[a]n organization that receives a permit".

Defined term:

"Person"	§ 1-101

§ 13-2627. Accounting.

Within 30 days after a fundraiser conducted under this part, the organization that received the permit for the fundraiser shall submit to the county commissioners:

(1) an accounting of all funds received or pledged;

(2) an accounting of all expenses paid or incurred; and

(3) a statement under oath of the application of the net profits. (An. Code 1957, art. 27, § 251B(k); 2002, ch. 26, § 2.)

REVISOR'S NOTE

This Revisor's note comprises information related to the revision by Acts 2002, ch. 26.

This section is new language derived without substantive change from former Art. 27, § 251B(k).

In the introductory language of this section, the reference to a fundraiser "conducted under this part" is added for clarity.

Also in the introductory language of this section, the reference to the organization that "received the permit for the fundraiser" is sub-

stituted for the former reference to the organization that "is issued a permit under this section" for consistency with § 13-2626 of this subtitle.

Also in the introductory language of this section, the reference to "submit[ting]" an accounting is substituted for the former reference to "send[ing]" an accounting for consistency within this title.

Defined term:
"County commissioners"   § 13-2601

§ 13-2628. Penalty.

(a) *Violation of part.* — A person who violates this part is guilty of a misdemeanor and on conviction is subject to imprisonment not exceeding 1 year or a fine not exceeding $1,000 or both.

(b) *Separate violation.* — Each day on which a violation of this part occurs is a separate violation. (An. Code 1957, art. 27, § 251B(m); 2002, ch. 26, § 2.)

REVISOR'S NOTE

This Revisor's note comprises information related to the revision by Acts 2002, ch. 26.

This section is new language derived without substantive change from former Art. 27, § 251B(m).

In subsection (a) of this section, the former reference to an "organization" is deleted as included in the defined term "person". *See* § 1-101 of this article.

In subsection (b) of this section, the reference to each day "on which a violation of this part

occurs" is substituted for the former reference to each day "of violation" for clarity and consistency with similar provisions throughout this article.

Also in subsection (b) of this section, the reference to a separate "violation" is substituted for the former reference to a separate "offense" for consistency within this article. *See* General Revisor's Note to article.

Defined term:
"Person"   § 1-101

Subtitle 1. Sentencing.

§ 14-101. Mandatory sentences for crimes of violence.

(a) *"Crime of violence" defined.* — In this section, "crime of violence" means:

(1) abduction;

(2) arson in the first degree;

(3) kidnapping;

(4) manslaughter, except involuntary manslaughter;

(5) mayhem;

(6) maiming, as previously proscribed under former Article 27, §§ 385 and 386 of the Code;

(7) murder;

(8) rape;

(9) robbery under § 3-402 or § 3-403 of this article;

(10) carjacking;

(11) armed carjacking;

(12) sexual offense in the first degree;

(13) sexual offense in the second degree;

(14) use of a handgun in the commission of a felony or other crime of violence;

(15) child abuse in the first degree under § 3-601 of this article;

(16) sexual abuse of a minor under § 3-602 of this article if:

(i) the victim is under the age of 13 years and the offender is an adult at the time of the offense; and

(ii) the offense involved:

1. vaginal intercourse, as defined in § 3-301 of this article;

2. a sexual act, as defined in § 3-301 of this article;

3. an act in which a part of the offender's body penetrates, however slightly, into the victim's genital opening or anus; or

4. the intentional touching, not through the clothing, of the victim's or the offender's genital, anal, or other intimate area for sexual arousal, gratification, or abuse;

(17) an attempt to commit any of the crimes described in items (1) through (16) of this subsection;

(18) continuing course of conduct with a child under § 3-315 of this article;

(19) assault in the first degree;

(20) assault with intent to murder;

(21) assault with intent to rape;

(22) assault with intent to rob;

(23) assault with intent to commit a sexual offense in the first degree; and

(24) assault with intent to commit a sexual offense in the second degree.

(b) *Scope of section.* — This section does not apply if a person is sentenced to death.

(c) *Fourth conviction of crime of violence.* — (1) Except as provided in subsection (g) of this section, on conviction for a fourth time of a crime of violence, a person who has served three separate terms of confinement in a correctional facility as a result of three separate convictions of any crime of violence shall be sentenced to life imprisonment without the possibility of parole.

(2) Notwithstanding any other law, the provisions of this subsection are mandatory.

(d) *Third conviction of crime of violence.* — (1) Except as provided in subsection (g) of this section, on conviction for a third time of a crime of violence, a person shall be sentenced to imprisonment for the term allowed by law but not less than 25 years, if the person:

(i) has been convicted of a crime of violence on two prior separate occasions:

1. in which the second or succeeding crime is committed after there has been a charging document filed for the preceding occasion; and

2. for which the convictions do not arise from a single incident; and

(ii) has served at least one term of confinement in a correctional facility as a result of a conviction of a crime of violence.

(2) The court may not suspend all or part of the mandatory 25-year sentence required under this subsection.

(3) A person sentenced under this subsection is not eligible for parole except in accordance with the provisions of § 4-305 of the Correctional Services Article.

(e) *Second conviction of crime of violence.* — (1) On conviction for a second time of a crime of violence committed on or after October 1, 1994, a person shall be sentenced to imprisonment for the term allowed by law, but not less than 10 years, if the person:

(i) has been convicted on a prior occasion of a crime of violence, including a conviction for a crime committed before October 1, 1994; and

(ii) served a term of confinement in a correctional facility for that conviction.

(2) The court may not suspend all or part of the mandatory 10-year sentence required under this subsection.

(f) *Compliance with Maryland Rules.* — If the State intends to proceed against a person as a subsequent offender under this section, it shall comply with the procedures set forth in the Maryland Rules for the indictment and trial of a subsequent offender.

(g) *Eligibility for parole after age 65.* — (1) A person sentenced under this section may petition for and be granted parole if the person:

(i) is at least 65 years old; and

(ii) has served at least 15 years of the sentence imposed under this section.

(2) The Maryland Parole Commission shall adopt regulations to implement this subsection. (An. Code 1957, art. 27, § 643B; 2002, ch. 26, § 2; 2004, ch. 25; 2006, ch. 261; 2007, chs. 524, 525.)

REVISOR'S NOTE

This Revisor's note comprises information related to the revision by Acts 2002, ch. 26.

This section is new language derived without substantive change from former Art. 27, § 643B(b) through (g) and the first sentence of (a).

In subsection (a)(5) of this section, the phrase "as previously proscribed under [§] 384. . . of this article", which formerly modified "mayhem", is deleted as unnecessary and inaccurate because former Art. 27, § 384 did not proscribe mayhem but merely stated the penalties for it. Similarly, in subsection (a)(16) through (21) of this section, the phrase "as these crimes were previously proscribed under former § 12 of this article", which formerly modified "assault with intent to murder, assault with intent to rape, assault with intent to rob, assault with intent to commit a sexual offense in the first degree, and assault with intent to commit a sexual offense in the second degree", is deleted as unnecessary and inaccurate because Art. 27, § 12 did not proscribe those crimes but merely stated the penalties for them.

In subsection (a)(6) of this section, the phrase "as previously proscribed under Article 27, §§ 385 and 386 of the Code", which modifies "maiming", is retained because these former provisions included specific elements of the crimes of maiming.

In subsections (d)(1)(i) and (e)(1)(i) of this section, the references to a "crime" are substituted for the former references to an "offense" for consistency within this article. *See* General Revisor's Note to article.

In subsection (d)(3) of this section, the reference to a person "sentenced under this subsection" is added for clarity.

Defined terms:

"Correctional facility"	§ 1-101
"Person"	§ 1-101

I. General Provisions.
II. Crimes of Violence.
III. Factors Affecting Enhancement.
IV. Third and Fourth Convictions.

I. GENERAL PROVISIONS.

Effect of amendments. — Chapter 25, Acts 2004, approved April 13, 2004, and effective from date of enactment, inserted "former" in (a)(6).

Chapter 261, Acts 2006, effective October 1, 2006, added (a)(15) and made related changes.

Chapters 524 and 525, Acts 2007, effective October 1, 2007, made identical changes. Each added (a)(16) and (a)(18), redesignated accordingly and made related changes.

Editor's note. — Section 3, ch. 288, Acts 2000, provides that "this Act shall only apply to offenses committed on or after October 1, 2000 and may not be construed to apply in any way to offenses committed before October 1, 2000."

Maryland Law Review. — For article, "Survey of Developments in Maryland Law, 1983-84," see 44 Md L. Rev. 317, 508 (1985).

For article, "Survey of Developments in Maryland Law, 1986-87," see 47 Md. L. Rev. 739 (1988).

For note, *"State v. Davis:* A Proportionality Challenge to Maryland's Recidivist Statute," see 48 Md. L. Rev. 520 (1989).

For note, "The Maryland Survey: 1994-1995," see 55 Md. L. Rev. 529 (1996).

University of Baltimore Law Review. — For comment, "Rights of the Maryland Probationer: A Primer for the Practitioner," see 11 U. Balt. L. Rev. 272 (1982).

For note discussing the constitutionality of life sentence without parole imposed on recidivist guilty of nonviolent crimes, see 14 U. Balt. L. Rev. 175 (1984).

For article concerning the hearsay exception for child abuse victims, see 17 U. Balt. L. Rev. 1 (1987).

For note discussing the mandatory sentencing statute requiring life imprisonment without parole for habitual offenders of violent crimes, see 17 U. Balt. L. Rev. 572 (1989).

For article, "Judicial Modification of Sentences in Maryland," see 33 U. Balt. L. Rev. 1 (2003).

University of Baltimore Law Forum. — For note on *"Muir v. State:* Clarifying Predicate Crimes of Violence Under Maryland's Enhanced Punishment Statute," see 17, No. 3 U. Balt. Law Forum 21 (1987).

For a 1994 development: "*Jones v. State:* It is Within the Trial Judge's Discretion to Determine Which Crime of Violence Constitutes the Third Conviction for the Purpose of Imposing an Enhanced Sentence under Article 27, § 643B(C)," 25.2 U. Balt. Law Forum 65 (1994).

For a 2009 development, "McGlone v. State: A Mandatory Sentence Enhancement for Conviction of a Third Crime Of Violence Does Not Require Intervening Terms of Confinement or Sequentiality Between Predicate Convictions," see 39 U. Balt. L. F. 243 (2009).

Constitutionality. — Former Art. 27, § 643B (see now this section) is constitutional. Hawkins v. State, 302 Md. 143, 486 A.2d 179 (1985).

Due process. — Where State informed defendant that it would pursue the mandatory sentence under former Art. 27, § 643B (see now this section) and complied with the notice requirements of Maryland Rule 4-245 (c), the fact that defendant was not given notice prior to his trial was not a denial of due process. Horsman v. State, 82 Md. App. 99, 570 A.2d 354, cert. denied, 321 Md. 225, 582 A.2d 531 (1990).

Use of convictions under this section not a consequence of guilty pleas. — The possible use of the present convictions as predicate convictions for sentencing under this section in the future is not a "consequence" of his guilty pleas that defendant must be made aware of under Maryland Rule 4-242 (c) (1) before the pleas can be accepted. Moore v. State, 72 Md. App. 524, 531 A.2d 1026 (1987).

Purpose. — The purpose of former Art. 27, § 643B (see now this section) is twofold: To protect the public from assaults upon people and property and to deter those with criminal records from perpetrating other criminal acts under the threat of an extended period of confinement. Hawkins v. State, 58 Md. App. 91, 472 A.2d 482 (1984), aff'd, 302 Md. 143, 486 A.2d 179 (1985).

The purpose of former Art. 27, § 643B (see now this section) is not merely to punish. Hawkins v. State, 58 Md. App. 91, 472 A.2d 482 (1984), aff'd, 302 Md. 143, 486 A.2d 179 (1985).

The dual purposes of public protection and deterrence do not require conversion of every life imprisonment sentence into a sentence of life imprisonment without parole; both purposes are sufficiently served by 25 years' mandatory imprisonment without parole. Montone v. State, 308 Md. 599, 521 A.2d 720 (1987).

Requirements for application of section. — Former Art. 27, § 643B (see now this section) requires more than merely "previous" convictions; it requires separate convictions. Moreover, the statute's scope is narrowed by the fact that it requires not only that an individual shall have received separate convictions, but that he shall have been sentenced to, and shall have actually served, a term of confine-

ment under the jurisdiction of the correctional system. Minor v. State, 313 Md. 573, 546 A.2d 1028 (1988).

Former Art. 27, § 643B (c) (see now subsection (d) of this section) only governs the use of prior convictions in meeting the requirements for imposition of mandatory sentences; that subsection has nothing to do with the general admissibility of prior convictions at capital sentencing proceedings. Grandison v. State, 341 Md. 145, 670 A.2d 398 (1995).

Section limited to repeat offenders whose crimes involve force or violence. — The language used by the General Assembly shows an intent to limit the application of former Art. 27, § 643B (see now this section) to repeat offenders of crimes actually involving force or violence. Temoney v. State, 290 Md. 251, 429 A.2d 1018 (1981).

"Conviction." — Former Art. 27, § 643B (see now this section) refers to a defendant's prior "convictions" and not to the "act" the defendant may have committed; a conviction within the meaning of former Art. 27, § 643B (see now this section) is a final judgment that the defendant is guilty of the crime charged beyond a reasonable doubt. Brown v. State, 311 Md. 426, 535 A.2d 485 (1988).

Validity of prior convictions. — A prior conviction cannot be collaterally attacked in a sentencing proceeding in a subsequent case. Simms v. State, 83 Md. App. 204, 574 A.2d 12, cert. denied, 321 Md. 68, 580 A.2d 1077 (1990).

Defendant was not entitled to mount a collateral attack on a facially valid prior conviction during recidivist sentencing proceedings when the defendant was represented by counsel at the earlier trial, and where the grounds of the attack involved only the question of whether he was properly advised of his rights before waiving his right to a jury trial. Fairbanks v. State, 331 Md. 482, 629 A.2d 63 (1993).

Convictions in other jurisdictions. — The validity of a conviction is determined not under Maryland law, but under the law of the jurisdiction in which the conviction was rendered. If a foreign jurisdiction indicates that a conviction is valid, Maryland will recognize that conviction. Hubbard v. State, 76 Md. App. 228, 544 A.2d 346, cert. denied, 313 Md. 688, 548 A.2d 128 (1988).

As far as the corpus delicti of the crime is concerned, as a general rule, proof of the offense under another state's laws as a crime of violence under this section must be within the four corners of the evidence received to establish the conviction. Bowman v. State, 314 Md. 725, 552 A.2d 1303 (1989).

Constitutionality of (c). — As applied to the particular defendant, former Art. 27, § 643B (see now this section) was unconstitutional on the grounds that the sentence was disproportionate to the offense committed where the section's operation on a fourth conviction for daytime housebreaking resulted in life imprisonment without parole, where the daytime housebreakings, although classified as crimes of violence, when committed by this defendant, were neither violent nor involved the threat of violence to any person. Davis v. State, 68 Md. App. 581, 514 A.2d 1229 (1986), modified, 310 Md. 611, 530 A.2d 1223 (1987).

Sentence of life imprisonment without parole is proportionate, in Eighth Amendment cruel and unusual punishment purposes, for a fourth housebreaking conviction, following three separate and unsuccessful attempts at rehabilitation through incarceration. State v. Davis, 310 Md. 611, 530 A.2d 1223 (1987).

Constitutionality of (d). — Former Art. 27, § 643B (c) (see now (d) of this section) is not unconstitutional as violative of the Eighth Amendment. Bryan v. State, 63 Md. App. 210, 492 A.2d 644, cert. denied, 304 Md. 296, 498 A.2d 1183 (1985).

The provisions of former Art. 27, § 643B (c) (see now (d) of this section) do not violate federal or State constitutional proscriptions against cruel and unusual punishment, nor federal or State constitutional guarantees of due process and equal protection. Teeter v. State, 65 Md. App. 105, 499 A.2d 503 (1985).

Offense committed before that offense was added to (a). — Former Art. 27, § 643B (see now this section) does not explicitly or impliedly limit an offense as a crime of violence to only such of those offenses as are committed on or after the effective date of an amendment adding the offense to the list of predicate offenses in former Art. 27, § 643B (a) (see now (a) of this section); predicate violent offenses included within (a) are to be taken into account as qualifying crimes of violence for enhanced punishment purposes irrespective of when the offenses were committed or the convictions obtained. Hawkins v. State, 302 Md. 143, 486 A.2d 179 (1985).

Constitutionality of (e). — The lack of a uniform standard in Maryland for application of prosecutor's discretion under former Art. 27, § 643B (d) (see now (e) of this section) does not deny equal protection of the law without evidence that the lack of uniformity is motivated by a discriminatory purpose. Middleton v. State, 67 Md. App. 159, 506 A.2d 1191, cert. denied, 308 Md. 146, 517 A.2d 771 (1986), overruled on other grounds by Fairbanks v. State, 331 Md. 482, 629 A.2d 63 (1993).

Effect of constitutional flaw subsequently discovered in general process by which conviction obtained. — The fact that the general process by which a conviction was obtained is later, in another case, found to be constitutionally flawed does not necessarily taint the otherwise valid conviction. Whether the conviction is tainted depends on the nature of the defect, primarily whether that defect touches the integrity of the factfinding process that led to the conviction. Raiford v. State, 52 Md. App. 163, 447 A.2d 496 (1982), aff'd in part, rev'd in part, 296 Md. 289, 462 A.2d 1192 (1983).

Due process. — Due process does not require prosecutor, during plea negotiations, to disclose his intent to invoke former Art. 27, § 643B (see now this section) if the plea negotiating failed and the defendant is convicted by the jury. State v. Loveday, 48 Md. App. 478, 427 A.2d 1087 (1981), aff'd, 296 Md. 226, 462 A.2d 58 (1983).

Notice of intent to seek mandatory sentence not required. — It is not necessary for the State to inform the defendant before trial that it intends to seek the mandatory sentence. Loveday v. State, 296 Md. 226, 462 A.2d 58 (1983).

Lack of notice claim meritless where notice set forth 5 prior convictions. — Appellant's claim that a timely notice under former Maryland Rule 734 c (now Rule 4-245 (c)) only alerted him to the possibility of a 25-year sentence as a three-time loser and not to the possibility of a mandatory life sentence as a four-time loser is meritless since the letter of notice set forth five prior convictions, any two of which could have served as the predicate for the lesser enhancement and any three of which could have served as the predicate for the greater enhancement. Davis v. State, 56 Md. App. 694, 468 A.2d 698 (1983), cert. denied, 299 Md. 656, 474 A.2d 218 (1984).

Notice timely given under Maryland Rule 4-245 not required again on remand. — Notice timely given under Maryland Rule 4-245 before the first sentencing hearing adequately put the defendant on the State's intention to seek mandatory sentencing under former Art. 27, § 643B (see now this section); notice was not required to be given again on remand. Gantt v. State, 73 Md. App. 701, 536 A.2d 135 (1988).

Withdrawal of plea upon remand. — Where defendant was made aware of the State's intention to seek a mandatory sentence based on prior convictions under former Art. 27, § 643B (see now this section) prior to the acceptance by the court of his guilty plea to other offenses, he could not withdraw his plea upon remand. Martin v. Allegany County Bd. of County Comm'rs, 73 Md. App. 695, 536 A.2d 132 (1988).

Defendant did not expressly waive defendant's right to counsel for Rule 4-215 purposes during a review under §§ 8-102 and 8-103 of the Criminal Procedure Article for violating former Art. 27, § 643B of the Code, now this section, as: (1) defendant asked the court for additional time so that defendant could consult with counsel; (2) the trial judge appeared to be suggesting representation by the Office of the Public Defender when the judge forwarded the letter requesting additional information to a public defender and addressed it to defendant and counsel; (3) it was unclear as to why such representation did not occur. Johnson v. State, 187 Md. App. 481, 979 A.2d 190 (Aug. 28, 2009).

Defendant had a right to appeal a sentence review panel's decision to leave defendant's sentence unchanged under former Art. 27, § 643B of the Code, now this section, as defendant claimed defendant was denied defendant's right to counsel under § 8-103 of the Criminal Procedure Article during the sentence review process; absent that denial, the panel might have been persuaded to decrease the sentence. Johnson v. State, 187 Md. App. 481, 979 A.2d 190 (Aug. 28, 2009).

Quoted in Deville v. State, 383 Md. 217, 858 A.2d 484 (2004).

Cited in Stouffer v. Staton, 152 Md. App. 586, 833 A.2d 33 (2003); Roary v. State, 385 Md. 217, 867 A.2d 1095 (2005); Demby v. Sec'y, Dep't of Pub. Safety & Corr. Serv., 163 Md. App. 47, 877 A.2d 187 (2005), aff'd, 390 Md. 580, 890 A.2d 310 (2006); Demby v. Sec'y, Dep't of Pub. Safety & Corr. Serv., 163 Md. App. 47, 877 A.2d 187 (2005), aff'd, 390 Md. 580, 890 A.2d 310 (2006); Brown v. Handgun Permit Review Bd., 188 Md. App. 455, 982 A.2d 830 (2009), cert. denied, 412 Md. 495, 988 A.2d 1008 (2010); Spencer v. State, 422 Md. 422, 30 A.3d 891 (2011); Adams v. State, 2012 Md. App. LEXIS 8, — A.3d — (Feb. 8, 2012).

II. CRIMES OF VIOLENCE.

"Crimes of violence" generally. — The term "crime of violence" in former Art. 27, § 643B (see now this section) includes daytime housebreaking under former Art. 27, § 30 (b) (see now § 6-203 of this article), burglary, and attempted robbery. Hubbard v. State, 76 Md. App. 228, 544 A.2d 346, cert. denied, 313 Md. 688, 548 A.2d 128 (1988).

Section 9-303(c)(1) of this article provides for a five-year maximum sentence. But, under § 9-303(c)(2), if the official proceeding or report against which a defendant retaliated relates to a felonious violation of Title 5 of this article or the commission of a crime of violence, as defined in this section, the defendant may be sentenced to a maximum of twenty years. Parker v. State, 185 Md. App. 399, 970 A.2d 968 (2009).

Section 1-209(d)(1) of the Criminal Procedure Article, requiring a "direct relationship" between a criminal conviction and an occupational license to revoke the license based on the conviction, did not bar the Maryland Real Estate Commission (Commission) from revoking a real estate broker's licenses due to the broker's convictions for sexual abuse of children because (1) the statute was not in effect when the licenses were revoked, and a presumption against retroactivity was not rebutted, and (2) the statute only applied to nonviolent crimes, and the broker's crimes were crimes of violence. Pautsch v. Md. Real Estate Comm'n, 423 Md. 229, 31 A.3d 489 (2011).

Crimes included in (a), subsequent to their commission, may serve as basis for enhanced punishment. — Appellant was properly sentenced to a 25-year term of imprisonment where his most recent crime of violence was preceded by two prior convictions for daytime housebreaking that were not crimes of violence under former Art. 27, § 643B(a) (see now (a) of this section) when committed, but were included in the statute prior to the commission of the third offense for which appellant is being sentenced. Hawkins v. State, 58 Md. App. 91, 472 A.2d 482 (1984).

A conviction of robbery or attempted robbery in any other state that defines robbery substantially as it is defined in Maryland, i.e., the taking or carrying away of the personal property of another, from his person or immediate presence, by violence or putting in fear, is a crime of violence within the meaning of this section, even if such conviction might have been based on taking or attempting to take property that was not deemed personalty under the common law but has been made personalty by statute. Hubbard v. State, 76 Md. App. 228, 544 A.2d 346, cert. denied, 313 Md. 688, 548 A.2d 128 (1988).

Housebreaking. — Housebreaking is a violent crime. Minor v. State, 313 Md. 573, 546 A.2d 1028 (1988).

Whether act constitutes "crime of violence" must be determined under former Art. 27, § 643B (see now this section), and it matters not whether the particular crime may be a violent act in a foreign state where it was committed. Mitchell v. State, 56 Md. App. 162, 467 A.2d 522 (1983).

Automobile manslaughter. — Automobile manslaughter under former Art. 27, § 388 (see now § 2-209 of this article) is not included on the list of "crimes of violence" in this section, and a prisoner is entitled to an award of ten days per month of good conduct credits. Sacchet v. Blan, 120 Md. App. 154, 706 A.2d 620 (1998), aff'd, 353 Md. 87, 724 A.2d 667 (1999).

Rape defined. — The term "rape," as employed in former Art. 27, § 643B(a) (see now (a) of this section) defining "crime of violence," includes both first and second degree rape so that defendant convicted of attempted rape in second degree may be sentenced as a subsequent offender. Blandon v. State, 60 Md. App. 582, 483 A.2d 1320 (1984), aff'd, 304 Md. 316, 498 A.2d 1195 (1985).

Rape in the second degree is "crime of violence" for purposes of sentencing under former

Art. 27, § 643B (see now this section). Blandon v. State, 304 Md. 316, 498 A.2d 1195 (1985).

Attempted rape in second degree is "crime of violence." — Defendant convicted of attempted rape in second degree may be sentenced as a subsequent offender. Blandon v. State, 60 Md. App. 582, 483 A.2d 1320 (1984), aff'd, 304 Md. 316, 498 A.2d 1195 (1985).

Daytime housebreaking. — The General Assembly intended that daytime housebreaking be taken into account as a qualifying crime of violence for enhanced punishment purposes irrespective of when the offense was committed or the conviction obtained. Hall v. State, 69 Md. App. 37, 516 A.2d 204 (1986), cert. denied, 308 Md. 382, 519 A.2d 1283 (1987).

The risk of personal harm and the right to be free of intrusion are the concerns underlying the inclusion of daytime housebreaking as a crime of violence. State v. Davis, 310 Md. 611, 530 A.2d 1223 (1987).

First degree assault. — When defendant was sentenced to ten years in prison for first degree assault, he had to serve five years of that sentence before becoming eligible for parole on that sentence (the greater of one-half the sentence imposed for the violent crime or one-fourth of his aggregate sentence for first degree assault and common law false imprisonment), pursuant to § 7-301(c)(1)(i) of the Correctional Services Article, because first degree assault was a crime of violence, under (a)(17) of this section. Cathcart v. State, 397 Md. 320, 916 A.2d 1008 (2007).

According to this section, second degree assault is not a crime of violence. Stouffer v. Holbrook, 417 Md. 165, 9 A.3d 25 (2010).

III. FACTORS AFFECTING ENHANCEMENT.

Use of foreign prior convictions. — Proof of a conviction of robbery under the law of the District of Columbia, standing alone, was not sufficient to establish a prima facie case that it was a crime of violence under Maryland law. Bowman v. State, 314 Md. 725, 552 A.2d 1303 (1989).

Proof of predicate offenses. — Trial court did not violate collateral estoppel, as embodied in the Double Jeopardy Clause, by allowing the State to proceed under former Art. 27, § 643B (b) (see now (b) of this section), when one of the predicate crimes to support that sentence had been ruled insufficient in another proceeding as the State is not foreclosed from reproving predicate offenses in subsequent sentencing proceedings. Simms v. State, 83 Md. App. 204, 574 A.2d 12, cert. denied, 321 Md. 68, 580 A.2d 1077 (1990).

Court has no discretion in sentencing where Maryland Rule 4-245(c) complied with. — There is no discretion in the trial court in sentencing under former Art. 27, § 643B (see now this section), provided the State complies with the procedure set forth in former Maryland Rule 734 c (now Rule 4-245 (c)). Loveday v. State, 296 Md. 226, 462 A.2d 58 (1983).

Factors to be considered by court. — In cases requiring proportionality review, the sentencing court should consider: (i) The gravity of the offense and the harshness of the penalty; (ii) the sentences imposed on other criminals in the same jurisdiction; and (iii) the sentences imposed for commission of the same crime in other jurisdictions. Minor v. State, 313 Md. 573, 546 A.2d 1028 (1988).

Notice of enhancement prosecution. — Where the maximum penalty for robbery with a dangerous and deadly weapon is ordinarily twenty years incarceration, but where defendant as a "three time loser" received an enhanced sentence of twenty-five years, the State was not required to charge the enhancing factor in the indictment, to submit the enhancing factor as an issue for the jury, or to require that the enhancing factor be proved beyond a reasonable doubt, because the decision in Apprendi v. New Jersey, 530 U.S. 466, 120 S. Ct. 2348, 147 L. Ed. 2d 435 (2000) made it very clear that the requirements stated above do not apply when the sentencing-enhancing factor is a prior conviction. Gibson v. State, 138 Md. App. 399, 771 A.2d 536 (2001).

Single incident. — A defendant who is convicted of more than one crime of violence arising out of a single incident is not entitled as a matter of law to have the former Art. 27, § 643B(c) (see now (d) of this section) mandatory minimum sentence imposed upon the offense that would otherwise carry the most severe statutory penalty. Jones v. State, 336 Md. 255, 647 A.2d 1204 (1994).

Where State relies upon prior convictions in another jurisdiction as the basis for the imposition of a mandatory sentence, the State must introduce evidence showing the convictions were for crimes of violence within the meaning of former Art. 27, § 643B (see now this section). Temoney v. State, 290 Md. 251, 429 A.2d 1018 (1981).

Enhanced sentencing under former Art. 27, § 643B(c) (see now (d) of this section) may not be imposed unless the State has demonstrated that prior convictions in another jurisdiction were in fact based on crimes of violence. Myers v. State, 48 Md. App. 420, 427 A.2d 1061 (1981).

A foreign conviction for sodomy is not a "crime of violence" under former Art. 27, § 643B(a) (see now (a) of this section). Dibartolomeo v. State, 61 Md. App. 302, 486 A.2d 256 (1985).

Where youthful offender treatment was not accorded in a foreign jurisdiction, the fact that defendant would have been eligible for youthful offender treatment had the offense been committed in Maryland does not preclude the use of such convictions in this State as a predicate felony for former Art. 27, § 643B(c)(see now (d) of this section) purposes. Muir v. State, 64 Md. App. 648, 498 A.2d 666 (1985), aff'd, 308 Md. 208, 517 A.2d 1105 (1986).

Mandatory sentence under former Art. 27, § 643B(c) (see now (d) of this section) must be vacated where State did not prove out-of-state offense was crime of violence. Powell v. State, 56 Md. App. 351, 467 A.2d 1052 (1983), cert. denied, 299 Md. 137, 472 A.2d 998 (1984).

Actual violence need not be established. — Under former Art. 27, § 643B (see now this section), when any of the predicate crimes listed are shown, actual violence need not be established. Teeter v. State, 65 Md. App. 105, 499 A.2d 503 (1985).

Concurrent sentences treated as separate terms of confinement. — The fact that a federal court imposed a sentence concurrent with a sentence imposed six years earlier does not preclude that "term of confinement" from being a separate one for the purpose of applying former Art. 27, § 643B(b) (see now (c) of this section). Simpkins v. State, 79 Md. App. 687, 558 A.2d 816 (1989).

Provisions mandatory. — Former Art. 27, § 643B(c) (see now (d) of this section) is mandatory and the trial judge must consider it when imposing sentence. State v. Loveday, 48 Md. App. 478, 427 A.2d 1087 (1981), aff'd, 296 Md. 226, 462 A.2d 58 (1983).

Prior convictions before effective date of section. — Two prior convictions of crimes of violence can be used to enhance defendant's sentence under former Art. 27, § 643B (see now this section) even though the prior convictions took place before the effective date of former Art. 27, § 643B (see now this section). Blandon v. State, 60 Md. App. 582, 483 A.2d 1320 (1984), aff'd, 304 Md. 316, 498 A.2d 1195 (1985).

Effect of conviction under statute later held unconstitutional. — Convictions, valid when entered, that are not subject to expungement, that do subject the defendant to legal disabilities as a result of them, and that may be used for impeachment purposes, may be regarded as valid and viable convictions for purposes of the mandatory sentence provisions of former Art. 27, § 643B (see now this section) even though defendant was tried for the convictions as an adult under a statute that was later found to be unconstitutional. Raiford v. State, 52 Md. App. 163, 447 A.2d 496 (1982), aff'd in part, rev'd in part, 296 Md. 289, 462 A.2d 1192 (1983).

Use of defendant's 1967 convictions to enhance his punishment for his 1981 robbery conviction constituted an unconstitutional deprivation of his right to equal protection where, at the time of the 1967 convictions, defendant was 17 years old and was tried as an adult under statutory provisions, later held to be in contravention of the equal protection and due process clauses of the Fourteenth Amendment, which exempted Baltimore City from the general statewide juvenile age limit of 18. Raiford v. State, 296 Md. 289, 462 A.2d 1192 (1983).

Prior conviction set aside under former Federal Youth Corrections Act. — A conviction under the former Federal Youth Corrections Act (see 18 U.S.C. § 5001 et seq.), which has been set aside pursuant to its provisions, may not be considered for purposes of enhanced punishment under former Art. 27, § 643B (see now this section). Smith v. State, 50 Md. App. 638, 440 A.2d 406 (1982).

Invalid prior convictions may not be used to enhance punishment. — While there is conflicting authority regarding whether or not invalid prior convictions may be used in some instances for impeachment purposes, it is well established that they may not be used to enhance punishment. Raiford v. State, 296 Md. 289, 462 A.2d 1192 (1983).

Accessory convictions includable under (a). — Since Maryland recognizes that accessories are equally culpable for a principal's act, appellant/cross-appellee's prior conviction as an accessory before the fact of robbery is tantamount to a conviction for robbery — a crime of violence according to former Art. 27, § 643B(a) (see now (a) of this section) and a crime to be considered by a trial judge when evaluating the propriety of imposing a sentence under former Art. 27, § 643B(c) (see now (d) of this section). Sanders v. State, 57 Md. App. 156, 469 A.2d 476, cert. denied, 299 Md. 656, 474 A.2d 1345 (1984).

Final convictions required. — Before the drastic effect of sentencing under former Art. 27, § 643B(c) (see now (d) of this section) can be allowed to stand, the supporting convictions must be final convictions. Butler v. State, 46 Md. App. 317, 416 A.2d 773 (1980).

Where the conviction of the accused was not a final conviction, it may not serve as a proper predicate for the application of sentencing under former Art. 27, § 643B(c) (see now (d) of this section). Butler v. State, 46 Md. App. 317, 416 A.2d 773 (1980).

Court-martial convictions. — General court-martial convictions may be included as predicate offenses for the purpose of imposing enhanced sentences under habitual offender statutes. Muir v. State, 308 Md. 208, 517 A.2d 1105 (1986).

Appropriateness of sentence. — Although a sentence of 25 years without parole may be considered harsh for a first offense of daytime housebreaking, the sentence was appropriate where defendant's criminal history revealed that he was a professional criminal in need of extended rehabilitation. Minor v. State, 313 Md. 573, 546 A.2d 1028 (1988).

Mandatory sentence imposed under (e)(1)(ii) at defendant's plea hearing was illegal because defendant did not serve a term of confinement for defendant's prior conviction for robbery within the meaning of (e)(1)(ii) as the sentence for the prior conviction was suspended. Instead, defendant served only a 45-day term of pretrial incarceration as defendant could not post bond. Stevenson v. State, 180 Md. App. 440, 951 A.2d 875 (2008).

Admissibility of hearsay in proceedings to increase punishment for charged offense. — Proceedings to increase punishment for a charged offense because of prior convictions are part of the sentencing procedure, and the rules of evidence applicable in a trial on the issue of innocence or guilt are not controlling; as a general rule hearsay is admissible at such a proceeding. Teeter v. State, 65 Md. App. 105, 499 A.2d 503 (1985).

Enhanced punishment permitted though second sentence imposed before completion of first. — The fact that the defendant had not finished serving his imposed period of confinement for one of the predicate offenses when a second sentence was imposed for a separate predicate offense did not render him ineligible for enhanced punishment. Davis v. State, 56 Md. App. 694, 468 A.2d 698 (1983), cert. denied, 299 Md. 656, 474 A.2d 218 (1984).

IV. THIRD AND FOURTH CONVICTIONS.

State may seek mandatory sentencing. — When a defendant has two prior convictions for crimes of violence and has served at least one term of confinement in a correctional institution as a result of such a conviction, then the State may seek mandatory sentencing. Calhoun v. State, 46 Md. App. 478, 418 A.2d 1241 (1980), aff'd, 290 Md. 1, 425 A.2d 1361 (1981).

Requirements of section. — It is not necessary that full sentence imposed be served in order to satisfy requirements of former Art. 27, § 643B (see now this section), so long as a term of incarceration has been completed. Teeter v. State, 65 Md. App. 105, 499 A.2d 503 (1985).

It is necessary that a defendant have served some portion of each of the three predicate sentences before being sentenced to life imprisonment without the possibility of parole under former Art. 27, § 643B(b) (see now (c) of this section). Creighton v. State, 70 Md. App. 124, 520 A.2d 382 (1987).

Where two convictions were not separated by an exposure to the correctional system, the convictions may not count as two predicate crimes for mandatory life sentencing. Montone v. State, 308 Md. 599, 521 A.2d 720 (1987).

For prior convictions to qualify for mandatory life sentencing they, except for the first conviction, must be for offenses committed after each preceding conviction, and all such prior convictions must precede the commission of the principal offense. Montone v. State, 308 Md. 599, 521 A.2d 720 (1987).

Prior convictions must precede commission of third offense. — In order for a defendant to be sentenced under former Art. 27, § 643B(c) (see now (d) of this section), the two convictions serving as the predicate for the enhanced sentence must precede, in time, the commission, and not the conviction, of the offense upon which the instant conviction is based. Garrett v. State, 59 Md. App. 97, 474 A.2d 931 (1984).

Two separate occasions. — Term "two separate occasions" in former Art. 27, § 643B(c) (see now (d) of this section) has a plain meaning and is not fairly susceptible of an interpretation other than that of two unconnected, distinct, or unique times. Lett v. State, 51 Md. App. 668, 445 A.2d 1050, cert. denied, 294 Md. 442 (1982).

Where the defendant was convicted of three additional separate offenses after the first charging document was filed, it was of no moment that the defendant pled guilty to all four offenses on the same day. Irby v. State, 66 Md. App. 580, 505 A.2d 552 (1986), cert. denied, 308 Md. 270, 518 A.2d 732 (1987).

In the context of former art. 27, § 643B(c) of the Code, now (d) of this section, a court may utilize as a predicate conviction, a second or succeeding conviction for a crime of violence if the underlying offense (to that second or succeeding conviction) occurred prior to the first predicate conviction of a crime of violence, but after the filing of the charging document as to the first offense. McGlone v. State, 406 Md. 545, 959 A.2d 1191 (2008).

In the context of former art. 27, § 643B(c) of the Code, now (d) of this section, art. 27, § 643B(c) of the Code only requires that the second or succeeding offense occur after the charging document in the first or proceeding offense has been filed. McGlone v. State, 406 Md. 545, 959 A.2d 1191 (2008).

Defendant's sentence under former art. 27, § 643B(c) of the Code, now (d) of this section, was not illegal. Defendant was subject to an enhanced sentence, under art. 27, § 643B(c) of the Code, because, prior to the most recent conviction for a crime of violence, he had been convicted of two crimes of violence on two separate occasions, arising from two separate incidents, and had served at least one term of confinement within the correctional system for those convictions. McGlone v. State, 406 Md. 545, 959 A.2d 1191 (2008).

Separate terms of confinement. — Plain language of former art. 27, § 643B(c) of the Code, now (d) of this section, did not mandate "separate terms of confinement," as art. 27, § 643B(b) of the Code, now (c) of this section, did; rather, art. 27, § 643B(c) of the Code required only that the offender serve at least one term of confinement. Thus, a defendant need only serve one term of confinement and receive two convictions to satisfy the eligibility requirements for imposition of a mandatory sentence under art. 27, § 643B(c); the required term of confinement could, therefore, occur after the first conviction, after the second conviction, or it could run concurrently with another sentence without affecting the offender's eligibility for an enhanced sentence. McGlone v. State, 406 Md. 545, 959 A.2d 1191 (2008).

Purpose of subsection. — Former Art. 27, § 643B(c) (see now (d) of this section) was enacted for the purpose of providing new and different alternatives for dealing with aggressive and violent offenders; the penological objectives of statutes such as former Art. 27, § 643B(c) (see now (d) of this section) which mandate the extended incarceration of recidivist criminals is to provide warning to those persons who have previously been convicted of criminal offenses that the commission of future offenses will be more harshly punished, and to impose the extended period of incarceration upon those who fail to heed that warning so as to protect society from violent recidivist offenders. Taylor v. State, 333 Md. 229, 634 A.2d 1322 (1994).

Applicability of section. — Plain language of former Art. 27, § 643B (see now this section) does not purport to cover third or subsequent offenses. Calhoun v. State, 46 Md. App. 478, 418 A.2d 1241 (1980), aff'd, 290 Md. 1, 425 A.2d 1361 (1981).

Applicability of (d). — Where the State proves the necessary predicates for the imposition of a 25-year, without the possibility of parole, mandatory sentence upon conviction for two crimes of violence, but only one 25-year sentence is imposed, on the lesser included offense, the sentences imposed on both crimes of violence must be vacated upon a finding of merger and the case remanded to the trial court for the imposition of a former § 643B(c) (see now (d) of this section) mandatory sentence of 25 years on the greater offense. State v. Taylor, 329 Md. 671, 621 A.2d 424 (1993).

Although defendant, who had been previously convicted and incarcerated for two crimes of violence, was convicted of two additional crimes of violence, the court could only impose one sentence under former Art. 27, § 643B(c) (see now (d) of this section). State v. Taylor, 329 Md. 671, 621 A.2d 424 (1993).

When it enacted former Art. 27, § 643B(c) (see now (d) of this section), the General Assembly did not exempt from its stern sanctions minors convicted in criminal court; nor did it exempt from the enhanced punishment calculation convictions that took place long ago. Stanley v. State, 313 Md. 50, 542 A.2d 1267

(1988), aff'd, 85 Md. App. 92, 582 A.2d 532 (1990).

The statutory limitations on suspension and eligibility for parole apply to only the first 25 years of a sentence of life imprisonment. Taylor v. State, 333 Md. 229, 634 A.2d 1322 (1994).

Prior convictions were predicate offenses even though they were not separated by a term of confinement; the plain, unambiguous language of former art. 27, § 643B(c) of the Code, now (d) of this section, did not mandate separate terms of confinement, as art. § 643B(b) of the Code did. Defendant only had to serve one term of confinement and receive two convictions to satisfy the requirements for a mandatory sentence under art. 27, § 643B(c) of the Code. McGlone v. State, 406 Md. 545, 959 A.2d 1191 (2008).

Requirements of (d). — Statutory criteria for mandatory sentence provided by former Art. 27, § 643B(c) (see now (d) of this section) are met where the accused had previously been convicted on two separate occasions of a crime of violence not arising from a single incident and where following conviction of his third crime of violence, he had served "at least one term of confinement" for prior offenses for which he was on parole. McLee v. State, 46 Md. App. 472, 418 A.2d 1238 (1980), cert. denied, 289 Md. 738 (1981).

Limitation of (d). — Former Art. 27, § 643B(c) (see now (d) of this section) permits the imposition of only one mandatory sentence without the possibility of parole. Calhoun v. State, 46 Md. App. 478, 418 A.2d 1241 (1980), aff'd, 290 Md. 1, 425 A.2d 1361 (1981); Mitchell v. State, 56 Md. App. 162, 467 A.2d 522 (1983).

Prerequisites to imposition of life imprisonment. — A sentence of life imprisonment without parole cannot be imposed under this section unless the sequence of commission of a crime of violence, as defined, conviction for that crime, sentence to imprisonment, and service of some part of the term of imprisonment has occurred three times before the fourth conviction for a crime of violence. State v. Davis, 310 Md. 611, 530 A.2d 1223 (1987).

Discretion of sentencing judge. — It is within the discretion of the judge to suspend all or part of a sentence of life imprisonment unless the power of the trial court to do so is limited by some other provision of law; former Art. 27, § 643B(c) (see now (d) of this section) is such a provision. Taylor v. State, 333 Md. 229, 634 A.2d 1322 (1994).

It is certainly within the trial judge's discretion to impose a sentence of life imprisonment without parole under former Art. 27, § 643B(c) (see now (d) of this section); it is also within his discretion, however, to impose a sentence of life imprisonment, and suspend all but 25 or more years thereof. Taylor v. State, 333 Md. 229, 634 A.2d 1322 (1994).

While the General Assembly clearly intended the confinement to encompass a minimum of 25 years, it did not intend to circumscribe a sentencing judge's discretion beyond that point. Taylor v. State, 333 Md. 229, 634 A.2d 1322 (1994).

Once the predicate requirements for imposition of the former Art. 27, § 643B(c) (see now (d) of this section) penalty have been established, a sentencing judge has no choice but to impose the mandatory minimum penalty upon the third crime of violence conviction. Jones v. State, 336 Md. 255, 647 A.2d 1204 (1994).

Where a defendant is convicted of more than one crime of violence arising out of a single incident, it is within the sound discretion of the sentencing judge to select any one of the predicate convictions to serve as the "third" conviction for the purposes of former Art. 27, § 643B(c) (see now (d) of this section). Jones v. State, 336 Md. 255, 647 A.2d 1204 (1994).

The trial court exceeded its authority when it reduced a sentence from twenty-five years to two concurrent ten year sentences. Where former Art. 27, § 643B(a) and (c) (see now (a) and (d) of this section), as codified on the date of sentencing, mandated that defendant be sentenced to a minimum of twenty-five years imprisonment, and where the sole reason given by defendant and the circuit court for the sentence modification was the October 1, 1994, definitional change, the trial court possessed no authority to deviate from the legislative mandate via the sentence modification/review process, and the court therefore acted in excess of its jurisdiction. State v. Webster, 119 Md. App. 585, 705 A.2d 151 (1998); Rush v. State, 403 Md. 68, 939 A.2d 689 (2008).

Statutory requirement of former art. 27, § 643B(c) of the Code, now (d) of this section, contemplated that a sentencing judge could exercise wide discretion in fashioning a defendant's sentence. McGlone v. State, 406 Md. 545, 959 A.2d 1191 (2008); Parker v. State, 193 Md. App. 469, 997 A.2d 912 (2010); Washington v. State, 200 Md. App. 641, 28 A.3d 164 (2011).

§ 14-102. Sentencing for crimes with minimum and maximum penalties.

(a) *In general.* — Subject to subsection (b) of this section, if a law sets a maximum and a minimum penalty for a crime, the court may impose instead of the minimum penalty a lesser penalty of the same character.

(b) *Exceptions.* — This section does not affect:

(1) a maximum penalty fixed by law; or

(2) the punishment for any crime for which the statute provides one and only one penalty. (An. Code 1957, art. 27, § 643; 2002, ch. 26, § 2.)

REVISOR'S NOTE

This Revisor's note comprises information related to the revision by Acts 2002, ch. 26.

This section is new language derived without substantive change from former Art. 27, § 643.

In subsection (a) of this section, the phrase "[s]ubject to subsection (b) of this section" is added for clarity and to reflect the deletion of the former phrase "provided, however" in subsection (b) of this section.

Also in subsection (a) of this section, the phrase "if a law" is substituted for the former phrase "[i]n all cases where the law prescribing a punishment" for brevity.

Also in subsection (a) of this section, the reference to the "court" is substituted for the former reference to the "several judges of the circuit courts of the counties and of the District Court of Maryland" for brevity.

Also in subsection (a) of this section, the reference to the "minimum penalty" is substituted for the former reference to the "minimum penalty so prescribed" for brevity.

Cross references. — As to constitutionality of death penalty, see § 2-303.

Section controls only laws existing at time of its adoption. — Former Art. 27, § 643 (see now this section) would only be controlling in the case of laws existing at the time of its adoption, for one General Assembly cannot prohibit repeal or modification by its successors, even where it purports to do so. State v. Fisher, 204 Md. 307, 104 A.2d 403 (1954).

Former Art. 27, § 643 (see now this section) would only be controlling in the case of laws existing at the time of its adoption (1906), although it might perhaps be given effect as to subsequently enacted laws by construction.

Woodfork v. State, 3 Md. App. 622, 240 A.2d 314 (1968).

Application to narcotics laws. — See Woodfork v. State, 3 Md. App. 622, 240 A.2d 314 (1968).

The General Assembly, in prescribing the penalty for first degree murder in 1916, did not intend to prescribe a maximum and a minimum (which would contemplate a range in between), but intended to prescribe two alternative penalties, each fixed by the General Assembly itself, without committing to the trial judge any

discretion except a choice between the two, with that choice available only when not precluded by the jury's verdict. Dodson v. State, 14 Md. App. 483, 287 A.2d 324 (1972).

Construction with other laws. — If there is a conflict between former Art. 27, § 36B (see now §§ 4-203 through 4-205 of this article) and former Art. 27, § 643 (see now this section), the General Assembly has mandated that former Art. 27, § 36B (see now §§ 4-203 through 4-205 of this article) prevail. State ex rel. Sonner v. Shearin, 272 Md. 502, 325 A.2d 573 (1974).

§ 14-103. Benefit of clergy abolished.

Any claim to dispensation from punishment by benefit of clergy is abolished. (An. Code 1957, art. 27, § 626; 2002, ch. 26, § 2.)

REVISOR'S NOTE

This Revisor's note comprises information related to the revision by Acts 2002, ch. 26.

This section formerly was Art. 27, § 626. No changes are made.

GENERAL REVISOR'S NOTE TO ARTICLE

The Department of Legislative Services is charged with revising the law in a clear, concise, and organized manner, without changing the effect of the law. One precept of revision has been that, once something is said, it should be said in the same way every time. To that end, the Criminal Law Article Review Committee conformed the language and organization of this article to that of previously enacted revised articles to the extent possible.

It is the manifest intent both of the General Assembly and the Criminal Law Article Review Committee that this bulk revision of the substantive criminal law of the State render no substantive change. The guiding principle of the preparation of this article is that stated in *Welch v. Humphrey*, 200 Md. 410, 417 (1952):

[T]he principal function of a Code is to reorganize the statutes and state them in simpler form. Consequently any changes made in them by a Code are presumed to be for the purpose of clarity rather than change of meaning. Therefore, even a change in the phraseology of a statute by a codification thereof will not ordinarily modify the law, unless the change is so radical and material that the intention of the Legislature to modify the law appears unmistakably from the language of the Code. (citations omitted)

Accordingly, except to the extent that changes, which are noted in Revisor's Notes, clarify the former law, the enactment of this article in no way is intended to make any change to the substantive criminal law of Maryland.

In this article, as in other revised articles, the word "regulation" is substituted for the former references to "rules and regulations" to distinguish, to the extent possible, between regulations of executive units and rules of judicial or legislative units and to establish consistency in the use of the words. This substitution conforms to the practice of the Division of State Documents.

Also throughout this article, to be consistent and to avoid unnecessary confusion, the singular verb "adopt" is used in relation to rules or regulations, and verbs such as "prescribe" and "promulgate" are deleted. Regulations of State units, in any event, are subject to Title 10, Subtitle 1 of the State Government Article.

Also throughout this article, the term "unit" is substituted for former references to State entities such as an "agency", "department", "administration", "commission", and "office" except when a former reference indicated a specific entity, or as part of a defined term. The term "unit" is used as the general term for an organization in the State government because it is broad enough to include all such entities.

References to current units and positions are substituted for obsolete references to entities and positions that have been abolished or have otherwise ceased to exist.

The forms of standard charging documents formerly contained in Article 27 were intended to provide a simple, clear method of charging the relevant crimes without the procedural difficulties attendant in pleading at common law. The revision of those charging documents merely states the same substance in more modern language.

References to a person found guilty of a misdemeanor being "subject to § 5-106(b) of the Courts Article" are substituted for the former references to a person being "subject to imprisonment in the penitentiary" for accuracy and consistency with the Criminal Procedure Article. Provisions that make persons who are convicted of certain crimes liable for imprisonment "in the penitentiary" are obsolete in light of the superseding law that commits all persons convicted of crimes to "the jurisdiction of the Division of Correction", notwithstanding any law requiring the imprisonment to be served at a specific State correctional facility. *See* CS § 9-103(a). The only remaining substantive effect of a reference to imprisonment "in the penitentiary" applies to "penitentiary misdemeanors", which: (1) are not subject to the 1-year limitation period for other misdemeanors; and (2) are subject to the right of in banc review under Md. Constitution, Art. IV, § 22. Section 5-106(b) of the Courts Article specifically addresses these two characteristics of penitentiary misdemeanors.

The former law used the terms "crime" and "offense" interchangeably to mean a felony or misdemeanor under the laws of the State, with no consistent rationale for choosing one or the other. In order to provide uniform language in this revision and for consistency with the Criminal Procedure Article, the Criminal Law Article Review Committee chose to use the term "crime" to mean a particular act prohibited as a felony or misdemeanor, and the term "violation" to refer to a particular instance of a crime. In a few instances, the term "offense" is retained because of common usage, such as the term "sexual offense", which is revised in Title 3, Subtitle 3 of this article.

The common-law distinction in pleading between charging a principal of a crime and an accessory before the fact to the crime has been abolished for most purposes by statute, in response to the holding of the Court of Appeals in *State v. Sowell*, 353 Md. 713 (1999). *See* CP § 4-204, enacted by Ch. 339, Acts of 2000. Accordingly, since most of the former references to an "accessory" in the material revised in this article referred only to accessories before the fact, and not to accessories after the fact, in those instances the references to an "accessory" are deleted. *See, e.g.*, § 3-503(a) (1) of this article; *cf.* § 8-408(c) (3) of this article.

Several provisions are repealed as unconstitutional in accordance with federal and State case law. Former Art. 27, § 20, which prohibited blasphemy, violated the Establishment and Free Exercise Clauses of the First Amendment of the United States Constitution. *State v. West*, 9 Md. App. 270 (1970). Former Art. 27, §§ 152 and 153, which prohibited employing or allowing "female sitters", violated Md. Decl. of Rights, Art. 46. *Turner v. State*, 299 Md. 565 (1984). Former Art. 27, §§ 558, 559, and 560, which prohibited "common thieves", a criminal sanction on the basis of status or reputation, would have constituted "a cruel or unusual punishment in violation of the Fourteenth Amendment" to the United States Constitution. *Robinson v. California*, 370 U.S. 660 (1962). *See* Letter of Advice from Attorney General J. Joseph Curran, Jr. to Judge Alan M. Wilner, pp. 1-2 (October 17, 2000).

The Committee considered several provisions involving minor penalties to be more suitable for revision in other articles relating to the same substantive law, or in the case of provisions applicable to one county or a few counties, in the Public Local Laws.

Former Art. 27, § 21, as it established speed limits on Seneca Creek in Montgomery County and on specified portions of the Monocacy River, respectively, is revised in NR §§ 8-725.5 and 8-725.6, respectively.

Former Art. 27, § 21, as it prohibited reckless boating, is revised in NR § 8-738.1.

Former Art. 27, § 79A, concerning debt adjusting, is revised in CL § 14-1316.

Former Art. 27, § 111A, concerning enclosed livestock, is revised in AG § 3-701.

Former Art. 27, § 120B, which prohibited the opening of food containers in stores, is revised in HG § 21-259.1.

Former Art. 27, § 134, concerning receiving consigned goods from a transporter, is revised in CL § 14-1317.

Former Art. 27, § 158A, as it prohibited fortune telling in Caroline County, is revised in § 109 of the Public Local Laws of Caroline County.

Former Art. 27, § 158A, as it prohibited fortune telling in Carroll County, is revised in § 4-103 of the Public Local Laws of Carroll County.

Former Art. 27, § 158A, as it prohibited fortune telling in Talbot County, is revised in § 8A-1 of the Public Local Laws of Talbot County.

Former Art. 27, § 159, concerning adulterated and mislabeled beer and related products, was revised by Ch. 26 in Art. 2B, § 22-201. However, Ch. 213, § 2, Acts of 2002, renumbered that section to be Art. 2B, § 22-101.

Former Art. 27, §§ 170 through 172, concerning consignment of farm articles and products, are revised in AG §§ 1-301 through 1-306.

Former Art. 27, § 172, as it related to consignment of goods other than farm articles and products, is revised in CL § 11-810.

Former Art. 27, §§ 181 through 190, concerning registration of and prohibited acts related to organizational insignia, are revised in BR §§ 19-201 through 19-207.

Former Art. 27, §§ 195 and 198, concerning false advertising and related practices, are revised in CL §§ 14-2901 through 14-2903.

Former Art. 27, § 233B, which prohibited racing horses under a false name, was revised by Ch. 26 in BR § 11-1002.

Similarly, former Art. 27, § 233C, which prohibited fraud in pari-mutuel betting, was revised by Ch. 26 in BR § 11-1003. However, Ch. 213, § 3, transferred those sections to be §§ 8-804 and 8-805 of this article. Also, Chs. 479 and 480 each renumbered Title 8, Subtitle 8 of this article to be Subtitle 9. Accordingly, those sections appear as §§ 8-904 and 8-905.

Former Art. 27, §§ 297C and 297D, concerning the Drug and Alcohol Grants Program and Fund, were revised by Ch. 26 in HG §§ 8-901 and 8-902. However, Ch. 213, §§ 4 and 5, Acts of 2002, renumbered Title 5, Subtitle 10 of this article to be Subtitle 11, and transferred HG §§ 8-901 and 8-902 to be §§ 5-1001 and 5-1002 of this article.

Former Art. 27, §§ 333A through 333D and AG § 4-123.1, concerning humane slaughter of livestock, are consolidated and revised in AG § 4-123.1.

Former Art. 27, §§ 336 and 336A, concerning required injury reports, are revised in HG §§ 20-701 through 20-703.

Former Art. 27, § 399 and FL § 5-503, concerning the authority of Maryland corporations for the care of minor children, are consolidated and revised in FL § 5-503.

Former Art. 27, § 399A, concerning alcoholic beverages in Worcester County, is revised in Art. 2B, § 18-104.

Former Art. 27, §§ 400 through 403A, concerning alcoholic beverages crimes and citations, were revised by Ch. 26 in Art. 2B, §§ 22-101 through 22-108. However, Ch. 213, § 1, Acts of 2002, transferred these provisions to be §§ 10-113 through 10-120 of this article.

Former Art. 27, § 434, which required the use of a ship-to-shore communication device on certain vessels operated on waters of the State, is revised in NR § 8-740.1.

Former Art. 27, § 465A, which prohibited certain real estate settlement practices, is revised in RP § 14-127.

Former Art. 27, § 469, concerning junkyards and related facilities, is revised in EN §§ 5-10A-01 through 5-10A-03.

Former Art. 27, §§ 471 through 480A, concerning registration of and prohibited acts related to returnable containers and returnable textiles, are revised in BR §§ 19-301 through 19-307.

Former Art. 27, §§ 482 and 483, which prohibited throwing certain waste materials into certain waters of the State, are revised in NR § 8-726.1.

Former Art. 27, § 484, which prohibited damaging or interfering with the use of a public wharf or landing, is revised in NR § 8-724.1.

Former Art. 27, § 582, which prohibited operating a vessel with number, name, or home port concealed, is revised in NR § 8-713.1.

A few provisions concerning transition from prior law are transferred to the Session Laws.

Former Art. 27, § 281(i), concerning initial registration of manufacturers, distributors, and dispensers of controlled dangerous substances engaged in those activities before July 1, 1970, is transferred to the Session Laws.

Former Art. 27, § 302(a) through (c), concerning controlled dangerous substances proceedings commencing before July 1, 1970, are transferred to the Session Laws.

In some instances, the staff of the Department of Legislative Services has created "Special Revisor's Notes" to reflect the substantive effect of legislation enacted during the 2002 Session on some provisions of this article.

Index

BUTANE —Cont'd
Possession of destructive device, CR
§§4-501 to 4-503.

BUTYL NITRATE.
Inhaling, CR §5-708.

C

CABLE TELEVISION COMPANIES.
Decoders, use, CR §7-303.
Fraud, receiving programing, CR §7-303.
Interference with service, CR §7-303.
Obstructing or delaying programing, CR
§7-303.
Receiving services without payment, CR
§7-303.
Telecommunications theft, CR §§7-313 to
7-318.
**Unauthorized transfer or recording or
sounds or images,** CR §§7-306 to 7-310.

CAIMANS.
Dangerous animals.
Importing, selling, or trading in, CR
§10-621.

CALVERT COUNTY.
Bingo, CR §§13-705 to 13-709.
Classes of licenses issued, CR §13-705.
Fees for licenses, CR §13-705.
Instant bingo considered bingo, CR §13-705.
License required, CR §13-705.
Limitations on issuing license, CR §13-705.
Organizations exempt from license
requirement, CR §13-706.
Prizes allowed, CR §13-707.
Public liability insurance required, CR
§13-705.
Regulations, adoption, CR §13-709.
Resident agent, designation, CR §13-705.
Revocation of license, CR §13-708.
Sunday bingo, limitation on license, CR
§13-705.
Cruelty to animals.
Humane society officers or animal control
officers, arrests by, CR §10-609.
Gaming, bazaar, carnival and raffles, CR
§§13-201 to 13-205, 13-701 to 13-709.
Bingo, CR §§13-705 to 13-709.
Conducting event for benefit of qualified
organization.
Allowed, CR §13-203.
Definitions, CR §§13-201, 13-701.
Gambling permit review committee, CR
§13-704.
Gaming event defined, CR §§13-201,
13-701.
Individual benefit prohibited, CR §13-203.
Management through organizations
members, CR §13-205.
Permit required for gaming event, CR
§13-703.

CALVERT COUNTY —Cont'd
Gaming, bazaar, carnival and raffles
—Cont'd
Prizes and gaming devices allowed, CR
§13-204.
Provisions applicable to county, CR
§§13-202, 13-301, 13-702.
Qualified organization defined, CR §13-201.
Qualified organizations to conduct, listed,
CR §13-703.

CAMERAS.
**Surveillance of individual in private
place,** CR §3-901.
With prurient intent, CR §3-902.
Surveillance of private residence, CR
§3-903.

CARD GAMES.
Carroll county.
Prohibition, CR §13-906.
Howard county.
Prohibited, CR §§13-1603, 13-1604.
Queen Anne's county, CR §§13-2001 to
13-2006.
St. Mary's county, CR §§13-2111 to 13-2115.

CARD PARTIES.
Prince George's county.
Benefit performance by qualified
organization, CR §§13-1901 to 13-1907.

CARGO.
Wrongful disposal, CR §8-405.

CARJACKING, CR §3-405.
Armed carjacking, CR §3-405.
**Intention not to permanently deprive
owner.**
Not defense, CR §3-405.
**Mandatory sentence for crime of
violence.**
Second, third or fourth conviction, CR
§14-101.

CARNIVAL.
Gaming events and gaming devices.
Acceptance of credit to play gaming event.
Prohibition, CR §12-108.
Anne Arundel county, CR §§13-401 to
13-408.
Baltimore City, CR §§13-501 to 13-510.
Baltimore county, CR §§13-601 to 13-607.
Calvert county, CR §§13-701 to 13-709.
Carroll county, CR §§13-901 to 13-909.
Cecil county, CR §§13-1001 to 13-1005.
Charles county, CR §§13-1101 to 13-1115.
Dorchester county, CR §§13-1201 to
13-1207.
Frederick county, CR §§13-1301 to 13-1307.
Prince George's county.
Benefit performance by qualified
organization, CR §§13-1901 to
13-1907.
Provisions applicable to several counties,
CR §§13-101 to 13-205.

I-71

PHONOGRAPH RECORDS.
Unauthorized recording of sounds or images, CR §§7-306 to 7-310.

PHOTOGRAPHS.
Obscenity and pornography.
Adult sexual displays, CR §§11-101 to 11-107.
Obscene matter generally, CR §§11-201 to 11-211.

PHYSICIANS.
Dispensers of controlled dangerous substances.
Registration, CR §§5-301 to 5-310.
Prescriptions.
Registration of dispensers of controlled dangerous substances, CR §§5-301 to 5-310.
Privileged communications.
Obtaining controlled substance by fraud or subterfuge.
Information communicated not privileged, CR §5-601.
Registration of dispensers of controlled dangerous substances, CR §§5-301 to 5-310.

PICKETING.
Firearm possessed at public demonstration, CR §4-208.
Funeral, burial, memorial service, funeral procession, CR §10-205.
Unlawful picketing and assembly, CR §3-904.

PICNIC.
Prince George's county.
Benefit performance by qualified organization, CR §§13-1901 to 13-1907.

PIERS.
Arson and burning, CR §§6-101 to 6-111.

PIGEONS.
Carrier pigeons.
Injuring or trapping, CR §10-622.

PIMPING.
Receiving earnings from prostitution, CR §11-304.

PIPE BOMB.
Possession of destructive device, CR §§4-501 to 4-503.

PIRACY.
Unauthorized transfer or recording or sounds or images, CR §§7-306 to 7-310.

PISTOLS.
Assault pistols, CR §§4-301 to 4-306.
Handguns.
Generally, CR §§4-201 to 4-209.

POISON GAS.
Possession of destructive device, CR §§4-501 to 4-503.

POISONS.
Attempted poisoning, CR §3-213.
Contaminating water supply or food or drink, CR §3-214.
Dogs, poisoning, CR §10-618.

POLICE.
Alcoholic beverages.
Issuance of citations to minors, CR §10-119.
False statement, report or complaint to officer, CR §9-501.
False statement as to identity, address or date of birth.
While under arrest, CR §9-502.
Fundraising to benefit police.
Fraudulent conduct, CR §8-520.

POLITICAL ACTION COMMITTEES.
Raffles.
Political committees or candidates conducting, CR §12-106.

POLITICAL COMMITTEES.
Raffles.
Political committees or candidates conducting, CR §12-106.

POLITICAL FUNDRAISERS.
Anne Arundel county.
Paddle wheel or wheel of fortune, CR §13-406.
Baltimore City.
Paddle wheel or wheel of fortune, CR §13-506.
Baltimore county.
Paddle wheel or wheel of fortune, CR §13-605.

POLLUTION.
Litter control law, CR §10-110.

PONZI SCHEMES, CR §8-404.

PORNOGRAPHY.
Adult sexual displays, CR §§11-101 to 11-107.
Obscene matter generally, CR §§11-201 to 11-211.

POSSESSING STOLEN PROPERTY, CR §7-104.

POSSESSION OF CONTROLLED DANGEROUS SUBSTANCE.
Counterfeit substances, CR §§5-604, 5-607.
Drug kingpins, CR §5-613.
Firearm possessed, used, worn, carried or transported.
Separate offense, enhanced sentence, forfeiture, CR §5-621.
Noncontrolled substance believing it to be controlled substance, CR §5-618.
Opium, CR §5-503.
Registrants.
Unauthorized possession, CR §5-902.
Schools.
Manufacturing, distributing, dispensing or possessing near, CR §5-627.

RELIGIOUS ORGANIZATIONS —Cont'd
Gaming, bazaar, carnival and raffles
—Cont'd
Carroll county, CR §§13-901 to 13-909.
Cecil county, CR §§13-1001 to 13-1005.
Charles county, CR §§13-1101 to 13-1115.
Frederick county, CR §§13-1301 to 13-1307.
Harford county.
  Raffles generally, CR §§13-1501 to
    13-1512.
Kent county.
  Raffles and other gaming devices, CR
    §§13-1701 to 13-1706.
Local gaming events generally, CR §§13-201
    to 13-205.
Montgomery county.
  Raffles generally, CR §§13-1801 to
    13-1815.
Prince George's county, CR §§13-1901 to
    13-1912.
Queen Anne's county.
  Raffles and other gaming devices, CR
    §§13-2001 to 13-2006.
Raffles, statewide provisions, CR §12-106.
St. Mary's county, CR §§13-2111 to 13-2115.
Wicomico county, CR §§13-2501 to 13-2508.
Worcester county, CR §§13-2619 to 13-2628.
**Hate crime to damage property of
  religious entity,** CR §10-302.
Slot machines.
Ownership and operation in certain
    counties, CR §12-304.
Tip jars and punch board.
Frederick county, CR §13-1305.
Washington county.
  Tip jars generally, CR §§13-2414 to
    13-2439.

RELIGIOUS SCHOOLS.
Hate crime.
Damaging property of religious entity, CR
    §10-302.

REMOVAL OF PERSONAL PROPERTY.
Intent to defraud, CR §8-403.

RENTING MOTOR VEHICLES.
Failure to return rental vehicle, CR
    §7-205.
Subleasing, CR §8-408.

REPEATED PHONE CALLS.
**Misuse of telephone facilities and
  equipment,** CR §3-804.

REPORTS.
Identity fraud, CR §8-304.

RESCUE SQUADS.
Bingo.
Charles county, CR §§13-1109 to 13-1115.
Frederick county, CR §13-1306.
Montgomery county, CR §§13-1801 to
    13-1815.
False alarms, CR §9-604.

RESCUE SQUADS —Cont'd
Gaming, bazaar, carnival and raffles.
Charles county, CR §§13-1101 to 13-1115.
Frederick county, CR §§13-1301 to 13-1307.
Montgomery county.
  Raffles generally, CR §§13-1801 to
    13-1815.
Tip jars and punch board.
Frederick county, CR §13-1305.
Washington county.
  Tip jars generally, CR §§13-2414 to
    13-2439.

RESEARCH FACILITIES.
Breaking and entering, CR §6-208.

RESERVOIRS.
Contaminated water supply, CR §3-214.

RESTAURANTS.
Bad checks.
Obtaining services by issuing or passing,
    CR §§8-101 to 8-108.
**Disturbing the peace, disorderly
  conduct,** CR §10-201.
**Theft of services available only for
  compensation,** CR §7-104.
Tip jars and punch board.
Washington county.
  Tip jars generally, CR §§13-2414 to
    13-2439.

RESTITUTION.
Cemeteries.
Destruction of funerary objects and other
    disorderly or indecent conduct, CR
    §10-404.
Controlled dangerous substances crimes,
    CR §5-610.
Destructive device violations, CR §4-503.
Disorderly conduct.
Cemeteries, CR §10-404.
Exploitation of vulnerable adult, CR
    §8-801.
**False statement or rumor concerning
  destructive device or toxic material,**
    CR §9-504.
Funerary objects, destruction of, CR
    §10-404.
Graffiti, CR §6-301.
Identity fraud, CR §8-301.
Leased or rented goods.
Fraudulent conversion, CR §8-407.
Public assistance fraud, CR §8-503.
Telecommunications services theft, CR
    §7-316.

RESTROOMS.
**Surveillance of individual in private
  place,** CR §3-901.
With prurient intent, CR §3-902.

**RETAIL ESTABLISHMENT THEFT
  DETECTION DEVICES.**
Code grabbing devices.
Manufacturing, selling or possessing, CR
    §7-301.